NORTHEAST
W9-BKP-672
WITHDRAWN

THE
Praxis
— *Series*™ —
Official Guide

COMMUNITY COLLEGE LIBRARY

WITHDRAWN

THE
Praxis
Series™
Official Guide

New York | Chicago | San Francisco | Lisbon
London | Madrid | Mexico City | Milan | New Delhi
San Juan | Seoul | Singapore | Sydney | Toronto

370.76
P919p

The *McGraw-Hill* Companies

Copyright © 2008 by Educational Testing Service. All rights reserved. Printed in the United States of America. Except as permitted under the United States Copyright Act of 1976, no part of this publication may be reproduced or distributed in any form or by any means, or stored in a database or retrieval system, without the prior written permission of the Publisher.

4 5 6 7 8 9 0 QPD/QPD 0 1 2 1 0 9 8

ISBN: 987-0-07-149423-6
MHID: 0-07-149423-5

ETS, the ETS logo, *Praxis I*, *Praxis II*, and *Praxis III* are registered trademarks of Educational Testing Service (ETS) in the United States of America and other countries throughout the world. *Praxis* and *The Praxis Series* are trademarks of Educational Testing Service (ETS).

CONTENTS

How to Use This Book ix

PART I. GETTING STARTED

1. Introducing the *Praxis* **3**
Praxis I: Pre-Professional Skills Tests (PPST®) 3
Praxis II: Principles of Learning and Teaching (PLT®), Elementary
    Education, and Subject Assessments 5
Praxis III 6
2. *Praxis* Practical Matters **9**
How to Register for The *Praxis* Assessments 9
Getting Your Scores 10
3. General Strategies for Test-Takers **11**
General Test Preparation Strategies 11
Strategies for Taking *Praxis* Tests 12

PART II. PREPARING FOR THE PPST

4. All About the PPST **19**
Planning Your Test Preparation Program 19
Tips for Taking the Computer Version 22
5. PPST Reading **27**
Purpose of the Reading Test 27
Format of the Reading Test 27
Strategies for the Reading Test 28
Guided PPST Reading Practice 29
6. PPST Mathematics **55**
Purpose of the Mathematics Test 55
Format of the Mathematics Test 55
Strategies for the Mathematics Test 55
PPST Math Review 66
Guided PPST Math Practice 73
7. PPST Writing: The Multiple-Choice Section **93**
Purpose of the Writing Multiple-Choice Section 93
Format of the Writing Multiple-Choice Section 93
Strategies for the Writing Multiple-Choice Section 94
English Grammar Review 95
Guided PPST Writing Multiple-Choice Practice 110

8. PPST Writing: The Essay **125**
Purpose and Format of the Essay...125
Overview of the Essay Section 125
How the Essay Is Scored...126
Strategies for Writing Your Essay 127
The Essay Topics 129
Writing Your Essay...134
Sample Essays with Scorers' Comments.......................................135
On Your Own: PPST Essay-Writing Practice 140

PART III. SIX REAL PPSTs FOR PRACTICE

9. PPST: Reading Test 1 .... **145**
Calculating Your Score 171
10. PPST: Reading Test 2 .... **175**
Calculating Your Score 201
11. PPST: Mathematics Test 1 .... **205**
Calculating Your Score 233
12. PPST: Mathematics Test 2 .... **237**
Calculating Your Score 261
13. PPST: Writing Test 1 .... **265**
Calculating Your Score 296
14. PPST: Writing Test 2 .... **301**
Calculating Your Score 334

PART IV. *PRAXIS II:* PRINCIPLES OF LEARNING AND TEACHING (PLT)

15. All About the PLT Tests... **341**
Purpose and Format of the PLT Tests 341
Preparing for the PLT Tests...342
PLT Study Topics 345
How to Read a Case Study...365
Case Study 1 367
Case Study 1 372
Case Study 2 375
Case Study 2 381
How to Answer Constructed-Response Questions......................385
16. Real PLT Questions for Practice **389**
Case Study 1 390
Strategies for Answering Constructed-Response Questions
    for Case Study 1 391
Case Study 2 413
Strategies for Answering Constructed-Response Questions
    for Case Study 2..416

PART V. *PRAXIS II:* ELEMENTARY EDUCATION

17. Elementary Education: Curriculum, Instruction, and Assessment 443

Preparing for the Curriculum, Instruction, and Assessment Tests............443

Real Questions for Practice..448

18. Elementary Education: Content Knowledge 453

Preparing for the Content Knowledge Test....................................453

Real Questions for Practice..455

19. Elementary Education: Content Area Exercises 463

Preparing for the Content Area Exercises Test 463

Real Questions for Practice..465

PART VI. *PRAXIS II:* SUBJECT ASSESSMENTS

20. All About the Subject Assessments 493

Fundamental Subjects: Content Knowledge (0511)..................................493

Education of Young Children (0021)..494

Special Education: Application of Core Principles Across

   Categories of Disability (0352) 494

Educational Leadership: Administration and Supervision (0410)..............495

School Psychologist (0400) 495

School Guidance and Counseling (0420) 496

Library Media Specialist (0310)..497

Real Questions for Practice..497

21. Reading, English, Language Arts..**503**

Middle School: English Language Arts (0049) 503

English Language, Literature, and Composition:

   Content Knowledge (0041) 503

English Language, Literature, and Composition: Essays (0042)................504

English Language, Literature, and Composition: Pedagogy (0043) 504

English to Speakers of Other Languages (0360) 505

Reading Across the Curriculum: Elementary (0201)................................506

Reading Across the Curriculum: Secondary (0202) 507

Real Questions for Practice..507

22. Social Studies, Math, Science **517**

Social Studies: Content Knowledge (0081)..517

Citizenship Education: Content Knowledge (0087) 518

Mathematics: Content Knowledge (0061) 518

Middle School: Science (0439)..519

Middle School: Social Studies (0089)..520

Middle School: Mathematics (0069) 520

Biology: Content Knowledge (0235)..521

Chemistry: Content Knowledge (0245) 521

Earth and Space Sciences: Content Knowledge (0571) 522

Physics: Content Knowledge (0265) 523
Real Questions for Practice...523
23. Other Subjects **531**
Spanish: Content Knowledge (0191) 531
French: Content Knowledge (0173)...531
German: Content Knowledge (0181) 532
Business Education (0100)...532
Art: Content Knowledge (0133)...533
Physical Education: Content Knowledge (0091) 533
Health Education (0550) 533
Audiology (0340) 534
Speech-Language Pathology (0330)..534
Parapro Assessment (0755)..535
Real Questions for Practice...535

APPENDIXES

Appendix A. State-by-State *Praxis* Passing Scores **543**
Appendix B. For More Information **551**

How to Use This Book

The *Praxis*™ tests are designed for three different testing populations. The test for which you prepare will depend on the population to which you belong.

If you are an undergraduate who is just starting out on the path toward becoming a prospective teacher, you will probably want to prepare for the PPST®, which tests your basic academic skills.

If you are in a teacher preparation program and are moving toward certification, you will most likely want to prepare for one or more of the *Praxis II* tests—the PLT®, the Elementary Education tests, and/or the Subject Assessments.

If you are in the classroom, you will want to prepare for *Praxis III*, which assesses your teaching skills.

This book will help you

- Familiarize yourself with the test formats.
- Review some key concepts that appear on the *Praxis* tests.
- Practice your test-taking skills, using real* *Praxis* test questions.

Here is a step-by-step plan for using this book.

Step 1: Determine Your Requirements

Appendix A on page 543 includes a state-by-state list of testing requirements for certification. The tests you must take vary depending on where you plan to teach. Use the list to determine which tests you must take. That will tell you which parts of this book to use as you prepare.

Step 2: Read Part I

This overview gives you practical information about the different *Praxis* tests, including how to register and how to get your scores. Part I is for everyone who plans to take a *Praxis* test.

Step 3: Focus on the Upcoming Test

Are you preparing for the PPST?
Read Part II and take the sample tests in Part III.

---

* When we refer to "real tests," we mean that literally. Since this book is prepared by ETS®, the same company that prepares the *Praxis* tests, all the questions you see in this book are taken directly from actual tests from years past. You will have a chance to answer the exact kinds of questions you will find on the *Praxis* test you are about to take.

Are you preparing for the PLT?

Read Part IV and work through the sample test questions in Chapter 16.

Are you preparing for the Elementary Education tests?

Read Part V and work through the sample test questions in Chapters 17–19.

Are you preparing for the Subject Assessments?

Read Part VI and work through the sample test questions in Chapters 20–23.

Working teachers who are preparing for evaluation and review via the *Praxis III* tests should visit www.ets.org/praxis to learn more about those in-class assessments.

Step 4: Review and Improve

Each set of the real test questions is followed by explanatory answers. Use the information you gain from these answers to figure out areas where you need to study and improve your skills.

THE
PRAXIS
SERIES™
Official Guide

PART I

Getting Started

Your Goals for This Part:

- Identify the purposes and components of *Praxis I, II,* and *III*® tests.
- Review basic information on test registration and scoring for *Praxis I* and *II*.
- Learn general test-preparation strategies to apply to *Praxis*™ tests.

CHAPTER 1

Introducing the *Praxis*

The Praxis Series™ Assessments provide tests and other services that states use as part of their teaching licensing certification process. The *Praxis I*® tests measure basic academic skills. The *Praxis II*® tests measure general and subject-specific knowledge and teaching skills. The *Praxis III*® tests assess classroom performance.

PRAXIS I: PRE-PROFESSIONAL SKILLS TESTS (PPST®)

The Pre-Professional Skills Tests (PPST) in Reading, Writing, and Mathematics are designed to be taken early in a student's college career. They measure whether the student has the academic skills needed to prepare for a career in education. The tests are available in a paper-based or computer-based format.

About the PPST

The PPST reflect the most current research and the professional judgment and experience of educators across the country. This group of tests includes the following:

Test Subject	Test Name and Code	Length of Test	Major Content Areas Covered and Approximate Number and Percentage of Questions in Each Area
Reading	*Computerized Pre-Professional Skills Test: Reading (5710)*	75 minutes	• Literal Comprehension (26 questions, 56.5%) • Critical and Inferential Comprehension (20 questions, 43.5%)
	Pre-Professional Skills Test: Reading (0710)	60 minutes	• Literal Comprehension (23 questions, 56.5%) • Critical and Inferential Comprehension (17 questions, 43.5%)

(Continued)

Test Subject	Test Name and Code	Length of Test	Major Content Areas Covered and Approximate Number and Percentage of Questions in Each Area
Writing	*Computerized Pre-Professional Skills Test: Writing (5720)*	68 minutes (38 minutes multiple-choice, 30 minutes essay)	• Grammatical Relationships (12 questions, 13%) • Structural Relationships (16 questions, 18.5%) • Idiom/Word Choice, Mechanics, and No Error (16 questions, 18.5%) • Essay (1 question, 50%)
	Pre-Professional Skills Test: Writing (0720)	60 minutes (30 minutes multiple-choice, 30 minutes essay)	• Grammatical Relationships (10 questions, 13%) • Structural Relationships (14 questions, 18.5%) • Idiom/Word Choice, Mechanics, and No Error (14 questions, 18.5%) • Essay (1 question, 50%) **Note:** A pencil or pen can be used to write the essay for the paper-based test.
Mathematics	*Computerized Pre-Professional Skills Test: Mathematics (5730)*	75 minutes	• Conceptual Knowledge and Procedural Knowledge (21 questions, 46%) • Representations of Quantitative Information (13 questions, 28%) • Measurement and Informal Geometry, Formal Mathematical Reasoning (12 questions, 26%) **Note:** Calculators are prohibited.

Test Subject	Test Name and Code	Length of Test	Major Content Areas Covered and Approximate Number and Percentage of Questions in Each Area
Mathematics	*Pre-Professional Skills Test: Mathematics (0730)*	60 minutes	• Conceptual Knowledge and Procedural Knowledge (18 questions, 45%) • Representations of Quantitative Information (12 questions, 30%) • Measurement and Informal Geometry, Formal Mathematical Reasoning (10 questions, 25%) **Note:** Calculators are prohibited.

PRAXIS II: PRINCIPLES OF LEARNING AND TEACHING (PLT®), ELEMENTARY EDUCATION, AND SUBJECT ASSESSMENTS

Praxis II is for individuals entering the teaching profession, who take these tests as part of the teacher licensing and certification process required by many states. These tests are different from the *Praxis I* tests. They assess both subject matter knowledge and teaching skills.

Principles of Learning and Teaching (PLT)

The Principles of Learning and Teaching (PLT) tests are designed to assess a prospective teacher's knowledge of a broad range of job-related topics. Students typically attain such knowledge in undergraduate courses in educational psychology, human growth and development, classroom management, instructional design and delivery techniques, evaluation and assessment, and other areas of professional preparation. Educational Testing Service (ETS) has aligned the content of this test with principles developed by INTASC (Interstate New Teacher Assessment and Support Consortium) and published in the *INTASC Model Standards*. To develop test questions for the PLT tests, ETS works in collaboration with teacher educators and higher education content specialists to keep the test updated and representative of current standards.

There are four Principles of Learning and Teaching tests:

Principles of Learning and Teaching: Early Childhood
Principles of Learning and Teaching: Grades K–6
Principles of Learning and Teaching: Grades 5–9
Principles of Learning and Teaching: Grades 7–12

Elementary Education

The Elementary Education tests are a series of three tests, two in multiple-choice format and one that requires written answers. The first test assesses prospective elementary teachers' understanding of curriculum, instruction, and assessment in the major K–5 subject areas. The second test measures knowledge of content in Language Arts and Reading, Mathematics, Social Studies, and Science—and the third test assesses content knowledge in a more open-ended, constructed-response format.

Subject Assessments

Praxis II: Subject Assessment tests measure knowledge of specific subjects that K–12 educators teach, as well as general and subject-specific teaching skills and knowledge.

Individuals entering the teaching profession take these tests as part of the teacher licensing and certification process required by many states. A number of professional associations and organizations require these tests as one criterion for professional licensing decisions.

Teaching Foundations tests, which are part of *Praxis II*: Subject Assessments, measure pedagogy in five areas: multisubject (elementary), English Language Arts, Mathematics, Science, and Social Science.

PRAXIS III

Praxis III: Classroom Performance Assessments comprise a system for assessing the skills of beginning teachers in classroom settings. ETS developed *Praxis III* for states or local agencies to use in teacher licensing decisions. Under the guidelines that govern its use, *Praxis III* may not be used to make employment decisions about teachers who are currently licensed.

This direct classroom assessment recognizes the importance of the teaching context as well as the many diverse forms that excellent teaching can take. The *Praxis III* system uses a three-pronged method to assess the beginning teacher's competence and success in the classroom. This includes direct observation of classroom practice, review of documentation prepared by the teacher, and semi-structured interviews.

Praxis III is an assessment system, not just a test. It is comprised of three separate, yet strongly interconnected components. Individually, each component augments the value of the assessment. Collectively, the system offers a thorough understanding of the teaching skills of a beginning teacher. *Praxis III* also provides insights into pedagogical areas in which a teacher may benefit from additional development.

- Component 1: Framework of knowledge and skills for a beginning teacher that assess the teaching performance across all grade levels and content areas.
- Component 2: Instruments used by trained assessors to collect data, analyze, and score the teacher's performance.
- Component 3: Training of assessors to facilitate consistent, accurate, and fair assessments of a beginning teacher.

Beginning teachers residing and planning to teach in states that require *Praxis III*: Classroom Performance Assessments as part of the criteria for teacher licensing decisions have their teaching skills assessed in classroom settings, by trained assessors.

CHAPTER 2

Praxis Practical Matters

HOW TO REGISTER FOR THE *PRAXIS* ASSESSMENTS

The *Praxis I*: Pre-Professional Skills Tests are offered as computer-based or paper-based tests. *Praxis II* tests are available only as paper-based tests. *Praxis III* is an in-class assessment authorized by state or local agencies.

> To find out which tests are required in your state, see Appendix A.

Registering for *Praxis* Computer-Based Testing

Computer-based testing (CBT) registration is made by appointment at more than 300 Prometric **test sites** throughout the United States.

To schedule an appointment, call Prometric Candidate Services Monday through Friday, 8 a.m.–8 p.m. Eastern Time (New York) (excluding holidays), at 1-800-853-6773, 1-443-751-4859, or call the test center directly. If you are deaf or hard of hearing and use a TTY, call 1-800-529-3590 to schedule an appointment.

- You must use an American Express®, Discover® Network, JCB®, Visa®, or MasterCard® credit card, or an authorization voucher.
- To obtain an authorization voucher, send payment to the Educational Testing Service (ETS) with a completed CBT Authorization Voucher Request Form.
- An authorization voucher will be sent to you. It is valid for 90 days from the date of issue. After receiving the voucher, make your test appointment.
- Be sure to take the voucher when you report for testing. It will be collected at the test center.

If you are a test taker with disabilities, refer to the Test Takers with Disabilities page or visit the Computer-Based Test Centers page.

You may test as a walk-in if space allows. Walk-in registrants may pay all test fees by check,* money order, credit card, or authorization voucher. If your check, money order, or credit card is declined, charged back, or returned for insufficient funds or stopped payment, you will be billed for the amount due plus an additional $20 processing fee.

You may take the Computerized PPST only once per calendar month, and no more than six times within a 12-month period. This applies even if you canceled

---

* When you pay by check, you authorize ETS to convert the check into an electronic fund transfer. Please be aware that your account may be debited as soon as the same day we receive your payment. Please also note that you will no longer receive a canceled check.

your scores on a test taken previously. If you violate this restriction, the scores from your retest will not be reported, and your test fees will not be refunded.

Registering for *Praxis* Paper-Based Testing

Register Online Register online for a paper-based test using a credit card, Monday–Friday, 7 a.m.–10 p.m. (EST) and Saturday, 7 a.m. through Sunday, 8 p.m. (EST).

Online registration is **not available** for the following:

- *Praxis I* computer-based testing
- Test-takers with disabilities
- Sabbath/Monday testing
- Examinees whose primary language is not English
- Fee waivers

Defense Activity for Nontraditional Education Support (DANTES) test takers: If you register for a national test date, you may not register to take a test at a DANTES center immediately prior to or following that date. If you register for and take a test, only the first answer sheet received by ETS will be scored and your fees will not be refunded.

Register by Mail   Download and complete the *Praxis* 2006-07 Registration Form (PDF) and follow the instructions in the *The Praxis Series 2006-07 Information Bulletin* (PDF).

GETTING YOUR SCORES

If you take a paper-and-pencil test, your official score report will arrive in the mail approximately four weeks after your test date. Your score report will contain your overall score and six area scores.

If you take the computer version of the PPST, you do not have to pre-register with ETS. To take the computer version, contact the appropriate person in your school or prospective district to find out how you can arrange a day and time for taking the test. Once you are seated at the computer and the school or district administrator has entered the correct codes to start the test, you will be asked to fill in your name, address, and other information on the registration screen. At the end of the testing session, you will receive an unofficial report of your score. Two weeks later, you will receive an official score report in the mail that will contain your overall score and six area scores.

CHAPTER 3

General Strategies for Test-Takers

GENERAL TEST PREPARATION STRATEGIES

Praxis tests contain a mixture of types of questions. Some of these are simple identification questions, such as "What is the name of the shape shown above?" Other questions require you to analyze situations, synthesize material, and apply knowledge to specific examples. In short, they require you to think and solve problems. This type of question is usually longer than a simple identification question and takes more time to answer. You may be presented with something to read (a description of a classroom situation, a sample of student work, a chart or graph) and then asked to answer questions based on your reading. Good reading skills are required, and you must read carefully.

Strengthen Your Reading Skills

Both on these tests and as a teacher, you will need to process and use what you read efficiently. If you know that your reading skills are not strong, you may want to take a reading course. Community colleges and night schools often have reading labs that can help you strengthen your reading skills.

Find Out the Test Specifications in Advance

Praxis multiple-choice test content specifications for a multiple-choice test can be found in the Tests at a Glance available on the *Praxis* Web site (www.ets.org/praxis) under "Prepare for a Test." You may have heard that there are several different test "forms" (different versions of the same test). It's true. You might take one version of the test in January, and your friend might take a different version of the test in April. The two of you will have different questions covering the same subject area. But the tests are "parallel"—they measure the same content domain, because both are built to the same specifications. ETS continually monitors the performance of test-takers to ensure that all test forms measure content knowledge in the same ways.

The specifications are like a recipe for the test: every version of the test covers the same specifications and contains the same proportion of questions on each topic. This coverage makes the test parallel from form to form. The actual questions may be different (a question on the Civil War may ask you about the surrender at Appomattox on one test form, and about Sherman's March to the Sea on another test form), but the content coverage will still be that required by the specifications (in this case, a question on a significant event of the Civil War).

The specifications lists within the Tests at a Glance, called "Topics Covered," contain the percent of the whole test that each topic will represent. The greater the percent, the more questions there will be on that topic, and the greater your knowledge of that area will need to be. Knowing the test specifications in advance can help you guide your study.

Learn to Pace Yourself as You Answer Questions

To help pace yourself through a test, try answering the practice questions in this study guide several times. You may want to use the practice questions to identify areas in which you need more studying, but you should also answer the practice questions several times without worrying about "content" issues. Instead, your goal should be simply to get used to taking the test. Time yourself, and notice the amount of concentration you need to stay focused on the test for the duration of the testing period. Discover the level of pacing that works best for you, and take the test until the pacing starts to feel natural.

STRATEGIES FOR TAKING *PRAXIS* TESTS

Useful Facts About the Tests

1. **You can answer the questions in any order.** You can go through the questions from beginning to end, as many test-takers do, or you can create your own path. Perhaps you will want to answer questions in your strongest subject first and then move from your strengths to your weaker areas. There is no right or wrong way. Use the approach that works for you.

2. **Don't worry about answer patterns.** One test-taking myth claims that answers on multiple-choice tests follow patterns. Another myth insists that there will never be more than two questions with the same lettered answer following each other. There is no truth to either of these myths. Select the answer you think is correct based on your knowledge of the subject.

3. **There is no penalty for guessing.** Your test score is based on the number of correct answers you have, and incorrect answers do not count against you. When you don't know the answer to a question on a multiple-choice test, try to eliminate any obviously wrong answers and then guess at the correct one.

4. **It's OK to write in your test booklet.** If you are taking the paper-and-pencil version of a test, you can work problems right on the pages of the booklet, make notes to yourself, or mark questions you want to review later. Your test booklet will be destroyed after you have finished with it, so use it in any way that is helpful to you. If you are taking the PPST test on a computer, you can work problems on scratch paper, and you can click the "Mark" button to note questions for later review.

Smart Tips for Taking the Tests

1. **Put your answers in the right "bubbles."** It seems obvious, but if you are taking the paper-and-pencil version of a multiple-choice test, you should make sure you are "bubbling in" the answer to the right question on your answer sheet. Check the question number each time you fill in an answer. Use a Number 2 lead pencil, and be sure that each mark is heavy and dark and completely fills the answer space. If you change an answer, be sure the previous mark is erased completely. For the PPST computer-based version, be sure that the circle next to your chosen answer is dark after you have clicked on it.

2. **Be prepared for questions that use the words *LEAST, EXCEPT,* or *NOT.*** Some questions may ask you to select the choice that doesn't fit or that contains information that is not true. Questions in this format use the words LEAST, EXCEPT, or NOT. The words are capitalized when they appear in test questions. This alerts you to the fact that you are looking for the single answer choice that is different in some specified way from the other answer choices. Here is an example of a question in this format that might be on the math part of the PPST:

> *Some values of x are less than 100.*

Which of the following is NOT consistent with the sentence above?

- (A) 5 is not a value of *x*.
- (B) 95 is a value of *x*.
- (C) Some values of *x* are greater than 100.
- (D) All values of *x* are less than 100.
- (E) No numbers less than 100 are values of *x*.

> *Note that the PPST offers you five answer choices. On most Praxis II tests, you will see four choices though some tests have five.*

In the question above, four of the five sentences are consistent with the boxed sentence, and one is NOT. The sentence that is NOT consistent is the correct answer choice—in this case, (E). If no numbers less than 100 are values of *x*, as stated in (E), there will not be at least one value of *x* less than 100, as stated in the boxed sentence.

When you encounter a *NOT, LEAST,* or *EXCEPT* question, it is a good idea to reread the question after you select your answer to make sure that you have answered the question correctly.

3. **Skip the questions you find to be extremely difficult.** There are bound to be some questions that you think are hard. Rather than trying to answer these on your first pass through the test, leave them blank and mark

them in your test booklet so that you can come back to them. (If you are taking the PPST on a computer, you can click the "Mark" button to mark a question and then use the "Review" listing to see which questions you have marked and/or left unanswered.) Pay attention to the time as you answer the rest of the questions on the test. Try to finish with 10 or 15 minutes remaining so that you can go back over the questions you that left blank. Even if you don't know the answers the second time around, see whether you can narrow down the possible answers, and then guess.

4. **Keep track of the time.** For paper-and-pencil tests, wear a watch, just in case the clock in the test room is difficult for you to see. (For the computer version of the PPST, there is a clock on the screen.) Remember that, on average, you have a little more than 1 ½ minutes to answer each of the questions. One and one-half (1 ½) minutes may not seem like much time, but you will be able to answer many questions in only a few seconds each. You will probably have plenty of time to answer all the questions, but if you find yourself becoming bogged down in one section, move on and come back to that section later.

5. **Read all the possible answers before selecting one.** Then reread the question to be sure the answer you have selected really answers the question being asked.

6. **Check your answers.** If you have extra time left over at the end of the test, look over each question. Make sure that you have filled in the "bubble" on the answer sheet (or on the computer screen) as you intended. Many test-takers make careless mistakes that could have been corrected if they had checked their answers.

7. **Don't worry about your score as you take the test.** No one expects you to get all the questions correct. This is not like the SAT or other similar tests, where a higher score means a better chance for success. On this test your score does not matter as long as you pass. If you meet the minimum passing scores for your state or district, you will have fulfilled the requirement.

Do Tests Make You Nervous? Try These Strategies

It's natural to be nervous before a test such as the *Praxis* tests. You can use your nervous energy to strengthen your performance if you approach the test with these facts in mind:

- There are no trick questions on the test. (Some questions may be difficult for you, but they were not written in order to trick you or other test-takers.)
- You should have plenty of time to complete the test. The times allotted for the tests are designed to be adequate. You should not feel rushed.

- Test developers have worded the test questions very carefully and reviewed them many times to make sure that they are clear. If a question seems confusing at first, take some time to reread it more slowly.
- You have choices during the test. You can skip a question and come back to it later. You can change your answer to any question at any time during the testing session. You can mark questions you want to return to later.

The Day of the Test. You should complete your review process a day or two before the actual test date. Remember, many clichés you may have heard about the day of the test are true. You should

- Be well rested
- Take photo identification with you
- Take a supply of No. 2 pencils (at least three) if you are taking a paper-and-pencil test
- Eat before you take the test
- Be prepared to stand in line to check in or to wait while other test-takers are being checked in

You can't control the testing situation, but you can control yourself. Stay calm. The supervisors are well trained and make every effort to provide uniform testing conditions, but don't let it bother you if the test doesn't start exactly on time. You will have the necessary amount of time once it does start.

Think of preparing for the test as you would train for an athletic event. Once you've trained and prepared and rested, give it everything you've got. Good luck.

PART II

Preparing for the PPST

Your Goals for This Part:

- Learn the purpose and format of the PPST.
- Review some strategies for approaching the PPST.
- Practice answering all types of PPST questions.

CHAPTER 4

All About the PPST

This chapter will give you an overview of the PPST, information about taking the test on computer, and general test-taking suggestions. The following three chapters present review courses in reading, math, and writing so you can refresh your understanding of the important principles you'll need to know for the test. These chapters also contain sample questions to help you become familiar with the question formats that actually appear on the test. The guided practice you'll get with these questions will help you understand the kinds of knowledge and reasoning you will need to choose correct answers.

PLANNING YOUR TEST PREPARATION PROGRAM

You will probably want to begin with the following steps:

Become familiar with the test content.

Consider how well you know the content in each subject area. You may already know that you need to build up your skills in a particular area—reading, math, or writing. If you're not sure, skim those sections to see what topics they cover. If you encounter materials that feel unfamiliar or difficult, tag them with sticky notes to remind yourself to spend extra time in these sections.

In addition, all users of this section of the book will probably want to end with these two steps:

Familiarize yourself with test taking. You can simulate the experience of the test by taking the practice questions within the specified time limits. Choose a time and place where you will not be interrupted or distracted. Then score your responses. Look over the explanations of the questions you missed, and see whether you understand them and could answer similar questions correctly. Next plan any additional studying according to what you've learned about your understanding of the topics.

Register for the test and consider last-minute tips. See the section in Part I on how to register for the test, and review the checklist on page 21 of this chapter to make sure you are ready for the test.

What you do between these first steps and last steps depends on whether you intend to use this book to prepare on your own or as part of a class or study group.

Preparing on Your Own

If you are working by yourself to prepare for the PPST, you may find it helpful to use the following approach:

Fill out the Study Plan Sheet. The worksheet on page 22 will help you to focus on what topics you need to study most, identify materials that will help you study, and set a schedule for doing the studying. The last item is particularly important if you tend to procrastinate.

Use other materials to reinforce your skills. The following chapters contain review courses in reading, math, and writing, but you may want to get additional help for the topics that give you the most trouble. For example, if you know you have a problem with spelling, you can find lists of frequently misspelled words in books and on the Internet. Math textbooks can provide instruction and give you additional practice with math problems. Computer-based instruction with a system such as the PLATO® PPST SimTest may also help you improve your skills in reading, math, and writing.

Preparing as Part of a Study Group

It is sometimes helpful to form a study group with others who are preparing for the same test. Study groups give members opportunities to ask questions and get detailed answers. In a group, some members may be good at some topics, while others may be better at other topics. As members take turns explaining concepts to one another, everyone builds self-confidence. If the group encounters a question that none of the members can answer well, the members can go as a group to a teacher or other expert and get answers efficiently. Because study groups schedule regular meetings, group members study in a more disciplined fashion. They also gain emotional support. The group should be large enough that various people can contribute various kinds of knowledge, but small enough that it stays focused. Often, three to six people is a good size.

Here are some ways to use this book as part of a study group:

Plan the group's study program. Parts of the Study Plan Sheet can help to structure your group's study program. By filling out the first five columns and sharing the worksheets, everyone will learn more about your group's mix of abilities and about the resources (such as textbooks) that members can share with the group. In the sixth column ("Dates planned for study of content"), you can create an overall schedule for your group's study program.

Plan individual group sessions. At the end of each session, the group should decide what specific topics will be covered at the next meeting and who will present each topic. Use the topic headings and subheadings to select topics. Some sessions might be based on topics from the review courses contained in these chapters; other sessions might be based on the sample questions from these chapters.

Prepare your presentation for the group. When it's your turn to present, prepare something that's more than a lecture. If you are presenting material from the review course part of a chapter, write 5 to 10 original questions to pose to the group. Writing questions can help you better understand the topics covered on the test as well as the types of questions you will encounter on the test. It will also give other members of the group extra practice at answering questions. If you are presenting material from the sample questions, use each sample question as a model for writing at least one original question.

Take the practice test together. To simulate actual administrations of the test, schedule a test session with the group to add to the realism and help boost everyone's confidence. Use practice tests from Part III of this book.

Learn from the results of the practice test. Score one another's answer sheets. Then plan one or more study sessions based on the questions that group members got wrong. For example, each group member may be responsible for a question that he or she got wrong and can use it as a model to create an original question to pose to the group, together with an explanation of the correct answer.

Whether you study alone or with a group, remember that the best way to prepare is to have an organized plan. The plan should set goals based on specific topics and skills that you need to learn, and it should commit you to realistic deadlines for meeting these goals. Then you must discipline yourself to stick with your plan and accomplish your goals on schedule.

PPST Checklist

- Do you have your appointment for the computer-based test or your admission ticket for the paper-and-pencil test?
- Do you know the topics that will be covered in each section of the test?
- Have you reviewed any textbooks, study notes, and course readings that relate to the topics covered?
- Do you know how long the test will take and the number of questions it contains? Have you considered how you will pace your work?
- Are you familiar with the test directions and the types of questions for the test?
- If you are taking the PPST, writing the test in paper-and-pencil format, are you aware that a pencil, not a pen, is the preferred way to write your essay?
- If you are taking a test on computer, have you familiarized yourself with the appearance of the screens and the use of the buttons?
- Are you familiar with the recommended test-taking strategies and tips?
- Have you practiced by working through the practice test questions at a pace similar to that of an actual test?
- If you are repeating a PPST, have you analyzed your previous score report to determine areas where additional study and test preparation could be useful?

PPST Study Plan Sheet

Content covered on test.	How well do I know the content?	What material do I have for study-ing this content?	What material do I need for study-ing this content?	Where could I find the materials I need?	Dates planned for study of content.	Dates completed.

TIPS FOR TAKING THE COMPUTER VERSION

You need only a beginner's level of computer skill to take the computer-based version of a PPST. The test runs in an Internet browser. If you have spent an hour surfing the Internet, you know how to work the mouse and how to click on buttons. If you do not have experience with computers, the mouse, and the Internet, visit your public library and ask someone to help you get started. Surf around until you feel comfortable making choices with the mouse.

What You Will See on the Screen

Most of the screens you will see when you take the computer-based version of a PPST will look like this:

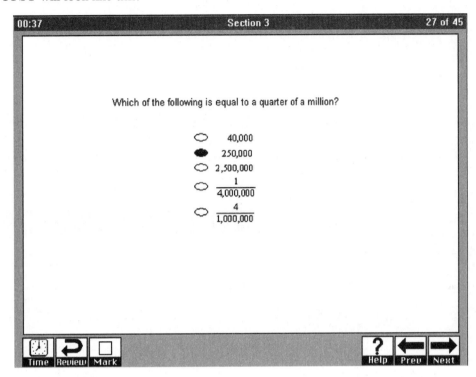

Note how the screen is laid out:

- In the upper right-hand corner, you can see which question you are now working on (question 27 of 45).
- In the upper left-hand corner, you can see how much time you have left (37 minutes). You can hide or display the clock by clicking [Time]. (During the last few minutes of the test, the clock remains on continuously.)
- The test questions appear in the middle of the screen. You simply click the oval ○ next to your answer choice, and it becomes blacked in. You can change your answer by clicking on another oval, which then becomes blacked in, while the oval you clicked earlier changes back to white.
- When you're ready to move to the next question, click [Next]. To move back to a previous question, click [Prev].
- To remind yourself of a question you want to check later, click [Mark]. When you return to the question, you'll see that the button has changed to [Mark].

- Help is always available. Just click 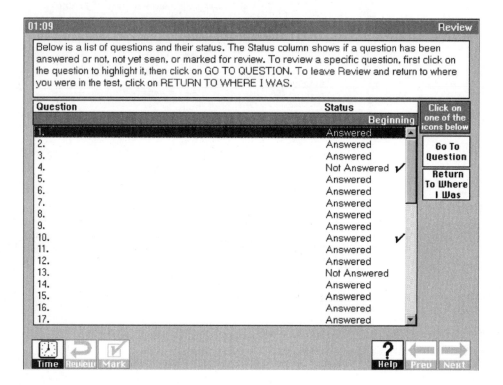 to see instructions about the PPST.
- When you reach the last question, or when time runs out, you will be able to exit the test and receive your score. Once you exit a test, you CANNOT return to it.
- If you want to review questions you have seen (such as those you have marked, or those you have left unanswered), click to review. You'll see a screen that looks like this:

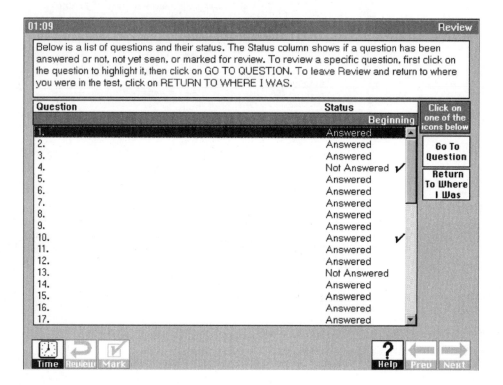

- Click on the question you want to review, then click Go To Question. To resume where you left off, click Return To Where I Was.

In the reading and writing sections, when you are given a long passage of text accompanied by several questions, the screen is divided and looks like this:

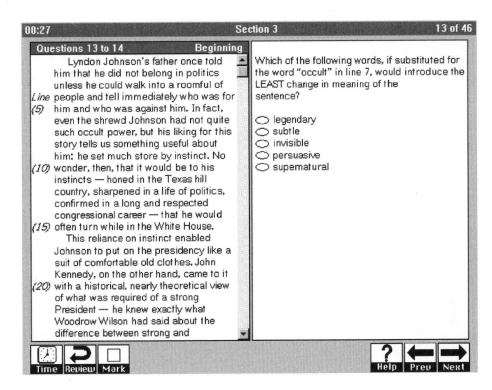

Note that the heading for the passage (above on the left) indicates that two questions (13 and 14) are based on the passage. After you answer the first question and click "Next," the right side of the screen changes to show you the next question about the passage.

After you complete the test and exit, you will be able to print your unofficial score report by using your Internet browser's Print button.

CHAPTER 5

PPST Reading

Pencil-and-Paper Version	Computer-Based Version
40 questions	46 questions
60 minutes	75 minutes

PURPOSE OF THE READING TEST

"Reading comprehension" refers to the ability to *understand, analyze,* and *evaluate* written material. The key to doing well on the PPST: Reading test is to read carefully and make correct judgments and conclusions about what you have read. You do not need to read fast to succeed on the test, but you do need to understand what you have read. You also need to evaluate how each author presents his or her arguments and the evidence used to support them.

FORMAT OF THE READING TEST

The test consists entirely of reading passages and questions related to the passages. There are no vocabulary questions on the test, such as antonyms (finding the word opposite in meaning) or analogies ("*X* is to *Y* as *Z* is to blank"). You do not have to memorize lists of hard words to prepare for the test. You simply need to be able to read 20 or so different reading selections and answer accompanying questions.

There are 40 questions on the test, and you will have 60 minutes to complete them. (If you are taking the computer version, you have 46 questions to answer in 75 minutes.) Your best preparation is to develop the ability to read *carefully*, but with strategies that help you move through the material quickly.

Reading Passages: Sources and Subject Matter

The reading passages are taken from a wide range of reading materials intended for the general reading public. Many passages come from magazines and journals such as *Scientific American, Smithsonian, Archaeology,* and *Psychology Today.*

Other reading passages in the PPST: Reading test come from nonfiction books published for general audiences, such as biographies, histories, and books of essays. A relatively small percentage of passages is taken from newspapers, usually from lengthy feature articles in major newspapers such as *The New York Times* or the *Washington Post.*

The subject matter of the passages varies. The passages cover a variety of subjects in the areas of social science, humanities, science, and general interest. You should expect to encounter a wide assortment of topics.

You may know a lot about some of the topics and next to nothing about others. That does not matter. *To answer the questions, you do not need to draw on any background or outside knowledge.* Everything you need to know to answer the questions is directly stated or implied in the passages.

In some cases, the information in the passage may conflict with knowledge you have about the subject. If it does, do not let your knowledge influence your choice of an answer. *Always answer each question on the basis of what is stated or implied in the given passage.*

The passages reflect various forms of writing: description, explanation, persuasion, narrative, and personal reflection. Most passages make a single central point and then back it up with supporting examples or observations. There will be a flow of logic or observation, often with transition words such as "but," "however," "therefore," and "in addition."

Reading Passages: Length

Each reading passage consists of one or more paragraphs on a single topic, followed by one or more questions.

The passages are of varying lengths:

- Long passages of roughly 200 words (with four to seven questions)
- Short passages of roughly 100 words (with two to three questions)
- Statements of a sentence or two (with one question)

Even the longest passages of 200 words are equivalent in length to a fairly brief newspaper article, so you can be confident that you can read each passage carefully and quickly without running out of time.

STRATEGIES FOR THE READING TEST

Once you've started a set of questions, answer all the questions in the set. When you take the reading comprehension test, work through each set of questions completely before moving on to the next set. For tests made up of discrete, unrelated questions, it might make sense to leave some questions unanswered and come back to them; however, once you have read a passage carefully, you should try to answer all the accompanying questions before going on to the next passage.

You may, however, read the passages in whatever order seems best to you. In other words, if a passage seems easy or interesting, you may prefer to begin with that one, and answer all the accompanying questions. If a passage seems difficult, you may want to save it for last.

Read through the passage once. For each passage, first read through it carefully but quickly. Then answer each question, referring to the passage as necessary.

Don't analyze the passage in great detail when you first read it. Analyze it only as needed to answer a question.

Cross out choices you think are wrong. When working on a question on the paper test, cross out choices you definitely know to be wrong. If you cross them out in your test booklet, you will not waste time rereading choices you've already decided are wrong. Once you eliminate the obviously wrong choices, you may increase the probability (improve your ability) to make an educated guess.

If it helps you focus, you may also want to mark parts of the passage that seem important. For instance, you might want to underline transition words, such as *however* or *therefore*, to call attention to the structure of the author's argument. Do not, however, spend too much time marking the passage.

Expect variety. Don't panic if you are not familiar with the topic of the passage. Even if the passage is on multicolored eels found near the New Zealand coast, don't be put off! Plunge in and read carefully. You will be given all the information you need to answer the questions.

Be prepared to shift your mindset between topics. You might encounter a dense passage describing a medical discovery and then a lighter passage about childhood memories of a hometown.

Pace yourself. Do not spend too much time on any one passage or question. If you find that a certain passage or question is taking up too much of your time, make an educated guess and move on to another question.

Answer all the questions. Be sure to answer every question. Because the test is scored according to the number of correct answers, you are not penalized for guessing. At the end of the test period, take a moment to check the answer sheet for any unanswered questions.

GUIDED PPST READING PRACTICE

The 12 Types of Questions on the PPST: Reading Test

It may look as if every question on the PPST: Reading test is different, but there are really only 12 question types. Below you'll see that the 12 types fall into two main categories. Read the in-depth explanation of each type and try the practice questions.

The 12 types of questions fall into two major categories:

- Literal comprehension skills (types 1–4)
- Critical and inferential comprehension skills (types 5–12)

Literal comprehension is the ability to understand accurately and completely what is explicitly stated in a passage. It also involves the ability to recognize how a passage is organized and how it uses language. To answer this kind of question, you must concentrate on what is written and how it is written. A little more than one-half of the questions measure this kind of comprehension.

The PPST: Reading test assesses the following literal comprehension skills:

Type 1: Recognizing the *main idea* or primary purpose of a passage
Type 2: Recognizing a *supporting idea* or detail in a passage
Type 3: Recognizing how particular *vocabulary* words or phrases are used in a passage
Type 4: Recognizing the *organization* of a passage

Critical and inferential comprehension questions test the ability to understand aspects of a passage that are not explicitly stated. When you read critically or inferentially, you must understand implications, make predictions, analyze an author's argument, and compare situations and arguments.

To answer this kind of question, you do not need any specialized knowledge. Clear and careful thinking is sufficient. A little less than one-half of the questions measure this kind of comprehension.

The PPST: Reading test assesses the following critical and inferential comprehension skills:

Type 5: Drawing an *inference* or implication from a passage
Type 6: Evaluating supporting *evidence*—its relevance or appropriateness
Type 7: Identifying an *assumption* made by the author
Type 8: Distinguishing *fact from opinion*
Type 9: Identifying the *attitude* of the author toward the topic
Type 10: *Extending and predicting* based on passage content
Type 11: Drawing a *conclusion*
Type 12: Making an *application* to another situation

In-Depth Preparation for All 12 Types of Questions

Type 1: Main Idea Questions

There are two kinds of Main Idea questions:

- Main idea
- Primary purpose

Main idea questions ask about the central point of a passage. The main idea may be explicitly stated, or you may have to figure it out. It might help first to identify the topic of the passage (in a few words) and then to identify the author's point about that topic (in a complete sentence). That will be the main idea. For example, the topic of a passage might be "the person who invented laptop computers," and the main idea might be "The person who invented laptop computers did not get support from coworkers when trying to sell the idea to the company's marketing department."

Primary purpose questions ask about the author's purpose. The author may explicitly state the purpose, or you may have to figure it out. Sometimes the question will ask you to identify a general phrase describing the purpose (using language such as "explain an event" or "refute an argument"). Sometimes the question will ask you to identify a specific statement describing the purpose (using language such as "refute a traditional theory about glaciers").

How to recognize Main Idea questions

Here are the ways in which Main Idea questions are usually asked:

- Which of the following statements best summarizes the main idea of the passage?
- Which of the following statements best expresses the main idea of the passage?
- The main idea of the passage is …

Here are the ways in which Primary Purpose questions are usually asked:

- In the passage, the author is primarily concerned with which of the following?
- The primary purpose of the passage is to …

Keep in mind that the question asks about the *main* idea and the *primary* purpose, not minor ideas and secondary purposes. For example, the way a harpsichord works might be described, but the author might do so *in order to* explain why pianos became more popular than harpsichords in the 1700s. So the primary purpose is not to describe harpsichords, but to explain the rising popularity of pianos.

Look for the choice that is a *complete* description of the main idea or primary purpose of the passage. This will require that you read the *entire* passage.

ETS TIPS for Main Idea Questions

- Don't just choose answers that are true. Some choices may be true, but they may not express the main idea of the given passage.
- Don't choose an answer just because you think the author would agree with the idea expressed; that may not be the main point the author was making in the passage.
- Don't look for the answer choice that has wording that is most similar to that used in the passage. Often, all choices will have wording similar to that used in the passage. You will have to read both the passage and the choices carefully to understand exactly what is meant by the words. Merely skimming the passage will not enable you to determine the main idea of the passage.
- For primary-purpose questions, pay attention to the specific meanings of words such as *compare, examine, explain,* and *refute,* which are often used in the answer choices.
- Be sure that the choice you select does not go *beyond* the passage. Sometimes a choice may present information that is not directly given in the passage. That choice will not, therefore, be the main idea or primary purpose.

Try a Main Idea question

Shakespeare wrote four types of plays: histories, comedies, tragedies, and tragicomedies. Some scholars contend that Shakespeare's choice of three of these types of dramatic forms reflects his various psychological states. As a young man making a name for himself in London, he wrote comedies. Then, saddened by the death of his son, he turned to tragedies. Finally, seasoned by life's joys and sorrows, he produced tragicomedies. But a look at the theater scene of his day reveals that Shakespeare was not so much writing out of his heart as into his pocketbook. When comedies were the vogue, he wrote comedies; when tragedies were the rage, he wrote tragedies; and when tragicomedies dominated the stage, he produced tragicomedies.

1. The primary purpose of the passage is to

    (A) examine Shakespeare's life in light of his dramatic works
    (B) contest a theory that attempts to explain why Shakespeare wrote the kinds of plays he did
    (C) explain the terms "comedy," "tragedy," and "tragicomedy" as they are used in discussions of Shakespeare's plays
    (D) compare Shakespeare's plays with the works of other dramatists of his day
    (E) discuss what is known about Shakespeare's psychological state

Explanation: The first two sentences classify Shakespeare's plays into four categories and offer a theory, endorsed by "some scholars," concerning why Shakespeare chose to write three of these four kinds of plays. The next three sentences provide support for this theory by showing correspondence between Shakespeare's likely psychological state and the plays he wrote at various times in his life. The word *But* in the next sentence indicates a change of direction in the passage: the author now suggests that the first theory may be wrong, and goes on to provide an alternate theory—that Shakespeare may well have written the kinds of plays he wrote not because they reflected a particular psychological state but because he thought they would be financially successful. The primary purpose of the passage, then, is best described in choice B, which states that the author's purpose is to "contest a theory" (and choice B correctly describes the theory being contested; that is, a theory about why Shakespeare wrote the kinds of plays he did).

Choice C can be eliminated because although the terms listed in choice C are used in the passage, they are not explained.

Choice D can be eliminated because the passage is not concerned with comparing Shakespeare's plays with those of another dramatist.

While choices A and E do to some extent reflect the content of the passage, neither expresses the complete primary purpose of the passage. (And, in fact, choice A has the examination backwards: Shakespeare's works are examined in light of his life, not the other way around.)

Type 2: Supporting Idea Questions

Supporting ideas are ideas used to support or elaborate on the main idea. Supporting Idea questions can focus on facts, details, definitions, or other information presented by the author. Whereas questions about the main idea ask you to determine the meaning of a passage or a paragraph as a whole, questions about supporting ideas ask you to determine the meaning of a particular part of the passage. Think of a lawyer during a court case examining an expert medical witness on the stand. The lawyer asks specific questions about supporting details: "What are the usual symptoms of the disease?" "What medicines are typically used to combat the disease?" "Why would some people take longer to be cured than others?" These specific questions do not comprise the main argument of the lawyer's case, which may be to show a hospital's negligence in the care of a patient, but they are critical supporting facts.

How to recognize Supporting Idea questions

Here are the ways in which Supporting Idea questions are usually asked:

- According to the passage, which of the following is true of X?
- The passage mentions all the following as characteristics of X EXCEPT …
- According to the author, the kinds of data mentioned in line n are significant because they …
- The author's description of X mentions which of the following?
- The passage states that one of the consequences of X was …
- According to the passage, X is immediately followed by …

ETS TIPS for Supporting Idea Questions

- You may need to refer to the passage to find out exactly what is said about the subject of the question. Since the question is asking about a specific detail, you may not recall the detail from your first reading of the passage.
- Eliminate the choices that present information contradictory to what is presented in the passage.
- Eliminate the choices that present information not given in the passage.
- Don't just select a choice that presents information that is given in the passage; your choice must answer the specific question that is asked.

Try two Supporting Idea questions

Predominantly Black land-grant colleges in the United States have a long tradition of supporting cooperative education programs. These programs combine academic courses with work experience that carries academic credit. This tradition has made these colleges the leaders in the recent movement in American education toward career-oriented curriculums.

2. According to the passage, predominantly Black land-grant colleges in the United States are leaders in career-oriented education because they

(A) have had cooperative education programs as part of their curriculums for many years
(B) were among the first colleges in the United States to shift away from career-oriented curriculums
(C) offer their students academic credit for their work experience prior to entering college
(D) have a long tradition of cooperation with local business and community leaders
(E) provide opportunities for students to work on campus to earn money for tuition

Explanation: The first sentence tells us that Black land-grant colleges have supported cooperative education programs for a long time. The second sentence describes cooperative education programs. The final sentence tells us that it is this tradition of support for cooperative education programs that has made these colleges leaders in the career-oriented education movement. Of the five choices, choice A best states the reason that the colleges are leaders in career-related education.

Choice B can be eliminated because it contradicts information in the passage.

Choice C can be eliminated because although it may be an accurate statement about these colleges, it does not account for their leadership in career-oriented education.

The passage says nothing about local business and community leaders; therefore, choice D can be eliminated.

Although choice E may be a correct statement about these colleges, this information is not explicitly stated in the passage. Even if the information were included, it would not help explain why the colleges are *leaders* in career-oriented education. Providing students with jobs on campus would not necessarily be beneficial to them in developing skills for a future career.

The women's movement emerged in the United States in the 1830s, a period of intense reform and evangelism. Women were encouraged to speak out at religious revival meetings, and many women thus gained public speaking experience. When women sought and were denied leadership and the right to speak out in the abolitionist and temperance societies to which they belonged, they organized their own reform groups and later worked to improve their own status.

3. According to the passage, women formed their own reform societies because women

(A) were denied membership in other reform societies
(B) disagreed with the aims of the societies to which they belonged
(C) were not permitted to act as leaders of the organizations of which they were members

(D) were preoccupied with issues that pertained only to the status of women

(E) wished to challenge the existing political order by questioning the political motives of their opponents

Explanation: This question asks you to identify information that is explicitly stated in the passage. The last sentence states that women formed their own reform societies because they were "denied leadership and the right to speak out" in the societies to which they already belonged. Thus, choice C is the best answer.

Choice A can be eliminated because the passage indicates that women were members of temperance and abolitionist societies.

Choices B, D, and E can be eliminated because the passage provides no information about the specific views of the women or about a desire on their part to challenge the existing political order.

Type 3: Vocabulary Questions

Vocabulary questions require you to identify the meanings of words as they are used in the context of a reading passage. These questions not only test your understanding of the meaning of a particular word, but also test your ability to understand how the word is being used in context. Authors make choices about the language they use, and they sometimes deliberately choose unusual words or figures of speech (words not intended to be understood literally). When you are asked about an unusual word or a figure of speech, you will be given sufficient context to help you identify the meaning of the word.

How to recognize Vocabulary questions

Here are the ways in which Vocabulary questions are usually asked:

- Which of the following words could be substituted for "Y" in line n without substantially altering the meaning of the statement?
- The author most probably uses the word "Y" in line n to mean …
- In line n, the word "Y" most nearly means …

ETS TIPS for Vocabulary Questions

- Remember that the question is not simply asking about the meaning of a specific word; it is asking about its meaning *in the context of the passage.* Therefore, do not simply choose the answer choice that provides a correct meaning; you must understand which meaning the author is using in the passage.
- Often all the choices will offer acceptable meanings of the word. Your job is to choose which meaning makes the most sense as the word is used in the passage.
- Reread the relevant sentence in the passage, using the word or phrase you have chosen. Confirm that the sentence makes sense in the context of the passage as a whole.

Try two Vocabulary questions

President Lyndon Johnson's father once told him that without the ability to walk into a roomful of people and tell immediately who was a supporter and who was an opponent, one did not belong in politics. In fact, even the shrewd younger Johnson never had such occult power, but his liking for this story tells us something useful about him: he set much store by instinct. No wonder, then, that it would be to his instincts—honed in the Texas hill country, sharpened in a life of politics, confirmed in a long and respected congressional career—that he would often turn while in the White House.

4. Which of the following words, if substituted for the word "occult" in line 4, would LEAST change the meaning of the sentence?

    (A) legendary
    (B) subtle
    (C) invisible
    (D) persuasive
    (E) supernatural

Explanation: The "occult" power described in the first sentence is clearly not a power that people ordinarily have. It could, therefore, best be described as "supernatural." Choice E is, therefore, the best answer.

Choices A and D can be eliminated because they are not synonyms of *occult* in any context.

Choice B can be eliminated because the process of dividing people into two categories, "for" and "against," is not "subtle," but rather a crude and direct means of dealing with others.

Choice C can be eliminated because powers of the mind are always "invisible" and there is no reason why the author would attribute a high degree of invisibility to one power when all are equally invisible.

In *Understanding Media*, Marshall McLuhan sheds a brilliant light, punctuated by occasional shadows of obscurity, on the essential nature of electronic media; the chapter on radio looks harder at that medium than anything since Arnheim's Radio.

5. The phrase "shadows of obscurity" most probably refers to McLuhan's

    (A) use of imagery
    (B) lack of clarity
    (C) depth of understanding
    (D) wide-ranging interests
    (E) waning reputation

Explanation: This question asks you to identify the meaning of a figure of speech (the author does not mean to suggest *real* shadows). The passage as a whole presents an evaluation of Marshall McLuhan's *Understanding Media*. The "brilliant light" shed by McLuhan is a figure of speech that can be interpreted as an illuminating discussion of electronic media. The passage states that this brilliant light is "punctuated by" something else, meaning that it is interrupted by something that contrasts with it. The "shadows of obscurity" can thus be interpreted as confusing or unclear parts of McLuhan's discussion. Thus choice B is the best answer.

Choice A can be eliminated because the passage is discussing McLuhan's work in general and not particular aspects of his style, such as imagery.

Choice C can be eliminated because while "shadows" might refer to "depths," "understanding" is *contrary* to "obscurity."

Choice D can be eliminated because "wide-ranging interests" captures the meaning of neither "shadows" nor "obscurity."

Choice E can be eliminated because the passage is about the merits of McLuhan's book rather than about McLuhan's reputation.

Type 4: Organization Questions

Organization refers to how the content of a reading passage is put together to achieve the author's purpose. The individual sentences and paragraphs that make up the passages have a logical and coherent relationship to one another.

Sometimes you will be asked to identify how a passage as a whole is constructed. For instance, a passage may introduce and then describe a theory. It may compare and then contrast two points of view. It may offer an idea and then refute it, and so on.

Sometimes you will be asked to identify how one paragraph is related to another. For instance, the second paragraph may give examples to support a statement offered in the first paragraph, or the second paragraph may refute a theory presented in the first paragraph. The answers may be expressed in general terms (e.g., a hypothesis is explained and then challenged) or in terms specific to the passage (e.g., how children learn one kind of activity is described and then this method is recommended for teaching children another kind of activity).

As another way of testing your ability to recognize organization, you may be asked to identify why an author mentions a particular piece of information or why an author quotes someone. For example, an author might mention a reason or example to support an assertion. An author might quote someone to provide an example of a person who holds a certain opinion.

To answer Organization questions, pay attention to how sentences and paragraphs are connected. Sometimes certain words make the connections explicit: *for example*, *however*, *a second reason*, *furthermore*, and so on. They may tell you whether a sentence or paragraph is giving an example, offering a contrast, offering additional information, or extending a point. You may even want to underline those kinds of words as you read through the passage for the first time. However, you should keep in mind that such key words might not always be present. When you cannot find key words, simply ask yourself how one sentence or paragraph is connected to another.

How to recognize Organization questions

Here are the ways in which Organization questions are usually asked:

- Which of the following statements best describes the organization of the passage?

- Which of the following best describes the way in which the claim is presented?
- The author mentions *X* most likely in order to …

ETS TIPS for Organization Questions

- Pay careful attention to the words used in the answer choices. They are usually the key to finding the right answer. Know the precise meanings of these terms: *definition, comparison, analogy, summary, refutation, chronological, controversial, criticism,* and *generalization*. These words are often used in the choices given for Organization questions.

   Sometimes it may help to recall the main idea or primary purpose of the passage—the organization of the whole as well as of the parts should serve that idea or purpose.

Try two Organization questions

One promising energy source would require sophisticated redesign of the basic windmills that have pumped water for centuries. Coupled with advanced storage batteries, large windmills might satisfy the total energy needs of rural areas and even small cities where strong and prevalent winds can be counted on. Wind power has several advantages. First, no new technology is really required. Second, the energy source is inexhaustible. Third, relatively little capital investment is needed to install or operate windmills.

But wind power has major disadvantages, too. Most obviously, it will work only in areas where wind is strong and prevalent. Furthermore, the amount of electricity that could be generated by wind power would simply be insufficient to meet major nationwide energy needs.

However, a network of sea-based windmills, placed on buoys and driven by the same prevailing winds that once powered sailing vessels, could provide a substantial fraction of the world's electrical energy—especially if the buoy-based windmills could be linked to land by superconducting power transmission cables.

6. Which of the following best describes the organization of the passage?

   (A) A series of interrelated events are arranged chronologically.
   (B) A controversial theory is proposed and then persuasively defended.
   (C) An unforeseen problem is described and several examples are provided.
   (D) A criticism is summarized, evaluated, and then dismissed.
   (E) A problematical issue is discussed and a partial solution is suggested.

Explanation: Choice E is the best answer. "A problematical issue is discussed" summarizes the first two paragraphs, in which both the positive and negative aspects of a complicated situation are examined. This discussion is followed, in the third paragraph, by the suggestion of "a partial solution," which may solve some of the problems involved in using windmills to generate electricity.

Choice A can be eliminated because the passage is concerned with examining an issue from different sides rather than with narrating specific events. Nor is there any sense of chronology in the passage.

Choice B attributes a one-sided approach to the author, who actually presents different points of view. Furthermore, although the passage implies that there may be disagreement about the usefulness of the windmills, it does not anywhere indicate that the issue is controversial. In addition, the passage focuses more on concrete aspects of a problem than on a theory.

Choice C can be eliminated because there is no evidence in the passage that the problems discussed in the second paragraph were unforeseen.

Choice D can be eliminated because the passage does not summarize, evaluate, or dismiss any criticism that is mentioned, nor does the entire passage deal with criticism.

Whatever their disadvantage with respect to distributing education tax dollars equally among school districts may be, in one respect at least, local property taxes are superior to state taxes as a means of funding public schools. Because local property taxes provide public schools with a direct source of revenue, these public schools are relatively free from competition with other government services for tax dollars. School administrators do not have to compete for a share of the state tax dollars, which are already being spent on health, criminal justice, public safety, and transportation. They are not placed in the position of having to argue that school programs must have priority over other public services financed by state taxes.

7. The author mentions the tax dollars spent on health, criminal justice, public safety, and transportation most likely in order to highlight the

(A) government services with which public schools do not have to compete for tax dollars
(B) unequal distribution of local property tax dollars among various public services
(C) high expense of maintaining schools as compared to other public services
(D) government services over which public schools have priority
(E) disadvantage of distributing education tax dollars among various public services

Explanation: The first sentence of this passage states that using local property taxes for schools has advantages over using state taxes. The second sentence explains this advantage: "public schools are relatively free from competition with other government services for tax dollars." The next sentence elaborates, listing some of those "other government services"—"health, criminal justice, public safety, and transportation." Thus, choice A is the best answer.

Choices B and E do not reflect the passage's content: the potentially unequal distribution of local property-tax dollars (a disadvantage) is among school districts, not among various public services.

Choice C can be eliminated because the author is not making a point about the relative cost of education.

Choice D can be eliminated with similar reasoning: the author does not say that public schools have priority over government services, merely that the freedom from competition frees school administrators from having to make that argument.

Type 5: Inference Questions

An inference is a statement that is clearly suggested or implied by the author. An inference is based on information given in the passage, but it is not directly stated in the passage. To answer inference questions, you may have to carry statements made by the author one step beyond what is presented in the passage. For example, if a passage explicitly states an effect, a question could ask you to infer its cause. Be ready, therefore, to concentrate not only on the explicit meanings of the author's words, but also on the logical implications of those words.

We make inferences in conversation all the time. Consider this conversation between two students:

Sean: "Did you get an A on the quiz?"

Chris: "Didn't you hear the professor say that no one got an A?"

Sean should be able to infer that Chris did not get an A on the quiz, even though Chris did not explicitly say so.

Here's another conversation that illustrates an inference:

Lee: "This is the first year that the university is offering a course in writing poetry."

Sara: "So my sister, who graduated last year, couldn't have taken a course here in writing poetry."

Sara can make an inference about her sister's particular situation from Lee's general statement.

How to recognize Inference questions

Pay special attention when you see words such as "infer," "suggests," and "implies" in a question. These are often signals for inference questions.

Here are the ways in which Inference questions are usually asked:

- Which of the following can be inferred about X from the passage?
- The passage strongly suggests that X would happen if …
- The author of the passage implies which of the following about X?
- It can be inferred from the passage that X is effective in all of the following ways EXCEPT …

ETS TIPS for Inference Questions

ETS TIPS for Inference Questions

- Make sure your answer doesn't contradict the main idea of the passage.
- Make sure your answer doesn't go too far and make assumptions that aren't included in the passage. (For example, in the conversation between Lee and Sara about poetry courses, Sara would have gone too far if she had said, "So all English majors will now be required to take the course in writing poetry." This cannot be inferred from Lee's statement.)
- Don't just choose a statement that sounds important or true. It must be inferable from the passage.
- You should be able to defend your selection by pointing to explicitly stated information in the passage that leads to the inference you have selected.
- Use the "if-then" test to verify your answers. To perform this test, complete the following statement: if X (information in the passage), then Y (your selected choice). Does your if-then statement make sense?

Try two Inference questions

Histories of the Middle East abound in stereotypes and clichés, particularly with respect to women. The position of women in the Middle East is frequently treated as though Middle Eastern societies formed a single unit that could be accurately represented in a simple description.

8. The author of the passage suggests which of the following about histories of the Middle East with regard to their treatment of women?

(A) A general problem with such histories was first noticed in their descriptions of the role of women.

(B) The experience of women in Middle Eastern societies is much more diverse than such histories have often assumed.

(C) The study of women's roles and experience has recently become a central focus in such histories.

(D) Such histories report that the position of women in Middle Eastern societies has undergone a major transformation.

(E) Until recently, such histories typically neglected to discuss the position of women.

Explanation: In the first sentence, the author asserts that histories of the Middle East are filled with oversimplified generalizations, particularly with regard to women. In the second sentence, the author explains that the error lies in the way historians of the Middle East discuss women as though all Middle Eastern societies were similar. By saying "as though," the author suggests that Middle Eastern societies are different and that the experiences of women in the countries are different, so that it is a mistake to assume that the experiences are similar. Thus, choice B is the best answer.

Choice A can be eliminated because the author does not suggest that the problem with histories of the Middle East was discovered as a result of the way those studies treat women.

Choices C and E can be eliminated because although the passage suggests that women are discussed in studies of the Middle East, it does not suggest that such studies either typically neglected or focused on women.

Choice D can be eliminated because the passage does not report that there has been a change in the position of women in the Middle East.

In the 1960's and 1970's, electoral support for public education was strong, mainly as a result of certain trends in the U.S. population. For example, enrollments in primary and secondary schools reached their zenith in these years, when public school students constituted one out of every four members of the U.S. population. Moreover, parents of children in public schools and public school employees comprised approximately 40 percent of eligible voters in the United States.

9. The author implies that one of the results of large enrollments in public schools in the 1960's and 1970's was

   (A) a deterioration in the quality of education offered by nonpublic schools
   (B) an increase in the demand for higher education
   (C) an increase in the number of eligible voters in the United States
   (D) broad electoral support for public education programs
   (E) overall improvement in the quality of higher education

Explanation: The author says that electoral support for public education was strong during the 1960's and 1970's because of certain trends in the United States population. The author then goes on to cite, as an example of those trends, the high levels of enrollment in public schools during this period. The author thus implies a cause-and-effect relationship between large enrollments in public schools and broad electoral support for education—implies, that is, that one of the results of large enrollment in public schools was broad electoral support for education. This answer is given in choice D.

Choices A, B, C, and E can be eliminated because the passage does not suggest anything about the quality of education offered in nonpublic schools, the demand for higher education, the number of eligible voters, or the quality of higher education.

Type 6: Evidence Questions

In the questions that assess your ability to evaluate supporting evidence, you will sometimes be given hypothetical pieces of evidence and asked which of them is relevant to supporting an argument made in a passage. To answer such a question, you must have a clear understanding of the argument made in the passage and must make a judgment about what kinds of acts, statistics, reasons, examples, or expert testimony would provide strong support for that argument.

For example, if a person argued that dancers experience fewer injuries than other athletes because they are more coordinated, then evidence about the injury rates of various athletes and their relative coordination would be relevant.

Other questions of this type ask you to identify which of several pieces of evidence strengthens or weakens an argument made in a passage. Evidence that provides support for the conclusion would strengthen an argument; evidence that contradicts or casts doubt on the conclusion would weaken an argument.

For example, in the case of the argument mentioned above about injury to dancers, evidence that dancers engage in more injury-reducing warm-up exercises than other athletes would weaken the argument, as it casts doubt on the conclusion that coordination (and not warm-up) is the reason for fewer injuries.

How to recognize Evidence questions

Here are the ways in which Evidence questions are usually asked:

- Which of the following, if true, would most weaken the author's argument concerning *X*?
- The author's argument would be strengthened if it could be proved that ...
- Which of the following facts, if true, would most help to explain *X*?
- Which of the following, if true, supports the conclusion drawn in the passage?
- In order to assess the claim made in the passage, it would be most useful to know which of the following?

ETS TIPS for Evidence Questions

- Remind yourself of the author's claim and the evidence used to support the claim.
- Then test each choice to see whether it provides an example that directly affects the chain of reasoning and supporting evidence.
- Usually a new piece of evidence will strengthen the author's claim, weaken the author's claim, or be irrelevant to whether the claim is valid or not.

Try an Evidence question

In our increasing awareness of ecological health, many industrial practices have come under close examination, and mining is no exception. Though drilling is required in both cases, base-metal mining involves toxic chemical leachates for separating the metal from the rock, whereas diamond mining does not—diamonds can be separated from surrounding rock using only crushers, screens, and all-natural water. Thus, base-metal mining is environmentally destructive, but diamond mining does not harm the environment.

10. Which of the following, if true, would most weaken the author's argument concerning the effect of diamond mining on the environment?

(A) The process of drilling and getting the drill rig to and from the site destroys ecological habitats.

(B) Base metals have utilitarian value, but diamonds are functionally almost worthless.

(C) Toxic chemical leachates contaminate not only soil, but groundwater as well.

(D) There have been proposals to use abandoned mine shafts as garbage dumps.

(E) Logging can be as ecologically destructive as mining.

Explanation: The author argues that whereas base-metal mining is harmful to the environment, diamond mining is not environmentally destructive. Therefore, evidence to the contrary would weaken the argument. Since choice A provides evidence indicating that diamond mining is harmful to the environment, it is the best answer.

Choices B, C, and E may well be true, but they are irrelevant to the argument made in the passage about the impact of diamond mining on the environment.

Choice D may seem at first reading to weaken the argument, but the statement describes environmental destruction caused not by the mining process itself, but by the use of the mines subsequent to mining. Furthermore, the destruction described is merely *potential* damage. Choice D is not, therefore, the best answer.

Type 7: Assumption Questions

These questions will ask you to recognize the ideas or perspectives that underlie an author's arguments. These assumptions are unstated ideas or facts that the author accepts as true or takes for granted. Indeed, they must be accepted as true in order for the author's argument to be valid.

If a person argued, "We could increase student performance if all students got eight hours of sleep every night," this person would be assuming that at least some students are not getting eight hours of sleep every night.

How to recognize Assumption questions

Here are the ways in which Assumption questions are usually asked:

- Which of the following assumptions is most likely made by the author of the passage?
- In arguing *X*, the author makes which of the following assumptions?
- The argument in the passage is based on which of the following assumptions?

> **ETS TIPS for Assumption Questions**
>
> - Ask yourself which choice would have to be true for the author's argument to be valid.
> - Sometimes the assumption is something you identified as a "missing step" as you were reading the passage.

Try an Assumption question

In 1888, just as its hospital was nearing completion, what was to become The Johns Hopkins School of Medicine ran out of funds; the Baltimore and Ohio Railroad, on which the parent university had been depending for money, was experiencing financial difficulty. The railroad's financial troubles proved a stroke of luck for the cause of women's rights. When the directors did open the school in 1893, it was because five women had raised more than $500,000 through a multi-city campaign. They had insisted, as a condition of this endowment, that Hopkins be the first school of medicine in the nation to admit men and women on equal terms.

11. Which of the following is an assumption made by the author of the passage?

    (A) Even if it had not experienced financial difficulties, the Baltimore and Ohio Railroad would not have furnished The Johns Hopkins University with additional funds.

    (B) The Johns Hopkins School of Medicine would have excluded women if the fund-raisers had not insisted that the school admit women.

    (C) In 1888 The Johns Hopkins University was suffering from a shortage of funds in all its schools.

    (D) The establishment of The Johns Hopkins School of Medicine would spur the development of other schools of medicine.

    (E) The women fund-raisers themselves wished to be trained as doctors.

Explanation: Choice B is the best answer. It is clearly supported by the last sentence of the passage: since the fund-raisers had to *insist* that Johns Hopkins admit women, we can tell that the author assumes that the admission of women was directly caused by the fund-raisers' insistence and would otherwise not have taken place. The author therefore makes the assumption stated in choice B.

Choices C and D are the easiest to eliminate because the passage neither states nor implies anything to support them. Neither choice is an *assumption* underlying the content of the passage.

Choice A is closer to the content of the passage, but it is clearly incorrect, since the phrase "on which the parent university had been depending" indicates that the railroad would, under normal circumstances, have furnished the funds.

Choice E is a plausible statement. It may possibly have been true—however, it could just as easily have been untrue. Nothing in the passage actually suggests it—all we know is that the fund-raisers insisted on a general policy of equal admissions opportunities. Therefore, choice E is not an assumption underlying the passage content.

Type 8: Fact/Opinion Questions

Often a piece of writing will contain both facts and opinions, and you will be asked to distinguish one from the other.

Facts can be verified (as objectively true or false) and are often presented in a straightforward fashion without emotion.

Opinions are beliefs or judgments that are subjective in nature and are sometimes presented with emotion.

Here are two statements, both related to music studies. One is an opinion about the effect of music studies; the other is a presentation of facts about music study.

- Opinion: "Nothing can match the sense of accomplishment a young person feels after mastering the basics of a musical instrument and playing in a first recital."
- Fact: "Studies have shown a positive correlation between learning to play a musical instrument and achieving above-average evaluations in other subjects."

How to recognize Fact/Opinion questions

Here is the way Fact/Opinion questions are usually asked:

- Which of the following statements, taken from the passage, is most clearly an expression of opinion rather than fact?

ETS TIPS for Fact/Opinion Questions

- Remember that you do not need to use any outside knowledge to answer the questions. You aren't expected to be able to verify facts with your own knowledge or with reference materials. However, you should be able to recognize pieces of evidence that are *presented* as facts versus judgments that have inadequate factual support.
- Ask yourself, "Could I reasonably argue with this statement?" If the answer is yes, then the statement is probably an opinion. If the statement seems to be presenting factual evidence, then it is probably a fact.
- Words such as "believe" or "probably" and comparisons such as "is more problematical" or "is the best of all" often indicate that authors are stating their opinions.
- Facts often are stated in terms of quantity or measurable qualities, such as dates or numbers.

Try a Fact/Opinion question

William Bailey, an American Realist painter, studied at Yale in the 1950's. His still lifes depict smooth, rounded containers that sit in a field of uniform color. Bailey denies a close connection to Giorgio Morandi, another American Realist, but admits that they share "a belief in the power of the mute object." While Morandi painted from direct observation, Bailey painted from memory. This difference in method makes Bailey's objects superior to Morandi's for they are thus purified, immutable, and mysterious.

12. Which of the following statements, taken from the passage, is most clearly an expression of opinion rather than fact?

(A) William Bailey, an American Realist painter, studied at Yale in the 1950s.

(B) His still lifes depict smooth, rounded containers that sit in a field of uniform color.

(C) Bailey denies a close connection to Giorgio Morandi, another American Realist, but admits that they share "a belief in the power of the mute object."

(D) While Morandi painted from direct observation, Bailey painted from memory.

(E) This difference in method makes Bailey's objects superior to Morandi's for they are thus purified, immutable, and mysterious.

Explanation: Choice E is the best answer because it expresses a subjective judgment about Bailey's objects (as well as about the effect of his method). One might disagree with the statement (and claim, e.g., that Bailey's objects are not "purified, immutable, and mysterious" or that they are so but not because of his method of painting from memory).

Choices A, B, C, and D are statements of fact. Each is either objectively true or false.

Type 9: Attitude Questions

Authors often have feelings about their subjects; that is, they may feel enthusiastic, angry, critical, uncertain, and so forth. The words an author chooses help you recognize her or his attitude. If, for example, an author describes a new invention as "unfortunate" and "misguided," you can say that the author's attitude toward the invention is critical or unfavorable.

How to recognize Attitude questions

Here are the ways in which Attitude questions are usually asked:

- The author's attitude toward *X* can best be described as …
- The author's attitude toward *X* is most accurately reflected in which of the following words, as they are used in the passage?

> **ETS TIP for Attitude Questions**
>
> Look for clue words in the passages. Words such as "successful," "fortunately," and "courageous" probably indicate a positive attitude toward the topic. Words or phrases such as "shortsighted," "inadequate," and "falls short" probably indicate a negative attitude toward the topic.

Try an Attitude question

Parents usually do not insist that their children learn to walk by a certain age. Parents feel confident that the children will learn to walk within a reasonable period of time, when their bodies are ready for such an undertaking. Teachers should adopt the same attitude when teaching children in school how to read. If teachers did this, children might learn to read much more quickly and experience less anxiety while doing so.

13. The author's attitude toward teachers who try to force children to learn to read once they reach a certain age can best be described as

    (A) sympathetic
    (B) accepting
    (C) disapproving
    (D) neutral
    (E) enthusiastic

Explanation: The word "should" in the third sentence indicates that the author is prescribing that, when teaching children how to read, teachers adopt the same attitude as that usually adopted by parents—not insisting that something be learned by a certain age, but rather letting the child do it when ready. The author would, therefore, disapprove of teachers who try to force children to read at a certain age, making choice C the best answer.

Choices B and E can be eliminated because they express positive attitudes toward teachers who force children to learn to read at a certain age.

Sympathy toward teachers who try to force children to learn to read at a certain age is not suggested by the author, so choice A can be eliminated.

Choice D, neutrality, is contradicted by the author's use of the word "should"—which clearly indicates an attitude of some sort.

Type 10: Extending/Predicting Questions

This type of question tests your ability to recognize ideas or situations that extend information that has been presented in the passage. For example, such questions can ask you to predict what is most likely to occur in the future if what the author says in the passage is accurate. These questions can also ask you to use information presented in the passage to determine whether the author or an individual mentioned in the passage would agree or disagree with a particular statement that has not been discussed in the passage.

This kind of extending or predicting occurs frequently in casual conversations. Consider this exchange:

Terry: "Did you like the concert last night?"

Rosalyn: "Yes, but it was much too loud for me. My ears hurt the whole time, and for hours afterward."

Terry could safely predict that Rosalyn would prefer *all* concerts she attends to be at comfortable noise levels. Terry could also generalize that Rosalyn's experience at the concert is similar to someone who attends an outdoor theater performance and finds the spotlights too bright, making his or her eyes uncomfortable. At both the concert and the outdoor theater performance, an aspect of the performance made the attendee physically uncomfortable.

To answer extending and predicting questions, you must do more than recall what you have read. You must be able to understand the essential nature or characteristics of ideas or situations appearing in the passage. You must then use that understanding to evaluate the choices in order to determine which choice is most consistent with information you have already been given in the passage.

How to recognize Extending/Predicting questions

Here are the ways in which Extending/Predicting questions are usually asked:

- On the basis of the description of X in the passage, the author would be most likely to make which of the following recommendations for future action regarding X?
- With which of the following statements about X would the author be most likely to agree?

ETS TIPS for Extending/Predicting Questions

- Make sure you find a choice that is highly consistent with the passage.
- For example, the passage might discuss the importance of providing an enriched environment for children, pointing out that interesting challenges stimulate the development of the child's cognitive capacities. One might predict, then, that children who have been raised in an enriched environment are likely to be more developmentally advanced than those children who have not been raised in an enriched environment.
- Don't choose an answer just because it sounds related and important. The answer choice may in fact overextend the principles expressed in the passage. Beware of choices that are overgeneralizations.

Try an Extending/Predicting question

Carl Filtsch, composer Frederic Chopin's favorite pupil, was once asked by a visitor why he played one of Chopin's compositions so differently from his teacher. His reply delighted Chopin: "I can't play with someone else's feelings."

14. The statement above suggests that Chopin would have agreed with which of the following ideas about musical performance?

(A) The most important element of a good performance is fidelity to the composer's intentions.
(B) The quality of a musical performance can be best judged by the composer of the piece.
(C) Performances of the same composition by two different musicians should sound different.
(D) A piano teacher must teach a student not only the notes in a composition but also their emotional interpretation.
(E) A composer's interpretation of his or her own compositions is not as profound as another musician's interpretation.

Explanation: The passage indicates that Chopin was pleased to hear his student say that the student's rendition of a musical composition differed from Chopin's because the student could play only with his own feelings and not with those of his teacher. Chopin's delight in this reply suggests that he would agree that each individual's rendition of a musical composition should sound different because each individual brings his or her own feelings to the piece. Thus, choice C is the best answer.

Choice A can be eliminated because the passage indicates that Chopin feels that each musician should play a piece with regard to his or her own feelings rather than with regard to the composer's intentions.

Choice B can be eliminated because the passage does not provide information from which to deduce Chopin's views on how a performance should be judged.

Choice D can be eliminated because Chopin's response to his student's remark suggests that Chopin believes that it is up to each individual, not a teacher, to bring his or her own emotional interpretation to a piece.

Choice E can be eliminated because Chopin's response to the student's remark suggests that Chopin would not necessarily agree that a composer's interpretation of a piece is more profound than another musician's interpretation.

Type 11: Conclusion Questions

This type of question asks you to determine which of several conclusions can best be drawn from the information presented in a passage, assuming that information is accurate. In other words, if everything the author says is true, what is a necessary consequence that follows from what the author says?

How to recognize Conclusion questions

Here are the ways in which Conclusion questions are usually asked:

- Given the information in the passage, which of the following must be concluded about *X*?
- Which of the following conclusions is best supported by the passage?

ETS TIPS for Conclusion Questions

- Be sure to find a choice that is highly consistent with the passage. Mentally add your choice to the end of the passage—does it fit?
- For example, the passage might present the findings of research that links an audience's comprehension of an advertisement with the advertisement's effectiveness: at the normal rate of 141 words per minute, listeners comprehend 100 percent of the advertisement; at 282 words per minute, listeners comprehend 90 percent of the advertisement; at 423 words per minute, listeners comprehend 50 percent of the advertisement. One might conclude that especially if advertisers incorporate some repetition of key points into their messages, their ads will be highly effective even if read at twice the normal rate—such a sentence would indeed fit well at the end of the passage.
- Don't choose an answer choice just because it sounds related and important. It may in fact overextend the principles expressed in the passage.

Try a Conclusion question

Scientists consider both landslides and surface-creep movement instrumental in the formation of rock glaciers. Evidence of landslides can be distinguished from that of surface-creep movement because landslides leave a more definite and deeper surface of rupture, partly due to their faster rate of movement. Those studying the origins of rock glaciers have noted that some glaciers are well-defined, while others are not, that is, some show evidence of deep ruptures, while others do not.

15. Given the information in the passage, which of the following must be concluded about rock glaciers?

   (A) Not all rock glaciers originate in the same way.
   (B) Landslides initiate the formation of rock glaciers, then surface-creep movement follows.
   (C) Neither landslides nor surface-creep movement can account for the formation of rock glaciers.
   (D) While the definition and depth of rupture can be measured at rock glacier sites, the rate of movement cannot.
   (E) Further study is required in order to determine the origins of rock glaciers.

Explanation: The passage suggests two possible mechanisms for the formation of rock glaciers (first sentence) and describes the effects that distinguish them (second sentence). Since observations reveal both kinds of effects (third and fourth sentences) at rock glacier sites, one can conclude that both formation mechanisms have been occurring. Thus, choice A is the best answer.

Choices C and E can be eliminated because the passage indicates that scientists believe that both landslides and surface-creep movement initiate rock glaciers.

There is no evidence given to support the conclusion that landslides, rock glaciers, and surface-creep movement occur consecutively. Hence, B can be eliminated.

Choice D can be eliminated because there is nothing in the passage to suggest that the rate of movement cannot be measured.

Type 12: Application Questions

This type of question requires you to recognize a general rule or idea that under-lies a specific situation described in the passage and apply that rule or idea to other situations not described in the passage. Specifically, this kind of question measures your ability to discern the relationships between situations or ideas presented by the author and other situations or ideas that might parallel those described in the passage. You might consider these questions "real-life application" questions.

How to recognize Application questions

Here are the ways in which Application questions are usually asked:

- The information in the passage suggests that *X* would be most useful to *Y* in which of the following situations?
- It can be inferred from the passage's description of certain *X*s that all *X*s must be …

ETS TIPS for Application Questions

- Look for the most reasonable and consistent choice. The principle from the passage must be directly applicable to the new situation.
- Look for a situation that has characteristics similar to those in the passage. For example, if the passage describes the problems associated with trying to locate the remains of ship-wrecks, look for a situation among the choices that has similar features (unknown locations, no eyewitnesses or maps, and some medium such as water that makes finding the object difficult).

Try an Application question

Part of the appeal of certain vacation sites is the solitude that can be experienced there. But as more people discover and visit such loca-tions, demand for vacations at those locations will likely decrease.

Paradoxically, as soon as the sites become popular, they will necessarily become unpopular.

16. If the analysis in the passage were applied to gemstones, one would expect the demand for certain gems to decrease when they became

    (A) rare
    (B) fashionable
    (C) beautiful
    (D) expensive
    (E) useful

Explanation: Choice B is correct because becoming fashionable implies becoming popular, and once that happens, according to the analysis in the passage, unpopularity follows (demand will decrease).

    Choice A reverses the logic of the passage. Choices C, D, and E are not relevant to the level of demand; they merely offer possible characteristics of the gems.

CHAPTER 6
PPST Mathematics

Pencil-and-Paper Version	Computer Version
40 questions	46 questions
60 minutes	75 minutes

PURPOSE OF THE MATHEMATICS TEST

The emphasis in the PPST: Mathematics test is on interpretation rather than computation. Thus, you will not be expected to carry out intricate calculations, but you may be asked to choose appropriate calculations or estimate answers. Many college courses involve some mathematics, but you are seldom required to do long division or add complicated fractions. You are more likely to find very large numbers or very small numbers to compare, a graph to interpret, or a formula to evaluate. The categories tested in the PPST represent the kinds of mathematics that might be encountered in any college course, not just in mathematics courses.

The mathematical preparation expected of you is limited to the usual topics of contemporary elementary school mathematics and at least one year of high school mathematics. The questions come from five broad content areas—arithmetic, algebra, geometry and measurement, data interpretation, and reasoning. They require the kind of mathematical competence that you may need in your course-work or in everyday life.

FORMAT OF THE MATHEMATICS TEST

You will have 60 minutes to complete 40 questions in the paper-and-pencil test. On the computerized test you will have 75 minutes to complete 46 questions. Approximately 45 percent of the questions test conceptual knowledge and procedural knowledge, 30 percent test representations of quantitative reasoning, and 25 percent test measurement and informal geometry and reasoning in a quantitative context. The test is scored on the basis of the number of correct answers. There is no penalty for incorrect answers.

STRATEGIES FOR THE MATHEMATICS TEST

The test questions are chosen from the following five categories, but questions may fit into more than one category. Reviewing the categories will help you prepare for the kinds of questions you will encounter on the test.

Category I: Conceptual Knowledge

This category includes knowledge of order, equivalence, numeration and place value, and number and operation properties.

Each number represents a particular value that determines its place when numbers are ordered. When we count "1, 2, 3, 4, 5, ...," we follow the order of the counting numbers. You should be familiar with the order not only of the counting numbers, but also of integers and fractions.

Integers   Integers consist of the counting numbers, zero, and the negatives of the counting numbers, as shown below:

$$\ldots, -4, -3, -2, -1, 0, 1, 2, 3, 4, 5, \ldots$$

Fractions and Decimals   Fractions, sometimes called rational numbers, include not only the integers but also the numbers between integers. A number line is a handy way to show how fractions are ordered. Here is an example:

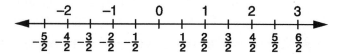

In this example, each unit has been partitioned into two equal parts, and the midpoint of each unit has been given a fraction name with 2 as the denominator. On the number line, you can see that $\frac{5}{2}$ is between 2 and 3 and that $-\frac{1}{2}$ is between 0 and −1. If each unit were partitioned into three equal parts, the number line would look like this:

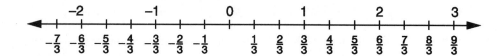

This number line shows, for example, that $\frac{5}{3}$ is between 1 and 2 and that $-\frac{4}{3}$ is less than −1. You should also notice that each integer has a fraction name. For example:

$$-1 = -\frac{2}{2} = -\frac{3}{3} \text{ and}$$
$$3 = \frac{6}{2} = \frac{9}{3}$$

If the units on a number line were partitioned into fourths, we could continue the sequence as follows:

$$-1 = -\frac{2}{2} = -\frac{3}{3} = -\frac{4}{4} \text{ and}$$
$$3 = \frac{6}{2} = \frac{9}{3} = \frac{12}{4}$$

Also, in this case $\frac{1}{2}$ would have the name $\frac{2}{4}$, $\frac{3}{2}$ would have the name $\frac{6}{4}$, and so on—that is, each number can be given many equivalent names. Here is another example that could come from other subdivisions:

$$\frac{1}{10} = \frac{10}{100} = \frac{100}{1000}$$

Number lines can be useful for showing both order and equivalence, and you might find it helpful to try some examples of your own, using various kinds of subdivisions.

We use two different systems of notation for numbers: fraction names, such as $\frac{6}{2}$ and $\frac{5}{10}$, and decimal names. In our number system, all numbers can be expressed in decimal form. A decimal point is used, and the place value for each digit depends on its position relative to the decimal point. For example, in the number 25.36, 25 means $(2 \times 10) + (5 \times 1)$ and .36 means $\left(3 \times \frac{1}{10}\right) + \left(6 \times \frac{1}{100}\right)$. (For decimals less than 1, use 0 to the left of the decimal point to make it more noticeable.)

Number Properties   Number properties include knowledge of factors and multiples, primes and divisibility, even and odd numbers, and zero and one.

Operation Properties   Operation properties include knowledge of the commutative, associative, and distributive principles.

Category II: Procedural Knowledge

This category includes the skills needed to match real-life problems with the appropriate mathematical procedures, operations, and quantities. It also includes finding the solution to applied problems, determining information needed, and interpreting and adjusting results of computation. Ratios, proportions, percents, equations and inequalities, computations, patterns, and simple probability are important in this skill category. Algorithmic thinking—for example, following or interpreting procedures and finding or applying patterns in sequences—is also tested in this category. Algorithms often involve repetition of an operation. The ability to estimate and to determine that a problem-solving method or a solution is reasonable is also important.

Estimation skills are useful in many situations. At the supermarket, for example, you might want to estimate the total cost of your groceries as you shop. When taking a test, you might want to estimate the average amount of time you want to spend on each question. In the case of shopping, you might want to *over*estimate the cost to be sure you have enough money. On the other hand, in the case of a test, you may want to estimate how much time you need per question and then try to work under that time to give yourself a little extra time at the end. Estimating means selecting some numbers "close to" the given numbers. It also means selecting numbers that will make the computation easy, because a lot of estimation is done mentally.

Comparisons may have to be more precise, as when you need to determine how much larger, or smaller, one number is than another, or how many times greater one number is than another. This may require some computation, but estimation skills can help you verify your answer.

You should be able not only to solve application problems but also to adjust your answer if the conditions of the problem change, and you should be able to select alternative methods of solution.

Although you will not be expected to know many formulas for the PPST: Mathematics test, you should be able to evaluate a given formula or equation, or interpret one. As an example of equivalence of equations, you should recognize that each of the following is equivalent to the equation: $2x = 4y + 6$

$$x = 2y + 3$$
$$2x - 4y = 6$$
$$2x + 1 = 4y + 7$$
$$2x - 2 = 4y + 4$$

Category III: Representations of Quantitative Information

This category includes reading and interpreting visual displays of quantitative information, such as graphs, tables, and diagrams; finding the average, range, mode, or median; making comparisons, predictions, extrapolations, or inferences; applying variation; and recognizing connections between symbols and words, tables, graphs, data, equations, number lines, and the coordinate plane.

Many college textbooks contain graphs to represent given sets of data, illustrate trends, and the like. Here are two examples:

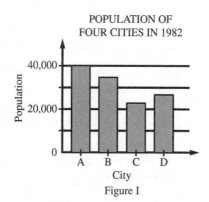

POPULATION OF
FOUR CITIES IN 1982

Figure I

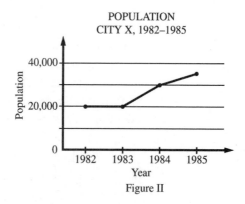

POPULATION
CITY X, 1982–1985

Figure II

Note that an appropriate kind of graph must be used to present data. From the bar graph in Figure I, it can be seen that the population of city B is approximately 35,000, and that the population of city C is less than that of the other three cities. The graph does not show trends, however. The line graph in Figure II does suggest that the population of city X, after showing no change from 1982 to 1983, began to increase. It also shows that the increase between 1983 and 1984 was greater than the increase between 1984 and 1985. The information on each graph could be presented in table form, but a graph provides an easy-to-read, visual representation of data.

Consider the following problems that illustrate variation:

1. If 1 ice-cream sundae takes 3 scoops of ice cream, how many scoops will 2 sundaes take?
2. If 1 person takes 3 hours to do a piece of work, how long will it take 2 people to do the work?

When events happen in a very regular way so that you can predict the outcome, it is sometimes possible to write an equation that fits. In the example of the ice cream sundaes, if every sundae is made with 3 scoops of ice cream, then the number of scoops N will be 3 times the number of sundaes S, and we can write

$$N = 3 \times S, \text{or just } N = 3S$$

Of course, this equation, which illustrates direct variation, would not fit the example of doing a piece of work. For one thing, the more people who work, the *less* time the job should take. Also, it is not likely that all the people will work at the same speed, so it is not as easy to predict how long the job will take even if you know how many workers there are. If everyone worked at the same speed, you would expect the job to take one-half as long if 2 people worked, one-third as long if 3 people worked, and so on. Assuming each person worked at the same speed, you would expect that

$$\text{Time } (T) = \frac{3 \text{ hours}}{\text{Number of workers } (N)}, \text{ or } T = \frac{3}{N}$$

This is an example of inverse variation.

Translating from words to symbols and from symbols to words is an important and useful skill. For example, if Ann is exactly 3 years older than Joe, she will always be 3 years older than Joe. We can express the relationship by the equation

$$A = J + 3$$

where A represents Ann's age and J represents Joe's age.

It follows that Joe will always be 3 years younger than Ann, so an equivalent equation would be

$$J = A - 3$$

The formula $D = 5t$ could represent the distance D traveled by someone or something moving at a constant speed of 5 miles per hour for t hours, and $t = \frac{D}{5}$ would be the time it takes to go D miles at 5 miles per hour.

Average, Median, Mode, and Range   Given a list of numbers, it is possible to find the average (arithmetic mean), median, mode, and range. For example, for the list of five variables

$$2, 10, 7, 3, 3$$

the average is

$$\frac{2+10+7+3+3}{5}=5$$

The median is 3, since it is the middle number when the numbers are ordered from least to greatest; the mode is 3, the number that appears most often; and the range is 8, the difference between the greatest number and the least number.

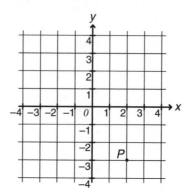

xy-Coordinate System The figure above shows the *xy-coordinate system*, or the *rectangular coordinate plane*. The horizontal number line is the *x*-axis, and the vertical number line is the *y*-axis; the point of intersection of the axes is the *origin*. Each point in the plane has an *x*-coordinate and a *y*-coordinate. A point is identified by an ordered pair (x, y) of numbers in which the *x*-coordinate is the first number. The *x*-coordinate gives the distance to the left (if negative) or to the right (if positive) of the *y*-axis, and the *y*-coordinate gives the distance below (if negative) or above (if positive) the *x*-axis. In the figure above, point *P* has coordinates $(2, -3)$.

Category IV: Measurement and Informal Geometry

This category includes knowledge of customary and metric systems of measurement; reading calibrated scales; using geometric concepts and properties, such as spatial relationships, symmetry, the Pythagorean theorem, and angles; and solving measurement problems, including linear, area, and volume formulas and rates.

There are two systems of measurement in common use: the U.S. Customary System and the metric, or SI, system. Many measurements today are given in the metric system, and you should know the basic units, together with common measures that are derived from them. In all scientific measurement, all units of measure are related to one another by powers of 10. This makes it easy to convert between units of measure.

Metric standard units:

- meter (length)
- gram (mass or weight)
- liter (volume)
- degrees Celsius (temperature)

Common prefixes:

- milli- (one one-thousandth, or 0.001)
- centi- (one one-hundredth, or 0.01)
- kilo- (one thousand, or 1,000)

The standard units of measure in the United States are called the U.S. Customary System. The U.S. Customary System does not use a common factor to convert from one unit to another, so it is important to know the relationships between the units of measure.

Length:

- 12 inches = 1 foot
- 3 feet = 1 yard
- 5,280 feet = 1 mile
- 1,760 yards = 1 mile

Weight:

- 16 ounces = 1 pound (lb)
- 2,000 pounds = 1 ton

Liquid capacity:

- 8 fluid ounces = 1 cup
- 2 cups = 1 pint
- 2 pints = 1 quart
- 4 quarts = 1 gallon

The following chart may be helpful:

Attribute Measured	U.S. Customary Units	Metric (SI)	
		Basic Units	Some Derived Units
Length or Distance	Inch Foot Yard Mile	Meter	Millimeter Centimeter Kilometer
Capacity or Volume	Pint Quart Gallon	Liter	Milliliter
Mass (Weight)	Ounce Pound Ton	Gram	Milligram Kilogram
Temperature	Degree Fahrenheit	Degree Celsius	

To solve measurement problems in everyday life, you need to know what characteristic or attribute to consider. If you have a square garden plot and want to know the amount of fence it will take to enclose it, you will be calculating the total *length* of the fence needed to go around the plot. But if you already have a fence and want to paint it, the amount of fence will have to include the *height* of the fence as well as its total length.

To select an appropriate unit of measure, you need to recognize the attribute that fits the problem and know the units used to measure that attribute. Different units of measurement are used for different attributes—weight and height, for example. These are familiar examples, and you probably know many of the units used to measure each of these. Within each attribute, there may be appropriate units as well. For example, you probably think of your age as being measured in years, but the ages of young children are sometimes expressed in months.

Sometimes different words are used for the same type of attribute. *Length*, *width*, and *height* are examples. These words are used to describe the position of an object in space or to indicate relative lengths. Each of the rectangles in the following figure can be said to have a length 4 and a width 3; the bottom of the box is also 4 by 3, and the height of the box is 2.

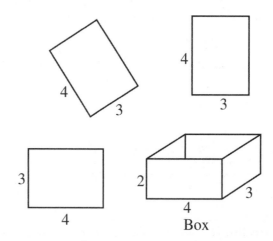

Units of linear measure—inches, feet, miles, meters, kilometers, and so on—are used to measure length, width, and height. Units of linear measure are also used to measure distance. Distance may be measured along a path, such as a highway or sidewalk, or it may be the "straight line" distance, as from point *A* to point *B* in the figure below.

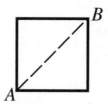

A box that is 2 feet by 3 feet by 4 feet can be thought of as a container with a certain *capacity* (also called *volume*). Capacity can be measured in units such as cubic inches, cubic feet, or cubic yards. If you had wooden blocks, each with a volume 1 cubic foot (1 foot by 1 foot by 1 foot), you could cover the bottom of the box with 12 of the blocks, as shown below.

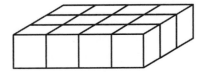

To find the capacity of the box, add another layer of blocks to fill the box, as shown below.

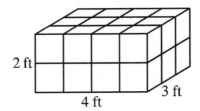

Since two layers contain 24 blocks, the volume of the box is 24 cubic feet.

The 24 blocks form a rectangular solid. If you wanted to paint it, you would need to measure its *surface area*, not its volume. The solid pictured has a top, a bottom, and four sides. The front and back sides of the solid are alike; they are rectangular and measure 4 feet by 2 feet. The two ends are also alike; they are rectangular and measure 3 feet by 2 feet. Finally, the top and bottom are alike; they measure 3 feet by 4 feet.

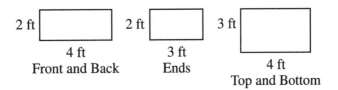

Area is equal to the measure of the length times the measure of the width, expressed in square units. The areas of the front and back are each 8 square feet, the area of each end is 6 square feet, and the areas of the top and the bottom are each 12 square feet. Therefore, the total area of the six surfaces is 8 + 8 + 6 + 6 + 12 + 12 = 52 square feet. We refer to this as the *surface area* of the box.

The lengths could also be in centimeters or meters. In that case, the volume would be in cubic centimeters or cubic meters, and the surface areas in square centimeters or square meters.

Spatial relationships are often important in solving everyday problems. Have you ever had to try several times to get all your belongings into the trunk of your car?

If you succeeded, you probably realize that the shape of the load can be as important as its size. Shape and arrangement may be of practical importance, as in packing the trunk of a car, or it may be important for artistic reasons. As a teacher, for example, you may want to prepare a worksheet for your students that includes charts or graphs. If you do not want the layout to look too crowded, you will be concerned with arrangement as well as with size. Making patterns for projects is an example of a situation in which you may need to be able to visualize certain spatial relations.

Some of the spatial relations with which you should be familiar are those among lines. Two lines in the same plane may be parallel, or they may intersect. Two intersecting lines may also be perpendicular. These relations are used to identify certain kinds of geometric figures, such as parallelograms and right triangles.

You will not be expected to know a great deal of the vocabulary of spatial relations for the PPST: Mathematics test, but you will need to recognize some of these relations. You may have noticed that beverages are now often sold by the liter, that labels on canned goods often give the mass (weight) in grams, and that the specifications for many late-model cars are expressed in metric units. You should know the meanings of the common metric prefixes: *milli-*, *centi-*, and *kilo-*. As illustrated in some of the sample problems, you may need to convert some units. For example, you should be able to convert 250 centimeters to other equivalent metric units.

Category V: Formal Mathematical Reasoning in a Quantitative Context

This category deals with connectives and quantifiers, Venn diagrams, validity, and conclusions, including generalizations and counterexamples.

The term *deductive reasoning* may not be as familiar as some other terms we have discussed, but you have probably had quite a bit of experience with the process, since it is an integral part of mathematics. For example, knowing that

$$\frac{1}{2} = \frac{3}{6} \text{ and}$$
$$\frac{1}{3} = \frac{2}{6}.$$

you can conclude that $\frac{1}{2} + \frac{1}{3} = \frac{3}{6} + \frac{2}{6}$.

In school, you probably first learned to add fractions with the same denominator. Then, using arguments such as that shown above, you developed a way to add fractions with different denominators.

As another example, you probably first learned you could find the area of a rectangular region by using the formula $A = lw$. Then you used this to develop a formula for the area of a region enclosed by any parallelogram. The reasoning is based on this series of diagrams:

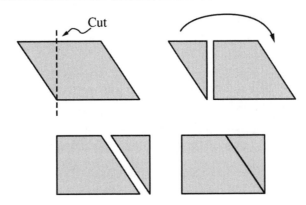

Because the region enclosed by the parallelogram in the first figure can be separated into two pieces that can be rearranged to form a rectangular region, the area can be calculated in the same way. The formula is written as $A = bh$, however, to emphasize that the measurement called the "width" of the rectangle is actually the *height* of the parallelogram and not the measurement of a side. The next step in this particular chain of reasoning would be to deduce the formula for the area of a triangular region. Many people find that following such chains of reasoning is an aid to memory because the chains show how topics are related.

You should note that certain basic assumptions were made in each of these examples, and the reasoning proceeded from them. These assumptions often take the form of generalizations. In the second example, the generalization was that "the area of any rectangular region can be calculated by the formula $A = lw$." As the examples show, generalizations can be useful, but only if they faithfully represent the mathematical situation. Thus, it is important to be able to tell whether a generalization is, in fact, valid. For example, the statement "all squares are rectangles" is valid because it agrees with the definitions of *square* and *rectangle*, but the statement is not valid if turned around—it is *in*valid that "all rectangles are squares." Not all generalizations are valid if reversed, as this example shows. It is sometimes difficult to verify that a general statement is *always* valid, because it would take too long to test every possible case. However, it takes only one false case to show that a generalization is invalid. The figure below, for example, shows that it is invalid that "all rectangles are squares."

Many generalizations are written with the words "if … then." For example, the statement "all squares are rectangles" can be expressed this way:

If a figure is a square, then it is a rectangle.

Sometimes it is easier to test a generalization when it is expressed in the "if … then" form, and sometimes it is easier to write a generalization very precisely by using that form.

Here is an example:

$$\text{if } x > 3, \text{ then } x^2 > 9$$

Note that neither of these if-then statements is valid if it is turned around. We have already seen that it is false to say that "if a figure is a rectangle, then it is a square." It is also false to say that "if $x^2 > 9$, then $x > 3$" because $(-5)^2 = 25$ and $25 > 9$ but $-5 < 3$. You should notice that each of the following is FALSE:

- If a figure is not a square, then it is not a rectangle.
- If x is not greater than 3, then x^2 is not greater than 9.

The following examples can be used to show that the statements are false:

- [   ] is not a square, but it *is* a rectangle.
- -5 is not greater than 3, but $(-5)^2$ *is* greater than 9.

It is easy to assume that when a generalization in an if-then form is valid, the negative of that generalization is also valid. Sometimes that is so, but, as we have just seen, it is not always so. As you study for the PPST: Mathematics test, it can be helpful to follow the chains of reasoning and test yourself on whether the generalizations you find are still true if turned around or changed to negative forms.

PPST MATH REVIEW

The following section provides a review of some of the mathematical concepts of arithmetic, algebra, and geometry. You should use it to familiarize yourself with the kinds of topics tested in the PPST: Mathematics test. If you want more detailed information, however, consult a textbook.

Symbols You Should Know

Some symbols that may be used on the test are as follows:

$=$ is equal to	$\leq$ is less than or equal to
$\neq$ is unequal to	$\geq$ is greater than or equal to
$<$ is less than	$\perp$ is perpendicular to
$>$ is greater than	$\llcorner$ is a right angle

Words and Phrases You Should Know

Integers	the numbers ..., -4, -3, -2, -1, 0, 1, 2, 3, 4, ...
Positive integers	the numbers 1, 2, 3, 4, ...
Negative integers	the numbers -1, -2, -3, -4, ...
Whole numbers	all positive integers, and zero
Zero	an integer that is neither positive nor negative
Odd numbers	the numbers ..., -3, -1, 1, 3, 5, 7, ...—that is, integers that are not divisible by 2

Even numbers	integers that are divisible by 2—that is, …, −4, −2, 0, 2, 4, 6, 8, …
Consecutive integers	integers in sequence, such as 3, 4, 5, or −1, 0, 1; they can be represented in general as n, $n + 1$, $n + 2$, … (where n is any integer)
Prime number	a positive integer that has exactly two different positive divisors, 1 and itself; for example, 2, 3, 5, 7, 11, 13
Real numbers	all numbers, including fractions, decimals, etc., that correspond to points on the number line
Factor	a divisor of an integer; for example, 1, 3, 5, and 15 are factors of 15, but 2 is not a factor of 15 (−1, −3, −5, and −15 are, however, factors of 15); zero is not a factor of any integer
Multiple	the product of an integer and another integer; some multiples of 4 are −8, −4, 0, 4, 8, 12, and 16, but 2 is not a multiple of 4 (2 is, however, a factor of 4); zero is a multiple of every integer
Mean	the average of a group of numbers—that is, the sum of n numbers divided by n
Median	the middle number of a list of numbers, when the numbers are ordered from least to greatest. For example, for the list 1, 3, 3, 4, 6, 9, 11, the median is 4. Note that when there are an even number of numbers, there is no single middle number. In such instances, the median is the average (arithmetic mean) of the *two* middle numbers. Thus, for example, for the list 1, 3, 3, 4, 6, 9, 11, 18, the median is $\frac{4+6}{2}$ or 5
Mode	the number that occurs most often in a group of numbers
Range	the greatest number minus the least number in a group of numbers
Reciprocal	the inverse of a number—that is, one of a pair of numbers whose product is 1; the reciprocal of 5 is $\frac{1}{5}$; the reciprocal of $\frac{2}{3}$ is $\frac{3}{2}$
Exponent	a superscript number that indicates the number of times a number is multiplied together; for example, 3^4 indicates $3 \times 3 \times 3 \times 3$
Square	a number multiplied by itself; for example, 5^2 or $5 \times 5 = 25$
Fraction	a number of the form $\frac{a}{b}$, where a and b are integers $(b \neq 0)$; a is the *numerator* and b is the *denominator*; if the numerator is larger than the denominator, the fraction is called an *improper fraction*
Variable	a letter, such as x or n, used to represent an unknown quantity

Ratio	a comparison of two or more quantities; for example, if there are 20 women and 15 men in a classroom, the ratio of the number of women to the number of men is 20 to 15, or 20:15, or $\frac{20}{15}$
Proportion	a statement of equality between two ratios; for example, if a second classroom contained 4 women and 3 men, the ratios of the number of women to the number of men in both classrooms would be equivalent; $20:15 = 4:3$ is a proportion. Proportions can be used to solve problems such as the following: If it takes a student 2 days to read 1 book, how many days will it take the student to read 5 books at the same rate? This can be expressed as $\frac{2}{1} = \frac{x}{5}$. Using cross-multiplication, we can see that if it takes 2 days to read 1 book, then it will take 10 days to read 5 books.
Percent	amount per hundred, or number out of 100; can be expressed as a fraction with a denominator of 100, or as a decimal. For example,

$$35\% = \frac{35}{100} = 0.35; \ 200\% = \frac{200}{100} = 2; \ 0.6\% = \frac{0.6}{100} = 0.006$$

Percent change	change represented as the amount changed divided by the original amount, or $\frac{\text{the amount of change}}{\text{the original amount}}$. For example, an increase from 100 to 150 is $\frac{50}{100}$, or 50%; a decrease from 150 to 100 is $\frac{50}{100}$, or $33\frac{1}{3}\%$.
Operation properties	*associative* (grouping): $(a+b)+c = a+(b+c)$; $\quad\quad\quad\quad\quad\quad\quad (a \times b) \times c = a \times (b \times c)$ *commutative* (order): $a+b = b+a$; $a \times b = b \times a$ *distributive*: $a \times (b+c) = (a \times b) + (a \times c)$

Some Key Mathematical Topics

Arithmetic—how and when to add, subtract, multiply, and divide; percents and ratios; average (arithmetic mean); odd and even numbers; primes, divisibility; simple ideas of probability; ordering and magnitude of whole numbers, fractions and decimals

Algebra—negative numbers; expressing relationships using variables and interpreting such expressions (for example, formulas and equations); use of positive integer exponents; square roots

Geometry—spatial relationships, such as parallel and perpendicular lines, intersections of sets of points (for example, a line and a circle), and order along a path; properties of common geometric figures (for example, rectangles and cubes); special triangles (isosceles, equilateral, right, etc.); locating points on a coordinate grid

Measurement—U.S. Customary System and common metric units; perimeters, areas, or volumes of common figures (triangles, circles, cubes, etc.); angle measure, comparisons among units of measurement; reading measuring instruments

Data Organization and Interpretation—interpretation of graphs, tables, stem-and-leaf plots, scatter plots, and other visual displays of data; mean, median, mode, and range

Other—reasoning; recognizing insufficient or extraneous data for problem solving; estimation

Algebra Review

Algebra is a generalization of arithmetic in which letters (variables) often represent numbers, and rules of arithmetic are followed. This allows words to be translated into algebraic expressions or equations. For example, "The sum of 8 and another number is 10" can be expressed as $8 + x = 10$. Similarly, the expression $1.04S$ can be used to represent a salary S after it is increased by 4 percent.

Rules to Remember in Solving Equations

- Combine like terms.
- Isolate the unknown term on one side of the equation (for example, x).
- When two fractions make up both sides of the equation, cross-multiply to solve the equation.
- When you multiply or divide two numbers, both of which have a positive sign or a negative sign, the result is positive.
- When you multiply or divide two numbers, one of which has a positive sign and the other of which has a negative sign, the result is negative.

Strategies for Solving Word Problems Decide what information is included in the problem and what information is unknown. Substitute a variable for the unknown quantity. Then write an equation to express the relationship given in the problem and solve the equation.

Probability

In probability problems you are asked to predict the outcome of events. The probability of a particular result is determined by dividing the total number of ways the outcome can occur by the total number of possible outcomes. For example, if there are 3 yellow balls and 2 red balls in a jar, the probability of drawing a red one at random is 2 out of 5.

Geometry and Measurement Review

Definitions of Common Terms

Line	A straight line extends infinitely in both directions.

Line segment	A segment has two endpoints. The part of line l from P to Q is a line segment.

Parallel lines	These are two lines in the same plane that do not intersect.
Perpendicular lines	These are two lines that intersect to form four angles of equal measure, each angle with a measure of 90°.
Ray	A ray has a single endpoint and extends infinitely from that point.

Angles	An angle is created by the intersection of two lines, rays, or segments. The point where they intersect is called the *vertex*. When two lines, rays, or segments intersect, the opposite angles have equal measure.
	A *straight angle* measures 180° and is a straight line. A 90° angle is called a *right angle*, an angle of less than 90° is an *acute angle*, and an angle of more than 90° is an *obtuse angle*. Angles whose measures total 90° are called *complementary angles*, while angles whose measures total 180° are called *supplementary angles*.
Triangles	The sum of the measures of the three angles of a triangle is 180°. *Equilateral triangles* have 3 equal sides, so that each angle is 60°. *Isosceles triangles* have 2 equal sides, giving them two angles of equal measure. *Right triangles* have a 90° angle, and the side opposite the right angle is called the *hypotenuse*.
Perimeter	Perimeter is a measurement of the distance around an object. To find an object's perimeter, add the measurements of all the sides.
Circumference	Circumference is the distance around a circle (its perimeter). Circumference can be found without measuring the distance around the circle if the length of the diameter or of the radius is known.

Linear units of measure	Linear units of measure are used to measure length. Examples of units include an inch, a foot, or a centimeter.
Square units of measure	Square units of measure are used to measure the area of a two-dimensional surface (such as a triangle, square, or circle) or the surface area of a three-dimensional figure (such as a prism, cone, or sphere).
Surface area	Surface area is the total area of all outside surfaces of three-dimensional objects. For example, a box has six outside surfaces—the sides, or faces, of the box. To find the surface area, you must find the area of each face and then add these values.

Formulas you should know:

$a^2 + b^2 = c^2$	The Pythagorean theorem: in a right triangle, the sum of the squares of the legs equals the square of the hypotenuse.
$A = \frac{1}{2}bh$	The area of a triangle is equal to one-half the base times the height.
$A = lw$	The area of a rectangle or square is equal to the length multiplied by the width.
$V = lwh$	The volume of a rectangular solid is equal to the length multiplied by the width, multiplied by the height.
$C = \pi d$	The circumference of a circle is found by multiplying the circle's diameter by pi.
$A = \pi r^2$	The area of a circle is found by multiplying the square of the radius by pi.
$\text{Distance} = \text{Rate} \times \text{Time}$, $\text{Time} = \frac{\text{Distance}}{\text{Rate}}$, $\text{Rate} = \frac{\text{Distance}}{\text{Time}}$	Use these formulas to solve word problems involving time, rate, and distance.

Helpful Advice for Taking the Mathematics Test

Review the mathematics topics, words and phrases, and symbols that you are expected to know, as listed above. Then work on any weaknesses you believe you have in those areas.

If you work through the practice questions carefully, you will probably find some mathematics that you already know, but you may also find some things that you need to review more closely. This should help you organize your review more efficiently.

You may need to consult some mathematics textbooks or other sources for assistance.

You will not be required to identify which type of question is being asked. However, being aware of the different types of questions as you prepare for the test may help you answer the questions correctly.

As you take the test, you should do the following carefully:

- Identify the specific task in each test question.
- Organize the given information in order to solve the problem.
- Execute each calculation carefully.
- Monitor your pace in order to remain on schedule.
- Use estimation as a means of checking your work.

The following suggestions may help you choose the best answer—and remember, try to answer every question.

ETS TIPS for Mathematics Questions

- In a question that involves both decimals and fractions, convert the decimals to fractions or the fractions to decimals. For example, converting $\frac{1}{2}$ to 0.5 may help you determine whether it is greater than or less than 0.7.
- You may also wish to convert given fractions to those with common denominators in order to compare them. For example, converting $\frac{1}{2}$ to $\frac{3}{6}$ may help you determine whether it is greater than or less than $\frac{5}{6}$. Likewise, to determine whether $\frac{1}{3}$ is greater than or less than $\frac{2}{5}$, convert both numbers to fractions with 15 as the denominator—that is, $\frac{5}{15}$ and $\frac{6}{15}$.
- Remember that negative numbers have values less than those of positive numbers.
- Drawing a number line often helps in determining "greater than," "less than," and "equivalent" questions.
- You may not need to perform time-consuming calculations to answer the question. If, for example, you are simply asked which of the given fractions is least, you may see at a glance that all are greater than 1 except one—that one being the correct answer. Or, if a question asks which of the given numbers is greatest, you need not calculate by how much it is greater than each of the others.
- Don't be intimidated by the visual presentation of data; take some time to figure out what the chart or graph is saying before you read the accompanying question.
- To solve irregular area measurement problems, try to visualize the piece that's not there—the piece that would make the area regular. Calculate the area of the missing piece and subtract it from the area as if it were regular; the difference will be the area

---

of the irregular piece. For example, if you have to figure out the area of a rectangle that has a corner missing, figure out the area of the missing corner (use the formula for calculating the area of triangles $A = \frac{1}{2}bh$, then subtract it from the area of the rectangle. You will then know the area of the rectangle with the missing corner.

- For word problems that ask you to calculate area measurements, draw a sketch. It does not have to be drawn to scale; the important thing is that you have a place in which to put the given numbers.
- Remember that some, but not all, general statements are valid if reversed. For example, it is true that "All squares are rectangles," but it is not true that "All rectangles are squares."
- It is often difficult to verify that a general statement is always valid, because it would take too long to test every possible case. However, it takes only one case to show that a generalization is false.
- Sometimes it is easier to test a generalization when it is expressed in the if-then form. For example, "If a figure is a square, then it is a rectangle" or "If $x > 3$, then $x^2 > 9$."

To succeed on the PPST: Mathematics test and many other mathematics tests, you will need to be able to apply mathematics to real-world situations. There are several things you can do to prepare for the test. You can review the mathematical skills that will be required for the test. You can work on any weaknesses you believe you have in those skills. You can study test-taking skills and practice working problems under a variety of self-imposed time limits. If you believe your performance will be hurt by a fear of tests or some other weakness, you can seek advice from your university testing center. Finally, plan to arrive at the test center relaxed and rested so that you do your best on the test.

You should note that no single test can cover all the topics listed here. Only a sample of the topics will be included on the test you take.

GUIDED PPST MATH PRACTICE

You should familiarize yourself with the following directions before taking the test.

Directions: Each of the questions or incomplete statements below is followed by five suggested answers or completions. Select the one that is best in each case and then fill in the corresponding lettered space on the answer sheet with a heavy, dark mark so that you cannot see the letter.

Special Note: Figures that accompany problems in the test are intended to provide information useful in solving the problem. They are drawn as accurately as possible, except when it is stated in a specific problem that its figure is not drawn to scale. Figures can be assumed to lie in a plane unless otherwise indicated. Position of points can be assumed to be in the order shown, and lines shown as straight can be assumed to be straight. The symbol ∟ denotes a right angle.

Remember, try to answer every question.

The following questions are representative of the questions in the test. They are arranged by category here, but they appear in random order in the test. Some of the questions that appear in this section are not multiple-choice questions; however, all the questions on the actual test are multiple-choice questions.

Category I: Conceptual Knowledge

1. Which of the following is equal to a quarter of a million?

(A) 40,000
(B) 250,000
(C) 2,500,000
(D) $\dfrac{1}{4,000,000}$
(E) $\dfrac{4}{1,000,000}$

Since one million is 1,000,000, a quarter of a million is $\dfrac{1}{4} \times 1,000,000$, or 250,000. The answer is choice B.

2. Which of the following fractions is least?

(A) $\dfrac{11}{10}$
(B) $\dfrac{99}{100}$
(C) $\dfrac{25}{24}$
(D) $\dfrac{3}{2}$
(E) $\dfrac{501}{500}$

It is not necessary to perform time-consuming calculations to answer the question. Of the five fractions given, four are greater than 1. Only one of the fractions, $\dfrac{99}{100}$, is less than 1, so it must be least. The answer is choice B.

3. Of the five numbers listed below, which is greatest?

(A) 0.02
(B) 0.009
(C) 0.036900
(D) 0.01078
(E) 0.0601

Choice E is the correct answer. If we write the expanded form of three of these, we begin to see why this is so:

(A) $0.02 = \left(0 \times \dfrac{1}{10}\right) + \left(2 \times \dfrac{1}{100}\right)$

(B) $0.009 = \left(0 \times \dfrac{1}{10}\right) + \left(0 \times \dfrac{1}{100}\right) + \left(9 \times \dfrac{1}{1,000}\right)$

(E) $0.0601 = \left(0 \times \dfrac{1}{10}\right) + \left(6 \times \dfrac{1}{100}\right) + \left(0 \times \dfrac{1}{1,000}\right) + \left(1 \times \dfrac{1}{10,000}\right)$

Which of the five numbers in the question is least? Choice B is correct, because there are zero $\dfrac{1}{100}$s, whereas each of the other numbers shown has at least one.

4. Which of the following numbers is between $\dfrac{1}{3}$ and $\dfrac{2}{5}$?

(A) $\dfrac{1}{2}$

(B) $\dfrac{1}{4}$

(C) $\dfrac{6}{15}$

(D) $\dfrac{11}{30}$

(E) $\dfrac{20}{60}$

The answer is choice D. If you think about the locations of $\dfrac{1}{3}$ and $\dfrac{2}{5}$ on a number line, you might notice that both $\dfrac{1}{3}$ and $\dfrac{2}{5}$ are less than $\dfrac{1}{2}$, so answer choice A can be ruled out. Also, $\dfrac{1}{4}$ is less than $\dfrac{1}{3}$, and $\dfrac{20}{60} = \dfrac{1}{3}$, so choices B and E can be eliminated. To check the remaining two choices, rewrite $\dfrac{1}{3}$ and $\dfrac{2}{5}$ as fractions with the denominators 15 and 30, respectively (or note that $\dfrac{6}{15} = \dfrac{2}{5}$, leaving only $\dfrac{11}{30}$).

5. In which of the following are the two numbers equivalent?

I. 0.7 and 0.70

II. $\dfrac{1}{3}$ and 1.3

III. 4.5 and $4\dfrac{1}{2}$

Examination of each of the pairs shows that I and III have two numbers that are equivalent:

I. $0.7 = 7 \times \dfrac{1}{10} = \left(7 \times \dfrac{1}{10}\right) + \left(0 \times \dfrac{1}{100}\right) = 0.70$ or just $0.7 = \dfrac{7}{10} = \dfrac{70}{100} = 0.70$

II. $\dfrac{1}{3}$ is less than 1, but $1.3 = 1 + \dfrac{3}{10}$, which is greater than 1, so $\dfrac{1}{3} < 1.3$. These are not equivalent.

III. $4.5 = 4 + \dfrac{5}{10} = 4 + \dfrac{1}{2} = 4\dfrac{1}{2}$

6. 1,200 is how many times 1.2?

    (A) 10

    (B) 100

    (C) 1,000

    (D) 10,000

    (E) 100,000

The answer is choice C. You can divide 1,200 by 1.2 or multiply 1.2 by each of the answer choices. You can verify your answer by noting that since 1.2 is a little more than 1, and 1,200 is a little more than 1,000, the answer must be 1,000.

Category II: Procedural Knowledge

7. Which of the sales commissions shown below is greatest?

    (A) 1% of $1,000

    (B) 10% of $200

    (C) 12.5% of $100

    (D) 15% of $100

    (E) 25% of $40

This problem can be solved by computing each of the commissions, but looking them all over first may save some time. Since 15% of $100 is greater than 12.5% of $100 (choices C and D), there is no need to consider choice C; and 10% of $200 (choice B) is $20, which is greater than 15% of $100, or $15. That leaves 1% of $1,000 (choice A) and $\frac{1}{4}$ of $40 (choice E) to consider, both of which equal $10. The answer is choice B.

8. For a certain board game, two number cubes are thrown to determine the number of spaces a player should move. One player throws the two number cubes, and the same number comes up on each of the cubes. What is the probability that the sum of the two numbers is 9?

    (A) 0

    (B) $\frac{1}{6}$

    (C) $\frac{2}{9}$

    (D) $\frac{1}{2}$

    (E) 1

If two number cubes are thrown and the same number appears on both, the sum will always be 2 times the number thrown on either of the cubes and thus must be an even number. Since 9 is an odd number, the sum cannot be 9; therefore, the probability is zero. The answer is choice A.

9. If $P \div 5 = Q$, then $P \div 10 =$

    (A) $10Q$
    (B) $2Q$
    (C) $Q \div 2$
    (D) $Q \div 10$
    (E) $Q \div 20$

$P \div 5 = Q$ can be expressed as $P = 5Q$. Since we are trying to determine what $P \div 10$ equals, we can divide both sides of the equation $P = 5Q$ by 10 as follows:

$$P \div 10 = \frac{P}{10} = \frac{5Q}{10}$$

Simplifying $\frac{5Q}{10}$ results in $\frac{Q}{2}$, and therefore $P \div 10 = \frac{Q}{2} = Q \div 2$. The answer is choice C.

10. Which of the following is closest to 34×987?

    (A) 25,000
    (B) 27,000
    (C) 30,000
    (D) 34,000
    (E) 40,000

The answer is choice D. 34×987 is a little less than $34 \times 1,000$, or approximately 34,000.

11. Which of the following is closest to 0.053×21?

    (A) 0.1
    (B) 1
    (C) 10
    (D) 100
    (E) 1,000

The answer is choice B. Since 0.053 is about $\frac{50}{1,000}$, which equals $\frac{5}{100}$, or $\frac{1}{20}$, and 21 is close to 20, we can estimate by finding $\frac{1}{20} \times 20 = 1$.

12. Mr. Jones discovered that his heating bill for the month of December was \$9.15 higher than his bill for the previous December. Since neither month was unusually warm or cold, he decided that the price of fuel had risen. If the bill for the previous December was \$50.00, what was the percent increase in the cost of fuel?

According to the problem, the cost for the cheaper month was \$50.00. That cost went up by \$9.15. Thus, the problem is to compare \$9.15 to \$50.00 and express that ratio as a percent:

$$\frac{9.15}{50.00} = \frac{18.3}{100.0}, \text{ which is } 18.3\%.$$

13. Two executives, Ms. Smith and Ms. Grambling, arrived at a restaurant, ordered, and were served their meal. A little later, Mr. Lucia, an important client of Ms. Smith's, walked into the dining room. The women invited Mr. Lucia to join them. As they prepared to leave, the waiter brought two checks: one for the earlier order, in the amount of $13.57, and one for Mr. Lucia's order, in the amount of $7.62. Ms. Smith planned to pay for all three meals and wanted to include a tip of about 15%. Approximately how much should she leave?

The problem involves both percent and estimation. The approximate cost of the three meals is $21—about $13.50 for the first two and $7.50 for the third. If Ms. Smith wants to leave about a 15% tip, the tip can be computed mentally as

10% of $21 is $2.10
so 5% of $21 is $1.05
and 15% of $21 is $3.15

The price of the meals plus tip, therefore, is approximately $25.

14. Carlos left Dallas with a full tank of gasoline and drove to Little Rock before stopping for fuel. He purchased 11.2 gallons of gas, refilling his tank. Since he had forgotten to write down the mileage on his odometer when he left Dallas, he consulted his map and found that the distance was reported as 330 miles. Using this information, he estimated his fuel consumption in miles per gallon. What would be a good estimate?

Without carrying out the actual computation, you can probably see that Carlos' car averaged a little less than 30 miles per gallon. If he had used exactly 11 gallons of gasoline and gone 330 miles, that would have represented a rate of 30 miles per gallon. Because he used a little more than 11 gallons, his car must have averaged a little less than 30 miles per gallon.

15. What if Carlos plans to drive 660 miles farther than he has traveled so far? What is the easiest way to calculate the amount of gas he will use?

There is no need for lengthy calculation; simply doubling what Carlos used for 330 miles (11.2 gallons) will result in the approximate amount he will need to go 660 miles (22.4 gallons).

16. As Carlos was completing his purchase in Little Rock, another motorist asked how far it was to Dallas. Carlos told her the distance was 330 miles, and the motorist wondered how much gas she would use getting there. Since the motorist said her pickup truck used 1 gallon of fuel every 15 miles, Carlos estimated her consumption as 22 gallons. What method might he have used?

Because the pickup truck gets 15 miles per gallon, it must use twice as much gas as Carlos' car, which gets about 30 miles per gallon. So, if Carlos' car required 11.2 gallons on the Dallas–Little Rock trip, the pickup should use about twice as much.

17. On a scale drawing of a room, the scale is to be 1 inch : 4 feet. If the room is 20 feet long, how long should the drawing be?

(A) 5 in.
(B) 16 in.
(C) 20 in.
(D) 24 in.
(E) 80 in.

The answer is choice A. If 1 inch represents 4 feet, then the proportion $\frac{1}{4} = \frac{x}{20}$ can be solved for x. By cross multiplication, $4x = 20$ and $x = 5$.

18. If the scale used on a scale drawing is 1 inch : 4 feet, and the drawing of the room is $3\frac{1}{2}$ inches wide, how wide is the room?

(A) $7\frac{1}{2}$ ft
(B) $12\frac{1}{2}$ ft
(C) 14 ft
(D) 15 ft
(E) $15\frac{1}{2}$ ft

The answer is choice C. Each inch represents 4 feet, so 3 inches would represent 12 feet, and $\frac{1}{2}$ inch would represent another 2 feet; $12 + 2 = 14$.

19. In a class of 25 students, 15 are girls. What percent of the students in this class are girls?

(A) 10%
(B) 15%
(C) 25%
(D) 30%
(E) 60%

The answer is choice E. Percent means per hundred, and $\frac{15}{25} = \frac{60}{100}$, or 60%.

20. In a certain class, there are 15 girls and 10 boys. What percent of the students in the class are girls?

(A) 10%
(B) 15%
(C) 60%
(D) $66\frac{2}{3}$%
(E) 150%

NORTHEAST COMMUNITY COLLEGE LIBRARY

The answer is choice C. This problem is the same as the one above, except that here you must first determine the number of students in the class. But the ratio of the number of girls to the number of students is still 15:25, which is 60:100, or 60%.

21. Correct methods for multiplying 399 by 19 include which of the following?

I.	II.	III.

III.
Step 1.
$400 \times 10 = 4,000$
$400 \times 9 = 3,600$

I.
$$\begin{array}{r} 399 \\ \times 19 \\ \hline 3591 \\ +399 \\ \hline \end{array}$$

II.
$$\begin{array}{r} 19 \\ \times 400 \\ \hline 7600 \\ -19 \\ \hline \end{array}$$

Step 2.
$4,000 + 3,600 = 7,600$

Step 3.
$7,600 - 19 =$

(A) I only
(B) III only
(C) I and II only
(D) II and III only
(E) I, II, and III

The answer is choice E. All the procedures are correct, and it is not necessary to complete each computation to determine this. Procedure I is the familiar procedure for multiplication. For II, the procedure is $19 \times 399 = 19 \times (400-1) = (19 \times 400) - (19 \times 1)$.

The procedure for III looks a bit more complicated because it includes extra steps for calculating 19×400.

22. Susan says that the probability that a certain traffic light will be green when she gets to it is 0.20. What is her best prediction of the number of times the light will be green for the next 30 times she gets to it?

(A) 5
(B) 6
(C) 7
(D) 10
(E) 15

The answer is choice B. A probability of 0.20 means that she would expect a green light 20 out of every 100 times, or $\frac{1}{5}$ of the time. Since $\frac{1}{5}$ of 30 is 6, the light would probably be green 6 times out of the next 30 times she gets to it.

23. There are 3 red marbles, 4 yellow marbles, and 3 blue marbles in a bag. If one of these marbles is to be selected at random, what is the probability that the marble chosen will be yellow?

(A) $\frac{1}{10}$

(B) $\frac{1}{4}$

(C) $\frac{1}{3}$

(D) $\frac{2}{5}$

(E) $\frac{2}{3}$

The answer is choice D. There are 10 marbles in the bag, and 4 of them are yellow. Therefore, there are 4 out of 10 chances of selecting a yellow one, $\frac{4}{10}$ or $\frac{2}{5}$.

24. 1. How many 10-foot lengths of rope can be cut from a coil of rope that is 42 feet long?
2. How many boxes are needed to transport 42 plants if no more than 10 plants can be placed in a box?
3. If 10 people share equally in the cost of a gift, what is each person's share for a gift costing $42?
4. If a 42-foot length of rope is cut into 10 pieces of equal length, how long is each of the pieces?

Notice that the *computation* $42 \div 10$ is appropriate for each of these examples. However, a different interpretation of the *answer* is needed for each of the situations:

1. At most, 4 pieces of rope 10 feet long can be cut from a 42-foot length.
2. At least 5 boxes are needed to transport the 42 plants if no more than 10 can be placed in a box.
3. Each of 10 people should pay $4.20 to cover the cost of a $42 gift.
4. Each of the 10 pieces of rope cut from a 42-foot length would be $4\frac{1}{5}$ feet long.

These examples illustrate the fact that in a real-life setting, the "answer" to "$42 \div 10$" may be 4 or 5 or 4.20 or $4\frac{1}{5}$, depending on the context.

25. If $A = 6s^2$ and $s = 3$, then $A =$

(A) 12
(B) 15
(C) 36
(D) 54
(E) 324

The answer is choice D, because if $s = 3$, then $s^2 = 9$, so $6s^2$ is 6×9, or 54.

26. If $D = 5t$ and $D = 20$, then $t =$

(A) $\frac{1}{4}$

(B) 4

(C) 15

(D) 25

(E) 100

The answer is choice B, because if $D = 20$, then 5 must be multiplied by 4 to get this.

Category III: Representations of Quantitative Information

Car Model	Frequency
K	7
X	9
W	7
J	8

27. The chart above gives data about the distribution of four compact-car models in a company parking lot. Which of the following figures best represents the data given?

(A)

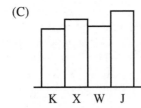

K X W J

(B)

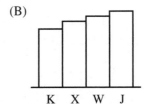

K X W J

(C)

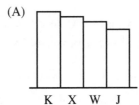

K X W J

(D)

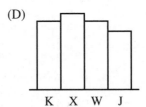

K X W J

(E)

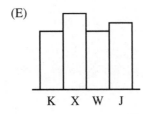

K X W J

The chart shows that one frequency is greater than the others and that two frequencies are equal. A quick look at the choices shows that only choices C, D, and E have both one bar that is taller than the others and two bars of equal height. According to the chart, the frequency of model X is greatest, which eliminates choice C. Model J is second greatest, so only choice E shows bars whose relative heights all agree with the information in the chart. The best answer is choice E.

x	y
0	5
2	11
6	23
7	26
10	35

28. Which of the following equations expresses the relationship between x and y in the table above?

(A) $y = x + 5$
(B) $y = x + 6$
(C) $y = 3x + 5$
(D) $y = 4x - 1$
(E) $y = 4x - 5$

Although you may see the relationship between x and y by carefully examining the values in the table, a more systematic approach may be helpful. The correct equation must hold when each of the pairs of values from the table is substituted for x and y in the equations given. Choice A holds for $x = 0$, $y = 5$, but not for $x = 2$, $y = 11$. Choices B, D, and E do not hold for $x = 0$. Choice C holds for all the values given:

If $x = 0$, then $y = 3(0) + 5 = 5$
If $x = 2$, then $y = 3(2) + 5 = 11$
If $x = 6$, then $y = 3(6) + 5 = 23$, and so forth.

The answer is choice C.

WIND-CHILL CHART

Temp. (F)	Wind Speed (m.p.h.)							
	5	10	15	20	25	30	35	40
50°	48	40	36	32	30	28	27	26
40°	37	28	22	18	16	13	11	10
30°	27	16	9	4	0	–2	–4	–6
20°	–16	4	–5	–10	–15	–18	–20	–21
10°	–6	–9	–18	–25	–29	–33	–35	–37
0°	–5	–21	–36	–39	–44	–48	–49	–53
–10°	–15	–33	–45	–53	–59	–63	–67	–69
–20°	–26	–46	–58	–67	–74	–79	–82	–85
–30°	–36	–58	–72	–82	–88	–94	–98	–100
–40°	–47	–70	–85	–96	–104	–109	–113	–116
–50°	–57	–83	–99	–110	–118	–125	–129	–132

29. The temperature today is 10°F, but it feels as cold as it did last week when the temperature was −10 and the wind speed was 10 miles per hour. According to the chart above, what is the wind speed today?

(A) 10 m.p.h.
(B) 15 m.p.h.
(C) 20 m.p.h.
(D) 25 m.p.h.
(E) 30 m.p.h.

According to the chart, if the temperature is −10°F and the wind speed is 10 miles per hour, then the wind-chill factor is −33. The problem states that it feels this cold today although the temperature is 10°F. To solve this problem, look at the row of the chart for 10°F and find the wind-chill factor −33. This factor corresponds to a wind speed of 30 miles per hour. The answer is choice E.

CHILDREN'S FAVORITE
CARTOONS

Billy Beagle	😃 😃 😃
Sergeant Starch	😃 😃 ◖
Kitty Kitty	😃 😃 😃 😃

Each 😃 represents 10 children.

30. According to the graph above, how many children chose "Sergeant Starch" as their favorite cartoon?

(A) $2\frac{1}{2}$
(B) 3
(C) $20\frac{1}{2}$
(D) 25
(E) 30

The answer is choice D. If each face in the pictograph represents 10 children, then one-half a face represents 5 children. There are $2\frac{1}{2}$ faces for Sergeant Starch, and $2\frac{1}{2} \times 10 = 25$.

MARKET SHARE

31. Based on the graph above, if Acme's share is $2,519,000, approximately what was Beta's share?

(A) $3,000,000
(B) $4,000,000
(C) $5,000,000
(D) $6,000,000
(E) $7,000,000

The answer is choice C. This is a circle graph or pie chart. Because the sector for Beta is about double that for Acme, you can double $2,500,000 for an estimate of Beta's share.

Category IV: Measurement and Informal Geometry

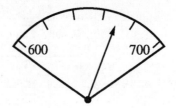

32. On the scale above, the arrow most likely indicates

(A) $630\frac{1}{2}$
(B) 635
(C) $660\frac{1}{2}$
(D) 670
(E) 685

The scale given in the problem shows the numbers 600 and 700, which means that the interval between them represents 100 units. The interval is marked off in fifths, so each subdivision represents 20 units, and the reading at each mark can be written on the scale.

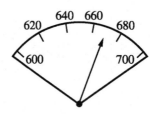

The arrow marks a point approximately halfway between 660 and 680, or 670. The best answer is choice D.

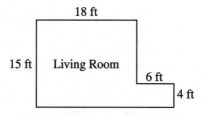

33. The de Falco family wanted to replace the carpet in their living room. The room was shaped as shown in the diagram above. The carpet they liked was available in 12-inch-square carpet tiles that were sold in cartons of 12 per carton. How many cartons of carpet did they need to buy?

The first thing to note, because the room dimensions are in feet (abbreviated as ft), is that the carpet tiles are 1 foot square. You also need to recognize that the floor space can be separated into two rectangular parts. The main part of the living room is a rectangle 15 feet by 18 feet that would require 15 × 18, or 270 carpet tiles to completely cover the floor. The area in the lower right of the diagram is 4 feet by 6 feet and requires another 24 tiles; so the de Falcos need a total of 294 tiles. Because the tiles come in units of 12 tiles per carton, you must divide 294 by 12 to determine the number of cartons needed. Since the answer is 24.5, the de Falcos must buy 25 cartons.

34. On a trip from Chicago to Seattle, the Bergen family drove westward on Interstate route I-90. At a rest area just before Spearfish, Ms. Bergen examined the route from Spearfish to Billings on the map. This is what she saw:

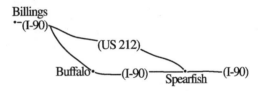

What could Ms. Bergen conclude from the map about the relative distances along US 212 and I-90 from Spearfish to Billings?

An important relation in a triangle is that any one of its sides is always shorter than the sum of the other two. Since the routes shown here form a rough triangle, the route along US 212 is shorter than the route along I-90.

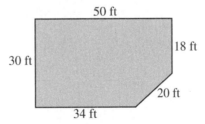

35. Suppose you want to buy sod to make a lawn on the plot of ground pictured above. How much sod would you need?

This is an example of a measurement problem you might encounter in everyday life. To solve it, you must first recognize that it is the *area* of the plot that is to be found. The plot is an odd shape, one for which you did not learn a formula in school, so a bit of work needs to be done. The plot is almost rectangular, but it has a corner missing. This is where spatial visualization comes in, because the missing corner is in the shape of a right triangle:

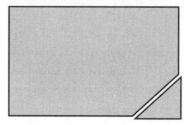

That is, the area of the plot can be found by calculating the area of a rectangular plot and then subtracting the area of the triangular piece. The area of a rectangular plot 50 feet by 30 feet is 1,500 square feet, but what is the area of the corner? You need to recall that the formula for the area of a triangular region is $A = \frac{1}{2}bh$, so all that is needed now is to determine the base and height of the piece. It is a right triangle, so its base and height can be considered to be as shown here:

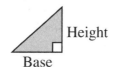

The completed rectangle is 50 by 30, and we know some other measurements:

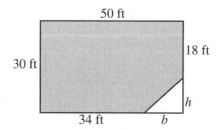

Thus, $h = 30 - 18 = 12$ feet
Thus, $b = 50 - 34 = 16$ feet

Therefore, the area of the plot to be sodded is $1,500 - 96$, which is 1,404 square feet. You should notice that to solve the problem, you need spatial skills to visualize the missing piece, and you also need knowledge of formulas and how to evaluate them. You should also note that the figure of 20 feet given in the problem was not needed for the solution.

36. Ramon wants to buy fabric for drapes in his den. He has one window 60 inches wide. The top of the window is 6 feet 8 inches above the floor. He wants the drapes to hang from 2 inches above the window to 1 inch from the floor. He also wants the drapes to extend 4 inches on either side of the window. He needs to allow 6 inches at the top and the bottom for hems, and he plans to add 50% to the width to allow for pleats and side hems. What are the dimensions of the piece of fabric needed before it is hemmed and pleated?

Without a picture to guide you, this may seem just a jumble of numbers, so the most helpful thing to do first might be to make a sketch. You don't need to draw the sketch to scale; the important thing is that you have a place to put in the numbers given. Beginning with the figure on the left, you can see what some of these numbers represent:

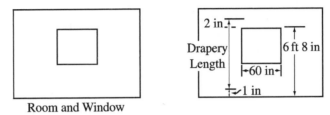

Room and Window

With the help of the sketch, you see that the height of the piece of fabric would be 6 feet 8 inches plus 2 inches (extra at the top) less 1 inch (height from the floor), but plus 12 inches (hem allowance). So the vertical dimension is 7 feet 9 inches. The horizontal dimension is 60 inches plus 8 inches (in order to allow for the extra coverage), or 68 inches. However, you must increase this by 50% to allow for pleats and side hems. That is, the width must be 68 inches plus $\frac{1}{2}$ (68 inches), which is 102 inches, or 8 feet 6 inches. Thus, the dimensions of the piece of fabric to be bought are 7 feet 9 inches by 8 feet 6 inches.

37. About how many cubic yards of coal can be stored in a silo 20 feet in diameter and 40 feet high? (A silo is a storage tower having the shape of a cylinder.)

In this problem you need to use the formula for the *volume* of a cylinder, $V = Ah$, where A represents the area of the base and h represents the height of the cylinder. The base is circular, and the formula for the area of a circular region is $A = \pi r^2$, where r represents the radius. You are given that the diameter is 20 feet, so you need to recall that a diameter is twice the length of a radius. You also need to recall that π is approximately 3.14. You should also notice that the problem asks, "How many cubic yards?" while the dimensions of the silo are given in feet.

Before you substitute into the formula, convert the dimensions from feet to yards, as shown below, recalling that 3 feet = 1 yard.

Diameter = 20 feet = $\frac{20}{3}$ yards

Radius = $\frac{1}{2}$ (diameter) = $\frac{1}{2}\left(\frac{20}{3}\text{ yards}\right)$ = $\frac{10}{3}$ yards

Height = 40 feet = $\frac{40}{3}$ yards

The area of the base of the silo is 3.14 × the square of the radius, or 3.14 × $\frac{100}{9}$, or $\frac{314}{9}$ square yards.

The silo is $\frac{40}{3}$ yards tall, so the volume is $\frac{314}{9}$ square yards = $\frac{314}{9}$ × $\frac{40}{3}$, or approximately 35 × $\frac{40}{3}$ = $\frac{1,400}{3}$, or approximately 467 cubic yards.

38. To convert centimeters to millimeters, you should

    (A) divide by 10
    (B) multiply by 10
    (C) divide by 100
    (D) multiply by 100
    (E) multiply by 1,000

The answer is choice B. Now 100 centimeters = 1 meter and 1,000 millimeters = 1 meter; 100 centimeters = 1,000 millimeters; so 1 centimeter = 10 millimeters.

39. If pesos are exchanged at 600 to the dollar, how do you convert pesos to dollars?

    (A) divide by 6
    (B) multiply by 6
    (C) divide by 600
    (D) multiply by 600
    (E) multiply by 100

The answer is choice C. 600 pesos = 1 dollar. 1 peso = $\frac{1}{600}$ dollar.

40. On the scale above, the arrow most likely points to

    (A) $60\frac{1}{2}$

    (B) $62\frac{1}{2}$

    (C) $63\frac{1}{2}$

    (D) 65

    (E) 70

The answer is choice E. The arrow points to a number that is about halfway between 60 and 80. Alternatively, each subinterval on the scale represents 4 units; so the arrow is pointing halfway between 68 and 72, at 70.

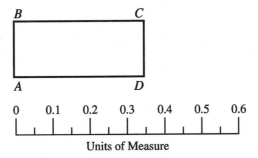

Units of Measure

41. According to the scale shown above, approximately how long is rectangle *ABCD*?

(A) 0.225 unit
(B) 0.300 unit
(C) 0.325 unit
(D) 0.350 unit
(E) 3.25 units

The answer is choice C. Each subinterval on the scale represents 0.5 unit. *AD* extends from 0 to about halfway between 0.30 and 0.35, or 0.325.

Category V: Formal Mathematical Reasoning in a Quantitative Context

Some values of *x* are less than 100.

42. Which of the following is NOT consistent with the sentence above?

(A) 5 is not a value of *x*.
(B) 95 is a value of *x*.
(C) Some values of *x* are greater than 100.
(D) All values of *x* are less than 100.
(E) No numbers less than 100 are values of *x*.

The sentence says that *some* values of *x* are less than 100, which means that there is *at least one* value of *x* that is less than 100. This value can be 5, but it does not have to be, or it can be 95, so choices A and B both are consistent. While at least one value of *x* must be less than 100, some values can be greater than 100, or all values can be less than 100, without contradicting the sentence. Thus choices C and D are consistent. If no numbers less than 100 are values of *x*, however, there will not be at least one value of *x* less than 100, so choice E is not consistent with the sentence. The best answer is choice E.

Now That You've Prepared

Now that you have worked through the five categories of questions, you are ready to apply your preparation to the real test. In the real *PPST: Mathematics* test, the questions appear in no particular order by category, and they are not labeled by category. You will likely recognize the category of question, though, and you can put your preparation to work.

The practice tests in Part III of this book are actual *PPST: Mathematics* tests from the past. You can simulate actual test conditions, take the test, and then see how you scored. Good luck!

CHAPTER 7

PPST Writing: The Multiple-Choice Section

Pencil-and-Paper Version	Computer Version
38 questions	44 questions
30 minutes	38 minutes

PURPOSE OF THE WRITING MULTIPLE-CHOICE SECTION

The multiple-choice section of the PPST: Writing test is designed to measure your ability to recognize correct standard written English, which is the language of most college textbooks and the language you will be expected to use as a professional. You will not need to define grammatical terminology or label particular elements of grammar. You will simply need to recognize what is correct and what is incorrect.

This chapter contains a review course on basic grammar and sentence construction, a close-up examination of the two types of questions (**Usage** and **Sentence Correction**), and practice questions with explanatory answers.

FORMAT OF THE WRITING MULTIPLE-CHOICE SECTION

The multiple-choice section of the test consists entirely of individual sentences. There are no essays or long paragraphs.

There are 38 sentences, and each is the basis of a single multiple-choice question. You have 30 minutes to complete these 38 questions. (If you are taking the computer version, you have 38 minutes in which to answer 44 questions.) You will need to develop the ability to work carefully and confidently, at a fairly quick pace.

Sentences: Sources and Subject Matter

The sentences used in the PPST: Writing test are rarely written from scratch by the question writers. The vast majority are taken from college-level books, magazines, and newspapers.

The sentences cover a wide variety of topics, ranging from science, history, and social sciences to literature and the arts. You should not be worried about or intimidated by their content. Each sentence makes a statement or presents an idea that you can understand without having any specialized knowledge. Do not be put off by subjects that seem foreign to you or names that are unfamiliar. Your task is to understand how the different parts of the sentence work together.

The Two Types of Questions

The multiple-choice section of the test consists of two subsections.

- The first subsection (**Usage**) consists of sentences that contain four underlined parts. Appearing after each sentence is a fifth underlined choice, "No error." For each sentence, you have to determine which underlined part, if any, contains an error. Some of the sentences will not contain any errors; that is, all the underlined parts will be correct. If this is the case, you should select the fifth choice, "No error," as your answer.
- The second subsection (**Sentence Correction**) gives you sentences in which some of or all of the words have been underlined. Each sentence is followed by five choices. The first choice is the same as the underlined part, and the other choices are rewrites. Your job is to decide whether the original is the best way to express the meaning of the sentence or whether one of the other four choices would be better.

An in-depth look at each question type, with specific ETS TIPS for each, can be found after the review course.

STRATEGIES FOR THE WRITING MULTIPLE-CHOICE SECTION

It is important to know what's being tested in the Writing multiple-choice section. The two question types, **Usage** and **Sentence Correction**, are the basis for assessing a whole range of skills and knowledge in standard written English.

The following list indicates the major areas covered by the questions. Each element in the list is covered in the review course that follows. Study the review course to refresh your knowledge of the basics of English grammar, usage, and mechanics.

Parts of speech:
- Noun
- Verb
- Adjective
- Adverb
- Pronoun
- Preposition
- Conjunction
- Interjection

Parts of sentences:
- Subject
- Predicate
- Phrases and clauses

Grammar:
- Forms of adjectives and adverbs
- Comparisons
- Subject–verb agreement

- Verb tense
- Parallelism
- Noun–pronoun agreement
- Negation
- Modification

Sentence fragments and run-on sentences

Punctuation:
- Comma usage
- Colon usage
- Semicolon usage
- Apostrophe usage

Capitalization

Word usage (diction)

Idiomatic expressions

Clarity of expression:
- Wordiness
- Redundancy

It is also important to know what is **not** tested on the multiple-choice section of the test.

- Spelling is not tested. Everything on the test is spelled correctly. Don't be tempted to choose an answer based on what you think is a spelling error.
- Extremely subtle and often-ignored distinctions, such as the difference between "shall" and "will" or the difference between "due to" and "because," are not tested.

You cannot study for the multiple-choice section of the PPST: Writing test, but you can use these strategies to help improve your score.

- "Say" test sentences in your head as you read them. Often, you will notice errors more readily by "hearing" them than by seeing them.
- Use the English Grammar Review below to assess your knowledge. If you find terms or concepts you do not know, practice on exercises from a grammar handbook until you are comfortable with those concepts.
- Edit your own written work, using the rules listed in the English Grammar Review. Decide whether most problems in your writing occur in the area of grammar, punctuation, capitalization, or diction. Recognizing your own errors will help you identify sentence errors on the test.

ENGLISH GRAMMAR REVIEW

This review course covers many of the common elements of grammar and sentence construction you must know to do well on this test. The review course may use some grammar terms that are new to you. You do **not** need to know these terms to do well on the PPST: Writing test. These terms are mentioned in case you want to consult a grammar handbook for more help.

Parts of Speech

Every word in a sentence can be classified as a part of speech. There are eight parts of speech:

- Noun
- Verb
- Adjective
- Adverb
- Pronoun
- Preposition
- Conjunction
- Interjection

In the PPST: Writing test, you will need to know how to identify the first six parts of speech on this list (you will not need to know how to identify conjunctions or interjections). However, it is helpful to recognize conjunctions and interjections because they often serve as signals for particular kinds of punctuation. Let's review the parts of speech and how to recognize them.

Noun   A **common noun** is a word that names a person, place, thing, or concept. Examples of nouns include "nurse" (person), "office" (place), "book" (thing), and "happiness" (concept).

A **proper noun** is a noun that names a specific person, place, thing, or concept; it is always capitalized. Examples of proper nouns include "Ellen" (person), the "Grand Canyon" (place), the "Washington Monument" (thing), and "Buddhism" (concept).

You will need to know when a noun should be a proper noun, and when it should not. For example, "judge," when used by itself, is a common noun and should not be capitalized. However, if "judge" is used as a part of someone's title, as in "Judge Harry Jones," it then becomes a proper noun and should be capitalized.

Verb   A **verb** is a word that tells what a subject does or is. Examples of verbs include "walk," "feel," "led," "is running," and "had eaten." The base, or infinitive, form of a verb is the phrase "to + verb": "to show," "to fall," "to seek," "to read." From this base form, the verb can change its form for one of several purposes. These include the following:

A verb can show time through its tense.

Example:	to <u>learn</u>	Present tense:	Tammy <u>learns</u>.
		Past tense:	Tammy <u>learned</u>.
		Past perfect tense:	Tammy <u>has learned</u>.
		Future tense:	Tammy <u>will learn</u>.

An **irregular verb** does not follow this pattern; the base form changes in different ways. Here are some common irregular verbs you should know for the PPST: Writing test:

Present	Past	Past Participle
be	was/were	(have/had) been
do	did	(have/had) done
go	went	(have/had) gone
lay	laid	(have/had) laid
lie	lay	(have/had) lain
rise	rose	(have/had) risen
swim	swam	(have/had) swum

The following verb pairs are often confused. The difference between those in each pair is that the first one takes a direct object and the second one does not.

Present	Past	Past Participle	
set (put)	set	set	*Set the glass down.*
sit (be seated)	sat	sat	*Please sit down.*
lay (put)	laid	laid	*She laid the papers down.*
lie (recline)	lay	lain	*An hour ago I lay down for a nap.*
raise (lift)	raised	raised	*The glasses have been raised.*
rise (get up)	rose	risen	*The sun has risen.*

A verb can indicate the number of the nouns engaging in the action—singular (one) or plural (more than one).

Example: to sprint   Singular: The runner sprints to the finish line.

Plural: The runners sprint to the finish line.

Adjective   An **adjective** is a word that describes a noun or pronoun. Adjectives are said to *modify* nouns and pronouns because they help change a reader's understanding of a noun. Notice how your image of the dog changes in the following sentences:

Examples: A <u>tired</u> dog sat on the porch next to the door.

An <u>angry</u> dog sat on the porch next to the door.

A <u>happy</u> dog sat on the porch next to the door.

Adverb   An **adverb** is a word that modifies a verb, an adjective, another adverb, or a clause. Adverbs are used to add detail and specificity to the action of a sentence.

Examples:	The adverb modifies a verb:	Dan finished his dessert <u>quickly</u>.
	The adverb modifies an adjective:	The puzzle left him <u>completely</u> confused.
	The adverb modifies another adverb:	The cat climbed the tree <u>very</u> quickly.

Most adverbs end in -ly. They are often formed by adding -ly to an adjective.

Pronoun   A **pronoun** is a word that stands in for or refers to a noun. A pronoun can be personal (stands in for a noun) or possessive (refers to a noun).

Examples: <u>He</u> baked a cake. (The pronoun "he" stands in for a noun, so it is a personal pronoun.)
Leticia fixed <u>her</u> car. (The pronoun "her" shows Leticia's possession of her car, so it is a possessive pronoun.)

Personal pronouns usually change their form depending on whether they are used as the subject (the person or thing performing the action) or object (the person or thing receiving the action) of a sentence.

Personal pronouns to use as subjects: *I, we, you, he, she, it, they*

Personal pronouns to use as objects: *me, us, you, him, her, it, them*

Examples: <u>He</u> fell out of the boat. ("He" is the subject of the sentence.)
Alice gave <u>me</u> the extra ticket. ("Me" is an object of the sentence.)

Possessive pronouns usually change form depending on whether they are used as adjectives or stand alone.

Possessive pronouns to use as adjectives: *my, our, your, his, her, its, their*

Possessive pronouns to use standing alone: *mine, ours, yours, his, hers, its* (rarely used), *theirs*

Examples: <u>Her</u> book won the Pulitzer Prize. ("Her" modifies *book* and thus acts as an adjective.)
Alice took my sandwich and gave me <u>hers</u>. ("Hers" stands alone; it is an object of the sentence and is being used in place of the phrase "her sandwich.")

Pronouns must agree in number with the noun they are replacing or to which they are referring. If a pronoun is used to replace "the students," it should be a plural pronoun (e.g., "they" or "them") because it is referring to more than one student.

Example: General Motors is one of our biggest companies. <u>It</u> has about 365,000 employees. ("It" refers to "General Motors," which is a single company even though the name ends with the letter s. Therefore the singular pronoun "it" is used, rather than the plural pronoun "they.")

Pronouns must also agree in gender with the noun for which they are standing in or to which they refer. If a pronoun is used to replace the male name "Mark," it should be a masculine pronoun, "he" or "him."

Following is an explanation of the most often confused pronouns.

"Who" and "whoever" are used as subjects.
Who is it?

"Whom" and "whomever" are used as objects.
Whom did you invite?

"Its" is a possessive pronoun.
The dog ate its dinner.

"It's" is not a pronoun, but a contraction.
It's not my dog.

Anytime you encounter the word "it's," substitute "it is" and check whether that makes sense.

Pronouns are often used to introduce information about the nouns to which they refer. We call such words **restrictive** and **nonrestrictive pronouns**.

Examples: Bring me the pear <u>that</u> looks ripest.

I do not like *Romeo and Juliet,* <u>which</u> is too sad for me to enjoy.

In the first example, the sentence does not make much sense without the information that follows the pronoun. "Bring me the pear" does not explain <u>which</u> pear is desired. The information "that looks ripest" limits or restricts the reader's understanding of the "pear" being referred to; therefore, the pronoun is **restrictive**.

By contrast, note that in the second example, *Romeo and Juliet* is very clearly a particular play, and the information that follows ("which is too sad for me to enjoy") is nice to know, but not necessary. (The fact that "which is too sad for me to enjoy" is set off by a comma is another clue that it is extra information.) *Romeo and Juliet* does not need any additional restrictive information, so the pronoun that follows is **nonrestrictive**.

Most pronouns can be either restrictive or nonrestrictive without any change in form.

Examples: My cousin <u>who</u> lives in Dallas called me last week. ("Who" is restrictive, because we assume that the writer has more than one cousin and is giving the information to indicate which cousin is being discussed.)

Charles Dickens, <u>who</u> wrote *David Copperfield*, was born in 1814. ("Who" is nonrestrictive, because the famous name indicates exactly which person is being discussed.)

On the other hand, with "that" (restrictive) and "which" (nonrestrictive), you do need to be careful to use the correct pronoun.

Preposition   A preposition is a word used most often in front of a noun or pronoun to identify a relationship such as time or space. Prepositions help provide more details about an action.

Examples: Portia drove <u>to</u> the bank. (The preposition "to" helps to show *where* Portia was driving.)

Josh hasn't seen Ken <u>since</u> Friday. (The preposition "since" helps to indicate *when* Josh last saw Ken.)

Common prepositions include "about," "at," "before," "for," "in," "like," "of," "on," "to," and "with." Consult a grammar handbook for a more detailed list of prepositions.

Conjunction   There are two types of conjunctions: **coordinate** and **subordinate**.

Coordinate conjunctions join two coordinate elements—for example, two independent nouns, verbs, phrases, or clauses. Coordinate conjunctions include "and," "but," "or," "nor," "for," and "also."

Example: I brought a notebook <u>and</u> a pen.

Subordinate conjunctions join subordinate elements to the principal elements of sentences.

Example: I will go <u>because</u> you asked.

Correlative conjunctions are conjunctions that are used in pairs. Correlative conjunctions include "either … or," "neither … nor," etc.

Example: <u>Either</u> he <u>or</u> I must go.

Interjection   An **interjection** is a word that expresses emotion. It is inserted into a sentence or stands alone. Interjections are usually punctuated by exclamation points.

Examples: <u>Wow!</u> Dante received an A on his research paper.

Trina lost control of her sled—<u>look out</u>!

Examples of interjections include "*wow!*," "*oh my!*," "*ha!*," and "*neat!*"

Parts of Sentences

Subject and Predicate   Every complete sentence needs two essential parts to be a complete sentence: a **subject** (a person, place, or thing that is performing an action) and a **predicate** (what the subject does or is).

For example, in the sentence

Raoul has been working in his garden.

"Raoul" is the **subject** of the sentence. Raoul is performing an action (he *has been working* in his garden).

"… has been working in his garden" is the **complete predicate**. It tells what Raoul does. As a complete predicate, it includes both the main verb ("has been working") and any modifiers of the action, or anyone or anything receiving the action of the verb. In this case "in his garden" modifies the action by saying where it happened.

"… has been working …" is the **simple predicate**. It consists only of the main and auxiliary verbs in the sentence.

The subject of a sentence may be a common noun ("book," "table," "lamp"); a proper noun ("Reggie," "Janet," "the Secretary of Education"); or a pronoun ("I," "you," "they"). It may consist of a word, phrase, clause, or combination of nouns ("Tyrone and Laura," "the first person who comes into the room," "the woman wearing the baseball cap"). The **simple subject** is the noun or pronoun about whom the sentence is written. The **complete subject** is the simple subject plus any descriptive or related words, phrases, or clauses.

Phrases and Clauses   Phrases and clauses are both parts of sentences. A **phrase** is a group of words that does not contain a subject and a predicate. "According to Susan" is a phrase.

A **clause** is a group of words that contains both a subject and predicate and that is used as part of a sentence.

Example: If she is late, we will miss the movie.

The example is made up of two clauses. The first clause ("If she is late") is grammatically and logically incomplete on its own. This is called a **dependent**, or **subordinate**, clause. The second clause ("we will miss the movie") is an **independent**, or **principal**, clause. It could stand alone as a sentence, but the sentence would not have the same meaning as in the example, which requires the dependent clause to express a complete thought.

The dependent, or subordinate, clause is introduced by a subordinating word that relates it to another clause. "She is late" would be an independent clause or a simple sentence. Adding the word "if" makes the clause subordinate to the second part of the sentence.

Grammar

Grammar is a system of rules that governs how words are used to form sentences. Grammar can be intimidating because it is often discussed using a highly specialized vocabulary. However, you do not need to know all the grammar rules and vocabulary to identify and correct grammar mistakes effectively. Here are some of the aspects of grammar that are most important for students who are learning how to write and speak effectively.

Forms of Adjectives and Adverbs   Adjectives and adverbs usually have three forms: the **positive**, the **comparative**, and the **superlative**. The comparative form is used to compare two things, and the superlative is used to compare three or more.

Positive	*Comparative*	*Superlative*
big	bigger	biggest
interesting	more interesting	most interesting
good	better	best
badly	worse	worst

Examples: She was <u>good</u> at tennis.
Of the two, she was the <u>better</u> player.
She is the <u>best</u> tennis player on the team.

The used car ran <u>badly</u>.
The ancient truck ran even <u>worse</u>.
The beat-up van ran <u>worst</u> of all.

Subject–Verb Agreement   Subjects and verbs have to indicate the same number. If a noun names a single thing, then the verb that goes with the noun must also be in singular form. A sentence has a **subject–verb agreement error** when one word in a subject–verb pair is singular and the other word is plural.

Incorrect: Birds flies.   This sentence is incorrect because the subject, "Birds," is in a plural form while the verb, "flies," is in singular form.

You can correct sentences by changing the form of one of the words to make both words singular or both words plural.

Correct: Birds fly.   (Both the subject and the verb are plural.)

A bird flies.   (Both the subject and the verb are singular.)

For the most part, English speakers have internalized this grammar point, and subject–verb agreement just "sounds" right. Speakers tend to make subject–verb agreement errors when the subject and verb are separated by a clause.

Example: Many employees at the law firm take long lunches.

Even though "law firm" is the noun next to the verb, "employees" is the subject, and "take" agrees with the plural subject.

Compound subjects are sometimes tricky. When two subjects are joined by "and," the subject is generally plural.

Example: Coffee and tea are available.

On the other hand, some words and phrases, such as "plus," "as well as," or "in addition to," do not make true compound subjects.

Example: Coffee, as well as tea, is available.

The commas around the phrase "as well as tea" are another hint that only "coffee" is the subject of the verb.

When compound subjects are joined by "or" or "nor," the verb agrees with the closest subject.

Example: Neither cookies nor tea is available.

Verb Tense   Each verb in a sentence must be in the proper tense. If two or more actions in a sentence occur at the same time, the verbs that indicate those actions must be in the same tense. Both verbs may be past-tense verbs, or both verbs may be present-tense verbs, but they must be consistent. A sentence has a **verb tense error** if a verb in the sentence is in the wrong tense. Keeping all the verbs in the same tense clarifies when the action in a sentence is taking place.

Incorrect: During the committee meeting last week, Jessie <u>suggested</u> going to the beach, while Tracy <u>votes</u> for going to a museum. (Both underlined verbs should be in the past tense because the phrase "During the committee meeting last week" indicates that both actions occurred in the past.)

You can correct the sentence by changing "votes" to the past tense.

Correct: During the committee meeting last week, Jessie <u>suggested</u> going to the beach, while Tracy <u>voted</u> for going to a museum. (Both verbs are now in the past tense. Verbs in the past tense often end in -ed.)

Parallelism   When a sentence contains a series of items, all the items should be in parallel form. Keeping all phrases and clauses in the same form creates **parallelism** by clarifying the relationship among the parts of the sentence.

Incorrect: Nadia enjoys <u>traveling</u> and <u>to visit</u> friends. (This sentence is not parallel because "traveling" and "to visit" are not in the same form.)

You can correct sentences by putting both expressions in the same form.

Correct: Nadia enjoys <u>traveling</u> and <u>visiting</u> friends. (Both words are now in an -ing form.)

Parallel grammatical structure is crucial for clear and concise sentences.

Incorrect: He was good at English, history, and playing soccer.
Correct: He was good at English, history, and soccer.

Noun–Pronoun Agreement All pronouns and the nouns to which they refer must have the same number; both words must be singular or both words must be plural. If both words do not have the same number, the sentence has a **noun-pronoun agreement** error.

> Example: I tried to go to the <u>supermarket</u> near my house, but <u>they</u> were closed.
> (The sentence is incorrect because the noun "supermarket" is singular, and the pronoun, "they," is plural.)

You can correct the sentence by making the pronoun singular.

> Example: I tried to go to the <u>supermarket</u> near my house, but <u>it</u> was closed.
> (Both noun and pronoun are singular. Note that the verb "were" also had to become singular to agree with the pronoun.)

Negation The negative particles are "not" and "no." The negative particle is placed after the auxiliary verb in a sentence.

> Example: The dog **will** *not* **come** when called.

"Come" is the verb, "will" is the **auxiliary verb** (it "helps" the verb "come" by putting it into the future tense), and "not" is the negative particle.

A form of the verb "to do" often performs an auxiliary function in forming the negative.

> Example: I **do** *not* **want** dessert.

"Never" can be used with the main verb.

> Example: I *never* **want** dessert.

Contractions are common in negation: "don't," "haven't," "isn't," "can't." In English, only one negative is allowed per sentence.

> Example: I *don't* **go** to school.

If a double negative is used, the expression becomes affirmative.

> Example: I *never don't* **go** to school.

"I never don't go to school" means "I always go to school."

Modification *Adjectives* modify nouns, and *adverbs* modify verbs.

> Examples: Her smile looked happy. (adjective)
> She smiled happily. (adverb)

Speakers often confuse the pairs of modifiers "good" (adjective) and "well" (adverb), and "bad" (adjective) and "badly" (adverb).

Examples: Peach cobbler tastes so good. (adjective)

She throws the ball well. (adverb)

He played tennis badly. (adverb)

I feel bad for his partner. (adjective)

A modifier should be placed as close as possible to the word it modifies. It should be clear which word in the sentence the modifier is modifying.

Examples: The copyeditor only found two errors.

The copyeditor found only two errors.

The first sentence suggests that the copyeditor did nothing with the errors except to find them. The second sentence suggests that there were only two errors to be found.

Adjectives usually precede the nouns they modify.

Example: I heard a loud noise.

If a modifier does not have a clear subject, it is called a **dangling modifier**.

Incorrect: As an adult, childhood was a happy memory.

It is not clear what or who the phrase "as an adult" modifies. The sentence seems to imply a subject.

Correct: As an adult, Marty remembered his childhood fondly.

Sentence Fragments and Run-On Sentences

Run-on sentences and **sentence fragments** are punctuated as sentences, but they have either too much or too little information to be a single sentence. Run-on sentences should be split into two or more sentences. Sentence fragments need to have their missing elements added in order to form complete sentences.

Incorrect: A new blender. Absolutely free!

These two sentence fragments can be made into a sentence with the addition of a verb:

Correct: Customers will receive a new blender absolutely free.

Run-on sentences occur when two independent clauses are joined with no connecting word or punctuation between them.

Incorrect: She called he didn't answer.

Correct: She called, but he didn't answer.

Comma splices occur when two independent clauses are joined by a comma. The two clauses must be separated by a semicolon.

Incorrect:	He wasn't at home, therefore he didn't answer the phone.
Correct:	He wasn't at home; therefore, he didn't answer the phone.

Punctuation

Punctuation separates the different parts of a sentence and distinguishes between sentences. While there are many rules for punctuation, we will concentrate on three of the most common punctuation errors: comma usage, colon and semicolon usage, and use of apostrophes to show possession.

Comma Usage Commas are used to separate elements of a sentence. For example, they may be used to separate a series of words in a list or two separate clauses. A **clause** is a group of words that contains both a subject and a verb. Below are the four most common ways to use commas.

1. Use commas between two independent clauses that are connected by a **conjunction** such as "and," "but," "yet," "or," "nor," "so," or "for." An **independent clause** is a clause that can stand alone as a complete sentence.

Incorrect:	Gemma won the election for student body president but Dana has more experience in leadership roles.
Correct:	Gemma won the election for student body president, but Dana has more experience in leadership roles.

The sentence above should have a comma because it contains two independent clauses connected by the word "but" (a coordinating conjunction). You can tell that it has two independent clauses because each clause has a subject paired with its own verb: the independent clause "Gemma won the election for student body president" has a subject ("Gemma") paired with a verb ("won"), and the independent clause "Dana has more experience in leadership roles" also has a subject ("Dana") paired with a verb ("has").

A good test to determine whether a sentence requires a comma is to break it into two sentences where you think the comma might need to go (before the coordinating conjunction). If you end up with two complete sentences ("Gemma won the election for student body president." "Dana has more experience in leadership roles."), then you need a comma. Make sure you don't forget about the coordinating conjunction; a sentence of this type with a comma but no coordinating conjunction is incorrect.

Note: In very short sentences, the comma may be omitted, but it is not incorrect to put a comma as long as there are two independent clauses connected by a coordinating conjunction.

2. Use commas after an introductory element for a sentence when that element appears before the subject of the sentence.

Incorrect:	Before the race started Cliff stretched his muscles.
Correct:	Before the race started, Cliff stretched his muscles.

Some writers do not use a comma after very short introductory elements. However, you should use a comma if the introductory element is long or if the comma would help clarify the meaning of the sentence.

3. Use commas before and after a clause or phrase that provides additional information that is not essential to the meaning of the sentence.

Incorrect:	My cousin an experienced pilot landed the plane safely.
Correct:	My cousin, an experienced pilot, landed the plane safely.

Since the phrase "an experienced pilot" is not essential to understanding that the speaker's cousin landed the plane safely, it should be surrounded by commas.

4. Use commas to separate items in a series. When three or more items are used in a series, commas should separate the items.

Incorrect:	Seth has traveled to France Italy and the Czech Republic.
Correct:	Seth has traveled to France, Italy, and the Czech Republic.

Some writers omit the comma before the last item in a series (before "and the Czech Republic"), but it is not incorrect to use a comma there.

Colon Usage   The **colon** (:) means "as follows." The colon is used to introduce a list or to anticipate a statement. It is also used after the salutation of a business letter: "Dear Madam or Sir:"

Example:	There is one main challenge for the new dog owner: house-breaking.

Semicolon Usage   The **semicolon** (;) is used to separate two independent clauses that are closely related in subject matter. (Remember, an **independent**

clause is a clause with a subject and verb that does not depend on another part of the sentence to clarify its meaning. It can stand alone as a complete sentence.)

Incorrect: Darrell wanted to wear his lucky tie for his job interview, unfortunately, the tie was at the cleaners.

Correct: Darrell wanted to wear his lucky tie for his job interview; unfortunately, the tie was at the cleaners.

The sentence contains two complete independent clauses: "Darrell wanted to wear his lucky tie for his job interview" and "unfortunately, the tie was at the cleaners." You can tell that they are independent clauses because either clause could stand alone as a sentence. Therefore, they should be separated by a semicolon, not a comma.

Apostrophe Usage   The **apostrophe** (') can be used to show that a noun belongs to someone or something. Here are some common rules for using apostrophes.
Use apostrophes in the following situations:

1. To show possession for singular nouns: add *'s*.

Examples: the bird's wing, the host's party

2. To show possession for plural nouns that do not end in s: add 's.

Examples: men's shoes, the mice's cheese

3. To show possession for plural nouns that end in s: add '.

Examples: the dogs' howling, the players' rivalry

Do not use apostrophes in the following situations:

1. *Do not* use apostrophes for possessive pronouns:

Examples: Use "yours," not "your's," to show possession: *This coat must be yours.*

2. *Do not* use apostrophes to make nouns plural:

Examples: Use "ten fingers," not "ten finger's."

Capitalization

Capitalization is used to mark the beginning of a sentence. The first letter of the first word of a sentence is capitalized. A quoted sentence within a sentence also begins with a capital letter.

Capitalization is also used to distinguish proper nouns and titles. A proper noun is the individual title of a person, place, or thing.

Examples: United States
Rutgers University

Nathaniel Hawthorne
The Scarlet Letter
Lake Erie
the Victorian Age
The New York Times

Word Usage (Diction)

Word usage refers to using words with meanings and forms that are appropriate for the context and structure of a sentence. A common error in word usage occurs when a word's meaning does not fit the context of the sentence. This often occurs with homophones (words that sound alike but have different meanings).

Incorrect:	Mark likes candy better then gum.
Correct:	Mark likes candy better than gum.
Incorrect:	The dog chased it's tail.
Correct:	The dog chased its tail.

In addition to "than/then" and "it's/its," some other commonly misused words include "they/their/they're," "your/you're," "except/accept," and "affect/effect."

For contractions ("it's," "they're," "you're"), you can spell out the contraction to make sure you are using the correct word ("it's" = "it is"; "they're" = "they are"; "you're" = "you are"). For other words, however, you will need to learn the correct usage by looking up the word in the dictionary to find out its meaning.

Idiomatic Expressions

Some words take particular prepositions in idiomatic usage. To English speakers, the correct form should "sound" right.

Incorrect:	similar as
Correct:	similar to
Incorrect:	different than
Correct:	different from

You should be able to identify when a certain preposition should be used. For example, dinner is *in* the oven, but *on* the table. A person is *in* love, but *at* home.

Clarity of Expression

Wordiness, redundancy, and awkwardness impede clarity of expression.

Wordiness   Always express your meaning in the clearest way possible. Omit unnecessary words. Wordy phrases should be simplified or eliminated.

Incorrect:	We missed our appointment due to the fact that the train was late.
Correct:	We missed our appointment because the train was late.

Incorrect:	at that point in time	for the purpose of	at all times
Correct:	then	for	always

Vague nouns and modifiers such as "factor," "situation," "really," and "very" can simply be deleted from most sentences in which they are used.

Redundancy

Incorrect:	I was really exhausted.
Correct:	I was exhausted.

"Really exhausted" is redundant because "exhausted" is already an extreme state.

Incorrect:	Combine the butter and sugar together in a bowl.
Correct:	Combine the butter and sugar in a bowl.

"Combine" already means to mix together.

GUIDED PPST WRITING MULTIPLE-CHOICE PRACTICE

Type 1: Usage Questions

In each **Usage** question, four elements of the sentence are underlined. Here is an example:

> The larger fireflies of eastern <u>North</u> America belong, <u>for the most part,</u>
>   A   B
> to the genus *Photurus*, a group <u>in which</u> the males show much more vari-
>   C
> ation in flash pattern <u>as</u> in body structure and color. <u>No error</u>
>   D   E

To answer the question, you have to determine whether there is an error and, if so, where it is. You are not required to specify what the error is, nor do you have to suggest a way to fix it. You just have to identify where the error is, if an error exists.

Note that choice E is "No error." You should choose E if you think the sentence is correct as shown. In every **Usage** question, E is the "No error" choice.

In the question about fireflies above, choice A tests capitalization: Is the continent correctly referred to as "North America" or "north America?" Choice B tests diction—is the phrase used correctly? Choice C tests subordination—does the wording "in which" correctly link the idea "group" to the following information about males in that group? Choice D tests a comparative construction: Should the phrase beginning with "more" be completed by a phrase beginning with "as" or "than?" The error is in choice D. Substituting "than" for "as" at D would make the sentence grammatically correct ("… the males show much greater variation in flash pattern *than* in body structure and color"). Choice D is the answer.

Usage questions typically present specific, discrete errors rather than expressions that may be ineffective. Stylistic problems, such as wordiness and vagueness, are generally tested in **Sentence Correction** questions.

ETS TIPS for Usage Questions

- Before you choose an answer, look at all parts of the sentence to see how they fit together.
- If you see a line under a blank space, it means that you must decide whether a punctuation mark is needed there.
- If you see a line under a single punctuation mark, you must consider three possibilities: (a) no punctuation mark is needed in that spot, so the mark shown is an error; (b) a punctuation mark is needed, but not the one shown; and (c) the punctuation mark is correct.
- The underlined part may consist of a single word or more than one word. Remember, where an underlined part is several words long, not all the underlined elements need be wrong for that part to be incorrect. The error may depend on only one word or element.
- The "No error" answer choice is always E in a Usage question. Do not be afraid to choose E if, after careful consideration, you think the sentence looks and sounds correct. Not every sentence has an error; there are some E answers in every Usage section.
- If you think that an answer choice contains an error, you should be able to correct the error mentally in one of the following ways.
  - You can delete an element, such as one of the words in an underlined phrase.
  - You can change the form of an element that is already there, such as changing *it's* to *its*.
  - You can replace an element, such as changing *than* to *then*.
  - You can add an element, such as a comma.

Try Usage Questions

> 1. The club members <u>agreed</u> that <u>each would contribute</u> ten days of
>   A   B
> volunteer work <u>annually each year</u> at the <u>local hospital</u>. <u>No error</u>
>   C   D   E

The error in this sentence occurs at choice C. The phrase "annually each year" is redundant, because "annually" and "each year" convey the same information. The sentence would be correct with either "annually" or "each year" at choice C. The error is one of redundancy.

> 2. Tennis players <u>have complained</u> for years <u>about</u> the surly crowds and
>   A   B
> the raucous noise at matches <u>,</u> distractions that seriously affect their ability
>   C
> to concentrate and <u>for playing</u> well. <u>No error</u>
>   D   E

The error occurs at choice D. The phrases "to concentrate" and "for playing" are connected by "and"; therefore, they should be parallel verb forms. The correct phrase at choice D is "to play."

> 3. Anesthesiologists are in <u>so short supply</u> that operating rooms <u>are used</u>
>   A   B
> <u>only three or four days</u> a week in <u>some</u> hospitals. <u>No error</u>
>   C   D   E

The error in this sentence occurs at choice A. The correct modifier for the noun phrase "short supply" is "such." "Such" is used to modify nouns or noun phrases, which may include nouns that are modified by adjectives (for example, "such tall trees"), whereas *so* is used to modify adjectives alone (for example, "so tall").

> 4. The school magazine will print <u>those who win</u> prizes for poetry, short
>   A
> stories, and drama <u>;</u> nonfiction, however, <u>will not</u> be <u>accepted for</u>
>   B   C   D
> publication. <u>No error</u>
>   E

The error occurs at choice A. In the phrase "those who win," the pronoun "those" indicates the people who win prizes. But the magazine will not print the *people* who win; it will print what the winners have written, or the names or submissions of those who win prizes. The error in this question is the illogical use of a pronoun.

---

5. Fireworks, which were probably <u>first created</u> in ancient China in
         A   B

order to frighten off devils, were not used <u>as</u> entertainment purposes
                                      C

<u>until around</u> A.D. 1500. <u>No error</u>
     D   E

The error occurs at choice C. The phrase "used as … purposes" is unidiomatic. The correct word at choice C is "for."

---

6. If <u>smaller amounts</u> of pesticide <u>would have</u> been used by the farmers,
         A   B

the streams <u>around</u> Merchantville would not now be <u>so polluted</u>. <u>No error</u>
          C   D   E

The error in this sentence occurs at choice B. The conditional "would," when used as it is here with "if," suggests that a specific action can still be performed ("if only the farmers would use smaller amounts of pesticide"). But the actions of the farmers were completed in the past and cannot be changed. Consequently, "would" is incorrect here. The correct verb form here is "had been used."

---

7. <u>Plagued by</u> robbers, Paris in 1524 passed an <u>ordinance</u> <u>requiring citizens</u>
    A   B   C
to burn candles _ in windows fronting on the streets. <u>No error</u>
          D   E

Because this sentence contains no grammatical, idiomatic, logical, or structural errors, the best answer is choice E. Note that at choice B a single letter is underlined in order to test whether that letter should be a capital. In this case a capital letter is incorrect. Also note that at D the underline of a blank space is designed to test the need for a mark of punctuation at that point. In this particular case no punctuation is needed.

---

8. Diabetes mellitus is <u>a disorder of</u> carbohydrate metabolism that
                              A

<u>inflicts</u> <u>approximately</u> 3 percent <u>of the population</u>. <u>No error</u>
   B   C   D   E

The error in this sentence occurs at choice B. The verb "inflict" means "to cause to be suffered" and is used to describe a step that is *actively* taken by a person or similar agent. (Example: "He inflicted punishment on the prisoners.") Diabetes mellitus, however, does not cause something to be suffered in this way; rather, it is a disease that *is* suffered. The correct word here is "afflicts," which means "distresses" or "affects." The error in this question is one of diction.

---

9. For a writer, the <u>rarest</u> privilege <u>is not merely</u> <u>to describe</u> her country
               A   B   C
and time but to help shape <u>it</u>. <u>No error</u>
                         D   E

The error in this sentence occurs at choice D. The pronoun "it" is wrongly used to refer to two nouns, "country" and "time." The pronoun required here is the plural "them."

---

10. Researchers in the United States say _ that a diet rich in fish oils
                                   A
<u>reduces</u> the <u>amount</u> of fat in the blood as <u>effective</u> as a diet rich in
  B   C   D
vegetable oils. <u>No error</u>
               E

The error in this sentence occurs at choice D. The word at choice D describes (or modifies) the verb "reduces," and because verbs are modified by adverbs, the word at choice D should be in the form of an adverb. In this sentence, the correct word would be "effectively."

---

11. The company is under pressure to sell <u>its</u> assets <u>to avoid</u> difficulties
                                     A   B
<u>in making</u> future interest payments <u>on</u> outstanding loans. <u>No error</u>
  C   D   E

This sentence contains no grammatical, idiomatic, logical, or structural errors, so the best answer is choice E, "No error."

---

12. The famous portraitist ⌄ John Singer Sargent <u>learned</u> the art
                          A   B
<u>of sketching</u> from his mother ⌄ an enthusiastic amateur. <u>No error</u>
  C   D   E

The comma at choice A is incorrect. The name "John Singer Sargent" is necessary to identify *which* "famous portraitist" is referred to in the preceding phrase. Elements that are necessary to the sentence in this way are **restrictive** and are not set off by commas. At choice D, the comma is correct because the phrase that follows "mother" is not needed to identify who his mother is.

---

13. The oldest remains <u>of cultivated</u> rice, <u>dating from</u> about 5000 B.C.E.,
                               A   B

<u>has been found</u> in eastern China, and northern India. <u>No error</u>
     C   D   E

This sentence presents a problem in subject–verb agreement. The plural subject "remains" requires a plural form of the conjugated verb at choice C. The phrase "have been found" would be correct.

---

14. <u>No one</u> is quite sure where the Moon came from , but it is clear that
     A   B

the Apollo lunar samples <u>are</u> very similar <u>with the rocks</u> of the Earth's
                            C   D

outer mantle. <u>No error</u>
            E

Choice D presents an error of idiom. The correct expression for the sentence would be "to the rocks."

---

15. The town council is applying <u>for funds</u> from the agency that
                              A

<u>has been established</u> two years ago <u>to coordinate</u> environmental
          B   C

projects in the state. <u>No error</u>
             D   E

The error in this sentence occurs at choice B. The tense of the verb should indicate that the action of establishing the agency was completed at a definite time in the past (two years ago). You could correct the sentence by changing choice B to "was established."

---

16. Movies, <u>like</u> fairy tales, <u>embody</u> powerful myths <u>that help</u> children
          A   B   C

<u>struggle against</u> unexpected difficulties. <u>No error</u>
     D   E

This sentence contains no grammatical, idiomatic, logical, or structural errors, so the best answer is choice E, "No error."

Type 2: Sentence Correction Questions

In **Sentence Correction** questions, you will not evaluate the underlined choices for a discrete grammatical error; instead, you will look at an entire portion of a sentence to determine how it should best be worded. **Sentence Correction** questions look different from **Usage** questions. One or more words in the sentence are underlined, as shown in this example:

By analyzing the wood used in its construction, <u>the settlement was dated by scientists to the seventh century</u>.

(A) the settlement was dated by scientists to the seventh century

(B) the dating of the settlement by scientists has been to the seventh century

(C) scientists dated the settlement to the seventh century

(D) the seventh century was the date of the settlement by scientists

(E) the settlement has been dated to the seventh century by scientists

---

The five choices provide five different ways that the underlined portion could be expressed. Your job is to decide whether the sentence is correct as is or whether one of the other four choices is the correct way to express the meaning of the underlined portion.

Note that choice A is the same as the original underlined portion. This is true for all **Sentence Correction** questions. If the sentence is correct as is, you should select choice A.

In the example about old wood above, the original sentence is not correct. The introductory phrase of the sentence, "By analyzing the wood used in its construction," should modify "scientists" because they do the analyzing; therefore, "scientists" should immediately follow the phrase. Choice C, the best answer, is the only choice in which "scientists" appears in this position.

The underlined portion of a **Sentence Correction** question may be as short as one or two words or as long as the entire sentence. It is important to read each of the choices carefully. More than one element may change from choice to choice, and if you do not read all choices carefully, you may miss some of these changes.

ETS TIPS for Sentence Correction Questions

- Choice A always repeats the underlined portion of the original sentence. Do not be reluctant to select choice A if you think that the original is better than any of the variations, but do not choose any answer until you have read every choice.

- If you detect one or more errors in the original sentence, you should be able to correct the sentence mentally, and, in most cases, you should find your corrections among the answer choices.

Do not spend more than a few seconds trying to make the corrections before you start reading the choices; you may very well recognize the corrections when you see them, even if you cannot come up with them yourself.

- Don't be alarmed if you mentally correct the sentence but then fail to find an answer choice that would correct it in exactly the same way. Sometimes there are several possibilities for correcting a faulty sentence; however, only one will appear among the answer choices. As long as you can recognize what is correct, you should still be able to answer the question.

- Read all the way through each answer choice. Don't stop at the first corrected element. Individual choices may correct some errors while also introducing new errors that do not appear in the original sentence.

- Remember that the answer you choose not only should be error-free but also should fit correctly and logically with the part of the original sentence that is not underlined.

- Don't be tempted into thinking that you can answer a question by looking at the relative lengths of the choices. A long choice does not necessarily signal a sophisticated statement. It may in fact be less effective than other possibilities because of wordiness or awkwardness. Conversely, don't assume that the shortest answer is as correct as it is concise.

- Once again, be sure to read all the choices before you choose an answer. It frequently happens that a version strikes you as being correct until something in another choice makes you realize that you have overlooked an error.

Try Sentence Correction Questions

1. <u>To try and appeal</u> to consumers who prefer no additives, some food companies are making unneeded changes in products.

(A) To try and appeal

(B) With the intention to appeal

(C) In an effort to appeal

(D) Because they made an effort to try appealing

(E) In that they made an effort to be appealing

The original sentence is incorrect because it includes the phrase "try and appeal" instead of "try to appeal." Choice B is incorrect, because "intention to appeal" should be "intention of appealing." Choices D and E are wordy and present an action, "made an effort," that took place in the past—incorrect in this sentence, because both parts of the sentence need to be in the same tense. Only choice C, the best answer, creates a logical and idiomatic statement.

2. Shunning astrologers and fortune-tellers, she insisted that life would be less interesting <u>were we in the possession of knowledge of the future</u>.

(A) were we in the possession of knowledge of the future

(B) were we to possess knowledge of the future

(C) if we were to possess the future's knowledge

(D) if we possess future knowledge

(E) if we can possess knowledge of the future

The original sentence is incorrect because the phrase "in the possession of knowledge of the future" is an awkward string of prepositional phrases and because it permits an ambiguous reading—that the people ("we") would be "possessed" *by* the knowledge. Choices C and D inaccurately replace "knowledge of the future" (knowledge *about* the future) with "the future's knowledge" (knowledge that the future possesses) and "future knowledge" (knowledge that exists in the future). Choices D and E are wrong because "we possess" and "we can possess" fail to indicate that the discussion is hypothetical. Choice B, the best answer, is both clear and grammatically correct.

3. Conservationists want to preserve stretches of "wild" rivers, those whose banks are still unobstructed by buildings and <u>uncontaminated by wastes in their waters</u>.

(A) uncontaminated by wastes in their waters

(B) whose waters are uncontaminated by wastes

(C) whose waters are without wastes contaminating them

(D) by wastes contaminated their waters

(E) wastes contaminating their waters

The problem in this sentence is faulty parallelism. Two attributes of "wild" rivers are named in the clause beginning with "those whose." Both parts of the clause should have the same grammatical structure. Choices B and C are therefore the only possibilities. Choice C is awkward, and "them" does not have a clear referent (it could refer to "waters" or "banks"). Choice B, "whose waters are uncontaminated by wastes," has the same grammatical structure as the first part of the clause, "whose banks are still unobstructed by buildings," and is clear and correct.

4. The fact that some mushrooms are perfectly safe for one person <u>but not for another</u> probably accounts for differences of opinion as to which species are edible and which are not.

(A) but not for another

(B) but not for the other

(C) and not for the other

(D) and unsafe for some other

(E) and some are unsafe for others

The original sentence is clear and grammatically correct. Therefore choice A is the correct answer. Choices B, C, and D change "another" to "the other" or "some other," suggesting incorrectly that one particular person is being discussed. In choices C, D, and E the appropriate conjunction "but" is changed to "and."

5. In the celery fields of Florida, <u>chameleons are welcome by the growers: they</u> feed upon caterpillars and moths.

(A) chameleons are welcome by the growers, they

(B) the chameleon is welcome to the growers, since they

(C) the chameleons are welcomed by the growers, since they

(D) the growers are welcoming of chameleons, which

(E) the growers welcome chameleons, which

The original sentence is incorrect and confusing. The phrase "are welcome by" is wrong (it should be "are welcomed by"). In addition, it is not clear whether the pronoun "they" refers to the chameleons or the growers. Choices B and C are wrong because the noun referent of the pronoun "they" is still "growers" instead of "chameleons." Choices D and E are correct with regard to the referent, but D uses an unidiomatic form of "welcome." Choice E, the best answer, is clear, idiomatic, and grammatically correct.

6. Martin Luther King, Jr., <u>spoke out passionately</u> for the poor of all races.

(A) spoke out passionately

(B) spoke out passionate

(C) did speak out passionate

(D) has spoke out passionately

(E) had spoken out passionate

This sentence presents no problem of structure or logic. The verb tense is correct, and the use of the adverb "passionately" is also correct in this context. In choices

B, C, and E, the adjective "passionate" is incorrectly used instead of the adverb. Choice D, while it uses the correct adverb, introduces an incorrect verb form, "has spoke out." Thus, the best answer is choice A.

7. The king preferred accepting the republican flag <u>than giving</u> up the throne altogether.

(A) than giving
(B) than to giving
(C) than to give
(D) rather than give
(E) to giving

The correct form for this kind of comparative statement is "preferred *X* to *Y*." Choices B, C, and E have the correct "to," but choices B and C can be eliminated because they add "than" before the "to." Only choice E, the best answer, presents the correct construction.

8. <u>The agent, passing through the crowd without being noticed by hardly anyone.</u>

(A) The agent, passing through the crowd without being noticed by hardly anyone.
(B) The agent passed through the crowd without hardly being noticed by anyone.
(C) The agent's passing through the crowd was not hardly noticed by anyone.
(D) No one hardly noticed how the agent passed through the crowd.
(E) The agent was hardly noticed as she passed through the crowd.

This sentence presents two major problems: it is not a complete sentence and the phrase "without … hardly" is not idiomatic. Although choices B, C, and D are complete sentences, each retains the problem of using "hardly" in an unidiomatic construction. The best correction is choice E.

9. <u>As a consumer, one can accept</u> the goods offered to us or we can reject them, but we cannot determine their quality or change the system's priorities.

(A) As a consumer, one can accept
(B) We the consumer either can accept
(C) The consumer can accept
(D) Either the consumer accepts
(E) As consumers, we can accept

The main problem in this sentence concerns agreement in pronoun number. In the portion of the sentence that is not underlined, the first person plural, "we," is used as the subject of the second part of the compound sentence. The underlined portion of the sentence is therefore wrong in the original, since it uses the singular "consumer" and the singular pronoun "one." To create a sentence free of agreement faults, you must look for a choice that contains "we" and the plural of "consumer." Choice E is the only one that corrects the agreement problem and has a phrase parallel to "we can reject them."

---

10. Since 1977, Mexico has <u>had a building code comparable to California</u>.

(A) had a building code comparable to California

(B) had a building code comparable to that of California

(C) had a building code that is similar to California

(D) a building code comparable to California's

(E) a building code comparable to that of California's

This sentence is correct in its verb tense (present perfect tense, "has had"), but it illogically compares Mexico's building code to the whole state of California rather than to California's building code. Choices D and E are wrong because they use the simple present tense, "has," alone. Choice C preserves the illogical comparison. Choice B correctly uses "has had" and creates a logical comparison.

---

11. <u>That its collection of ancient manuscripts can be preserved</u>, the museum keeps them in a room where temperature and humidity are carefully controlled.

(A) That its collection of ancient manuscripts can be preserved

(B) So they can preserve the collection of ancient manuscripts

(C) For preserving its collection of ancient manuscripts

(D) In order that they can preserve the collection of ancient manuscripts

(E) To preserve its collection of ancient manuscripts

This sentence presents an awkward and unidiomatic expression but is correct in that the pronoun "its" agrees with the singular noun "museum." Choices B and D have pronoun reference agreement problems: the plural pronoun "they" doesn't match the singular noun "museum." Between choices C and E, choice E presents the clearer and more idiomatic expression.

12. The flow of the Hudson River was so reduced by the drought of 1985 that salt water borne on ocean tides moved upstream to within six miles of Poughkeepsie, New York.

(A) The flow of the Hudson River was so reduced by the drought of 1985 that

(B) So reduced was the flow of the Hudson River by the drought of 1985 as to make

(C) The drought of 1985 made such a reduction of the flow of the Hudson River that

(D) Of such a reduction was the flow of the Hudson River by the drought of 1985 that

(E) There was such a reduction of the flow of the Hudson River by the drought of 1985 as to make

The original sentence is correct; therefore, choice A is the answer. Choices B, C, D, and E are unidiomatic, wordy, and awkward.

---

13. Neon glows red-orange upon placing it in a glass tube and charged with electricity.

(A) upon placing it

(B) when placed

(C) as placed

(D) on its placement

(E) after placement

This sentence suffers from lack of parallelism. Both verbs in the sentence ("place" and "charge") should be in the same form. Choices B and C use correct forms of "place," but the "as" in choice C is unidiomatic. Choice B is best.

---

14. The conflict between somatic and psychological interpretations of mental disorder rage as noisily as ever, and each side make tragic errors of diagnosis and treatment.

(A) rage as noisily as ever, and each side make

(B) rage as noisily as ever, and each side makes

(C) rages as noisily as ever, and each side make

(D) rages as noisily as ever, with each side making

(E) have raged as noisily as ever, with each side making

There are two subject–verb agreement errors in the original sentence. The subject of the first part of the sentence is "conflict," a singular noun. The correct form of the conjugated verb is "rages." Therefore, "rage" in choices A and B and "have raged" in choice E (which also inappropriately changes the tense of the verb) are all wrong. The second part of choice C contains a second subject–verb agreement error (it should be "each side *makes*"). Only choice D avoids errors in subject–verb agreement in both parts of the sentence. Therefore, choice D is the best answer.

---

15. Jazz is a rigorous and <u>technical demanding music, deeply affecting such composers like Stravinsky and Gershwin</u>.

(A) technical demanding music, deeply affecting such composers like Stravinsky and Gershwin

(B) technical demanding music, one that deeply affected such composers like Stravinsky and Gershwin

(C) technically demanding music, which deeply affected such composers like Stravinsky and Gershwin

(D) technically demanding music, and such composers as Stravinsky and Gershwin were being deeply affected by it

(E) technically demanding music, one that deeply affected such composers as Stravinsky and Gershwin

---

In the original sentence there are two errors. The first is the word "technical": since it modifies an adjective ("demanding"), it should be in adverbial form ("technically," as in choices C, D, and E). The second error is "like" (preceded by "such"): the correct modifier is "as." Choices D and E use "as," but choice D is awkward and also uses the past progressive tense unidiomatically. Choice E, which is clear as well as grammatically and idiomatically correct, is the best answer.

CHAPTER 8

PPST Writing: The Essay

30 minutes

PURPOSE AND FORMAT OF THE ESSAY

The essay counts toward one-half of your score on the PPST: Writing test, so it is crucial that you maximize your success on this section. Of all parts of the three PPST tests, you have probably had the most experience with the essay format. The purpose of the examination is to test your ability to write effectively within a limited time. The term "writing sample" is often used to describe the kind of writing you will be asked to produce, and it is useful to think of your response in this way. If you were trying out for a part in a play or for a sports team, you might be asked to read a small section of dialogue or to demonstrate some aspect of your athletic skills. Your overall ability would be evaluated on the basis of samples of what you can do. The writing sample works in the same way. You are not expected to turn out a well-researched, comprehensive essay about a highly specific, specialized topic.

This chapter discusses the scoring criteria and offers some strategies for using your time effectively during the test. The chapter also includes a list of 71 sample essay topics that show the kind of topics you will encounter when you take the test.

OVERVIEW OF THE ESSAY SECTION

In the essay section of the PPST: Writing test, you have 30 minutes to write on an assigned topic. Thirty minutes should allow you sufficient time to read the topic carefully, organize your thoughts prior to writing, write a draft with reasonable care and precision, and briefly check over your response. Note that the result is considered a *draft*, not the kind of highly polished document you would be expected to produce if you were given the assignment to do as homework.

After your draft essay is returned to ETS, it will be evaluated by experienced teachers of writing. Every essay is graded by at least two scorers, neither of whom knows what score the other has given. Each scorer gives a score ranging from 1 (low) to 6 (high). (Essays that do not respond to the specified topic are given a score of 0, regardless of the quality of the writing.) If the two scorers differ by more than one point in the score they assign, the essay is scored independently by a third scorer, who is not given any information about what other scores the essay has received. Your essay score is then combined with your multiple-choice Writing score to give you a total PPST: Writing score.

HOW THE ESSAY IS SCORED

The easiest way to find out what skills are being tested in the essay portion of the test is to look at the PPST: Writing scoring guide below, which scorers use to assign a score of 1 to 6 to each paper. You should also look at the sample essays and scorers' comments included at the end of this chapter.

The ETS Scoring Guide

Here is the official ETS scoring guide used by the PPST: Writing essay scorers:

---

6 A 6 essay demonstrates a *high degree of competence* in response to the assignment but may have a few minor errors.

An essay in this category
- states or clearly implies the writer's position or thesis
- organizes and develops ideas logically, making insightful connections between them
- clearly explains key ideas, supporting them with well-chosen reasons, examples, or details
- displays effective sentence variety
- clearly displays facility in the use of language
- is generally free from errors in grammar, usage, and mechanics

5 A 5 essay demonstrates *clear competence* in response to the assignment but may have minor errors.

An essay in this category
- states or clearly implies the writer's position or thesis
- organizes and develops ideas clearly, making connections between them
- explains key ideas, supporting them with relevant reasons, examples, or details
- displays some sentence variety
- displays facility in the use of language
- is generally free from errors in grammar, usage, and mechanics

4 A 4 essay demonstrates *competence* in response to the assignment. An essay in this category
- states or implies the writer's position or thesis
- shows control in the organization and development of ideas
- explains some key ideas, supporting them with adequate reasons, examples, or details
- displays adequate use of language
- shows control of grammar, usage, and mechanics, but may display errors

---

3 A 3 essay demonstrates *some competence* in response to the assignment but is obviously flawed. An essay in this category reveals *one or more* of the following weaknesses:
- limitation in stating or implying a position or thesis
- limited control in the organization and development of ideas
- inadequate reasons, examples, or details to explain key ideas
- an accumulation of errors in the use of language
- an accumulation of errors in grammar, usage, and mechanics

2 A 2 essay is *seriously flawed*.

An essay in this category reveals *one or more* of the following weaknesses:
- no clear position or thesis
- weak organization or very little development
- few or no relevant reasons, examples, or details
- frequent serious errors in the use of language
- frequent serious errors in grammar, usage, and mechanics

1 A 1 essay demonstrates *fundamental deficiencies* in writing skills.

An essay in this category
- contains serious and persistent writing errors, or
- is incoherent, or
- is undeveloped

0 A 0 essay is off topic; that is, it is not a response to the topic specified.

STRATEGIES FOR WRITING YOUR ESSAY

While you are preparing for the test, maximize your chances for success by focusing on the same characteristics that the scorers look for when scoring the essays. To help you do this, let's closely dissect the scoring guide—that's where the strategies for success lie.

Strategy 1: Respond to the Specific Topic

In the scoring guide, the characteristics of a "6-point" versus a "1-point" essay are described in terms of the degree of competence the writer shows in *responding to the assignment*. Notice the description of a score of zero: "not a response to the specified topic." This is the goal of strategy 1: staying focused on the exact question being asked. It sounds simple, but this focus is critical for success.

Strategy 2: State Your Position Clearly

The first bullet under the description of each score point, from 6 to 1, makes it clear that responses with higher scores *state their position or thesis clearly*. As you will see in the next section of this chapter, the essay assignment in PPST: Writing always involves stating to what extent you agree or disagree with a given statement. The scoring guide specifies that it is critical to make sure you communicate clearly whether or not to what extent you agree or disagree—don't leave the reader guessing.

Strategy 3: Organize Your Essay Before You Write

The second bullet under the description of each score point addresses *organization* and *development*. You should strive for logical organization, not just a loose collection of ideas. You might consider taking a few minutes to make an outline or notes before you write.

Strategy 4: Create a Logical Flow from Idea to Idea

In addition to organization, you must consider the development of ideas within your draft. Think about the logical flow from idea to idea. A reader should be able to predict where you are going from where you have been. You should consider using transition phrases to link ideas both within and between paragraphs.

Strategy 5: Develop Each Key Idea with Examples or Clarifying Statements

The third bullet under the description of each score point mentions the use of reasons, examples, or details. Depending on the topic you're given and the arguments you're making, this could take the form of particular examples (such as, "For example, there are literally thousands of species of spiders") or clarifying explanations (such as, "The enforcement of such a policy would put an undue burden on teachers, who already have a great many responsibilities to attend to during the school day"). Be alert for opportunities to expand your key ideas or provide specific details or examples.

Strategy 6: Use Variety in Sentence Construction

The fourth bullet under the two highest score points refers to "sentence variety." This means that in high-scoring papers, the sentences are not all structured in the same way. Try to vary the length and type of sentences. For example, don't start every sentence with "There is …." Transition words and phrases (*Finally, At the same time*) can add variety to your sentence beginnings. You might begin some sentences with modifying phrases (such as, "Remaining true to their profession, teachers often…"). Consider occasionally combining simple sentences in order to vary the length and rhythm of your sentences.

Strategy 7: Follow the Rules of Standard Written English

The remaining bullets encompass the large territory known as "correct written English." This means correct subject-verb agreement, correct use of modifiers, correct parallelism, correct idiomatic expressions, and so on—all the elements discussed earlier in Chapter 7. Try to get these elements correct, especially as you look through your draft before turning in your test. However, do not sacrifice organization, development, details, and sentence variety by spending all your time thinking about mechanics.

Now that you have considered the strategies, let's examine the types of topics to which you'll apply the strategies.

THE ESSAY TOPICS

ETS has published the list of topics that is printed below. One of these exact topics, or a similar topic, will be presented to you when you take the test. This is the official ETS list of essay topics, so it makes sense to examine it carefully.

The format for every essay question is the same: you will be asked to discuss the extent to which you *agree* or *disagree* with the opinion presented in the topic and to *support your position* with specific reasons and examples from your own experience, observations, or reading.

It does not matter whether you agree or disagree with the topic. The scorers are trained to accept all varieties of opinions. What matters are the skills we've discussed in the section above: taking a clear stand that responds directly to the question and writing a draft essay that is characterized by good organization, complete development, sentence variety, and correct written English.

None of the topics requires specialized academic knowledge. Most topics are general and are based on common educational experiences or issues of public concern. Don't be intimidated by the topic. Just decide quickly whether or to what extent you agree or disagree with the statement, and then begin working on your essay.

What should you do with this list of 71 topics? To prepare for the essay portion of the test, you should practice writing essays in response to these topics. Try to make your practice conditions as much like the actual testing conditions as possible. Make sure to time yourself, giving yourself 30 minutes to read a question and write a response. After you complete an essay, read it over and compare it with the scoring guide. Better yet, have a friend, professor, or teacher evaluate the essay against the scoring criteria and give you feedback. Identify the skills with which you have trouble, and try to practice them in future writing. Composition professors and staff at college writing labs can also recommend useful textbooks on how to improve your writing.

Here are the official directions that precede each topic in the test:

Read the opinion stated below. Discuss the extent to which you agree or disagree with this point of view. Support your position with specific reasons and examples from your own experience, observations, or reading.

Each of the following 71 topics is an opinion statement. You will be asked to agree or disagree with one of them (or a statement like one of them) when you take the PPST: Writing test.

1. "Celebrities have a tremendous influence on the young, and for that reason, they have a responsibility to act as role models."
2. "Our society is overly materialistic. We center our lives on acquiring material things at the expense of such traditional values as family and education."
3. "Censorship of song lyrics, television shows, and offensive speech is necessary in order to protect the rights of all members of society."
4. "Young people who attend college immediately after high school often lack a clear sense of direction and seriousness about learning. Before hurrying into college, it's better to get a taste of the real world by working or serving in the military for a few years."
5. "Although routines may seem to put us in a rut and stifle creativity, in fact routines make us more efficient and allow creativity to blossom."
6. "An effective leader of any organization—from the military to businesses to social organizations—is someone who is decisive, acts quickly, and remains committed to certain key principles."
7. "Advances in computer technology have made the classroom unnecessary, since students and teachers are able to communicate with each other from computer terminals at home or at work."
8. "Schools should be open for classes all year long."
9. "Schools should focus more on preparing students for specific careers and vocations, and less on teaching subjects such as literature, art, and history."
10. "Although the marvels of technology surround us every day, there are moments when we all would give anything to be freed from that technology."
11. "Colleges should require all students, regardless of their individual majors, to take a common set of required courses."
12. "Schools should require all students to participate in field trips since these outings are an essential part of the curriculum for all grade levels."
13. "In order to prepare students to live in a culturally diverse society, schools should formally require all students to study other cultures and societies in depth."

14. "One clear sign that our society has improved over the past 100 years is the development of disposable products whose convenience has made our lives easier."

15. "The best way to understand the true nature of a society is to study its dominant trends in art, music, and fashion."

16. "Because the traditional grading scale of A through F fosters needless competition and pressure, colleges and universities should use a simple pass/fail system."

17. "To address the problem of chronic truancy, schools should fine the parents of students who are frequently absent from school."

18. "Studying a foreign language should be a college requirement for anyone planning to be a teacher."

19. "We are constantly bombarded by advertisements—on television and radio, in newspapers and magazines, on highway signs and the sides of buses. They have become too pervasive. It's time to put limits on advertising."

20. "In order to understand other societies, all college students should be required to spend at least one of their undergraduate years studying or working in a foreign country."

21. "Every member of society should be required before the age of 21 to perform at least one year of community or government service, such as in the Peace Corps, AmeriCorps, USA Freedom Corps, the military, a hospital, a rural or inner-city school, or some equivalent organization."

22. "Citizens of the United States should be allowed to designate how a portion of their tax dollars should be spent."

23. "The only important criterion by which to judge a prospective teacher is his or her ability to get along with the widest possible variety of students."

24. "Rather than relying on taxes, communities should be directly responsible for raising any required funds to pay for all extracurricular public school activities, including after-school sports."

25. "School activities not directly related to course work, such as assemblies and pep rallies, should not be part of the regular school day."

26. "School children should be required to participate in a variety of extracurricular activities so that they can become well-rounded individuals."

27. "All schools should have student dress codes."

28. "It is well within the capability of society to guarantee that all public schools are entirely drug-free."

29. "Opinion polls should not play an important role in the political decision-making process because they indicate only what is popular, not what is the right or wrong position for our leaders to take."

30. "Childhood is a time for studying and playing, not working. Parents should not force their children to do chores."

31. "We are all influenced in lasting ways—whether positive or negative—by the particular kind of community in which we grow up."

32. "Television has had an overwhelmingly negative impact on society."

33. "Grading systems should be replaced with some other method of measuring students' performance because giving grades to students puts too much emphasis on competition and not enough emphasis on learning for its own sake."

34. "Political candidates should not be allowed to use popular actors in their advertising campaigns. Candidates too often win elections because they have actors for friends rather than because they are honestly qualified to represent the public interest."

35. "Television programming should be limited and strictly monitored for offensive content by a governmental supervising agency."

36. "Although we say we value freedom of expression, most of us are not really very tolerant of people who express unpopular ideas or act in nonconforming ways."

37. "Job satisfaction is more important in a career than a high salary and fringe benefits."

38. "College students should not have to decide on a major until after they have taken several classes and examined the various career fields the school has to offer."

39. "Schools should make a greater effort to teach ethics and moral values to students."

40. "Colleges and universities should ban alcoholic beverages on campus, even for students who are of legal drinking age."

41. "Teachers and parents should be more concerned than they are about the gradual trend among high school students toward part-time employment and away from participation in school-sponsored extracurricular activities."

42. "It is the responsibility of the government rather than the individual citizen to find a solution to the growing problem of homelessness in the United States."

43. "Federal regulations should entirely ban all advertising of alcoholic beverages in all media, including television, radio, and magazines."

44. "Schools should put as much emphasis on such subjects as music, physical education, and visual arts as they do on traditional academic courses such as English or math."

45. "Materialism and consumerism have gone too far in American society. We often buy things that we do not need, and we even buy things that we do not especially enjoy."

46. "The failure of public schools is not ruining society. The failure of society has ruined the public schools."

47. "Honesty is universally valued, at least in principle. In practice, however, there are many cases in which governments, businesses, and individuals should not be completely honest."

48. "All employers should institute mandatory drug testing for employees."

49. "All high school students should be required to take some classes in vocational education."

50. "School administrators should regulate student speech in school-sponsored publications."

51. "Computer training should be mandatory for anyone planning to become a teacher, no matter what subject the person will teach."

52. "The world offers us abundant places to learn. We should not expect all of our most important lessons to be learned in the buildings we call schools."

53. "Many public buildings and transportation systems in the United States prohibit or restrict smoking. These restrictions are unfair because they deny smokers their individual rights."

54. "Public schools should be required to offer socially oriented courses, such as sex education and personal finance, because such courses help students cope with problems in society."

55. "Our lives today are too complicated. We try to do too much and, as a result, do few things well."

56. "The United States government has become so corrupt that people who vote in national elections are wasting their time."

57. "The increasing involvement of businesses in the schools, ranging from the establishment of apprenticeships and grants to the donation of equipment and facilities, is a cause for concern because this involvement gives the businesses too much influence over school policy and curriculum."

58. "One of the biggest troubles with colleges is that there are too many distractions."

59. "The best way to improve the quality of public schools in the United States is to institute a national curriculum with national standards so that students, parents, and teachers all across the country know exactly what is expected at each grade level."

60. "Instead of making our lives simpler, computers cause more problems than they solve."

61. "Children learn responsibility and the value of work by being required to do household chores such as making beds, washing dishes, and taking care of pets."

62. "We should ban any speech—whether on the radio, in the movies, on television, or in public places such as college campuses—that encourages violent behavior."

63. "In today's society, the only real function of a college education is to prepare students for a career."

64. "Students suffer from participating in highly competitive extracurricular activities such as debate and sports."

65. "We live in a passive society in which few people take a stand or become involved in social issues."

66. "Students should be required to meet certain academic standards, such as passing all courses or maintaining a C average, in order to participate in extracurricular activities."

67. "Increasing reliance on the use of new technologies in the classroom has distracted from, rather than contributed to, the learning process."

68. "We find comfort among those who agree with us—growth among those who don't."

69. "Film and television studios in the United States nearly always want to dish up a sunny view of life because American audiences would rather not be reminded of problems in society."

70. "Competition is a destructive force in society."

71. "All 18- to 21-year-olds should be required to perform government or community service."

After you have carefully read the topic, you may find it helpful to jot down notes about the points you plan to cover or even to make a brief outline. Space for notes is provided in the test booklet. These notes will not be considered when your essay is evaluated. The space is for your own use, and the kind of outline you write or the kind of notes you make is up to you. You do not have time to make an elaborate outline, but you should take time to plan what you are going to write. Skilled writers typically plan first. Even when time is an issue, as it is in timed writing tests, spending five minutes on some kind of outline or notes is often a good investment. A simple list of the major points (and supporting examples or reasons) you want to cover can be very helpful as you write your essay. Suppose that you are writing on topic 71 from the list above ("All 18- to 21-year-olds should be required to perform government or community service.")

This kind of outline might be all you need to jog your memory as you write.

WRITING YOUR ESSAY

On the paper version of the test, some people try to write out their essays in the section for notes and then copy them over into the designated answer area. In these cases, the writers usually run out of time before they can complete the copying, and they are forced to turn in incomplete essays. It is usually best to use the answer area to write out your essay once, writing as legibly as you can. You might plan to give yourself five minutes near the end of the allotted time period for editing and proofreading your essay. Such editing might include checking that the essay is organized—that is, that it proceeds from one point to another in a way that your readers can follow—that your sentences are clearly stated, and that your spelling and punctuation are correct.

The people who evaluate your essay need to be able to read your handwriting, but neatness, as such, does not count. It is expected that you might cross out words and make insertions. Also, it is not necessary for papers to be mechanically perfect: a misspelled word or a forgotten comma in an otherwise well-written paper will not lower your score. Still, careless mistakes can be corrected if you use your time well; you do not want to give your scorers the impression that you do not understand the rules that govern written English. Plan on spending three to five minutes cleaning up your draft and making corrections.

SAMPLE ESSAYS WITH SCORERS' COMMENTS

Let's return to topic 71 in the list of ETS topics, "All 18- to 21-year-olds should be required to perform government or community service," and look at actual test-taker responses at each score level, from a high score of 6 to a low score of 1.

Response That Received a Score of 6

Essay	Explanation of Score
"We wanted her car." This simple reason of wanting a certain car was several teenagers' reason for killing a young nursing student. Several years ago, a woman named Pam was getting out of her car which she had parked at her apartment. She was attacked, stabbed, and left for dead while a group of teenagers took her car. This is one example of young people's way of thinking here in the U.S. This "Generation X" seems to have a lack of morals, low esteem, apathy, and no vision or goals for the future. Perhaps this generation needs a taste of the real world, a chance to see people who are needy and have nothing tangible in life. Perhaps if these young people could see others who are in a poorer state than they are, they themselves would see how much they have, and in turn, treat others with more respect. Is this a job the government can do, or does the decision to see and help others who are in need have to come from the individual "X-ers?"

The government's role in the community is to protect the liberty of the people, not to form morals or create better people. Although forcing young people, specifically between the ages of eighteen and twenty-one, to do community service, volunteer at a hospital or inner-city school, or participate in other outreach projects could help society as a whole, several consequences could occur. First of all the act of forcing individuals to participate in acts is unconstitutional and the government would be stepping over the bounds created for it. The government also declares the age of eighteen as an adult. This is seen through the right to vote, the right to marry without parental consent, and the right to smoke as well. By these two examples alone, the government could not possibly force any and every adult to do community work.

Besides the fact of unconstitutionality, another reason why government could not require all people between eighteen and twenty-one years of age to do community projects is simply because of human nature. What benefit in life comes from force? In many times throughout history, when force is used, rebellion follows. An example of this is seen nearly two thousand years ago. | The writer lures the reader into this debate with an intriguing introduction. Think about how more engaging an introduction this is than the normal "I'm against community service." In this essay, the writer uses this first anecdote to show that kids today do need to change their ways, although he goes on to say that he is against mandatory community service. The reasons the writer is against it are clearly stated (it is unconstitutional and against human nature), and each reason is fully explained in a paragraph of its own. Having stated a position and explained the supporting reasons, the essay concludes with a reasonable explanations why mandated community service will not work. The essay is clear and organized, with transitions linking together both ideas and sentences, and there are varied sentences (long and short) and precise word choices ("apathy, compassion, commendable") Errors are rare and do not interfere with understanding. |

Essay	Explanation of Score
After the death of Jesus, his followers proclaimed his name as the Messiah, and they proclaimed him as God. Some of the followers were commanded by authorities to not even mention the name of Jesus. However, since the followers believed in Him with all they had, they could not obey the authorities. As a result, Christianity, the religion of following Jesus, is one of the most well-known religions in the world. Examples such as this one permeate history, and if government were to force people to do outreach projects, it could face the opposite effect of what was intended. One cannot change the heart of a person, even if this person is shown the most helpless being in the world. Helping others will not create compassion. Compassion comes from within, and it is compassion which motivates one to help others. Young people today need to see beyond themselves. How can this be done? Can any person, government, or thing cause anyone to see that more lies beyond the selfish intentions that most humans have, or does that "seeing beyond themselves" come from within? Seeing and helping the lives of others who are less fortunate is a commendable thing and must come from a loving heart. What success is there when it comes out of duty, out of government law? If the government were to ever create a law that makes young adults participate in some type of outreach project, the government would be replacing compassion with law. There is no doubt that the young adults of today need morals. They need role models. They need to see beyond their selfish selves. Government's responsibility, however, is limited to only project man's God-given rights of liberty, so perhaps hopefully one day these young people will be able to taste true love that gives and serves from the heart.	

Response That Received a Score of 5

Essay	Explanation of Score
Our Founding Fathers obviously thought that each American citizen should be responsible and accountable. Along with the rights that we have as Americans, there are also responsibilities that go along with those rights. However, I do not believe these rights can be mandated or legislated by the government. The definition of a good citizen might be one who is patriotic, a contributor to society, one who obeys the law, and who seeks to live peaceably among other men, as our constitution implies when it reads, "…the pursuit of happiness." The pursuit of happiness cannot be forced upon an individual. It must come from within. If one does not want to be a good citizen of America, that is his or her choice. Rather than the government mandating community or government service upon individuals, the most logical and reasonable thing to do would be to begin teaching citizenship early in a child's life; teaching children what good citizens are and what good citizens do. The home should be the first place citizenship should be taught. Parents ought to serve as examples to their children. They ought to be good citizens themselves and give to their communities and to their country. Teachers should also teach citizenship as soon as students come into the public schools. They should teach responsibility, respect for others, patriotism, and contribution to society. Facts prove that young people are not being taught good citizenship. The greatest number of people who fail to vote but are eligible falls in the category of those between the ages of 18 and 24. Generally speaking, have these young people been taught that along with their rights as Americans, they also have many responsibilities? If these young people will not even vote, how can we expect them to serve the community or their country? And why are they not voting? Because they are against freedom and responsibility? No. In most cases, it is because they have not been taught the core democratic values of what a good citizen is. Can this be blamed upon them? Absolutely not. The fault lies upon the older adults, the parents, teachers, ministers, and business-people. Values in this democracy are being destroyed from within, by the same people who are advocating them. It is certain that young people from 18–21 need to be good citizens and serve their communities and their country. It is just as certain that government legislation is not needed to facilitate this change. All that is needed is caring parents, teachers, and other community leaders who will stand upon their foundations in America, upon the basic core values of democracy, and who will teach America's youth the same good things. I believe this change would bring a refreshing national revival to America's youth and compel them to desire to serve their communities and their country with feverency of mind and zealousness of heart.	This essay is very well written, with precise word choices ("facilitate, revival, zealousness") and sentences that are fluid and rhythmic (for example, varying lengths of sentences from long to short and asking questions to add punch: "Can this be blamed upon them? Ansolutely not. The fault lies upon the older adults, the parents, teachers, ministers and business people"). The essay clearly states that there should NOT be mandatory community service, and works hard to give reasons to support that position. However, the essay could be better organized, as the position is never originally stated until a third of the way down the first page, and then much of the explanation to support the position against mandatory community service rambles into a discussion of whose fault it is that kids today are lacking morals. While the essay has a clear position with support, better organization, and more focus could help the essay score even higher.

Response That Received a Score of 4

Essay	Explanation of Score
I teach in a vocational high school setting. After instructing the students how the business world works, the students are ready to experience what they have been trained to do. The students want the ability to purchase products without the help of their parents or guardians. They also want to find a good job, and the ability to make decisions on their own. I have many students who are also contemplating marraige.	This essay has few errors and is easy to follow. Although there are some interesting ideas (service work could reduce crime, or could broaden the horizons of many underprivileged kids), these ideas are not presented in support of a position. The
I feel that these students should be involved in community service, but not a full year of their lives. Requiring these young adults to perform community service work a certain amount of hours each week would be adequate. Many of these people have their lives planned and they are certain what they want to do.	writer says limited community service should be required, but then says some students wouldn't need it at all and others could use lots of it. This lack of a clear position takes away from the piece as a
In the classroom, I also have students that have no goals or direction. When questioned what they will do upon graduation, many of them reply, "Get a job at McDonalds" or "Hang around awhile". These students would possibly benefit from community or Peace Corps service work. It would allow the students to see what is happening in the community around them. Some of these students have not had the opportunity to travel or experience anything outside their little world. Many students, when given the opportunity to see other regions of the country or world, would now find a direction to aim their lives.	whole, even though the writer can write very well and has offered some intriguing ideas. By the final sentence one can infer the writer is for mandatory service, but this is an assumption the reader has to make. This essay would benefit from a more clear main idea (a stance, clearly stated, for or against mandatory community service) and an explanation organized in support of that.
Once these students are involved with an organization, they will be given the chance to see how other parts of the world function. Most young people do not realize until they experience what life is like in under-developed countries. This might help them realize they need to work for what they receive. Also, their training in a high school vocational program can be put to use, such as carpentry skills, computer skills, etc. This will allow the students to gain experience and confidence when they return to the work sector in our country.	
If young adults are used for service work, a study should be done to see if the crime rate among young adults drops. Once a person has a goal or job, I feel they will be less likely to have the free time to commit robbery or get involved with illegal drugs. When a person is bored, I feel they are more likely to get into trouble with the law.	
When a young adult does get involved in something constructive, instead of destructive, the person, the community and the world will be better off.	

Response That Received a Score of 3

Essay	Explanation of Score
Requiring 18–21 year olds to participate in government or community service for one year is an excellent idea. However, this type of a program may not be suitable for all young adults, it may only be beneficial to those that plan to continue on to college or some sort of specialty school. This would provide these young adults with a broad experience of different cultures in the world, help to prepare them for making future career choices, and also help them to develop into better young adults by learning to relate to others.

Today many students who have graduated from high school and are continuing on to college are not prepared to decide on a particular field of study. In many cases we as seventeen year olds do not have the experience or foresight to make a decision on our future, I did not make a final decision on my field of study untill late into my sophomore year. As I look back on my college experience I feel I could have learned more by having that extra year and a half of time dedicated to my major field of study.

The more an individual can experience in life, the better off he or she will be in the long run. Our life experience can help us to see things from many perspectives instead of strictly one perspective and this makes life a little easier. With this type of experience in community or government service, the young adults will be more well rounded in their view of the world in which we live.

I think this idea will help the world to be a better place as well as save much money on wasted college tuition. | This essay states that mandatory community service is an "excellent idea" and defends that position with a discussion of the benefits of that year of work for college-bound students. It explains that a year of work may help students to decide on their field of study, an argument that supports the writer's reasoning. But this is the only support given, and while it is clear and helps the writer's main point, additional similar support would make the essay stronger. The essay has few errors and is clear, but it would be better if it supported its idea with more explanation. |

Response That Received a Score of 2

Essay	Explanation of Score
Developing a community outreach or government service for young adults for one year I think is a great idea. If organized well it could only make the United States a better country. Young people could learn responsibility, accountability, and character.

Since we live in a democracy something like this could not be enforced, but it could be highly encouraged. For example if from the time they start school until they finish they are taught the opportunities and benefits of doing an outreach project. The government could provide financial assistance for the young adults. They could provide an opportunity for the student to do one year of community service and in return one full year of school.

This kind of community service would not have to mean leaving the country or state; although this could be an option. | This essay states a clear position in favor of mandatory community service ("I think is a great idea") and gives reasons that support it (the U.S. will be "a better country," students could learn responsibility, accountability, and character"). But instead of explaining those ideas, the essay goes on to explain how the program would work, not why it should be adopted. This means the reasons to support the position are not explained at all, even though they could do |

(*Continued*)

Essay	Explanation of Score
It could be done right in their own community. I also think that there could be options of the length of time the student would put in.	a great deal to help the writer's argument. This leaves the essay feeling incomplete and causes it to earn a much lower score than it would have if the writer had explained the ideas. Vague language also occasionally makes the essay hard to follow.

Response That Received a Score of 1

Essay	Explanation of Score
The government already tells us too much what we should and shouldn't do. They shouldn't also be able to tell us how much we have to help the community, thats something we should just be able to decide on our own. What good does it do if the government decides we should be good people if we don't feel like it. They can't make laws which tell people to be nice, that's crazy. Weather or not people are nice is gonna be there choice, not the Presidents or anyone else's. If people want to do a good thing they ought to but I can't see someone making them do it. Community service is not something that should be legilized or illegal because its against human nature.	This essay is against mandatory community service, but its reasons why the government "shouldn't also be able to tell us how much we have to help the community" is just that mandatory service is "against human nature." How it is against human nature is never explained, so no clear reasons are ever given why this writer is against the idea. No reasons equals no explanation, and no explanation means the essay can earn little credit. It is possible to understand the sentences in this essay, but they are disorganized, lack explanation, and add up to little.

ON YOUR OWN: PPST ESSAY-WRITING PRACTICE

30 minutes

Directions: You will have 30 minutes to plan and write an essay on the topic presented.

Read the topic carefully. You will probably find it best to spend a little time considering the topic and organizing your thoughts before you begin writing. DO NOT WRITE ON A TOPIC OTHER THAN THE ONE SPECIFIED. An essay on a topic of your own choice will not be acceptable. In order for your test to be scored, your response must be in English.

The essay question is included in this test to give you an opportunity to demonstrate how well you can write. You should, therefore, take care to write clearly and effectively, using specific examples where appropriate. Remember that how well you write is much more important than how much you write, but to cover the topic adequately, you will probably need to write more than a paragraph.

Your essay will be scored on the basis of its total quality—i.e., holistically. Each essay score is the sum of points (0-6) given by two readers. When your total writing score is computed, your essay score will be combined with your score for the multiple-choice section of the test.

You are to write your essay on the answer sheet; you will receive no other paper on which to write. Please write neatly and legibly. To be certain you have enough space on the answer sheet for your entire essay, please do NOT skip lines, do NOT write in excessively large letters, and do NOT leave wide margins. You may use the bottom of the next page for any notes you may wish to make before you begin writing.

SECTION 2
ESSAY
Time—30 minutes

Read the opinion stated below.

"Letter grading systems should be replaced by pass/fail grading systems."

Discuss the extent to which you agree or disagree with this point of view. Support your position with specific reasons and examples from your own experience, observations, or reading.

The space below is for your NOTES. Write your essay in the space provided on the answer sheet.

PART III

Six Real PPSTs for Practice

Your Goals for This Part:

- Take real PPSTs under actual testing conditions.
- Read explanations for all test questions, focusing especially on those you answered incorrectly.
- Use your scores to help determine your test readiness.

CHAPTER 9

PPST: Reading Test 1

Professional Assessments for Beginning Teachers®

TEST NAME:
Pre-Professional Skills Test Reading

Time—60 minutes

40 Questions

THE PRAXIS SERIES™

Answer Sheet B

DO NOT USE INK

Use only a pencil with soft black lead (No. 2 or HB) to complete this answer sheet.
Be sure to fill in completely the oval that corresponds to your answer choice.
Completely erase any errors or stray marks.

1. NAME
Enter your last name and first initial.
Omit spaces, hyphens, apostrophes, etc.

Last Name (first 6 letters)   F I

2.

YOUR NAME: (Print)
Last Name (Family or Surname)   First Name (Given)   M. I.

MAILING ADDRESS: (Print)
P.O. Box or Street Address   Apt. # (if any)

City   State or Province

Country   Zip or Postal Code

TELEPHONE NUMBER: ( )   Home   ( )   Business

SIGNATURE: _____   **TEST DATE:** _____

3. DATE OF BIRTH
Month   Day

Jan.
Feb.
Mar.
April
May
June
July
Aug.
Sept.
Oct.
Nov.
Dec.

4. SOCIAL SECURITY NUMBER

5. CANDIDATE ID NUMBER

6. TEST CENTER / REPORTING LOCATION

Center Number   Room Number

Center Name

City   State or Province

Country

7. TEST CODE / FORM CODE

8. TEST BOOK SERIAL NUMBER

9. TEST FORM

10. TEST NAME

Educational Testing Service, ETS, the ETS logo, and THE PRAXIS SERIES:PROFESSIONAL ASSESSMENTS FOR BEGINNING TEACHERS and its design logo are registered trademarks of Educational Testing Service. The modernized ETS logo is a trademark of Educational Testing Service.

ETS. Copyright © 1993 by Educational Testing Service. Princeton, NJ 08541. Printed in U.S.A.

MH99232   Q2572-06   51055 • 08916 • CV99M500
I.N. 202973
1   2   3   4

CERTIFICATION STATEMENT: (Please write the following statement below. DO NOT PRINT.)
"I hereby agree to the conditions set forth in the *Registration Bulletin* and certify that I am the person whose name and address appear on this answer sheet."

_____

_____

_____

SIGNATURE: _____ DATE: _____/_____/_____
                                                                          Month   Day   Year

---

BE SURE EACH MARK IS DARK AND COMPLETELY FILLS THE INTENDED SPACE AS ILLUSTRATED HERE: ●

1 Ⓐ Ⓑ Ⓒ Ⓓ Ⓔ	41 Ⓐ Ⓑ Ⓒ Ⓓ Ⓔ	81 Ⓐ Ⓑ Ⓒ Ⓓ Ⓔ	121 Ⓐ Ⓑ Ⓒ Ⓓ Ⓔ
2 Ⓐ Ⓑ Ⓒ Ⓓ Ⓔ	42 Ⓐ Ⓑ Ⓒ Ⓓ Ⓔ	82 Ⓐ Ⓑ Ⓒ Ⓓ Ⓔ	122 Ⓐ Ⓑ Ⓒ Ⓓ Ⓔ
3 Ⓐ Ⓑ Ⓒ Ⓓ Ⓔ	43 Ⓐ Ⓑ Ⓒ Ⓓ Ⓔ	83 Ⓐ Ⓑ Ⓒ Ⓓ Ⓔ	123 Ⓐ Ⓑ Ⓒ Ⓓ Ⓔ
4 Ⓐ Ⓑ Ⓒ Ⓓ Ⓔ	44 Ⓐ Ⓑ Ⓒ Ⓓ Ⓔ	84 Ⓐ Ⓑ Ⓒ Ⓓ Ⓔ	124 Ⓐ Ⓑ Ⓒ Ⓓ Ⓔ
5 Ⓐ Ⓑ Ⓒ Ⓓ Ⓔ	45 Ⓐ Ⓑ Ⓒ Ⓓ Ⓔ	85 Ⓐ Ⓑ Ⓒ Ⓓ Ⓔ	125 Ⓐ Ⓑ Ⓒ Ⓓ Ⓔ
6 Ⓐ Ⓑ Ⓒ Ⓓ Ⓔ	46 Ⓐ Ⓑ Ⓒ Ⓓ Ⓔ	86 Ⓐ Ⓑ Ⓒ Ⓓ Ⓔ	126 Ⓐ Ⓑ Ⓒ Ⓓ Ⓔ
7 Ⓐ Ⓑ Ⓒ Ⓓ Ⓔ	47 Ⓐ Ⓑ Ⓒ Ⓓ Ⓔ	87 Ⓐ Ⓑ Ⓒ Ⓓ Ⓔ	127 Ⓐ Ⓑ Ⓒ Ⓓ Ⓔ
8 Ⓐ Ⓑ Ⓒ Ⓓ Ⓔ	48 Ⓐ Ⓑ Ⓒ Ⓓ Ⓔ	88 Ⓐ Ⓑ Ⓒ Ⓓ Ⓔ	128 Ⓐ Ⓑ Ⓒ Ⓓ Ⓔ
9 Ⓐ Ⓑ Ⓒ Ⓓ Ⓔ	49 Ⓐ Ⓑ Ⓒ Ⓓ Ⓔ	89 Ⓐ Ⓑ Ⓒ Ⓓ Ⓔ	129 Ⓐ Ⓑ Ⓒ Ⓓ Ⓔ
10 Ⓐ Ⓑ Ⓒ Ⓓ Ⓔ	50 Ⓐ Ⓑ Ⓒ Ⓓ Ⓔ	90 Ⓐ Ⓑ Ⓒ Ⓓ Ⓔ	130 Ⓐ Ⓑ Ⓒ Ⓓ Ⓔ
11 Ⓐ Ⓑ Ⓒ Ⓓ Ⓔ	51 Ⓐ Ⓑ Ⓒ Ⓓ Ⓔ	91 Ⓐ Ⓑ Ⓒ Ⓓ Ⓔ	131 Ⓐ Ⓑ Ⓒ Ⓓ Ⓔ
12 Ⓐ Ⓑ Ⓒ Ⓓ Ⓔ	52 Ⓐ Ⓑ Ⓒ Ⓓ Ⓔ	92 Ⓐ Ⓑ Ⓒ Ⓓ Ⓔ	132 Ⓐ Ⓑ Ⓒ Ⓓ Ⓔ
13 Ⓐ Ⓑ Ⓒ Ⓓ Ⓔ	53 Ⓐ Ⓑ Ⓒ Ⓓ Ⓔ	93 Ⓐ Ⓑ Ⓒ Ⓓ Ⓔ	133 Ⓐ Ⓑ Ⓒ Ⓓ Ⓔ
14 Ⓐ Ⓑ Ⓒ Ⓓ Ⓔ	54 Ⓐ Ⓑ Ⓒ Ⓓ Ⓔ	94 Ⓐ Ⓑ Ⓒ Ⓓ Ⓔ	134 Ⓐ Ⓑ Ⓒ Ⓓ Ⓔ
15 Ⓐ Ⓑ Ⓒ Ⓓ Ⓔ	55 Ⓐ Ⓑ Ⓒ Ⓓ Ⓔ	95 Ⓐ Ⓑ Ⓒ Ⓓ Ⓔ	135 Ⓐ Ⓑ Ⓒ Ⓓ Ⓔ
16 Ⓐ Ⓑ Ⓒ Ⓓ Ⓔ	56 Ⓐ Ⓑ Ⓒ Ⓓ Ⓔ	96 Ⓐ Ⓑ Ⓒ Ⓓ Ⓔ	136 Ⓐ Ⓑ Ⓒ Ⓓ Ⓔ
17 Ⓐ Ⓑ Ⓒ Ⓓ Ⓔ	57 Ⓐ Ⓑ Ⓒ Ⓓ Ⓔ	97 Ⓐ Ⓑ Ⓒ Ⓓ Ⓔ	137 Ⓐ Ⓑ Ⓒ Ⓓ Ⓔ
18 Ⓐ Ⓑ Ⓒ Ⓓ Ⓔ	58 Ⓐ Ⓑ Ⓒ Ⓓ Ⓔ	98 Ⓐ Ⓑ Ⓒ Ⓓ Ⓔ	138 Ⓐ Ⓑ Ⓒ Ⓓ Ⓔ
19 Ⓐ Ⓑ Ⓒ Ⓓ Ⓔ	59 Ⓐ Ⓑ Ⓒ Ⓓ Ⓔ	99 Ⓐ Ⓑ Ⓒ Ⓓ Ⓔ	139 Ⓐ Ⓑ Ⓒ Ⓓ Ⓔ
20 Ⓐ Ⓑ Ⓒ Ⓓ Ⓔ	60 Ⓐ Ⓑ Ⓒ Ⓓ Ⓔ	100 Ⓐ Ⓑ Ⓒ Ⓓ Ⓔ	140 Ⓐ Ⓑ Ⓒ Ⓓ Ⓔ
21 Ⓐ Ⓑ Ⓒ Ⓓ Ⓔ	61 Ⓐ Ⓑ Ⓒ Ⓓ Ⓔ	101 Ⓐ Ⓑ Ⓒ Ⓓ Ⓔ	141 Ⓐ Ⓑ Ⓒ Ⓓ Ⓔ
22 Ⓐ Ⓑ Ⓒ Ⓓ Ⓔ	62 Ⓐ Ⓑ Ⓒ Ⓓ Ⓔ	102 Ⓐ Ⓑ Ⓒ Ⓓ Ⓔ	142 Ⓐ Ⓑ Ⓒ Ⓓ Ⓔ
23 Ⓐ Ⓑ Ⓒ Ⓓ Ⓔ	63 Ⓐ Ⓑ Ⓒ Ⓓ Ⓔ	103 Ⓐ Ⓑ Ⓒ Ⓓ Ⓔ	143 Ⓐ Ⓑ Ⓒ Ⓓ Ⓔ
24 Ⓐ Ⓑ Ⓒ Ⓓ Ⓔ	64 Ⓐ Ⓑ Ⓒ Ⓓ Ⓔ	104 Ⓐ Ⓑ Ⓒ Ⓓ Ⓔ	144 Ⓐ Ⓑ Ⓒ Ⓓ Ⓔ
25 Ⓐ Ⓑ Ⓒ Ⓓ Ⓔ	65 Ⓐ Ⓑ Ⓒ Ⓓ Ⓔ	105 Ⓐ Ⓑ Ⓒ Ⓓ Ⓔ	145 Ⓐ Ⓑ Ⓒ Ⓓ Ⓔ
26 Ⓐ Ⓑ Ⓒ Ⓓ Ⓔ	66 Ⓐ Ⓑ Ⓒ Ⓓ Ⓔ	106 Ⓐ Ⓑ Ⓒ Ⓓ Ⓔ	146 Ⓐ Ⓑ Ⓒ Ⓓ Ⓔ
27 Ⓐ Ⓑ Ⓒ Ⓓ Ⓔ	67 Ⓐ Ⓑ Ⓒ Ⓓ Ⓔ	107 Ⓐ Ⓑ Ⓒ Ⓓ Ⓔ	147 Ⓐ Ⓑ Ⓒ Ⓓ Ⓔ
28 Ⓐ Ⓑ Ⓒ Ⓓ Ⓔ	68 Ⓐ Ⓑ Ⓒ Ⓓ Ⓔ	108 Ⓐ Ⓑ Ⓒ Ⓓ Ⓔ	148 Ⓐ Ⓑ Ⓒ Ⓓ Ⓔ
29 Ⓐ Ⓑ Ⓒ Ⓓ Ⓔ	69 Ⓐ Ⓑ Ⓒ Ⓓ Ⓔ	109 Ⓐ Ⓑ Ⓒ Ⓓ Ⓔ	149 Ⓐ Ⓑ Ⓒ Ⓓ Ⓔ
30 Ⓐ Ⓑ Ⓒ Ⓓ Ⓔ	70 Ⓐ Ⓑ Ⓒ Ⓓ Ⓔ	110 Ⓐ Ⓑ Ⓒ Ⓓ Ⓔ	150 Ⓐ Ⓑ Ⓒ Ⓓ Ⓔ
31 Ⓐ Ⓑ Ⓒ Ⓓ Ⓔ	71 Ⓐ Ⓑ Ⓒ Ⓓ Ⓔ	111 Ⓐ Ⓑ Ⓒ Ⓓ Ⓔ	151 Ⓐ Ⓑ Ⓒ Ⓓ Ⓔ
32 Ⓐ Ⓑ Ⓒ Ⓓ Ⓔ	72 Ⓐ Ⓑ Ⓒ Ⓓ Ⓔ	112 Ⓐ Ⓑ Ⓒ Ⓓ Ⓔ	152 Ⓐ Ⓑ Ⓒ Ⓓ Ⓔ
33 Ⓐ Ⓑ Ⓒ Ⓓ Ⓔ	73 Ⓐ Ⓑ Ⓒ Ⓓ Ⓔ	113 Ⓐ Ⓑ Ⓒ Ⓓ Ⓔ	153 Ⓐ Ⓑ Ⓒ Ⓓ Ⓔ
34 Ⓐ Ⓑ Ⓒ Ⓓ Ⓔ	74 Ⓐ Ⓑ Ⓒ Ⓓ Ⓔ	114 Ⓐ Ⓑ Ⓒ Ⓓ Ⓔ	154 Ⓐ Ⓑ Ⓒ Ⓓ Ⓔ
35 Ⓐ Ⓑ Ⓒ Ⓓ Ⓔ	75 Ⓐ Ⓑ Ⓒ Ⓓ Ⓔ	115 Ⓐ Ⓑ Ⓒ Ⓓ Ⓔ	155 Ⓐ Ⓑ Ⓒ Ⓓ Ⓔ
36 Ⓐ Ⓑ Ⓒ Ⓓ Ⓔ	76 Ⓐ Ⓑ Ⓒ Ⓓ Ⓔ	116 Ⓐ Ⓑ Ⓒ Ⓓ Ⓔ	156 Ⓐ Ⓑ Ⓒ Ⓓ Ⓔ
37 Ⓐ Ⓑ Ⓒ Ⓓ Ⓔ	77 Ⓐ Ⓑ Ⓒ Ⓓ Ⓔ	117 Ⓐ Ⓑ Ⓒ Ⓓ Ⓔ	157 Ⓐ Ⓑ Ⓒ Ⓓ Ⓔ
38 Ⓐ Ⓑ Ⓒ Ⓓ Ⓔ	78 Ⓐ Ⓑ Ⓒ Ⓓ Ⓔ	118 Ⓐ Ⓑ Ⓒ Ⓓ Ⓔ	158 Ⓐ Ⓑ Ⓒ Ⓓ Ⓔ
39 Ⓐ Ⓑ Ⓒ Ⓓ Ⓔ	79 Ⓐ Ⓑ Ⓒ Ⓓ Ⓔ	119 Ⓐ Ⓑ Ⓒ Ⓓ Ⓔ	159 Ⓐ Ⓑ Ⓒ Ⓓ Ⓔ
40 Ⓐ Ⓑ Ⓒ Ⓓ Ⓔ	80 Ⓐ Ⓑ Ⓒ Ⓓ Ⓔ	120 Ⓐ Ⓑ Ⓒ Ⓓ Ⓔ	160 Ⓐ Ⓑ Ⓒ Ⓓ Ⓔ

FOR ETS USE ONLY	R1	R2	R3	R4	R5	R6	R7	R8	TR	CS

Directions: Each statement or passage in this test is followed by a question or questions based on its content. After reading a statement or passage, choose the best answer to each question from among the five choices given. Answer all questions following a statement or passage on the basis of what is *stated* or *implied* in that statement or passage; you are not expected to have any previous knowledge of the topics treated in the statements and passages.

Be sure to mark all your answers on your answer sheet and completely fill in the lettered space with a heavy, dark mark so that you cannot see the letter.

Remember, try to answer every question.

1. In 1976 a powerful earthquake devastated the city of Tangshan, China. Scientists had failed to predict the earthquake. But if people had paid attention to the unusual animal behavior that

Line

5

preceded the earthquake, they would have known it was coming. For animals can often sense an impending earthquake when scientists cannot.

Which of the following, if true, indicates a weakness of the argument above?

(A) A wide variety of phenomena can cause animals to behave strangely.

(B) Scientists use a variety of sophisticated tools to monitor and predict earthquakes.

(C) Many domestic as well as farm animals behaved strangely the day before the Tangshan earthquake.

(D) The city of Tangshan is near a major fault line and will probably be hit by an earthquake again.

(E) Scientists had correctly predicted three major earthquakes in China in the eighteen months prior to the Tangshan earthquake.

Questions 2–3

James Baldwin's eloquent, forceful style has given his work its wide recognition. The intricate sentences, the lyrical prose, the dramatic stance—all these characteristics contribute to a style that is unique and thus immediately recognizable. But Baldwin's style is more than simply

Line

5

unique; it is a living illustration of what can be achieved in a difficult environment; and when he uses it to discuss oppression, racial segregation, and inadequate social and cultural opportunities, its sophisticated grace serves as ironic commentary on the problems he considers.

2. Which of the following statements best summarizes the main idea of the passage?

(A) James Baldwin's ironic commentary about racial oppression fills his writings with life and excitement.

(B) James Baldwin has a highly original style that exemplifies what an individual can accomplish even in the face of a difficult environment.

(C) James Baldwin is widely regarded as one of the most important writers of the twentieth century because of his innovations in literary technique.

(D) James Baldwin has often turned to matters with which he is intimately familiar, like racial segregation and inadequate social opportunities, as the subject for his work.

(E) James Baldwin has dedicated his literary work to educating the public at large about the problems that Black Americans face.

3. The passage mentions all of the following as characteristic elements of Baldwin's style EXCEPT

(A) lyrical prose
(B) ironic illustrations
(C) dramatic stance
(D) intricate sentences
(E) sophisticated grace

4. A recent article has argued at length that the power of factory supervisors over workers increased after 1900; this point of view, however, completely ignores the fact that, after 1900, personnel departments and seniority systems diminished the power of the supervisors by introducing legal restrictions.

The statement above is primarily concerned with

(A) summarizing a point of view
(B) proposing a compromise
(C) settling a dispute
(D) refuting an argument
(E) exposing a falsification of data

Questions 5–7

Modern medicine has not yet devised any widely accepted treatment that actively promotes the healing of wounds. Rather, by closing wounds and keeping them moist and sterile, physicians can only try to make it as easy as possible for nature to take its course. That may soon change: researchers are now exploiting recombinant-DNA technology to produce in large quantities substances that occur naturally in the body and have a potent stimulatory effect on cell migration and cell division, two processes central to wound healing. These substances,

Line

5

called growth factors, can attach themselves to cells and stimulate cell
10　growth or movement.

5. Which of the following best summarizes the main idea of the passage?

(A) Natural cell migration and cell division contribute to wound healing.
(B) New technological developments may soon alter the way physicians can treat wounds.
(C) The artificial stimulation of cell growth may have unpredictable consequences.
(D) Wounds should be kept clean and moist if they are to heal properly.
(E) In general, physicians have not kept current with the latest developments in the treatment of wounds.

6. The passage implies that growth factors contribute to wound-healing by

(A) keeping the wound moist and sterile
(B) making it easier for physicians to encourage the proper treatment of wounds
(C) encouraging new cell growth and cell movement
(D) circumventing recombinant-DNA technology
(E) changing the way physicians treat wounds

7. The primary purpose of the passage is to

(A) evaluate the efforts of researchers working with recombinant-DNA technology
(B) summarize the methods physicians use to treat wounds
(C) examine in detail the biological mechanisms involved in cell division and migration and the way these mechanisms affect wound healing
(D) stimulate medical researchers to investigate new approaches to the treatment of wounds
(E) outline the current treatment for wounds and announce new research that seeks to promote wound healing

Questions 8–12

The Native Americans sometimes referred to as "Plains Indians" typically painted the hides they used as robes with designs that either were abstract or depicted scenes from their lives.

Line

5　　The robes with abstract designs represent the oldest stylistic tradition and were painted by women. These designs seem to follow a distinct tradition: they are simple and symmetrical, contain geometric elements, and follow conventional patterns. The design generally covers only the back of the robe and seldom appears without a surrounding border pattern.

Abstract designs contain primarily the colors red, yellow, blue, and green, flatly and evenly applied. The most striking aspect of the abstract designs is the contrast in scale and texture they produce— the discrepancy between the delicate tracery of the designs and the thick, bulky hides on which they are painted.

Life scenes are even better suited to the bulky hides. Most of these scenes are dynamic and, taken together, they form patterns of great animation that completely cover the robe. Figures are placed on a background lacking sky or earth, are flatly painted in a wide variety of colors, and are sometimes outlined in dark paint. The main subjects are warriors and horses shown in battles and epic events. These designs usually serve to illustrate the exploits of the men who painted them.

10

15

20

8. The passage provides information for answering most fully which of the following questions?

(A) What were the sources of the colors that the Plains Indians used to paint the hides?
(B) When did abstract designs first appear on Plains Indian robes?
(C) What color did the Plains Indians paint the surface of the hides?
(D) What colors generally appeared in the abstract designs on Plains Indian robes?
(E) How did the Plains Indians modify traditional abstract designs to fit specific robes?

9. The phrase "the contrast in scale and texture" (line 12) refers to the contrast between the

(A) weight of the hide and the quality of the leather
(B) symmetry of the design and the effect of the colors
(C) size of the hide and the extent of the design
(D) complexity of the design and the pattern that the design creates
(E) delicacy of the design and the bulkiness of the hide

10. It can be inferred from the passage that robes with abstract designs and robes with life scenes differ in all of the following ways EXCEPT the

(A) amount of the hide covered by the design
(B) range of colors used in the design
(C) pattern of the design
(D) sex of the artist who painted the robe
(E) type of hide used

11. Which of the following descriptions of life scenes could the author best use to support her claim that such scenes are "dynamic" (line 15)?

(A) The scenes are arranged in horizontal rows.
(B) Horses and riders are often depicted in motion.
(C) A scene containing more than one figure often shows all the figures in the same pose.
(D) The horses are painted in colors that are contrary to those seen in nature.
(E) The figures are represented in varying degrees of realism.

12. Which of the following facts, if true, would most help to explain why abstract designs of robes such as those described in the passage originated before life scenes?

(A) Pottery, a very early Plains Indian art form, was decorated with abstract designs that later reappeared in other art forms.
(B) The abstract designs used by the Plains Indians are not derived from the shapes of living creatures.
(C) The Plains Indians, like their predecessors, probably used highly realistic drawings of animals in ceremonies performed to assure successful hunting.
(D) The realistic depiction of animals in Plains Indian art occurred before the realistic depiction of people.
(E) The Plains Indians decorated the surfaces of even the most ordinary household objects with a wide variety of colors.

Questions 13–14 are based on the following excerpt from a commentary on children's literature.

The publishing of children's books today is not unlike the cookie business: a profitable side avenue of a major industry, turning out, in unprecedented volume and variety, what was once a high-quality product. But most of these new varieties are only sugar and hot air.

13. Which of the following best describes the way in which the claim above is presented?

(A) A generalization is made and is supported with specific details.
(B) Irony is used to suggest the opposite of what is stated in the passage.
(C) An analogy is used to clarify a qualitative judgment.
(D) Highly emotional language is used to hide the real issue.
(E) An argument derived from one situation is applied to a variety of other situations.

14. The author's attitude toward the current publishing of children's books can best be described as

(A) enthusiastic
(B) tolerant
(C) uncertain
(D) uninterested
(E) disapproving

15. Although not the equal of Ibsen or Chekhov, Elmer Rice was one of the most innovative and imaginative dramatists the United States ever produced. But since socially relevant drama of the 1920s will be remembered primarily for fiery rhetoric rather than for the unemotional intellectualism that characterized Rice's plays, Rice will probably endure as an anonymous and unseen influence rather than as a towering name.

Which of the following can be inferred about Rice from the statement above?

(A) His style was too fiery to be considered great.
(B) He wrote many of his plays anonymously.
(C) He was once as well known as Ibsen or Chekhov.
(D) He did not fully understand the society of the 1920s.
(E) He wrote socially relevant dramas.

16. In the earliest electronic computers, space for the storage of information was a precious resource. Computer programs were therefore written in the most compact form possible. As the cost of computer memory has decreased, the need for succinctness in programs has diminished, and programs have grown increasingly large.

According to the statement above, the decrease in the cost of computer memory has led to

(A) less compact computer programs
(B) an increase in the number of computer programs
(C) the general availability of low-cost personal computers
(D) an increase in the cost of information storage
(E) less computer space being available for information storage

17. In making her crucial contributions to the Civil Rights movement, Ella Baker never sought public attention, nor did many of the other Black women who were important leaders of the movement. Their main concern was not stardom but the well-being of all Black Americans.

The passage above is mainly concerned with which of the following?

(A) Identifying the best-known leaders of the Civil Rights movement.

(B) Explaining why many women who were important leaders of the Civil Rights movement are not well known.

(C) Describing the most important achievements of the Civil Rights movement.

(D) Determining how many of the leaders of the Civil Rights movement were women.

(E) Analyzing why public attention to social movements generally focuses more on individuals than on organizations.

Questions 18–23

Historians who study middle-class Victorian women have difficulty finding reliable sources of information. The significant lack of extensive autobiographical data has led them to rely heavily on the serious *Line* fiction of the day. But an undiscriminating reliance on such fiction 5 has led some historians, incorrectly, to see the social circumstances of literary characters as typical of those of actual middle-class Victorian women and has unfortunately reinforced the false image of the idle Victorian woman. Although most popular Victorian novels (those without serious literary ambitions) get closer to the reality of middle-class 10 women's lives than do the serious novels, the problem of typicality remains. Even household manuals—written for and by middle-class women—must be scrutinized closely to determine the degree to which their depictions of women's roles are representative of women's actual lives.

15 A more promising source of information is census and wage data. These throw into doubt the image of the idle woman by undermining the assumption made by some historians that most middle-class Victorian families employed several domestic servants. The data strongly imply that these households could rarely afford to hire more 20 than a single servant. This information suggests that, in fact, most middle-class Victorian women had to spend considerable time and energy themselves to maintain their households.

18. According to the author, the uncritical reliance on serious fiction by some historians has resulted in which of the following?

(A) Outright rejection of information from popular Victorian novels.

(B) Inaccurate generalizations about middle-class Victorian women as a group.

(C) Insufficient consideration of autobiographical data about middle-class Victorian women.

(D) The unsubstantiated assumption that middle-class Victorian households employed no domestic servants.

(E) Overly high estimates of the amount of time that middle-class Victorian women spent on managing their households.

19. It can be inferred from the passage that historians might have relied less heavily on serious Victorian fiction as a source of data if which of the following had been available in greater numbers?

(A) Victorian household manuals.
(B) Popular Victorian novels.
(C) Works of serious fiction from pre-Victorian times.
(D) Autobiographical accounts of Victorian women's lives.
(E) Census and wage data from Victorian times.

20. According to the passage, one advantage for historians that popular Victorian novels have over the serious fiction of the day is that the popular novels

(A) are a more complete source of wage data
(B) attracted a greater and more diverse readership
(C) more often portray women drawn from all economic classes
(D) give a more accurate picture of the lives of middle-class women
(E) convey a more thorough sense of the circumstances of female domestic servants

21. According to the passage, the kinds of data mentioned in line 15 are significant because they

(A) emphasize the unique economic circumstances of middle-class households
(B) call into question the image of the idle Victorian woman
(C) suggest that the importance of such data in the study of history is debatable
(D) support the descriptions of middle-class women found in serious Victorian fiction
(E) undermine the assertion that Victorian household manuals were written by middle-class women

22. The passage strongly suggests that the employment of several domestic servants was uncharacteristic of the

(A) ideal Victorian family described in household manuals
(B) typical middle-class household prior to Victorian times
(C) middle-class families described in Victorian women's autobiographies
(D) fictional middle-class households described in serious Victorian fiction
(E) typical middle-class household of Victorian times

23. Which of the following statements best describes the organization of the passage?

(A) A theory is advanced and then arguments in its favor are introduced.

(B) A current debate among historians is described and then the author's position is introduced.

(C) Difficulties regarding the use of certain sources by historians are described and then an alternative source is recommended.

(D) Individual facts about a historical period are revealed and then a generalization about these facts is made.

(E) A new approach to historical sources is summarized and then the drawbacks of that approach are suggested.

24. Rembrandt seems to have been his own favorite model. Seventy self-portraits or representations of his face have been preserved, and no moment in the artist's biography is not vividly represented. Such personal statements, expressed with feeling and intensity, are a record of Rembrandt's view of the world and his relationship to it.

The passage implies which of the following about Rembrandt's self-portraits?

(A) They were used to illustrate Rembrandt's autobiography.

(B) They accurately depict the world in which Rembrandt lived.

(C) They reveal Rembrandt's personality and outlook at many times in his life.

(D) They are more carefully crafted than Rembrandt's portraits of other people.

(E) They are similar to Rembrandt's paintings of other subjects.

25. Science fiction films often achieve weird effects by simply exaggerating the size of a familiar creature, such as an insect. But that change in size would probably be far more bizarre than any science fiction movie if it actually happened, because the law of gravity dictates that a major change in size means a change in form as well.

If the statements above are true, which of the following must also be true of a bird that became as large as a cow?

(A) It would be recognizable as a familiar form.

(B) Its form would resemble that of a cow.

(C) It would no longer be bizarre.

(D) Its body would be altered in form.

(E) The law of gravity would prevent it from moving.

26. In 1932 many of the highest political leaders in Britain feared that the greatest military threat to Britain was from the air. However, by 1939 a chain of twenty radar stations had been put into operation along the British coast. After the Battle of Britain, in 1941, many of those same leaders believed that radar had succeeded in making Britain an island again.

By the phrase "making Britain an island again," the author most probably means which of the following?

(A) Enabling Britain to remain relatively invulnerable to attacks.

(B) Isolating Britain from technological developments taking place in other countries.

(C) Enabling Britain to avoid going to war in neighboring countries.

(D) Establishing Britain as the most technologically advanced country.

(E) Preventing radio communication between Britain and other countries.

Questions 27–31

Some very successful advertising campaigns rely on creating what advertisers call "resonance"—the campaigns link a particular product with some widely recognized positive symbol to induce a favorable
Line
5
view of the product. Consider the recent advertising campaign for personal computers featuring a Charlie Chaplin look-alike as the Little Tramp who, by using his personal computer, brings order to several comically chaotic business settings. By linking its product with the Little Tramp, beloved for his combination of naive innocence and indomitable spirit, the computer company acquires a human face and
10
grafts a soul onto its new machine.

The irony of these advertisements and the resonance they create is that Chaplin himself was expressly opposed to mechanization and the technological goals of speed and efficiency. Those views, evident throughout much of his work, are nowhere more clearly expressed than
15
in the film *Modern Times*, where the Little Tramp as factory worker is driven mad by the soul-destroying monotony and inhuman pace of the assembly line, comically reducing an entire factory to chaos. The company claims its advertisements "stand fear of technology on its head." In reality, it is the Chaplin character who is being stood on his
20
head. His original meaning has been expunged, leaving behind only an appealing image to be exploited by the advertiser.

27. Which of the following best expresses the main idea of the first paragraph?

(A) The use of resonance in advertising is well-illustrated by a recent advertising campaign featuring the Little Tramp character.

(B) The Little Tramp character is a good example of a widely recognized cultural symbol with positive associations.

(C) Computers are generally viewed unfavorably by consumers, so advertisements for them often rely on linking them to a positive symbol.

(D) Because computers often help to reduce chaos in the workplace, consumers associate them with the Little Tramp character.

(E) The computer advertisements featuring the Little Tramp character were very successful primarily because the actor appearing in them looked so much like Charlie Chaplin.

28. According to the author, which of the following is true of advertising campaigns that rely on creating resonance?

(A) They are particularly useful in combating consumer resistance to new products.

(B) They usually feature historical and cultural figures who would, in fact, have objected to the product advertised.

(C) They usually rely on irony and humor to achieve their effect.

(D) They try to induce consumers to associate the product advertised with some appealing and widely known image or person.

(E) They are more successful than most other kinds of advertising campaigns.

29. Which of the following, if true, would most weaken the author's argument concerning the irony of the computer advertisements?

(A) *Modern Times* is not considered to be one of Chaplin's best films, because its political and social message overshadows the humorous elements it contains.

(B) The advertisers who created the campaign doubted that many consumers would recognize their inversion of the plot of *Modern Times*.

(C) *Modern Times* condemns only the mechanization that dehumanizes the workplace; computerization significantly reduces the drudgery of office work.

(D) The theme of *Modern Times* is not limited to the effects of mechanization; the film also addresses other social changes.

(E) *Modern Times* is not the only film by Chaplin in which machines appear as comic props.

30. According to the author, which of the following is true of the actor Charlie Chaplin?

(A) He expressly opposed the use of computers.

(B) He was beloved for his simplicity and lack of sophistication.

(C) He disapproved of increasing speed and efficiency through technology.

(D) His films featuring the Little Tramp character are usually serious political or social inquiries.

(E) His films are generally quite chaotic and disorganized, but are, nonetheless, very funny.

31. Which of the following best summarizes the passage?

(A) It is ironic that most successful advertisements rely on creating appealing images rather than on informing consumers about the product itself.

(B) The original meaning of an image or symbol usually changes over time, especially if it is often used in advertising.

(C) Although advertisements that use a positive symbol to create resonance can be quite successful, they may also violate the original meaning of that symbol.

(D) Linking an advertised product with a widely known positive symbol is called "creating resonance" and is often a successful advertising technique.

(E) Advertisements that try to create resonance are most successful when the images they use are familiar to a large number of consumers.

32. In 1843, Emil Du Bois-Reymond became the first person to prove that electricity runs through the nervous system. Working with nerves from animals and with electrodes, he demonstrated the existence of what is now called the action potential, the electrochemical pulse in our neurons that is nothing less than the language of the brain.

According to the statement above, Emil Du Bois-Reymond was the first person to

(A) demonstrate that electrical pulses exist in the nervous system
(B) insert electrodes into the nerves of animals
(C) coin the term "action potential"
(D) discover the existence of neurons
(E) measure the strength of the electrochemical pulse

33. For the school of painting known as Photorealism, the painter's only function was to "transfer information" from a photograph to a canvas. Photo-realists sought to remove all evidence of the artist's hand or interpretive vision from their works. However, they did not succeed; even devout Photo-realists "cleaned up" photographs as they painted—sharpening outlines, emphasizing important details, eliminating others.

According to the author, Photo-realist artists tended to produce works that

(A) were indistinguishable from the photographs on which they were based
(B) were based on photographs that had been skillfully retouched before the artists began to work
(C) displayed sharper outlines than did the photographs from which the artists worked

(D) lacked any evidence that they were produced through the interpretive vision of an artist

(E) demonstrated convincingly that the primary function of the artist should be to transfer information from one medium to another

Questions 34–36

Stating that there was "no English precedent for the admission of women to the bar" (i.e., for women to act as lawyers in a courtroom), the United States Supreme Court in 1878 denied lawyer Belva Lockwood permission to argue cases before the Court, pending the enactment of "special legislation." In response Lockwood herself drafted the necessary legislation and successfully argued it before the House Judiciary Committee. In February 1879, it was signed into law, and the following month Lockwood became the first woman to argue a case before the Supreme Court. For Lockwood this would be only one distinction in a lifetime of ground-breaking achievements; in 1884, she became the first woman to appear on a ballot in a presidential election.

Line
5

10

34. According to the passage, Lockwood was the first woman in the United States to do which of the following?

(A) Become a lawyer.
(B) Draft legislation.
(C) Serve on the House Judiciary Committee.
(D) Argue a case before the Supreme Court.
(E) Vote in a presidential election.

35. Which of the following criticisms, if true, would undermine the Supreme Court's argument that "special legislation" was necessary before Lockwood could be allowed to argue before the Supreme Court?

(A) The Supreme Court has the power to override precedent and to establish new judicial procedures.
(B) Being admitted to the bar is not a necessary prerequisite for drafting legislation.
(C) Legislation is more important than precedent in determining who may argue before a United States court.
(D) Most members of the House Judiciary Committee had less experience as lawyers than did Lockwood.
(E) The Supreme Court has no jurisdiction over who may present legislation before the House Judiciary Committee.

36. The author mentions Lockwood's appearance on a presidential ballot as an example of which of the following?

(A) The way Lockwood used legislation to change social conditions.

(B) The role of the Supreme Court in the advancement of women's rights.

(C) The power of the House Judiciary Committee to review judicial decisions.

(D) Lockwood's accomplishments in pursuits previously closed to women.

(E) Lockwood's skill in the courtroom.

Questions 37–38

During the 1970s a book-banning epidemic broke out in the United States. Statistics collected by associations of teachers and librarians showed an alarming rise in the incidence of attempts to remove books from the shelves of school and public libraries. In the early 1970s, the American Library Association received reports of about 100 such attempts per year. By the late 1970s the number had tripled; by 1981 it had tripled again. In a 1982 survey of school librarians, 34 percent reported having had a book challenged by a parent or a community group that year. What was worse, over half of those protests met with success—the challenged book was finally removed from the library.

Line

5

10

37. According to the passage, in the 1982 survey, school librarians reported which of the following?

(A) Fewer attempts were made to ban books from school libraries than were made in 1981.

(B) Almost all challenged books were removed from school library shelves.

(C) About 100 attempts were made to ban books from school libraries during the year.

(D) Many of the attempts to ban books from school libraries were made by associations of teachers.

(E) More than half of the reported attempts to ban books from school libraries were successful.

38. The author's attitude toward book banning is most clearly revealed in which of the following lists of words?

(A) "epidemic" (line 1); "alarming" (line 3); "worse" (line 9)

(B) "book-banning" (line 1); "attempts" (line 3); "challenged" (line 8)

(C) "Statistics" (line 2); "protests" (line 9); "success" (line 10)

(D) "associations" (line 2); "survey" (line 7); "finally" (line 10)

(E) "incidence" (line 3); "public libraries" (line 4); "removed" (line 10)

39. Slang originates in the effort of ingenious individuals to make language more pungent and picturesque and thus serves to increase the store of striking words, widen the boundaries of metaphor, and provide for new shades of difference in meaning. As some have argued, this is also the aim of poets.

The author attempts to persuade the reader to adopt a positive attitude toward slang by doing which of the following?

(A) Pointing out that most slang is devised by intellectuals.
(B) Providing examples of the slang used in normal speech.
(C) Refuting a standard criticism of slang.
(D) Making a comparison between slang and poetry.
(E) Supporting the observation that poets often use slang.

40. To this day, the idea that the mass of the materials involved in a chemical reaction remains constant, that matter is conserved, governs the practice of modern chemistry; it would be ridiculous to teach physics and chemistry without this concept, even though, of course, it is not strictly true according to our knowledge of relativity.

With which of the following statements concerning scientific concepts would the author be most likely to agree?

(A) Outmoded scientific concepts are more likely to be abandoned than modified.
(B) In science, old rules of thumb must be used carefully and with many qualifications.
(C) There is no more important task in science than the reconciliation of theory and practice.
(D) The sciences of physics and chemistry are so complicated that explaining them by using simplified concepts introduces unacceptable distortions.
(E) Certain concepts used in practical applications of chemistry are not strictly and unequivocally true.

PPST: Reading Test 1
Answers and Explanations

1. **Choice A is the best answer.** The author of the passage argues that people would have known that an earthquake was about to occur if they had paid attention to the unusual animal behavior that preceded the earthquake. This argument is weakened, however, if unusual animal behavior can occur for a wide variety of reasons. If there is no necessary link between unusual animal behavior and earthquakes, there would be no sure way for people to know that an earthquake was about to occur on the basis of animal behavior.

2. **Choice B is the best answer.** It summarizes the points the passage makes about Baldwin's style. The passage as a whole discusses the characteristics of Baldwin's writing style. It describes Baldwin's style as unique or original, and also states that Baldwin's style illustrates or exemplifies what someone can achieve in a difficult environment.

3. **Choice B is the best answer.** The passage mentions "intricate sentences," "lyrical prose," and "dramatic stance" as characteristic elements of Baldwin's style in lines 2–3. In lines 7–8, "sophisticated grace" is also mentioned as a characteristic element of Baldwin's style. Choice B, "ironic illustrations," is the best response because such illustrations are not mentioned in the passage as a characteristic element of Baldwin's style.

4. **Choice D is the best answer.** The passage begins by stating the conclusion of an argument made in a recent article: factory supervisors had increased power over workers after 1900. The passage then goes on to dispute that conclusion by mentioning that the power of supervisors was actually diminished after 1900 by the introduction of legal restrictions. Thus, the passage is primarily concerned with refuting an argument.

5. **Choice B is the best answer.** It summarizes the main idea of the passage. The passage begins by discussing the current treatment of wounds. The passage then states that these treatment procedures may soon change and goes on to discuss the new technology that may lead to a change in the way physicians treat wounds. Choices A and D can be eliminated because they focus on only part of the passage; choices C and E can be eliminated because they make claims that are not supported by the passage.

6. **Choice C is the best answer.** The passage states that growth factors stimulate cell growth and movement. The passage also states that cell migration or movement and cell division or growth

are central to wound-healing. From these two statements it can be inferred that growth factors contribute to wound-healing by encouraging new growth and cell movement.

7. **Choice E is the best answer.** It summarizes the primary purpose of the passage. The passage begins by briefly describing the current treatment of wounds followed by physicians. It then goes on to announce new research into the promotion of wound-healing.

8. **Choice D is the best answer.** Lines 9–10 state that abstract designs were painted in "red, yellow, blue, and green." Thus, only the question posed in choice D can be answered fully on the basis of the information in the passage. The passage does not provide enough information to answer the questions in the other options.

9. **Choice E is the best answer.** The phrase "contrast in scale and texture" is found in line 11 of the passage. Lines 11–12 indicate the nature of the contrast mentioned in line 11. These lines state that there is a discrepancy between the delicacy of the design and the thickness of the hides.

10. **Choice E is the best answer.** Choice A can be eliminated because line 8 states that abstract designs cover the back of the robe only, whereas line 16 states that life scenes cover the whole robe. Choice B can be eliminated because lines 9–10 states that abstract designs "contain primarily the colors red, yellow, blue, and green," whereas lines 17–18 state that life scenes are painted in a "wide variety of colors." Choice C can be eliminated because lines 7–8 state that the robes with abstract designs follow conventional patterns and usually appear with a surrounding border pattern, whereas lines 15–16 state that the robes with life scenes "form patterns of great animation that completely cover the robe." Choice D can be eliminated because lines 4–5 state that abstract designs were painted by women, whereas line 20 states that life scenes were painted by men. Choice E is the best answer because the passage does NOT state that the type of hide used in abstract designs differs from the type used in life scenes. In fact, the passage suggests that abstract designs and life scenes were painted on the same type of hide.

11. **Choice B is the best answer.** The word "dynamic" means active, showing energy and force. The motion of horses and riders, which the passage tells us are depicted in battle, is active and shows energy and force. Thus, choice B best supports the claim in line 15 that the scenes are dynamic.

12. **Choice A is the best answer.** The question asks for the answer choice reporting a fact that, if true, would best help to explain why the use of abstract designs predated the use of life scenes

on painted robes. One plausible explanation is that the Native Americans sometimes referred to as "Plains Indians" were already using abstract designs in some other art form and transferred the use of these designs when they first began to paint robes. This explanation is made even more plausible by line 4 of the passage, which states that abstract designs represent the oldest stylistic tradition of the Plains Indians. Thus, choice A is best because it offers a plausible explanation for why the use of abstract designs on painted robes predated the use of life scenes.

13. **Choice C is the best answer.** The author compares the publishing of children's books to the cookie business and then states that, although the publishing industry once turned out a high-quality product, it now turns out a product that is devoid of any real content—"sugar and hot air." Thus, the author uses the comparison between publishing children's books and the cookie business to make a judgment about the quality of the children's books being published today.

14. **Choice E is the best answer.** The author compares the books published by current publishers of children's books to cookies made only of "sugar and hot air." This comparison suggests that the author finds current children's books to be devoid of any important or useful content. Choice E correctly describes the author's attitude—"disapproving."

15. **Choice E is the best answer.** In offering a reason why Rice's name will not endure, the passage states that a certain class of plays—socially relevant dramas of the 1920s—will be remembered for fiery rhetoric rather than for unemotional intellectualism. The reason offered would be irrelevant if Rice had not written plays that belonged to this particular class of plays. Therefore, the passage suggests that Rice's plays were socially relevant dramas.

16. **Choice A is the best answer.** The author states that the earliest electronic computers had very little space for the storage of information and, as a result, computer programs were written in very compact forms. However, the author goes on to say that because computer memory does not cost as much as it did originally, computer programs have grown increasingly large.

17. **Choice B is the best answer.** The passage states that neither Ella Baker nor many other Black women who played an important role in the Civil Rights movement sought public attention because they were more concerned with making contributions to the Civil Rights movement than with becoming famous. The information contained in the passage thus explains why many women who were important civil rights leaders are not well known. The other

answer choices can be eliminated because the passage does not identify the best-known leaders of the Civil Rights movement, specify how many of the movement's leaders were women, or analyze public response to social movements.

18. Choice B is the best answer. Lines 2–4 state that historians of middle-class Victorian women have had to rely heavily on the serious fiction of the day because of the lack of extensive autobiographical data. Because Victorian women in serious fiction were typically idle, some historians have incorrectly concluded that actual middle-class Victorian women were idle. This reliance has therefore led some historians to make inaccurate generalizations about middle-class Victorian women.

19. Choice D is the best answer. In lines 2–4 the passage states that historians relied on serious Victorian fiction because there was a lack of extensive autobiographical data about women. Therefore, the passage suggests that they would have been less likely to rely on serious Victorian fiction if there had been a significant amount of autobiographical data.

20. Choice D is the best answer. Lines 8–10 state that middle-class women are portrayed more realistically in popular Victorian novels than in serious fiction. This more realistic portrayal of middle-class women is an advantage to historians studying the actual conditions of women's lives.

21. Choice B is the best answer. Line 15 introduces a source of data about middle-class Victorian women's lives that is more promising than is the fiction of the day. Lines 20–23 indicate that the data mentioned in line 15 (census and wage data) are significant because they undermine the assumption that middle-class Victorian families employed several servants, and thus throw into doubt the image of the idle Victorian woman.

22. Choice E is the best answer. Lines 19–20 indicate that census and wage data strongly imply that middle-class Victorian families "could rarely afford to hire more than a single servant." Thus, the passage suggests that it was uncharacteristic for middle-class Victorian families to employ several domestic servants.

23. Choice C is the best answer. In the first paragraph, the author points out the weakness in using either serious or popular fiction as a source of information about middle-class Victorian women. Serious fiction has presented a portrait of middle-class women that has led historians to conclude inaccurately that middle-class Victorian women were idle; and popular fiction, even though it provides a more realistic portrait of middle-class women's lives than does serious fiction, is still not completely reliable. However, census and wage data, which the author introduces in the second paragraph, are alternate sources of information about middle-class Victorian women that can provide an accurate picture of the actual circumstances of middle-class Victorian women's lives. Thus, choice C best describes the organization of the passage.

24. **Choice C is the best answer.** The passage indicates that Rembrandt painted self-portraits at many points in his life. It also indicates that Rembrandt's self-portraits expressed personal feelings about the world and his place in it. Thus, the passage suggests that Rembrandt's self-portraits show his personality and his attitudes at many different periods in his life.

25. **Choice D is the best answer.** It is supported by the statements in the passage. The passage says that a major change in the size of a creature would also always mean a change in its form. Thus, if a bird were to change its size and become as large as a cow, it follows that the bird's form would change as well.

26. **Choice A is the best answer.** The first sentence states that British rulers in 1932 worried about wartime aerial threats to their country. The next sentence states that in 1939 the British built radar stations along their coast. It can be inferred that the purpose of the radar stations was to detect enemy airplanes. The last sentence of the passage suggests that the radar was successful in helping to protect Britain from aerial attacks. Thus, with the phrase "making Britain an island again" the author suggests that the radar chain around its coast defended Britain from attacks by air in the same way that the ocean around Britain defended it from attack before the invention of the airplane.

27. **Choice A is the best answer.** It most accurately describes the main topic of the first paragraph, which introduces the concept of resonance in advertising and illustrates it with the specific example of the Little Tramp ads. The other answer choices are incorrect because they incorrectly identify the main topic of the paragraph as being computers or the computer advertising campaign or the Little Tramp, rather than the general advertising strategy under discussion.

28. **Choice D is the best answer.** Lines 1–2 of the passage discuss advertising campaigns that rely on creating resonance. The passage states that in these campaigns, advertisers link a product with some positive image or symbol to create a favorable view of that product in the public's mind.

29. **Choice C is the best answer.** The author argues that the computer advertisements discussed in the passage are ironic because they use Charlie Chaplin to create favorable feelings about a machine

used in the workplace, when in reality Chaplin was opposed to "mechanization and the technological goals of speed and efficiency" (lines 12–13). In the film *Modern Times*, according to the author, Chaplin sees the "soul-destroying monotony and inhuman pace of the assembly line" (lines 16–17) as forces that drive workers mad. However, if computers make work less monotonous and reduce drudgery, they make the workplace better. Because Chaplin presumably would have been in favor of an improved workplace, the author's argument would thus be weakened.

30. Choice C is the best answer. In lines 12–13, the author states that Chaplin was "opposed to mechanization and the technological goals of speed and efficiency."

31. Choice C is the best answer. It best summarizes the whole passage, whose first paragraph explains the concept of resonance by using the Little Tramp campaign as an example, and whose second paragraph argues that the use of Charlie Chaplin in the ad campaign is ironic because the original meaning of the symbol has been completely changed in the ads. The other answer choices are incorrect either because they accurately describe only a part of the passage (choice D) or because they introduce information or ideas not included in the passage (choices A, B, and E).

32. Choice A is the best answer. The first sentence in the passage indicates that Emil Du Bois-Reymond was the first person "to prove that electricity runs through the nervous system," and the second sentence states that he "demonstrated the existence of … the electrochemical pulse in our neurons."

33. Choice C is the best answer. The first two sentences of the passage indicate that Photorealist artists sought to produce works that resembled as closely as possible the photographs on which they were based. However, the last sentence of the passage indicates that the Photorealists did not succeed in doing so. They did change aspects of the photographs they were working from; the passage states that they included sharper outlines in their paintings than the outlines in the original photographs.

34. Choice D is the best answer. Lines 8–9 of the passage state that Lockwood became the first woman to argue a case before the Supreme Court.

35. Choice A is the best answer. The Supreme Court's argument was that legislation was needed before Lockwood could argue a case before the Court because there was no English precedent for women to act as lawyers in a courtroom. However, if the Supreme Court has the power to override precedent and to establish new judicial procedures, it does not matter that there was no precedent.

The Court can on its own establish that women can argue cases before the court.

36. Choice D is the best answer. In lines 8–9, the author states that Lockwood was the first woman to argue a case before the Supreme Court. In lines 9–10, the author adds that for Lockwood this was "only one distinction in a lifetime of ground-breaking achievements." By "ground-breaking achievements" the author means that Lockwood was the first woman to accomplish certain things. Immediately after this statement, the author mentions that Lockwood was the first woman to appear on a presidential ballot. Thus, the author mentions Lockwood's appearance on a presidential ballot to provide another example of Lockwood's accomplishments in pursuits previously closed to women.

37. Choice E is the best answer. Lines 7–8 of the passage give the percentage of librarians in a 1982 survey who reported having a book challenged. Lines 9–10 state that in over one-half of such cases, the challenged book was removed from the library. Thus, the passage indicates that more than one-half of the reported attempts to ban books from libraries were successful.

38. Choice A is the best answer. The three words listed in choice A reveal the author's attitude toward book-banning. The word "epidemic" suggests diseases, "alarming" suggests something dangerous, and "worse" suggests something bad—all carry a negative tone. The author of the passage has a disapproving attitude toward book-banning that is revealed by the choice of these negative words.

39. Choice D is the best answer. In the first sentence of the passage, the author makes several positive statements about slang, including statements about its effects on vocabulary, metaphor, and meaning. In the second sentence, the author suggests that poets aim for the same results. The passage therefore suggests that the writing of poets—poetry—and slang have some elements in common. By comparing slang to something valuable such as poetry, the author is attempting to convince the reader that slang is positive.

40. Choice E is the best answer. According to the passage, the principle that matter is conserved is important in the practice of modern chemistry. However, the passage ends by stating that this principle is not strictly true. Therefore, it can be inferred that the author would be likely to agree that some concepts used in practical applications of chemistry are not necessarily true.

CALCULATING YOUR SCORE

To score PPST: Reading Test 1:

- Count the number of questions you answered correctly. The correct answers are in Table 1.
- Use Table 2 to find the scaled score corresponding to the number of questions answered correctly. You can compare your scaled score to the passing score required by your state or institution. (Passing state scores are available on the Praxis Web site at www.ets.org/praxis.)
- Score report category R-1 contains 25 questions measuring literal comprehension. The 15 questions in category R-2 assess reading skills in critical and inferential comprehension. Count the number of questions you answered correctly in each of these categories. This may give you some idea of your strengths and weaknesses.

Table 1—PPST: Reading Test 1

Answers to Practice Test Questions and Percentages
of Examinees Answering Each Question Correctly

Question	Score Report Category	Correct Answer	Percentage of Examinees Choosing Correct Answer
1	R-2	A	73%
2	R-1	B	75
3	R-1	B	85
4	R-1	D	55
5	R-1	B	91
6	R-2	C	86
7	R-1	E	84
8	R-1	D	63
9	R-1	E	81
10	R-2	E	52
11	R-2	B	60
12	R-2	A	41
13	R-1	C	67
14	R-2	E	91
15	R-2	E	53
16	R-1	A	50
17	R-1	B	88
18	R-1	B	88
19	R-2	D	67
20	R-1	D	84
21	R-1	B	66
22	R-2	E	75
23	R-1	C	71
24	R-2	C	72
25	R-2	D	90
26	R-1	A	80
27	R-1	A	69
28	R-1	D	83
29	R-2	C	53
30	R-1	C	72
31	R-1	C	57

(Continued)

Table 1—PPST: Reading Test 1 (*Continued*)

*Answers to Practice Test Questions and Percentages
of Examinees Answering Each Question Correctly*

Question	Score Report Category	Correct Answer	Percentage of Examinees Choosing Correct Answer
32	R-1	A	91
33	R-1	C	68
34	R-1	D	90
35	R-2	A	42
36	R-1	D	85
37	R-1	E	75
38	R-2	A	83
39	R-1	D	51
40	R-2	E	55

NOTE: Percentages are based on the test records of 2,231 examinees who took the 60-minute version of the PPST: Reading test in June 2003.

* In general, questions may be considered as easy, average, or difficult based on the following percentages:

Easy questions = 75% or more answered correctly.

Average questions = 55%–74% answered correctly.

Difficult questions = less than 55% answered correctly.

Table 2—PPST: Reading Test 1

Score Conversion Table

Number Right	Scaled Score
40	187
39	186
38	186
37	185
36	184
35	183
34	182
33	181
32	180
31	179

(Continued)

Table 2—PPST: Reading Test 1 (*Continued*)

Score Conversion Table

Number Right	Scaled Score
30	178
29	177
28	177
27	176
26	175
25	174
24	173
23	172
22	171
21	170
20	169
19	168
18	168
17	167
16	166
15	165
14	164
13	163
12	162
11	161
10	160
9	159
8	159
7	158
6	157
5	156
4	155
3	154
2	153
1	152
0	151

CHAPTER 10

PPST: Reading Test 2

DO NOT USE INK

Use only a pencil with soft black lead (No. 2 or HB) to complete this answer sheet.
Be sure to fill in completely the oval that corresponds to your answer choice.
Completely erase any errors or stray marks.

THE PRAXIS SERIES™

Answer Sheet B PAGE 1

2.

YOUR NAME: _____
(Print) Last Name (Family or Surname) First Name (Given) M. I.

MAILING ADDRESS: _____
(Print) P.O. Box or Street Address Apt. # (if any)

City State or Province

Country Zip or Postal Code

TELEPHONE NUMBER: (___) _____ (___) _____
Home Business

SIGNATURE: _____ **TEST DATE:** _____

1. NAME

Enter your last name and first initial.
Omit spaces, hyphens, apostrophes, etc.

Last Name (first 6 letters) F I

3. DATE OF BIRTH

Month Day

Jan.
Feb.
Mar.
April
May
June
July
Aug.
Sept.
Oct.
Nov.
Dec.

4. SOCIAL SECURITY NUMBER

5. CANDIDATE ID NUMBER

6. TEST CENTER / REPORTING LOCATION

Center Number Room Number

Center Name

City State or Province

Country

7. TEST CODE / FORM CODE

0
1

8. TEST BOOK SERIAL NUMBER

9. TEST FORM

10. TEST NAME

Educational Testing Service, ETS, the ETS logo, and THE PRAXIS SERIES:PROFESSIONAL
ASSESSMENTS FOR BEGINNING TEACHERS and its design logo are registered trademarks of
Educational Testing Service. The modernized ETS logo is a trademark of Educational Testing Service.

Copyright © 1993 by Educational Testing Service. Princeton, NJ 08541. Printed in U.S.A.

MH99232 Q2572-06

51055 • 08916 • CV99M500
I.N. 202973

1 2 3 4

CERTIFICATION STATEMENT: (Please write the following statement below. DO NOT PRINT.)
"I hereby agree to the conditions set forth in the *Registration Bulletin* and certify that I am the person whose name and address appear on this answer sheet."

_____

_____

_____

SIGNATURE: _____ DATE: _____ / _____ / _____
                                                                                                 Month   Day   Year

BE SURE EACH MARK IS DARK AND COMPLETELY FILLS THE INTENDED SPACE AS ILLUSTRATED HERE: ●

1 Ⓐ Ⓑ Ⓒ Ⓓ Ⓔ	41 Ⓐ Ⓑ Ⓒ Ⓓ Ⓔ	81 Ⓐ Ⓑ Ⓒ Ⓓ Ⓔ	121 Ⓐ Ⓑ Ⓒ Ⓓ Ⓔ
2 Ⓐ Ⓑ Ⓒ Ⓓ Ⓔ	42 Ⓐ Ⓑ Ⓒ Ⓓ Ⓔ	82 Ⓐ Ⓑ Ⓒ Ⓓ Ⓔ	122 Ⓐ Ⓑ Ⓒ Ⓓ Ⓔ
3 Ⓐ Ⓑ Ⓒ Ⓓ Ⓔ	43 Ⓐ Ⓑ Ⓒ Ⓓ Ⓔ	83 Ⓐ Ⓑ Ⓒ Ⓓ Ⓔ	123 Ⓐ Ⓑ Ⓒ Ⓓ Ⓔ
4 Ⓐ Ⓑ Ⓒ Ⓓ Ⓔ	44 Ⓐ Ⓑ Ⓒ Ⓓ Ⓔ	84 Ⓐ Ⓑ Ⓒ Ⓓ Ⓔ	124 Ⓐ Ⓑ Ⓒ Ⓓ Ⓔ
5 Ⓐ Ⓑ Ⓒ Ⓓ Ⓔ	45 Ⓐ Ⓑ Ⓒ Ⓓ Ⓔ	85 Ⓐ Ⓑ Ⓒ Ⓓ Ⓔ	125 Ⓐ Ⓑ Ⓒ Ⓓ Ⓔ
6 Ⓐ Ⓑ Ⓒ Ⓓ Ⓔ	46 Ⓐ Ⓑ Ⓒ Ⓓ Ⓔ	86 Ⓐ Ⓑ Ⓒ Ⓓ Ⓔ	126 Ⓐ Ⓑ Ⓒ Ⓓ Ⓔ
7 Ⓐ Ⓑ Ⓒ Ⓓ Ⓔ	47 Ⓐ Ⓑ Ⓒ Ⓓ Ⓔ	87 Ⓐ Ⓑ Ⓒ Ⓓ Ⓔ	127 Ⓐ Ⓑ Ⓒ Ⓓ Ⓔ
8 Ⓐ Ⓑ Ⓒ Ⓓ Ⓔ	48 Ⓐ Ⓑ Ⓒ Ⓓ Ⓔ	88 Ⓐ Ⓑ Ⓒ Ⓓ Ⓔ	128 Ⓐ Ⓑ Ⓒ Ⓓ Ⓔ
9 Ⓐ Ⓑ Ⓒ Ⓓ Ⓔ	49 Ⓐ Ⓑ Ⓒ Ⓓ Ⓔ	89 Ⓐ Ⓑ Ⓒ Ⓓ Ⓔ	129 Ⓐ Ⓑ Ⓒ Ⓓ Ⓔ
10 Ⓐ Ⓑ Ⓒ Ⓓ Ⓔ	50 Ⓐ Ⓑ Ⓒ Ⓓ Ⓔ	90 Ⓐ Ⓑ Ⓒ Ⓓ Ⓔ	130 Ⓐ Ⓑ Ⓒ Ⓓ Ⓔ
11 Ⓐ Ⓑ Ⓒ Ⓓ Ⓔ	51 Ⓐ Ⓑ Ⓒ Ⓓ Ⓔ	91 Ⓐ Ⓑ Ⓒ Ⓓ Ⓔ	131 Ⓐ Ⓑ Ⓒ Ⓓ Ⓔ
12 Ⓐ Ⓑ Ⓒ Ⓓ Ⓔ	52 Ⓐ Ⓑ Ⓒ Ⓓ Ⓔ	92 Ⓐ Ⓑ Ⓒ Ⓓ Ⓔ	132 Ⓐ Ⓑ Ⓒ Ⓓ Ⓔ
13 Ⓐ Ⓑ Ⓒ Ⓓ Ⓔ	53 Ⓐ Ⓑ Ⓒ Ⓓ Ⓔ	93 Ⓐ Ⓑ Ⓒ Ⓓ Ⓔ	133 Ⓐ Ⓑ Ⓒ Ⓓ Ⓔ
14 Ⓐ Ⓑ Ⓒ Ⓓ Ⓔ	54 Ⓐ Ⓑ Ⓒ Ⓓ Ⓔ	94 Ⓐ Ⓑ Ⓒ Ⓓ Ⓔ	134 Ⓐ Ⓑ Ⓒ Ⓓ Ⓔ
15 Ⓐ Ⓑ Ⓒ Ⓓ Ⓔ	55 Ⓐ Ⓑ Ⓒ Ⓓ Ⓔ	95 Ⓐ Ⓑ Ⓒ Ⓓ Ⓔ	135 Ⓐ Ⓑ Ⓒ Ⓓ Ⓔ
16 Ⓐ Ⓑ Ⓒ Ⓓ Ⓔ	56 Ⓐ Ⓑ Ⓒ Ⓓ Ⓔ	96 Ⓐ Ⓑ Ⓒ Ⓓ Ⓔ	136 Ⓐ Ⓑ Ⓒ Ⓓ Ⓔ
17 Ⓐ Ⓑ Ⓒ Ⓓ Ⓔ	57 Ⓐ Ⓑ Ⓒ Ⓓ Ⓔ	97 Ⓐ Ⓑ Ⓒ Ⓓ Ⓔ	137 Ⓐ Ⓑ Ⓒ Ⓓ Ⓔ
18 Ⓐ Ⓑ Ⓒ Ⓓ Ⓔ	58 Ⓐ Ⓑ Ⓒ Ⓓ Ⓔ	98 Ⓐ Ⓑ Ⓒ Ⓓ Ⓔ	138 Ⓐ Ⓑ Ⓒ Ⓓ Ⓔ
19 Ⓐ Ⓑ Ⓒ Ⓓ Ⓔ	59 Ⓐ Ⓑ Ⓒ Ⓓ Ⓔ	99 Ⓐ Ⓑ Ⓒ Ⓓ Ⓔ	139 Ⓐ Ⓑ Ⓒ Ⓓ Ⓔ
20 Ⓐ Ⓑ Ⓒ Ⓓ Ⓔ	60 Ⓐ Ⓑ Ⓒ Ⓓ Ⓔ	100 Ⓐ Ⓑ Ⓒ Ⓓ Ⓔ	140 Ⓐ Ⓑ Ⓒ Ⓓ Ⓔ
21 Ⓐ Ⓑ Ⓒ Ⓓ Ⓔ	61 Ⓐ Ⓑ Ⓒ Ⓓ Ⓔ	101 Ⓐ Ⓑ Ⓒ Ⓓ Ⓔ	141 Ⓐ Ⓑ Ⓒ Ⓓ Ⓔ
22 Ⓐ Ⓑ Ⓒ Ⓓ Ⓔ	62 Ⓐ Ⓑ Ⓒ Ⓓ Ⓔ	102 Ⓐ Ⓑ Ⓒ Ⓓ Ⓔ	142 Ⓐ Ⓑ Ⓒ Ⓓ Ⓔ
23 Ⓐ Ⓑ Ⓒ Ⓓ Ⓔ	63 Ⓐ Ⓑ Ⓒ Ⓓ Ⓔ	103 Ⓐ Ⓑ Ⓒ Ⓓ Ⓔ	143 Ⓐ Ⓑ Ⓒ Ⓓ Ⓔ
24 Ⓐ Ⓑ Ⓒ Ⓓ Ⓔ	64 Ⓐ Ⓑ Ⓒ Ⓓ Ⓔ	104 Ⓐ Ⓑ Ⓒ Ⓓ Ⓔ	144 Ⓐ Ⓑ Ⓒ Ⓓ Ⓔ
25 Ⓐ Ⓑ Ⓒ Ⓓ Ⓔ	65 Ⓐ Ⓑ Ⓒ Ⓓ Ⓔ	105 Ⓐ Ⓑ Ⓒ Ⓓ Ⓔ	145 Ⓐ Ⓑ Ⓒ Ⓓ Ⓔ
26 Ⓐ Ⓑ Ⓒ Ⓓ Ⓔ	66 Ⓐ Ⓑ Ⓒ Ⓓ Ⓔ	106 Ⓐ Ⓑ Ⓒ Ⓓ Ⓔ	146 Ⓐ Ⓑ Ⓒ Ⓓ Ⓔ
27 Ⓐ Ⓑ Ⓒ Ⓓ Ⓔ	67 Ⓐ Ⓑ Ⓒ Ⓓ Ⓔ	107 Ⓐ Ⓑ Ⓒ Ⓓ Ⓔ	147 Ⓐ Ⓑ Ⓒ Ⓓ Ⓔ
28 Ⓐ Ⓑ Ⓒ Ⓓ Ⓔ	68 Ⓐ Ⓑ Ⓒ Ⓓ Ⓔ	108 Ⓐ Ⓑ Ⓒ Ⓓ Ⓔ	148 Ⓐ Ⓑ Ⓒ Ⓓ Ⓔ
29 Ⓐ Ⓑ Ⓒ Ⓓ Ⓔ	69 Ⓐ Ⓑ Ⓒ Ⓓ Ⓔ	109 Ⓐ Ⓑ Ⓒ Ⓓ Ⓔ	149 Ⓐ Ⓑ Ⓒ Ⓓ Ⓔ
30 Ⓐ Ⓑ Ⓒ Ⓓ Ⓔ	70 Ⓐ Ⓑ Ⓒ Ⓓ Ⓔ	110 Ⓐ Ⓑ Ⓒ Ⓓ Ⓔ	150 Ⓐ Ⓑ Ⓒ Ⓓ Ⓔ
31 Ⓐ Ⓑ Ⓒ Ⓓ Ⓔ	71 Ⓐ Ⓑ Ⓒ Ⓓ Ⓔ	111 Ⓐ Ⓑ Ⓒ Ⓓ Ⓔ	151 Ⓐ Ⓑ Ⓒ Ⓓ Ⓔ
32 Ⓐ Ⓑ Ⓒ Ⓓ Ⓔ	72 Ⓐ Ⓑ Ⓒ Ⓓ Ⓔ	112 Ⓐ Ⓑ Ⓒ Ⓓ Ⓔ	152 Ⓐ Ⓑ Ⓒ Ⓓ Ⓔ
33 Ⓐ Ⓑ Ⓒ Ⓓ Ⓔ	73 Ⓐ Ⓑ Ⓒ Ⓓ Ⓔ	113 Ⓐ Ⓑ Ⓒ Ⓓ Ⓔ	153 Ⓐ Ⓑ Ⓒ Ⓓ Ⓔ
34 Ⓐ Ⓑ Ⓒ Ⓓ Ⓔ	74 Ⓐ Ⓑ Ⓒ Ⓓ Ⓔ	114 Ⓐ Ⓑ Ⓒ Ⓓ Ⓔ	154 Ⓐ Ⓑ Ⓒ Ⓓ Ⓔ
35 Ⓐ Ⓑ Ⓒ Ⓓ Ⓔ	75 Ⓐ Ⓑ Ⓒ Ⓓ Ⓔ	115 Ⓐ Ⓑ Ⓒ Ⓓ Ⓔ	155 Ⓐ Ⓑ Ⓒ Ⓓ Ⓔ
36 Ⓐ Ⓑ Ⓒ Ⓓ Ⓔ	76 Ⓐ Ⓑ Ⓒ Ⓓ Ⓔ	116 Ⓐ Ⓑ Ⓒ Ⓓ Ⓔ	156 Ⓐ Ⓑ Ⓒ Ⓓ Ⓔ
37 Ⓐ Ⓑ Ⓒ Ⓓ Ⓔ	77 Ⓐ Ⓑ Ⓒ Ⓓ Ⓔ	117 Ⓐ Ⓑ Ⓒ Ⓓ Ⓔ	157 Ⓐ Ⓑ Ⓒ Ⓓ Ⓔ
38 Ⓐ Ⓑ Ⓒ Ⓓ Ⓔ	78 Ⓐ Ⓑ Ⓒ Ⓓ Ⓔ	118 Ⓐ Ⓑ Ⓒ Ⓓ Ⓔ	158 Ⓐ Ⓑ Ⓒ Ⓓ Ⓔ
39 Ⓐ Ⓑ Ⓒ Ⓓ Ⓔ	79 Ⓐ Ⓑ Ⓒ Ⓓ Ⓔ	119 Ⓐ Ⓑ Ⓒ Ⓓ Ⓔ	159 Ⓐ Ⓑ Ⓒ Ⓓ Ⓔ
40 Ⓐ Ⓑ Ⓒ Ⓓ Ⓔ	80 Ⓐ Ⓑ Ⓒ Ⓓ Ⓔ	120 Ⓐ Ⓑ Ⓒ Ⓓ Ⓔ	160 Ⓐ Ⓑ Ⓒ Ⓓ Ⓔ

FOR ETS USE ONLY	R1	R2	R3	R4	R5	R6	R7	R8	TR	CS

Directions: Each statement or passage in this test is followed by a question or questions based on its content. After reading a statement or passage, choose the best answer to each question from among the five choices given. Answer all questions following a statement or passage on the basis of what is <u>stated</u> or <u>implied</u> in that statement or passage; you are not expected to have any previous knowledge of the topics treated in the statements and passages.

Be sure to mark all your answers on your answer sheet and completely fill in the lettered space with a heavy, dark mark so that you cannot see the letter.

Remember, try to answer every question.

1. From the outside, plants seem to be the silent inhabitants of a noisy planet. But this impression is deceptive. Plants harbor an alien world of animal signals—eerie vibrational songs transmitted through stems and leaves by insects, spiders, and even some frogs and lizards. Some of these creatures serenade potential mates, while others sound strident notes of alarm. In fact, so many species send messages through plants that these songs may outnumber all other animal sounds on Earth.

   According to the passage, the impression that plants are silent is deceptive because plants

   (A) vibrate with sounds produced by animals
   (B) transmit audible signals to other plants
   (C) vibrate as part of their reproductive strategy
   (D) emit noises to ward off predatory insects
   (E) create friction with their leaves and stems

2. They talked with a candor induced by the knowledge that there was nothing left to conceal. They remembered what Elizabeth had been like, what they had loved about her and what they had never understood, the mysterious motivations, the oddities of her individual temperament. For long periods, they were quiet, exhausted, but with a sense that something had happened in its proper place. They were made silent by awe.

Which of the following best expresses what is described in the passage?

(A) People disagreeing with each other about a person they knew.
(B) People speaking about a dramatic encounter involving their friend.
(C) People conversing honestly about a mutual friend.
(D) People talking about a famous person they had recently met.
(E) People remembering a person whom none of them truly liked.

Questions 3–4

What is it about exercise that can make people more inventive thinkers? Exercise has the ability to alter factors that inhibit creativity. One such factor is a lack of energy. When people exercise, they experience physiological changes such as increased metabolism and cardiac activity; these changes increase energy. Another factor is mood: depression and anxiety often inhibit creativity, and both are decreased when the body gets exercise. A third factor is mental preoccupation: exercise produces a state Zen Buddhists call the "empty mind," and when the mind empties, preoccupations slip away. During those moments of silence, creative thoughts have a chance to develop.

Line

5

10

3. The primary purpose of the passage is to

(A) present three theories about factors that affect creativity
(B) explain how exercise increases creativity
(C) refute a theory about the mind's effect on the body
(D) argue that people who exercise tend to be creative only in certain fields
(E) show how little is understood about the mental effects of exercise

4. The author uses the term "empty mind" in line 8 as an example of which of the following?

(A) A mind that lacks energy.
(B) A mind that is not creative.
(C) An effect of exercise.
(D) A cause of depression and anxiety.
(E) A mind that is like a child's.

Questions 5–9

From 1952 to 1959, jazz singer Billie Holiday recorded dozens of songs. In these last years, her voice was not what it had been. Her range had narrowed and deepened, and much of the sparkle and buoyancy were gone. But she continued to develop as an artist. She remade many of her previous successes, now in a voice that was so edged with emotional intensity that at times it seemed almost too much to bear. For me, contrary to today's popular wisdom, her last years were her greatest.

Line

5

Some otherwise dependable music historians have been shockingly confused on the matter of Holiday as an artist and have persisted in
10 presenting her art as if it were little more than data in a psychological or sociological profile. Her greatness as a singer did not derive—as many people seem to believe—from the hard life she led. Like any real artist, she transmuted what she could use of her sorrows into the pure gold of her singing. She became an artist not because she was in trouble
15 (it takes more than a sad heart to sing a sad song effectively), but because she worked hard to achieve her artistic voice and to master the timbres, turns of phrase, timings, and thousand other nuances that made her a singer whose records live on.

5. The passage is mainly concerned with

(A) tracing the effect of Holiday's everyday life on her music
(B) contrasting Holiday's voice with that of other artists
(C) arguing that jazz is a complex art form comparable to classical music
(D) contrasting techniques used by singers with those used by instrumentalists
(E) challenging beliefs held about Holiday and her work

6. Which of the following best describes the author's opinion about the recordings Holiday made between 1952 and 1959?

(A) Though some qualities of Holiday's voice had deteriorated, her expressiveness had increased.
(B) Though Holiday sang well, inferior musical accompaniment weakened the overall effect.
(C) Holiday's ability to find new material was the recordings' greatest asset.
(D) The recordings did not match the intensity of Holiday's live performances.
(E) The recordings are of interest only to historians and other specialists.

7. Which of the following best describes the author's view concerning the "music historians" mentioned in line 8?

(A) Their assessment of Holiday's early work is more accurate than their assessment of her later work.
(B) Their interpretation of Holiday's music was common in the 1950s but is not popular today.
(C) They are less reliable in their assessment of Holiday's artistry than they are on other topics.
(D) They agree with the author's own opinion about the significance of Holiday's music.
(E) They disagree among themselves about the effect of Holiday's life on her work.

8. According to the passage, the author believes which of the following to be true of "real" artists (lines 12–13)?

(A) They transform some aspects of their emotional life into great art.

(B) They forget their troubles in order to produce their art.

(C) They are able to maintain a consistent standard of quality over an entire career.

(D) Their work is characterized by technical virtuosity rather than emotional significance.

(E) They are so far ahead of their time that their significance can be evaluated only in retrospect.

9. The passage suggests which of the following about Holiday's reputation today?

(A) She is more widely admired today than she was during her lifetime.

(B) She is admired by music historians, but not by the general public.

(C) She is widely known for her music, but few people know much about her life.

(D) She is admired more for her early work than for her later work.

(E) She is admired primarily by those jazz musicians who have been influenced by her work.

Questions 10–11

Eighteenth-century biographer James Boswell's *The Life of Samuel Johnson* is an innovative work of English literature. It shifts biography from what the writer says about a subject to what the writer shows a subject doing. Boswell does not simply describe, chronologize, and comment; he presents his friend, the formidable, famous writer, Dr. Samuel Johnson, quite dramatically, in living speech and action.

Boswell, a failure in law and politics, had only his friendship with Johnson. Without Johnson as his subject, Boswell's talent as a writer would have been unrealized. Without Boswell's artistry, Johnson's genius would not come alive for today's readers.

Line

5

10

10. According to the passage, Boswell's biography of Samuel Johnson is considered innovative primarily because Boswell

(A) described only those facets of his subject's life considered complimentary

(B) relied on knowledge that only a friend would have access to

(C) brought his subject to life by describing him in action

(D) developed the chronological approach to biographical writing

(E) attributed greater skill to his subject than did other biographers of the time

11. The author of the passage would be most likely to agree with which of the following statements about Boswell?

(A) Boswell had little impact on later writers of biography.
(B) If Boswell had not written his biography, Johnson's work would never have been acknowledged.
(C) The relationship between Boswell and Johnson was mutually beneficial.
(D) Many of the descriptions of Johnson in Boswell's biography are inaccurate.
(E) Boswell was too close to Johnson to be an objective observer.

12. The ancient Babylonians were obsessed with tables. And the abundance of clay allowed them to create many tablets containing tables. Because of the clay tablets' durability, many survive today. From one location alone, the site of ancient Nippur, over 50,000 tablets were recovered and are now in collections at the museums of Yale, Columbia, and the University of Pennsylvania, among others. Many of these tablets are in the basements of the museums, gathering dust, lying there unread and undeciphered.

Line

5

Which of the following phrases is most likely a statement of the author's opinion rather than a statement of fact?

(A) "obsessed with tables" (line 1)
(B) "abundance of clay" (lines 2–3)
(C) "create many tablets" (line 2)
(D) "survive today" (line 3)
(E) "lying there unread" (line 7)

13. Sailors in the North Sea were slow to feel a need for the magnetic compass. They primarily sailed shallow waters where sailors had long been feeling their way along the bottom using depth soundings. Thus, experienced sailors could effectively navigate by the shape of the North Sea floor. Even after the compass arrived, sailors in these waters still felt more secure when they could combine the new device with their old, familiar methods.

According to the passage, experienced sailors in the North Sea had

(A) a dependable means of navigation before the arrival of the compass
(B) a method of navigation that used the North Sea's currents
(C) a great need for the compass, even though they were slow to accept it
(D) long actively sought a more reliable method of navigation
(E) a difficult time navigating the unpredictable North Sea during bad weather

14. Delmonico's restaurant in New York is credited with introducing the first printed menu in the United States in 1834. That menu and others of the period were simple in design, offering straightforward information. By the 1930s, however, menus were seen as part of a restaurant's program to create a memorable meal. Their elaborate language could whet an appetite, tell a joke, explain a food item, create a mood, and above all, sell some food.

The evolution of the menu as described in the passage is most similar to which of the following?

(A) Grocery trucks, which originally delivered items in nondescript vehicles, later utilized bright graphics on their vans to identify the origins of the grocer.

(B) Catalogues, which were once mere lists of products available for sale, later became a persuasive descriptive format for marketing retailers' goods and ideas.

(C) Early dental practitioners, in an attempt to overcome negative feelings about dentistry, found advertising handbills effective in dispelling fears of patients.

(D) Educators, who once taught core curricula in one-room schoolhouses, promoted proposals for new buildings and expanded staffs.

(E) Newspapers, in an effort to compete with the electronic media, eventually utilized color photos and bold graphics to interest casual readers.

Questions 15–16

At the height of Mayan civilization, in what is now Mexico, kings fervently believed in the power of the pen. Whether they thought it mightier than the sword is doubtful, but a growing body of evidence from Mayan writing and art shows that scribes, or writers, played a central role in magnifying their king's reputation and solidifying his political hold on the realm.

No royal court in Mayan civilization was without scribes of high rank. Scribes were depicted in paintings and sculptures, accompanied by inscriptions identifying them as keepers of the royal library or as chief scribes. Court scribes came from the noble class, sometimes from the royal family itself—younger sons and even some daughters. Their duty was to prepare art and text for elaborate public displays glorifying the king's triumphs.

Line

5

10

15. The passage states which of the following about the position of scribes in Mayan civilization?

(A) They were the keepers of all written materials and, in some cases, even more powerful than the king.

(B) They prepared art and texts for the exclusive enjoyment of the royal family.

(C) They created art and text displaying a king's achievements, thus helping to solidify the position of the king.

(D) As highly skilled male members of the aristocratic ruling class, they were singled out for political favors.

(E) They were rewarded by royalty for being the only recorders of information about the daily lives of ordinary Mayans.

16. The passage suggests which of the following about Mayan kings?

(A) They were not overly concerned with their reputation.

(B) They discouraged the depiction of scribes by Mayan artists.

(C) They believed that only the elite should view art.

(D) They recognized the power of propaganda.

(E) They valued the power of the pen over military power.

Questions 17–21

Most people know that vitamins are essential to good health; a blood test that measures vitamin levels might therefore be a welcome option at one's annual physical checkup. In fact, biochemist Bruce Ames calls such testing the future of preventive medicine. Someday, he says, vitamins and minerals will be measured routinely, just as cholesterol is today. Such testing would benefit people by providing guidance on how to improve their diets; it would also prevent those who take vitamin supplements from taking overdoses. Critics of such testing point out, however, that the ideal levels of the various vitamins and minerals are not really known: we know how much our bodies should have daily to avoid deficiency illnesses like scurvy, but when it comes to defense against cancer and heart disease, researchers are mostly guessing. Furthermore, vitamins and minerals in the bloodstream do not necessarily reflect levels in the rest of the body. Further still, the test measures what is present at the moment one's blood is drawn, but levels can vary from day to day. Because of these difficulties, one lab has developed a test that measures not simply vitamin levels, but the speed at which white blood cells divide when a vitamin is added; if the rate increases, that indicates that the cell was deficient in that nutrient.

Line
5

10

15

17. The primary purpose of the passage is to

(A) illustrate the value of vitamins to good health

(B) describe and evaluate the practice of testing for levels of vitamins in the blood

(C) present several theories regarding the ideal levels of various vitamins

(D) compare various tests that can be used to establish the levels of vitamins in the blood

(E) advocate testing for levels of vitamins in the blood as part of annual physical checkups

18. Which of the following words could be substituted for "reflect" in line 14 without substantially altering the meaning of the sentence?

(A) Meditate
(B) Rebound
(C) Indicate
(D) Ponder
(E) Reverberate

19. The author mentions the fact that vitamin levels in the blood "can vary from day to day" (line 16) most likely in order to

(A) suggest that testing the effect of vitamins on white blood cells is unnecessary
(B) suggest that people should take vitamin supplements on a daily basis
(C) point out a limitation of the usefulness of testing the level of vitamins in the blood
(D) provide evidence that many people have poor diets
(E) explain why the ideal levels of various vitamins are unknown

20. According to the passage, Bruce Ames believes which of the following?

(A) The cholesterol test used routinely today is unreliable.
(B) Most people need more vitamins and minerals in their diets.
(C) Preventive medicine is of questionable value.
(D) Testing for vitamins will eventually become part of regular checkups.
(E) Vitamin supplement overdoses are an important but unrecognized problem.

21. The passage suggests which of the following about the test mentioned in the last sentence?

(A) It has similar limitations to tests that measure levels of vitamins in the blood.
(B) It is more often used than tests that measure levels of vitamins in the blood.
(C) It is helping doctors determine the amount of vitamins needed to avoid deficiency illnesses.
(D) It has been found controversial by biochemists such as Bruce Ames.
(E) It was developed in response to the drawbacks associated with tests that measure vitamin levels in the blood.

Questions 22–23

Most people believe Guglielmo Marconi invented the radio; he did not. His contribution was the wireless telegraph, which permitted the transmission of coded messages through the air. Radio made a huge *Line* leap beyond the coded confines of the telegraph. It brought to the 5 human ear the sounds of the human voice and music, sounds it seemed to pluck magically from the air. While the telegraph and telephone were instruments for private communication between two individuals, the radio was democratic—it directed its message to the masses and allowed one person to communicate with many.

22. The passage is primarily concerned with

(A) correcting a misconception about the early uses of the radio
(B) discussing the significance of the development of the radio
(C) arguing that the telegraph had important effects on private communication
(D) providing information about the inventor of the telegraph
(E) describing the inventions of the telegraph and the telephone

23. The last sentence of the passage serves mainly to create a contrast between

(A) Guglielmo Marconi and Alexander Graham Bell
(B) coded telegraph messages and spoken voice messages
(C) communication of news and communication of opinions
(D) private and public forms of communication
(E) Marconi's reputation and his actual accomplishment

24. One of the art forms of the pre-Columbian Pueblo culture is "dry painting." Made with colored sands, pollen, and cornmeal, dry paintings usually formed part of the altar arrangements in religious ceremonies. Although a great deal of time and labor went into producing the paintings, they were destroyed immediately after their use. Such paintings were inherently impermanent, but a stronger explanation for this destruction lies in the Pueblos' concern that such powerful art might be misused.

The primary purpose of the passage is to

(A) challenge the claim that the production of dry paintings required much time and labor
(B) discuss Pueblo dry paintings and the significance of their immediate destruction
(C) state the fundamental beliefs of the Pueblo religion
(D) describe the various art forms of the Pueblo culture
(E) discuss the various uses of dry paintings in Pueblo culture

25. Novelist Willa Cather, like Emily Dickinson, forged an art out of precise observation, wide reading, and idiosyncratic certainty. Like Dickinson, she had a perfect ear and made new rhythms for American prose. Unlike Dickinson, she has had neither a wide influence among fellow authors nor a place in histories of American literature commensurate with her power. In her lifetime she sold many books, but her work has been ludicrously misrepresented and misused by modern critics, even when they appear to admire it.

According to the passage, Cather differed from Dickinson in that Cather

(A) had a perfect ear
(B) has had an important place in histories of American literature
(C) created new rhythms for American prose
(D) sold few books in her lifetime
(E) was not widely influential on other authors

26. Memphis in autumn has not the moss-hung oaks of Natchez. Nor, my dear young man, have we the exotic, the really exotic orange and yellow and rust foliage of the maples at Rye or Saratoga. When our five-month summer season burns itself out, the foliage is left a cheerless brown; the leaves under your feet are mustard and khaki-colored; and the air, the atmosphere, is virtually a sea of dust.

The speaker's language emphasizes which of the following characteristics about Memphis in autumn?

(A) Freshness
(B) Belligerence
(C) Grandeur
(D) Brilliance
(E) Bleakness

Questions 27–29

Heroes are often those who come to the rescue in moments of crisis. During the American Revolution, on August 29, 1776, under the cover of night and a fortuitous fog, John Glover and his Massachusetts
Line
5 mariners rescued George Washington's army from certain defeat and capture, ferrying them across the turbulent East River from Long Island to New York, a feat of exceptional bravery and nautical skill. Later it was Glover and his men who transported Washington across the Delaware to launch the surprise Christmas attack at Trenton. In Boston, a statue of Glover stands on Commonwealth Avenue, but probably not
10 one passerby in a thousand has any idea how much is owed to him.

27. Which of the following best describes the organization of the passage?

(A) A generalization followed by a series of exceptions.
(B) A definition of a term followed by an illustrative example.

(C) A description of a problem followed by a proposed solution.

(D) A description of an event followed by an outline of its causes.

(E) A description of a viewpoint followed by a description of an opposing viewpoint.

28. The passage implies that the two exploits in which Glover was involved had which of the following in common?

(A) They were critical moments for the success of Washington's army during the war.

(B) Their importance has been exaggerated by historians in recent years.

(C) They highlight Washington's extraordinary gifts as a military commander.

(D) They illustrate the unexpected importance of weather in military operations.

(E) They were hastily arranged, unplanned maneuvers that nearly ended in disaster.

29. Which of the following is most similar to the statue of John Glover and the passersby mentioned in the last sentence of the passage?

(A) A much-admired painting whose painter's identity is unknown.

(B) An old building that is razed to make way for a new one.

(C) A doctor working in a hospital where no one knows the contributions he made to an important cure.

(D) A championship team honored with a ticker-tape parade.

(E) A local politician who is well known in her home district but not outside of it.

Questions 30–34

Japan is a nation built entirely on the tips of giant, suboceanic volcanoes. Little of the land is flat and suitable for agriculture. Terraced hillsides make use of every available square foot of arable land.

Line

5

Single-family dwellings are usually built very close together to further conserve the land. Japan has often been struck by natural disasters, such as earthquakes and hurricanes. Traditional Japanese dwellings were built of light construction materials, so that a house falling down during a disaster would not crush its occupants and also could be quickly and inexpensively rebuilt. During the feudal period, feudal

10

lords sought to discourage their subjects from moving from one village to the next for fear that such mobility would threaten the balance of power. Apparently bridges were not commonly built across rivers and streams until the late nineteenth century, since bridges increased mobility between villages. Taken all together, this characteristic style

15

of living explains why the Japanese have long valued teamwork and collective effort. For generations people lived in the same village next door to the same neighbors. Living in close proximity and in dwellings that gave very little privacy, the traditional Japanese villagers developed an extraordinary capacity to work together in harmony.

30. Which of the following statements best summarizes the main idea of the passage?

(A) Features of Japan's land and history led to an emphasis on cooperation.
(B) Topographical and political barriers hindered progress in feudal Japan.
(C) The instability of Japan's terrain led to instability in its social fabric.
(D) Japan's stability was jeopardized by the competing interests of cities and farms.
(E) Japan's susceptibility to natural disasters led to an emphasis on personal independence.

31. According to the passage, Japanese homes were built small and close together in order to

(A) conserve building materials
(B) make housing affordable to everyone
(C) foster cooperation
(D) deal with frequent natural disasters
(E) maximize land use

32. The passage suggests that few bridges were built in Japan until the late nineteenth century because

(A) feudal lords wished to restrict the mobility of their subjects
(B) frequent natural disasters made investment in infrastructure prohibitive
(C) communities sought to isolate themselves from potential enemies
(D) Japan's typically light construction materials were not suitable for bridges
(E) mobility was associated with natural disaster in the minds of the feudal lords

33. In line 10, the word "discourage" most nearly means

(A) caution
(B) stagger
(C) divert
(D) deter
(E) distract

34. With which of the following statements about Japanese culture would the author be most likely to agree?

(A) Feudal lords encouraged cooperation between villages.
(B) Natural disasters inspired mobility.
(C) Mountainous terrain made construction of bridges difficult.
(D) Enduring neighborhoods led to an unstable balance of power.
(E) Limited resources and reduced privacy led to cooperation.

Questions 35–38

Given that a salesperson's goal is to sell a product, potential customers have reason to question the sincerity of the salesperson's comments. Researchers suggest that two factors determine customers' propensity to do this. The first is accessibility of ulterior motives. For example, the motive behind the car salesperson's "This is a great car!" is easily accessible as the ulterior one of selling the car. In such a case, the customer is apt to question the salesperson's sincerity. However, the motive behind the less relevant "That's a cute dog!" is less easily accessible: the comment may be an insincere compliment intended to make the customer like the salesperson and thus buy the car, or it may be a genuine observation of a dog-loving car salesperson. In this case, we are more apt to take the comment at face value.

The second factor that determines customers' propensity to question the sincerity of salespeople is cognitive "busy-ness": when customers are engaged in a complex task (for example, processing difficult-to-understand information about the car) or when they have competing demands (listening to the salesperson and controlling a curious dog), they are less apt to question the sincerity of comments, as that requires further cognitive effort. They are even less apt to do so when the motive is not easily accessible, as that requires even more effort.

Line
5

10

15

20

35. The primary purpose of the passage is to

(A) criticize the insincerity of salespeople's comments
(B) discuss factors that determine customers' inclinations to question salespeople's sincerity
(C) describe the techniques used by salespeople to sell a product
(D) suggest that salespeople today are more likely to be insincere than were salespeople in the past
(E) justify salespeople's use of insincere comments

36. According to the passage, which of the following is true of customers who are cognitively "busy?"

(A) They are less likely to purchase the product that salespeople are trying to sell.

(B) They are less likely to question the sincerity of salespeople's comments.

(C) They are more likely to be subject to insincere comments by salespeople.

(D) They are more likely to be distracted by factors unimportant to the product, such as other customers.

(E) They are more likely to end up focusing on one issue, such as price.

37. The author mentions "controlling a curious dog" in line 17 as an example of an activity that

(A) places a competing cognitive demand on a customer

(B) provides an opportunity to the salesperson to offer a compliment

(C) makes it less likely that a customer will purchase a product

(D) encourages salespeople to be sincere in their compliments

(E) allows the customer to distinguish sincere salespeople from insincere salespeople

38. The researchers mentioned in line 3 of the passage would be most likely to agree with which of the following about customers and salespeople's comments?

(A) Customers find salespeople's comments insincere whether the comments are related to the product or not.

(B) Customers are more likely to find salespeople's comments insincere if the information about a product is difficult to understand.

(C) Customers rely on salespeople's comments as the most important source of information about a product.

(D) Customers are likely to be less suspicious of salespeople's comments when those comments are not directly relevant to the product.

(E) Customers are more affected by the prices of products than by the perceived sincerity of salespeople's comments.

39. French film critics in the 1950s were the first to acclaim filmmaker Alfred Hitchcock as a tragic metaphysician, at a time when the English-speaking world still considered him to be no more than a shrewd commercial operator. Even today it is French art historians and cinephiles who hold him to be one of the indispensable modern masters—a creator of form, as French filmmakers Claude

Chabrol and Eric Rohmer called him, who altered the way we see the world.

The passage asserts which of the following about French film critics' views of Hitchcock?

(A) They were the first to recognize Hitchcock's artistic talents as a filmmaker.
(B) They were the first to believe that Hitchcock's films would be a strong commercial success.
(C) They failed to see the influence Hitchcock's films had on other films.
(D) They believed that Hitchcock's films were interesting for their form and not for their content.
(E) They were more likely than the English to acknowledge Hitchcock's popularity as a filmmaker.

40. Researchers can use computer simulations of rock glaciers to learn about past climate conditions. Though computer simulations are based on many simplified assumptions (such as a uniformly sloping bed, which real glaciers probably never have), they have led to two hypotheses: small rock glaciers are more sensitive indicators of climate than previously thought, especially if short-term climate changes are of interest; large rock glaciers are good indicators of long-term climate changes because they filter out the small disturbances.

According to the passage, which of the following is true about computer-simulated rock glaciers?

(A) They have confirmed the hypothesis that small rock glaciers are good indicators of long-term climate change.
(B) They cannot be used to simulate past climate conditions.
(C) They are useful because they can simulate a real glacier's irregularly sloping bed.
(D) They can be used only to learn about short-term climate changes.
(E) They are based on certain assumptions that are probably not true of real glaciers.

STOP

If you finish before time is called, you may check your work on this test.

1. **Choice A is the best answer.** According to the third sentence in the passage, the "animal signals" transmitted through plants are "vibrational songs." The last sentence in the passage makes even clearer the idea that these signals are "animal sounds." Choices B, C, D, and E all suggest that the noises come from the plants themselves, not from outside sources.

2. **Choice C is the best answer.** In the first sentence in the passage, the phrase "talked with a candor" indicates that the people described were speaking honestly with one another. The second sentence in the passage indicates that Elizabeth was loved and was well known to the people in the passage. Thus, even though they did not completely understand her, she was most likely a friend. There is no indication in the passage that the people disagreed with one another (choice A) or that they disliked Elizabeth (choice E). No specific encounter with Elizabeth is mentioned (choice B), and there is no indication that Elizabeth was a famous person (choice D).

3. **Choice B is the best answer.** The passage describes the effect that exercise has on each of three factors that in turn affect creativity, thus answering the question posed at the beginning of the passage regarding the relationship between exercise and creativity.

4. **Choice C is the best answer.** The passage indicates that exercise leads to a state called "empty mind," a period of time when the mind is not preoccupied. This lack of preoccupation can encourage creativity.

5. **Choice E is the best answer.** The phrases "contrary to today's popular wisdom" (line 7) and "as many people seem to believe" (lines 16–17) indicate that the author's own beliefs about Holiday and her work are different from the beliefs of other people. In addition, the author's description of some music historians as "shockingly confused" (lines 8–9) about Holiday's artistry indicates that the historians' beliefs are being challenged.

6. **Choice A is the best answer.** The author of the passage acknowledges that Holiday's voice "was not what it had been" (line 2), suggesting that it had deteriorated in some way. However, the author goes on to say that Holiday's emotional intensity, her expressiveness, had increased. No mention is made in the passage of Holiday's musical accompaniment, new material, or live performances (choices B, C, and D). The statement at the end of the passage that she is a singer "whose records live on" indicates that choice E is incorrect.

7. **Choice C is the best answer.** The author of the passage comments that these historians are "otherwise dependable" (line 8) but "shockingly confused on the matter of Holiday as an artist" (lines 8–9). This indicates that, in the author's opinion, the historians are less reliable in their assessment of Holiday's artistry than they are when they discuss other subjects. Since no other information is given in the passage about these particular historians, choices A, B, and E cannot be correct. The author's characterization of the historians as "shockingly confused" indicates that he disagrees with them, so choice D is also incorrect.

8. **Choice A is the best answer.** The passage states that Holiday transmuted, or transformed, her sorrows, an aspect of her emotional life, into gold, or great art. The phrase "Like any real artist" (lines 12–13) indicates that "real" artists must be able to do the same.

9. **Choice D is the best answer.** Line 7 state that the author's opinion—that "her last years were her greatest"—is contrary to current popular opinion. Therefore, it can be inferred that most people today prefer Holiday's early work.

10. **Choice C is the best answer.** The first paragraph in the passage describes Boswell's approach to writing biography as "innovative" (line 2), and indicates that descriptions of the subject's actions were central to that innovation. The last sentence in the passage confirms that Boswell's work made his subject "come alive."

11. **Choice C is the best answer.** The second paragraph in the passage describes the particular way in which the biographer, Boswell, and his subject, Johnson, each benefited the other. Choice A is incorrect because it is contradicted by information in the passage. Choice B is also incorrect: although the passage states that "Without Boswell's artistry, Johnson's genius would not have come alive" (lines 9–10), the passage does not go so far as to suggest that no acknowledgment of Johnson's work would ever have been made. There is no information in the passage to indicate that Boswell's descriptions are inaccurate, so choice D can be eliminated. Choice E is incorrect because, although it is possible that Boswell was not an objective observer, there is nothing in the passage to indicate that the author would agree with that assessment.

12. **Choice A is the best answer.** Since the author of the passage could not have had first-hand knowledge of the Babylonians themselves, the statement that they were "obsessed with tables" must be an opinion based on the large number of tables they created. Each of the other choices could possibly be verified by observation as a fact.

13. **Choice A is the best answer.** The statement that "experienced sailors could effectively navigate" using depth soundings indicates that the sailors already had a dependable method for finding their way. Choice B is incorrect because the method described in the passage was based on depth soundings, not currents. Because the sailors had a dependable navigation method, they did not have a great need for the compass, so choice C cannot be correct. Choices D and E may have been true, but there is no support for either one in the passage.

14. **Choice B is the best answer.** Each of the choices describes an attempt to make a product or service more attractive to buyers. However, catalogues, as they are described in choice B, are most similar to the menu, which evolved from a "mere list" to a more complex form. The menu and the catalogue each use detailed descriptions in an attempt to sell particular items.

15. **Choice C is the best answer.** The last sentence in the passage summarizes the role of the scribes in Mayan civilization, indicating that they prepared both art and text, the purpose of which was to glorify the king, thus making his position more secure.

16. **Choice D is the best answer.** The passage asserts that the scribes' writing and art were used for "magnifying their king's reputation and solidifying his political hold" (lines 5–6). This use suggests that the kings understood the power of propaganda, information used by a government or a ruler to promote particular ideas among the population.

17. **Choice B is the best answer.** In the first paragraph, the author provides arguments for the testing of levels of vitamins in the blood; in the second paragraph, arguments against such testing are presented. As part of this evaluation of the usefulness of the practice, a current testing method and a possible new method for testing vitamin levels in blood are described.

18. **Choice C is the best answer.** The word "reflect" has several meanings. In the context of the sentence, certain blood test results cannot "reflect" vitamin levels in other parts of the body. Thus, "indicate" is the substitution that would least change the meaning of the sentence. Since vitamin levels cannot meditate or ponder, choices A and D are incorrect. The results of tests do not directly affect what is going on in the body, so choices B and E are also incorrect.

19. **Choice C is the best answer.** The statement that vitamin levels can vary from day to day is one of a list of difficulties, each of which, critics point out, might limit the usefulness of testing for the level of vitamins in the blood.

20. Choice D is the best answer. In line 4, Bruce Ames is said to have called testing for vitamins "the future of preventive medicine" and to have compared the measurement of vitamins and minerals to the measuring of cholesterol levels, a test commonly performed as part of a regular checkup.

21. Choice E is the best answer. The description of the new test in the last sentence in the passage follows a list of the difficulties encountered in testing for blood levels of vitamins. The phrase "Because of these difficulties" in line 16 indicates that the test was developed in an attempt to overcome these difficulties.

22. Choice B is the best answer. Although the passage begins by mentioning the wireless telegraph and its inventor, most of the passage describes how the radio differed from the telegraph, discussing its impact on communication. The misconception mentioned in the passage has to do with the invention of the radio, not its early uses, so choice A is not correct. Although the use of the telegraph in private communication is mentioned in the passage, no argument regarding its importance is made. Therefore, choice C is not correct. The passage does provide some information about the inventor of the telegraph, but only as a way to introduce the discussion of the radio, so choice D is incorrect. Since the passage does not describe the actual invention of either the telegraph or the telephone, choice E is also incorrect.

23. Choice D is the best answer. In the last sentence, the author contrasts the contributions of telephone and telegraph (means of private communication between individuals) and radio, which had the capacity to reach many people at a time (public communication).

24. Choice B is the best answer. The passage describes the making and use of dry paintings and suggests two possible explanations for their immediate destruction. Contrary to choice A, the passage confirms that much time and labor was required to make the paintings. Since the passage discusses only dry paintings, and not other aspects of the religion or culture of which they were a part, choices C, D, and E are not correct.

25. Choice E is the best answer. The third sentence in the passage states that Cather is unlike Dickinson in that Cather did not have a wide influence among fellow authors. According to the passage Cather is like Dickinson in having a perfect ear and in creating new rhythms for American prose, so choices A and C are not correct. Although Cather differs from Dickinson with regard to her place in histories of American literature, it is Dickinson, and not Cather, who has had an important place in those histories, so choice B is incorrect. Choice D is incorrect because, according to the passage, Cather sold many books in her lifetime, not few books.

26. Choice E is the best answer. The author's mention of "cheerless brown" and "mustard and khaki-colored" as the dull colors found in Memphis in autumn suggests that the city is dull and cheerless, characterized by bleakness.

27. Choice B is the best answer. In line 1, the author provides one possible definition of heroes—"those who come to the rescue in moments of crisis." The rest of the passage describes the actions of John Glover, an example of a hero who rescued Washington's army at a critical time.

28. Choice A is the best answer. The author of the passage cites Glover as an example of a hero, one who acts in times of crisis—times that are especially important, or critical. The information that Washington's army was saved from "certain defeat and capture" (lines 4–5) in one case and was helped to "launch the surprise Christmas attack at Trenton" (line 8) in the other makes clear that both rescues by Glover occurred at important times during the American Revolution.

29. Choice C is the best answer. Like the anonymous contribution made by a doctor doing his job, John Glover's contribution is unrecognized by most people.

30. Choice A is the best answer. The passage describes the effects on the Japanese people of the limited amount of usable land and the effects of Japan's history of natural disasters and feudal restrictions. As a result of these features, the people developed "an extraordinary capacity to work together in harmony" (line 19); in other words, they placed an emphasis on cooperation. Choice B is incorrect, since no mention is made of the effects of topography or politics on progress in feudal Japan. There is no indication that Japanese society was or is unstable, so choices C and D are incorrect. Choice E suggests a style of living quite different from that described in the passage.

31. Choice E is the best answer. The passage states that houses were constructed in a way that would "conserve the land" (line 5). Small houses built close together would take up little land. Choice A is incorrect because, although small houses would use little building material, building houses close together would have no such effect. There is no indication in the passage that making housing affordable and fostering cooperation were actually goals in Japan, so choices B and C are incorrect. Choice D is incorrect because use of light construction materials, not spacing or building size, is mentioned as being important in dealing with the effects of natural disasters.

32. Choice A is the best answer. According to the passage, feudal lords feared that mobility would "threaten the balance of power" (lines 11–12), and "bridges increased mobility between villages" (lines 13–14). Therefore, it can be concluded that few bridges were built because feudal lords wanted to restrict their subjects' mobility.

33. Choice D is the best answer. The feudal lords wanted to discourage, or prevent, their subjects from moving from one village to the next.

34. Choice E is the best answer. Throughout the passage, the author discusses the limited availability of land in Japan, and the lack of privacy that led the Japanese to "work together in harmony" (line 19), a form of cooperation.

35. Choice B is the best answer. After stating in the first sentence in the passage that customers "have reason to question the sincerity of the salesperson's comments," the author points out two factors that affect the likelihood that a customer will do so. Discussion of these factors includes examples relating to a particular situation in which the factors might occur. Since the passage does not say that salespeople's comments actually are insincere, choices A, D, and E are incorrect. Although the passage suggests that salespeople may use insincere comments in the course of a sale, discussing a variety of techniques is not the primary purpose of the passage, so choice C is incorrect.

36. Choice B is the best answer. According to line 14, cognitive "busy-ness" is a factor that affects a customer's perception of a salesperson's sincerity. A cognitively "busy" person is "less apt to question the sincerity of comments" (line 18).

37. Choice A is the best answer. The author of the passage uses parentheses in line 17 to indicate that controlling a curious dog while listening to a salesperson is an example of a situation in which demands are competing. Such competition requires increased cognitive effort on the part of the customer.

38. Choice D is the best answer. Since the passage is primarily a discussion about the two factors suggested by the researchers mentioned in line 3, those researchers would be likely to agree with statements made or implied in the passage. According to the passage, when a salesperson makes a comment that is not directly relevant to the product being sold, a customer may have difficulty deciding whether the comment is sincere. When the motivation for the comment is unclear, the customer is "more apt to take the comment at face value" (line 12), and thus is less likely to suspect an ulterior motive.

39. Choice A is the best answer. The passage states that French film critics were the first to "acclaim filmmaker Alfred Hitchcock" for his artistry, rather than for his ability to make a profit, as choice B suggests.

40. Choice E is the best answer. The passage states that computer simulations of rock glaciers are based on simplified assumptions. It provides an example that suggests that some of the assumptions are probably untrue.

CALCULATING YOUR SCORE

To score PPST: Reading Test 2:

- Count the number of questions you answered correctly. The correct answers are in Table 1.
- Use Table 2 to find the scaled score corresponding to the number of questions answered correctly. You can compare your scaled score to the passing score required by your state or institution. (Passing state scores are available on the Praxis Web site at www.ets.org/praxis.)
- Content category I contains 24 questions measuring literal comprehension. The 16 questions in category II assess reading skills in critical and inferential comprehension. Count the number of questions you answered correctly in each of these categories. This may give you some idea of your strengths and weaknesses.

Table 1—PPST: Reading Test 2
Answers to Practice Test Questions

Sequence Number	Correct Answer	Content Category	Sequence Number	Correct Answer	Content Category
1	A	I	21	E	II
2	C	II	22	B	I
3	B	I	23	D	I
4	C	I	24	B	I
5	E	I	25	E	I
6	A	I	26	E	II
7	C	II	27	B	I
8	A	II	28	A	II
9	D	II	29	C	II
10	C	I	30	A	I
11	C	II	31	E	I
12	A	II	32	A	II
13	A	I	33	D	I
14	B	II	34	E	II
15	C	I	35	B	I
16	D	II	36	B	I
17	B	I	37	A	I
18	C	I	38	D	II
19	C	II	39	A	I
20	D	I	40	E	I

Table 2—PPST: Reading Test 2
Score Conversion Table

Raw Score	Scaled Score	Raw Score	Scaled Score	Raw Score	Scaled Score
0	151	14	161	28	173
1	151	15	162	29	174
2	151	16	163	30	175
3	151	17	164	31	176
4	151	18	165	32	177
5	151	19	165	33	178
6	152	20	166	34	179
7	152	21	167	35	180
8	154	22	168	36	181
9	156	23	169	37	182
10	157	24	170	38	183
11	158	25	170	39	185
12	159	26	171	40	186
13	160	27	172		

Next, assess your strengths in the two content categories. Use the content category information in Table 1 to determine whether you need to prepare more intensely in any of the two areas covered by the test. The content categories are represented in Table 1 by Roman numerals, which correspond to the following descriptions:

I. Literal Comprehension

II. Critical and Inferential Comprehension

Fill in Table 3 to see where you have the most room for improvement.

Table 3—Assessment of Strengths in Each Category

Content Category	Number of Correct Answers Possible	Number of Incorrect Answers
I	24	
II	16	

Focus on the content area or areas in which you have the most incorrect answers (the rightmost column in Table 3). The *Praxis Pre-Professional Skills Tests (PPST): Reading Study Guide* can help you review these content areas. (The guide can be purchased at www.ets.org/store.html or in your local bookstore.)

Measure of Question Difficulty

The values in Table 4 are the percentage of examinees that answered each question correctly. This is used as a measure of question difficulty. In general, the higher the percentage the easier the question.

Table 4—Percentage of Examinees Choosing Correct Answers for the PPST Reading Practice Test

Sequence Number	Percentage of Examinees Choosing Correct Answer	Sequence Number	Percentage of Examinees Choosing Correct Answer
1	91%	21	69%
2	70%	22	76%
3	75%	23	87%
4	79%	24	92%
5	87%	25	92%
6	95%	26	86%
7	56%	27	66%
8	88%	28	94%
9	60%	29	87%
10	87%	30	90%
11	66%	31	78%
12	78%	32	88%
13	88%	33	70%
14	84%	34	85%
15	94%	35	86%
16	74%	36	89%
17	64%	37	82%
18	95%	38	53%
19	79%	39	71%
20	88%	40	66%

NOTE: Percentages are based on the test records of 2,331 examinees who took the 60-minute version of the PPST Reading test in June 2003.

In general, questions may be considered as easy, average, or difficult based on the following percentages:

Easy questions = 75% or more answered correctly
Average questions = 55%–74% answered correctly
Difficult questions = less than 55% answered correctly

Using Your Practice Test Score to Estimate Your Future Score

When you take the Pre-Professional Skills Test: Reading at an actual administration, the questions you will be presented with will be similar to the questions in this practice test, but they will not be identical. Because of the difference in questions, the test that you actually take may be slightly more or less difficult. Therefore, you should not expect to get exactly the same score that you achieved on this practice test.[*]

Good luck on your test!

---

[*] To make all editions of the test comparable, there is a statistical adjustment for the difference in difficulty among editions of the test. This adjustment for difficulty makes it possible to give the same interpretation to identical scaled scores on different editions of the test.

CHAPTER 11

PPST: Mathematics Test 1

THE PRAXIS SERIES

Professional Assessments for Beginning Teachers®

TEST NAME:
Pre-Professional Skills Test Mathematics

Time—60 minutes

40 Questions

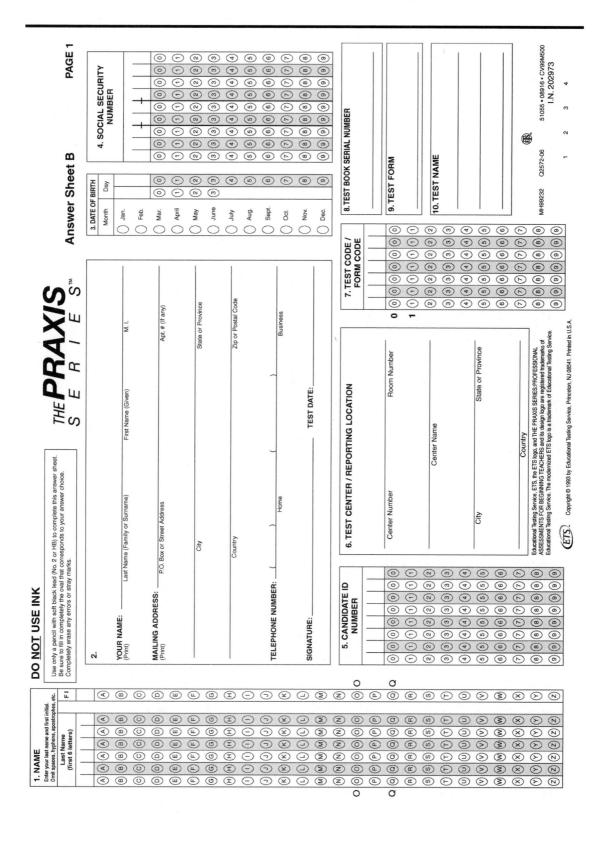

CERTIFICATION STATEMENT: (Please write the following statement below. DO NOT PRINT.)

"I hereby agree to the conditions set forth in the *Registration Bulletin* and certify that I am the person whose name and address appear on this answer sheet."

_____

_____

_____

SIGNATURE: _____ DATE: _____/_____/_____
                                                                                                Month   Day   Year

BE SURE EACH MARK IS DARK AND COMPLETELY FILLS THE INTENDED SPACE AS ILLUSTRATED HERE: ●

1 Ⓐ Ⓑ Ⓒ Ⓓ Ⓔ	41 Ⓐ Ⓑ Ⓒ Ⓓ Ⓔ	81 Ⓐ Ⓑ Ⓒ Ⓓ Ⓔ	121 Ⓐ Ⓑ Ⓒ Ⓓ Ⓔ
2 Ⓐ Ⓑ Ⓒ Ⓓ Ⓔ	42 Ⓐ Ⓑ Ⓒ Ⓓ Ⓔ	82 Ⓐ Ⓑ Ⓒ Ⓓ Ⓔ	122 Ⓐ Ⓑ Ⓒ Ⓓ Ⓔ
3 Ⓐ Ⓑ Ⓒ Ⓓ Ⓔ	43 Ⓐ Ⓑ Ⓒ Ⓓ Ⓔ	83 Ⓐ Ⓑ Ⓒ Ⓓ Ⓔ	123 Ⓐ Ⓑ Ⓒ Ⓓ Ⓔ
4 Ⓐ Ⓑ Ⓒ Ⓓ Ⓔ	44 Ⓐ Ⓑ Ⓒ Ⓓ Ⓔ	84 Ⓐ Ⓑ Ⓒ Ⓓ Ⓔ	124 Ⓐ Ⓑ Ⓒ Ⓓ Ⓔ
5 Ⓐ Ⓑ Ⓒ Ⓓ Ⓔ	45 Ⓐ Ⓑ Ⓒ Ⓓ Ⓔ	85 Ⓐ Ⓑ Ⓒ Ⓓ Ⓔ	125 Ⓐ Ⓑ Ⓒ Ⓓ Ⓔ
6 Ⓐ Ⓑ Ⓒ Ⓓ Ⓔ	46 Ⓐ Ⓑ Ⓒ Ⓓ Ⓔ	86 Ⓐ Ⓑ Ⓒ Ⓓ Ⓔ	126 Ⓐ Ⓑ Ⓒ Ⓓ Ⓔ
7 Ⓐ Ⓑ Ⓒ Ⓓ Ⓔ	47 Ⓐ Ⓑ Ⓒ Ⓓ Ⓔ	87 Ⓐ Ⓑ Ⓒ Ⓓ Ⓔ	127 Ⓐ Ⓑ Ⓒ Ⓓ Ⓔ
8 Ⓐ Ⓑ Ⓒ Ⓓ Ⓔ	48 Ⓐ Ⓑ Ⓒ Ⓓ Ⓔ	88 Ⓐ Ⓑ Ⓒ Ⓓ Ⓔ	128 Ⓐ Ⓑ Ⓒ Ⓓ Ⓔ
9 Ⓐ Ⓑ Ⓒ Ⓓ Ⓔ	49 Ⓐ Ⓑ Ⓒ Ⓓ Ⓔ	89 Ⓐ Ⓑ Ⓒ Ⓓ Ⓔ	129 Ⓐ Ⓑ Ⓒ Ⓓ Ⓔ
10 Ⓐ Ⓑ Ⓒ Ⓓ Ⓔ	50 Ⓐ Ⓑ Ⓒ Ⓓ Ⓔ	90 Ⓐ Ⓑ Ⓒ Ⓓ Ⓔ	130 Ⓐ Ⓑ Ⓒ Ⓓ Ⓔ
11 Ⓐ Ⓑ Ⓒ Ⓓ Ⓔ	51 Ⓐ Ⓑ Ⓒ Ⓓ Ⓔ	91 Ⓐ Ⓑ Ⓒ Ⓓ Ⓔ	131 Ⓐ Ⓑ Ⓒ Ⓓ Ⓔ
12 Ⓐ Ⓑ Ⓒ Ⓓ Ⓔ	52 Ⓐ Ⓑ Ⓒ Ⓓ Ⓔ	92 Ⓐ Ⓑ Ⓒ Ⓓ Ⓔ	132 Ⓐ Ⓑ Ⓒ Ⓓ Ⓔ
13 Ⓐ Ⓑ Ⓒ Ⓓ Ⓔ	53 Ⓐ Ⓑ Ⓒ Ⓓ Ⓔ	93 Ⓐ Ⓑ Ⓒ Ⓓ Ⓔ	133 Ⓐ Ⓑ Ⓒ Ⓓ Ⓔ
14 Ⓐ Ⓑ Ⓒ Ⓓ Ⓔ	54 Ⓐ Ⓑ Ⓒ Ⓓ Ⓔ	94 Ⓐ Ⓑ Ⓒ Ⓓ Ⓔ	134 Ⓐ Ⓑ Ⓒ Ⓓ Ⓔ
15 Ⓐ Ⓑ Ⓒ Ⓓ Ⓔ	55 Ⓐ Ⓑ Ⓒ Ⓓ Ⓔ	95 Ⓐ Ⓑ Ⓒ Ⓓ Ⓔ	135 Ⓐ Ⓑ Ⓒ Ⓓ Ⓔ
16 Ⓐ Ⓑ Ⓒ Ⓓ Ⓔ	56 Ⓐ Ⓑ Ⓒ Ⓓ Ⓔ	96 Ⓐ Ⓑ Ⓒ Ⓓ Ⓔ	136 Ⓐ Ⓑ Ⓒ Ⓓ Ⓔ
17 Ⓐ Ⓑ Ⓒ Ⓓ Ⓔ	57 Ⓐ Ⓑ Ⓒ Ⓓ Ⓔ	97 Ⓐ Ⓑ Ⓒ Ⓓ Ⓔ	137 Ⓐ Ⓑ Ⓒ Ⓓ Ⓔ
18 Ⓐ Ⓑ Ⓒ Ⓓ Ⓔ	58 Ⓐ Ⓑ Ⓒ Ⓓ Ⓔ	98 Ⓐ Ⓑ Ⓒ Ⓓ Ⓔ	138 Ⓐ Ⓑ Ⓒ Ⓓ Ⓔ
19 Ⓐ Ⓑ Ⓒ Ⓓ Ⓔ	59 Ⓐ Ⓑ Ⓒ Ⓓ Ⓔ	99 Ⓐ Ⓑ Ⓒ Ⓓ Ⓔ	139 Ⓐ Ⓑ Ⓒ Ⓓ Ⓔ
20 Ⓐ Ⓑ Ⓒ Ⓓ Ⓔ	60 Ⓐ Ⓑ Ⓒ Ⓓ Ⓔ	100 Ⓐ Ⓑ Ⓒ Ⓓ Ⓔ	140 Ⓐ Ⓑ Ⓒ Ⓓ Ⓔ
21 Ⓐ Ⓑ Ⓒ Ⓓ Ⓔ	61 Ⓐ Ⓑ Ⓒ Ⓓ Ⓔ	101 Ⓐ Ⓑ Ⓒ Ⓓ Ⓔ	141 Ⓐ Ⓑ Ⓒ Ⓓ Ⓔ
22 Ⓐ Ⓑ Ⓒ Ⓓ Ⓔ	62 Ⓐ Ⓑ Ⓒ Ⓓ Ⓔ	102 Ⓐ Ⓑ Ⓒ Ⓓ Ⓔ	142 Ⓐ Ⓑ Ⓒ Ⓓ Ⓔ
23 Ⓐ Ⓑ Ⓒ Ⓓ Ⓔ	63 Ⓐ Ⓑ Ⓒ Ⓓ Ⓔ	103 Ⓐ Ⓑ Ⓒ Ⓓ Ⓔ	143 Ⓐ Ⓑ Ⓒ Ⓓ Ⓔ
24 Ⓐ Ⓑ Ⓒ Ⓓ Ⓔ	64 Ⓐ Ⓑ Ⓒ Ⓓ Ⓔ	104 Ⓐ Ⓑ Ⓒ Ⓓ Ⓔ	144 Ⓐ Ⓑ Ⓒ Ⓓ Ⓔ
25 Ⓐ Ⓑ Ⓒ Ⓓ Ⓔ	65 Ⓐ Ⓑ Ⓒ Ⓓ Ⓔ	105 Ⓐ Ⓑ Ⓒ Ⓓ Ⓔ	145 Ⓐ Ⓑ Ⓒ Ⓓ Ⓔ
26 Ⓐ Ⓑ Ⓒ Ⓓ Ⓔ	66 Ⓐ Ⓑ Ⓒ Ⓓ Ⓔ	106 Ⓐ Ⓑ Ⓒ Ⓓ Ⓔ	146 Ⓐ Ⓑ Ⓒ Ⓓ Ⓔ
27 Ⓐ Ⓑ Ⓒ Ⓓ Ⓔ	67 Ⓐ Ⓑ Ⓒ Ⓓ Ⓔ	107 Ⓐ Ⓑ Ⓒ Ⓓ Ⓔ	147 Ⓐ Ⓑ Ⓒ Ⓓ Ⓔ
28 Ⓐ Ⓑ Ⓒ Ⓓ Ⓔ	68 Ⓐ Ⓑ Ⓒ Ⓓ Ⓔ	108 Ⓐ Ⓑ Ⓒ Ⓓ Ⓔ	148 Ⓐ Ⓑ Ⓒ Ⓓ Ⓔ
29 Ⓐ Ⓑ Ⓒ Ⓓ Ⓔ	69 Ⓐ Ⓑ Ⓒ Ⓓ Ⓔ	109 Ⓐ Ⓑ Ⓒ Ⓓ Ⓔ	149 Ⓐ Ⓑ Ⓒ Ⓓ Ⓔ
30 Ⓐ Ⓑ Ⓒ Ⓓ Ⓔ	70 Ⓐ Ⓑ Ⓒ Ⓓ Ⓔ	110 Ⓐ Ⓑ Ⓒ Ⓓ Ⓔ	150 Ⓐ Ⓑ Ⓒ Ⓓ Ⓔ
31 Ⓐ Ⓑ Ⓒ Ⓓ Ⓔ	71 Ⓐ Ⓑ Ⓒ Ⓓ Ⓔ	111 Ⓐ Ⓑ Ⓒ Ⓓ Ⓔ	151 Ⓐ Ⓑ Ⓒ Ⓓ Ⓔ
32 Ⓐ Ⓑ Ⓒ Ⓓ Ⓔ	72 Ⓐ Ⓑ Ⓒ Ⓓ Ⓔ	112 Ⓐ Ⓑ Ⓒ Ⓓ Ⓔ	152 Ⓐ Ⓑ Ⓒ Ⓓ Ⓔ
33 Ⓐ Ⓑ Ⓒ Ⓓ Ⓔ	73 Ⓐ Ⓑ Ⓒ Ⓓ Ⓔ	113 Ⓐ Ⓑ Ⓒ Ⓓ Ⓔ	153 Ⓐ Ⓑ Ⓒ Ⓓ Ⓔ
34 Ⓐ Ⓑ Ⓒ Ⓓ Ⓔ	74 Ⓐ Ⓑ Ⓒ Ⓓ Ⓔ	114 Ⓐ Ⓑ Ⓒ Ⓓ Ⓔ	154 Ⓐ Ⓑ Ⓒ Ⓓ Ⓔ
35 Ⓐ Ⓑ Ⓒ Ⓓ Ⓔ	75 Ⓐ Ⓑ Ⓒ Ⓓ Ⓔ	115 Ⓐ Ⓑ Ⓒ Ⓓ Ⓔ	155 Ⓐ Ⓑ Ⓒ Ⓓ Ⓔ
36 Ⓐ Ⓑ Ⓒ Ⓓ Ⓔ	76 Ⓐ Ⓑ Ⓒ Ⓓ Ⓔ	116 Ⓐ Ⓑ Ⓒ Ⓓ Ⓔ	156 Ⓐ Ⓑ Ⓒ Ⓓ Ⓔ
37 Ⓐ Ⓑ Ⓒ Ⓓ Ⓔ	77 Ⓐ Ⓑ Ⓒ Ⓓ Ⓔ	117 Ⓐ Ⓑ Ⓒ Ⓓ Ⓔ	157 Ⓐ Ⓑ Ⓒ Ⓓ Ⓔ
38 Ⓐ Ⓑ Ⓒ Ⓓ Ⓔ	78 Ⓐ Ⓑ Ⓒ Ⓓ Ⓔ	118 Ⓐ Ⓑ Ⓒ Ⓓ Ⓔ	158 Ⓐ Ⓑ Ⓒ Ⓓ Ⓔ
39 Ⓐ Ⓑ Ⓒ Ⓓ Ⓔ	79 Ⓐ Ⓑ Ⓒ Ⓓ Ⓔ	119 Ⓐ Ⓑ Ⓒ Ⓓ Ⓔ	159 Ⓐ Ⓑ Ⓒ Ⓓ Ⓔ
40 Ⓐ Ⓑ Ⓒ Ⓓ Ⓔ	80 Ⓐ Ⓑ Ⓒ Ⓓ Ⓔ	120 Ⓐ Ⓑ Ⓒ Ⓓ Ⓔ	160 Ⓐ Ⓑ Ⓒ Ⓓ Ⓔ

FOR ETS USE ONLY	R1	R2	R3	R4	R5	R6	R7	R8	TR	CS

Directions: Each of the questions or incomplete statements below is followed by five suggested answers or completions. Select the one that is best in each and then fill in the corresponding lettered space on the answer sheet with a heavy, dark mark so that you cannot see the letter.

Remember, try to answer every question.

Special note: Figures that accompany problems in the test are intended to provide information useful in solving the problem. The figures are drawn as accurately as possible except when it is stated in a specific problem that its figure is not drawn to scale. Figures can be assumed to lie in a plane unless otherwise indicated. Position of points can be assumed to be in the order shown, and lines shown as straight can be assumed to be straight. The symbol ∟ denotes a right angle.

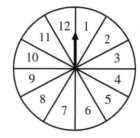

1. On the spinner above, the probability of spinning a number that is a multiple of 3 is

(A) $\frac{1}{12}$ (D) $\frac{5}{12}$

(B) $\frac{3}{12}$ (E) $\frac{8}{12}$

(C) $\frac{4}{12}$

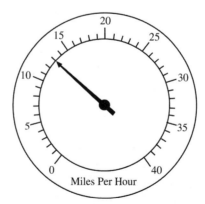

Miles Per Hour

2. A gauge on an exercise bicycle is shown above. The reading on the gauge, in miles per hour, is

(A) 10.3   (D) 12
(B) 10.5   (E) 13
(C) 10.6

3. Which of the following numbers is <u>least</u>?

(A) $\dfrac{1}{7}$

(B) $\dfrac{11}{70}$

(C) $\dfrac{101}{700}$

(D) $\dfrac{1,001}{7,000}$

(E) $\dfrac{10,001}{70,000}$

4. A 10-gallon tank contains $6\frac{1}{8}$ gallons of gasoline. How many more gallons are needed to fill the tank?

(A) A little less than 3 gallons
(B) A little more than 3 gallons
(C) A little less than 4 gallons
(D) A little more than 4 gallons
(E) A little less than 5 gallons

5. A map is drawn to the scale of $\frac{3}{4}$ inch = 50 miles. What is the actual distance between two towns that are $1\frac{1}{2}$ inches apart on the map?

(A) 75 miles
(B) 100 miles
(C) 125 miles
(D) 150 miles
(E) 200 miles

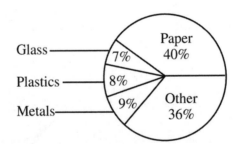

6. The graph above shows the distribution of the content, by weight, of a county's trash. If approximately 60 tons of the trash consists of paper, approximately how many tons of the trash consists of plastics?

(A) 24
(B) 20
(C) 15
(D) 12
(E) 5

7. A certain soccer league reported that 12.5 percent of its injured players received ankle injuries last season. There were 128 injured players. Which computation shows the number of players who received ankle injuries?

(A) 0.0125×128
(B) 0.125×128
(C) 1.25×128
(D) 12.5×128
(E) 125×128

x	y
−4	−2
−3	$-\dfrac{3}{2}$
−2	−1
−1	$-\dfrac{1}{2}$
0	0

8. Which of the following is true about the data in the table above?

(A) As x decreases, y increases.
(B) As x decreases, y does not change.
(C) As x increases, y does not change.
(D) As x increases, y decreases.
(E) As x increases, y increases.

NUMBER OF COPIES OF FOUR BOOKS
SOLD IN ONE DAY IN A BOOKSTORE

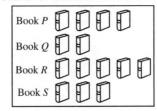

9. If the bookstore sold 60 more copies of book R than book Q, how many books does each in the pictograph represent?

(A) 3
(B) 10
(C) 20
(D) 30
(E) 60

7

10. If the perimeter of the rectangle above is 50, what is its length?

(A) 43
(B) 36
(C) 28
(D) 26
(E) 18

11. If $3a = 18 - 3b$ what is the value of $a + b$?

(A) 0
(B) 6
(C) 9
(D) 12
(E) 15

Questions 12–13 refer to the following graph.

NUMBER OF STUDENTS IN MEDICAL SCHOOLS
IN THE UNITED STATES, 1950–1985
(in thousands)

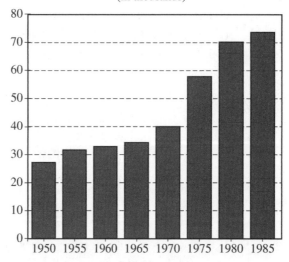

12. In how many of the years shown were there more than twice as many students in medical schools as there were in 1950?

(A) None
(B) One
(C) Two
(D) Three
(E) Five

13. The number of students in medical schools increased by approximately what percent from 1970 to 1980?

(A) 75%
(B) 60%
(C) 50%
(D) 45%
(E) 30%

14. The number 1,000 is how many times 0.1?

(A)   10
(B)   100
(C)   1,000
(D)   10,000
(E) 100,000

15. Which of the following shows a circle with center at (1,1) and a radius of 2?

(A)
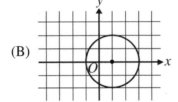

(B)
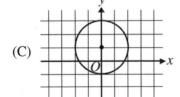

(C)
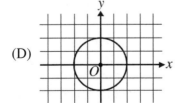

(D)
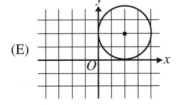

(E)
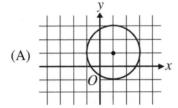

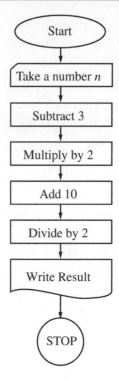

16. If $n = 2$, what is the result of the computation outlined in the chart above?

(A) −6
(B) −4
(C) 4
(D) 5
(E) 6

17. A vending machine containing school supplies offers pencils at 2 for a quarter and notebooks at 50 cents each. If the machine accepts only quarters, how many quarters are needed to buy 6 pencils and 2 notebooks?

(A) 16
(B) 10
(C) 8
(D) 7
(E) 5

18. Which of the following numbers, if any, are the same?

I. 1 million
II. 1,000 thousands
III. 10,000 tens

(A) None of them
(B) I and II only

(C) I and III only

(D) II and III only

(E) I, II, and III

19. Which of the following does NOT leave a remainder of 5 when divided into 141?

(A) 136

(B) 68

(C) 34

(D) 16

(E) 8

20. Which of the following is greater than 18.7%?

(A) 0.05

(B) 0.15

(C) $\frac{1}{10}$

(D) 0.01875

(E) $\frac{1}{5}$

21. There are 8 boys and 13 girls in a choir. What fractional part of the choir is boys?

(A) $\frac{8}{13}$

(B) $\frac{8}{21}$

(C) $\frac{13}{21}$

(D) $\frac{5}{8}$

(E) $\frac{13}{8}$

22. To find 400 times 30, one could multiply 12 by

(A) 10

(B) 100

(C) 1,000

(D) 10,000

(E) 100,000

23. If 30% of $W = 483$, then $W =$

(A) 1,610

(B) 627.9

(C) 513

(D) 338.1

(E) 144.9

24. A set of three points on a line could be a subset of any of the following EXCEPT a

(A) square
(B) triangle
(C) cube
(D) cylinder
(E) circle

ROBIN'S TEST SCORES

88, 86, 98, 92, 90, 86

25. In an ordered set of numbers, the median is the middle number if there is a middle number; otherwise, the median is the average of the two middle numbers. If Robin had the test scores given in the table above, what was her median score?

(A) 86
(B) 89
(C) 90
(D) 92
(E) 95

Questions 26–27 refer to the following table.

**DAYTIME RATES
FOR DIRECT-DIALED CALLS**

Miles Between Parties	First Minute	Each Additional Minute
1–10	$0.23	$0.15
11–22	$0.28	$0.19
23–55	$0.31	$0.21
56–124	$0.33	$0.24
125–292	$0.33	$0.26
293–430	$0.34	$0.28
431–925	$0.36	$0.30
926–1,910	$0.37	$0.31
1,911–3,000	$0.40	$0.32

26. The cost of a 50-minute direct-dialed daytime call between two parties 500 miles apart is

(A) $14.00
(B) $14.70
(C) $15.06
(D) $15.36
(E) $17.00

27. If the cost of a 20-minute direct-dialed daytime call was \$6.26, which of the following could be the distance between the parties?

(A)   50 miles
(B)   360 miles
(C)   480 miles
(D)   900 miles
(E) 1,250 miles

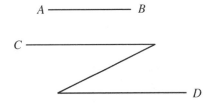

28. If the length of *AB* in the figure above represents 0.3 mile, which of the following is most likely the length, in miles, of the road shown from *C* to *D*?

(A) 0.012
(B) 0.12
(C) 1.2
(D) 0.9
(E) 3

29. If $B = 2(G - 5)$, then $G =$

(A) $2(B-5)$

(B) $\dfrac{B+10}{2}$

(C) $\dfrac{B}{2}$

(D) $2(B+5)$

(E) $\dfrac{B-5}{2}$

30. Which of the following expressions is NOT equivalent to the others?

(A) $2^2 \times 10 \times 12$
(B) $2^3 \times 6 \times 10$
(C) $2^4 \times 5 \times 6$
(D) $2^5 \times 3 \times 10$
(E) $4^2 \times 5 \times 6$

31. In one year, a funding agency spent the following amounts on five projects.

Project 1: $19,256,413
Project 2: $ 7,986,472
Project 3: $11,010,218
Project 4: $ 754,194
Project 5: $ 4,918,975

The total amount spent on these five projects, in millions of dollars, was most nearly

(A) 40
(B) 41
(C) 42
(D) 43
(E) 44

32. A square-topped cake is uniformly iced on its top and sides. Which of the following figures shows a way to slice the cake so that each piece has the same amount of icing?

(A)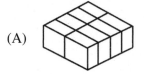

(D)

(B)

(E)

(C)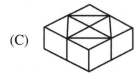

33. If $\boxed{\begin{array}{cc} T & S \\ & R \end{array}} = \dfrac{T - S}{R}$, then $\boxed{\begin{array}{cc} 12 & -4 \\ & 8 \end{array}} =$

(A) 2
(B) 1
(C) −1
(D) −2
(E) −5

34. The four shapes below are made up of identical squares and identical right triangles. If two sides of each triangle have equal length, which of the four shapes, if any, has the <u>least</u> perimeter?

(A)

(D)

(B)

(E)   All have the same perimeter.

(C)

35. On a certain day, high tide occurred at 8:54 a.m. and again at 9:26 p.m. What was the length of time between the two high tides?

(A) 11 hr 12 min
(B) 12 hr 32 min
(C) 13 hr 12 min
(D) 13 hr 20 min
(E) 14 hr 20 min

36. Which of the figures below could be used to <u>disprove</u> the statement "If all sides of a polygon are equal in length, then all angles of the polygon are equal in measure?"

(A)

(D)

(B)

(E)

(C)

37. If the width of the rectangle above is doubled and its length is halved, then the area of the new rectangle is given by the formula

(A) $A = 2\frac{1}{2}x$

(B) $A = 5x$

(C) $A = 7\frac{1}{2}x$

(D) $A = 10x$

(E) $A = 20x$

In a design all isosceles triangles are shaded.
In the design some isosceles triangles are
right triangles.

38. Which of the following conclusions about the design is valid if the statements above are true?

(A) All right triangles are shaded.
(B) All right triangles are isosceles.
(C) Some right triangles are shaded.
(D) No right triangles are shaded.
(E) No right triangles are isosceles.

39. What number is halfway between $\frac{2}{3}$ and $\frac{3}{4}$?

(A) $\frac{5}{14}$

(B) $\frac{7}{12}$

(C) $\frac{13}{18}$

(D) $\frac{17}{24}$

(E) $\frac{8}{9}$

40. Which of the following numbers is written in scientific notation?

(A) $4{,}136.28 \times 10^2$
(B) 413.628×10^3
(C) 41.3628×10^4
(D) 4.13628×10^5
(E) 0.413628×10^6

1. **Choice C is the best answer.** The multiples of 3 shown on the spinner are 3, 6, 9, and 12, so there are 4 chances in 2 of the spinner stopping on a multiple of 3.

2. **Choice E is the best answer.** The reading on the gauge shown is between 10 and 15. Since the interval between 10 and 15 is marked off in fifths, each subdivision represents 1, and the reading is thus 13.

3. **Choice A is the best answer.** Fractions are easy to compare if they have the same denominator. Convert each fraction to one with a denominator of 7 by dividing the numerator and the denominator by the same number.

$$\frac{1}{7} = \frac{1}{7}$$
$$\frac{11 \div 10}{70 \div 10} = \frac{1.1}{7}$$
$$\frac{101 \div 100}{700 \div 100} = \frac{1.01}{7}$$
$$\frac{1,001 \div 1,000}{7,000 \div 1,000} = \frac{1.001}{7}$$
$$\frac{10,001 \div 10,000}{70,000 \div 10,000} = \frac{1.0001}{7}$$

Since $\frac{1}{7}$ has the smallest numerator, $\frac{1}{7}$ is less than the other four fractions.

4. **Choice C is the best answer.** If there were 6 gallons in the tank, 4 more gallons would be needed to fill the 10-gallon tank. Since $6\frac{1}{8}$ is a little more than 6, a little less than 4 gallons is needed.

5. **Choice B is the best answer.** The scale is the relation between a distance on a map and the distance it represents on the ground. If $\frac{3}{4}$ inch represents 50 miles, then $1\frac{1}{2}$ inches, which is $2 \times \frac{3}{4}$ inch, represents $2 \times 50 = 100$ miles.

6. **Choice D is the best answer.** The circle graph shows the distribution of the trash content *in percentages*, but the question asks for the *weight* of the plastic content in tons. From the graph we see that plastics account for 8% of the total weight of the trash. The problem states that 60 tons of the trash consist of paper; the graph shows that this amount equals 40% of the total, so

$$60 = 0.4 \times \text{(total weight)}$$

and the total weight is $\frac{60}{0.4} = 150$ tons.

The weight of plastics equals 8% of 150 tons, or $(0.08)(150) = 12$ tons.

There is another, slightly faster, way to solve this problem. We use the fact that the *ratio* of plastics to paper in the trash is the same, whether the two amounts are given as percents or in tons. This gives us the proportion.

$$\frac{\text{tons of plastic}}{\text{tons of paper}} = \frac{8\%}{40\%} = \frac{1}{5}$$

Or

$$\frac{\text{tons of plastic}}{60} = \frac{1}{5}$$

$$\text{tons of plastic} = \frac{60}{5} = 12$$

7. Choice B is the best answer. The problem tells us that 128 players were injured and that the number of players with ankle injuries was 12.5% of this total. Since $12.5\% = \frac{12.5}{100} = 0.125$, the problem is solved by multiplying 0.125×128.

8. Choice E is the best answer. The numbers in the table follow a pattern, and you are asked to select a description of that pattern. The values of x in the table correspond to points on the number line. As x moves from -4 to 0, that is, from left to right on the number line, its value increases.

Similarly, the value of y increases from -2 to 0. Thus, it can be seen that as x increases, y increases.

9. Choice C is the best answer. In a pictograph, each symbol represents the same quantity, and there are 3 more book symbols in the row for book R than in the row for book Q. Since the bookstore sold 60 more copies of book R than book Q, the 3 book symbols represent 60 books. Therefore, 1 book symbol represents 20 books.

10. Choice E is the best answer. The opposite sides of a rectangle are equal in length, and the perimeter of a rectangle is the sum of those lengths. If you label the given figure and write an equation for the perimeter, you can find the length l of the rectangle.

$$\text{Perimeter} = 7 + 7 + l + l = 50$$
$$2l = 50 - 14$$
$$2l = 36$$
$$l = 18$$

The length of the given rectangle is therefore 18.

11. **Choice B is the best answer.** To find $a + b$, add $3b$ to both sides of the equation.

$$3a + 3b = 18 - 3b + 3b$$
$$3a + 3b = 18$$
$$3(a + b) = 18$$

Divide both sides of the equation by 3.

$$\frac{3(a+b)}{3} = \frac{18}{3}$$
$$a + b = 6$$

12. **Choice D is the best answer.** There is information for eight different years in the bar graph. The vertical scale goes from 0 to 80,000. The zeros are left off the scale because the title tells you to read the numbers in thousands. To find the number of students in any one year, read the height of the corresponding bar off the left-hand scale and multiply that height by 1,000.

The bar for 1950 has a height of about 27, so the number of students in 1950 was about 27,000. You have to find the number of years in which there were more than twice as many—that is, more than 54,000 students. To do this, count the number of bars that are higher than 54. These are the bars for 1975, 1980, and 1985. Thus, there were three years in which there were more than twice as many students as in 1950.

13. **Choice A is the best answer.** To compute a percent increase, you need the increase in the number of students and the number of students before the increase. The graph shows that the number of students in 1970 was 40,000 and the number of students in 1980 was 70,000, an increase of 30,000 students. To find the percent increase, divide this number by the base number, that is, the number of students before the increase, or 40,000.

$$\frac{30,000}{40,000} = \frac{3}{4} = 0.75 = 75\%$$

14. **Choice D is the best answer.** Since $0.1 = \frac{1}{10}$, you can multiply each of the answer choices by $\frac{1}{10}$.

10 times $\frac{1}{10}$ is 1.

100 times $\frac{1}{10}$ is 10.

1,000 times $\frac{1}{10}$ is 100.

10,000 times $\frac{1}{10}$ is 1,000.

100,000 times $\frac{1}{10}$ is 10,000.

1,000 is 10,000 times $\frac{1}{10}$, or 0.1.

15. Choice A is the best answer. The question asks you to look at each of the circles and find the one that has a center at (1,1) and radius 2, but the scale is not given. First, find a point that could be (1,1). In the rectangular coordinate system, the point (1,1) is 1 unit to the right of the origin O along the x-axis, and 1 unit up along the y-axis. The circles in choices A and E could have their center at (1,1), because in each the distances along the x-axis and the y-axis are equal; but then the radius of the circle in choice E would be 1, with each grid line representing $\frac{1}{2}$. In choice A, with each grid line representing 1 unit, the radius of the circle is 2.

16. Choice C is the best answer. The problem gives a set of instructions to follow, one step at a time, in the order given, and you are told the number $n = 2$. Thus, if you start with the second step, the computation is as follows.

$$2 - 3 = -1$$
$$-1 \times 2 = -2$$
$$-2 + 10 = 8$$
$$8 \div 2 = 4$$

The result is 4.

17. Choice D is the best answer. This is what you are given in this problem.

- 2 pencils cost 1 quarter (25¢).
- 1 notebook costs 2 quarters (50¢).
- The machine takes only quarters.

To find the number of quarters needed to buy 6 pencils and 2 notebooks, you can draw a picture and then count the number of quarters needed.

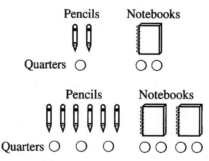

You need 7 quarters.

18. Choice B is the best answer. 1 million (I) is the same as 1,000,000.

1,000 thousands (II) is the same as
$$1,000 \times 1,000 = 1,000,000.$$

10,000 tens (III) is the same as
$$10,000 \times 10 = 100,000.$$

1 million and 1,000 thousands are the same.

19. Choice D is the best answer. One way of doing this problem is to divide 141 by each of the given numbers and find the remainder that is different from 5.

$$\frac{141}{136} = 1R5$$

$$\frac{141}{68} = 2R5$$

$$\frac{141}{34} = 4R5$$

$$\frac{141}{16} = 8R13$$

$$\frac{141}{8} = 17R5$$

If 141 is divided by 16, the remainder is NOT equal to 5.

20. Choice E is the best answer. Numbers are easy to compare if they are written in the same form. Each of the numbers in the problem can be converted to a decimal, and then the decimal can be compared to $0.187 = 18.7\%$. Remember that adding zeros at the end of a decimal does not change the value of the decimal.

0.05 = 0.050 and is less than 0.187.
0.15 = 0.150 and is less than 0.187.
$\frac{1}{10}$ = 0.100 and is less than 0.187.
0.01875 is less than 0.18700.
$\frac{1}{5}$ = 0.200 and is greater than 0.187.
0.187 is less than $0.200 = \frac{1}{5}$.

21. Choice B is the best answer. You are given that there are 8 boys and 13 girls in a choir, so the total number of boys and girls in the choir is 21, as represented in the picture.

ⓑⓑ G ⓑⓑ
ⓑⓑ G G G ⓑⓑ
G G G G G G G G G

The fraction of the choir that is boys is, therefore, $\frac{\text{number of boys}}{\text{total}} = \frac{18}{21}$

22. Choice C is the best answer. This question asks you to think of 400×30 as 12 times some number. Because $400 = 4 \times 10$ and $30 = 3 \times 10$, you can write 400×30 as $4 \times 100 \times 3 \times 10$. Since the order in which you multiply does not matter, you can write 400×30 as $(4 \times 3)(100 \times 10)$, which is $12 \times 1,000$.

23. Choice A is the best answer. You are told that 483 is 30% of a number W. This means that 483 is $\frac{30}{100}$, or $\frac{3}{10}$, of W, so $W = \frac{10}{3}(483) = \frac{10(483)}{3} = 10(161) = 1,610$.

24. Choice E is the best answer. The question asks you to think of three points on a line and, if possible, to visualize the three points on each of the given figures. You can visualize the three points on a square.

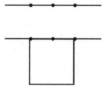

You can visualize the three points on a triangle.

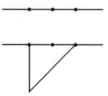

You can visualize the three points on a cube.

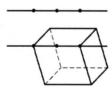

You can visualize the three points on a cylinder.

If you think about a circle, you CANNOT visualize the three points on a circle.

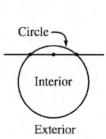

Two of the points on the line can be on the circle, but the third one cannot be.

25. Choice B is the best answer. The problem gives a set of test scores and the definition of median. The first part of the definition tells you to order the scores, that is, to arrange them in order from smallest to largest. Here are the numbers ordered from smallest to largest:

$$86, 86, 88, 90, 92, 98$$

Because there are an even number of scores (6), there are two middle numbers in the set, 88 and 90, and the average of the two middle numbers is

$$\frac{88 + 90}{2} = \frac{178}{2} = 89$$

Thus the median of Robin's scores is 89. (Notice that the median of a set of numbers need not be one of the numbers in the set.)

26. Choice C is the best answer. The question asks you to compute the cost of a 50-minute call when the parties are 500 miles apart. The range 431–925 miles in the table gives the rates for parties 500 miles apart. The cost of the first minute is $0.36, and the cost of each additional minute is $0.30. This information can be represented in an equation. Cost = $0.36 + 49($0.30) where 49 is the number of additional minutes.

27. Choice E is the best answer. In this question, you are given that the cost of a 20-minute call was $6.26, and you have to find the distance between the parties who were on the phone for 20 minutes. If the additional-minute rate for the whole 20 minutes is used, the approximate cost of each minute is the cost of the call divided by the number of minutes, or $6.26 ÷ 20, which is about $0.31 per minute. The row in which each additional minute costs $0.31 is the row with 926–1910 miles between the parties. Only the distance given in choice E could be the miles between the parties.

This result can be checked by using the cost of the first minute and the cost of each additional minute listed in the eighth row to compute the total cost of the call.

$$\$0.37 + 19(\$0.31) = \$6.26$$

28. Choice C is the best answer. You are given a line segment AB that represents 0.3 mile—that is, about $\frac{1}{3}$ of a mile—and are asked to estimate the distance from C to D. By inspection you can see that each of the 3 segments of the road is a little longer than AB; so the distance from C to D is greater than $3 \times \frac{1}{3}$, or 1 mile. Only two choices are greater than 1 mile: 1.2 and 3. For the distance to be 3, each of the segments would have to be about 3 times as long as AB.

29. Choice B is the best answer. One way to solve the equation $B = 2(G - 5)$ for G is to multiply $(G - 5)$ by 2.

$$B = 2G - 10$$

Add 10 to both sides of the equation.

$$B + 10 = 2G - 10 + 10 = 2G$$

Divide both sides of the equation by 2.

$$\frac{B + 10}{2} = \frac{2G}{2} = G$$

30. Choice D is the best answer. All five choices can be easily compared if they are expressed in the same form. One way to do this is to factor all choices completely.

(A) $2^2 \times 10 \times 12 =$
$2^2 \times 2 \times 5 \times 2 \times 2 \times 3$
$2^5 \times 3 \times 5$

(B) $2^3 \times 6 \times 10 =$
$2^3 \times 2 \times 3 \times 2 \times 5 =$
$2^5 \times 3 \times 5$

(C) $2^4 \times 5 \times 6 =$
$2^4 \times 5 \times 2 \times 3 =$
$2^5 \times 3 \times 5$

(D) $2^5 \times 3 \times 10 =$
$2^5 \times 3 \times 2 \times 5 =$
$2^6 \times 3 \times 5$

(E) $4^2 \times 5 \times 6 =$
$(2 \times 2)^2 \times 5 \times 2 \times 3 =$
$2^2 \times 2^2 \times 5 \times 2 \times 3 =$
$2^5 \times 3 \times 5$

Choice D is NOT equivalent to the others and therefore is the answer.

Another way to express all choices in the same form is to perform all the indicated operations.

(A) $2^2 \times 10 \times 12 = 4 \times 10 \times 12 = 480$
(B) $2^3 \times 6 \times 10 = 8 \times 6 \times 10 = 480$
(C) $2^4 \times 5 \times 6 = 16 \times 5 \times 6 = 480$
(D) $2^5 \times 3 \times 10 = 32 \times 35 \times 10 = 960$
(E) $4^2 \times 5 \times 6 = 16 \times 5 \times 6 = 480$

Choice D is NOT equivalent to the others and therefore is the answer.

31. Choice E is the best answer. This problem gives five amounts and asks for an estimate of the sum of the amounts to the nearest million dollars. You can round each amount in the list and then add these rounded numbers. Because the answer choices are consecutive numbers, however, it is advisable to round to the nearest tenth of a million dollars before adding.

Project 1:	$19.3
Project 2:	8.0
Project 3:	11.0
Project 4:	0.8
Project 5:	4.9
Total:	$44.0 million

32. Choice B is the best answer. You are given five different ways to slice a cake and are asked to pick the one way that gives pieces each with the same amount of icing. By examining each of the ways, you can see that only choice B shows that each slice of the cake has the same size and is iced on top and on one side only.

Each slice of the cake cut this way has the same amount of icing.

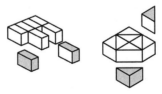

In choices A and C, it can be seen that a corner piece of the cake has more icing than a piece that is not a corner.

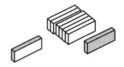

In choice D, the two end slices have more icing than any of the other slices.

In choice E, a slice from the middle of the cake has more icing than a slice closer to the corner pieces of the cake.

33. **Choice A is the best answer.** Although this problem has an unusual look, it requires only the substitution of the given values $T = 12$, $S = -4$, and $R = 8$, in the expression $\frac{T-S}{R}$. Substituting gives

$$\frac{T-S}{R} = \frac{12-(-4)}{8} = \frac{12+4}{8} = \frac{16}{8} = 2$$

34. **Choice A is the best answer.** The problem asks you to examine four shapes and decide if the distance around any one of them—the perimeter—is less than the distance around any of the other three. When we think about perimeter, we think about the lengths of the line segments that are joined at endpoints to make up the shape. We do not think about any of the line segments drawn inside. Each shape can be thought of as being made from 6 lengths, and each length is either short or long. The shapes in choices B, C, and D are made from 4 short lengths and 2 long lengths, and the shape in choice A is made from 6 short lengths. Thus, the perimeter of the shape in choice A is least.

35. **Choice B is the best answer.** Two times within a 24-hour period are given, and you are asked to find the number of hours and minutes between the two times. From high tide in the morning at 8:54 a.m. to noon is 3 hours 6 minutes, and from noon to high tide at 9:26 p.m. in the evening is 9 hours 26 minutes. Adding the two times gives 12 hours 32 minutes. The problem can also be solved by subtraction, but you must be careful when subtracting times because you cannot regroup in the usual way. Since there are 24 hours in a day, 9:26 p.m. can be expressed as 21 hours 26 minutes and the subtraction problem can be solved as follows.

Hours	Minutes
20	
~~21~~	$26+60$
-8	-54
12	32

The amount of time between the two high tides was 12 hours 32 minutes.

Alternatively, you can estimate. You know that from 8:54 a.m. to 8:54 p.m. is 12 hours. From 8:54 p.m. to 9:54 p.m. would be 13 hours. So the answer must lie between 12 and 13, making choice B the only logical answer.

36. **Choice B is the best answer.** You are given five figures, called polygons, to look at. One of them shows that the statement in the question is not always true. Examine the first part of the statement, "If all sides of a polygon are equal in length." This means that you have to look at only the figures in which the sides are equal in length. (The little marks on the sides of the figures tell which sides are equal in length.) Choices D and E do not have sides that are equal in length and can therefore be eliminated. You now look at the three figures that remain to find the one that does not have angles all equal in measure. That figure is the one example needed to disprove the statement. The figure in choice A is an equilateral triangle, so all angles have equal measure. The figure in choice C is a square with all right angles. By carefully looking at the figure in choice B, you see that the angles in the figure do not all have equal measure.

37. Choice B is the best answer. The formula for the area A of a rectangle is $A = \text{length} \times \text{width}$. The length of the rectangle shown is 5, and the width is x. The area of a rectangle with length $\frac{1}{2}(5)$ and width $2(x)$ is $A = \frac{1}{2}(5) \times 2(x) = 5x$.

38. Choice C is the best answer. In this question you are asked to use logical reasoning to draw a conclusion. An isosceles triangle has two equal sides, and a right triangle has one 90° angle. A triangle can be both an isosceles triangle and a right triangle.

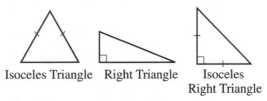

Isoceles Triangle   Right Triangle   Isoceles Right Triangle

One way to represent the two statements in the box is by a Venn diagram.

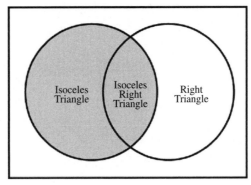

From the Venn diagram you see that only the statement in choice C is true.

39. Choice D is the best answer. The question asks you to find the number halfway between two fractions. The number you are looking for is greater than $\frac{2}{3}$ and less than $\frac{3}{4}$. Write $\frac{2}{3}$ and $\frac{3}{4}$ as fractions with a common denominator in order to find the fraction that is halfway between them. Common denominators of 3 and 4 include 12 and 24, so you can write

$$\frac{2}{3} = \frac{8}{12} = \frac{16}{24} \qquad \frac{3}{4} = \frac{9}{12} = \frac{18}{24}$$

The fraction $\frac{17}{24}$ is halfway between $\frac{16}{24}$ and $\frac{18}{24}$.

Alternatively, the problem can be solved by finding the average of $\frac{2}{3}$ and $\frac{3}{4}$, since the average of two numbers is halfway between the numbers.

$$\frac{\frac{2}{3} + \frac{3}{4}}{2} = \frac{\frac{8}{12} + \frac{9}{12}}{2} = \frac{17}{12} \times \frac{1}{2} = \frac{17}{24}$$

40. Choice D is the best answer. In scientific notation, a positive number is written as a number between 1 and 10 multiplied by a power of 10. For example, 125,000 can be written as 1.25×10^5.

$$125,000 = 1.25 \times 10^5$$

A power of 10

A number between 1 and 10

Although 125,000 is also equal to 12.5×10^4 or 125×10^3, neither is written in scientific notation because neither 12.5 nor 125 is a number between 1 and 10. All the answer choices are numbers multiplied by a power of 10, but only 4.13628 is a number between 1 and 10.

CALCULATING YOUR SCORE

To score PPST: Mathematics Test 1:

- Count the number of questions you answered correctly. The correct answers are in Table 1.
- Use Table 2 to find the scaled score corresponding to the number of questions answered correctly. You can compare your scaled score to the passing score required by your state or institution. (Passing state scores are available on the Praxis Web site at www.ets.org/praxis.)
- Score report category M-1 contains 20 questions measuring conceptual knowledge and procedural knowledge, category M-2 contains 10 questions measuring understanding of and use of representations of quantitative information, and category M-3 contains 10 questions measuring understanding and use of informal geometry and measurement and reasoning in a quantitative context.
- Count the number of questions you answered correctly in each of the categories. This may give you some idea of your strengths and weaknesses.

Table 1—PPST: Mathematics Test 1
Answers to Practice Test Questions and Percentages of
Examinees Answering Each Question Correctly

Question	Score Report Category	Correct Answer	Percentage of Examinees Choosing Correct Answer
1	M-1	C	81%
2	M-3	E	89
3	M-1	A	54
4	M-1	C	71
5	M-3	B	82
6	M-2	D	63
7	M-1	B	73
8	M-2	E	74
9	M-2	C	89
10	M-3	E	71
11	M-1	B	72
12	M-2	D	79
13	M-2	A	28
14	M-1	D	69
15	M-2	A	88
16	M-1	C	84

(Continued)

Table 1—PPST: Mathematics Test 1 (*Continued*)

Answers to Practice Test Questions and Percentages of Examinees Answering Each Question Correctly

Question	Score Report Category	Correct Answer	Percentage of Examinees Choosing Correct Answer
17	M-1	D	92
18	M-1	B	58
19	M-1	D	81
20	M-1	E	69
21	M-1	B	81
22	M-1	C	90
23	M-1	A	63
24	M-3	E	67
25	M-2	B	48
26	M-2	C	88
27	M-2	E	50
28	M-3	C	66
29	M-1	B	61
30	M-1	D	79
31	M-1	E	75
32	M-3	B	80
33	M-1	A	68
34	M-3	A	33
35	M-3	B	80
36	M-3	B	45
37	M-1	B	51
38	M-3	C	61
39	M-2	D	51
40	M-1	D	37

NOTE: Percentages are based on the test records of 2,231 examinees who took the 60-minute version of the PPST: Mathematics test in June 2003.

* In general, questions may be considered as easy, average, or difficult based on the following percentages:

Easy questions = 75% or more answered correctly.

Average questions = 55%–74% answered correctly.

Difficult questions = less than 55% answered correctly.

Table 2—PPST: Mathematics Test 1
Score Conversion Table

Number Right	Scaled Score
40	190
39	189
38	188
37	187
36	186
35	185
34	184
33	183
32	182
31	181
30	180
29	179
28	178
27	177
26	176
25	175
24	174
23	173
22	172
21	171
20	170
19	169
18	168
17	167
16	166
15	165
14	164
13	163
12	162
11	161
10	160
9	159

(Continued)

Table 2—PPST: Mathematics Test 1 (*Continued*)
Score Conversion Table

Number Right	Scaled Score
8	158
7	157
6	155
5	154
4	153
3	152
2	151
1	150
0	150

CHAPTER 12

PPST: Mathematics Test 2

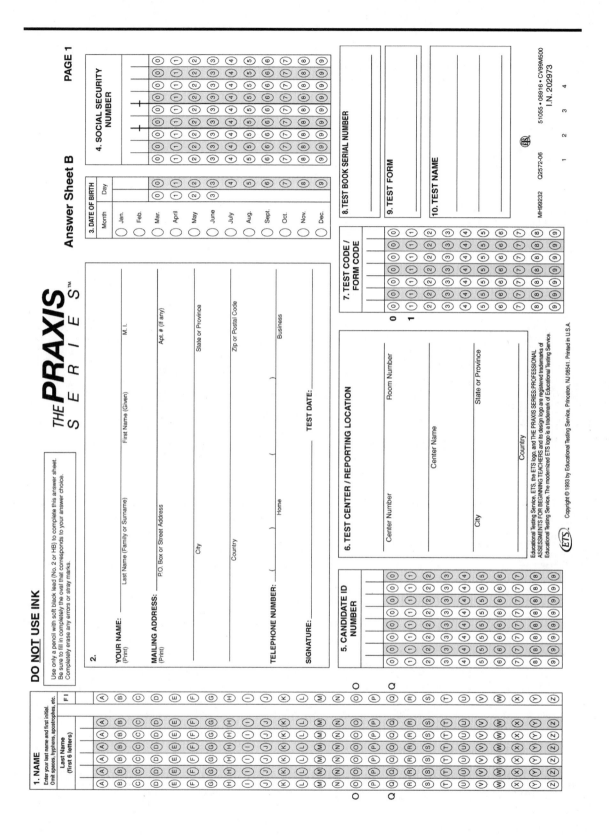

CERTIFICATION STATEMENT: (Please write the following statement below. DO NOT PRINT.)

"I hereby agree to the conditions set forth in the *Registration Bulletin* and certify that I am the person whose name and address appear on this answer sheet."

_____

_____

_____

SIGNATURE: _____ DATE: _____ / _____ / _____

Month   Day   Year

BE SURE EACH MARK IS DARK AND COMPLETELY FILLS THE INTENDED SPACE AS ILLUSTRATED HERE: ●

1 Ⓐ Ⓑ Ⓒ Ⓓ Ⓔ	41 Ⓐ Ⓑ Ⓒ Ⓓ Ⓔ	81 Ⓐ Ⓑ Ⓒ Ⓓ Ⓔ	121 Ⓐ Ⓑ Ⓒ Ⓓ Ⓔ
2 Ⓐ Ⓑ Ⓒ Ⓓ Ⓔ	42 Ⓐ Ⓑ Ⓒ Ⓓ Ⓔ	82 Ⓐ Ⓑ Ⓒ Ⓓ Ⓔ	122 Ⓐ Ⓑ Ⓒ Ⓓ Ⓔ
3 Ⓐ Ⓑ Ⓒ Ⓓ Ⓔ	43 Ⓐ Ⓑ Ⓒ Ⓓ Ⓔ	83 Ⓐ Ⓑ Ⓒ Ⓓ Ⓔ	123 Ⓐ Ⓑ Ⓒ Ⓓ Ⓔ
4 Ⓐ Ⓑ Ⓒ Ⓓ Ⓔ	44 Ⓐ Ⓑ Ⓒ Ⓓ Ⓔ	84 Ⓐ Ⓑ Ⓒ Ⓓ Ⓔ	124 Ⓐ Ⓑ Ⓒ Ⓓ Ⓔ
5 Ⓐ Ⓑ Ⓒ Ⓓ Ⓔ	45 Ⓐ Ⓑ Ⓒ Ⓓ Ⓔ	85 Ⓐ Ⓑ Ⓒ Ⓓ Ⓔ	125 Ⓐ Ⓑ Ⓒ Ⓓ Ⓔ
6 Ⓐ Ⓑ Ⓒ Ⓓ Ⓔ	46 Ⓐ Ⓑ Ⓒ Ⓓ Ⓔ	86 Ⓐ Ⓑ Ⓒ Ⓓ Ⓔ	126 Ⓐ Ⓑ Ⓒ Ⓓ Ⓔ
7 Ⓐ Ⓑ Ⓒ Ⓓ Ⓔ	47 Ⓐ Ⓑ Ⓒ Ⓓ Ⓔ	87 Ⓐ Ⓑ Ⓒ Ⓓ Ⓔ	127 Ⓐ Ⓑ Ⓒ Ⓓ Ⓔ
8 Ⓐ Ⓑ Ⓒ Ⓓ Ⓔ	48 Ⓐ Ⓑ Ⓒ Ⓓ Ⓔ	88 Ⓐ Ⓑ Ⓒ Ⓓ Ⓔ	128 Ⓐ Ⓑ Ⓒ Ⓓ Ⓔ
9 Ⓐ Ⓑ Ⓒ Ⓓ Ⓔ	49 Ⓐ Ⓑ Ⓒ Ⓓ Ⓔ	89 Ⓐ Ⓑ Ⓒ Ⓓ Ⓔ	129 Ⓐ Ⓑ Ⓒ Ⓓ Ⓔ
10 Ⓐ Ⓑ Ⓒ Ⓓ Ⓔ	50 Ⓐ Ⓑ Ⓒ Ⓓ Ⓔ	90 Ⓐ Ⓑ Ⓒ Ⓓ Ⓔ	130 Ⓐ Ⓑ Ⓒ Ⓓ Ⓔ
11 Ⓐ Ⓑ Ⓒ Ⓓ Ⓔ	51 Ⓐ Ⓑ Ⓒ Ⓓ Ⓔ	91 Ⓐ Ⓑ Ⓒ Ⓓ Ⓔ	131 Ⓐ Ⓑ Ⓒ Ⓓ Ⓔ
12 Ⓐ Ⓑ Ⓒ Ⓓ Ⓔ	52 Ⓐ Ⓑ Ⓒ Ⓓ Ⓔ	92 Ⓐ Ⓑ Ⓒ Ⓓ Ⓔ	132 Ⓐ Ⓑ Ⓒ Ⓓ Ⓔ
13 Ⓐ Ⓑ Ⓒ Ⓓ Ⓔ	53 Ⓐ Ⓑ Ⓒ Ⓓ Ⓔ	93 Ⓐ Ⓑ Ⓒ Ⓓ Ⓔ	133 Ⓐ Ⓑ Ⓒ Ⓓ Ⓔ
14 Ⓐ Ⓑ Ⓒ Ⓓ Ⓔ	54 Ⓐ Ⓑ Ⓒ Ⓓ Ⓔ	94 Ⓐ Ⓑ Ⓒ Ⓓ Ⓔ	134 Ⓐ Ⓑ Ⓒ Ⓓ Ⓔ
15 Ⓐ Ⓑ Ⓒ Ⓓ Ⓔ	55 Ⓐ Ⓑ Ⓒ Ⓓ Ⓔ	95 Ⓐ Ⓑ Ⓒ Ⓓ Ⓔ	135 Ⓐ Ⓑ Ⓒ Ⓓ Ⓔ
16 Ⓐ Ⓑ Ⓒ Ⓓ Ⓔ	56 Ⓐ Ⓑ Ⓒ Ⓓ Ⓔ	96 Ⓐ Ⓑ Ⓒ Ⓓ Ⓔ	136 Ⓐ Ⓑ Ⓒ Ⓓ Ⓔ
17 Ⓐ Ⓑ Ⓒ Ⓓ Ⓔ	57 Ⓐ Ⓑ Ⓒ Ⓓ Ⓔ	97 Ⓐ Ⓑ Ⓒ Ⓓ Ⓔ	137 Ⓐ Ⓑ Ⓒ Ⓓ Ⓔ
18 Ⓐ Ⓑ Ⓒ Ⓓ Ⓔ	58 Ⓐ Ⓑ Ⓒ Ⓓ Ⓔ	98 Ⓐ Ⓑ Ⓒ Ⓓ Ⓔ	138 Ⓐ Ⓑ Ⓒ Ⓓ Ⓔ
19 Ⓐ Ⓑ Ⓒ Ⓓ Ⓔ	59 Ⓐ Ⓑ Ⓒ Ⓓ Ⓔ	99 Ⓐ Ⓑ Ⓒ Ⓓ Ⓔ	139 Ⓐ Ⓑ Ⓒ Ⓓ Ⓔ
20 Ⓐ Ⓑ Ⓒ Ⓓ Ⓔ	60 Ⓐ Ⓑ Ⓒ Ⓓ Ⓔ	100 Ⓐ Ⓑ Ⓒ Ⓓ Ⓔ	140 Ⓐ Ⓑ Ⓒ Ⓓ Ⓔ
21 Ⓐ Ⓑ Ⓒ Ⓓ Ⓔ	61 Ⓐ Ⓑ Ⓒ Ⓓ Ⓔ	101 Ⓐ Ⓑ Ⓒ Ⓓ Ⓔ	141 Ⓐ Ⓑ Ⓒ Ⓓ Ⓔ
22 Ⓐ Ⓑ Ⓒ Ⓓ Ⓔ	62 Ⓐ Ⓑ Ⓒ Ⓓ Ⓔ	102 Ⓐ Ⓑ Ⓒ Ⓓ Ⓔ	142 Ⓐ Ⓑ Ⓒ Ⓓ Ⓔ
23 Ⓐ Ⓑ Ⓒ Ⓓ Ⓔ	63 Ⓐ Ⓑ Ⓒ Ⓓ Ⓔ	103 Ⓐ Ⓑ Ⓒ Ⓓ Ⓔ	143 Ⓐ Ⓑ Ⓒ Ⓓ Ⓔ
24 Ⓐ Ⓑ Ⓒ Ⓓ Ⓔ	64 Ⓐ Ⓑ Ⓒ Ⓓ Ⓔ	104 Ⓐ Ⓑ Ⓒ Ⓓ Ⓔ	144 Ⓐ Ⓑ Ⓒ Ⓓ Ⓔ
25 Ⓐ Ⓑ Ⓒ Ⓓ Ⓔ	65 Ⓐ Ⓑ Ⓒ Ⓓ Ⓔ	105 Ⓐ Ⓑ Ⓒ Ⓓ Ⓔ	145 Ⓐ Ⓑ Ⓒ Ⓓ Ⓔ
26 Ⓐ Ⓑ Ⓒ Ⓓ Ⓔ	66 Ⓐ Ⓑ Ⓒ Ⓓ Ⓔ	106 Ⓐ Ⓑ Ⓒ Ⓓ Ⓔ	146 Ⓐ Ⓑ Ⓒ Ⓓ Ⓔ
27 Ⓐ Ⓑ Ⓒ Ⓓ Ⓔ	67 Ⓐ Ⓑ Ⓒ Ⓓ Ⓔ	107 Ⓐ Ⓑ Ⓒ Ⓓ Ⓔ	147 Ⓐ Ⓑ Ⓒ Ⓓ Ⓔ
28 Ⓐ Ⓑ Ⓒ Ⓓ Ⓔ	68 Ⓐ Ⓑ Ⓒ Ⓓ Ⓔ	108 Ⓐ Ⓑ Ⓒ Ⓓ Ⓔ	148 Ⓐ Ⓑ Ⓒ Ⓓ Ⓔ
29 Ⓐ Ⓑ Ⓒ Ⓓ Ⓔ	69 Ⓐ Ⓑ Ⓒ Ⓓ Ⓔ	109 Ⓐ Ⓑ Ⓒ Ⓓ Ⓔ	149 Ⓐ Ⓑ Ⓒ Ⓓ Ⓔ
30 Ⓐ Ⓑ Ⓒ Ⓓ Ⓔ	70 Ⓐ Ⓑ Ⓒ Ⓓ Ⓔ	110 Ⓐ Ⓑ Ⓒ Ⓓ Ⓔ	150 Ⓐ Ⓑ Ⓒ Ⓓ Ⓔ
31 Ⓐ Ⓑ Ⓒ Ⓓ Ⓔ	71 Ⓐ Ⓑ Ⓒ Ⓓ Ⓔ	111 Ⓐ Ⓑ Ⓒ Ⓓ Ⓔ	151 Ⓐ Ⓑ Ⓒ Ⓓ Ⓔ
32 Ⓐ Ⓑ Ⓒ Ⓓ Ⓔ	72 Ⓐ Ⓑ Ⓒ Ⓓ Ⓔ	112 Ⓐ Ⓑ Ⓒ Ⓓ Ⓔ	152 Ⓐ Ⓑ Ⓒ Ⓓ Ⓔ
33 Ⓐ Ⓑ Ⓒ Ⓓ Ⓔ	73 Ⓐ Ⓑ Ⓒ Ⓓ Ⓔ	113 Ⓐ Ⓑ Ⓒ Ⓓ Ⓔ	153 Ⓐ Ⓑ Ⓒ Ⓓ Ⓔ
34 Ⓐ Ⓑ Ⓒ Ⓓ Ⓔ	74 Ⓐ Ⓑ Ⓒ Ⓓ Ⓔ	114 Ⓐ Ⓑ Ⓒ Ⓓ Ⓔ	154 Ⓐ Ⓑ Ⓒ Ⓓ Ⓔ
35 Ⓐ Ⓑ Ⓒ Ⓓ Ⓔ	75 Ⓐ Ⓑ Ⓒ Ⓓ Ⓔ	115 Ⓐ Ⓑ Ⓒ Ⓓ Ⓔ	155 Ⓐ Ⓑ Ⓒ Ⓓ Ⓔ
36 Ⓐ Ⓑ Ⓒ Ⓓ Ⓔ	76 Ⓐ Ⓑ Ⓒ Ⓓ Ⓔ	116 Ⓐ Ⓑ Ⓒ Ⓓ Ⓔ	156 Ⓐ Ⓑ Ⓒ Ⓓ Ⓔ
37 Ⓐ Ⓑ Ⓒ Ⓓ Ⓔ	77 Ⓐ Ⓑ Ⓒ Ⓓ Ⓔ	117 Ⓐ Ⓑ Ⓒ Ⓓ Ⓔ	157 Ⓐ Ⓑ Ⓒ Ⓓ Ⓔ
38 Ⓐ Ⓑ Ⓒ Ⓓ Ⓔ	78 Ⓐ Ⓑ Ⓒ Ⓓ Ⓔ	118 Ⓐ Ⓑ Ⓒ Ⓓ Ⓔ	158 Ⓐ Ⓑ Ⓒ Ⓓ Ⓔ
39 Ⓐ Ⓑ Ⓒ Ⓓ Ⓔ	79 Ⓐ Ⓑ Ⓒ Ⓓ Ⓔ	119 Ⓐ Ⓑ Ⓒ Ⓓ Ⓔ	159 Ⓐ Ⓑ Ⓒ Ⓓ Ⓔ
40 Ⓐ Ⓑ Ⓒ Ⓓ Ⓔ	80 Ⓐ Ⓑ Ⓒ Ⓓ Ⓔ	120 Ⓐ Ⓑ Ⓒ Ⓓ Ⓔ	160 Ⓐ Ⓑ Ⓒ Ⓓ Ⓔ

FOR ETS USE ONLY	R1	R2	R3	R4	R5	R6	R7	R8	TR	CS

PPST: MATHEMATICS Test 2
Time—60 minutes
40 Questions

Directions: Each of the questions or incomplete statements below is followed by five suggested answers or completions. Select the one that is best in each case and then fill in the corresponding lettered space on the answer sheet with a heavy, dark mark so that you cannot see the letter.

Remember, try to answer every question.

Special Note: Figures that accompany problems in the test are intended to provide information useful in solving the problem. The figures are drawn as accurately as possible except when it is stated in a specific problem that its figure is not drawn to scale. Figures can be assumed to lie in a plane unless otherwise indicated. Position of points can be assumed to be in the order shown, and lines shown as straight can be assumed to be straight. The symbol ⌐ denotes a right angle.

1. The Lopez family plan to drive 250 miles on the first day of their vacation and at most 70 miles on each of the next 4 days to allow time for sightseeing. At most, how many miles do they plan to drive during their 5 days of vacation?

   (A) 320
   (B) 530
   (C) 600
   (D) 1,280
   (E) 1,600

2. Which of the following is equivalent to 2.75 ?

   (A) $\dfrac{9}{4}$ (D) $\dfrac{11}{4}$

   (B) $\dfrac{12}{5}$ (E) $\dfrac{14}{5}$

   (C) $\dfrac{8}{3}$

3. Donald planted more than 8 bushes and more than 4 trees on his new lot. What is the minimum total number of bushes and trees that Donald planted?

   (A) 10
   (B) 11
   (C) 12
   (D) 13
   (E) 14

BUDGET DISTRIBUTION

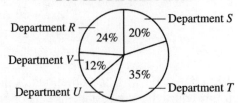

4. The graph above shows the percent of a company's yearly budget distributed to each of its five departments. What percent of the company's yearly budget is distributed to Department *U*?

(A) 8%
(B) 9%
(C) 10%
(D) 11%
(E) 12%

5. Jackie wants to make bags of candy so that each bag contains 25 pieces of candy. If Jackie has a total of 562 pieces of candy, what is the greatest number of bags of candy that she can make?

(A) 19
(B) 20
(C) 21
(D) 22
(E) 25

6. Which of the following units of measure is most appropriate for reporting the distance between City *A* and City *Z*?

(A) Kilometer
(B) Centimeter
(C) Millimeter
(D) Liter
(E) Light-year

School	Number of Classrooms
A	18
B	36
C	24

7. The table above shows the number of classrooms in each of the three schools in a certain school district. A fourth school is to be built in the district. How many classrooms should be in the fourth school if the average (arithmetic mean) number of classrooms per school is to be 30?

(A) 40
(B) 41
(C) 42
(D) 43
(E) 44

8. What digit is in the tenths place of the number 543.712?

(A) 2
(B) 3
(C) 4
(D) 5
(E) 7

9. A map is drawn with a scale of 1 inch representing 6 feet. How many inches on the map would represent 18 feet?

(A) 2
(B) 3
(C) 6
(D) 9
(E) 12

10. Of the following, which is the closest approximation of 72,059 ÷ 794?

(A)   30
(B)   90
(C)   300
(D)   900
(E) 3,000

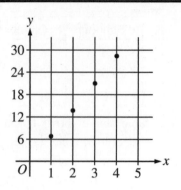

11. The relationship between which of the following could be represented by the four points in the graph above?

(A) Seconds and minutes
(B) Minutes and hours
(C) Hours and days
(D) Days and weeks
(E) Weeks and years

$$49, 50, 24, x, 58, 37, 29$$

12. If the range for the data listed above is 34, which of the following CANNOT be the value of x? (The range is the difference between the greatest and the least numbers in a set of data.)

(A) 54
(B) 43
(C) 38
(D) 29
(E) 21

Specialty	Ten Years or Less		More Than Ten Years	
	Male	Female	Male	Female
Internists	7	7	9	7
Cardiologists	4	5	5	6
Surgeons	3	3	6	8
Pediatricians	2	1	4	3

13. The table above lists the specialties of the 80 doctors in a certain medical group by length of time in the group and by gender. What fraction of the doctors in the group are female surgeons who have been in the group for more than ten years?

(A) $\frac{3}{40}$ (D) $\frac{1}{5}$

(B) $\frac{1}{10}$ (E) $\frac{3}{10}$

(C) $\frac{11}{80}$

14. If $3x + 5y = 30$ and $x + y = 5$, then $2x + 4y =$

(A) 35
(B) 25
(C) 20
(D) 15
(E) 10

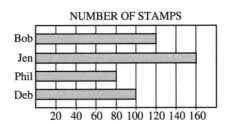

NUMBER OF STAMPS

15. Four stamp collectors met to trade stamps. The number of stamps each collector brought to trade is shown in the graph above. At the end of trading, Bob had 105 stamps, Jen had 165, and Phil had 75. How many stamps did Deb have?

(A) 100
(B) 110
(C) 115
(D) 120
(E) 125

16. Each of the students in two classes applied for a merit award. One of the classes had 30 students, 1 of whom received a merit award. The other class had 33 students, 2 of whom received a merit award. If no student is in both classes, what fraction of the students in the two classes received a merit award?

(A) $\dfrac{1}{30}$

(B) $\dfrac{1}{21}$

(C) $\dfrac{2}{33}$

(D) $\dfrac{1}{11}$

(E) $\dfrac{1}{10}$

17. Claire bought 6 packages of pencils, with 24 pencils in each package. Claire would have had the same number of pencils if she had bought

(A) 9 packages with 16 pencils each
(B) 10 packages with 14 pencils each
(C) 12 packages with 10 pencils each
(D) 16 packages with 8 pencils each
(E) 18 packages with 6 pencils each

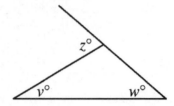

18. In the figure above, if $v = 30$ and $z = 70$, then $w =$

(A) 100
(B) 80
(C) 50
(D) 40
(E) 30

19. Which of the following numbers can be used to show that the square root of a number is NOT always less than or equal to the number?

(A) 0
(B) 0.25
(C) 2.25
(D) 4.9
(E) 10

$$0.215632156321563\ldots$$

20. In the decimal number above, the first five digits to the right of the decimal point are 2, 1, 5, 6, and 3. These digits repeat indefinitely in that order. What is the 87th digit to the right of the decimal point?

(A) 1
(B) 2
(C) 3
(D) 5
(E) 6

21. In a high school club, 42 members own a bike and 36 members own in-line skates. Of the club members who own a bike or in-line skates, 24 own both a bike and in-line skates. If there are 56 members in the club, how many members own neither?

(A) 0
(B) 2
(C) 4
(D) 5
(E) 6

NUMBER OF PEOPLE OUT OF 100 WHO REGULARLY PLAY VIDEO GAMES				
Age-Group	10 and Younger	11–18	19–25	26–40	41 and Older
Number of People	30	20	11	10	2

22. A total of 100 people responded to the survey question "Do you regularly play video games?" The table above shows the number of "yes" responses for various age-groups. What is the probability that a person chosen at random from the 100 people who responded to the survey is age 26 or older and plays video games regularly?

(A) $\frac{1}{50}$

(B) $\frac{1}{10}$

(C) $\frac{3}{25}$

(D) $\frac{10}{73}$

(E) $\frac{12}{73}$

23. Norbert took a job selling magazines. The first week he earned x dollars. The second week he earned two dollars less than he earned the first week, and the third week he earned one dollar less than three times what he earned the second week. Which of the following represents the amount of money, in dollars, that Norbert earned the third week?

(A) $3(x - 1)$
(B) $3(x - 3)$
(C) $3x - 4$
(D) $3x - 5$
(E) $3x - 7$

Year	Net Income
2000	$80,000
2001	$88,000

24. The table above shows the net income of a small company in 2000 and 2001. For each of the next two years, the percent increase of the company's net income is equal to the percent increase from 2000 to 2001. Which of the following is closest to the company's net income in 2003?

(A) $100,000
(B) $104,000
(C) $106,000
(D) $110,000
(E) $112,000

25. A club has a total of n members. If k of the members play chess, which of the following represents the fraction of the club membership that does NOT play chess?

(A) $\dfrac{n-k}{n}$ (D) $\dfrac{k-n}{k}$

(B) $\dfrac{k-n}{n}$ (E) $\dfrac{n-k}{n+k}$

(C) $\dfrac{n-k}{k}$

26. In the formula $M = \dfrac{x^2}{y}$, if x is tripled, then the value of M will be

(A) $\dfrac{1}{3}$ as great
(B) 2 times as great
(C) 3 times as great
(D) 6 times as great
(E) 9 times as great

x	$x-1$	8
	5	
2		

27. In the table above, the sum of the numbers in each row, column, and diagonal is 15. What number should be in the box directly below the box containing 5 ?

(A) 3
(B) 4
(C) 6
(D) 7
(E) 9

> Ms. Smith wants to give 5 nickels to each of 5 children. She has 75 cents worth of nickels. How many more nickels does she need?

28. Which of the following can be used to find the answer to the question above?

I. $(5 \times 5) - \dfrac{75}{5}$

II. $(5 \times 5) - \dfrac{0.75}{0.05}$

III. $(0.05 \times 0.05) - \dfrac{0.75}{0.05}$

(A) I only
(B) II only
(C) I and II only
(D) II and III only
(E) I, II, and III

STUDENT CLUB MEMBERSHIP

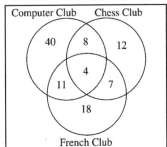

29. Each of the circles in the Venn diagram above represents a club, whose membership is given by the numbers shown. How many students are members of at least two of the three clubs?

(A) 26
(B) 30
(C) 35
(D) 38
(E) 40

30. If $p = 0.4997 \times 0.5003 \times 0.4998$, which of the following is true?

(A) $\dfrac{1}{3} < p < \dfrac{1}{2}$

(B) $\dfrac{1}{5} < p < \dfrac{1}{4}$

(C) $\dfrac{1}{7} < p < \dfrac{1}{5}$

(D) $\dfrac{1}{9} < p < \dfrac{1}{7}$

(E) $\dfrac{1}{14} < p < \dfrac{1}{12}$

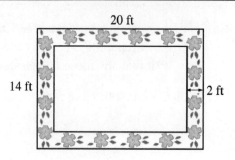

20 ft

14 ft

2 ft

31. The figure above represents a rectangular rug with a solid center and 2-foot-wide flowered border. What is the area, in square feet, of the rug's flowered border?

(A)　64
(B)　120
(C)　160
(D)　212
(E)　264

32. Which of the following is greatest in value?

(A)　$\dfrac{1}{19^2}$

(B)　$\dfrac{1}{19^2 + 1}$

(C)　$\dfrac{1}{19^2 - 1}$

(D)　$\dfrac{1}{19^3 + 1}$

(E)　$\dfrac{1}{19^3 - 1}$

33. Luann multiplied 129 by 312 instead of by 3.12. Which of the following can she do to her result to get the correct answer?

(A)　Subtract 308.88 from her result.
(B)　Multiply her result by 10.
(C)　Multiply her result by 100.
(D)　Divide her result by 10.
(E)　Divide her result by 100.

34. If a store sold 45 chairs last month and 30 chairs this month, what was the percent decrease in the number of chairs sold?

(A)　15%
(B)　20%
(C)　$33\frac{1}{3}\%$
(D)　50%
(E)　$66\frac{2}{3}\%$

35. *F*, *H*, *J*, *N*, and *Q* are positive numbers. *F* is less than *J* but greater than *N*. *J* is less than *H* but greater than *Q*. If *Q* is less than *F* but greater than *N*, which of the following orders the numbers from least to greatest?

(A) *F*, *J*, *H*, *N*, *Q*
(B) *N*, *F*, *H*, *Q*, *J*
(C) *N*, *Q*, *F*, *J*, *H*
(D) *Q*, *H*, *N*, *F*, *J*
(E) *Q*, *N*, *F*, *J*, *H*

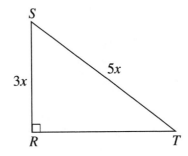

36. What is the length of *RT* in right triangle *RST* above?

(A) $8x^2$
(B) $4x^2$
(C) $2x^2$
(D) $4x$
(E) $2x$

> A total of 15 salespeople had an average (arithmetic mean) of 16 sales each during a 3-day sale. The total price for the purchases was $132,000. What was the average purchase price during the sale?

37. Which of the numbers in the problem above are needed to answer the question?

(A) 15 and 16 only
(B) 15 and $132,000 only
(C) 16 and $132,000 only
(D) 15, 16, and $132,000 only
(E) 3, 15, 16, and $132,000

$$-2 < a$$
$$b < 8$$
$$a < c < b$$

38. According to the inequalities above, if a, b, and c are integers, which of the following could be the value of c?

(A) −6
(B) −4
(C) −2
(D) 3
(E) 7

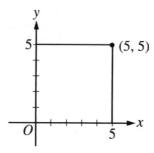

39. Inside the square above, how many points have integer coordinates (x, y) such that x is greater than y?

(A) Six
(B) Eight
(C) Ten
(D) Twelve
(E) Fourteen

40. If a, b, and c are positive numbers, which of the following must be true?

I. $a(b + c) = ab + ac$
II. $a \div (b + c) = a \div b + a \div c$
III. $(b − c)a = ba − ca$

(A) I only
(B) I and II only
(C) I and III only
(D) II and III only
(E) I, II, and III

STOP

If you finish before time is called, you may check your work on this test.

PPST: Mathematics Test 2
Answers and Explanations

1. **Choice B is the best answer.** The greatest number of miles that the Lopez family plans to drive for the last 4 days of vacation is 70×4, or 280 miles. Since the plan is to drive 250 miles on the first day, the greatest number of miles the family plans to drive during all 5 days is $250 + 280$ miles, or 530 miles.

2. **Choice D is the best answer.** Another way of writing 2.75 is $2\frac{3}{4}$. Changing $2\frac{3}{4}$ to an improper fraction gives $\frac{11}{4}$.

3. **Choice E is the best answer.** If Donald planted more than 8 bushes, the least number of bushes that he could have planted is 9. If he planted more than 4 trees, the least number of trees that he could have planted is 5. Therefore, the minimum total number of bushes and trees that Donald planted is $9 + 5 = 14$.

4. **Choice B is the best answer.** A circle graph like the one shown represents 100% of something. In this case, it represents how the entire 100% of a company's yearly budget is distributed. If the percents of the budget for Departments R, S, T, and V are totaled, the result is $24\% + 20\% + 35\% + 12\% = 91\%$. Thus, the remaining percent of the budget, $100\% - 91\% = 9\%$, is the percent of the yearly budget that is distributed to Department U.

5. **Choice D is the best answer.** Since there are to be 25 pieces of candy in each bag, to find the greatest number of bags that can be made, divide the total number of pieces of candy available by 25 and ignore any remainder. In this case, $562 \div 25 = 22$ with a remainder of 12. A 23rd bag cannot be made with the leftover 12 pieces because 25 pieces are required.

6. **Choice A is the best answer.** Through a process of elimination, centimeter and millimeter can quickly be ruled out. Both of these measurements are very small. They are hundredths and thousandths of a meter, respectively. A liter is a liquid measurement, and a light-year is a huge distance for measuring distances in space, so both can also be eliminated. One kilometer is 1,000 meters, and thus kilometer is the only reasonable answer.

7. **Choice c is the best answer.** To find the average number of classrooms per school, divide the total number of classrooms by the number of schools. In this question, the average is to be 30, but only three of the four schools' numbers of classrooms are given. Since $30 = \frac{120}{4}$, the total number of classrooms must be 120. The total number of classrooms for schools A, B, and C is $18 + 36 + 24 = 78$. Thus, the number of classrooms in the fourth school is determined by subtracting 78 from 120, which gives 42.

8. **Choice E is the best answer.** In the number 543.712, the digit 5 is in the hundreds place, 4 is in the tens place, and 3 is in the ones place. The digits that come after the decimal point have values less than 1 and so have place values that end in "th." The digit 7 is in the tenths place, the 1 is in the hundredths place, and the 2 is in the thousandths place.

9. **Choice B is the best answer.** If 1 inch on the map represents 6 feet, then 18 feet, which is 3×6 feet, is represented by $3 \times 1 = 3$ inches on the map.

10. **Choice B is the best answer.** The number 72,059 is very close to 72,000, and 794 is very close to 800. Since $72,000 \div 800 = 90$, it can be seen that $72,059 \div 794$ is approximately equal to 90.

11. **Choice D is the best answer.** For every 1 space on the x-axis, there is an increase of about 7 on the y-axis; that is, 1 corresponds to 7, 2 corresponds to 14, 3 corresponds to 21, and 4 corresponds to 28. Since 1 week contains 7 days, the relationship between days and weeks could be represented by the four points in the graph.

12. **Choice E is the best answer.** As stated in the question, the range is computed by using only the greatest and the least numbers in a set. Therefore, only numbers that are greater than or less than all the others need be considered. The greatest number in the set is 58, and the least is 24. Of the five choices listed, 21 is the only one that would have an impact on the range. If $x = 21$, it would then be the least number and the range would be $58 - 21 = 37$, not 34.

13. **Choice B is the best answer.** The question asks about doctors who are female and have been in the group for more than 10 years. This means that the information lies in the last column of data on the right of the table. Since the question is asking about only surgeons, it narrows the search to the third row of data. Eight female surgeons have been in the group for more than 10 years. There are a total of 80 doctors in the group, so the fraction is $\frac{8}{80}$ which reduces to $\frac{1}{10}$.

14. To find $2x + 4y$, write the two equations one above the other and subtract:

$$\begin{array}{r} 3x + 5y = 30 \\ -(x + y = 5) \\ \hline 2x + 4y = 25 \end{array}$$

15. **Choice C is the best answer.** Based on the bar graph shown, Bob initially had 120 stamps, Jen had 160 stamps, Phil had 80 stamps, and Deb had 100 stamps. The total number of stamps is thus $120 + 160 + 80 + 100 = 460$ stamps. At the end of trading,

the total number of Bob's, Jen's, and Phil's stamps was 105 + 165 + 75 = 345. Since the collectors are only trading, the total number of stamps remains the same. Thus, Deb must have ended the trading with 460 − 345 = 115 stamps.

16. **Choice B is the best answer.** There are a total of 63 students in the two classes, all of whom applied for a merit award. Since only 3 of them received a merit award, the fraction of the students who did is $\frac{3}{63}$, which reduces to $\frac{1}{21}$.

17. **Choice A is the best answer.** The total number of pencils that Claire has is 6 × 24, or 144 pencils. By using the same procedure and going through the possible answer choices, 9 packages of 16 pencils each would also give her a total of 9 × 16, or 144, pencils.

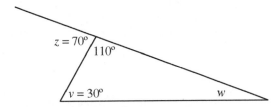

18. **Choice D is the best answer.** The numerical values for v and z have been substituted into the figure. The angle next to z has a measure of 110° since the two angles form a straight angle, which has a measure of 180°. Since the sum of the measures of the three interior angles of a triangle is 180°, 30° + 110° + w° = 180° and w = 40.

   Another way to look at this question is to realize that angle z is an exterior angle to the triangle in the figure. Thus, its measure is equal to the sum of the measures of the two interior angles that are farthest from it; that is, 30° + w° = 70° and w = 40.

19. **Choice B is the best answer.** Any number that is between 0 and 1 has a square root that is greater than itself. Answer choice B is such a number. You can also find the square roots of all the answer choices: the square roots of 0, 0.25, 2.25, 4.9, and 10 are, respectively, 0, 0.5, 1.5, ≈2.2, and ≈3.16. All the square roots are less than or equal to the numbers except the square root of 0.25.

20. **Choice A is the best answer.** In the series of numbers shown, there is a group of 5 repeating digits. Dividing 87 by 5 tells us that this block of digits repeats 17 times evenly and begins again but does not make it through another cycle. The remainder of 2 is the important number to consider. This means that the second digit of the repeating group lies in the 87th position to the right of the decimal point. Since the group of numbers that repeat consists of 2, 1, 5, 6, and 3, the number 1 is in the 87th position.

21. Choice B is the best answer. This question is a written description of a Venn diagram. Here is what it would look like:

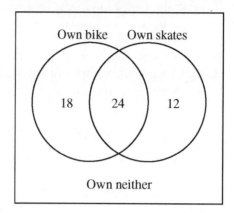

The values 18 and 12 in the diagram are computed by taking the number of members for each group and subtracting 24 (those who are in both groups) from each. If there are a total of 56 members in the club, those who own neither a bike nor a pair of skates are calculated by using the values shown: $56 - 18 - 24 - 12 = 2$.

22. Choice C is the best answer. Based on the table shown, there are 12 people from the surveyed group who are aged 26 or older and play video games regularly. Therefore, there are 12 chances in 100 that a person chosen at random will be in that category, $\frac{12}{100} = \frac{3}{25}$

23. Choice E is the best answer. Here is an algebraic translation for what Norbert earned each week:

1st week:	x
2nd week:	$x - 2$
3rd week:	$3(x - 2) - 1$

Since the question is concerned with Norbert's earnings for the third week, we must distribute the 3:

$$3x - 6 - 1$$

and combine like terms:

$$3x - 7$$

24. Choice C is the best answer. To find the percent increase between two amounts, find the difference and compare that with the starting amount. In this case, the percent increase from 2000 to 2001 is $\frac{\$8,000}{\$80,000} \times 100\%$, which is $\frac{1}{10} \times 100\%$, which equals 10%.

This means that there is a 10% increase from each year to the next. For the year 2002, the increase will be 10% of $88,000, which is $8,800. Thus, the company's net income in 2002 was $88,000 + $8,800 = $96,800.

The question is asking for the net income in 2003, so the process must be repeated: 10% of 96,800 is $9,680, and so $96,800 + $9,680 = $106,480. This is closest to $106,000.

25. **Choice A is the best answer.** If the club has n members, of which k play chess, this means that $n - k$ of them do NOT play chess. To find the fraction of the club members who do NOT play chess, simply compare those who do not play to the total number of members, which is n.

Therefore, the fraction is $\frac{n-k}{n}$.

26. **Choice E is the best answer.** Since the value of x is being tripled, it should be replaced in the equation with $(3x)$. The equation then becomes

$$M = \frac{(3x)^2}{y} \text{ or } M = \frac{9x^2}{y} \text{ which is 9 times as great as } \frac{x^2}{y}$$

27. **Choice D is the best answer.** The first horizontal row contains all three entries and should be considered initially. The question states that the sum of the numbers in every row is 15, so you can write the equation $x + x - 1 + 8 = 15$. Combining like terms gives $2x + 7 = 15$. Subtracting 7 from both sides and dividing by 2 gives $x = 4$.

However, the question asks for the value that should be in the box directly below the box containing the 5, which is in the middle column. Substituting the value of 4 that was determined to be x into the expression $x - 1$, you can see that the first box in the middle column contains the number 3. Adding the values down the column results in $3 + 5 + ? = 15$, where ? represents the missing number. The number in the box should be 7.

28. **Choice C is the best answer.** The question asks how many *more* nickels Ms. Smith needs, so you must find out how many she wants to give and how many she already has. The difference between these numbers will answer the question. Since she wants to give 5 nickels to each of 5 children, she will need 5×5 nickels. She has 75 *cents* worth of nickels, and each nickel has a value of 5 cents.

The computation $\frac{75}{5}$ will tell you how many nickels she already has. As mentioned previously, the difference between these two amounts is the answer to the question. Statement I, therefore, can be used to answer the question. Statement II is almost identical to statement I. In statement II, $\frac{75}{5}$ has been replaced with $\frac{0.75}{0.05}$. If the top and bottom of this fraction are each multiplied by 100, the fraction is equivalent to $\frac{75}{5}$. Thus, statement II also answers the question. Statement III matches statement II with the exception that 5×5 has been replaced with 0.05×0.05, which is equal to $\frac{5}{100} \times \frac{5}{100}$, not 5×5. Only statements I and II can be used to answer the question.

29. Choice B is the best answer. In a Venn diagram, when two circles intersect, their intersection represents members that belong to both sets. To answer this question, add all the numbers for every intersection of two or more of the circles: $8 + 4 + 11 + 7 = 30$. The 4 is included in the total because the question is asking for students who are members of *at least* two of the clubs. Since those 4 members belong to all three of the clubs, they meet the criterion.

30. Choice D is the best answer. Each of the numbers 0.4997, 0.5003, and 0.4998 is approximately equal to 0.5, which is equal to $\frac{1}{2}$. Thus, p is approximately equal to $\frac{1}{2} \times \frac{1}{2} \times \frac{1}{2} = \frac{1}{8}$, and the value of p is between $\frac{1}{9}$ and $\frac{1}{7}$; that is, $\frac{1}{9} < p > \frac{1}{7}$.

31. Choice B is the best answer. The area of the rug's flowered border can be calculated by subtracting the area of the solid center from the area of the entire rug. Since the rug is rectangular, its area is equal to its length times its width. Thus, the area of the entire rug is 20 ft $\times$ 14 ft = 280 square feet. To get the area of the solid center, you must first obtain its dimensions. If the outer length of the rug is 20 ft, and the border is 2 ft wide on either side, the length of the solid center is 20 ft − 4 ft = 16 ft.

Using the same idea, the width of the solid center is 14 ft − 4 ft = 10 ft. Thus, the area of the solid center is its length times its width, or 16 ft $\times$ 10 ft = 160 square feet.

The area of the flowered border is therefore 280 square feet minus 160 square feet, or 120 square feet.

32. Choice C is the best answer. Since all the fractions in this question have a numerator of 1, the fraction that has the least denominator will actually be the greatest in value. Choices D and E can be eliminated, since 19^3 is much greater than 19^2, and $19^2 - 1$ is the least of 19^2, $19^2 + 1$, and $19^2 - 1$.

33. Choice E is the best answer. Since 312 is 100 times greater than 3.12, Luann multiplied a number that was 100 times as great as what she really intended. To correct this error, she needs to undo this multiplication error by using the opposite mathematical operation—that is, division. She needs to divide her result by 100 to get the correct answer.

34. Choice C is the best answer. To find a percent decrease, compare the change in numbers with the original number as a fraction and then multiply by 100% to change it into a percent. Here the change is 45 chairs − 30 chairs = 15 chairs. The number of chairs sold last month was 45, so the percent decrease was $\frac{15}{45} \times 100\%$. This reduces to $\frac{1}{3} \times 100\%$, or $33\frac{1}{3}\%$.

35. **Choice C is the best answer.** The problem states that four numbers are positive and gives three statements that can be used to order these numbers from least to greatest. The relationship among F, J, and N can be determined by symbolizing the statement "F is less than J but greater than N" on a number line:

$$\xleftarrow{\hspace{3cm}}\xrightarrow{\hspace{3cm}}$$

$$N \qquad\qquad F \qquad J$$

Next, "J is less than H but greater than Q" lets you add H to the number line:

$$\xleftarrow{\hspace{3cm}}\xrightarrow{\hspace{3cm}}$$

$$N \qquad\qquad F \qquad J \;\; H$$

You know that Q is to the left of J, but you can't be sure where to place it just yet.

Finally, "Q is less than F but greater than N" allows you to add Q to the number line:

$$\xleftarrow{\hspace{3cm}}\xrightarrow{\hspace{3cm}}$$

$$N \;\; Q \qquad F \qquad J \;\; H$$

The order of the numbers from least to greatest is their order as it appears on the number line from left to right.

36. **Choice D is the best answer.** Since the triangle shown is a right triangle, use the Pythagorean theorem $a^2 + b^2 = c^2$ to get the answer. The variables a and b represent the legs of the triangle, while the variable c represents the side opposite the right angle (the hypotenuse). Substituting the expressions given in the diagram and solving for RT:

$$(3x)^2 + (RT)^2 = (5x)^2$$
$$9x^2 + (RT)^2 = 25x^2$$
$$(RT)^2 = 16x^2$$
$$RT = 4x$$

37. **Choice D is the best answer.** Because the question asks for the average purchase price, you need to divide the total price for all purchases by the number of purchases. Therefore, the total price for the purchases, \$132,000, is needed. To find the number of purchases, multiply the average number of sales for each salesperson by the number of salespeople. The average number of sales is 16, and there are 15 salespeople. By dividing \$132,000 by this total number of purchases, you obtain the average purchase price per sale. The fact that the sale lasted 3 days is not needed to solve the problem.

38. **Choice D is the best answer.** According to the inequalities given, since a, b, and c are integers, $a \geq -1$, $b \leq 7$, and c is between a and b. Of the answer choices given, only 3 is greater than -1 and less than 7.

39. Choice A is the best answer. There are 16 points that have integer coordinates within the square shown:

$$(1,4) \quad (2,4) \quad (3,4) \quad (4,4)$$
$$(1,3) \quad (2,3) \quad (3,3) \quad (4,3)$$
$$(1,2) \quad (2,2) \quad (3,2) \quad (4,2)$$
$$(1,1) \quad (2,1) \quad (3,1) \quad (4,1)$$

All you must do is to compare their x and y values. The six points outlined below all have x values that are greater than the corresponding y values:

$$(1,4) \quad (2,4) \quad (3,4) \quad (4,4)$$
$$(1,3) \quad (2,3) \quad (3,3) \quad \boxed{(4,3)}$$
$$(1,2) \quad (2,2) \quad (3,2) \quad (4,2)$$
$$(1,1) \quad (2,1) \quad (3,1) \quad (4,1)$$

40. Choice C is the best answer. By choosing some positive values for a, b, and c, you can quickly determine the statements that are true. Suppose that $a = 6$, $b = 1$, and $c = 2$. Plugging these values into statement I:

$$a(b + c) = ab + ac$$
$$6(1 + 2) = 6 \times 1 + 6 \times 2$$
$$6(3) = 6 + 12$$
$$18 = 18$$

Statement I appears to be true.

Using the same values, evaluate statement II:

$$a \div (b + c) = a \div b + a \div c$$
$$6 \div (1 + 2) = 6 \div 1 + 6 \div 2$$
$$6 \div (3) = 6 + 3$$
$$2 = 9$$

Since statement II produces a false result, it is not true.

Finally, evaluate statement III:

$$(b - c)a = ba - ca$$
$$(1 - 2)6 = 1 \times 6 - 2 \times 6$$
$$(-1)6 = 6 - 12$$
$$-6 = -6$$

Statement III appears to be true.

Another way to solve this problem is to use the distributive principle. Statements I and III are true by the distributive principle, but statement II is not true.

CALCULATING YOUR SCORE

To score PPST: Mathematics Test 2

- Count the number of questions you answered correctly. The correct answers are in Table 1.
- Use Table 2 to find the scaled score corresponding to the number of questions answered correctly. You can compare your scaled score to the passing score required by your state or institution. (Passing state scores are available on the Praxis Web site at www.ets.org/praxis.)
- Content category I contains 18 questions measuring conceptual knowledge and procedural knowledge, category II contains 12 questions measuring understanding of and use of representations of quantitative information, and category III contains 10 questions measuring understanding and use of measurement and informal geometry and formal mathematical reasoning.
- Count the number of questions you answered correctly in each of the categories. This may give you some idea of your strengths and weaknesses.

Table 1—PPST: Mathematics Test 2

Answers and Content Categories for Practice Test Questions

Sequence Number	Correct Answer	Content Category	Sequence Number	Correct Answer	Content Category
1	B	III	21	B	III
2	D	I	22	C	I
3	E	III	23	E	II
4	B	II	24	C	II
5	D	I	25	A	I
6	A	III	26	E	I
7	C	II	27	D	II
8	E	I	28	C	I
9	B	III	29	B	III
10	B	I	30	D	I
11	D	II	31	B	III
12	E	II	32	C	I
13	B	II	33	E	I
14	B	I	34	C	I
15	C	II	35	C	II
16	B	I	36	D	III
17	A	I	37	D	I
18	D	III	38	D	I
19	B	III	39	A	II
20	A	II	40	C	I

Table 2—PPST: Mathematics Test 2

Score Conversion Table

Raw Score	Scaled Score
0	150
1	150
2	150
3	150
4	152
5	153
6	154
7	156
8	157
9	158
10	160
11	161
12	162
13	163

Raw Score	Scaled Score
14	165
15	166
16	167
17	169
18	170
19	171
20	173
21	174
22	175
23	177
24	178
25	179
26	180
27	181

Raw Score	Scaled Score
28	182
29	183
30	184
31	185
32	186
33	186
34	187
35	188
36	189
37	189
38	190
39	190
40	190

Table 3—Assessment of Strengths in Each Category

Content Category	Number of Correct Answers Possible	Number of Incorrect Answers
I	18	
II	12	
III	10	

Table 4—Percentage of Examinees Choosing Correct Answers for the PPST Mathematics Practice Test

Sequence Number	Percentage of Examinees Choosing Correct Answer	Sequence Number	Percentage of Examinees Choosing Correct Answer
1	94%	21	59%
2	81%	22	41%
3	51%	23	25%
4	91%	24	31%
5	95%	25	75%
6	96%	26	26%
7	78%	27	52%
8	77%	28	34%
9	98%	29	66%
10	76%	30	25%
11	64%	31	35%
12	73%	32	45%
13	60%	33	60%
14	32%	34	48%
15	80%	35	73%
16	68%	36	42%
17	86%	37	35%
18	53%	38	66%
19	32%	39	25%
20	78%	40	36%

NOTE: Percentages are based on the test records of 3,346 examinees who took the 60-minute version of the PPST Mathematics test in June 2003.

In general, questions may be considered as easy, average, or difficult based on the following percentages:

Easy questions = 75% or more answered correctly
Average questions = 55%–74% answered correctly
Difficult questions = less than 55% answered correctly

CHAPTER 13

PPST: Writing Test 1

THE PRAXIS SERIES

Professional Assessments for Beginning Teachers ®

TEST NAME:
Pre-Professional Skills Test Writing

Time—60 minutes

38 Multiple-Choice Questions

1 Essay

THE *PRAXIS* SERIES™

Answer Sheet A

DO NOT USE INK

Use only a pencil with soft black lead (No. 2 or HB) to complete this answer sheet.
Be sure to fill in completely the oval that corresponds to the proper letter or number.
Completely erase any errors or stray marks.

1. NAME
Enter your last name and first initial.
Omit spaces, hyphens, apostrophes, etc.

Last Name
(first 6 letters)   F I

2.

YOUR NAME: _____
(Print)

Last Name (Family or Surname)   First Name (Given)   M. I.

MAILING ADDRESS: _____
(Print)

P.O. Box or Street Address   Apt. # (if any)

City   State or Province

Country   Zip or Postal Code

TELEPHONE NUMBER: (____) ____   (____) ____
Home   Business

SIGNATURE: _____   **TEST DATE:** _____

3. DATE OF BIRTH

Month	Day
Jan.	
Feb.	
Mar.	
April	
May	
June	
July	
Aug.	
Sept.	
Oct.	
Nov.	
Dec.	

4. SOCIAL SECURITY NUMBER

5. CANDIDATE ID NUMBER

6. TEST CENTER / REPORTING LOCATION

Center Number   Room Number

Center Name

City   State or Province

Country

7. TEST CODE / FORM CODE

8. TEST BOOK SERIAL NUMBER

9. TEST FORM

10. TEST NAME

51055 • 09244 • TF72R200 • Printed in U.S.A.
MH98334   Q2570-06   I.N. 203230

1   2   3   4

Educational Testing Service, ETS, the ETS logo and THE PRAXIS SERIES:PROFESSIONAL
ASSESSMENTS FOR BEGINNING TEACHERS and its design logo are registered trademarks of
Educational Testing Service. The modernized ETS logo is a trademark of Educational Testing Service.

CERTIFICATION STATEMENT: (Please write the following statement below. DO NOT PRINT.)
"I hereby agree to the conditions set forth in the Registration Bulletin and certify that I am the person whose name and address appear on this answer sheet."

_____

_____

_____

SIGNATURE: _____   DATE: _____ / _____ / _____
                                                          Month   Day   Year

---

BE SURE EACH MARK IS DARK AND COMPLETELY FILLS THE INTENDED SPACE AS ILLUSTRATED HERE: ● .

1 Ⓐ Ⓑ Ⓒ Ⓓ Ⓔ	13 Ⓐ Ⓑ Ⓒ Ⓓ Ⓔ	25 Ⓐ Ⓑ Ⓒ Ⓓ Ⓔ	37 Ⓐ Ⓑ Ⓒ Ⓓ Ⓔ
2 Ⓐ Ⓑ Ⓒ Ⓓ Ⓔ	14 Ⓐ Ⓑ Ⓒ Ⓓ Ⓔ	26 Ⓐ Ⓑ Ⓒ Ⓓ Ⓔ	38 Ⓐ Ⓑ Ⓒ Ⓓ Ⓔ
3 Ⓐ Ⓑ Ⓒ Ⓓ Ⓔ	15 Ⓐ Ⓑ Ⓒ Ⓓ Ⓔ	27 Ⓐ Ⓑ Ⓒ Ⓓ Ⓔ	39 Ⓐ Ⓑ Ⓒ Ⓓ Ⓔ
4 Ⓐ Ⓑ Ⓒ Ⓓ Ⓔ	16 Ⓐ Ⓑ Ⓒ Ⓓ Ⓔ	28 Ⓐ Ⓑ Ⓒ Ⓓ Ⓔ	40 Ⓐ Ⓑ Ⓒ Ⓓ Ⓔ
5 Ⓐ Ⓑ Ⓒ Ⓓ Ⓔ	17 Ⓐ Ⓑ Ⓒ Ⓓ Ⓔ	29 Ⓐ Ⓑ Ⓒ Ⓓ Ⓔ	41 Ⓐ Ⓑ Ⓒ Ⓓ Ⓔ
6 Ⓐ Ⓑ Ⓒ Ⓓ Ⓔ	18 Ⓐ Ⓑ Ⓒ Ⓓ Ⓔ	30 Ⓐ Ⓑ Ⓒ Ⓓ Ⓔ	42 Ⓐ Ⓑ Ⓒ Ⓓ Ⓔ
7 Ⓐ Ⓑ Ⓒ Ⓓ Ⓔ	19 Ⓐ Ⓑ Ⓒ Ⓓ Ⓔ	31 Ⓐ Ⓑ Ⓒ Ⓓ Ⓔ	43 Ⓐ Ⓑ Ⓒ Ⓓ Ⓔ
8 Ⓐ Ⓑ Ⓒ Ⓓ Ⓔ	20 Ⓐ Ⓑ Ⓒ Ⓓ Ⓔ	32 Ⓐ Ⓑ Ⓒ Ⓓ Ⓔ	44 Ⓐ Ⓑ Ⓒ Ⓓ Ⓔ
9 Ⓐ Ⓑ Ⓒ Ⓓ Ⓔ	21 Ⓐ Ⓑ Ⓒ Ⓓ Ⓔ	33 Ⓐ Ⓑ Ⓒ Ⓓ Ⓔ	45 Ⓐ Ⓑ Ⓒ Ⓓ Ⓔ
10 Ⓐ Ⓑ Ⓒ Ⓓ Ⓔ	22 Ⓐ Ⓑ Ⓒ Ⓓ Ⓔ	34 Ⓐ Ⓑ Ⓒ Ⓓ Ⓔ	
11 Ⓐ Ⓑ Ⓒ Ⓓ Ⓔ	23 Ⓐ Ⓑ Ⓒ Ⓓ Ⓔ	35 Ⓐ Ⓑ Ⓒ Ⓓ Ⓔ	
12 Ⓐ Ⓑ Ⓒ Ⓓ Ⓔ	24 Ⓐ Ⓑ Ⓒ Ⓓ Ⓔ	36 Ⓐ Ⓑ Ⓒ Ⓓ Ⓔ	

FOR ETS USE ONLY	R	ESSAY	R / ESSAY	CS

LAST NAME (first two letters) ☐☐   FIRST INITIAL ☐   DATE OF BIRTH (month and day <u>only</u>)   MONTH ☐☐   DAY ☐☐

TEST DATE: ___/___/___
Mo.   Day   Year

CANDIDATE ID NUMBER: _____

TEST BOOK SERIAL NUMBER: _____

TEST CODE / FORM CODE

I agree to give Educational Testing Service permission to use my responses anonymously in its educational research and for instructional purposes. I understand that I am free to mark "No," with no effect on my score or its reporting.

◯ Yes   ◯ No

(ESSAY) Begin your essay on this page. If you need more space, continue on page 4.

_____
_____
_____
_____
_____
_____
_____
_____
_____
_____
_____
_____
_____
_____
_____
_____
_____
_____
_____
_____
_____
_____
_____
_____
_____
_____
_____
_____

36-3 MH98308

Continuation of essay from page 3. Write below only if you need more space.

THE AREA BELOW IS FOR ETS USE ONLY. DO NOT MARK.

1 READER NO.	⓪①②③④⑤⑥⑦⑧⑨ ⓪①②③④⑤⑥⑦⑧⑨ ⓪①②③④⑤⑥⑦⑧⑨	**1**	ⒶⒷⒸⒹⒺⒻⒼⒽⒾⒿⓀⓁⓂ ⓃⓄⓅⓆⓇⓈⓉⓊⓋⓌⓍⓎⓏ
2 READER NO.	⓪①②③④⑤⑥⑦⑧⑨ ⓪①②③④⑤⑥⑦⑧⑨ ⓪①②③④⑤⑥⑦⑧⑨	**2**	ⒶⒷⒸⒹⒺⒻⒼⒽⒾⒿⓀⓁⓂ ⓃⓄⓅⓆⓇⓈⓉⓊⓋⓌⓍⓎⓏ
3 READER NO.	⓪①②③④⑤⑥⑦⑧⑨ ⓪①②③④⑤⑥⑦⑧⑨ ⓪①②③④⑤⑥⑦⑧⑨	**3**	ⒶⒷⒸⒹⒺⒻⒼⒽⒾⒿⓀⓁⓂ ⓃⓄⓅⓆⓇⓈⓉⓊⓋⓌⓍⓎⓏ

ETS®

Directions: In each of the sentences below four portions are under-lined and lettered. Read each sentence and decide whether any of the underlined parts contains a grammatical construction, a word use, or an instance of incorrect or omitted punctuation or capitalization that would be inappropriate in carefully written English. If so, note the letter printed beneath the underlined portion and completely fill in the corresponding lettered space on the answer sheet with a heavy, dark mark so that you cannot see the letter.

If there are no errors in any of the underlined portions, fill in space E. No sentence has more than one error.

Remember, try to answer every question.

Examples:

1. He spoke <u>bluntly</u> and <u>angrily</u>
            A   B

to <u>we</u> <u>spectators</u>. <u>No error</u>
   C   D   E

2. Margaret <u>insists</u> <u>that</u> this hat <u>,</u>
              A   B   C

coat, and scarf <u>,</u> are hers.
                D

<u>No error</u>
E

Sample Answers:

1. (A) (B) ● (D) (E)

2. (A) (B) (C) ● (E)

1. In some of the new computer industries , more problems result from
     A   B   C

poor business decisions as from lack of technical expertise.
                 D

No error
  E

2. Although the amount of registered nurses in the United States has
              A   B

increased every year since 1983, there are still not enough nurses
                   C   D

to meet the demand for their services. No error
                             E

3. Chairs as we know them today were virtually unheard of until the
                                 A   B

sixteenth century, when they began to replace stools and benches
                                   C

as a more comfortable mode of seating. No error
D   E

4. Contrary to its reputation for aggressive brutality, the sperm
              A

whales that were observed around the Galápagos Islands proved
                 B   C

to be timid and sociable. No error
            D   E

5. Some experts believe that unless the number of vehicles on the
              A

road is regulated, neither the improved combustion engines or
                                          B

the new fuels now being tested by automobile manufacturers will
                C

significantly reduce air pollution in the next decade. No error
                                D   E

6. Born in 1887, Marcus Garvey came to the United States in 1916,
    A

two year's after founding the Universal Negro Improvement
     B   C

Association in his native Jamaica. No error
          D   E

7. $\underline{\text{That women}}$ generally live $\underline{\text{longer than}}$ men has been reflected not
   $\hspace{3.2cm}$ A $\hspace{4.1cm}$ B

only in lower annuity $\underline{\text{payments}}$ to women $\underline{\text{and}}$ also in higher life
   $\hspace{5.4cm}$ C $\hspace{2.8cm}$ D

insurance premiums for men. $\underline{\text{No error}}$
   $\hspace{6.3cm}$ E

8. $\underline{\text{The plan to preserve}}$ the prison $\underline{\text{as a national monument}}$ led to objec-
   $\hspace{2.2cm}$ A $\hspace{4.6cm}$ B

tions from $\underline{\text{those who believe that its}}$ cell blocks represent a sordid
   $\hspace{2.0cm}$ C

part of the nation's history, one that $\underline{\text{is best forgotten}}$. $\underline{\text{No error}}$
   $\hspace{6.3cm}$ D $\hspace{2.6cm}$ E

9. Between $\underline{1947}$ to 1973, the average worker's earnings, when adjusted
   $\hspace{2.9cm}$ A

for inflation, $\underline{\text{rose}}$ 61 percent, $\underline{\text{reflecting}}$ $\underline{\text{a rise}}$ in productivity.
   $\hspace{3.4cm}$ B $\hspace{3.4cm}$ C $\hspace{1.4cm}$ D

$\underline{\text{No error}}$
   E

10. $\underline{\text{Because}}$ federal Superfund dollars are used to clean up hazardous
   $\hspace{1.3cm}$ A

waste sites, states that have large numbers of $\underline{\text{such sites}}$ $\underline{\text{will suffer from}}$
   $\hspace{8.0cm}$ B $\hspace{1.9cm}$ C

cuts in appropriations more than $\underline{\text{those that are not}}$. $\underline{\text{No error}}$
   $\hspace{6.2cm}$ D $\hspace{2.5cm}$ E

11. The first documented human flight in a balloon took place

in 1783, $\underline{\text{in which}}$ two men $\underline{\text{sailed over}}$ Paris, covering five and
   $\overline{\text{A}}$ $\hspace{1.2cm}$ B $\hspace{2.4cm}$ C

one-half miles $\underline{\text{in}}$ about 23 minutes. $\underline{\text{No error}}$
   $\hspace{2.9cm}$ D $\hspace{3.3cm}$ E

12. In their study *Women in Europe from Prehistory to the Present,*

Bonnie Anderson and Judith Zinsser insist that, $\underline{\text{although}}$ differ-
   $\hspace{8.1cm}$ A

ences of historical era, class, and nationality $\underline{\text{are crucial}}$ to the study
   $\hspace{8.3cm}$ B

of women $\underline{\text{,}}$ these differences are all outweighed $\underline{\text{by what they call}}$
   $\hspace{2.1cm}$ C $\hspace{5.0cm}$ D

"similarities of gender." $\underline{\text{No error}}$
   $\hspace{4.1cm}$ E

13. The bank's reputation for making $\underline{\text{both}}$ safe and profitable investments
   $\hspace{6.5cm}$ A

has been shaken by scandals $\underline{\text{,}}$ $\underline{\text{that have forced}}$ $\underline{\text{the resignations of}}$
   $\hspace{4.3cm}$ B $\hspace{1.5cm}$ C $\hspace{2.6cm}$ D

several prominent bank officials. $\underline{\text{No error}}$
   $\hspace{5.3cm}$ E

14. A preliminary study suggests that alcoholism and drug abuse are

most prevalent in rural than in urban areas. No error
‾‾‾‾A‾‾‾‾ ‾‾B‾ C‾ ‾‾‾‾‾‾D‾‾‾‾‾‾ ‾‾‾E‾‾‾

15. Anita Brookner, an art historian known for her work on eighteenth-
‾‾‾‾‾‾‾‾‾‾‾‾
A

century french painting, has also recently earned a reputation
‾‾‾‾‾‾
B   ‾‾‾‾‾‾‾‾
C

as a major novelist. No error
‾‾‾‾‾‾‾‾
D   ‾‾‾E‾‾‾

16. In an effort to compensate for diminished vacation traffic , many
‾‾‾‾‾‾‾‾‾‾‾‾‾
A   ‾
B

airlines now direct their advertising at the business traveler.
‾‾‾‾‾‾‾‾‾‾‾
C   ‾‾‾‾‾‾‾‾‾‾‾‾‾‾‾
D

No error
‾‾‾‾‾
E

17. Early in the century, many travelers went from Pittsburgh to
‾‾‾‾‾‾‾‾‾
A   ‾‾‾‾‾‾‾‾‾‾
B

Cincinnati on a 1,200-ton riverboat, the Virginia ; a steamer that
‾‾
C

regularly provided transportation along the Ohio River. No error
‾‾‾‾‾‾‾‾‾‾‾‾‾‾‾
D   ‾‾‾E‾‾‾

18. First published in 1949, Simone de Beauvoir's *The Second Sex*
‾‾‾‾‾‾‾‾‾‾‾‾‾
A

remains a penetrating and relevant interpretation of the relationship
‾‾‾‾‾‾‾‾
B   ‾‾‾‾‾‾‾‾‾‾‾‾‾‾‾
C

among women and men. No error
‾‾‾‾‾‾
D   ‾‾‾E‾‾‾

19. Mayan astronomers developed a precise calendar that permitted
‾‾‾‾‾‾‾‾‾‾‾‾
A

rulers and priests to predict with great accuracy such phenomena
‾‾‾‾‾‾‾‾‾‾‾‾‾‾‾‾‾‾‾‾‾‾‾‾‾‾‾‾
B

like eclipses of the Sun and Moon. No error
‾‾‾‾
C   ‾‾‾‾‾‾‾‾‾‾
D   ‾‾‾E‾‾‾

20. Horace Pippin, an African American artist worked on several
‾‾
A

drafts of a war narrative before he turned from writing to drawing
‾‾‾‾‾‾
B   ‾‾‾‾‾‾‾‾‾‾‾
C

and finally to painting. No error
‾‾‾‾‾‾‾
D   ‾‾‾E‾‾‾

21. The giant trees of the rain forest absorb carbon dioxide as they grow
‾‾‾‾‾‾‾‾‾‾‾‾‾‾‾
A   ‾‾‾‾‾‾‾‾
B

but release it into the atmosphere when they burn or rot. No error
‾‾‾‾‾‾‾‾‾
C   ‾‾‾‾‾‾‾‾‾‾
D   ‾‾‾E‾‾‾

Part B
17 Questions
(Suggested Time—20 minutes)

Directions: In each of the following sentences some part of the sentence or the entire sentence is underlined. Beneath each sentence you will find five ways of writing the underlined part. The first of these repeats the original, but the other four are all different. If you think the original sentence is better than any of the suggested changes, you should choose answer A; otherwise you should mark one of the other choices. Select the best answer and completely fill in the corresponding lettered space on the answer sheet with a heavy, dark mark so that you cannot see the letter.

This is a test of correctness and effectiveness of expression. In choosing answers, follow the requirements of standard written English; that is, pay attention to acceptable usage in grammar, diction (choice of words), sentence construction, and punctuation. Choose the answer that expresses most effectively what is presented in the original sentence; this answer should be clear and exact, without awkwardness, ambiguity, or redundancy.

Remember, try to answer every question.

Examples:

1. <u>While waving</u> goodbye to our friends, the airplane took off, and we watched it disappear in the sky.

(A) While waving
(B) Waving
(C) As we were waving
(D) While we are waving
(E) During waving

2. Modern travelers seem to prefer speed <u>to comfort</u>.

(A) to comfort
(B) than comfort
(C) rather than being comfortable
(D) instead of being comfortable
(E) more than comfort

Sample Answers:

1.

2.

22. The successful effort to clean the Thames has allowed the authorities to rescind the law that made it mandatory <u>for you to spend a night in the hospital for observation if one happened to fall into the river</u>.

    (A) for you to spend a night in the hospital for observation if one happened to fall into the river

    (B) for one to spend a night for observation in the hospital if you happened to fall into the river

    (C) that you should spend a night in the hospital for observation should you have happened to fall into the river

    (D) for people happening to fall into the river that they should spend a night in the hospital for observation

    (E) for people who happened to fall into the river to spend a night in the hospital for observation

23. In many areas water was long considered a free commodity, available to the farmer <u>at not any more than the price to transport it</u>.

    (A) at not any more than the price to transport it

    (B) at no more than costs of transportation

    (C) for not any more than are the costs of its transportation

    (D) for no more than the price of transporting it

    (E) only for the price that it costs to transport it

24. Completing seven triple-jumps, <u>Kristi Yamaguchi's performance was the most technically difficult free-style program</u> of any of the female competitors at the 1989 United States National Figure Skating Championships.

    (A) Kristi Yamaguchi's performance was the most technically difficult free-style program

    (B) Kristi Yamaguchi's free-style program was of the most technical difficulty

    (C) Kristi Yamaguchi performed the most technically difficult free-style program

    (D) the free-style program of Kristi Yamaguchi was the most technically difficult

    (E) the performance of Kristi Yamaguchi's free-style program was of the most technical difficulty

25. During the seventh and eighth centuries A.D., Damascus <u>flourished as</u> the capital of the Umayyad Empire, which stretched from Spain to India.

    (A) flourished as

    (B) flourishes, being

    (C) has flourished, being

    (D) flourishes, since it was

    (E) flourished in that it was

26. Lithography was invented in Germany by a Bavarian playwright, Aloys Senefelder, who found that <u>his scripts can be duplicated cheap</u> by printing them from greasy crayons and inks applied to slabs of local limestone.

(A) his scripts can be duplicated cheap
(B) he can duplicate his scripts cheap
(C) he can cheaply duplicate his scripts
(D) he could duplicate his scripts cheap
(E) he could duplicate his scripts cheaply

27. The curator of the new art exhibit believes that Max Ernst is to Dada and Surrealism <u>the way that Picasso is to</u> twentieth-century art as a whole.

(A) the way that Picasso is to
(B) what Picasso is to
(C) what Picasso means for
(D) the way that Picasso has meaning for
(E) how Picasso has been for

28. The lynx is endowed with a heavy <u>coat and is enabled by it</u> to function well in extreme cold.

(A) coat and is enabled by it
(B) coat by which it is enabled
(C) coat that enables it
(D) coat, thus enabled by it
(E) coat, and thus it is enabled

29. There is some evidence that garlic <u>may be capable to</u> play a role in providing protection against vascular disease.

(A) may be capable to
(B) may be can
(C) can maybe
(D) can perhaps
(E) perhaps can be capable to

30. <u>As against what government analysts had expected</u>, the drop in home mortgage interest rates did not stimulate the housing market.

(A) As against what government analysts had expected
(B) Contrary with what government analysts were expecting
(C) In contrast to the expectations government analysts had
(D) Opposite of government analysts' expectations
(E) Contrary to the expectations of government analysts

31. Advocates of women's rights have accused the regulatory agencies <u>with being lax as to enforcing</u> antidiscrimination laws.

(A) with being lax as to enforcing
(B) of being lax in enforcing
(C) with being lax on the enforcement of
(D) as to being lax for the enforcement of
(E) with laxness on enforcing

32. Because freight rates for grain are subsidized in Canada, it costs no more to ship 100 pounds of grain 700 miles from Saskatchewan to ports on the Great Lakes <u>as sending</u> a letter.

(A) as sending
(B) as it does to send
(C) as to send
(D) than sending
(E) than it does to send

33. In the 1950s and 1960s, the acceptance by employers of substantial health and pension plans <u>which were part of a contract settlement made union officials to be</u> the executive officers of large funds requiring investment expertise.

(A) which were part of a contract settlement made union officials to be
(B) which were part of contract settlements converted union officials into
(C) included in the contract settlement made union officials to be
(D) as part of contract settlements made union officials
(E) as part of a contract settlement converted union officials into

34. Unlike the United States, <u>in Japan there is no</u> tax incentive for art patronage in the form of a charitable deduction.

(A) in Japan there is no
(B) Japan does not offer a
(C) Japanese law provides no
(D) the Japanese do not have a
(E) Japan's laws do not provide for

35. Before it was known to be a carcinogen, asbestos was widely used <u>to be insulation and fireproofing</u>.

(A) to be insulation and fireproofing
(B) for insulation and fireproof
(C) as insulation and for fireproofing
(D) to be insulation and for fireproofing
(E) as insulation and as fireproof

36. Defendants in Florida do not have the right to close their trials to television cameras, <u>as defendants in some other states do</u>.

(A) as defendants in some other states do
(B) as defendants have it in some other states
(C) which they do in some other states
(D) which in some other states they have
(E) like defendants have in some other states

37. <u>To play wind instruments, it requires not only manual dexterity but also breath control as well</u>.

(A) To play wind instruments, it requires not only manual dexterity but also breath control as well.
(B) To play wind instruments requires both manual dexterity and breath control as well.
(C) Playing wind instruments requires not manual dexterity only but breath control too.
(D) Playing wind instruments, it requires manual dexterity and breath control.
(E) Playing wind instruments requires both manual dexterity and breath control.

38. <u>As recent as 30 years ago there were</u> no Saudi universities for women.

(A) As recent as 30 years ago there were
(B) Just as recent as 30 years ago there was
(C) As recently as 30 years ago was there
(D) As recently as 30 years ago there were
(E) Just as recent as 30 years ago there were

Section 2
Essay
Time—30 minutes

Directions: You will have 30 minutes to plan and write an essay on the topic presented on page 277. Read the topic carefully. You will probably find it best to spend a little time considering the topic and organizing your thoughts before you begin writing. DO NOT WRITE ON A TOPIC OTHER THAN THE ONE SPECIFIED. An essay on a topic of your own choice will not be acceptable. In order for your test to be scored, your response must be in English.

The essay question is included in this test to give you an opportunity to demonstrate how well you can write. You should, therefore, take care to write clearly and effectively, using specific examples where appropriate. Remember that how well you write is much more important than how much you write, but to cover the topic adequately, you will probably need to write more than a paragraph.

Your essay will be scored on the basis of its total quality—i.e., holistically. Each essay score is the sum of points (0–6) given by two readers. When your total writing score is computed, your essay score will be combined with your score for the multiple-choice section of the test.

You are to write your essay on the answer sheet; you will receive no other paper on which to write. Please write neatly and legibly. To be certain you have enough space on the answer sheet for your entire essay, please do NOT skip lines, do NOT write in excessively large letters, and do NOT leave wide margins. You may use the bottom of page 277 for any notes you may wish to make before you begin writing.

Section 2
Essay
Time—30 minutes

Read the opinion stated below.

"Letter grading systems should be replaced by pass/fail grading systems."

Discuss the extent to which you agree or disagree with this point of view. Support your position with specific reasons and examples from your own experience, observations, or reading.

The space below is for your **NOTES.** Write your essay in the space provided on the answer sheet.

DO NOT TURN BACK TO SECTION 1 OF THIS TEST.

PPST: Writing Test 1
Answers and Explanations
Part A

1. **Choice D is the best answer.** A grammatical error occurs at choice D, where the word "as" is incorrectly used. A comparative construction beginning with "more" should be completed by a phrase beginning with "than" rather than with "as": "more *X* than *Y*." The word at choice D should be "than."

2. **Choice A is the best answer.** The word "amount" is used to refer to quantities that can be measured but not counted, and is normally followed by a singular noun (e.g., "large amount of snow"). The word required at choice A is "number," which is used for quantities that can be counted, and is usually followed by a plural noun ("number of registered nurses").

3. **Choice E is the best answer.** There are no grammatical, idiomatic, logical, or structural errors in this sentence.

4. **Choice A is the best answer.** A noun–pronoun agreement error occurs at choice A. The possessive pronoun that is used to refer to the plural noun "whales" must also be plural. Thus, the singular pronoun "its" should be replaced by "their."

5. **Choice B is the best answer.** The correct form for an expression of negation that includes "neither" is "neither *X* nor *Y*." The error can be corrected by substituting "nor" for "or" at choice B.

6. **Choice B is the best answer.** An apostrophe should not be used to form the plural of "year." The correct plural of "year" is "years."

7. **Choice D is the best answer.** An error of idiom occurs at choice D. The construction begun by "not only" is correctly completed by "but also." The "and" at choice D therefore produces an unidiomatic expression. The word at choice D should be "but."

8. **Choice E is the best answer.** There are no grammatical, idiomatic, logical, or structural errors in this sentence.

9. **Choice A is the best answer.** An error of idiom occurs at choice A. Because the idiomatic form of this expression is "between *X* and *Y*," the correct word at choice A would be "and."

10. **Choice D is the best answer.** In this sentence, the construction "more than" is used to compare those districts that "have large numbers" of certain kinds of students with those districts that do not have large numbers of them. "Are" cannot grammatically substitute for "have" because it would produce the implied construction "those that are not have large numbers," which is

ungrammatical and nonsensical here. Thus, the phrase "those that do not" is called for at choice D.

11. **Choice B is the best answer.** The conjunction "when" is needed to refer to 1783 and to introduce a clause that describes that date as the time when something occurred; "in which" is not an idiomatic way to refer to dates.

12. **Choice E is the best answer.** There are no grammatical, idiomatic, logical, or structural errors in this sentence.

13. **Choice B is the best answer.** The clause "that have forced..." is a restrictive clause, one that is essential to the meaning of the sentence. A restrictive clause is not preceded by a comma, because it is part of the main idea and should not be separated from it; thus, the comma at choice B is incorrect. On the other hand, a nonrestrictive clause, one that is not essential and could be removed from the sentence without altering its meaning, must be preceded by a comma to indicate that it is not essential to the main idea and can be separated from it. A nonrestrictive clause would also normally use the relative pronoun "which" rather than "that."

14. **Choice A is the best answer.** The construction "most... than" is incorrect because "most" is a superlative, whereas "than" functions as part of a comparison. A construction in which "than" is used to make a comparison usually begins with "more"; thus, the word at choice A should be "more," not "most."

15. **Choice B is the best answer.** An error in capitalization occurs at choice B. Because words that name nationalities should be capitalized, the letter at choice B should be a capital F.

16. **Choice E is the best answer.** There are no errors of grammar, idiom, logic, or structure in this sentence.

17. **Choice C is the best answer.** An error of punctuation occurs at choice C. The semicolon is typically used to separate independent clauses; a comma is needed at choice A to set off the noun phrase "a steamer...," which renames "the *Virginia*."

18. **Choice D is the best answer.** When a "relationship" involves only two elements, the appropriate connecting word is "between"; the word "among" is used with three or more elements. Therefore, the error at choice D can be corrected by changing "among" to "between."

19. **Choice C is the best answer.** In phrases presenting examples, the word that should normally be used in combination with "such" is "as," not "like." The use of "like" is unidiomatic here.

20. **Choice A is the best answer.** The phrase "a Black American artist" is not the subject of the verb "worked"; "Horace Pippin" is the subject. The phrase "a Black American artist" is an appositive

phrase that provides additional information about Horace Pippin, and as such it should be set off by commas from the rest of the sentence. Therefore, a comma should be placed at choice A.

21. **Choice E is the best answer.** There are no errors in grammar, idiom, logic, or structure in this sentence.

Part B

22. **Choice E is the best answer.** Choices A and B lack consistency in the use of pronouns: "you" and "one" should not be used together in a sentence to refer to the same person. In addition, the wording of A is awkward and confusing because "one happened to fall into the river" is closer to "hospital" and to "observation" than to any word it could logically modify. Choices C and D are incorrect because they use the unidiomatic "that you should spend" and "that they should spend," respectively. The appropriate way of completing the phrase "made it mandatory" is with the infinitive "to spend." Choice E uses both the idiomatic "to spend" and avoids the "you-one" confusion by using "people."

23. **Choice D is the best answer.** Choice D, is idiomatic, logical, and unambiguous. Choices A and C are wordy and awkward, and both use a phrase that is unidiomatic in this context—"not any more," rather than "no more." Choice B is awkwardly and unclearly phrased: "available at… costs of" should be "available for… the price of," and the word "transportation" does not clearly refer to "water." In choice E, "the price that it costs" is redundant, and "only" confusingly suggests that water will be available "only" if the farmer pays a price equal to the costs of transportation.

24. **Choice C is the best answer.** The opening phrase, "Completing seven triple-jumps," should be completed by a noun that identifies the person who performed the jumps. Only choice C supplies that noun. In the other four choices, either the "program" (choices B and D) or the "performance" (choices A and E) are illogically credited with completing the jumps, and are thus illogically compared with "female competitors."

25. **Choice A is the best answer.** Because this sentence discusses only past time ("During the seventh and eighth centuries"), the appropriate tense for the verb is the past tense "flourished." Choices B and D use the present tense "flourishes," and choice C uses the present perfect tense "has flourished." Also, in choice D, "since it was" changes the meaning of the sentence by introducing the idea of a cause–effect relationship—that is, that Damascus flourished *because* it was the capital. Similarly, in choice E, the phrase "in that" is roughly equivalent to "since" or "because." Choice A, which uses the past tense and is logically clear and grammatically correct, is the best choice.

26. Choice E is the best answer. There should be consistency of verb tenses in the sentence. Because the first two verbs, "was invented" and "found," are in the past tense, the next verb should be the past tense "could" rather than the present tense "can." In addition, the word that modifies the verb "duplicated" should be an adverb such as "cheaply," not an adjective such as "cheap." The only choice that contains both the past tense "could" and the adverb "cheaply" is choice E.

27. Choice B is the best answer. This sentence requires that the comparison between Ernst and Picasso be completed by a parallel construction beginning with "what": "*W* is to *X* what *Y* is to *Z*." Choices A and D are wrong because they use "the way that." Choice E is wrong because it uses "how" instead of "what." Choice C begins with "what" but uses "means for" rather than "is to." Similarly, choices D and E substitute "means for" and "has meaning for," respectively, for "is to." Choice B is the only option in which this parallel construction is used correctly.

28. Choice C is the best answer. Choices A, B, D, and E are wordy and use a weak passive voice, "(is) enabled." Furthermore, choice D is incomplete: the words following the comma bear no clear grammatical relationship to the rest of the sentence. Choice C is clear and to the point and uses the active voice.

29. Choice D is the best answer. Choice D is both grammatically and idiomatically correct. Choices A and E use the incorrect phrase "capable to"; the correct form is "capable of." Choice C is redundant. Choice B is incorrect on two counts: grammatically, the adverb "maybe" rather than the verb form "may be," is required to modify the verb "can"; but even if this error were corrected, "maybe can" would still be unidiomatic.

30. Choice E is the best answer. The opening phrase of choice A, "As against what," and the opening phrase of choice D, "Opposite of," are awkward and unidiomatic in this context. Choice B uses "Contrary with," which is unidiomatic in this context; "contrary to" is required. Choice C is awkward and wordy. Choice E is clear, idiomatic, and grammatically correct.

31. Choice B is the best answer. Choice B is the only choice to use the correct phrasing. The correct construction is "to accuse (a party) of" an offense. Also, it is appropriate to say that one is lax "in performing" an action. Thus, the prepositions "with" in choices A, C, and E and "as to" in choice D are incorrect. Similarly, choice A uses "as to enforcing," choice C uses "on the enforcement of," choice D uses "for the enforcement of," and choice E uses "on enforcing"—all wordy or unidiomatic in context.

32. **Choice E is the best answer.** A comparative construction beginning with "more" is properly completed by a phrase beginning with "than": "more *X* than *Y*." Thus, choices A, B, and C are incorrect because they use "as" instead of "than." Also, the "no more... than" comparison requires a parallel construction: "it costs no more to *ship*... than (it does) *to send*." In choices A and D, "sending" is not parallel to "to ship." Choice E preserves the parallelism and uses "than" rather than "as."

33. **Choice D is the best answer.** The phrase "as part of contract settlements" is clearer than the more awkward and wordy phrasing of choices A, B, C, and E. Also, the "made... to be" construction is ungrammatical as used in choices A and C, and "converted... into" in choices B and E misleadingly implies a total change in the functions of the officials, rather than the addition of a new function to their existing duties.

34. **Choice B is the best answer.** In a comparison using "like" or "unlike," the things being compared must be of the same type. Because the first noun in this comparison is the name of a country, "the United States," the second term must also be the name of a country, "Japan." Only choice B follows this logical structure. Choice A lacks the parallel construction of a proper comparison because it introduces the preposition "in." Choices C and E substitute the laws of the country, and choice D its people, for the name of the country itself.

35. **Choice C is the best answer.** When "used" is followed by a noun such as "insulation" or "fireproofing," the correct idioms are "used as" and "used for." Thus, in choices A and D, the infinitive "to be" is incorrect. In choices B and E, the adjective or verb form "fireproof" is incorrectly used as a noun, instead of the proper form of the noun, "fireproofing." Choice C uses both this noun and the correct idioms.

36. **Choice A is the best answer.** The sense of this sentence is that defendants in Florida *do not* have a right that defendants in some other states *do*. The verb "do" must be repeated in the second part of the sentence to parallel the verb "do" in the first part. It is not necessary to repeat "have." Choices B, D, and E fail to repeat "do," and the referent of "it" is unclear in choice B. In choices C and D, the pronoun "they" lacks a logical antecedent; grammatically, it refers to "Defendants in Florida," not to defendants in other states. Choice E is also wrong because the correct usage before comparisons containing a subject and verb ("defendants have") is "as," not "like." Choice A maintains the "do" parallel and contains no unclear reference.

37. Choice E is the best answer. To be grammatically correct, this sentence must provide one clear subject and a concise indication of the two requirements, "manual dexterity" and "breath control." Choices A and D are ungrammatical because "it" wrongly introduces a second grammatical subject for the verb "requires." In choice A, the use of both "also" and "as well" is redundant, since both have the same meaning. In choice B, "as well" used with "both" is unidiomatic; only "both" is required. In choice C, "only" should be placed immediately after "not." In choice E, "Playing" makes a better subject for "requires" than does "To play...," and the rest of the sentence is clear and concise.

38. Choice D is the best answer. The subject of the sentence is "universities," a plural noun. Because the verb must agree with the subject, the singular verb "was," as used in choices B and C, should be "were." The adjective "recent" in choices A, B, and E is incorrect; because the word modifies the verb "were," the adverb form, "recently," is correct. Also in choice C, the correct word order, "there was," is reversed. Choice D correctly uses the adverb and the plural verb.

Essay
Response That Received a Score of 6

Essay	Explanation of Score
The debate as to whether a precise grading system, or the development of a pass/fail system in the schools would be better is a discussion which is a topic of great consideration in today's educational system. There are many questions which need to be asked when considering this debate. In what ways are children learning differently in the late 1990s as compared to any other time? Are teachers teaching differently, and in what ways are teachers organizing their classrooms? Most importantly, where is the motivation coming from for children to learn? All of these issues need to be addressed before a decision can be made about the grading systems used, and whether or not there needs to be one unanimous choice made on the issue. However, while there is support for both precise grading systems and pass/fail grading systems, precise grading systems seem to provide more motivation for academic achievement among students in America.	This essay begins by considering both sides of the debate, then ends the first paragraph in favor of "precise grading systems." Three clear reasons are given in support of that choice (new educational techniques, teacher organization, motivation), each well explained in its own paragraph. The essay is very clear, very well organized, and its reasons in support of a precise grading system are fully developed. It builds logically from beginning to end, with ideas and sentences nicely linked together. There are sentences of varied lengths and rhythm (including both simple and complex sentences), providing a fluent and enjoyable read; precise word choices ("consideration, unanimous, academic achievement, conjure, flying colors") help to keep the reader interested.
Today, children learn much differently than they did even ten years ago. Mostly, this is because of the increase in resources and their accessibility. The improvement in the public library systems and the introduction of computers as the norm in schools, as well as the continually increasing popularity of the internet, makes learning much more of an every day activity, if not something that is enjoyable. Because of the availability of these resources every student is on equal ground when it comes to projects, papers, and other tasks. In this case, a precise grading system seems to be in order, because if everyone has the same opportunities, then everyone should be taking advantage of those opportunities. In communities where these resources might not be as readily available to students, it is important that parents and teachers encourage the discovery and use of these tools for education.	

(Continued)

Essay	Explanation of Score
The way in which a teacher organizes his or her classroom is also a factor to consider in this debate. While no one should praise only the excellent students for the achievement and ignore the struggling students, it is important that success is recognized. If success is not recognized, then where is the motivation for learning? Most children at a young age, and maybe not until college, do not appreciate learning for learning's sake. It takes something more than the information a book has to offer to make a student want to read it. It is how the teacher presents it and what the student will be expected to learn from the book which makes reading the book a task which will be completed. The biggest factor, though, is probably what the other students will know that drives one student to learn. Motivation to do well in school comes mainly from competition. No one student wants to be left behind the others when he or she knows he can do well. The word competition may conjure negative images in people's minds, but in reality it is probably the biggest driving force leading to academic achievement among America's students. There are scholarships and awards given to those who achieve in various areas of their school experience. Things like this make learning something worthwhile. When a student can get an A, B, C, D or F in a class, the motivation for getting an A is high. An A is definitely better than a C (average) or a D (barely passing) and obviously better than an F. In a pass/fail system however, a student can only pass or fail. There is no distinction between passing with flying colors or barely passing. In many cases, a student might do just enough work to pass, whereas in a precise grading system, a student might work diligently to earn an A. The motivation is obvious: everyone can see how hard a student worked to earn that A. In a pass/fail system, however, every student that passes is on equal ground—just where they were when they began the class.	

(Continued)

Essay	Explanation of Score
Pass/fail systems can definitely work in some classrooms, depending on the subject and age level. In beginning classrooms where the focus is learning basic concepts, a pass/fail system would be appropriate and applicable. In a more advanced classroom, however, where the emphasis is on applying basic concepts to different tasks and forming new ideas, the use of a precise grading system would definitely produce more effort from the students, and better results in the end. Precise grading systems encourage learning based on the outcome, and those who are successful in grade school and high school understand the expectations that university will hold, and work more diligently to meet those expectations.	

Response That Received a Score of 5

Essay	Explanation of Score
My experiences in school lead me to believe that letter grading systems should not be replaced with pass/fail grading systems. I feel this way for three reasons. First, in a pass/fail system students will only be motivated to do the minimum amount required to pass. Second, the uses of letter scores gives motivation to a student to perform at a high level. Finally, letter grading gives feedback to a student so the student determine what her strengths and weaknesses are.

A pass/fail system will only motivate a student to do enough work to pass. I have directly experienced this effect in the past semester at my university. I took a racquetball class pass/fail while I took the rest of my classes under a letter grading system. I am a person who is intrinsically motivated to achieve high grades in my classes. In my letter graded classes I never missed a class and studied many hours a night. However, in my pass/fail class I skipped several classes and never did any work beyond what was required to pass. In this case I was not motivated to go beyond what was required to pass and therefore | This essay begins with a clear and explicit thesis: "My experiences in school lead me to believe that letter grading systems should not be replaced with pass/fail grading systems." The main idea is followed by three specific reasons for this position, each reason providing the topic sentence for the three body paragraphs and each paragraph elaborating on these topic sentences with a variety of relevant details and examples to support key ideas.

In the first body paragraph, the essay presents the writer's personal school experience—taking a racquetball course—and explains the results of taking the course on |

(Continued)

Essay	Explanation of Score
do not know as much about racquetball as I would had I taken it for a letter grade.	a pass/fail basis: "I was not motivated to go beyond what was required to pass." In the second paragraph, the essay continues explaining the connection between letter grades and motivation, speculating that "a student who received a B- in Math can give herself the goal of shooting for a B+," a situation not possible with the pass/fail system. In the final body paragraph, the essay notes that students can receive more feedback from letter grades and once again provides a personal experience to support this main idea. All paragraphs contribute to the overall clear organization of the paper.
A scoring scale gives a student motivation to achieve a higher grade. A letter grade system has built-in goals set for a student while a pass/fail only has one goal, to pass. In a letter grade system a student who received a B- in Math can give herself the goal of shooting for a B+ next semester. In a pass/fail system, a B- would be passing and the student would not have anything to shoot for, thereby decreasing her motivation and not causing her to work harder. This lack of motivation is cheating the student out of possible learning experiences that maybe achieved through education to improve herself.	
Finally, a pass/fail system does not provide a student with as in depth of feedback as a letter grade system does. In a letter grade system, a student is given a score in many areas such as Grammar, Math, and Science. These scores are on the same letter scale and can allow the student to compare across areas to see where her strengths are. While I personally pass all areas, I am better in Math than in Grammar. This knowledge of my strengths leads me to work on improving my grammar and also gives me direction in life. Instead of trying to become an English teacher, I am trying to become a Business teacher, an occupation that lends itself to my mathematical abilities. A pass/fail system would not have allowed me to compare these abilities and would have made my decision more difficult.	This well-organized and developed paper is also generally free from errors. However, while the paper is well organized, the repetition and paraphrasing of the key ideas in the introduction and topic sentences, even though making effective connections between paragraphs, does not demonstrate the type of sentence variety and language facility that might appear in a stronger paper.
In conclusion, I feel that a letter grade system gives students more motivation and allows them to be better prepared for the world after their schooling is completed. Without a system to compare and rank abilities, it would be difficult for a student to identify their strengths and weaknesses. A pass/fail system would also fail to give students something to shoot for. Therefore a letter grading system should be favored over a pass/fail grading system.	

(*Continued*)

Response That Received a Score of 4

Essay	Explanation of Score
Grades play an important role in school. I think that a precise grading scale would work better for students than a pass/fail system. Any type of grading system will cause competition, but I think a little competition is good for students. Competition, if controlled, teaches students how to get along with others and also pushes them to try harder. A precise grading system would cause a little more competition than any other type of grading system. Precise grades motivate students to work their hardest. A precise grading system not only gives students motivation, it also gives them a reasonable goal to work towards. Say for instance, an average student could aim for a B, while an above average student could set their goal for an A. Instead of both just trying to pass. I personally think that a pass/fail grading system would put more strain and pressure on a student than a precise grading system. If I were on a pass/fail system then I would feel that if I made one mistake then I would be that much closer to failing. This would make me nervous and I would second guess myself more often then usual and I wouldn't perform as well. If I was on a precise grading system, I would feel that I had a little room for mistakes. Another reason I think precise grading is important, is because it is a good way of telling where a student stands. In a pass/fail grading system the teacher would only know if you passed of failed, but in a precise grading system teachers would be able to see how well a student did on an assignment or test and they could see how they stand with the rest of the class. I have seen students that were graded both by pass/fail and by a precise scale. One teacher assigned the students a paper, they were graded on a pass/fail. These students were happy with passing. This seemed reasonable, because they did pass. But in another classroom where the teacher assigned the same paper and graded	This essay is for the "precise grading system" and says why (to motivate students). The explanation for choosing letter grades discusses motivating students, but also includes a specific example from the writer's life when he or she saw the effect of letter grading versus pass/fail; this example helps bring the writer's argument to life. The essay is organized—building from its clear introduction through its explanation of ideas—and easy to follow. More specifics and more explanation would help the piece, as would variety in language; there are few interesting words, and the constant repetition of certain phrases ("precise grading system...grades... teachers...students...pass/fail") makes the reading somewhat monotonous. Better word choices and sentences of different lengths would help to give this essay a little more sparkle.

(Continued)

Essay	Explanation of Score
these student's using a precise scale. These students were not happy unless they got a grade higher than a C. These papers were way above passing, yet they were unhappy. This made me realize that students are and will be more motivated with letter grades rather than pass/fail. 　Students decide for themselves how hard they are going to try, but by using a precise grading system, students will compete a little with each other and try to better themselves. A precise grading system would not only be useful for the students, but for teachers as well. Teachers would be able to tell how each student was doing in each subject and then could offer whatever help was needed for that student.	

Response That Received a Score of 3

Essay	Explanation of Score
What is happening in schools is it is getting to easy for kids to get out of working hard. Going to a pass/fail grading system would play right into their hands. They want the easy way out, and what is easier then passing or failing? Here are someways that we can get the kids back into the grading system. First lets challlenge the kids to do better. Then we make the children want to get a higher grade. Finally we can relax on the grading scale. I will explain in detail what I mean in my steps below. 　Let's go back to the days when kids wanted to learn, ok that was never true. If we can not make them want to go to school, we can at least make them want to learn. We can start to change the classroom to make it more challenging and to bring back the energy to do well in school. This gets the kids to stop thinking some much on the grades, but rather on the learning. That would be the first step to reintroducing the grading scale. 　Making the classroom fun will hopefully get the kids minds of the grades and learning will take place and the grades will go up and they will not worry about pass/fail. Rather they will be thinking A or B. Taking the hassle out of learning will promote the kids to learn rather then to force them to learn.	This writer has an obvious position ("I am totally in favor of keeping the grading scale"), but the reasons explaining why the writer feels this way are not very clear. Instead of approaching the argument with a clear starting point, the essay instead seems to be jumping around. Many ideas are like the following sentence, which changes in mid-thought: "Let's go back to the days when kids wanted to learn, ok that was never true." The writer has obviously not thought his or her position through, which is evident from the lack of organization and unclear explanation. While there is focus and explanation in this essay, better organization could certainly have helped it.

(Continued)

Essay	Explanation of Score
The final step for the kids and the teachers to keep the grade scale is to relax on the grading. I feel that you have to grade appriately for the student. If he is a little slower, do not be as harsh as with your honor student. Also give more credit for group work. Group work will promote energy in learning because you are a part of something and you feel more at liberty to speak and interact. So I am in totally favor of keeping the grading scale because I feel that it promotes self worth and motivation to work harder. I do not think it would be in anyone's best interest to go to the pass/fail method. That just promotes laziness. Because if you can get away with medicore work, then why try hard. If you really think about the current grading system, it is almost the same idea. You have four letter grades which are passing and only one that is failing. I think you have a better chance with the grading system rather then without. To make the children to stop thinking about failing you should make the class fun, interest them in things that will strike an interest, and finally take the grading system for what it is worth, a degree of passing.	

Response that Received a Score of 2

Essay	Explanation of Score
Some people argue that giving grades to students puts too much emphasis on competition and not enough emphasis on learning. While, others argue that without a precise grading system, students would not work as hard to excel. Students receiving grades in school encourages them to suceed and prepares them for their future. Receiving grades will continue throughout the students lives. For example when entering the work force you will be graded on your job preformance. In school if a students strived to achieve then this will continue in their job preformance.	This essay may be a discussion of the benefits of grades, but it never discusses whether or not letter grades should be replaced by a pass/fail system. That is the topic addressed in the prompt, so this essay lacks a clear position or thesis. The arguments make sense, but they are not being given to support a thesis; the writer is rambling. Odd word choices

(Continued)

Essay	Explanation of Score
Some students might not of been motivated in school to achieve high grades but they are outstanding in the job field that they have choosen. The aspect of grading will still be a part of them because they were graded for preformance in school. Grades are important in our lives they give us encouragement to achieve. This process will continue through out our lives.	and mistakes in grammar also confuse the reader, and it is often not easy to understand the writer's point. This essay needs a more clear focus, better explanation, and language that is easier to follow.

Response that Received a Score of 1

Essay	Explanation of Score
I think we should use the same grading system we already have, not Pass/Fail. That way kids will keep working at their homework. I believe the only thing that would happen the other way would be terribul. People would just skip school all the time because, students wouldnt have to worry about there grades. Instead the schools should remain having the grades they way they always have.	This brief essay does have a clear position ("we should use the same grading system…not Pass/Fail"), but gives only one vague reason to support it ("the other way would be terrible"). The writer does tell us the terrible result would be that kids would skip school, but never tells us why they would skip. We are told students "wouldn't have to worry about their grades" any longer, but again we are not told why. Language problems do not interfere with the reader's understanding in this essay, but a lack of explanation does make it hard for the reader to know what the writer is getting at.

CALCULATING YOUR SCORE

Follow these instructions to score PPST: Writing Test 1. When you actually take the PPST, you will have questions that are very similar to the questions in the sample tests in this book, but they will not be identical. Because of the difference in questions, the tests you actually take may be slightly more or less difficult than the tests printed in this book. Therefore, you may not get the same number of questions right on an actual test as on the sample tests.

NOTE: The **data** in Tables 1 and 2 apply to only the PPST: Writing Test 1. The actual test you take will have a different answer table and a different conversion table.

To score PPST: Writing Test 1:

- Count the number of questions you answered correctly in the multiple-choice section of the test. The correct answers are in Table 1. Score report category W-1 contains 9 questions measuring knowledge of grammatical relationships; category W-2 contains 12 questions assessing understanding of structural relationships; and category W-3 contains 17 questions assessing understanding of idiom and word choice, mechanics, and correct usage. Count the number of questions you answered correctly in each of these categories. This may give you some idea of your strengths and weaknesses.

- Essays from actual administrations of the PPST: Writing test are read and rated by at least two writing experts. The readers use a rating scale of 1 to 6, where 6 is best. (Zero is used for "off-topic" essays.) The essay score is the sum of the two ratings and can therefore range from 2 to 12. Because it is impossible for you to score your own essay, you might want to try using three different values of essay scores in combination with your score on the multiple-choice section to see how your overall score would vary depending on how well you did on the essay. A score of 8 would be about average. You might also want to try a low score of 3 or 4, for example, and a high score, say, of 11 or 12.

- Use Table 2 to find your possible scaled scores. In the column on the left, find the number of questions you answered correctly on the multiple-choice section. Look across the top of Table 2 to the column with the essay score you are using. Go across the row and down the column to find the scaled scores for different combinations of multiple-choice section and essay scores. You can compare your scaled score to the passing score required by your state or institution. (Passing state scores are available on the Praxis website at www.ets.org/praxis.)

Table 1—PPST: Writing Test 1

*Answers to Practice Test Questions and Percentages of
Examinees Answering Each Question Correctly*

Question	Score Report Category	Correct Answer	Percentage of Examinees Choosing Correct Answer
1	W-2	D	83%
2	W-3	A	33
3	W-3	E	68
4	W-1	A	57
5	W-2	B	70
6	W-3	B	73
7	W-2	D	69
8	W-3	E	63
9	W-2	A	83
10	W-1	D	54
11	W-1	B	52
12	W-3	E	46
13	W-3	B	73
14	W-2	A	68
15	W-3	B	78
16	W-3	E	67
17	W-3	C	65
18	W-2	D	60
19	W-1	C	70
20	W-3	A	92
21	W-3	E	68
22	W-1	E	67
23	W-3	D	66
24	W-2	C	56
25	W-3	A	87
26	W-1	E	68
27	W-2	B	63
28	W-1	C	89
29	W-3	D	84
30	W-3	E	70

(Continued)

Table 1—PPST: Writing Test 1 (*Continued*)

Question	Score Report Category	Correct Answer	Percentage of Examinees Choosing Correct Answer
31	W-3	B	75
32	W-2	E	54
33	W-2	D	45
34	W-2	B	70
35	W-1	C	69
36	W-3	A	48
37	W-2	E	80
38	W-1	D	64

NOTE: Percentages are based on the test records of 2,250 examinees who took the 60-minute version of the PPST: Writing test in November 1992.

* In general, questions may be considered as easy, average, or difficult based on the following percentages:

Easy questions   = 75% or more answered correctly.
Average questions = 55%–74% answered correctly.
Difficult questions = less than 55% answered correctly.

Table 2—PPST: Writing Test 1
Score Conversion Table

Multiple-Choice Section (# Right)	Essay Score (Sum of Two Readings)												
	0	**1**	**2**	**3**	**4**	**5**	**6**	**7**	**8**	**9**	**10**	**11**	**12**
0	150	150	152	154	155	157	158	160	162	163	165	166	168
1	150	151	152	154	156	157	159	160	162	164	165	167	168
2	150	151	153	155	156	158	159	161	163	164	166	167	169
3	150	152	153	155	157	158	160	161	163	165	166	168	169
4	151	152	154	156	157	159	160	162	164	165	167	168	170
5	151	153	154	156	158	159	161	162	164	166	167	169	170
6	152	153	155	157	158	160	161	163	165	166	168	169	171
7	152	154	155	157	159	160	162	163	165	167	168	170	172
8	153	154	156	158	159	161	162	164	166	167	169	170	172
9	153	155	157	158	160	161	163	165	166	168	169	171	173
10	154	155	157	159	160	162	163	165	167	168	170	171	173
11	154	156	158	159	161	162	164	166	167	169	170	172	174
12	155	156	158	160	161	163	164	166	168	169	171	172	174
13	155	157	159	160	162	163	165	167	168	170	171	173	175
14	156	157	159	161	162	164	165	167	169	170	172	173	175
15	156	158	160	161	163	164	166	168	169	171	172	174	176
16	157	158	160	162	163	165	166	168	170	171	173	174	176
17	157	159	161	162	164	165	167	169	170	172	173	175	177
18	158	159	161	163	164	166	167	169	171	172	174	175	177
19	158	160	162	163	165	166	168	170	171	173	174	176	178
20	159	160	162	164	165	167	168	170	172	173	175	176	178
21	159	161	163	164	166	167	169	171	172	174	175	177	179
22	160	161	163	165	166	168	169	171	173	174	176	177	179
23	160	162	164	165	167	168	170	172	173	175	176	178	180
24	161	162	164	166	167	169	170	172	174	175	177	178	180
25	161	163	165	166	168	169	171	173	174	176	177	179	181
26	162	163	165	167	168	170	172	173	175	176	178	180	181
27	162	164	166	167	169	170	172	174	175	177	178	180	182
28	163	165	166	168	169	171	173	174	176	177	179	181	182
29	163	165	167	168	170	171	173	175	176	178	179	181	183
30	164	166	167	169	170	172	174	175	177	178	180	182	183

(Continued)

Table 2—PPST: Writing Test 1 (*Continued*)

Multiple-Choice Section (# Right)	Essay Score (Sum of Two Readings)												
	0	1	2	3	4	5	6	7	8	9	10	11	12
31	164	166	168	169	171	172	174	176	177	179	180	182	184
32	165	167	168	170	171	173	175	176	178	179	181	183	184
33	165	167	169	170	172	173	175	177	178	180	181	183	185
34	166	168	169	171	172	174	176	177	179	180	182	184	185
35	166	168	170	171	173	174	176	178	179	181	182	184	186
36	167	169	170	172	173	175	177	178	180	181	183	185	186
37	167	169	171	172	174	175	177	179	180	182	183	185	187
38	168	170	171	173	174	176	178	179	181	182	184	186	187

CHAPTER 14

PPST: Writing Test 2

THE PRAXIS SERIES™

Answer Sheet B

PAGE 1

DO NOT USE INK

Use only a pencil with soft black lead (No. 2 or HB) to complete this answer sheet.
Be sure to fill in completely the oval that corresponds to your answer choice.
Completely erase any errors or stray marks.

1. NAME
Enter your last name and first initial.
Omit spaces, hyphens, apostrophes, etc.

Last Name (first 6 letters) | F.I.

2.

YOUR NAME: _____
(Print) Last Name (Family or Surname) — First Name (Given) — M.I.

MAILING ADDRESS: _____
(Print) P.O. Box or Street Address — Apt. # (If any)

_____ City — State or Province

_____ Country — Zip or Postal Code

TELEPHONE NUMBER: (____) Home (____) Business

SIGNATURE: _____

TEST DATE: _____

3. DATE OF BIRTH
Month | Day

Jan., Feb., Mar., April, May, June, July, Aug., Sept., Oct., Nov., Dec.

4. SOCIAL SECURITY NUMBER

5. CANDIDATE ID NUMBER

6. TEST CENTER / REPORTING LOCATION

Center Number — Room Number

Center Name

City — State or Province

Country

7. TEST CODE / FORM CODE

8. TEST BOOK SERIAL NUMBER

9. TEST FORM

10. TEST NAME

Educational Testing Service, ETS, the ETS logo, and THE PRAXIS SERIES: PROFESSIONAL ASSESSMENTS FOR BEGINNING TEACHERS and its design logo are registered trademarks of Educational Testing Service. The modernized ETS logo is a trademark of Educational Testing Service.

Copyright © 1993 by Educational Testing Service, Princeton, NJ 08541. Printed in U.S.A.

MH99232   Q2572-06   51055 • 08916 • CV99M500
I.N. 202973

1   2   3   4

CERTIFICATION STATEMENT: (Please write the following statement below. DO NOT PRINT.)

"I hereby agree to the conditions set forth in the Registration Bulletin and certify that I am the person whose name and address appear on this answer sheet."

_____

_____

_____

SIGNATURE: _____ DATE: _____/_____/_____
                                                                Month   Day   Year

---

BE SURE EACH MARK IS DARK AND COMPLETELY FILLS THE INTENDED SPACE AS ILLUSTRATED HERE: ● .

1 Ⓐ Ⓑ Ⓒ Ⓓ Ⓔ	13 Ⓐ Ⓑ Ⓒ Ⓓ Ⓔ	25 Ⓐ Ⓑ Ⓒ Ⓓ Ⓔ	37 Ⓐ Ⓑ Ⓒ Ⓓ Ⓔ
2 Ⓐ Ⓑ Ⓒ Ⓓ Ⓔ	14 Ⓐ Ⓑ Ⓒ Ⓓ Ⓔ	26 Ⓐ Ⓑ Ⓒ Ⓓ Ⓔ	38 Ⓐ Ⓑ Ⓒ Ⓓ Ⓔ
3 Ⓐ Ⓑ Ⓒ Ⓓ Ⓔ	15 Ⓐ Ⓑ Ⓒ Ⓓ Ⓔ	27 Ⓐ Ⓑ Ⓒ Ⓓ Ⓔ	39 Ⓐ Ⓑ Ⓒ Ⓓ Ⓔ
4 Ⓐ Ⓑ Ⓒ Ⓓ Ⓔ	16 Ⓐ Ⓑ Ⓒ Ⓓ Ⓔ	28 Ⓐ Ⓑ Ⓒ Ⓓ Ⓔ	40 Ⓐ Ⓑ Ⓒ Ⓓ Ⓔ
5 Ⓐ Ⓑ Ⓒ Ⓓ Ⓔ	17 Ⓐ Ⓑ Ⓒ Ⓓ Ⓔ	29 Ⓐ Ⓑ Ⓒ Ⓓ Ⓔ	41 Ⓐ Ⓑ Ⓒ Ⓓ Ⓔ
6 Ⓐ Ⓑ Ⓒ Ⓓ Ⓔ	18 Ⓐ Ⓑ Ⓒ Ⓓ Ⓔ	30 Ⓐ Ⓑ Ⓒ Ⓓ Ⓔ	42 Ⓐ Ⓑ Ⓒ Ⓓ Ⓔ
7 Ⓐ Ⓑ Ⓒ Ⓓ Ⓔ	19 Ⓐ Ⓑ Ⓒ Ⓓ Ⓔ	31 Ⓐ Ⓑ Ⓒ Ⓓ Ⓔ	43 Ⓐ Ⓑ Ⓒ Ⓓ Ⓔ
8 Ⓐ Ⓑ Ⓒ Ⓓ Ⓔ	20 Ⓐ Ⓑ Ⓒ Ⓓ Ⓔ	32 Ⓐ Ⓑ Ⓒ Ⓓ Ⓔ	44 Ⓐ Ⓑ Ⓒ Ⓓ Ⓔ
9 Ⓐ Ⓑ Ⓒ Ⓓ Ⓔ	21 Ⓐ Ⓑ Ⓒ Ⓓ Ⓔ	33 Ⓐ Ⓑ Ⓒ Ⓓ Ⓔ	45 Ⓐ Ⓑ Ⓒ Ⓓ Ⓔ
10 Ⓐ Ⓑ Ⓒ Ⓓ Ⓔ	22 Ⓐ Ⓑ Ⓒ Ⓓ Ⓔ	34 Ⓐ Ⓑ Ⓒ Ⓓ Ⓔ	
11 Ⓐ Ⓑ Ⓒ Ⓓ Ⓔ	23 Ⓐ Ⓑ Ⓒ Ⓓ Ⓔ	35 Ⓐ Ⓑ Ⓒ Ⓓ Ⓔ	
12 Ⓐ Ⓑ Ⓒ Ⓓ Ⓔ	24 Ⓐ Ⓑ Ⓒ Ⓓ Ⓔ	36 Ⓐ Ⓑ Ⓒ Ⓓ Ⓔ	

FOR ETS USE ONLY	R	ESSAY	R / ESSAY	CS

LAST NAME (first two letters)   FIRST INITIAL   DATE OF BIRTH (month and day **only**)   MONTH   DAY

TEST CODE / FORM CODE

TEST DATE: ___ / ___ / ___
Mo.   Day   Year

CANDIDATE ID NUMBER: _____

TEST BOOK SERIAL NUMBER: _____

I agree to give Educational Testing Service permission to use my responses anonymously in its educational research and for instructional purposes. I understand that I am free to mark "No," with no effect on my score or its reporting.

◯ Yes   ◯ No

(ESSAY) Begin your essay on this page. If you need more space, continue on page 4.

36-3 MH98308

Continuation of essay from page 3. Write below only if you need more space.

THE AREA BELOW IS FOR ETS USE ONLY. DO NOT MARK.

1 READER NO.

2 READER NO.

3 READER NO.

Section 1
Multiple Choice
Time—30 minutes
38 Questions

Part A
21 Questions
(Suggested Time—10 minutes)

Directions: In each of the sentences below four portions are underlined and lettered. Read each sentence and decide whether any of the underlined parts contains a grammatical construction, a word use, or an instance of incorrect or omitted punctuation or capitalization that would be inappropriate in carefully written English. If so, note the letter printed beneath the underlined portion and completely fill in the corresponding lettered space on the answer sheet with a heavy, dark mark so that you cannot see the letter.

If there are no errors in any of the underlined portions, fill in space E. No sentence has more than one error.

Remember, try to answer every question.

Examples: **Sample Answers**

1. He spoke <u>bluntly</u> and <u>angrily</u> to <u>we</u>
           A   B   C

   <u>spectators</u>. <u>No error</u>
     D   E

1. Ⓐ Ⓑ ● Ⓓ Ⓔ

2. Margaret <u>insists</u> <u>that</u> this hat <u>,</u> coat,
           A   B   C

   and scarf <u>,</u> are hers. <u>No error</u>
        D   E

2. Ⓐ Ⓑ Ⓒ ● Ⓔ

1. In the 1920s and 1930s, the Harlem Renaissance , an
                                              A
   intellectually and artistic movement centered in the African-
        B   C
   American community of Harlem, New York, stimulated significant cultural and creative activity in many authors, musicians,
                    D
   and painters. No error
                  E

2. The number of Herman Melville's personal letters and
   A
   diaries that have been preserved is so large that biographers
                                  B
   could chronicle virtually every week of the authors life.
        C   D
   No error
   E

3. A blend of West African and English languages, Gullah (it's
                                                       A
   name possibly deriving from the Gola tribe of West Africa), is
                 B
   spoken by up to a quarter of a million people, most of whom live
        C   D
   on the Sea Islands of Georgia and South Carolina. No error
                                                     E

4. Documentary photographer Dorothea Lange (1895–1965)
               A
   was best known for her photographs of the unemployed and uprooted
        B   C
   victims of the Great Depression. No error
                 D   E

5. When Hawaii became the fiftieth State in August 1959, Hiram
                                   A
   Leong Fong became the first person of Chinese ancestry to be
              B   C
   elected to the United States Senate. No error
                               D   E

6. After American and Arctic peregrine falcons became protected
   under the Endangered Species Act of 1973, The Peregrine Fund ,
             A   B
   a private organization, was beginning the release of falcons in
                           C   D
   New York State. No error
                   E

7. Migrating in the circular system of currents known to be the
                                                            A

North American gyre , hatchling loggerhead sea turtles start
                   B

off from the shore of eastern Florida, head east toward Portugal,
                                           C

then past the coast of Morocco, and finally back to Florida. No error
                                    D   E

8. Because there are more than six hundred species of endemic
        A   B

birds and many easily accessible birding areas in Costa Rica, it
                    C

is possible for one to see several dozen species in a single day.
                            D

No error
   E

9. Both Abraham Lincoln's Gettysburg Address and even Francis
                                          A   B

Scott Key's "The Star-Spangled Banner" were written on the
                                        C   D

backs of envelopes. No error
                        E

10. An unusually vast coral reef, the Great Barrier Reef runs for
           A

1,250 miles along the coast of Queensland, Australia , however, it
                                                     B

then breaks into countless islands, some awash, some submerged,
        C

others perfectly habitable. No error
                   D   E

11. The Silk Road Ensemble, a group of musicians from seventeen
        countries , weaves together elements from many cultures,
                  A

drawing from Sufi trance music, lively Uzbek folk chants, and
powerful Korean drumming, they updated musical traditions
         B   C

that go back more than three thousand years. No error
              D   E

12. The succession of an old queen bee by a younger queen occurs
                                                               A

infrequent because queen bees secrete a pheromone that is
   B

given to worker bees to inhibit the normal development of their
                                                             C

reproductive systems and thereby <u>prevent</u> the birth of other
D
queens. <u>No error</u>
      E

13. The rings of the planet Saturn <u>is made</u> of ice crystals and meteorite
                                        A
particles <u>locked</u> in circular orbits <u>around</u> the <u>planet's</u> equator.
         B   C   D
<u>No error</u>
E

14. Contemporary architect <u>,</u> Frank Gehry conceived a bold
                               A
experimental design <u>for</u> his new building; <u>its</u> vivid colors and
                    B   C
unusual structure <u>dominate</u> the center of Seattle. <u>No error</u>
                 D   E

15. In the English <u>language</u>, the lack of perfect correspondence
                 A
<u>between</u> letters and sounds <u>are</u> a source of confusion, and a
    B   C
potential <u>roadblock</u> for beginning readers. <u>No error</u>
         D   E

16. Centuries after Ice Age <u>glaciers</u> retreated, a great abundance of
                      A
precipitation and a mildly cool maritime climate created a vast
rain forest <u>in</u> the broad <u>western</u> valleys of the United States,
          B   C
which are now collectively known as Olympic National Park, in
the <u>state</u> of Washington. <u>No error</u>
    D   E

17. By the fifth century B.C., neither the scribes of the courts <u>or</u>
                                          A
<u>those</u> of the temples were the sole practitioners of the art of
B
writing; <u>members of the general population</u> were also <u>gradually</u>
                      C   D
acquiring this skill. <u>No error</u>
            E

18. In traditional <u>Chinese</u> paintings, separateness is an essential
               A
quality of a garden, which <u>is</u> always private and <u>removed</u> <u>to</u> the
                         B   C D
business of public life. <u>No error</u>
                  E

19. A motion picture is a sequence of <u>a still image</u>, each of which
   A

pauses for a split second before the <u>next</u> moves into view,
   B

<u>presented at a speed of</u> 24 frames <u>per</u> second. <u>No error</u>
   C   D   E

20. In his ground-breaking work, *Origin of Species* <u>,</u> British
   A

<u>naturalist</u> Charles Darwin <u>used</u> the phrases, "survival of the
   B   C

fittest" and "struggle for existence," which <u>have since become</u>
   D

common terms. <u>No error</u>
   E

21. Marine and freshwater environments together cover more than
75 percent of <u>Earth's</u> surface and, since <u>it</u> can be occupied at any
   A   B

depth, offer a <u>much</u> greater volume of living space than <u>does the</u>
   C   D

land. <u>No error</u>
   E

Part B
17 Questions
(Suggested Time—20 minutes)

Directions: In each of the following sentences some part of the sentence or the entire sentence is underlined. Beneath each sentence you will find five ways of writing the underlined part. The first of these repeats the original, but the other four are all different. If you think the original sentence is better than any of the suggested changes, you should choose answer A; otherwise you should mark one of the other choices. Select the best answer and completely fill in the corresponding lettered space on the answer sheet with a heavy, dark mark so that you cannot see the letter.

This is a test of correctness and effectiveness of expression. In choosing answers, follow the requirements of standard written English; that is, pay attention to acceptable usage in grammar, diction (choice of words), sentence construction, and punctuation. Choose the answer that expresses most effectively what is presented in the original sentence; this answer should be clear and exact, without awkwardness, ambiguity, or redundancy.

Remember, try to answer every question.

Examples: **Sample Answer**

1. <u>While waving</u> goodbye to our friends,   1. Ⓐ Ⓑ ● Ⓓ Ⓔ
    the airplane took off, and we watched it
    disappear in the sky.

    (A) While waving
    (B) Waving
    (C) As we were waving
    (D) While we are waving
    (E) During waving

2. Modern travelers seem to prefer speed   2. ● Ⓑ Ⓒ Ⓓ Ⓔ
    <u>to comfort</u>.

    (A) to comfort
    (B) than comfort
    (C) rather than being comfortable
    (D) instead of being comfortable
    (E) more than comfort

22. The second English settlement in North America at Roanoke Island, Virginia, disappeared within a few years, <u>and the fate of their people remain</u> a mystery.

(A) and the fate of their people remain
(B) and the fate of its people remains
(C) and the fate of its people remaining
(D) with the fate of their people remaining
(E) while the fate of its people remain

23. Among the first of the trees to grow in a recently burned or cleared forest, pines, in addition to <u>a production of</u> strong and durable wood perfect for a variety of building purposes, are an important source of pitch and tar.

(A) a production of
(B) their producing of
(C) producing
(D) the fact of producing
(E) the fact that it produces

24. Martians have figured regularly in the cast of science fiction literature and films, <u>if it be</u> as invaders trying to colonize Earth, as in H.G. Wells' *War of the Worlds* (1898), or as an extinct civilization that left its monuments behind, as in Ray Bradbury's *Martian Chronicles* (1950).

(A) if it be
(B) if it is
(C) whether or not it is
(D) whether or not it be
(E) be it

25. <u>Whereas formerly we believed light</u> essential to life, but we now know that bacteria dwell in scalding hot springs on the seafloor where the light of the Sun does not reach.

(A) Whereas formerly we believed light
(B) Whereas formerly believing in light to be
(C) Formerly believing light as
(D) Formerly we believed that light was
(E) Formerly we believed in light to be

26. <u>Since</u> Louis Pasteur had earlier recognized the dangers of infection, Joseph Lister, a Scottish surgeon, is generally given credit for developing and systematizing the notion of antiseptic surgery to curb the infections that followed wounds or surgery.

(A) Since
(B) Even when
(C) Even though
(D) Inasmuch as
(E) For as much as

27. Contrary to what one might expect, the deepest waters of the Atlantic Ocean, <u>as</u> other oceans, are along its edges.

(A) as
(B) like
(C) as are
(D) as those of
(E) like those of

28. In recent decades, as human population has grown, <u>water shortages in many of the regions of the world become</u> a major constraint on agricultural productivity.

(A) water shortages in many of the regions of the world become
(B) water shortages in many regions of the world have become
(C) there are water shortages in many regions of the world and they have become
(D) there have been water shortages in many regions of the world and have become
(E) there were water shortages in many regions of the world and they became

29. Not until <u>up to the latter half of the nineteenth century was it that medical investigators began to develop</u> an awareness of the health risks posed by coal mining.

(A) up to the latter half of the nineteenth century was it that medical investigators began to develop
(B) up to the latter half of the nineteenth century did medical investigators begin the developing of
(C) the latter half of the nineteenth century, when medical investigators began to develop
(D) the latter half of the nineteenth century was it that medical investigators began the developing of
(E) the latter half of the nineteenth century did medical investigators begin to develop

30. The Federal Reserve Regulatory Commission ordered the electricity transmission grid for the eastern United States to be put under the control of two regional authorities: one group overseeing New England and the Middle Atlantic states, <u>with another</u> responsible for the Southeast.

(A) with another
(B) with the other that would be
(C) and another
(D) and the other
(E) and the other that would be

31. Being able to think critically means <u>the ability to examine ideas, evaluate arguments, as well as to recognize the existence of other points of view other</u> than our own: that is, learning to examine and to evaluate our own thinking processes.

(A) the ability to examine ideas, evaluate arguments, as well as to recognize the existence of other points of view other
(B) the ability to examine ideas, evaluate arguments, as well as recognizing the existence of other points of view
(C) the ability of examining ideas, evaluating arguments, and recognizing the existence of other points of view other
(D) being able to examine ideas, evaluate arguments, as well as recognizing the existence of other points of view
(E) being able to examine ideas, evaluate arguments, and recognize the existence of other points of view

32. In 1858 gold was discovered in the area that became Denver, Colorado, prompting twice as many people to pick up and cross the continent <u>as did it</u> in 1849.

(A) as did it
(B) as had done so
(C) as those who did it
(D) than had done it
(E) than those that did so

33. When the European colonists arrived in what is now New England, forest was the dominant form of vegetative cover and was the main obstacle <u>to stand between them and their quest for remaking the region into</u> an agricultural utopia.

(A) to stand between them and their quest for remaking the region into
(B) to stand between them and their quest to remake the region into what would become
(C) that stood between them and their quest for remaking the region into what would become
(D) standing between them and their quest to remake the region into
(E) standing between them and their quest of remaking the region into what would become

34. Contrary to popular belief, taste buds in humans are located not only on the tongue, but also they are inside the cheeks, on the roof of the mouth, and in the throat.

(A) Contrary to popular belief, taste buds in humans are located not only on the tongue, but also they are

(B) Contrary to popular belief, taste buds in humans are located not only on the tongue but also

(C) Contrasted with popular belief, taste buds in humans are not only located on the tongue, but they are also

(D) Contrasting to popular belief, taste buds in humans not only are located on the tongue but also

(E) Contrasting to popular belief, taste buds in humans are located not only on the tongue but also are

35. If the West Antarctic Ice Sheet, estimated to contain one million cubic miles of ice, were to melt, it will lead to global flooding, most ports disappearing around the world, and an average rise in the oceans of some fifteen feet.

(A) it will lead to global flooding, most ports disappearing around the world, and an average rise in the oceans of some fifteen feet

(B) it will lead to global flooding, most ports disappearing around the world, and an average rise of some fifteen feet in the oceans

(C) the event would lead to global flooding, the disappearance of most ports around the world, and an average rise in the oceans of some fifteen feet

(D) there will be as a consequence global flooding, the disappearance of most ports around the world, and the oceans would rise some fifteen feet on the average

(E) there would be as a consequence global flooding, most ports around the world disappearing, and some fifteen feet as an average rise in the oceans

36. Discovered by scientists aboard the research submersible Alvin in 1977 at a depth of 8,200 feet in the Galapagos Rift Zone of the eastern Pacific, hydrothermal vents that are cracks in the seafloor at the juncture of two tectonic plates.

(A) hydrothermal vents that are cracks in the seafloor at the juncture of two tectonic plates

(B) hydrothermal vents are cracks in the seafloor at the juncture of two tectonic plates

(C) at the juncture of two tectonic plates, hydrothermal vents that are cracks in the seafloor

(D) there are cracks in the seafloor at the juncture of two tectonic plates, which are hydrothermal vents

(E) hydrothermal vents, that is, cracks in the seafloor at the juncture of two tectonic plates

37. Buffalo face winter on their feet: plodding through the deepening <u>snow, sweeping it away from last summer's dry grass with their muzzle, and they eat</u> what they uncover to stretch out their dwindling store of fat.

(A) snow, sweeping it away from last summer's dry grass with their muzzle, and they eat

(B) snow, they sweep it away from last summer's dry grass with their muzzle, and eating

(C) snow, sweeping it away from last summer's dry grass with their muzzle, and eating

(D) snow and sweeping it away from last summer's dry grass with their muzzle, eating

(E) snow and sweeping it away from last summer's dry grass with their muzzle, and they eat

38. One of the nineteenth century's leading critics of progress and its impact on the natural world, Henry David Thoreau came of age in a region <u>thoroughly transformed by human action, that it was a place of fields and fences so devoid of forest and animal habitat so</u> that the largest mammal commonly encountered was the muskrat.

(A) thoroughly transformed by human action, that it was a place of fields and fences so devoid of forest and animal habitat so

(B) thoroughly transformed by human action, a place of fields and fences so devoid of forest and animal habitat

(C) so thoroughly transformed by human action so that it was a place of fields and fences so devoid of forest and animal habitat

(D) that human action transformed thoroughly, that it was a place of fields and fences so devoid of forest and animal habitat

(E) that human action had transformed thoroughly, which was a place of fields and fences so devoid of forest and animal habitat so

STOP

If you finish before time is called, you may check your work on this test.

Directions: You will have 30 minutes to plan and write an essay on the topic presented on page 317. Read the topic carefully. You will probably find it best to spend a little time considering the topic and organizing your thoughts before you begin writing. DO NOT WRITE ON A TOPIC OTHER THAN THE ONE SPECIFIED. An essay on a topic of your own choice will not be acceptable. In order for your test to be scored, your response must be in English.

An essay question is included in this test to give you an opportunity to demonstrate how well you can write. You should, therefore, take care to write clearly and effectively, using specific examples where appropriate. Remember that how well you write is much more important than how much you write, but to cover the topic adequately, you will probably need to write more than a paragraph.

Your essay will be scored on the basis of its total quality—i.e., holistically. Each essay score is the sum of points (0–6) given by two readers. When your total writing score is computed, your essay score will be combined with your score for the multiple-choice section of the test.

You are to write your essay on the answer sheet; you will receive no other paper on which to write. Please write neatly and legibly. To be certain you have enough space on the answer sheet for your entire essay, please do NOT skip lines, do NOT write in excessively large letters, and do NOT leave wide margins. You may use the bottom of page 317 for any notes you may wish to make before you begin writing.

Read the opinion stated below.

"Advances in computer technology have made the classroom unnecessary, since students and teachers are able to communicate with each other from computer terminals at home or at work."

Discuss the extent to which you agree or disagree with this point of view. Support your position with specific reasons and examples from your own experience, observations, or reading.

The space below is for your **NOTES**. Write your essay in the space provided on the answer sheet.

STOP

If you finish before time is called, you may check your work on this test.

1. **Choice B is the best answer.** The noun "movement" is modified both by "artistic" and by "intellectually." Therefore, both words should take the adjectival form, since they are modifying a noun. The correct adjectival form in choice B is "intellectual."

2. **Choice D is the best answer.** When you are forming the possessive of a singular noun, most instances require that an apostrophe and the letter "s" be used (e.g., the ocean's tides). In choice D, there is no apostrophe given, even though "authors" is modifying "life." The correct word in choice D is "author's."

3. **Choice A is the best answer.** "It's" is a contraction for the phrase "it is." In choice A, substituting "it is" for "it's" renders the phrase unintelligible. The correct form is "its," without the apostrophe, which is the possessive form of the pronoun "it."

4. **Choice E is the best answer.** There are no grammatical, idiomatic, logical, or structural errors in this sentence.

5. **Choice A is the best answer.** While "Hawaii" is a proper noun and is therefore capitalized, "State" is considered a common noun in this instance. Therefore, choice A contains the error, as "State" should be lowercase.

6. **Choice C is the best answer.** The verb form in choice C should be in the past tense because the act of releasing the falcons has been completed. The verb form currently in choice C, "was beginning," is incorrect because this use implies a continuing action. The correct verb in choice C is "began."

7. **Choice A is the best answer.** The phrase "known to be" is typically used when referring to a particular action (e.g., "The company was known to be developing a new product"), whereas the phrase "known as" is used when renaming something. In this case, the phrase "circular system of currents" is used as to rename "the North American gyre." The phrase in choice A should be "known as."

8. **Choice E is the best answer.** There are no grammatical, idiomatic, logical, or structural errors in this sentence.

9. **Choice B is the best answer.** The use of the word "even" is redundant, since the word "Both" already lets the reader know that there will be two things addressed. "Even" should not be included in the sentence.

10. **Choice B is the best answer.** Compound sentences contain two coordinate clauses. When the two coordinate clauses are linked through the use of a conjunctive adverb (e.g., "however," "therefore," "thus," "consequently"), a semicolon should precede the adverb. In this sentence, the two coordinate clauses are linked by the word "however." A semicolon, not a comma, should appear in choice B.

11. **Choice C is the best answer.** "They updated" is incorrect because it is in the past tense. The phrase should most likely parallel the construction in the phrase that begins "Drawing from," making the correct word in choice C "updating."

12. **Choice B is the best answer.** In this sentence, "occurs" is modified by "infrequent." Adverbs are the part of speech that modifies verbs, adjectives, and other adverbs. Choice B contains the error, as the correct word should be the adverbial form, "infrequently."

13. **Choice A is the best answer.** Choice A contains an error in subject–verb agreement. The subject of the verb "is made" is "rings." Because "rings" is a plural noun, the verb should be plural as well. The phrase in choice A should be "are made."

14. **Choice A is the best answer.** The comma in choice A is unnecessary. The phrase "contemporary architect" functions here as Frank Gehry's title (similar to "General" in "General George Washington"). Just as there would not be a comma separating "General" from "George Washington," no comma is needed between "contemporary architect" and "Frank Gehry."

15. **Choice C is the best answer.** Choice C contains an error in subject–verb agreement. The subject of the verb "are" is "lack." Because "lack" is a singular noun, the accompanying verb should be the singular "is."

16. **Choice E is the best answer.** There are no grammatical, idiomatic, logical, or structural errors in this sentence.

17. **Choice A is the best answer.** The correct form for an expression of negation that includes "neither" is "neither X nor Y." The error in choice A can be corrected by replacing "or" with "nor."

18. **Choice D is the best answer.** The phrase "removed to" implies movement from one place to another, which is not true according to the sentence. The garden is not moving anywhere; it's only being removed *from* "public life." "Removed from" is the correct idiomatic usage that should appear in choice D.

19. **Choice A is the best answer.** Both "sequence" and "each of which" imply plurality. The error in choice A, "a still image," is one in number. "A still image" is only one discrete thing, and you

can't have a sequence of one thing, nor can you refer to one thing with the phrase "each of which." The correct phrase in choice A should be the plural "still images."

20. **Choice E is the best answer.** There are no grammatical, idiomatic, logical, or structural errors in this sentence.

21. **Choice B is the best answer.** Choice B contains an error in agreement between a pronoun and its antecedent. The singular pronoun in choice B, "it," refers to the antecedent "marine and freshwater environments," which is plural. The pronoun and antecedent should agree in number. Thus, the correct pronoun in choice B should be the plural "they."

Part B

22. **Choice B is the best answer.** Choice B contains both the correct pronoun referent ("its") for "settlement" and the correct verb form, "remains." The other options contain an incorrect use of at least one of these.

23. **Choice C is the best answer.** Choices D and E are wordy because they contain the unnecessary construction "the fact of/that." Both choices A and B use the unidiomatic "production/producing of" phrases.

24. **Choice E is the best answer.** Choices A and B add the conditional "if," which does not fit with the sentence, and choices C and D are both wordy and contain an incorrect pronoun–antecedent reference ("Martians . . . it").

25. **Choice D is the best answer.** Choices A and B use "whereas," which is unnecessary in a construction that already uses "but." Choice C omits the pronoun "we" that is needed for parallelism. Choice E contains the phrase "in light to be," which is unidiomatic.

26. **Choice C is the best answer.** "Even though" signals that the succeeding clause is an exception to the achievement of Pasteur, which is true in this sentence. "Since" is incorrect because it signals an addition to the clause, not an exception. "Even when" sets up an exception for time, not for Pasteur's achievement. "Inasmuch as" and "For as much as" are unidiomatic.

27. **Choice E is the best answer.** The comparison must include parallel constructions. Since the first term in the comparison is "waters of the Atlantic Ocean," the correct answer has to be parallel to this. Choices A, B, and C are not parallel. Choice D uses the right construction, but incorrectly uses "as."

28. **Choice B is the best answer.** Choices A and E use the incorrect verb forms "become/became." Although choices C and D use the correct verb form "have become," they introduce the incorrect adverb "there."

29. **Choice E is the best answer.** Choice E contains the correct verb form and tense. The use of "up to" in choices A and B is vague and does not fit with the use of "Not until." Choice C does not make a complete sentence. Choice D uses the unidiomatic phrase "developing of" and inserts a vague pronoun reference, "it."

30. **Choice D is the best answer.** In choice D, "and the other" preserves the meaning that both regional authorities are equally responsible. Choices A and C use "another," which is not needed when talking about only two things. Choices B and E introduce the conditional "would," which is not parallel with the verb "ordered."

31. **Choice E is the best answer.** The construction in choice E is parallel with the introductory phrase "Being able to think critically," and it also uses the present tense for each item in the option. Choice D is also parallel with the introductory phrase "Being able to think critically," but it incorrectly uses "recognizing" and "as well as." Choices A, B, and C are not parallel with the introductory phrase.

32. **Choice B is the best answer.** In a comparison, when the first thing being compared is introduced by "as," the second thing being compared must also be introduced by "as." Choices D and E do not follow this rule. Choices A and C do follow this rule, but they use the incorrect pronoun referent "it."

33. **Choice D is the best answer.** Choices A and B contain the infinitive "to stand," which is incorrect. Choice C confuses tenses—"that stood" and "would become"—creating a confusing sentence. Choice E contains "of remaking," an unidiomatic use of this phrase, and also uses the wrong tense, "would become."

34. **Choice B is the best answer.** Choice B correctly uses the "not only … but also" correlation and the correct form of "Contrary to popular belief." Choices C, D, and E use an incorrect and unidiomatic version of "Contrary to popular belief." Choice A uses the correct form of "Contrary to popular belief," but it incorrectly adds the pronoun "they" and the verb "are."

35. **Choice C is the best answer.** Choice C is the only option that uses both the correct conditional verb ("would lead") and correct parallelism among the items in the series ("flooding ... disappearance ... rise"). Choices A, B, and D use incorrect verb forms ("will be/lead"), and although choice E uses the correct verb, it does not maintain parallelism among the items in the series.

36. Choice B is the best answer. The beginning of the underlined section should start with the phrase "hydrothermal vents," because the non-underlined part of the sentence describes this term. Choice A does start with this term, but it uses "that are" instead of the correct "are"; as such, choice A does not make a complete sentence. Choice C also uses "that are" and is not a complete sentence. While choice E does start with the correct term, there is no verb present, so choice E is a sentence fragment. Choice D is an awkward construction that does not make sense.

37. Choice C is the best answer. To maintain parallelism, all the verbs in the final phrase must be parallel with those that come before it ("plodding" ... "sweeping" ... "eating"). Only choice C does this correctly. Although choice D uses the proper "-ing" ending for each verb, because it uses "and" instead of the comma, "eating" is no longer the correct verb form; it would have to change to "they eat" to be correct. Choices A, B, and E all contain an error of parallelism; choices A and B use "eat" and choice E uses "sweep."

38. Choice B is the best answer. Choice B is the only option that does not include the word "that" at the beginning. "That" is unnecessary there because the word is already present directly after the underlined section in the sentence; using it again creates an awkward construction. All the other options include some other use of "that."

Essay

Sample 1: Score of 1 (out of a possible 6)

Computer technology has advanced drastically within the last decade. Society has gotten acustom to handling everyday transactions and interacting with computerized machines all the time. Schools have taken advantage of the new information age.

Commentary on Sample 1:

This paper has a promising start with a description of advancing technology and the acceptance of computers by society. However, the paper only states, "Schools have taken advantage of the new information age" and does not address the topic of whether computers "have made the classroom unnecessary." Because of this lack of development, this paper is given a score of 1.

Sample 2: Score of 2 (out of a possible 6)

I agree that computer technology has advanced. However, I do not feel that the classroom is unnecessary. The classroom is a very important part of a student's learning. Students need to have personal communication with their teachers. I think they would learn much more through oral communication, than reading a lesson off of the computer. Besides, what would happen if the student had a question about the lesson? Sure he/she could write back to the teacher and ask the question, but how long would it take to receive the reply? Also, not all students own a personal computer or have the transportation to get to one. In conclusion, I think it would be much more effective, for the student, to keep the classroom communication alive.

Commentary on Sample 2:

This paper starts with a clear thesis disagreeing with the statement. It continues with some support of the thesis, stating that students "need to have personal communication with their teachers" and that students "would learn much more through oral communication, than reading a lesson off of the computer." However, the paper does little more than list these positions, rather than providing supporting examples and details, as in a stronger paper.

While the paper poses interesting questions concerning interaction between students and teachers, the paper provides only limited development of the main ideas, and therefore limited support of the thesis, keeping the paper to a score of 2.

Sample 3: Score of 3 (out of a possible 6)

I have to agree with the point that technology has made the classroom unnecessary. Although the classroom has become unnessary it will not be done away with. Children still have to have a place to go in order to learn and the classroom will always be there. Given that subject teacher may not be there any more. There will always be a supervising teacher in the room to maintain order with in the classroom. I think if you take the class room away then children will no longer want to learn or have a place to go to learn that is familiar to them. Using the technology to allow different teacher to teach more students the subject they, the teachers, are most interested in will allow the students to gain better knowledge of each subject. With in my old high school we had a distance learning room where students from all over the area where linked together in order to learn one subject for a qualified teacher. I guess one of the biggest fears of taking the teacher out of the classroom will be the disruption of the student culture. Every student has to come to the norm where a classroom is taught by a teacher who stands up front as teaches. By taking out that teacher up front and placing a television set or computer there, students may not pay attention to the subject matter. I think that there are limitations to the using technology in the classroom, and using it so teachers can teach from home is crossing those limitations. Use the technology to help students further their education, but do it with the teacher in the room.

Commentary on Sample 3:

This paper shows some competence, starting with the thesis that even though technology has advanced so that "the classroom has become unnecessary" it will not be done away with.

The paper offers some development of the thesis, explaining why the classroom is important and explaining the need for supervised learning stating, "If you take the class room away then children will no longer want to learn," however, there is no further support of this idea. Later in the essay is the statement that "students may not pay attention to the subject matter" if the teacher is on television.

The writer does have some personal experience with distance learning for a specialized subject but doesn't expand on that idea to support the thesis. Continuing, the paper talks of the "disruption of the students culture" but just states that students are used to having a teacher in the classroom, rather than describing the importance of student culture and learning, as a stronger paper would.

While the paper does have a logical conclusion, the lack of development and connections in this paper keep this essay to a score of 3.

Sample 4: Score of 4 (out of a possible 6)

In my opinion no amount of computer technology could make the classroom unnecesary. All of the technological advances should make the teachers' and students' jobs easier but not eliminate them altogether. Students still need structure and teaching. They need someone there when they have a question about a subject. Children also need the positive reinforcement from their teacher to do well in school. A computer may be able to do many things but it is not able to extrinsically motivate a child the way a teacher can. School provides many essential things that meet childrens' needs. Without school, children would not be able to have as much social interaction. Social interaction is what the classroom is all about. Teachers have started to stray away from paper -pencil assesments and are moving more towards cooperative learning. In cooperative learning the students are able to teach each other and in return their knowledge about the subject material is enhanced. Sitting at home on a computer will not manufacture the same results. Also teachers are incorporating Garner's Eight Intelligences into their curriculum. All children learn in different ways and excel in different areas. Learning material through a computer would only blind them from the true potential that they have. However, I do feel that computers should be integrated into the classroom. The most recent school that I have observed at incorporated computers into their language arts program. The program was called Accelerated Reader. The students loved reading books because they got to use the computer when they were finished and take a quiz. For every book they read and passed, they recieved a prize. Computers also allow the children to research material at a much faster pace and they make communication between faculty and parents much easier. Using computers in this way is imperative but replacing the classroom is ignorant as well as unethical. Children need to be around children on a daily basis and actually experience childhood.

Commentary on Sample 4:

This paper, which shows competence in response to the assignment, has the clear thesis: "no amount of computer technology could make the classroom unnecesary."

The paper shows control of development when describing various things that children need: "structure and teaching," "someone there when they have a question," and "positive reinforcement." In a stronger paper these needs would have been gathered together in one sentence, rather than placed individually in simple staccato sentences.

Continuing, the paper mentions "social interaction" but only states, "Social interaction is what the classroom is all about," which is not very informative. However, the paper explains the cooperative-learning technique effectively.

The strongest part of the essay is where the writer describes how the "most recent school that I have observed at incorporated computers into their language arts program." The program is described in detail, especially how it inspired students to read. The writer then comes to the conclusion that computers should be integrated into school programs but should not replace them.

Despite the lack of paragraphing, the paper still shows control of organization and development, and it generally supports the thesis. The paper lacks the overall language facility, however, which would lift this essay above the 4 level.

Sample 5: Score of 5 (out of a possible 6)

The opinion that advances in computer technology have made the classroom obsolete is one that I strongly disagree with. Although technology has helped to connect people in ways unheard of previously and provides new opportunites for supplementing learning in and out of the classroom, it will never replace the benefits of a real rather than virtual classroom. A real classroom provides important social interaction, real-time and personal interaction in the progress of our students, and acts as a baseline for social equity for the students who lack the resources and comfort of other students.

One goal of universal education is to create responsible and intelligent citizens in our democracy. If this is the case, which I believe it is, then the social interaction our students recieve is invaluable. Students learn how to live with one another and accept differences in appearance, as well as opinion. This social interaction also helps to fulfill our own need for personal touch and personal connection that a computer will never be able to satisfy.

I also believe that the benefit of the real classroom really revolves around our being able to be involved in the minute by minute and second by second progress of our students. From the moment that our students begin math examples, the writing process and reading, we are able to monitor the process they're using and the progress they're making. This happens in real time and we can work with small groups and individuals. We can switch fluidly from student to student in a way that may be impossible for a technology such as computers.

Lastly, schools are the one place where students are all equal for 8 hours of their day. As many in the government and media have pointed out, there is a digital divide. How can we ensure that all students have the very same equiptment? Even if we exclude equiptment issues from this discussion, school is the one place where all students are provided a safe place. Some children live in tumultous or even dangerous places that can make it impossible for schoolwork to be completed and learning to take place. Additionally, all students have access to the same learning materials when they walk into a real classroom; they all have access to the same school or classroom library, supplemental materials, and the teacher's attention. This is perhaps the best reason to allow the real classroom to endure. It is the one place where all children are treated equally and given access to the same materials.

> In conclusion, despite the many benefits new computer technologies offer us, they will never truly replace the benefits that our country and our children derive from a real classroom. The social interactions and the personal attention and equal access given to students are factors that can never be replaced by a virtual classroom. Our children deserve the best and most personalized curriculum we can give them. We can do that best together in the real classroom.

Commentary on Sample 5:

This paper starts with a clear thesis disagreeing with the statement. It then proceeds to list the benefits of a classroom: "important social interaction, real-time and personal interaction in the progress of our students" and its function "as a baseline for social equity."

That leads to a natural organization to develop ideas as well as clear transitions. In the second paragraph, the paper states, "One goal of universal education is to create responsible and intelligent citizens in our democracy" and supports this idea with examples of how social interaction in schools helps students develop into such citizens. The paper then links to the thesis with: "This social interaction also helps to fulfill our own need for personal touch and personal connection that a computer will never be able to satisfy."

The next paragraph is developed well as the paper moves from "minute by minute" to "second by second" to "real time" and finally to "fluidly" in the description of how a teacher may watch the progress of students. Those transitions in the description of time draw the reader in and are persuasive, as the paper then states, "We can switch fluidly from student to student in a way that may be impossible for a technology such as computers."

The fourth paragraph discusses how schools can be a basis for equality in society. The support of this statement is well explained, starting with, "schools are the one place where students are all equal for 8 hours of their day" and "they all have access to the same school or classroom library, supplemental materials, and the teacher's attention." It is also explained that it would be difficult to achieve parity of computer equipment and access.

In the conclusion, the paper effectively reexamines the key ideas and provides a clear conclusion: "despite the many benefits new computer technologies offer us, they will never truly replace the benefits that our country and our children derive from a real classroom." Though lacking the language facility and sentence variety of a paper earning a score of 6, this paper shows clear competence in addressing the prompt and develops ideas clearly, earning it a score of 5.

Sample 6: Score of 6 (out of a possible 6)

Advancements in computer technology today have made society a close network of people—making it easier to get wired and access vast amounts of information than ever before. Some colleges and universities have taken advantage of this and have created networked classrooms, allowing students and teachers to communicate via computer terminals, thus eliminating much classroom time. However, I disagree with the statement that this new technology will completely make the classroom unnecessary, for three reasons. First, eliminating the classroom would eradicate interaction between student and teacher, creating a steril learning environment. Secondly, students who learn best via kinesthetic or audio methods would be disadvantaged. Finally, individuals who choose not to "get wired" would miss out on opportunities to advance their education because instruction is offered only on the Internet.

Humans are social beings—we thrive on interaction with one another. If students and teachers interacted via only the computer screen, it would eliminate the social aspect so important to the learning process. One strategy of educators is to generate response from the students. Discussions allow students to actively process information given, vocalize what they are learning, and gain additional insight from the educator by asking questions. This interaction cannot take place through a computer screen; even live chats are void of the face-to-face contact that makes learning interactive and interesting.

We as humans also learn and process information very differently. Some learn best through audio instruction, others visually, and others through kinesthetic methods. Computer-based teaching would cater best to those who learn visually. Audio-students might cope, if the on-line classroom included some audio downloads. However, kinesthetic learners would be put to a complete disadvantage; the only hands-on interaction that would take place would be on their keyboard. I have personally witnessed in my tutoring experiences that kinesthetic learners, especially younger ones, need to classroom to interact hands-on in the learning process—taking what they have learned to create something in order to better understand the implications of the lesson.

Finally, regardless of how dependent our society becomes on technology, not everyone will jump at the opportunity to "get wired." My mother works in the healthcare profession, and is constantly surrounded by technology. However, she utilizes it just enough to "get by," and simply checking her e-mail is not an easy task. Though the younger generation is quick to catch on and take advantages of the opportunities posed by technology, the older generation is being left behind; many will not take the initiative to get acquainted with technology unless their occupation demands it. If classrooms were eliminated, many would-be, older, non-traditional students not familiar or interested in technology, would not have the opportunity to continue their education, because they would be discouraged at the prospect of taking courses online.

Technology today is fascinating, and has created numerous opportunities for people to get wired and reach out to the world in new ways. Though I agree that computer-based learning adds to the dimensions of a classroom, it can not totally replace the classroom. Complete computer-based learning would eliminate student-teacher interaction, and would put to disadvantage students of alternative learning styles, and non-traditional students not familiar with technology. Students learn best by utilizing a variety of educational sources, but one should not completely replace the other.

Commentary on Sample 6:

This well-written paper begins with a strong thesis disagreeing with the statement for three reasons: computer learning would "eradicate interaction between student and teacher," "students who learn best via kinesthetic or audio methods would be disadvantaged," and those without computers would "miss out on opportunities to advance their education." Listing these three reasons leads to natural organization. However, this paper has more logical connections than a paper earning a score of 5.

The second paragraph begins with a discussion of the "social aspect so important to the learning process." The paper uses well-chosen reasons to support the idea, including a description of educational strategy.

Transitioning from the "face-to-face contact" of the preceding paragraph to how people "learn and process information very differently," the paper describes how some students learn "through audio instruction, others visually, and others through kinesthetic methods." Each of these methods is explained clearly, with a description of "kinesthetic" learning as "hands-on" learning, which the writer has used personally in a classroom.

Moving to society as a whole, the paper mentions that not everyone has the inclination to use a computer and that "if classrooms were eliminated, many would-be, older, non-traditional students not familiar or interested in technology, would not have the opportunity to continue their education." Again, this idea is explained clearly with examples.

The concluding paragraph distills the various arguments and logically states, "Students learn best by utilizing a variety of educational sources, but one should not completely replace the other." Because this paper shows a high degree of competence, organizes and develops ideas logically, supports ideas with details and examples, uses a variety of sentence structures, and shows a high degree of language facility, this paper is appropriately given a score of 6.

CALCULATING YOUR SCORE

Follow these instructions to score PPST: Writing Test 2. When you actually take the *PPST*, you will have questions that are very similar to the questions in the sample tests in this book, but they will not be identical. Because of the difference in questions, the tests you actually take may be slightly more or less difficult than the tests printed in this book. Therefore, you may not get the same number of questions right on an actual test as on the sample tests.

NOTE: The **data** in Tables 1 and 2 apply to only PPST: Writing Test 2. The actual test you take will have a different answer table and a different conversion table.

To score PPST: Writing Test 2:

- Count the number of questions you answered correctly in the multiple-choice section of the test. The correct answers are in Table 1. Content category I contains 10 questions measuring knowledge of grammatical relationships; category II contains 13 questions assessing understanding of structural relationships; and category III contains 14 questions assessing understanding of idiom and word choice, mechanics, and correct usage. Count the number of questions you answered correctly in each of these categories. This may give you some idea of your strengths and weaknesses.

- Essays from actual administrations of the PPST: Writing test are read and rated by at least two writing experts. The readers use a rating scale of 1 to 6, where 6 is best. (Zero is used for "off-topic" essays.) The essay score is the sum of the two ratings and can therefore range from 2 to 12. Because it is impossible for you to score your own essay, you might want to try using three different values of essay scores in combination with your score on the multiple-choice section to see how your overall score would vary depending on how well you did on the essay. A score of 8 would be about average. You might also want to try a low score of 3 or 4, for example, and a high score, say, of 11 or 12.

- Use Table 2 to find your possible scaled scores. In the column on the left, find the number of questions you answered correctly on the multiple-choice section. Look across the top of Table 2 to the column with the essay score you are using. Go across the row and down the column to find the scaled scores for different combinations of multiple-choice section and essay scores. You can compare your scaled score to the passing score required by your state or institution. (Passing state scores are available on the *Praxis* website at www.ets.org/praxis.)

Table 1—PPST: Writing Test 2
Answers to Practice Test Questions

Sequence Number	Correct Answer	Content Category	Sequence Number	Correct Answer	Content Category
1	B	I	20	E	III
2	D	III	21	B	I
3	A	III	22	B	II
4	E	III	23	C	III
5	A	III	24	E	II
6	C	I	25	D	II
7	A	III	26	C	III
8	E	III	27	E	II
9	B	III	28	B	I
10	B	III	29	E	II
11	C	I	30	D	I
12	B	I	31	E	II
13	A	I	32	B	II
14	A	III	33	D	II
15	C	I	34	B	II
16	E	III	35	C	II
17	A	II	36	B	II
18	D	III	37	C	II
19	A	I	38	B	II

Table 2—PPST: Writing Test 2
Score Conversion Table

Multiple-Choice Section (# Right)	Essay Score (Sum of Two Readings)												
	0	1	2	3	4	5	6	7	8	9	10	11	12
0	152	153	155	157	158	160	161	163	164	166	168	169	171
1	152	154	155	157	159	160	162	163	165	167	168	170	171
2	153	154	156	158	159	161	162	164	165	167	169	170	172
3	153	155	156	158	160	161	163	164	166	168	169	171	172
4	154	155	157	159	160	162	163	165	166	168	170	171	173
5	154	156	157	159	161	162	164	165	167	169	170	172	173
6	155	156	158	160	161	163	164	166	167	169	171	172	174
7	155	157	158	160	162	163	165	166	168	170	171	173	174
8	156	157	159	161	162	164	165	167	168	170	172	173	175
9	156	158	159	161	163	164	166	167	169	171	172	174	175
10	157	158	160	162	163	165	166	168	169	171	173	174	176
11	157	159	160	162	164	165	167	168	170	172	173	175	176
12	158	159	161	163	164	166	167	169	170	172	174	175	177
13	158	160	161	163	165	166	168	169	171	173	174	176	177
14	159	160	162	164	165	167	168	170	171	173	175	176	178
15	159	161	162	164	166	167	169	170	172	174	175	177	178
16	160	161	163	165	166	168	169	171	172	174	176	177	179
17	160	162	163	165	167	168	170	171	173	175	176	178	179
18	161	162	164	166	167	169	170	172	173	175	177	178	180
19	161	163	164	166	168	169	171	172	174	176	177	179	180
20	162	163	165	167	168	170	171	173	174	176	178	179	181
21	162	164	165	167	169	170	172	173	175	177	178	180	181
22	163	164	166	168	169	171	172	174	175	177	179	180	182
23	163	165	166	168	170	171	173	174	176	178	179	181	182
24	164	165	167	169	170	172	173	175	176	178	180	181	183
25	164	166	167	169	171	172	174	175	177	179	180	182	183
26	165	166	168	170	171	173	174	176	177	179	181	182	184
27	165	167	168	170	172	173	175	176	178	180	181	183	184
28	166	167	169	171	172	174	175	177	178	180	182	183	185
29	166	168	169	171	173	174	176	177	179	181	182	184	185
30	167	168	170	172	173	175	176	178	179	181	183	184	186

(Continued)

Multiple-Choice Section (# Right)	Essay Score (Sum of Two Readings)												
31	167	169	170	172	174	175	177	178	180	182	183	185	186
32	168	169	171	173	174	176	177	179	180	182	184	185	186
33	168	170	171	173	175	176	178	179	181	183	184	186	187
34	169	170	172	174	175	177	178	180	181	183	185	186	187
35	169	171	172	174	176	177	179	180	182	184	185	186	188
36	170	171	173	175	176	178	179	181	182	184	186	187	188
37	170	172	173	175	177	178	180	181	183	185	186	187	189
38	171	172	174	176	177	179	180	182	183	185	186	188	189

Table 3—Assessment of Strengths in Each Category

Content Category	Number of Correct Answers Possible	Number of Incorrect Answers
I	10	
II	14	
III	14	

Table 4—Percentage of Examinees Choosing Correct Answers for the PPST Mathematics Practice Test

Sequence Number	Percentage of Examinees Choosing Correct Answer	Sequence Number	Percentage of Examinees Choosing Correct Answer
1	49%	20	40%
2	58%	21	40%
3	71%	22	61%
4	70%	23	68%
5	85%	24	40%
6	65%	25	81%
7	46%	26	84%
8	44%	27	40%
9	82%	28	75%
10	64%	29	68%
11	64%	30	62%
12	79%	31	27%
13	87%	32	25%
14	52%	33	36%
15	55%	34	71%
16	53%	35	57%
17	57%	36	30%
18	64%	37	50%
19	63%	38	53%

NOTE: Percentages are based on the test records of 1,398 examinees who took the 60-minute version of the PPST Writing test in June 2003.

In general, questions may be considered as easy, average, or difficult based on the following percentages:

Easy questions   = 75% or more answered correctly
Average questions = 55%–74% answered correctly
Difficult questions = less than 55% answered correctly

PART IV

Praxis II: Principles of Learning and Teaching (PLT)

Your Goals for This Part

- Identify the purpose and format of the PLT tests.
- Review PLT study topics.
- Learn how to read a case study and how to answer constructed-response questions.
- Practice answering PLT questions.

CHAPTER 15

All About the PLT Tests

This chapter will give you instruction and test-taking advice to help you prepare for the Principles of Learning and Teaching (PLT) tests. Here you'll find an overview of the tests and a comprehensive outline of the areas of knowledge covered to guide your study. You'll learn how to read a case study, and you'll explore two expert strategies for answering questions based on case studies. Then, in the chapter that follows, you'll be able to test yourself with 12 sample short-answer questions just like the ones on the actual test. Sample answers and scoring guides will help you understand just what it takes to succeed on the PLT tests.

PURPOSE AND FORMAT OF THE PLT TESTS

The Principles of Learning and Teaching (PLT) tests are designed to assess a prospective teacher's knowledge of a variety of job-related topics. Students typically obtain such knowledge through undergraduate courses in educational psychology, human growth and development, classroom management, instructional design and delivery techniques, evaluation and assessment, and other areas of professional preparation.

There are four Principles of Learning and Teaching tests:

Principles of Learning and Teaching: Early Childhood
Principles of Learning and Teaching: Grades K–6
Principles of Learning and Teaching: Grades 5–9
Principles of Learning and Teaching: Grades 7–12

While the four tests cover the same fundamental topics and concepts, each test differs from the others by featuring developmentally appropriate cases and scenarios.

The PLT Tests at a Glance

Format	4 case histories, each followed by 3 short-answer questions 24 multiple-choice questions in 2 sections of 12 questions each

Contents	Students as Learners (approximately 35% of total score)
	  • Student development and the learning process
	  • Students as diverse learners
	  • Student motivation and the learning environment
	Instruction and Assessment (approximately 35% of total score)
	  • Instructional analysis
	  • Planning instruction
	  • Assessment strategies
	Communication Techniques (approximately 15% of total score)
	  • Effective verbal and nonverbal communication
	  • Cultural and gender differences
	  • Stimulating discussion and responses in the classroom
	Teacher Professionalism (approximately 15% of total score)
	  • The reflective practitioner
	  • The larger community

Time	2 hours Plan on 25 minutes per case study and 10 minutes per multiple-choice section

PREPARING FOR THE PLT TESTS

You will probably want to begin with the following step:

Become familiar with the test content. Learn what will be tested, as covered in the study topics. Assess your knowledge in each area. How well do you know the material? In which areas do you need to learn more before you take the test?

In addition, you will probably want to end with these two steps:

Familiarize yourself with test taking. You can simulate the experience of the test by answering the practice questions within specified time limits. Choose a time and a place where you will not be interrupted or distracted. When you have completed the test, check the sample responses to the constructed-response questions and learn how they were scored. Plan any additional studying according to what you've learned about your understanding of the topics.

Register for the test and consider last-minute tips. See the section in Part I on how to register for the test, and review the checklist on page 344 to make sure you are ready for the test.

What you do between the first step and these last steps depends on whether you intend to use this book to prepare on your own or as part of a study group.

Preparing on Your Own

If you are working by yourself to prepare for a Principles of Learning and Teaching test, you may find it helpful to use the following approach:

Fill out the Study Plan Sheet. This worksheet will help you to focus on what topics you need to study most, identify materials that will help you study, and set a schedule for doing the studying.

Identify study materials. Most of the material covered by the test is contained in standard introductory textbooks in the field. If you do not own introductory texts, borrow the texts from friends or from a library. Don't rely heavily on information provided by friends or from searching the Web. Neither of these sources is as uniformly reliable as textbooks.

Work through your study plan. Work through the topics and questions. Be able to define and discuss the topics in your own words rather than memorizing definitions from books.

Preparing as Part of a Study Group

Sometimes it is helpful to form a study group with others who are preparing for the same test. Study groups give members opportunities to ask questions and get detailed answers. In a group, some members usually have a better understanding of certain topics, while others in the group may be better at other topics. As members take turns explaining concepts to one another, everyone builds self-confidence. If the group encounters a question that none of the members can answer well, the members can go as a group to a teacher or other expert and get answers efficiently. Because study groups schedule regular meetings, group members study in a more disciplined fashion. They also gain emotional support. The group should be large enough that various people can contribute various kinds of knowledge but small enough that it stays focused. Often, three to six people is a good size.

Here are some ways to use this book as part of a study group:

Plan the group's study program. Parts of the Study Plan Sheet can help to structure your group's study program. By filling out the first five columns and sharing the work sheets, everyone will learn more about your group's mix of abilities and about the resources (such as textbooks) that members can share with the group. In the sixth column ("Dates planned for study of content"), you can create an overall schedule for your group's study program.

Plan individual group sessions. At the end of each session, the group should decide what specific topics will be covered at the next meeting and who will present each topic. Use the topic headings and subheadings in the study topics section to select topics.

Prepare your presentation for the group. When it's your turn to present, prepare something that's more than a lecture. Write five to ten original questions to pose to the group. Practicing writing actual questions can help you better understand the topics covered on the test as well as the types of questions you will encounter on the test. It will also give other members of the group extra practice at answering questions. If you are presenting material from the sample questions, use each sample question as a model for writing at least one original question.

Take a practice test together. Scheduling a test session with the group will add to the realism and boost everyone's confidence. Practice questions are available in this study guide and online at the Praxis Web site (www.ets. org/praxis).

Learn from the results of the practice test. Use a scoring matrix to score one another's tests. Then plan one or more study sessions based on the questions that group members got wrong or on the constructed-response questions that members did not answer well. For example, each group member might be responsible for a question that he or she got wrong and could use it as a model to create an original question to pose to the group, together with an explanation of the correct answer.

Whether you decide to study alone or with a group, remember that the best way to prepare is to have an organized plan. The plan should set goals based on specific topics and skills that you need to learn, and it should commit you to realistic deadlines for meeting those goals. Then if you stick to your plan, you will accomplish your goals on schedule.

What's the best way to use the section on case studies?

Become familiar with case studies. Learn what a case study is and how to read one carefully and analytically in preparation for answering questions about it. Think about possible applications of situations and issues in the case studies to your own teaching experience. What information does your own teaching background provide for answering the questions?

Sharpen your skills on short-answer questions. Understand how short-answer questions are scored and how to write high-scoring responses.

Decide whether you need more review. After you have looked at your results, decide if there are areas that you need to brush up on before taking the actual tests. Go back to your textbooks and reference materials to see if the topics are covered there. You might also want to go over your questions with a friend or teacher who is familiar with the subjects.

Assess your readiness. Do you feel confident about your level of understanding in each of the subject areas? If not, where do you need more work? If you feel ready, complete the checklist to double-check that you've thought through the details.

PLT Checklist

- Do you know the testing requirements for your teaching field in the state(s) where you plan to teach?
- Have you followed all the test registration procedures?
- Do you know how long the test will take and the number of questions it contains? Have you considered how you will pace your work?
- Are you familiar with the test directions and the types of questions for the test?

- Are you familiar with the recommended test-taking strategies and tips?
- Have you practiced by working through the practice test questions at a pace similar to that of an actual test?
- If you are repeating a Praxis Series Assessment, have you analyzed your previous score report to determine areas in which additional study and test preparation could be useful?

PLT Study Plan Sheet

Content covered on test.	How well do I know the content?	What materials do I have for studying this content?	What materials do I need for studying this content?	Where could I find the materials I need?	Dates planned for study of content.	Dates completed.

PLT STUDY TOPICS

Here is an overview of the areas of knowledge covered in the Principles of Learning and Teaching tests:

Students as Learners

- Student development and the learning process
- Students as diverse leaders
- Student motivation and the learning environment

Instruction and Assessment

- Instructional strategies
- Planning instruction
- Assessment strategies

Communication Techniques

- Effective verbal and nonverbal communication
- Cultural and gender differences in communication
- Stimulating discussion and responses in the classroom

Profession and Community

- The reflective practitioner
- The larger community

Using the topic lists that follow. You are not expected to be an expert on the topics that follow. But you should understand the major characteristics or aspects of each topic and be able to relate the topic to various situations presented in the test questions. For instance, here is one of the topic lists in "Instructional Strategies," under the "Instruction and Assessment" category:

Major categories of instructional strategies, including

- Cooperative learning
- Direct instruction
- Discovery learning
- Whole-group discussion
- Independent study
- Interdisciplinary instruction
- Concept mapping
- Inquiry method
- Questioning

Using textbooks and other sources as needed, make sure you can describe each of these strategies in your own words. Find materials that will help you identify examples of each and situations for which each is appropriate. On the test you may be asked direct questions on one or more of these topics, or you may be asked to evaluate the use or appropriateness of a strategy in a particular context.

Special questions marked with stars. Interspersed throughout the list of topics are questions that are preceded by stars (☆). These questions are intended to help you test your knowledge of fundamental concepts that apply to typical classroom situations. Most of the questions require you to combine several pieces of information in order to formulate an integrated understanding and response. Answering these questions will help you gain increased understanding of the subject matter covered on the test. You might want to discuss these questions and your answers with a teacher or mentor.

Note that the questions marked with stars are not short-answer or multiple-choice. These questions are intended as *study* questions, not practice questions. Thinking about the answers can improve your understanding of fundamental concepts and help you answer a broad range of questions on the test. For example, the following starred question appears in the list of study topics under "Planning Instruction."

If you think about the relationships among curriculum goals, scope, and sequence frameworks, and unit and lesson plans, you have probably prepared yourself to answer multiple-choice questions similar to the one below, which asks you to link a curricular goal with the most appropriate performance objective.

The goal of a particular mathematics curriculum is for students to use computational strategies fluently and estimate appropriately. Which of the following objectives for students best reflects that goal?

(A) Students in all grades will use calculators for all mathematical tasks.

(B) Students in all grades will be drilled daily on basic number facts.

(C) Students in all grades will know the connections between the basic arithmetic operations.

(D) Students in all grades will evaluate the reasonableness of their answers.

The correct answer is choice D. To "evaluate the reasonableness of their answers," students must understand the computational strategies involved in mathematical solutions before they are able to estimate or to evaluate estimated answers.

Teachers are responsible for connecting scope and sequence frameworks and curriculum goals into classroom lessons and groups of lessons. How does a teacher translate curriculum goals and disciplines-specific scope and sequence frameworks into units and lesson plans with objectives, activities, and assessments appropriate for the students being taught? Give an example of a curriculum goal and then write a lesson objective, one activity, and an idea for an assessment of student learning that would accomplish that goal.

Outline of Study Topics

I. Students as Learners

A. Student Development and the Learning Process

You will notice that in this section, the names of important theorists appear in more than one category. This is so because the work of these theorists has implications for multiple domains that are important to effective teaching.

▷ Theoretical foundations about how learning occurs: how students construct knowledge, acquire skills, and develop habits of mind.

Knowing each theorist's major ideas and being able to compare and contrast one theory with another comprises basic professional knowledge for teachers. In addition, knowing how these ideas actually can be applied to teaching practice is important professional knowledge for teachers.

What are the major differences between Jerome Bruner's and Jean Piaget's theories of cognitive development in young children?

How might a teacher apply some of Lev Vygotsky's ideas about scaffolding and direct instruction in the classroom?

What does Gardner's work on multiple intelligences suggest about planning instruction?

What does Abraham Maslow's hierarchy of needs suggest about motivation for learning in the classroom?

▷ Examples of important theorists
- Albert Bandura
- Jerome Bruner
- John Dewey
- Jean Piaget
- Lev Vygotsky
- Howard Gardner
- Abraham Maslow
- B. F. Skinner

Important terms that relate to learning theory

- Constructivism
- Metacognition
- Readiness
- Schemata
- Transfer
- Scaffolding
- Loom's taxonomy
- Zone of proximal development
- Instrinsic and extrinsic motivation

Human development in the physical, social, emotional, moral, and cognitive domains

- The theoretical contributions of important theorists such as Erik Erikson, Lawrence Kohlberg, Carol Gilligan, Jean Piaget, Abraham Maslow, Albert Bandura, and Lev Vygotsky
- The major progressions in each developmental domain and the ranges of individual variation within each domain
- The impact of students' physical, social, emotional, moral, and cognitive development on their learning and how to address these factors when making instructional decisions.
- How development in one domain, such as physical, may affect performance in another domain, such as social.

Go beyond memorization of definitions: try to apply the terms to the theories behind them and think of applications in the classroom.

What are some specific classroom-based examples of extrinsic and intrinsic motivators for students?

Make sure you can recognize the differences between lower-order and higher-order thinking in classroom activities, using Bloom's taxonomy as a guide.

What is an example of a schema, and what good is it?

What is scaffolding, and why is it important for both teachers and students?

When responding to case studies, you will be asked to perform the following kinds of tasks related to the area of human development and the learning process:

Identify and describe strengths and/or weaknesses in

- the instruction described in the case, in terms of its appropriateness for students at a particular age

Propose a strategy for

- instruction that would be appropriate for students at the age described in the case

☆ Give a specific example from your own classroom experience of the effects of differences in learning styles on how people understand and express what they know.

☆ What is an example of the way cultural expectations from a particular geographical region or ethnic group might affect how students learn or express what they know?

☆ What does the research reveal about gender differences and how they might affect learning?

☆ Know the major types of challenges in each category (e.g., dyslexia under "Learning Disabilities"), know the major symptoms and range of severity, and know the major classroom and instructional issues related to each area.

☆ Know the basic rights or responsibilities that the legislation established.

B. Students as Diverse Learners

▷ Differences in the ways students learn and perform

- Learning styles
- Multiple intelligences
- Performance modes
  ○ Concrete operational thinkers
  ○ Visual and aural learners
- Gender differences
- Cultural expectations and styles

▷ Areas of exceptionality in student learning

- Visual and perceptual differences
- Special physical or sensory challenges
- Learning disabilities
- Attention Deficit Disorder (ADD); Attention Deficit-Hyperactivity Disorder (ADHD)
- Functional mental retardation
- Behavioral disorders
- Developmental delays

▷ Legislation and institutional responsibilities relating to exceptional students

- Americans with Disabilities Act (ADA)
- Individuals with Disabilities Education Act (IDEA)
- Inclusion, mainstreaming, and "Least Restrictive Environment"
- IEP (Individual Education Plan), including what, by law, must be included in each IEP
- Section 504 of the Rehabilitation Act
- Due process
- Family involvement

▷ Approaches for accommodating various learning styles, intelligences, or exceptionalities, including:

- Differentiated instruction
- Alternative assessments
- Testing modifications

▶ The process of second-language acquisition, and strategies to support the learning of students for whom English is not a first language

▶ How students' learning is influenced by individual experiences, talents, and prior learning, as well as language, culture, family, and community values, including:

- Multicultural backgrounds
- Age-appropriate knowledge and behavior
- The student culture at the school
- Family backgrounds
- Linguistic patterns and differences
- Cognitive patterns and differences
- Social and emotional issues

When responding to case studies, you will be asked to perform the following kinds of tasks related to the area of students as diverse learners:

Identify and describe strengths and/or weaknesses in

- a lesson plan for meeting needs of individual students with identified special needs, as described in the case . . .
- the interaction described in the case between the teacher and students in terms of culturally responsive teaching . . .

Propose a strategy for

- helping the students with attention deficit problems described in the case stay on task (e.g., in listening to a lecture, following a demonstration, doing written work)
- improving performance of students in the case who do not perform well on homework, original compositions, or other assignments
- helping students in the case for whom English is not the first language to build literacy skills and/or improve in academic areas
- meeting the needs of a wide range of students (especially students with learning difficulties and students who are accelerated)
- building positive relationships with a student the case shows is very turned off to school
- adapting instruction and/or assessment for an individual student with identified needs described in the case
- helping the student described in the case see issues from different points of view

C. Student Motivation and the Learning Environment

▷ Theoretical foundations about human motivation and behavior

- Abraham Maslow
- Albert Bandura
- B. F. Skinner

▷ Important terms that relate to motivation and behavior

- Hierarchy of needs
- Correlational and casual relationships
- Instrinsic motivation
- Extrinsic motivation
- Learned helplessness
- Self-efficacy
- Operant conditioning
- Reinforcement
- Positive reinforcement
- Negative reinforcement
- Shaping successive approximations
- Prevention
- Extinction
- Punishment
- Continuous reinforcement
- Intermittent reinforcement

▷ How knowledge of human motivation and behavior should influence strategies for organizing and supporting individual and group work in the classroom

▷ Factors and situations that are likely to promote or diminish students' motivation to learn; how to help students become self-motivated

☆ Go beyond memorization of definitions; try to apply the terms to the theories behind them and think of applications in the teaching situations.

Principles of effective classroom management and strategies to promote positive relationships, cooperation, and purposeful learning, including:

- Establishing daily procedures and routines
- Establishing classroom rules
- Using natural and logical consequences
- Providing positive guidance
- Modeling conflict resolution, problem solving, and anger management
- Giving timely feedback
- Maintaining accurate records
- Communicating with parents and caregivers
- Using objective behavior descriptions
- Responding to student misbehavior
- Arranging of classroom space
- Pacing and structuring the lesson

Why is each of the principles on the left a good practice for teachers to cultivate and maintain in terms of its effect on student learning? How can each help you to be a more effective teacher? What are the characteristics of effective implementation of each of these practices? How can you structure your instructional planning to include these?

What are the choices a teacher has in each of the last three bulleted items to the left? What are the most important considerations when you are making decisions about each one?

Pacing and structuring of a lesson is a particularly challenging aspect of instruction. What factors can change the pace and structure of a lesson as it unfolds? How can you prepare *in advance* for adjusting the pace and the structure of a lesson for each of these factors?

When responding to case studies, you will be asked to perform the following kinds of tasks related to the area of student motivation and the learning environment:

Identify and describe a strength and/or weakness in

- a lesson plan or instructional strategy described in the case with the intention of building a positive classroom environment

Propose a strategy for

- revising a lesson that is described in the case for improving student motivation and engagement
- improving motivation through means other than negative strategies described in the case
- addressing behavioral problems that are described in the case

What are some specific instructional goals in a particular content area that would be associated with each of these cognitive processes?

How are these cognitive processes connected with the developmental level of students?

How are these processes different from one another?

What are some ways that teachers can simulate each of these cognitive processes in a lesson?

What are the primary advantages of each of these strategies? In general terms, describe the kinds of situations or the kinds of goals and objectives for which each of these strategies is appropriate. What kinds of information about students' levels does each of these offer? When would you NOT use a particular instructional strategy?

II. Instruction and Assessment

A. Instructional Strategies

▶ The major cognitive processes associated with student learning, including:

- Critical thinking
- Creative thinking
- Higher-order thinking
- Inductive and deductive thinking
- Problem-structuring and problem-solving
- Invention
- Memorization and recall
- Social reasoning
- Representation of ideas

▶ Major categories of instructional strategies, including:

- Cooperative learning
- Direct instruction
- Discovery learning
- Whole-group discussion
- Independent study
- Interdisciplinary instruction
- Concept mapping
- Inquiry method
- Questioning
- Play
- Learning centers
- Small group work
- Revisiting
- Reflection
- Project approach

Principles, techniques, and methods associated with various instructional strategies, including:

- Direct instruction

  Madeline Hunter's "Effective Teaching Model"

  David Ausubel's "Advance Organizers"

  Mastery learning

  Demonstrations

  Mnemonics

  Note taking

  Outlining

  Use of visual aids

- Student-centered models

  Inquiry model

  Discovery learning

  Cooperative learning (pair-share, jigsaw, STAD, teams, games, tournaments)

  Collaborative learning

  Concept models (concept development, concept attainment, concept mapping)

  Discussion models

  Laboratories

  Project-based learning

  Simulations

What are some examples of appropriate situations for grouping students heterogeneously? What are some for grouping students homogeneously? Besides grouping by performance level, what are other characteristics that a teacher should sometimes consider when grouping students?

What is wait time? What does research suggest about wait time?

How might a teacher promote critical thinking among students in a discussion?

How can a teacher encourage student-to-student dialogue in a class discussion?

What kinds of classroom management procedures and rules would tend to make class discussion more productive?

How does the development level of students affect the way a teacher might handle classroom discussion?

In what kinds of discussions or situations should a teacher name a specific student before asking a question? When is it best *not* to name a specific student?

What should a teacher consider when planning to incorporate various resources into a lesson design?

What are the advantages of these different resources?

When responding to case studies, you will be asked to perform the following kinds of tasks related to the area of instructional planning:

Identify and describe a strength and/or weakness in

- specific activities that are described in the case

Propose a strategy for

- teaching critical thinking skills in a specific lesson described in the case
- achieving effectiveness with group work in a particular situation described in the case
- helping students stay on task in the situation described in the case
- helping students learn material presented through various media introduced in the case
- assigning students to group work appropriate to the case
- bringing closure to a lesson that stops abruptly as presented in the case
- improving student interaction during class discussion as described in the case
- addressing a "missed opportunity" during instruction that is described in the case

A. Instructional Strategies (continued)

Methods for enhancing student learning through the use of a variety of resources and materials

- Computers, Internet resources, Web pages, e-mail
- Audiovisual technologies such as videotapes and compact discs
- Local experts
- Primary documents and artifacts
- Field trips
- Libraries
- Service learning

B. Planning Instruction

▷ Techniques for planning instruction to meet curriculum goals, including the incorporation of learning theory, subject matter, curriculum development, and student development

- National and state learning standards
- State and local curriculum frameworks
- State and local curriculum guides
- Scope and sequence in specific disciplines
- Units and lessons—rationale for selecting content topics
- Behavioral objectives: affective, cognitive, psychomotor
- Learner objectives and outcomes
- Emergent curriculum
- Antibias curriculum
- Themes/projects
- Curriculum webbing

▷ Techniques for creating effective bridges between curriculum goals and students' experiences

- Modeling
- Guided practice
- Independent practice, including homework
- Transitions

☆ Teachers are responsible for connecting scope and sequence frameworks and curriculum goals into classroom lessons and groups of lessons. How does a teacher translate curriculum goals and disciplines-specific scope and sequence frameworks into units and lesson plans with objectives, activities, and assessments appropriate for the students being taught? Give an example of a curriculum goal, and then write a lesson objective, one activity, and an idea for an assessment of student learning that would accomplish that goal.

☆ How do behavioral objectives and learner objectives and outcomes fit into a teacher's planning for units and lessons?

☆ What criterion or criteria does a teacher use to decide when to use each of these techniques?

☆ Why is it so important for a teacher to plan carefully for transitions? What are the risks if transitions are not thought through and executed with care?

☆ Why is each of these actions a principle of effective instruction?

☆ What tools and techniques can a teacher plan to use to accomplish each one?

☆ What strategies can a teacher employ to monitor student understanding as a lesson unfolds?

☆ What evidence should the teacher observe in order to know whether to reteach a topic, move more quickly, or go back to material previously covered?

☆ When responding to case studies, you will be asked to perform the following kinds of tasks related to the area of instructional planning:

Identify and describe a strength and/or weakness in

- a unit plan that is described in the case
- specific strategies used in instruction (e.g., using lecture, using class discussion) in the case
- a sequence of lessons described in the case designed to achieve a goal or set of objectives
- one or more written assignments given to students in the case

Propose a strategy for

- meeting what may appear to be conflicting goals or objectives described in the case
- incorporating activities that will have students described in the case draw on their own experiences to understand the instruction
- stimulating prior knowledge in the situation described in the case

B. Planning Instruction (continued)

- Activating students' prior knowledge
- Anticipating preconceptions
- Encouraging exploration and problem-solving
- Building new skills on those previously acquired
- Predicting

C. Assessment Strategies

Measurement theory and assessment-related issues

- Types of assessments
  - Standardized tests, norm-referenced or criterion-referenced
  - Achievement tests
  - Aptitude tests
  - Structure observations
  - Anecdotal notes
  - Assessments of prior knowledge
  - Student response during a lesson
  - Portfolios
  - Essays written to prompts
  - Journals
  - Self-evaluations
  - Performance assessments
- Characteristics of assessments
  - Validity
  - Reliability
  - Norm-referenced
  - Criterion-referenced
  - Mean, median, mode
  - Sampling strategy
- Scoring assessments
  - Analytical scoring
  - Holistic scoring
  - Rubrics
  - Reporting assessment results
  - Percentile rank
  - Stanines
  - Mastery levels

☆ What are the characteristics, uses, advantages, and limitations of each of the formal and informal types of assessments to the left?

☆ When might you use "holistic scoring"?

☆ Under what circumstances would "anecdotal notes" give a teacher important assessment information?

☆ How might a teacher effectively use student self-evaluation?

☆ What are some examples of informal assessments of prior knowledge that a teacher can easily use when a new topic is introduced?

☆ What kind of assessment information can a teacher gather from student journals?

☆ What is a structured observation in a classroom setting?

When responding to case studies, you will be asked to perform the following types of tasks related to the area of assessment:

Propose a strategy for

- assessing progress for students described in the case who are working toward specified goals or objectives
- assessing class progress toward achievement of specified goals or objectives
- gathering information to use to help understand classroom performance that is different from what was expected at the beginning of the year
- assessing language fluency of a student for whom English is not the first language

Propose a hypothesis or explanation for

- a student's strength's and/or weaknesses as a learner based on the evidence presented
- what might be important to explore in working with a student described in the case who is having difficulties academically, socially, or emotionally

C. Assessment Strategies (continued)

- ○ Raw score
- ○ Scaled score
- ○ Grade equivalent score
- ○ Standard deviation
- ○ Standard error of measurement
- Use of assessments
  - ○ Formative evaluation
  - ○ Summative evaluation
  - ○ Diagnostic evaluation
- Understanding measurement theory and assessment-related issues
- Interpreting and communicating results of assessments

III. Communication Techniques

A. Basic effective verbal and nonverbal communication techniques

B. Effect of cultural and gender differences on communications in the classroom

C. Types of questions that can stimulate discussion in different ways for particular purposes

- Probing for learner understanding
- Helping students articulate their ideas and thinking processes
- Promoting risk-taking and problem-solving
- Facilitating factual recall
- Encouraging convergent and divergent thinking
- Stimulating curiosity
- Helping students to question
- Promoting a caring community

What are some ways that a teacher's raising his or her voice might be interpreted differently by students with different cultural backgrounds?

What are specific examples of gestures and other body language that have different meanings in different cultures (e.g., looking someone directly in the eye, disagreeing openly during a discussion, pointing)

What is an example of a question in a particular content area that probes for understanding?

What is an example of a question that would help a student articulate his or her ideas?

What is an example of a comment a teacher might make that would promote risk-taking? Problem-solving?

How would a teacher encourage divergent thinking on a particular topic?

How would a teacher encourage students to question one another and the teacher?

When responding to case studies, you will be asked to perform the following kinds of tasks related to the area of communication:

Identify and describe a strength and/or weakness in

- the teacher's oral or written communication with students in the case (e.g., feedback on assignments, interaction during class)

Propose a strategy for

- improving the self-image of a student described in the case or the student's sense of responsibility for his or her own learning

- involving all students in a class discussion described in the case in a positive way, showing respect for others

- helping a student described in the case to develop social skills in a specified situation

IV. Profession and Community

A. The Reflective Practitioner

▷ Types of resources available for professional development and learning

- Professional literature
- Colleagues
- Professional associations
- Professional development activities

▷ Ability to read, understand, and apply articles and books about current research, views, ideas, and debates regarding best teaching practices

▷ Why personal reflection on teaching practices is critical, and approaches that can be used to reflect and evaluate

- Code of ethics
- Advocacy for learners

B. The Larger Community

▷ The role of the school as a resource to the larger community

- Teachers as a resource

▷ Factors in the students' environment outside of school (family circumstances, community environments, health and economic conditions) that may influence students' life and learning

▷ Basic strategies for developing and utilizing active partnerships among teachers, parents/guardians, and leaders in the community to support the educational process

- Shared ownership
- Shared decision making
- Respectful/reciprocal communication

☆ Be able to read and understand articles and books about current views, ideas, and debates regarding best teaching practices.

☆ What types of help or learning can each of these resources offer a new teacher?

☆ What are the titles of two professional journals of particular interest to you in your chosen field of teaching to which you might subscribe?

☆ What professional association or associations offer professional meetings and publications and opportunities for collaborative conversation with other teachers?

☆ What might be a professional development plan for the first two years of a teacher's career that would support her or his learning and growth?

When responding to case studies, you will be asked to perform the following kinds of tasks related to the area of the larger community:

Identify and describe a strength and/or weakness in

- the communication with parents used by a teacher described in the case
- the approach taken by a teacher described in the case to involve parents

Propose a strategy for

- using parent volunteers during a lesson that is described in a case
- involving all parents or other caregivers
- in helping students in areas specified in the case
- helping the family of a student described in the case work with the student's learning or other needs

A. The Reflective Practitioner (continued)

Major laws related to students' rights and teacher responsibilities

- Equal education
- Appropriate education for students with special needs
- Confidentiality and privacy
- Appropriate treatment of students
- Reporting in situations related to possible child abuse

HOW TO READ A CASE STUDY

ETS uses case studies as the basis for the assessment of a beginning teacher's professional and pedagogical knowledge for several important reasons.

- First, professional educators frequently use case studies of teaching situations as a method for representing the complex domain of professional practice. Carefully constructed, case studies can simulate actual teaching contexts, issues, and challenges. They also provide a platform for thinking about theoretical and practical pedagogical concerns, making them a professionally credible method for assessing an educator's knowledge.
- Second, case studies allow the presentation of sufficient detail about a particular teaching situation or series of classroom events. By identifying strengths and weaknesses in the teaching presented, case studies provide a medium in which hypotheses, conclusions, and suggestions for strategies that might accomplish particular pedagogical goals can be thoughtfully supported and explained.
- Third, case studies encourage questions that demand application of knowledge across a broad range of professional knowledge bases —developmental psychology, motivation, communication strategies, pedagogical methods and strategies, instructional design principles and strategies—rather than simple recognition and recall of facts without a meaningful context.

Simulations of teaching situations like those presented in the Principles of Learning and Teaching case studies offer the opportunity to ask questions that may have several acceptable answers. The open-ended questions that follow each case study encourage the beginning teacher to synthesize knowledge much as he or she will have to in the day-to-day work of teaching. Because the open-ended questions can be satisfactorily answered from many different perspectives, they acknowledge that teachers have extremely varied backgrounds and experiences with students, and that there are often many possible effective responses in a given teaching situation.

Two Kinds of Cases: Teacher-Based and Student-Based

You may encounter either or both of two kinds of cases in the Principles of Learning and Teaching test. The first is a "teacher-based" case, and the second is a "student-based" case. A teacher-based case focuses on the teaching practice of one or more teachers. The case will present sufficient information about the teaching context, goals, objectives, lesson plans, assignments, teaching strategies, assessments, and interactions with students to enable you to identify the issues involved in the case and to respond fully to the questions about the teachers' practices. However, the information is carefully restricted to only what is required to understand the issues and respond to the questions. Additional information might be interesting to have but is not essential for understanding and responding. A response that says the question cannot be answered because more information is needed is not acceptable.

A student-based case focuses on one student, with information about the student's background, where appropriate, and the student's strengths and weaknesses. In addition, there may be examples of the student's work as well as excerpts of conversations between the student and a teacher, counselor, or interviewer.

Excerpts of a class discussion in which the student participated may also be provided. Again, the information provided is all you need to understand the issues involved and to respond to the questions. As with teacher-based cases, you might want to know more about the student, but all the information you need to respond fully to each question is presented.

Although cases are termed "student-based" and "teacher-based," both kinds of cases often have questions that deal with both teachers and students as learners. For example, one of the cases presented below is termed a student-based case because one student is the focus of the case. However, the teacher's practice is clearly an essential part of the case, and there are questions that focus both on the student as a learner and on the teacher's practice.

All case studies are approximately the same length, 800–850 words, and each is followed by three questions requiring a "constructed response." This means that for each question, you need to write one or two paragraphs to answer the question. In no case are there questions that require knowledge specific to academic disciplines such as language arts, history, science, or mathematics.

Expert Strategies for Reading Case Studies

There are two different strategies you can use for reading case studies. The key to both of them is a close and careful reading of the case, with attention focused on the important information in each paragraph or document. You will also want to consider how each paragraph or document relates to the central issues addressed in the case and in the questions.

Strategy 1. Read the case study with the major content categories clearly in mind. (You'll find those categories in the PLT Tests at a Glance chart on page 333.) Remember that each case and the questions are based directly on these categories. You will also want to keep in mind that each paragraph of the narrative or each document is included specifically to elicit understanding of an issue or to provide information for responding to the questions.

Therefore, for each section, narrative, or document, ask the following questions as you read:

- What issues about the teacher's planning, instruction, and assessment does this raise?
- What issues are raised about the student as a learner and the way teachers and others do and/or do not understand and address the student's strengths and needs?
- What specific information is presented here that addresses the way issues were faced and resolved? How else might they have been resolved?
- How, specifically, does this information address one or more of the questions?

Strategy 2. Read the questions that follow the case first—before you read the case. Once you have carefully examined the questions and made mental notes about what kinds of issues to look for in the case, then you can read the case and take notes about how each paragraph, section, and/or document relates to particular questions.

Case Study 1: Content Category Approach

To help you understand more about what case studies look like and how the first expert approach might work for you, look at the sample case with annotations that follows. This narrative, about Sara, is a student-based case that involves issues about Sara as a learner and about Ms. Mercer, her first-grade teacher. Follow the case in the left column and note the questions raised in the marginal notes in the right column. These questions relate to the major content categories covered on the test.

CASE STUDY 1

SARA

Information Presented

Scenario

Six-year-old Sara lives with her mother, who has a relaxed schedule. Ms. Mercer, Sara's teacher, notes that Sara is often tired and inattentive after arriving late. Sara says she frequently stays up past midnight if others are up. Ms. Mercer, a second-year teacher, has asked her mentor to observe Sara and suggest ways to help Sara achieve Ms. Mercer's purposes.

Observation: Ms. Mercer's Class, April 30

Pre-observation interview notes

Ms. Mercer says, "The purposes of first grade are to teach children 'school survival skills' and reading, writing, and arithmetic." She adds, "Sara needs help with 'survival skills,' including following directions, concentrating on a task to its completion, and being attentive to the lessons I present."

Mentor Classroom Observation—Focus on Sara Porter

As Ms. Mercer's class begins, the children play with puzzles and other activities requiring construction or manipulation. Two children "write" on a flannel board, using letters kept in alphabetical stacks in a box. They return the letters so they fit exactly over their counterparts. Ms. Mercer praises them for neatness. She instructs them to return to their previously assigned groups as Sara enters the room.

Notes

What possible issues does this section suggest about Sara as a learner? How might this information be useful in thinking about these issues?

What possible issues are raised about Ms. Mercer's approach to teaching first grade? How might these affect Sara?

What does this section tell us about Ms. Mercer's approach and how it might impact Sara?

What issues about Ms. Mercer's approach does this section raise? What strengths and/or areas for improvement in her use of group work might this suggest?

What information does this section present about Sara as a learner? How might this information be used?

What additional information about Sara as a learner is presented? What issues might this information raise? How does Ms. Mercer interact with Sara? How might this be important?

The students are seated at six tables, four students at each table. Ms. Mercer explains, "Tables one and two will work on reading first, while tables three and four will solve math problems, and tables five and six will draw page illustrations for your collaborative Big Book. After 25 minutes, the groups will stop the first activity and begin working on a second task without changing seats. Twenty-five minutes later, you will change again to work on the activity each group has not yet done. The math groups and those doing illustrations will hand in their work when time is called. I will work with the two groups who are reading aloud." She plans to monitor progress of students in the reading group.

Sara is at table one. Ms. Mercer begins with this table and table two, working on reading. Several children read aloud. Ms. Mercer praises them. When Ms. Mercer calls on Sara, she begins reading in the wrong place. Joyce, seated next to Sara, points to where they are. Ms. Mercer says, "Sara, you would know where we are if you were paying attention." She calls on another child. Sara looks hurt, but soon starts to follow along in the book. Subsequently, Ms. Mercer calls on Sara, who now has the right place. Ms. Mercer then calls on another child.

During the math activity, Sara, yawning frequently, is the last to open her workbook and write her name. When she completes the page, she waits. She seems puzzled, although Ms. Mercer has already given directions. Sara gets up, sharpens a pencil, and returns to the wrong seat. "That's MY seat," accuses an angry boy. Sara apologizes and returns to her seat. Later, she waits to have her workbook checked. She has not torn out pages as Ms. Mercer instructed. Sara is told to "do it right." Sara has not creased the paper as Ms. Mercer demonstrated, so the pages do not tear out easily. Sara sucks her thumb and holds her ear for a minute. Suddenly, she yanks the paper and the pages come out with jagged edges. She receives three dots for her work. Ms. Mercer says, "Sara, this is good. I wish you could earn four dots" (the maximum). Sara slaps herself on the forehead. During the illustration activity, Sara helps several others who have trouble thinking of ideas. Sara's illustration is among the best handed in.

After the group work, Ms. Mercer places a large pad on an easel and says, "Now we're going to write about our trip to the art museum yesterday. Raise your hand and tell me something you saw or did in the museum." No one responds. She says, "Tell me the first thing we did at the museum." Sara raises her hand, offering a first sentence. After each response, Ms. Mercer asks, "What happened next?" or "What did we see next?" She prints each child's contribution.

Our Trip to the Art Museum

We rode the elevator to the second floor. We looked at different shapes on the ceiling. We saw a statue with a white triangle. We went to another room where we saw some pictures. We rode back down to the first floor. On our way out, we saw a painting of a grandfather and a boy.

During the writing of the group story, Sara fidgets in her seat, stares out the window, and makes a face at her neighbor.

Post-observation interview notes

Ms. Mercer says, "Sara is a top performer in academic achievement and on standardized tests, consistently scoring among the top five students in the class. She's so bright. It's a shame she's late and distracted so much." The mentor replies, "There may be something else bothering Sara. Although she is easily distracted, there may be other explanations for her behavior. Let's talk more."

> What additional information about Sara is presented? How might this be important in addressing her strengths and needs? How might the information about Ms. Mercer's writing lesson be important? What strengths or areas for improvement might it suggest? How might it be built upon?

> What are the implications of the mentor's comment?

Case Study 1: Question Approach

Now let's examine the same case using the second expert method. First read through the questions below, then read through the case again with question-related notes. Notice that this time the notes next to the case show how each paragraph or section relates to a particular question and propose some ideas that will eventually go into the actual response to the questions.

Questions related to Case Study 1. Sara

1. Suppose that Ms. Mercer and her mentor discuss how to connect school and Sara's home environment for the benefit of Sara's learning.

- Identify TWO specific actions Ms. Mercer might take to connect school and Sara's home environment for the benefit of Sara's learning.
- Explain how each action you identified could benefit Sara's learning. Base your response on principles of fostering school-parent relationships to support student learning.

2. Review the preobservation notes in which Ms. Mercer explains the purposes of first grade as she sees them. Suppose that her mentor suggests that Ms. Mercer consider other purposes of first grade and how she might modify her instruction to address those purposes and the related needs of Sara and her other students.

- Identify TWO additional purposes of first grade that Ms. Mercer could consider when planning her instruction, in order to meet the needs of Sara and/or her other students.
- For each purpose you identified, explain how Ms. Mercer might modify her instruction to address the purpose and meet the needs of Sara and/or her other students. Base your response on principles of planning instruction and learning theory.

3. Assume that the groups working on mathematics and illustrations for the Big Book become very noisy and unproductive over the course of the activity.

- Suggest TWO changes Ms. Mercer could have made in the planning and/or implementation of the group work that would have made the activity more successful.
- Explain how each change you suggested could have made the group work activity more successful. Base your response on principles of planning instruction and human development.

4. In the activities described in the Mentor Classroom Observation, Ms. Mercer demonstrates understanding of developmentally appropriate instruction.

- Identify TWO strengths in the instructional approaches Ms. Mercer uses in the activities that reflect understanding of the principles of developmentally appropriate instruction.
- Explain how each of these strengths you identified provides evidence of an understanding of the principles of developmentally appropriate instruction. Base your response on principles of planning instruction and human development.

5. Assume that the day after the lesson was observed, Ms. Mercer's objective is to use the story about the museum visit to continue building students' literacy.

- Identify TWO strategies and/or activities involving the story about the museum visit that Ms. Mercer could use to continue building students' literacy.
- For each strategy and/or activity you identified, explain how it could help build literacy. Base your response on principles of language development and acquisition.

6. In the post-observation notes, Ms. Mercer's mentor suggests that they explore explanations for Sara's inattentive behavior.

- Suggest TWO hypotheses other than lack of sleep that Ms. Mercer and her mentor might explore to learn more about why Sara behaves as she does in class.
- For each hypothesis you suggested, describe at least one action that Ms. Mercer and her mentor might take to see if the hypothesis might be correct. Base your response on principles of human development, motivation, and diagnostic assessment.

SARA

Information Presented

Scenario

Six-year-old Sara lives with her mother, who has a relaxed schedule. Ms. Mercer, Sara's teacher, notes that Sara is often tired and inattentive after arriving late. Sara says she frequently stays up past midnight if others are up. Ms. Mercer, a second-year teacher, has asked her mentor to observe Sara and suggest ways to help Sara achieve Ms. Mercer's purposes.

Observation: Ms. Mercer's Class, April 30

Pre-observation interview notes:

Ms. Mercer says, "The purposes of first grade are to teach children 'school survival skills' and reading, writing, and arithmetic." She adds, "Sara needs help with 'survival skills,' including following directions, concentrating on a task to its completion, and being attentive to the lessons I present."

Mentor classroom observation—focus on Sara Porter

As Ms. Mercer's class begins, the children play with puzzles and other activities requiring construction or manipulation. Two children "write" on a flannel board, using letters kept in alphabetical stacks in a box. They return the letters so they fit exactly over their counterparts. Ms. Mercer praises them for neatness. She instructs them to return to their previously assigned groups as Sara enters the room.

The students are seated at six tables, four students at each table. Ms. Mercer explains, "Tables one and two will work on reading first, while tables three and four will solve math problems, and tables five and six will draw page illustrations for your collaborative Big Book. After 25 minutes, the groups will stop the first activity and begin working on a second task without changing seats. Twenty-five minutes later you will change again to work on the activity each group has not yet done. The math groups and those doing illustrations will hand in their work when time is called. I will work with the two groups who are reading aloud." She plans to monitor progress of students in the reading group.

Notes

Question 1: Conference with mother about lateness and tiredness and their effects on learning. School nurse—advise mother about healthful sleep. Document Sara's behavior.

Question 2: First grade is also for building self-esteem, learning responsibility, beginning higher-order thinking skills, and dealing with the "whole child."

Question 2: Could praise students for something more demanding than neatness—beginning to "write."

Question 4: Puzzles and other manipulatives are good for this age, as is "writing" on flannel board.

Question 3:

- Could shorten the activity time
- Could have them move seats between activities
- Could make directions and expectations clearer

Sara is at table one. Ms. Mercer begins with this table and table two, working on reading. Several children read aloud. Ms. Mercer praises them. When Ms. Mercer calls on Sara, she begins reading in the wrong place. Joyce, seated next to Sara, points to where they are. Ms. Mercer says, "Sara, you would know where we are if you were paying attention." She calls on another child. Sara looks hurt, but soon starts to follow along in the book. Subsequently, Ms. Mercer calls on Sara, who now has the right place. Ms. Mercer then calls on another child.

During the math activity, Sara, yawning frequently, is the last to open her workbook and write her name. When she completes the page, she waits. She seems puzzled, although Ms. Mercer has already given directions. Sara gets up, sharpens a pencil, and returns to the wrong seat. "That's MY seat," accuses an angry boy. Sara apologizes and returns to her seat. Later, she waits to have her workbook checked. She has not torn out pages as Ms. Mercer instructed. Sara is told to "do it right." Sara has not creased the paper as Ms. Mercer demonstrated, so the pages do not tear out easily. Sara sucks her thumb and holds her ear for a minute. Suddenly, she yanks the paper and the pages come out with jagged edges. She receives three dots for her work. Ms. Mercer says, "Sara, this is good. I wish you could earn four dots" (the maximum). Sara slaps herself on the forehead.

During the illustration activity, Sara helps several others who have trouble thinking of ideas. Sara's illustration is among the best handed in.

Question 6: Hypothesis: ADHD?

Question 6:
- Physical/emotional problems?
- K–1 instruction so different she can't follow?
- Sara angry?—what about?
- Sara needs positive reinforcement?

Question 4: Connecting a writing activity to the field trip is good; questioning and prompting during the discussion is also good.

Question 5:

- Groups revise for another group of students, provide more information, share, present orally—writing, speaking, listening.
- Writing revision lesson—brainstorm ideas for specific part of story, rewrite.
- Pictures or discussion to identify more objects; revise, read aloud—writing, listening, speaking.

Question 6: Note hypotheses must be in addition to lack of sleep.

After the group work, Ms. Mercer places a large pad on an easel and says, "Now we're going to write about our trip to the art museum yesterday. Raise your hand and tell me something you saw or did in the museum." No one responds. She says, "Tell me the first thing we did at the museum." Sara raises her hand, offering a first sentence. After each response, Ms. Mercer asks, "What happened next?" or "What did we see next?" She prints each child's contribution.

Our Trip to the Art Museum

We rode the elevator to the second floor. We looked at different shapes on the ceiling. We saw a statue with a white triangle. We went to another room where we saw some pictures. We rode back down to the first floor. On our way out, we saw a painting of a grandfather and a boy.

During the writing of the group story, Sara fidgets in her seat, stares out the window, and makes a face at her neighbor.

Post-observation interview notes:

Ms. Mercer says, "Sara is a top performer in academic achievement and on standardized tests, consistently scoring among the top five students in the class. She's so bright. It's a shame she's late and distracted so much." The mentor replies, "There may be something else bothering Sara. Although easily distracted, there may be other explanations for her behavior. Let's talk more."

These two versions of the same student-based case show that you should be well prepared to respond to each of the questions by following these steps:

- Read each case carefully, raising questions about each section as you read.
- After reading the questions, reread the section and make notes.

These questions call on your knowledge of effective teaching and learning as conceptualized in the content categories and also on theories that support teaching and learning. With this foundation of knowledge, and careful reading and annotation of the case, you should find that you can respond to each of the questions fully.

Case Study 2: Content Category Approach

Below is a second case, this time a document-based, teacher-based case. It is presented first using strategy 1—reading and annotating with questions based on the major content categories covered in the test.

CASE STUDY 2

MS. RILEY

Information Presented

Scenario

Ms. Riley is a third-year teacher in an urban elementary school. She has a heterogeneously mixed class of twenty-six 9- and 10-year-olds. At the beginning of the second month of school, she introduces a long-term project called "Literature Logs." She plans the project to support her long-term goals. The following documents relate to that project.

Document 1
Literature Log Project Plan

Long-term goals:

1. Improve reading, writing, speaking, and listening abilities.
2. Develop critical-thinking skills.
3. Address students' individual differences.
4. Build a positive classroom community.

Notes

What information is given in this section that might be relevant to Ms. Riley's instruction?

What details about the planning might be significant?

- Appropriateness of goals and objectives?
- Strengths and weaknesses of the assignment?
- Strengths and weaknesses of assessment?
- Match of goals and objectives, activities, and assessment?
- Ways to expand or build on goals and objectives beyond the assignment?

Objectives:

1. Students will use writing to link aspects of a text with experiences and people in their own lives.

2. Students will write accurate summaries of what they have read.

Project assignment:

**Independent Reading Assignment
Literature Logs**

You are expected to read independently for about 2 hours each week (25 to 30 minutes every school night).

You may choose the book.

You are also expected to write four entries in your literature logs every two weeks.

Each entry should be about one handwritten page in your log.

At the beginning of each entry you are to write the following:

- The title and author of the book you are reading
- The numbers of the pages you are writing about
- A summary of the part of the book you have just read

In addition to writing a summary, you are to include one or more of the following:

- Similar things that have happened in your life
- What you think might happen next in the story
- Dilemmas the characters are facing and how they solve them or how you would solve them

HAPPY READING!

Assessment:

Each week, each student's literature log will be assessed on the following criteria:

- Number of pages read during week
- Number of entries in literature log during week
- Ability to write effective summaries of what has been read

Document 2
Entries from Sharon's literature log and
Ms. Riley's comments

Sharon
October 13, 2002
pp. 240–267

Beth died. I almost didn't notice because the book didn't really say she died. The way I noticed was because they started talking about how everyone missed her humming when she did house-work and how she played the piano and all kinds of things. My mother explained to me about <u>yufamisms</u>, which are words people use for things they really don't like to talk about. Well, we don't like to talk about it either but we say died. My aunt came to live with us because she was very sick and last year she died. I wonder what it felt like. I wonder how she felt when she was <u>dieing</u>? I miss her lots of times too.

I think you are reading *Little Women* by Louisa May Alcott. Remember to state the book title, author, and pages read every time.

Euphemisms

I'm sorry.
dying

Sharon
October 27, 2002
Little Women
by Louisa May Alcott
pp. 268–296

Jo <u>realy likd</u> to write and she started selling her stories to the <u>newspapper</u>. But one of her <u>frends didnt</u> like that kind of story so she <u>stoped</u> signing her name.

Sharon—
I'm disappointed with your spelling in this entry in your log. You need to be more careful.

really liked

newspaper
friends didn't

stopped

Don't you have any thoughts about your own life to add?

- Why are there two different entries? Are there changes?
- Do the entries meet the assignment and/or the goals and objectives?
- Why are the teacher's comments given?

- What does the conversation show about Kenny as a learner?
- How does Ms. Riley interact with Kenny?
- How might Ms. Riley address Kenny as a learner based on what is learned?

Document 3
A conversation with Kenny

Ms. Riley: Kenny, in my grade book I noticed I don't have a check for your literature logs. But I'm sure you've been reading, since I've seen you read at least two books a week since the beginning of the year.

Kenny: Yeah, I read three books last week.

Ms. Riley: I noticed how much you enjoyed one of them, at least you were laughing as you read during silent reading. Did you choose one you wanted to write about in your literature log?

Kenny: Well, right now I'm reading an interesting one that takes place in a museum.

Ms. Riley: Oh, what book is that?

Kenny: It's a long name, From the Mixed-Up Files of Mrs. Basil E. Frankenweiler. I just started it last night.

Ms. Riley: Oh, I know that book. It's very good.

Kenny: Great, because I have a question about it.

Ms. Riley: Is it a question that could help with your reading?

Kenny: Well, someone keeps explaining things to Saxonberg and I don't know who is explaining. I don't know who Saxonberg is either.

Ms. Riley: You know, Kenny, I think if you read a few more chapters you will probably find out, and then you can write about it in your lit log.

Kenny: Well, I can tell you about it tomorrow. It has a long name, but it's a small book. I'll finish it tonight.

Ms. Riley: Well, I'd really love to see it written in your lit log, or I won't be able to fill in that you've completed your homework.

Kenny: That's O.K.—I don't read to get credit. I just read for fun.

Case Study 2: Question Approach

Questions related to Case Study 2. Ms. Riley

1. Review Document 1, the Literature Log Project Plan. The plan demonstrates both strengths and weaknesses.

   - Identify ONE strength and ONE weakness of the Literature Log Project Plan.
   - Describe how each strength or weakness you identified demonstrates a strength or weakness in planning instruction. Base your response on principles of effective instructional planning.

2. Review Sharon's first entry (dated October 13) in Document 2, her literature log. Suppose that Ms. Riley wants to evaluate how well the entry demonstrates achievement of her long-term goals and/or her objectives.

   - Identify TWO aspects of Sharon's October 13 entry in her literature log that an effective evaluation would identify as achieving one or more of Ms. Riley's goals and/or her objectives.
   - For each aspect you identified, explain how it demonstrates achievement of one or more of Ms. Riley's goals and/or her objectives. Base your response on principles of effective assessment and evaluation.

3. In Document 2, Sharon's literature log, there are significant differences between Sharon's entry dated October 13 and her entry dated October 27. It appears that Sharon is having less success meeting the objectives for the project in the October 27 entry than in the October 13 entry.

   - Identify TWO significant differences between the first and second entries that indicate that Sharon is having less success in meeting the objectives of the project in the second entry.
   - For each difference you identified, suggest how Ms. Riley might have responded differently to Sharon in order to help Sharon continue to meet the objectives of the project. Base your response on principles of communication, assessment, and/or effective instruction.

4. In Document 3, Kenny's conversation with Ms. Riley, Kenny reveals characteristics of himself as a learner that could be used to support his development of literacy skills.

   - Identify ONE characteristic of Kenny as a learner, and then suggest ONE strategy Ms. Riley might use to address that characteristic in a way that will support his development of literacy skills.
   - Describe how the strategy you suggested addresses the characteristic of Kenny as a learner and how the strategy could support Kenny's development of literacy skills. Base your response on principles of varied instructional strategies for different learners and of human development.

5. Review Ms. Riley's long-term goals at the beginning of Document 1, the Literature Log Project Plan.

- Select TWO long-term goals and for each goal, and identify one strategy Ms. Riley might use to expand the literature log unit beyond the stated assignment and assessment plan to address the goal.
- Explain how the use of each strategy you identified could expand the literature log unit to address the selected goal. Base your response on principles of planning instruction and/or language development and acquisition.

6. Review the two objectives of the Literature Log Project Plan included in Document 1. Suppose that at the end of the project, as a culminating activity, Ms. Riley wants her students to use their literature logs to help them do a self-assessment of the two objectives.

- For each of the TWO project objectives described in Document 1, suggest one assignment Ms. Riley could give the students that would serve as a self-assessment.
- For each assignment you suggested, des-cribe how Ms. Riley's students could use it as a self-assessment. Base your response on principles of effective assessment.

With these questions in mind, reread the text of the case and note marginal comments that would directly help in responding to the questions.

CASE STUDY 2

MS. RILEY

Scenario

Ms. Riley is a third-year teacher in an urban elementary school. She has a heterogeneously mixed class of twenty-six 9- and 10-year-olds. At the beginning of the second month of school, she introduces a long-term project called "Literature Logs." She plans the project to support her long-term goals. The following documents relate to that project.

Document 1

Literature Log Project Plan

Long-term goals:

1. Improve reading, writing, speaking, and listening abilities.
2. Develop critical-thinking skills.
3. Address students' individual differences.
4. Build a positive classroom community.

Objectives:

1. Students will use writing to link aspects of a text with experiences and people in their own lives.
2. Students will write accurate summaries of what they have read.

Questions 1 and 5: In evaluating project plan and ways to expand the unit, bear in mind the following:

- urban elementary
- heterogeneous
- 26 nine-/ten-year-olds
- second month of school

Question 1:

Strengths

- Independent reading two hours per week—strengthens reading skills, literacy
- Student choice of book—individual differences
- Four entries per week—writing practice, known topic
- Including summary—meets objective, builds specific writing/thinking skills
- Link to lives—student-based instruction
- Prediction—builds thinking skills
- Dilemmas of characters—thinking skills, individual differences

Weaknesses

- Assessing number of pages—unimportant, doesn't meet any objectives
- Assessing number of entries per week doesn't meet objectives, suggests low-level expectations

Question 5:

- Speaking/listening: report aloud, students listen and question
- Critical thinking: rubric for self- and teacher assessment
- Positive community: cooperative groups to share
- Individual differences: find ways students differ
- All skills: folders, students present two favorites, revise in response to input

Question 6:

- For Objective 1, could have class develop a rubric together for evaluating entries in terms of linking with personal experience—students use rubric to evaluate selected entries.
- For Objective 2, could have students write an essay about strengths and weaknesses they see in five or six of their own summaries.

Project Assignment:

Independent Reading Assignment

Literature Logs

You are expected to read independently for about 2 hours each week (25 to 30 minutes every school night).

You may choose the book.

You are also expected to write four entries in your literature log every two weeks.

Each entry should be about one handwritten page in your log.

At the beginning of each entry you are to write the following:

- The title and author of the book you are reading
- The numbers of the pages you are writing about
- A summary of the part of the book you have just read

In addition to writing a summary, you are to include one or more of the following:

- Similar things that have happened in your life
- What you think might happen next in the story
- Dilemmas the characters are facing and how they solve them or how you would solve them

HAPPY READING!

- Objective of building positive community never addressed
- Assessment doesn't match goals/objectives except for summaries—no critical thinking, individual differences, positive community, using writing to link reading and personal experience

Assessment:

Each week, each student's literature log will be assessed on the following criteria:

- Number of pages read during week
- Number of entries in literature log during week
- Ability to write effective summaries of what has been read

Document 2

Entries from Sharon's literature log and Ms. Riley's comments.

Sharon
October 13, 2002
pp. 240–267

Beth died. I almost didn't notice because the book didn't really say she died. The way I noticed was because they started talking about how everyone missed her humming when she did housework and how she played the piano and all kinds of things. My mother explained to me about <u>yufamisms</u>, which are words people use for things they really don't like to talk about.

I think you are reading Little Women by Louisa May Alcott. Remember to state the book title, author, and pages read every time.

euphemisms

Well, we don't like to talk about it either but we say died. My aunt came to live with us because she was very sick and last year she died. I wonder what it felt like. I wonder how she felt when she was <u>dieing</u>? I miss her lots of times too.

I'm sorry.
dying

Sharon
October 27, 2002
Little Women
by Louisa May Alcott
pp. 268 – 296

Sharon—
I'm disappointed with your spelling in this entry in your log. You need to be more careful.

Jo <u>realy likd</u> to write and she started selling her stories to the <u>newspapper</u>.
But one of her <u>frends didnt</u> like that kind of story so she <u>stoped</u> signing her name.

really liked

newspaper
friends didn't
stopped

Don't you have any thoughts about your own life to add?

Question 2:

- Uses critical thinking to figure out Beth is dead.
- Uses mother's definition connecting to family.
- Writes accurate brief summary.
- Wrestles with dilemma: what is it like to die?
- Strong personal voice: individual differences

Question 3:

- Oct. 27 entry, no dilemmas of characters. Positive comment in Oct. 13 entry might have encouraged more.
- Oct. 27 entry, no reference to own life.
- Oct. 27 entry, no speculation; needed positive comment in Oct. 13 entry from teacher to encourage more.
- Oct. 27 entry is a short summary; no critical thinking. Positive reinforcement on Oct. 13 needed.
- Oct. 27 entry minimal; comments on Oct. 13 entry almost all on routine requirements and not on accurate summary or personal response.

Question 4:

- Loves to read; doesn't waste time writing about it—make writing more creative or provide alternate response mode like taping.
- Loves to read—ask to imitate book he likes to write own story.
- Loves to read—review favorites for other students.
- Insightful, curious reader—suggest reviews he might read to see how others respond.
- Enthusiastic about books—act out a scene from favorite for others.
- Curious mind—use the Internet for articles with interesting facts about books he likes.

Document 3

A conversation with Kenny

Ms. Riley:	Kenny, in my grade book I noticed I don't have a check for your literature logs. But I'm sure you've been reading, since I've seen you read at least two books a week since the beginning of the year.
Kenny:	Yeah, I read three books last week.
Ms. Riley:	I noticed how much you enjoyed one of them, at least—you were laughing as you read during silent reading. Did you choose one you wanted to write about in your literature log?
Kenny:	Well, right now I'm reading an interesting one that takes place in a museum.
Ms. Riley:	Oh, what book is that?
Kenny:	It's a long name, From the Mixed-Up Files of Mrs. Basil E. Frankenweiler. I just started it last night.
Ms. Riley:	Oh, I know that book. It's very good.
Kenny:	Great, because I have a question about it.
Ms. Riley:	Is it a question that could help with your reading?
Kenny:	Well, someone keeps explaining things to Saxonberg and I don't know who is explaining. I don't know who Saxonberg is either.
Ms. Riley:	You know, Kenny, I think if you read a few more chapters you will probably find out, and then you can write about it in your lit log.
Kenny:	Well, I can tell you about it tomorrow. It has a long name, but it's a small book. I'll finish it tonight.
Ms. Riley:	Well, I'd really love to see it written in your lit log. Or I won't be able to fill in that you've completed your homework.
Kenny:	That's O.K.—I don't read to get credit. I just read for fun.

With these strategies in mind, you may now want to go on to the next section, which takes a different focus: writing your answers to questions based on cases.

HOW TO ANSWER CONSTRUCTED-RESPONSE QUESTIONS

The previous section focused on strategies for reading, analyzing, and taking notes on case studies and how to relate each question to a particular section or concept in the case study. This section focuses on producing your response—making sure you understand what the question is asking and then using advice from experts to formulate a successful response.

Advice from the Experts

Scorers who have scored thousands of real tests were asked to give advice to students taking the Principles of Learning and Teaching test. Here is what they said.

1. **Answer all parts of the question.** This seems simple, but many test-takers fail to provide a complete response. If the question asks for two activities, don't forget the second one. If the question asks for a strength and a weakness, don't describe just a weakness. No matter how well you write about one activity or about a weakness, you will not get full credit for an answer that does not cover all aspects of the question.

2. **Show that you understand the pedagogical concepts related to the question.** This is a more subtle piece of advice. The scorers are looking to see not only that you can read the case study and make good observations, but also that you can relate those good observations to pedagogical concepts such as the principles of human development, the principles of motivation, the principles of effective instructional design, and the principles of diagnostic and evaluative assessment. To show that you understand these concepts, you have to do more than just mention that the concepts exist. You must also relate them to the specifics of your response. For example, in answering a question about identifying a weakness in a teacher's approach to assessment, instead of stating that "Mr. Taft didn't give the students very good tests," you could improve on this answer and state instead, "Given that assessment of student performance is most effective when evidence is gathered frequently and through a variety of exercises and assignments, Mr. Taft's reliance on end-of-chapter tests did not give students such as Paige adequate opportunities to demonstrate achievement."

3. **Show that you have a thorough understanding of the case.** Some answers receive partial credit because they are vague—they address the issues brought up in the case study at too general a level rather than at a level that takes into consideration the particulars given about a teacher, student, or assignment. If you are asked, for example, about the boy with learning disabilities whose patterns of behavior are described specifically in several sentences in the case study, don't answer the question in terms of children with disabilities in general, but, instead, focus on the boy in the case study and all the particulars you know about him.

4. **Support your answers with details.** This advice overlaps, to some extent, with numbers 2 and 3 above. The scorers are looking for some justification of your answers. If you are asked to state a "strength" shown by the teacher in a case study, don't just state the strength in a few words. Write why this is a strength—perhaps because of a particular principle of effective instructional design, which you should briefly summarize, or perhaps because of a good outcome described in the case, to which you should refer.

5. **Do not change the question or challenge the basis of the question.** Stay focused on the question that is asked, and do your best to answer it. You will receive no credit or, at best, a low score if you choose to answer another question or you state that, for example, there really aren't any activities that could be proposed, or there aren't any strengths to mention, or in some other way deny the basis of the question.

How PLT Constructed-Response Questions Are Scored

The following guide provides the overarching framework that guides how constructed-response questions on the Principles of Learning and Teaching tests are scored and the method by which the Question-Specific Scoring Guide for each question is created and revised.

Principles of Learning and Teaching General Scoring Guide.

All questions will be scored on a 0, 1, 2 scale.

A response that receives a score of score 2

- demonstrates a thorough understanding of the aspects of the case that are relevant to the question
- responds appropriately (see next page) to all parts of the question
- if an explanation is required, provides a strong explanation that is well supported by relevant evidence
- demonstrates a strong knowledge of pedagogical concepts, theories, facts, procedures, or methodologies relevant to the question

A response that receives a score of 1

- demonstrates a basic understanding of the aspects of the case that are relevant to the question
- responds appropriately (see next page) to one portion of the question
- if an explanation is required, provides a weak explanation that is well supported by relevant evidence
- demonstrates some knowledge of pedagogical concepts, theories, facts, procedures, or methodologies relevant to the question

A response that received a score of 0

- demonstrates misunderstanding of the aspects of the case that are relevant to the question
- fails to respond appropriately (see next page) to the question
- is not supported by relevant evidence
- demonstrates little knowledge of pedagogical concepts, theories, facts, procedures, or methodologies relevant to the question

No credit is given for blank or off-topic response.

The criteria for evaluating whether a response is "appropriate" are established through a "model answers" methodology, which consists of the following steps:

- After a case and questions are written, three or four knowledgeable experts are asked to read the case and answer the questions, addressing each question exactly as it is worded. These experts are carefully chosen to represent the diverse perspectives and situations relevant to the testing population.
- The case writer uses these "model answers" to develop a Question-Specific Scoring Guide for each question, creating a list of specific examples that would receive full credit. This list is considered to contain examples of correct answers, not all the possible correct answers.

- These question-specific scoring guides based on model answers provide the basis for choosing the papers that serve as benchmark and sample papers for the purpose of training the scorers at the scoring session.
- During the scoring sessions, while reading student papers, scorers can add new answers to the scoring guide as they see fit.
- Training at the scoring session is aimed to ensure that scorers do not score papers on the basis of their opinions or their own preferences but rather make judgments based on the carefully established criteria in the scoring guide.

CHAPTER 16
Real PLT Questions for Practice

Now you can practice writing your own responses to the 12 questions based on the case studies you read in Chapter 15. When you read a question for the first time, it is helpful to think about what the question is really asking and then to think about which of the content categories the question assesses. Note in the samples below that the last sentence of each question contains a reference to the content category addressed. This is nearly always the case in the constructed-response questions on the Principles of Learning and Teaching test, although there may be instances when the category is not explicitly stated.

As you plan and evaluate your response to the question, think about the scoring criteria used by the scorers, and think about the advice given by the experts.

The two cases and 12 practice questions, with accompanying advice and commentary, begin on the next page.

CASE STUDY 1

SARA

Scenario

Six-year-old Sara lives with her mother, who has a relaxed schedule. Ms. Mercer, Sara's teacher, notes that Sara is often tired and inattentive after arriving late. Sara says she frequently stays up past midnight if others are up. Ms. Mercer, a second-year teacher, has asked her mentor to observe Sara and suggest ways to help Sara achieve Ms. Mercer's purposes.

Observation: Ms. Mercer's Class, April 30

Pre-observation interview notes

Ms. Mercer says, "The purposes of first grade are to teach children 'school survival skills' and reading, writing, and arithmetic." She adds, "Sara needs help with 'survival skills,' including following directions, concentrating on a task to its completion, and being attentive to the lessons I present."

Mentor Classroom Observation—Focus on Sara Porter

As Ms. Mercer's class begins, the children play with puzzles and other activities requiring construction or manipulation. Two children "write" on a flannel board, using letters kept in alphabetical stacks in a box. They return the letters so they fit exactly over their counterparts. Ms. Mercer praises them for neatness. She instructs them to return to their previously assigned groups as Sara enters the room.

The students are seated at six tables, four students at each table. Ms. Mercer explains, "Tables one and two will work on reading first, while tables three and four will solve math problems, and tables five and six will draw page illustrations for your collaborative Big Book. After 25 minutes, the groups will stop the first activity and begin working on a second task without changing seats. Twenty-five minutes later, you will change again to work on the activity each group has not yet done. The math groups and those doing illustrations will hand in their work when time is called. I will work with the two groups who are reading aloud." She plans to monitor progress of students in the reading group.

Sara is at table one. Ms. Mercer begins with this table and table two, working on reading. Several children read aloud. Ms. Mercer praises them. When Ms. Mercer calls on Sara, she begins reading in the wrong place. Joyce, seated next to Sara, points to where they are. Ms. Mercer says, "Sara, you would know where we are if you were paying attention." She calls on another child. Sara looks hurt, but soon starts to follow along in the book. Subsequently, Ms. Mercer calls on Sara, who now has the right place. Ms. Mercer then calls on another child.

During the math activity, Sara, yawning frequently, is the last to open her workbook and write her name. When she completes the page, she waits. She seems puzzled, although Ms. Mercer has already given directions. Sara gets up, sharpens a pencil, and returns to the wrong seat. "That's MY seat," accuses an angry boy. Sara apologizes and returns to her seat. Later, she waits to have her workbook checked. She has not torn out pages as Ms. Mercer instructed. Sara is told to "do it right." Sara has not creased the paper as Ms. Mercer demonstrated, so the pages do not tear out easily. Sara sucks her thumb and holds her ear for a minute. Suddenly, she yanks the paper and the pages come out with jagged edges. She receives three dots for her work. Ms. Mercer says, "Sara, this is good. I wish you could earn four dots" (the maximum). Sara slaps herself on the forehead.

During the illustration activity, Sara helps several others who have trouble thinking of ideas. Sara's illustration is among the best handed in. After the group work, Ms. Mercer places a large pad on an easel and says, "Now we're going to write about our trip to the art museum yesterday. Raise your hand and tell me something you saw or did in the museum." No one responds. She says, "Tell me the first thing we did at the museum." Sara raises her hand, offering a first sentence.

After each response, Ms. Mercer asks, "What happened next?" or "What did we see next?" She prints each child's contribution.

Our Trip to the Art Museum

We rode the elevator to the second floor. We looked at different shapes on the ceiling. We saw a statue with a white triangle. We went to another room where we saw some pictures. We rode back down to the first floor. On our way out, we saw a painting of a grandfather and a boy. During the writing of the group story, Sara fidgets in her seat, stares out the window, and makes a face at her neighbor.

Post-observation interview notes

Ms. Mercer says, "Sara is a top performer in academic achievement and on standardized tests, consistently scoring among the top five students in the class. She's so bright. It's a shame she's late and distracted so much." The mentor replies, "There may be something else bothering Sara. Although she is easily distracted, there may be other explanations for her behavior. Let's talk more."

STRATEGIES FOR ANSWERING CONSTRUCTED-RESPONSE QUESTIONS FOR CASE STUDY 1

The questions that follow are the same questions you read in Chapter 15. Read each question again, then complete the exercises below it. These exercises are designed to help you think critically about what is being asked.

Question 1

Suppose that Ms. Mercer and her mentor discuss how to connect school and Sara's home environment for the benefit of Sara's learning.

- Identify TWO specific actions Ms. Mercer might take to connect school and Sara's home environment for the benefit of Sara's learning.
- Explain how each action you identified could benefit Sara's learning. Base your response on principles of fostering school–parent relationships to support student learning.

How to Answer Question 1

Step 1. Think about what is being asked.

In the space below, state in your own words what you think the question is asking.

[ ]

Compare your impression of what is being asked with the explanation below.
The question asks for

- *two* things Ms. Mercer might do to help the school and parent work together to identify Sara's needs
- for *each* thing, an explanation of how it could help Sara's learning

Step 2. Think about the category being assessed.

- The larger community

The important aspect of this content category is fostering "relationships with . . . parents." Also, although they are not the focus of the question, you need to understand the underlying human development issues—the physical, social, emotional, moral, and cognitive development of children this age. Both aspects (fostering relationships . . . and human development) are critical in a teacher's responsibilities to meet the needs of all students, but especially students such as Sara.

Step 3. Write your response.

In the space below, write what you consider to be a response that directly addresses the question.

[ ]

Step 4. Reflect on your response in light of the scoring guide, sample responses, and commentary.

Note that the scoring guide that will be used to evaluate responses to this question specifies two actions and that they must be appropriate. Note that the rubric contains bulleted possible answers, but that they are introduced by the statement ". . . such as the following." The list is neither prescriptive nor restrictive; all appropriate responses are given full credit. The experienced educators who score the test can evaluate the appropriateness of responses that are not contained in this list.

ETS Scoring Guide for Question 1

Score of 2

The response presents two appropriate actions Ms. Mercer might take to connect school and Sara's home environment and explanations of how each could benefit Sara's learning, such as the following:

- Ms. Mercer can seek a conference with Sara's mother to determine why Sara often arrives late and appears tired in class. Together they can discuss strategies to address Sara's problems.
- Ms. Mercer might ask the school nurse to schedule a conference with Sara, her mother, and Ms. Mercer to explore the reasons for Sara's tiredness in class. With the mediation of the school nurse, the adults and Sara can discuss ways to improve Sara's attentiveness and ability to follow directions.
- Ms. Mercer might telephone Sara's mother and explain that Sara is doing very well on tests, but that she is falling behind in class because she arrives late, appears very tired, reports she often stays up late, and finds it hard to follow directions or to contribute to discussions in class. Together they can explore ways to address Sara's problematic behavior.
- Ms. Mercer can document one or two weeks of Sara's inability to follow directions or to arrive on time and then call Sara's mother or schedule a conference to discuss what can be done at home and in school to improve Sara's ability to follow directions and to arrive on time.
- Ms. Mercer could gather a few articles about the necessity of at least 8 hours of sleep each night for 6-year-olds. She could ask for a conference with Sara's mother and discuss with her the harmful effects Sara's apparent lack of sleep is having on her school performance. Together they can seek solutions to Sara's tiredness.
- Ms. Mercer can discuss with second- and third-grade teachers the importance of a student's ability to follow directions and to contribute in class. She could then seek a conference with Sara's mother to show the negative effects of Sara's inability to follow

directions and contribute in class, indicating why that might be important for her present and future well-being.

Score of 1

The response presents two appropriate actions Ms. Mercer might take to connect school and Sara's home environment for the benefit of Sara's learning, without sufficient explanations, or presents one appropriate action with explanation, such as those presented in score point 2.

Score of 0

The response fails to address the question, presents inappropriate actions, or is vague.

Sample Responses and Commentary

Response that would receive a score of 2

First, Ms. Mercer can collect as much information as possible to use in conferences with Sara's mother to help establish a positive relationship and to help identify Sara's strengths and needs. Ms. Mercer should do some systematic observation and objective description of Sara's performance and the effects of her late arrival and inattentiveness in class. Observation information should include Sara's good qualities. She might also gather information, with the help of the school nurse, about healthful habits for children Sara's age, including amount of sleep needed. Second, Ms. Mercer then needs to seek a parent conference to discuss the areas in which Sara shows strengths as a student and to address her concerns about Sara's performance in class. By showing a sincere interest in Sara's positive growth and development as well as identifying the youngster's problems, Ms. Mercer can work to establish a positive working relationship with Sara's mother.

Commentary on the above response

The response presents two appropriate actions in considerable detail. The actions are related to each other, but are still clearly two separate steps in building a positive home–school relationship. The actions are clearly presented and directly applicable to the situation. The response receives full credit.

Response that would receive a score of 1

Ms. Mercer needs to talk with Sara's mother in order to connect school and Sara's home environment for the benefit of Sara's learning. She should call her to make an appointment, and when Sara's mother comes to school for the meeting, they can begin to discuss Sara's behavior and the possible causes for it. In the same way, Ms. Mercer and perhaps the nurse or school psychologist know a lot about what Sara does at school and a lot of theory about child growth and development, and they can help Sara's mother understand what her problems are and how to approach them. In this way, Sara will benefit because both home and school will know more and be better able to help her.

Commentary on the above response

The response presents only one action. Calling the mother is not presented as a separate action that, in itself, would address the problem, but rather as a preliminary to the meeting. The response does present one action that is appropriate, clearly expressed, and applicable to the situation. The response receives partial credit.

Response that would receive a score of 0

Although it sounds like a good idea, probably very little if anything will be gained by trying to establish contact with Sara's mother. From the way Sara behaves in school, it appears that a very likely cause of her problems lies at home, especially if her mother keeps her up very late at night and has little regard for her welfare. Therefore, in the best interests of Sara, Ms. Mercer should rely on the school to help her try to figure out what's going on with Sara and how best to help her and should not involve Sara's mother.

Commentary on the above response

The response presents an inappropriate action. The INTASC standard that reads "the teacher fosters relationships with school colleagues, parents, and agencies in the larger community to support students' learning and well being" clearly indicates that deliberately not involving Sara's mother is an inappropriate course of action. The response receives no credit.

How to Answer Question 2

Question 2

Review the preobservation notes in which Ms. Mercer explains the purposes of first grade as she sees them. Suppose that her mentor suggests that Ms. Mercer consider other purposes of first grade and how she might modify her instruction to address those purposes and the related needs of Sara and her other students.

- Identify TWO additional purposes of first grade that Ms. Mercer could consider when planning her instruction, in order to meet the needs of Sara and/or her other students.
- For each purpose you identified, explain how Ms. Mercer might modify her instruction to address the purpose and meet the needs of Sara and/or her other students. Base your response on principles of planning instruction and learning theory.

Step 1. Think about what is being asked.

In the space below, state in your own words what you think the question is asking.

Compare your impression of what is being asked with the explanation below.
The question asks for

- *two* additional purposes that might indicate needs of Sara and the other students
- for *each* purpose, an explanation of how Ms. Mercer might modify her instruction to meet these needs

Step 2. Think about the categories being assessed.

- Planning instruction
- Learning theory

It is important to know how to establish appropriate purposes for specific groups of students, and how to plan instruction to meet those purposes in a way that will engage students fully in learning.

Step 3. Write your response.
In the space below, write what you consider to be a response that directly addresses the question.

Step 4. Reflect on your response in light of the scoring guide, sample responses, and commentary.
Remember, as you study the scoring guide below, that scorers use it as the primary means of evaluating responses, and use their professional knowledge to evaluate

the appropriateness of responses. Remember, too, that the words "such as" introducing the bulleted examples of possible appropriate responses mean that these possible responses are neither prescriptive nor restrictive.

ETS Scoring Guide for Question 2

Score of 2

The response presents two additional appropriate purposes for first grade. For each, the response offers one modification for the teacher's instruction to better meet the needs of Sara or the other students, such as the following:

- The mentor can suggest that another purpose for first grade is to build self-esteem and confidence by providing success for all students in a variety of learning situations. Instead of pointing out Sara's weaknesses, she could praise her in class when she does well. By building in opportunities for success and building self-esteem and confidence, she can increase the engagement of Sara and other students.
- The mentor can suggest that another purpose of first grade is to offer students multiple opportunities to recognize and accept their responsibilities. For example, she could have a student repeat the directions she gives to each group and could have students identify what they are responsible for doing.
- The mentor can suggest that first grade should also be about developing more challenging skills than those for "survival," and could recommend that rather than just having the students learn survival routines, Ms. Mercer could introduce higher-order tasks, including evaluation, analysis, and/or synthesis, at an appropriate level for students to perform as part of each task.
- The mentor can suggest that another purpose for first grade is for students to learn to support one another in their learning. Instead of reprimanding Sara and other students for not hearing the directions the first time, she can appoint a buddy for each student so they can check with each other when they're unsure of what to do.
- The mentor can suggest that another purpose of first grade is to develop "the whole child," addressing physical, emotional, and intellectual growth and development. For example, Ms. Mercer might learn more about Sara's talents, interests, and problems so she can address Sara's strengths and needs in all three areas.

Score of 1

The response presents two additional purposes, but does not explain how Ms. Mercer might modify her instruction, or presents one additional purpose and explains how she might modify her instruction, in keeping with the purposes and modifications presented in score point 2.

Score of 0

The response fails to address the question, presents inappropriate additional purposes and modifications, or is vague.

Sample Responses and Commentary

Response that would receive a score of 2

The mentor can point out to Ms. Mercer that an important additional purpose for first grade is to address the physical, emotional, and intellectual needs of all children. She could have modified her instruction by learning more about Sara and then addressing Sara's needs in a carefully planned way that supports Sara's growth and development. A second additional purpose for first grade is to build students' self-esteem and confidence. The mentor could point out that Ms. Mercer shows her concern about Sara to the mentor, but to Sara she generally shows her frustration and impatience with what Sara does wrong. If Ms. Mercer began by praising Sara for her ability and acknowledging her genuine contributions, she would take an important step toward building Sara's self-esteem and confidence.

Commentary on the above response

The response presents two appropriate additional purposes of first grade. For each, the response offers one modification for her instruction to better meet Sara's needs. The two purposes and the accompanying explanations of the modification are presented clearly and thoroughly. Therefore, the response receives full credit.

Response that would receive a score of 1

One additional purpose of first grade is to begin introducing some of the higher-order thinking skills at a level appropriate for the age and grade level. Ms. Mercer is right that reading, writing, and arithmetic are important, but she could help the students grow much more effectively by helping them begin to use some synthesis, analysis, and evaluation skills in the tasks they are doing. For example, in her oral reading activity, she could ask some questions related to what the students are reading that would require them to use these higher-order thinking skills. She could ask how characters are alike, or ask them to name two things they really like about the story.

Commentary on the above response

The response presents one appropriate additional purpose for first grade and suggests an appropriate modification Ms. Mercer might make in her instruction. Both the purpose and the modification are explained with sufficient appropriate detail. However, the response does not present two additional purposes with modifications as the question requires, and so it receives partial credit.

Response that would receive a score of 0

It seems to me that, with everything first-grade teachers are expected to do these days, Ms. Mercer has more than enough challenge with the purposes she has established. Yes, it might be nice if she could think of some "additional" purposes, but I think her students will be best served if she concentrates on the purposes she has established and works to give her students a solid foundation on which later grades can build.

Commentary on the above response

The response fails to address the question. Responses that argue with the premise of the question receive no credit.

How to Answer Question 3

Question 3

Assume that the groups working on mathematics and illustrations for the Big Book become very noisy and unproductive over the course of the activity.

- Suggest TWO changes Ms. Mercer could have made in the planning and/or implementation of the group work that would have made the activity more successful.
- Explain how each change you suggested could have made the group work activity more successful. Base your response on principles of planning instruction and human development.

Step 1. Think about what is being asked.

In the space below, state in your own words what you think the question is asking.

Compare your impression of what is being asked with the explanation below.

The question asks for

- *two* changes Ms. Mercer could have made that could have made the group work more successful
- for *each* change, an explanation of how the group work would have been more successful

Step 2. Think about the categories being assessed.

- Planning instruction
- Human development

Again, note the importance of addressing each of these two categories. These two are especially important when a teacher is thinking about planning specific instructional strategies for specific groups of students. Note again that knowledge from learning theory and human behavior and motivation should be utilized to develop strategies for organizing and supporting individual and group work.

Step 3. Write your response.

In the space below, write what you consider to be a response that directly addresses the question.

Step 4. Reflect on your response in light of the scoring guide, sample responses, and commentary.

Again, note that the scoring guide contains possible appropriate responses that are illustrative only and are neither prescriptive nor restrictive. Remember that there are many appropriate ways in which the question could be answered, and these are illustrations only.

Score of 2

The response presents two appropriate changes Ms. Mercer could have made in planning and implementing the group work, and explanations of how they could make the activity more successful, such as the following:

- Ms. Mercer could shorten the amount of time for each activity, so that the students would be more likely to stay ontask. Twenty-five minutes per activity is too much time for students this age to be expected to work independently or in small groups without direct supervision.
- Ms. Mercer should teach or review group work behavior and expectations before the work begins, so that her students would be more likely to participate appropriately in the activity.
- Ms. Mercer could have groups move seats between activities. Students this age need to move more frequently and have physical activity, rather than being expected to sit in the same seats for long periods.
- Ms. Mercer could use parent volunteers to help support and monitor the work of the two groups with whom she is not working directly.
- Ms. Mercer could give clear directions, with steps and models of what final products are to look like, before students begin to work, so that they would be more likely to understand and achieve the objectives of the activity.
- Ms. Mercer could display posters that illustrate what students are to do; posters can also indicate the location of each group activity. The posters would provide the students with clearer directions for completing the activity.

Score of 1

The response presents two appropriate changes Ms. Mercer could have made in planning and implementing the group work without explanations of how the changes make the activity more successful, or presents one change Ms. Mercer could have made with an explanation of how the activity could have been more successful, such as those presented in score point 2.

Score of 0

The response fails to address the question, presents inappropriate ways to introduce and implement the group work, or is vague.

Sample Responses and Commentary

Response that would receive a score of 2

First, Ms. Mercer should plan shorter times for the students to work on each activity, so that the students would be able to stay ontask. Twenty-five minutes is too long to expect students this age to work alone or even in small groups on one activity. Next, she should plan to review much more carefully what she expects students in each group to do, showing them examples of what their finished work is supposed to look like. Providing clearer expectations would increase the likelihood that the students would complete the activity as desired.

Commentary on the above response

The response presents two appropriate changes Ms. Mercer could have made in the planning and implementation of the group work. They take into account the students' developmental levels and present approaches that would strengthen the group activities. The response receives full credit.

Response that would receive a score of 1

Ms. Mercer should introduce the activity by teaching or reviewing rules for behavior and procedures for small group work. She can't expect students to know this, or even to remember it from day to day. She needs to explain rules for working independently, or rules for working cooperatively so students can help one another without disturbing other students. If she reviews these things, the groups will have a better chance of success.

Commentary on the above response

The response presents one appropriate change Ms. Mercer could have made in her planning. It is presented in detail, but constitutes only one change. The question requires two appropriate changes; the response receives partial credit.

Response that would receive a score of 0

Ms. Mercer should not try to use small group work with students this age. They are too young to be expected to work independently or even in small groups. She should keep the class together so that she can have direct supervision over them at all times.

Commentary on the above response

The response argues with the question, rather than responding to it in an appropriate way. Responses that argue with the premise of the question receive no credit.

How to Answer Question 4

Question 4

In the activities described in the Mentor Classroom Observation, Ms. Mercer demonstrates understanding of developmentally appropriate instructions.

- Identify TWO strengths in the instructional approaches Ms. Mercer uses in the activities that reflect understanding of the principles of developmentally appropriate instructions.

- Explain how each of these strengths you identified provides evidence of an understanding of the principles of developmentally appropriate instruction. Base your response on principles of planning instruction and human development.

Step 1. Think about what is being asked.

In the space below, state in your own words what you think the question is asking.

Compare your impression of what is being asked with the explanation below. The question asks for

- *two* strengths in Ms. Mercer's instructional approaches
- for *each* strength, an explanation of how it demonstrates understanding of developmentally appropriate instruction

Step 2. Think about the categories being assessed.

- Planning instruction
- Human development

Again, note the importance of addressing each of these two categories. These two are especially important in thinking about planning specific instructional strategies for specific groups of students. Note again that knowledge from learning theory and human behavior and motivation are utilized to develop strategies for organizing and supporting individual and group work.

Step 3. Write your response.

In the space below, write what you consider to be a response that directly addresses the question.

Step 4. Reflect on your response in light of the scoring guide, sample responses, and commentary.

ETS Scoring Guide for Question 4

Score of 2

The response presents two strengths in Ms. Mercer's instructional approaches, with evidence of understanding of developmentally appropriate instructions, such as the following:

- Having students engage in play with puzzles or other activities requiring construction and manipulation is very appropriate to the students' developmental levels.
- Having the students "write" on flannel boards is an appropriate language development activity for students this age.
- Having students work on a variety of tasks, rotating among three tasks, is an appropriate activity-centered approach for students this age.
- Connecting the writing activity to the students' previous experience on the field trip is an appropriate way to help students this age make connections and, therefore, perform well.
- Questioning and prompting students as they are developing the account of the trip is an appropriate way to help students this age develop writing fluency.

Score of 1

The response presents two strengths in Ms. Mercer's instructional approaches, without appropriate discussion of how they are developmentally appropriate, or presents one strength in Ms. Mercer's instructional approach with evidence of how it is developmentally appropriate, such as those presented in score point 2.

Score of 0

The response fails to address the question, presents inappropriate points as strengths, or is vague.

Sample Responses and Commentary

Response that would receive a score of 2

Ms. Mercer's lesson does display strengths. She is developing students' writing skills in an appropriate way for students this age by having students "write" at the flannel board. They are developing an enthusiasm for writing and a sense of what it means to put letters together to form words. Another strength is the way she connects the writing of the story to their previous trip to the museum. When teachers connect one activity to previous knowledge or experience of students, the students this age have a better opportunity to learn and demonstrate their learning. It was also a strength to prompt and question students as they were developing ideas for the story. They were having trouble remembering, but without just telling them what to say, she helped them develop ideas.

Commentary on the above response

The response presents more than two appropriate strengths. Each point presented is valid and explained in sufficient detail. No additional credit, however, is given for going beyond the requirement of the question. The response receives full credit.

Response that would receive a score of 1

Ms. Mercer's use of rotating group activities for the students is a strength of the lesson. This activity-centered approach is very effective in helping students develop skills and remain engaged in the work. The activities are varied enough to keep the students interested and are all appropriate for students this age.

Commentary on the above response

The response presents one appropriate strength of her approach. It is explained in sufficient detail. However, the response presents only one strength, and the question calls for two. It receives partial credit.

Response that would receive a score of 0

One appropriate strength in her approach is that she is very nice to the children. Boys and girls in first grade need lots of personal attention and a supportive classroom environment. Teachers who are enthusiastic and supportive of their students help students a lot more than teachers who are too stern and critical.

Commentary on the above response

The response refers to aspects for teaching first grade that are important. However, the discussion does not address the question of strengths of Ms. Mercer's instructional approaches. Discussing aspects of instruction stressed by the INTASC standards but not relevant to the question posed is not sufficient to receive credit.

How to Answer Question 5

Question 5

Assume that the day after the lesson was observed, Ms. Mercer's objective is to use the story about the museum visit to continue building students' literacy.

- Identify TWO strategies and/or activities involving the story about the museum visit that Ms. Mercer could use to continue building students' literacy.
- For each strategy and/or activity you identified, explain how it could help build literacy. Base your response on principles of language development and acquisition.

Step 1. Think about what is being asked.

In the space below, state in your own words what you think the question is asking.

Compare your impression of what is being asked with the explanation below. The question asks for

- *two* strategies or activities the teacher could use to meet this objective
- an explanation of how *each* strategy or activity helps build literacy

Step 2. Think about the category being assessed.

- Planning instruction

For students this age, building literacy skills is essential. The ability to address this need in practice is critical.

Step 3. Write your response.

In the space below, write what you consider to be a response that directly addresses the question.

Reflect on your response in light of the scoring guide, sample responses, and commentary.

ETS Scoring Guide for Question 5

Score of 2

The response offers two appropriate strategies Ms. Mercer could use and explains how each strategy meets her objective, such as the following:

- Ms. Mercer could tell the students their story is going to be shared with students in another class. Have them brainstorm ways to make the story more interesting for other children their age, including more information they remember that might be included. This activity would build their writing skills by adding information for a specific audience.
- Ms. Mercer could have copies of the story run off by the end of the day and give each student a copy of the story. She could ask them to have their parents read the story with them and ask questions about it. The next day they could use the questions they can remember to brainstorm more ideas. This activity would build their oral literacy through conversation with their parents and their writing skills through revision.
- Ms. Mercer can ask students to think about one thing they remember from the visit (the marble with the white triangle, the ceiling pictures, or the room full of statues) and draw a picture of it. She could post the pictures and use them as a basis for a word board of good descriptive language. This builds their writing skills by revising to add more specific, focused details about one aspect of the visit.
- Ms. Mercer might read the children a story about a visit. She could have children discuss what they liked about the story, and use this information to brainstorm ways to write about their own visit. This builds their writing skills by modeling an effective description,

and their speaking and listening skills as they share aloud ideas to revise their story.

- Ms. Mercer can show pictures of the various things the class saw at the museum. By asking the members of each group to identify an item that interests them and discuss what they could write to make another person their age interested in the item, Ms. Mercer could build on their discussion and listening skills and develop writing skills.

Score of 1

The response presents one appropriate strategy and explains how it meets the objective to develop students' literacy such as those presented in score point 2, or presents two appropriate strategies such as those presented in score point 2 but does not explain how the strategies meet the objective.

Score of 0

The response fails to address the question, presents inappropriate strategies and explanations of how the strategies meet the objective, or is vague.

Sample Responses and Commentary

Response that would receive a score of 2

Ms. Mercer has many opportunities to develop the speaking, reading, writing, and listening skills of her students by using the description of the museum visit in creative ways. By having students revise the story for a specific audience, say a group of children their age, and describe their visit in ways that would make the others want to go to the museum too, she can increase their ability to write for a specific audience. If she were to display pictures of things they saw, ask them to provide descriptive words, and then write the words beneath the pictures, she would help them develop vocabulary appropriate to their writing and to develop speaking and listening skills.

Commentary on the above response

The response identifies two specific ways in which Ms. Mercer could continue building students' literacy. The activities suggested are appropriate and described in detail. The response receives full credit.

Response that would receive a score of 1

Ms. Mercer could use two additional activities to build students' literacy. The next day they could return to the story they have written, and could brainstorm some additional details that could be added to make the story more interesting. Ms. Mercer might have to prompt them a bit, but by giving them some hints, she could help them remember things that would make the story fuller and more detailed. She could also develop literacy by having "listening stations" where students can listen to tape-recorded stories and follow along in books. By connecting the story read aloud (on tape) and the story as it appears in print, she can help them understand that the words on the page have real meaning.

Commentary on the above response

The question specifically says her objective is "to use the story about the museum visit to continue building students' literacy" and asks for two strategies or activities to meet this objective. One of the activities presented does extend the lesson and receives credit. However, the second activity is unrelated to the story about the museum and therefore is considered unresponsive to the question. The response receives partial credit.

Response that would receive a score of 0

I believe developing literacy is probably the most important academic objective first grade teachers can have. Literacy involves developing specifically the skills of reading, writing, speaking, and listening. There are many activities that first grade teachers can use to develop literacy. It is important to remember that for first graders, print is very confusing, and they often see little connection between ideas and print, so anything a teacher can do to help them make that connection will help.

Commentary on the above response

Merely selecting one word—even a critical word—from the question and writing about it does not constitute responding appropriately to the question. While the question does deal with developing literacy, the response does not address the specific requirements of the question and receives no credit.

How to Answer Question 6

Question 6

In the post-observation notes, Ms. Mercer's mentor suggests that they explore explanations for Sara's inattentive behavior.

- Suggest TWO hypotheses other than lack of sleep that Ms. Mercer and her mentor might explore to learn more about why Sara behaves as she does in class.
- For each hypothesis you suggested, describe at least one action that Ms. Mercer and her mentor might take to see if the hypothesis might be correct. Base your response on principles of human development, motivation, and diagnostic assessment.

Step 1. Think about what is being asked.

In the space below, state in your own words what you think the question is asking.

Compare your impression of what is being asked with the explanation below. The question asks for

- *two* hypotheses that Ms. Mercer and the mentor might explore to learn more about Sara's behavior in class
- for *each* hypothesis, a description of one action Ms. Mercer and the mentor might take to learn more about why Sara behaves as she does

Step 2. Think about the categories being assessed.

- Diagnostic and evaluative strategies in the areas of human development and learner motivation

The ability to make effective assessments, both of the needs of students and of the strengths and weaknesses in student performance, is essential. Here, the question asks for hypotheses to explore to learn more about Sara's behavior—in other words, for the beginning of a diagnostic assessment.

Step 3. Write your response.

In the space below, write what you consider to be a response that directly addresses the question.

Step 4. Reflect on your response in light of the scoring guide, sample responses, and commentary.

ETS Scoring Guide for Question 6

Score of 2

The response presents two appropriate hypotheses that the mentor and Ms. Mercer can explore to learn the causes for Sara's inattentiveness in class, and for each hypothesis, the response describes one action Ms. Mercer and her mentor could take to see if the hypothesis is correct, such as the following:

- One hypothesis is that Sara has ADHD or some other learning disability. They can have the nurse or a counselor observe Sara and determine whether she needs further testing.
- One hypothesis is that there are physical or emotional factors in Sara's background that affect her behavior now. They could look for information in Sara's background data that suggest causes for her inattentiveness. They can examine Sara's folder and find out if any potential causes are listed in the data.
- One hypothesis is that Sara had a very different kind of teacher in kindergarten, and she may miss the kind of instruction with which she was familiar. Ms. Mercer and the mentor could talk with Sara's kindergarten teacher to find out what behavior patterns she exhibited and what kinds of approaches worked well with her.
- One hypothesis is that Sara is angry about something, related either to school or to other areas of her life, as indicated by her angry gestures. They could explore a variety of sources including Sara's mother, Sara's records, or a discussion with Sara herself to determine if there is ongoing anger.
- One hypothesis is that Sara needs ongoing, frequent positive reinforcement in order to function well. They could try a program of greatly enhanced positive reinforcement and praise to see if Sara responds to this approach.
- One hypothesis is that Sara is bored. Ms. Mercer has noted her high test scores and identified her as very bright. She may be bored with activities that aren't challenging her. They could have a counselor or other trained staff member work with Sara to determine if she would respond to more intellectually challenging work.

Score of 1

The response presents two appropriate hypotheses that the mentor and Ms. Mercer can explore to learn the causes for Sara's inattentiveness in class, but no actions they could take to see if the hypotheses might be correct; or the response presents one appropriate hypothesis Ms. Mercer and the mentor could explore with one action they could take to see if the hypothesis might be correct, such as those presented in score point 2.

Score of 0

The response fails to address the question, presents inappropriate hypotheses, or is vague.

Sample Responses and Commentary

Response that would receive a score of 2

The mentor may suspect that Sara has ADHD or some other learning disability that prevents her from maintaining concentration on her work. They can work with the school nurse or counselor or other professional staff to explore this possibility. The mentor may also suggest that Sara needs consistent, ongoing positive reinforcement and performs poorly when exposed to criticism. She and Ms. Mercer could work together to provide consistent feedback to Sara that would build self-esteem and confidence, and see if this approach helps Sara be more fully engaged in the work.

Commentary on the above response

The response presents two appropriate hypotheses the mentor teacher and Ms. Mercer could explore to learn more about Sara's behavior. They are presented briefly, but are specific and presented in sufficient detail. Responses need not be lengthy nor elaborately written to receive full credit. This response does receive full credit.

Response that would receive a score of 1

The mentor teacher and Ms. Mercer could explore the possibility that Sara has some form of a learning disability that prevents her from paying attention. They could use a school psychologist to help them make this determination.

Commentary on the above response

The response presents only one hypothesis. It is appropriate and although very brief is sufficient for partial credit.

Response that would receive a score of 0

The mentor teacher and Ms. Mercer could look for the causes of Sara's behavior in class. The mentor teacher seems to understand that there may be more involved than Sara's lack of sleep. She can clearly help Ms. Mercer and together, they can brainstorm possibilities about what may be causes of Sara's behavior. A second thing they could do would be to consult some of the professional staff of the school and ask them for help in figuring out what's going on with Sara so they can help her.

Commentary on the above response

The response fails to address the question. A response that paraphrases the question or offers related information that does not directly address the requirements of the question receives no credit.

Now let's look at how the questions for the teacher-based, document-based case "Ms. Riley" might be analyzed, responded to, and evaluated. Again, the materials below are intended as illustrative of how you might prepare for practice cases and respond to actual cases. As you prepare, remember that the critical factors to bear in mind as you read and respond to the questions are what is being asked and the categories being assessed.

MS. RILEY

Scenario

Ms. Riley is a third-year teacher in an urban elementary school. She has a heterogeneously mixed class of twenty-six 9- and 10-year-olds. At the beginning of the second month of school, she introduces a long-term project called "Literature Logs." She plans the project to support her long-term goals. The following documents relate to that project.

Document 1

Literature Log Project Plan

Long-term goals:

1. Improve reading, writing, speaking, and listening abilities.
2. Develop critical-thinking skills.
3. Address students' individual differences.
4. Build a positive classroom community.

Objectives:

1. Students will use writing to link aspects of a text with experiences and people in their own lives.
2. Students will write accurate summaries of what they have read.

Project assignment:

Independent Reading Assignment

Literature Logs

You are expected to read independently for about 2 hours each week (25 to 30 minutes every school night).

You may choose the book.

You are also expected to write four entries in your literature logs every two weeks.

Each entry should be about one handwritten page in your log.

At the beginning of each entry you are to write the following:

- The title and author of the book you are reading
- The numbers of the pages you are writing about
- A summary of the part of the book you have just read

In addition to writing a summary, you are also to include one or more of the following:

- Similar things that have happened in your life
- What you think might happen next in the story
- Dilemmas the characters are facing and how they solve them or how you would solve them

HAPPY READING!

Assessment:

Each week, each student's literature log will be assessed on the following criteria:

- Number of pages read during week
- Number of entries in literature log during week
- Ability to write effective summaries of what has been read

Document 2

Entries from Sharon's literature log and Ms. Riley's comments

Sharon
October 13, 2002
pp. 240–267

Beth died. I almost didn't notice because the book didn't really say she died. The way I noticed was because they started talking about how everyone missed her humming when she did housework and how she played the piano and all kinds of things. My mother explained to me about yufamisms, which are words people use for things they really don't like to talk about. Well, we don't like to talk about it either but we say died. My aunt came to live with us because she was very sick and last year she died. I wonder what it felt like. I wonder how she felt when she was dieing? I miss her lots of times too.

I think you are reading *Little Women* by Louisa May Alcott. Remember to state the book title, author, and pages read every time.

euphemisms

I'm sorry.

dying

Sharon
October 27, 2002
Little Women
by Louisa May Alcott
pp. 268–296

Sharon—
I'm disappointed with your spelling in this entry in your log. You need to be more careful.

Jo <u>realy likd</u> to write and she started selling her stories to the <u>newspapper</u>. But one of her <u>frends didnt</u> like that kind of story so she <u>stoped</u> signing her name.

really liked
newspaper
friends didn't
stopped

Don't you have any thoughts about your own life to add?

Document 3

A conversation with Kenny

Ms. Riley:	Kenny, in my grade book I noticed I don't have a check for your literature logs. But I'm sure you've been reading, since I've seen you read at least two books a week since the beginning of the year.
Kenny:	Yeah, I read three books last week.
Ms. Riley:	I noticed how much you enjoyed one of them, at least you were laughing as you read during silent reading. Did you choose one you wanted to write about in your literature log?
Kenny:	Well, right now I'm reading an interesting one that takes place in a museum.
Ms. Riley:	Oh, what book is that?
Kenny:	It's a long name, *From the Mixed-Up Files of Mrs. Basil E. Frankenweiler*. I just started it last night.
Ms. Riley:	Oh, I know that book. It's very good.
Kenny:	Great, because I have a question about it.
Ms. Riley:	Is it a question that could help with your reading?
Kenny:	Well someone keeps explaining things to Saxonberg and I don't know who is explaining. I don't know who Saxonberg is either.
Ms. Riley:	You know, Kenny, I think if you read a few more chapters you will probably find out, and then you can write about it in your lit log.
Kenny:	Well, I can tell you about it tomorrow. It has a long name, but it's a small book. I'll finish it tonight.
Ms. Riley:	Well, I'd really love to see it written in your lit log or I won't be able to fill in that you've completed your homework.
Kenny:	That's O.K.—I don't read to get credit. I just read for fun.

STRATEGIES FOR ANSWERING CONSTRUCTED-RESPONSE QUESTIONS FOR CASE STUDY 2

The questions that follow are the same questions you read in Chapter 15. Read each question again, then complete the exercises below it. These exercises are designed to help you think critically about what is being asked. Here is the first question related to the Ms. Riley case.

How to Answer Question 1

Question 1

Review Document 1, the Literature Log Project Plan. The plan demonstrates both strengths and weaknesses.

- Identify ONE strength and ONE weakness of the Literature Log Project Plan.
- Describe how each strength or weakness you identified demonstrates a strength or weakness in planning instruction. Base your response on principles of effective instructional planning.

Step 1. Think about what is being asked.

In the space below, state in your own words what you think the question is asking.

Compare your impression of what is being asked with the explanation below.
   The question asks for

- *one* strength of the plan and one weakness of the plan
- explanations of why *each* is a strength or a weakness

Step 2. Think about the categories being assessed.

- Planning instruction

As you saw in studying the questions and domains for the first case presented, planning instruction is a very important category and is addressed in many of the questions in the cases. Planning instruction draws on an understanding of learning theory, subject matter, curriculum development, and student development and a sense of how to use that knowledge in planning instruction. In the Principles of Learning and Teaching test, rather than being asked to plan a unit or lesson plan of your own, you are asked to analyze existing plans in terms of strengths and weaknesses or in terms of how to modify them for specific purposes.

Step 3. Write your response.

In the space below, write what you consider to be a response that directly addresses the question.

Step 4. Reflect on your response in light of the scoring guide, sample responses, and commentary.

Now consider your response in light of the following scoring guide used to evaluate test-takers' responses. Remember that the guide contains illustrative possible responses that are neither restrictive nor prescriptive.

Score of 2

The response presents one appropriate strength of the plan and one appropriate weakness of the plan and explains why each is a strength or a weakness. Here are some examples:

Strengths:

- Having students read independently for over two hours a week is likely to help them improve their reading skills.
- Letting each student choose the books to read reinforces the notion that individual differences are worth respecting.
- Writing four entries a week gives each student a significant amount of writing practice and can improve each student's writing fluency.
- The assignment to include a summary of the part of the book just read supports the objective of having students write accurate summaries.
- Having students link events in their lives to events in what they read directly supports the first objective.
- Having each student indicate what will happen next can build a student's critical thinking ability.
- Focusing on the dilemmas the characters face and how the reader would solve them promotes critical thinking and acknowledgment of individual differences.

Weaknesses:

- Assessing the number of pages read each week does not necessarily support any of the long-term goals or the objectives. It is, therefore, an inappropriate criterion for assessment.
- Keeping track of the number of entries in the log each week suggests that the teacher really wants more than the four entries she requires. Although having the students read more each week supports the goal of building reading skills, it does not necessarily promote the joy of reading suggested by the caps in the assignment: HAPPY READING!
- There is no aspect of the project assignment or the assessment that addresses the long-term goal of building a positive classroom community.
- The assessment does not match the goals and objectives, with the exception of the assessment of writing effective summaries. The assessment does not address critical thinking skills, individual differences, building a positive classroom community, or using writing to link reading and personal experience.

Score of 1

The response offers one appropriate strength or one appropriate weakness and appropriate reasons why it is a strength or weakness, such as those presented in score point 2, or one strength and one weakness without appropriate reasons why each is a strength or a weakness.

Score of 0

The response fails to address the question, presents inappropriate strengths and weaknesses, or is vague.

Sample Responses and Commentary

Response that would receive a score of 2

Ms. Riley's goals and assignment are fairly well matched. She assigns a reasonable amount of reading for a week to address the goal of improving reading, attempts to help the students make personal connections to their lives, allows them to select their own books, and asks them to write regularly about what they read. Generally, her assignment develops her goals pretty well. However, her assessments are not well aligned with her goals. All her assessments focus on mechanical aspects of the tasks she assigns. By grading student summaries and the number of entries, and counting the number of pages, she is suggesting that she is not very interested in critical thinking or in helping students to acknowledge differences among people. She establishes these as her goals, but when it comes to assessing student performance in the project, most of the goals and objectives do not count toward a grade, and therefore they are undervalued.

Commentary on the above response

The response presents both: one appropriate strength and one appropriate weakness. The response is very fully developed; however, responses are evaluated on the appropriateness and/or accuracy of the information presented, not on the writing skill with which they are presented. The response receives full credit because it explains one appropriate strength and one appropriate weakness. Note that had the strength and weakness simply been named, without an explanation of why each was selected, the response would have received a score of 1.

Response that would receive a score of 1

Having the students include a summary of the part of the book just read supports one of the objectives, the one that says students should write accurate summaries. In addition, having students link events in their lives to events in the books helps students see connections between their lives and what occurs in literature, and so matches another of the objectives.

Commentary on the above response

The response presents two appropriate strengths of the assignment. However, the question calls for one strength and one weakness. It therefore receives partial credit.

Response that would receive a score of 0

I think having students keep literature logs is a very good idea. It helps them to think about what they have read, and gives them a chance to use their writing skills to write about something they know. A second good thing about these logs is that they give the teacher a way to assess what students have understood and are thinking.

Commentary on the above response

The response does not address the question. While a different question might have asked for advantages of this kind of assignment, the question as presented asks for one strength and one weakness of this specific plan. It therefore receives no credit.

How to Answer Question 2

Question 2

Review Sharon's first entry (dated October 13) in Document 2, her literature log. Suppose that Ms. Riley wants to evaluate how well the entry demonstrates achievement of her long-term goals and/or her objectives.

- Identify TWO aspects of Sharon's October 13 entry in her literature log that an effective evaluation would identify as achieving of one or more of Ms. Riley's goals and/or her objectives.
- For each aspect you identified, explain how it demonstrates achievement of one or more of Ms. Riley's goals and/or her objectives. Base your response on principles of effective assessment and evaluation.

Step 1. Think about what is being asked.

In the space below, state in your own words what you think the question is asking.

Compare your impression of what is being asked with the explanation below.
   The question asks for

- *two* aspects of the first entry that show achievement of one or more of Ms. Riley's long-term goals and/or her objectives
- for *each* aspect, an explanation of how it meets one or more of the goals and/or objectives

Step 2. Think about the categories being assessed.

- Assessment (diagnostic and evaluative)

An important aspect of this category is the ability to use formal and informal assessment strategies to evaluate the continuous intellectual development of the learner. This question asks for an assessment of Sharon's work and of Ms. Riley's ability to assess and respond to that work effectively.

Step 3. Write your response.

In the space below, write what you consider to be a response that directly addresses the question.

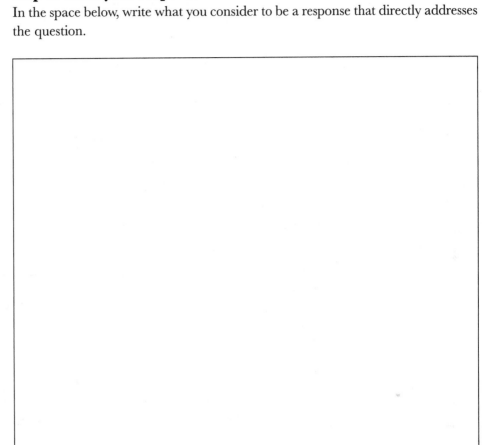

Step 4. Reflect on your response in light of the scoring guide, sample responses, and commentary.

ETS Scoring Guide for Question 2

Score of 2

The response identifies and explains two appropriate achievements of one or more instructional goals or objectives, such as the following:

- Sharon notes that characters miss hearing Beth humming. She figures out from this that Beth is dead. She is using her critical-thinking skills to figure out what is happening in the text.
- By including her mother's definition of "yufamisms" Sharon is connecting what happens in the book to her family, thereby making direct links between literature and her life.
- Sharon is writing an accurate summary of what happens in the book.
- By wondering what it is like to die, Sharon is indicating her own individuality and trying to wrestle with one of the dilemmas both she and the characters face.
- Sharon's entry is quite candid and unique, expressing her own unique point of view.
- Sharon trusts Ms. Riley to respect individual differences by "confessing" a great deal about her own private questions, family events, and dilemmas about the sensitive subject of death.

Score of 1

The response identifies and explains one appropriate achievement of one or more instructional goals or objectives, such as those presented in score point 2, or identifies but does not explain two aspects of the literature log entry that achieve one or more instructional goals or objectives.

Score of 0

The response fails to address the question, presents inappropriate achievements, or is vague.

Sample Responses and Commentary

Response that would receive a score of 2

Sharon is a sensitive, thoughtful reader who in her first response offers Ms. Riley many of the things Ms. Riley wants to promote in readers. She talks about her own personal links to the characters when she discusses the death of Beth and her aunt, uses her analytic powers to figure out the meaning of dilemmas that characters face when she uses clues to figure out that Beth has died, and suggests how personally she responds to key events in the novel when she notes that she wonders what it felt like to die.

Commentary on the above response

The response presents and explains at least two appropriate ways in which Sharon's entry demonstrates achievement of the objectives. Adding a third appropriate way neither adds to nor subtracts from the effectiveness of the response. It receives full credit.

Response that would receive a score of 1

In the first entry, Sharon does a wonderful job of connecting what she has read to her own life. When she talks about one of the characters dying and then connects that to her aunt's death, she has done a wonderful job of making a connection. She has really met her teacher's objective!

Commentary on the above response

The response presents and explains only one appropriate way in which Sharon's first entry demonstrates achievement of one or more of the objectives. It therefore receives partial credit.

Response that would receive a score of 0

Sharon's first entry is wonderful! I wish I could get my students to write reading log entries like this one. She does everything her teacher wanted, and more! I just wish Ms. Riley had given her a lot more positive feedback.

Commentary on the above response

The response does talk about the first entry, but it does not address the question, which asks for specific ways in which the entry demonstrates achievement of one or more of the objectives. It receives no credit.

How to Answer Question 3

Question 3

In Document 2, Sharon's literature log, there are significant differences between Sharon's entry dated October 13 and her entry dated October 27. It appears that Sharon is having less success meeting the objectives for the project in the October 27 entry than in the October 13 entry.

- Identify TWO significant differences between the first and second entries that indicate that Sharon is having less success in meeting the objectives of the project in the second entry.
- For each difference you identified, suggest how Ms. Riley might have responded differently to Sharon in order to help Sharon continue to meet the objectives of the project. Base your response on principles of communication, assessment, and/or effective instruction.

Step 1. Think about what is being asked.

In the space below, state in your own words what you think the question is asking.

```
[blank response box]
```

Compare your impression of what is being asked with the explanation below.
   The question asks for

- *two* specific differences between the first entry and the second
- for *each* difference, how Ms. Riley might have helped Sharon continue to meet her goals

Step 2. Think about the categories being assessed.

- Planning instruction
- Communication, social organization, classroom management
- Assessment

The question addresses all three of these important domains in one way or another. Part of planning instruction is using an understanding of student development. Communication addresses using knowledge of effective verbal communication techniques to foster active inquiry, while assessment involves formal and informal assessment strategies to evaluate the continuous intellectual development of the learner. The ways in which Ms. Riley thinks about her responses as she plans, the way in which she assesses the achievement of her objectives, and the way in which she communicates with Sharon all directly address these domains.

Step 3. Write your response.

In the space below, write what you consider to be a response that directly addresses the question.

Step 4. Reflect on your response in light of the scoring guide, sample responses, and commentary.

Score of 2

The response presents two significant differences between Sharon's October 13 and October 27 entries and offers appropriate suggestions about how Ms. Riley could have helped Sharon to meet the teacher's goals, such as the following:

- As Ms. Riley requested, Sharon's second entry summarizes what happened in the book, but doesn't discuss any of the dilemmas the characters face. Because Ms. Riley doesn't comment on the dilemma Sharon included in the first entry, Sharon probably believes that it is not important. Had Ms. Riley praised Sharon for including her remarks on the dilemmas faced in the first entry, Sharon might have included dilemmas in the second entry.

- Sharon's first entry draws connections to the student's life with her reference to her mother's definition and to her aunt's death. Had Ms. Riley noted how interesting those comments were, Sharon might have included similar comments in the second entry.

- Sharon's first entry engages in introspective speculation when she comments, "I wonder what it felt like." This is a kind of thinking skill Ms. Riley suggests she wants to develop. Had she commented positively about it, Sharon would have been more likely to continue doing this kind of thinking.

- The second entry is a minimal summary and does not give any evidence of Sharon's using critical-thinking skills, such as her ability to figure out Beth's death in the first entry. Had Ms. Riley praised Sharon's ability to think critically to figure out that Beth had died, Sharon would have been more likely to continue using this critical-thinking skill.

- By focusing her comments in response to the October 13 entry largely on matters of routine requirements (title, author, pages read) and on spelling, with only a two-word comment on a personal response, Ms. Riley implies that the routine requirements are much more important than the ability to write an accurate summary or to link aspects of the text with experiences and people in their own lives. Had she focused on the summary and the connections, Sharon would have been more likely to continue developing the skills to address these aspects of the assignment.

Score of 1

The response presents one significant difference between the October 13 and the October 27 entries and offers one appropriate way in which Ms. Riley could help Sharon to meet the teacher's goals, such as those presented in score point 2; or the response presents two significant differences between the October 13 and the October 27 entries with no ways in which Ms. Riley could have responded differently to Sharon.

Score of 0

The response fails to address the question, presents inappropriate differences, or is vague.

Sample Responses and Commentary

Response that would receive a score of 2
In Sharon's second entry, the student includes the kinds of things Ms. Riley says she wants to see when she comments on Sharon's first entry. She gives title and author and pages read, and does include a very short summary. However, she omits any personal connections to the literature or focusing on any dilemmas the characters face because Ms. Riley makes no comment on those aspects of Sharon's first entry. If Ms. Riley had sympathized with Sharon when she gave Ms. Riley what she asked for or praised her for including some of the aspects the teacher requested, Sharon might have included them in the second entry.

Commentary on the above response
The response presents two appropriate and significant differences (the second entry does include all the specific information the teacher says she wants about title, author, and pages read but omits any personal connections to literature or discussion of dilemmas the characters face). It also presents appropriate suggestions for how Ms. Riley might have responded in a way that would have helped Sharon meet the goals. The response receives full credit.

Response that would receive a score of 1
One significant difference is that Sharon stopped sharing ways that the book reminded her of her own life. If Ms. Riley had commented favorably and constructively on the connections Sharon made in the first entry, Sharon might have continued working in this way to achieve the objective. The second difference is that the first entry is a lot longer. If Ms. Riley had praised her for writing a lot, she might have continued developing her fluency in this way.

Commentary on the above response
The response presents one appropriate difference, but then discusses a difference that does not indicate that Sharon is having less success meeting the objectives for the project. The response therefore receives partial credit.

Response that would receive a score of 0
Ms. Riley is really missing an opportunity to help Sharon. Students this age are very sensitive and I suspect Sharon had a pretty negative reaction when she got her literature log back after the first entry. Ms. Riley could profit from a professional development workshop that helps teachers develop effective ways to respond to student logs.

Commentary on the above response

The response, while it makes some valid points, does not address the question which requires an identification of significant differences between the two entries and ways Ms. Riley might help Sharon continue to meet her goals. It therefore receives no credit.

How to Answer Question 4

Question 4

In Document 3, Kenny's conversation with Ms. Riley, Kenny reveals characteristics of himself as a learner that could be used to support his development of literacy skills.

- Identify ONE characteristic of Kenny as a learner, and then suggest ONE strategy Ms. Riley might use to address that characteristic in a way that will support his development of literacy skills.
- Describe how the strategy you suggested addresses the characteristic of Kenny as a learner and how the strategy could support Kenny's development of literacy skills. Base your response on principles of varied instructional strategies for different learners and of human development.

Step 1. Think about what is being asked.

In the space below, state in your own words what you think the question is asking.

Compare your impression of what is being asked with the explanation below.
The question asks for

- *one* characteristic of Kenny as a learner and *one* strategy Ms. Riley might use to address that characteristic to support his development of literacy skills
- descriptions of how the strategy addresses the characteristics of Kenny as a learner and supports development of his literacy skills

Step 2. Think about what is being assessed.

- Human development
- Varied instructional strategies for different kinds of learners

These two domains are both very important in understanding students and their needs and in planning instruction to meet those needs. Both are directly involved in understanding Kenny and his needs as a learner and in planning strategies to meet his specific needs.

Step 3. Write your response.

In the space below, write what you consider to be a response that directly addresses the question.

Step 4. Reflect on your response in light of the scoring guide, sample responses, and commentary.

ETS Scoring Guide for Question 4

Score of 2

The response identifies and describes one appropriate characteristic of Kenny as a learner and one appropriate strategy Ms. Riley can use to address that characteristic and support the development of Kenny's literacy skills.

- Kenny loves to read, but doesn't want to take the time to write about what he's read. Ms. Riley might make the writing more creative to match Kenny's interest in books. She could ask Kenny to think about what makes a book interesting to him, thereby supporting his critical thinking, or might provide an alternate mode, such as a tape-recording, for Kenny to record his thoughts.
- Ms. Riley might ask Kenny to imitate the plot of a book he likes in order to create his own story. That would link Kenny's love of reading with writing that would indicate what Kenny takes from the books he reads.
- Ms. Riley might ask Kenny to write a review of one of the books he likes so that others in the class will want to read it. That links Kenny's writing to a purpose supported by his inherent interest in books.
- Ms. Riley might give Kenny some reviews or analysis of the books he's read and ask him to analyze whether the reviews or analysis are accurate from his perspective. That will give Kenny insights into the act of reviewing as well as reading books.
- Because Kenny is intrigued by books, Ms. Riley might ask Kenny to select a small group and act out a scene from one of his favorite books. That will allow Kenny to develop a more critical perspective on a book he's reading.
- Ms. Riley might ask Kenny to search the Internet for articles about an author Kenny admires. She might then have him analyze the book from the perspective of the author. This activity might spark Kenny's interest in the connections between an author's life and some of the characters in her or his books.

Score of 1

The response identifies and describes one appropriate characteristic of Kenny as a learner such as those presented in score point 2, but does not present a strategy Ms. Riley can use to address that characteristic and support the development of Kenny's literacy skills, or identifies an appropriate characteristic of Kenny as a learner and a strategy Ms. Riley could use to address that characteristic, but does not sufficiently describe either the characteristic or the strategy.

Score of 0

The response fails to address the question, presents inappropriate identification of characteristics of Kenny as a learner and strategies to address those characteristics, or is vague.

Sample Responses and Commentary

Response that would receive a score of 2

Because Kenny is an avid reader, Ms. Riley needs to think of a strategy that might engage Kenny in critical thinking that can enhance his literacy. Since one of her long-term goals includes developing speaking abilities, she might offer him the opportunity to tape-record his comments about the book, moving the apparent focus from writing to talking about the book—something it appears he likes to do. To address her goal of developing critical-thinking skills, she might give him a few analyses of books by reviewers and ask Kenny to support or refute the reviews from his reading of the book.

Commentary on the above response

The response begins by identifying an appropriate characteristic of Kenny as a learner, and then presents and describes an appropriate strategy Ms. Riley might use to address that characteristic in a way that would address her first long-term goal. The response receives full credit, score point 2.

Response that would receive a score of 1

Kenny is a very interesting learner. He obviously loves to read; Ms. Riley comments she's seen him read at least two books a week, and he himself says he just reads "for fun." But he candidly admits he doesn't "read to get credit," and so he isn't concerned about the assignment Ms. Riley has given or about meeting her objectives. Students such as Kenny are a challenge: he loves reading (good for him!) but doesn't want to jump through Ms. Riley's hoops. She has to be creative to figure out how to challenge him!

Commentary on the above response

The response analyzes Kenny as a learner with appropriate commentary. However, simply saying that Ms. Riley "has to be creative to figure out how to challenge him" is not sufficient to meet the second requirement of the question. The response therefore receives partial credit.

Response that would receive a score of 0

There isn't really enough information given here to do an analysis of Kenny as a learner, or to suggest how his teacher could work to support his development of literacy skills. A much fuller presentation of his work, his thoughts, and his interactions with his teacher and the other students would be needed.

Commentary on the above response

As was pointed out earlier, saying that "more information is needed" is not an acceptable response or a viable excuse for not responding to the question. While it is true that more information could and would be sought to do a full analysis of Kenny or a complete plan for addressing his needs, there is sufficient information in the short conversation presented to warrant "one characteristic of Kenny as a learner" and one strategy to address that characteristic.

How to Answer Question 5

Question 5

Review Ms. Riley's long-term goals at the beginning of Document 1, the Literature Log Project Plan.

- Select TWO long-term goals, and for each goal, identify one strategy Ms. Riley might use to expand the literature log unit beyond the stated assignment and assessment plan to address the goal.
- Explain how the use of each strategy you identified could expand the literature log unit to address the selected goal. Base your response on principles of planning instruction and/or language development and acquisition.

Step 1. Think about what is being asked.

In the space below, state in your own words what you think the question is asking.

Compare your impression of what is being asked with the explanation below.
  The question asks for

- *two* goals
- for *each* goal, explanation of one strategy to expand the literature log

Step 2. Think about the categories being assessed.

- Planning instruction
- Language development and acquisition

Both planning instruction and planning strategies to support the language learning of all students are important skills. The literature log is a part of Ms. Riley's literacy program; by asking you to plan strategies she might use to expand the literature log assignment, the question directly assesses both categories.

Step 3. Write your response.

In the space below, write what you consider to be a response that directly addresses the question.

Step 4. Reflect on your response in light of the scoring guide, sample responses, and commentary.

Score of 2

The response selects two long-term goals and identifies an appropriate strategy to address each goal with explanations of how the use of each strategy could address the selected goal, such as the following:

- One goal is to develop speaking and listening abilities. To develop these skills, Ms. Riley can include activities such as having students report aloud about the books read while other students note what is important about each and ask questions about the books.

- One goal is to develop critical-thinking skills. Ms. Riley could have included in her assessment plan a rubric that would provide a means for student self-assessment and for her own assessment of the kinds of critical-thinking skills she has included in the assignment.

- One goal is to build a positive classroom community, but this goal is never addressed. Ms. Riley might form cooperative groups based on principles of teaching social skills and have the groups read members' literature logs, identifying positive ways to see the differences in how members of the group responded to what they read.

- One goal is to address students' individual differences. Ms. Riley could read all the logs and find significant differences among the ways students responded. She could then present those examples to the class and conduct a class discussion about how interesting and valuable those differences are.

- To address the goal of linking aspects of a text with experiences and people in their own lives, Ms. Riley could use an overhead projector to display features of the logs that presented intriguing ways in which individuals made connections between what they read and their own lives. In this case, she should check first with students to be sure she has not invaded their privacy. The class could discuss those connections and offer further suggestions about how individual class members might respond.

- To address the goal of improving reading, writing, speaking, and listening, Ms. Riley can have each student maintain a folder of literature log entries for several weeks and select two for public presentation. The student could then rewrite each entry to present to the class in published form. This adds audience and purpose to the assignment.

- To address the goal of improving speaking and listening skills, Ms. Riley can form groups and have students present an oral summary of their book and why it was important to them. They can also explain to their group why others might want to read the book as well. Each group could then select one or two books for presentation to the whole class. The activity could develop speaking and listening skills and generate greater interest in books that students might want to read.

- To address the goal of building a positive classroom community, Ms. Riley can form groups of those who have read the same or similar books. She could then have the members of the group explain some of the individual connections they made to what happened in the book, or comment about one or two things each finds interesting about each student's response to the characters. By sharing responses to books, students build a sense of a community.
- To address the goal of building critical-thinking skills, Ms. Riley can ask students who identified interesting dilemmas in books to explain what was problematic for the characters and why. Ms. Riley could use these dilemmas to begin a class discussion about human dilemmas all people face.
- To address her long-term goal of building a positive classroom community and her objectives of both linking reading to experience and developing summary writing skills, Ms. Riley can form response groups in which students share their logs. She could establish the principle that there are to be no "put downs," and that students must find one or two positive things to say about the connections others draw to the texts or about the summaries.

Score of 1

The response selects two long-term goals and, for each, identifies but does not explain an appropriate strategy to address the goal, such as those presented in score point 2, or selects one long-term goal and identifies and explains an appropriate strategy to address the goal.

Score of 0

The response fails to address the question, presents inappropriate goals and strategies, or is vague.

Sample Responses and Commentary

Response that would receive a score of 2

Ms. Riley has many valuable long-term goals that could be developed through additional activities or assessments. For example, one of her goals is to build a positive classroom community. To address this goal, she could create cooperative groups and have students respond in positive ways to the connections other students have made between their books and their own lives or to the summaries that are written. If several students have read the same book, she could have them share their summaries and personal responses, developing a sense of the commonality of their reading and personal experiences. Another of her goals is to address students' individual differences. After checking with students to be sure they are comfortable with sharing, she might discuss or present on an overhead projector a variety of kinds of connections students make between books and their own lives, to show how each reader responds in ways that are unique.

Commentary on the above response

The response presents two goals and fully discusses an appropriate strategy Ms. Riley might use to expand the literature log to implement the goal. The response fully and appropriately addresses the question and receives full credit.

Response that would receive a score of 1

One of her goals is to build critical-thinking skills. To address this goal, Ms. Riley can ask students who came up with some interesting dilemmas in books to explain what was difficult for the characters and to tell why they thought the situation was difficult. Ms. Riley could use these dilemmas to start a class discussion about problems all people face. In this way, she would be addressing one of her important goals and at the same time extending the lesson.

Commentary on the above response

The response only partially addresses the requirements of the question. The question calls for an identification of "two goals" and one strategy for each that can be used to expand the literature log unit. The response identifies only one goal and does present a strategy to address it in a way that would expand the unit. The response receives partial credit.

Response that would receive a score of 0

I don't think it would really be a good idea to try to expand the literature log unit at this time. Third-grade teachers have an enormous amount of material to cover. For each subject, there are state, district, and school standards of objectives to meet. If she adds to this unit, she is going to be taking away time and emphasis from other subjects like social studies, mathematics, or science. All of these need a lot of instructional time. I think she should leave well enough alone.

Commentary on the above response

Arguing with the question is not an acceptable way to respond. While the points made in the response may be seen as having some validity, it must be assumed that Ms. Riley could expand the unit within the time she has for her language arts program. Because the response does not address the question, it receives no credit.

How to Answer Question 6

Question 6

Review the two objectives of the Literature Log Project Plan included in Document 1. Suppose that at the end of the project, as a culminating activity, Ms. Riley wants her students to use their literature logs to help them do a self-assessment of the two objectives.

- For each of the TWO project objectives described in Document 1, suggest one assignment Ms. Riley could give the students that would serve as a self-assessment.
- For each assignment you suggested, describe how Ms. Riley's students could use it as a self-assessment. Base your response on principles of effective assessment.

Step 1. Think about what is being asked.

In the space below, state in your own words what you think the question is asking.

Compare your impression of what is being asked with the explanation below.

The question asks for two proposed assignments:

- *one* to serve as a self-assessment for students based on the *first* objective mentioned in Document 1
- *one* to serve as a self-assessment for students based on the *second* objective mentioned in Document 1

Step 2. Think about the categories being evaluated.

- Assessment

Part of the assessment domain involves teaching students how to assess their own work. Self-assessment can help students make connections between learning objectives and their own performance.

Step 3. Write your response.

In the space below, write what you consider to be a response that directly addresses the question.

Step 4. Reflect on your response in light of the scoring guide, sample responses, and commentary.

ETS Scoring Guide for Question 6

Score of 2

The response presents an explanation of two appropriate culminating activities: one that will help students do a self-assessment of the first objective and one that will help students do a self-assessment of the second objective, such as the following:

Objective 1

- She could have them select three entries that they believe meet the objective of linking aspects of their reading with experiences and people in their own lives. For each entry, explain why it meets the objective.
- She could have them write a new paragraph about a character or event that they felt strongly connected to, and explain why.
- She could have them select one entry that they feel they could improve in terms of making connections to their own lives and could have them write a revision and one entry that they feel meets the objective and tell why.
- She could have the class develop a rubric for evaluating entries in terms of making connections between reading and personal experience, and use the rubric to evaluate selected entries.

Objective 2

- She could have the class develop a rubric for an effective summary and have individuals use it to evaluate three of their own entries.
- She could have each student read five or six of their summaries and write a reflective assessment about the strengths or weaknesses she or he sees in the summaries.
- She could have the class write a summary of a short selection they all read and use a class-developed rubric to have them evaluate their own summaries.

Score of 1

The response presents an explanation of one appropriate culminating activity that will help students do a self-assessment of either the first objective or the second objective, such as those presented in score point 2; or the response suggests two culminating activities related to the objectives but does not describe how the students could use them as self-assessments.

Score of 0

The response fails to address the question, presents inappropriate culminating activities, or is vague.

Response that would receive a score of 2

For both objectives, her activity for the students to do self-assessment could begin with the development of a rubric for evaluating success in meeting the objective. Students could work together to develop both rubrics. Then, for the first objective, she could have students select three of their own entries and use the rubric to evaluate how well each student met the objective. For the second objective, Ms. Riley could have the students write a summary of a new selection, and then use the rubric to evaluate how well they have learned to write an effective summary.

Commentary on the above response

The response presents one appropriate assignment for each objective. Although the response begins by explaining something that both activities could have in common, it includes separate appropriate activities for each of the two objectives. It receives full credit.

Response that would receive a score of 1

Following up with a culminating self-assessment is a very good way to end the project. It will help students internalize what they have learned. There are many different activities she could use. One is that she could have them select one entry that they feel could be improved in terms of making connections to their own lives. They could then write a revision and one entry that they feel meets the objective and tell why. Doing these two things would really help them take a fresh look at what it means to connect literature to their own lives.

Commentary on the above response

The response suggests that there are two activities, but they address only one of the objectives. The question specifically calls for one activity for each of the two objectives. It therefore receives only partial credit.

Response that would receive a score of 0

In a sense, it's a very good idea for her to do a culminating activity. But, on the other hand, it's very possible that by now the students have learned everything there is to learn about writing literature logs. They have been doing it for several months, and I have found that students of this age get tired of activities after a while. I would therefore suggest that she just wrap up the literature logs with a celebration in which she praises them for what they have done well, and then move on to some other aspect of literature study.

Commentary on the above response

The response begins with what appears to be a direct response to the question, but moves off the point and fails to address the question, instead arguing with its premise. Responses that argue with the question are deemed nonresponsive and receive no credit.

PART V

Praxis II: Elementary Education

Your Goals for This Part

- Learn the purpose and format of Praxis Elementary Education Tests.
  - Curriculum, Instruction, and Assessment
  - Curriculum, Instruction, and Assessment (K–5)
  - Content Knowledge
  - Content Area Exercises
- Practice answering real test questions and see what it takes to choose the correct answers.

CHAPTER 17

Elementary Education: Curriculum, Instruction, and Assessment

The test titled: *Elementary Education: Curriculum, Instruction, and Assessment* (Test Code 0011) is designed for prospective teachers of students in the elementary grades. Most people who take the test have completed a bachelor's degree program in elementary/middle school education or have prepared themselves through some alternative certification program. (Note that the test titled *Elementary Education: Curriculum, Instruction, and Assessment K-5,* Test Code 0016, has been discontinued.)

PREPARING FOR THE CURRICULUM, INSTRUCTION, AND ASSESSMENT TEST

Questions on the Curriculum, Instruction, and Assessment test cover the breadth of material a new teacher needs to know and assess knowledge of both principles and processes. Some questions assess basic understanding of curriculum planning, instructional design, and assessment of student learning. Many questions pose particular problems that teachers routinely face in the classroom, and many are based on authentic examples of student work. Although some questions concern general issues, most questions are set in the context of the subject matter most commonly taught in elementary school: reading/language arts, mathematics, science, social studies, fine arts, and physical education.

In developing assessment material for this test, the ETS has worked in collaboration with educators, higher education content specialists, and accomplished practicing teachers to keep the tests updated and representative of current standards.

Elementary Education: Curriculum, Instructions, and Assessment (0011)
Test at a Glance

Time	2 hours	
Format	110 multiple-choice questions	
Content Categories	**Approximate Number of Questions**	**Approximate Percentage of Examination**
I. Reading and Language Arts Curriculum, Instruction, and Assessment	38	35%
II. Mathematics Curriculum, Instruction, and Assessment	22	20%

III. Science Curriculum, Instruction, and Assessment	11	10%
IV. Social Studies Curriculum, Instruction, and Assessment	11	10%
V. Arts and Physical Education Curriculum, Instruction, and Assessment	11	10%
VI. General Information about Curriculum, Instruction, and Assessment	17	15%

Elementary Education: Curriculum, Instruction, and Assessment (K–5) (0016) (*Discontinued*)

Test at a Glance

Time	2 hours	
Format	120 multiple-choice questions	
Content Categories	**Approximate Number of Questions**	**Approximate Percentage of Examination**
I. Reading and Language Arts Curriculum, Instruction, and Assessment	42	35%
II. Mathematics Curriculum, Instruction, and Assessment	24	20%
III. Science Curriculum, Instruction, and Assessment	12	10%
IV. Social Studies Curriculum, Instruction, and Assessment	12	10%
V. Arts and Physical Education Curriculum, Instruction, and Assessment	12	10%
VI. General Information about Curriculum, Instruction, and Assessment	18	15%

The *Elementary Education: Curriculum, Instruction, and Assessment* test may be structured in one of two ways:

- The questions will be grouped into the six content areas listed above (e.g., with all mathematics questions together), and in each content area you will answer questions that measure your understanding of curriculum, instruction, and assessment.

OR

- The questions will be grouped into three areas—curriculum, instruction, assessment—with content areas mixed throughout the test (e.g., a question about assessment in mathematics might be followed by a question about assessment in music).

You are not allowed to use a calculator during these tests.

Preparing on Your Own

As you use this chapter, set the following tasks for yourself:

- **Become familiar with the test content.** Learn what will be tested. You will find a list of topics covered in the Test at a Glance bulletins available on the Praxis Web site (www.ets.org/praxis).

- **Assess how well you know the content in each area.** After you learn what topics the test contains, you should assess your knowledge in each area. How well do you know the material? In which areas do you need to learn more before you take the test? It is quite likely that you will need to brush up on most of or all the areas. If you encounter material that feels unfamiliar or difficult, mark the pages with sticky notes to remind yourself to spend extra time reviewing these topics.

- **Read the section in this book on multiple-choice questions to sharpen your skills in reading and answering multiple-choice questions.** To succeed on questions of this kind, you must focus carefully on the question, avoid reading things into the question, pay attention to details, and sift patiently through the answer choices.

- **Develop a study plan.** Assess what you need to study and create a realistic plan for studying. You can develop your study plan in any way that works best for you. A Study Plan Sheet is included in this chapter as a possible way to structure your planning. Remember that you will need to allow time to find books and other materials, time to read the materials and take notes, and time to apply your learning to the practice questions.

- **Identify study materials.** Most of the material covered by the test is contained in standard textbooks in the field. If you no longer own the texts you used in your undergraduate course work, borrow texts from friends or from a library. Use standard textbooks and other reliable, professionally prepared materials. Information provided by friends or information obtained from searching the Web is not as uniformly reliable as information found in your textbooks and other relevant course materials.

- **Work through your study plan.** Whether you choose to work alone or with a study group, don't just memorize definitions from books. Instead, prepare to define and discuss the topics in your own words, and make sure you understand the relationships between diverse topics and concepts. If you are working with a group or mentor, you can also try informal quizzes and questioning techniques.

- **Proceed to the practice questions.** Once you have completed your review, you are ready to benefit from the practice questions on page 444. Use the Answers and Explanations to mark the questions you answered correctly and the ones you missed. Read the explanations of the questions you missed and see whether you understand them.

- **Decide whether you need more review.** After you have looked at your results, decide whether there are areas that you need to brush up on before taking the actual test. Go back to your textbooks and reference materials to see if the topics are covered there. You might also go over your questions with a friend or teacher who is familiar with the subjects.

- **Assess your readiness.** Do you feel confident about your level of understanding in each of the subject areas? If not, where do you need more work? If you feel ready, complete the checklist to double-check that you've thought through the details.

Readiness Checklist

- Do you know the testing requirements for your teaching field in the state(s) where you plan to teach?
- Have you followed all the test registration procedures?
- Do you know how long the test will take and the number of questions it contains? Have you considered how you will pace your work?
- Are you familiar with the test directions and the types of questions for the test?
- Are you familiar with the recommended test-taking strategies and tips?
- Have you practiced by working through the practice questions at a pace similar to that of an actual test?
- If you are repeating a Praxis Series Assessment, have you analyzed your previous score report to determine areas in which additional study and test preparation could be useful?

Preparing with a Study Group

There are several advantages to forming a study group with others preparing for the same test.

- Study groups give members opportunities to ask questions and get detailed answers.
- In a group, some members usually have a better understanding of certain topics, while others may be better at other topics. As members take turns explaining concepts to one another, everyone builds self-confidence.
- Because study groups schedule regular meetings, group members study in a more disciplined fashion.

The group should be large enough so that various people can contribute various kinds of knowledge, but small enough so that it stays focused. Often, three to six people makes a good-sized group.

Here are some ways to use this book as part of a study group:

- **Plan the group's study program.** Parts of the Study Plan Sheet on page 443 can help to structure your group's study program. By filling out the first five columns and sharing the work sheets, everyone will learn more about your group's mix of abilities and about the resources (such as textbooks) that members can share with the group. In the sixth column ("Dates planned for study of content"), you can create an overall schedule for your group's study program.

- **Plan individual group sessions.** At the end of each session, the group should decide what specific topics will be covered at the next meeting and who will present each topic.
- **Prepare your presentation for the group.** When it's your turn to present, prepare something that's more than a lecture. Write five to ten original questions to pose to the group. Writing test questions can help you better understand the topics covered as well as the types of questions you will encounter on the test. It will also give other members of the group extra practice at answering questions.
- **Take the practice test together.** The idea of the practice test is to simulate an actual administration of the test, so scheduling a test session with the group will add to the realism and will also help boost everyone's confidence.

Whether you decide to study alone or with a group, remember that the best way to prepare is to have an organized plan. The plan should set goals based on specific topics and skills that you need to learn, and it should commit you to a realistic set of deadlines for meeting these goals. Stick with your plan, and you will accomplish your goals on schedule.

Study Plan Sheet

Content covered on test.	How well do I know the content?	What materials do I have for studying this content?	What materials do I need for studying this content?	Where could I find the materials I need?	Dates planned for study of content.	Dates completed.

The questions that follow illustrate the kinds of questions on the test. They are not, however, representative of the entire scope of the test in either content or difficulty. Answers and Explanations follow the question section.

Directions: Each of the questions or statements below is followed by four suggested answers or completions. Select the one that is best in each case.

1. During a unit on folktales, a second-grade teacher wants to help students engage in higher-order thinking skills. After the students read *The Little Red Hen*, the teacher asks the students to justify the Little Red Hen's decision to eat the bread herself. Which of the levels of Bloom's taxonomy does this activity address?

   (A) Application
   (B) Analysis
   (C) Synthesis
   (D) Evaluation

2. As part of a language arts program, a first-grade teacher takes students on field trips, often reads aloud from books, and frequently equips the classroom with pictures and prints. Which of the following student needs is met by all these instructional practices?

   (A) Facilitated social adjustment
   (B) Expanded reading readiness
   (C) Increased motor development
   (D) Improved auditory ability

3. A fourth-grade teacher wants students to find some basic information for a short written report on an American Revolutionary War hero. The students may use encyclopedias, biographical profiles, and the Internet. Which of the following language arts strategies is LEAST likely to be used during this exercise?

   (A) Location of information using alphabetizing skills
   (B) Understanding information using skim-reading skills
   (C) Transcription of information using note-taking skills
   (D) Long-term recall of information using memorization skills

4. At the beginning of the school year, a first-grade teacher observes that a student is unable to use beginning and final consonants correctly while reading. Which of the following is most likely to help the student develop these skills?

   (A) Modeling words in context and teaching decoding skills
   (B) Showing a video of a popular children's story and stopping to discuss words that appear in the story

     (C) Pairing the student with another student who is able to use consonants correctly

     (D) Displaying pictures and corresponding printed words around the room

5. During which of the following stages in the writing process are students most likely to share their writing with the entire class?

     (A) Drafting

     (B) Revising

     (C) Editing

     (D) Publishing

6. At the end of a second-grade reading unit, the teacher reads the following sentences from the response journal of a student in the class:

> I liked the story. The boy wds d good Suh.

The student needs help with which of the following?

     (A) Synonyms

     (B) Antonyms

     (C) Phonics

     (D) Homophones

7. A class has finished reading a novel. Which of the following actions by the teacher is most likely to foster continued interest in reading fiction?

     (A) Calling on students to answer questions about the story's theme and setting

     (B) Having small groups of students discuss what they liked and disliked about the story

     (C) Telling students that there will be a follow-up assignment to compare the story with other stories they have read

     (D) Asking students to prepare a graphic organizer that shows the relationship between story parts

8. A teacher gives students two sets of cards to match. One set contains headlines, and the other contains news articles. Which of the following skills are students most likely to develop as a result of this activity?

     (A) Decoding text

     (B) Recognizing sight vocabulary

     (C) Identifying main ideas

     (D) Using context clues to determine the meaning of words

9. A first-grade student wrote, "R dg is bg n blk" and read aloud: "Our dog is big and black." Which of the following instructional activities is most likely to help the student become a more competent speller?

(A) Discussion of the difference between "our" and "are"
(B) Demonstration of left-to-right movement
(C) Explicit instruction in phonics and phonemic awareness
(D) Reviews of the rules of capitalization and punctuation

10. Some teachers require their students to give oral book reports. Which of the following is the best rationale for using oral book reports to motivate students to read?

(A) They provide students with practice in making formal presentations before a group.
(B) They show that students have read the books and know the plots.
(C) They require students to analyze every book they read.
(D) They encourage students to share their reading experiences with others.

Answers and Explanations

1. In asking the students to "justify the Little Red Hen's decision," the teacher is helping the students to reason and make judgments and is encouraging them to develop and defend their decisions based on criteria they establish. "Evaluation" is the level of this task. Therefore, choice D is the correct answer.

2. Teachers are expected to understand the relationship of "parts" to "wholes" in the subject they teach and to apply this knowledge in designing learning activities. Although the activities listed in this question have a number of possible benefits for students as part of a language arts program, they are designed to expand readiness for reading. Because all are "prereading" activities, choice B is the correct answer.

3. This question asks about the language arts strategy least likely to be used by students during a social studies assignment. All of the possible strategies might be employed, but the question asks which "is LEAST likely to be used." Although memorization skills can be important, the assignment here is to write a short report, so long-term recall by commitment to memory is not the goal. Therefore, choice D is the correct answer.

4. Choices B and D may be appropriate for building interest in reading and enhancing reading readiness. C might be appropriate for practicing new skills. Only choice A combines teaching of the needed skills with meaningful contexts in which to use them. The correct answer, therefore, is choice A.

5. During the publishing phase of the writing process, students make their writing public by reading, putting the writings in a booklet, and so on. The correct answer, therefore, is choice D.

6. In the scenario presented here, the student has confused the word "son" (which is the desired word) with the word "sun," a word that sounds the same. Homophones are words that sound alike but have different meanings and spellings. Therefore, choice D is the correct answer.

7. Teachers must always be aware of the consequences of the learning activities they select. In this question, for example, the teacher might have chosen any one of these activities to follow up the reading of the novel. However, discussion in class about what students liked and disliked about the story is the most likely of the options to foster continued interest in the reading of fiction. Therefore, choice B is the correct answer.

8. This question asks about the skills that are most likely to be developed as a result of a specific activity. Another way to look at this question is to ask: "What is the goal of this assignment?" Identifying main ideas is the likely result of this activity. Newspaper headlines usually summarize the main ideas of the articles they describe. Choice C is therefore the correct answer.

9. Analyzing student work can provide valuable insights into what a student can do and what additional work and activities are needed. A teacher needs to select developmentally appropriate strategies and adjust instructions accordingly to meet the needs of individual students. In this question, a first-grade student writes the words phonetically, as they are heard and not as they are spelled. Of all the options presented, "Explicit instruction in phonics and phonemic awareness" is most likely to assist the student in becoming a better speller. Therefore, choice C is the correct answer.

10. This question asks about oral book reports and the rationale for requiring students to present their reports orally. Note that it does not ask about other positive outcomes from oral presentations, but asks only which is the most likely motivator for reading. Oral book reports encourage students to share enjoyable reading experiences with others. This is a prime motivator both for the students who present reports and for the students who hear them. Therefore, choice D is the correct answer.

CHAPTER 18

Elementary Education: Content Knowledge

The *Elementary Education: Content Knowledge* test is designed for prospective teachers of children in primary through upper elementary school grades. The 120 multiple-choice questions focus on four major subject areas: language arts/reading, mathematics, social studies, and science. Test questions are arranged by subject area.

PREPARING FOR THE CONTENT KNOWLEDGE TEST

The Content Knowledge test is not intended to be a test of your teaching skills. Rather, it is intended to demonstrate that you possess fundamental knowledge in the subject areas you will be required to teach.

Elementary Education: Content Knowledge
Test at a Glance

Time	2 hours	
Format	120 multiple-choice questions, scientific or four-function calculator use permitted	
Content Categories	**Approximate Number of Questions**	**Approximate Percentage of Examination**
I. Language Arts	30	25%
II. Mathematics	30	25%
III. Social Studies	30	25%
IV. Science	30	25%

Advice from the Experts

The test makers recommend the following approach to prepare for the test.

- **Become familiar with the test content.** Learn what will be tested in the four sections of the test. Consult the Study Topics section of the Test at a Glance bulletin available at the *Praxis* Web site.
- **Assess how well you know the content in each area.** It is likely that you will need to study in most of or all the four content areas. After you learn what the test contains, assess your knowledge in each area. How well do you know the material? In which areas do you need to learn more before you take the test?

- **Develop a study plan.** Assess what you need to study and create a realistic plan for studying. You can develop your study plan in any way that works best for you. The Study Plan Sheet on page 443 is one possible way to structure your planning. Remember that this is a licensure test and covers a great deal of material. Plan to review carefully. You will need to allow time to find the books and other materials, time to read the material and take notes, and time to go over your notes.

- **Identify study materials.** Most of the material covered by the test is contained in standard introductory textbooks in each of the four fields. If you do not own an introductory text in each area, borrow one or more from friends or from a library. You should also obtain a copy of your state's standards for the subject areas for elementary-grade students. (One way to find these standards quickly is to go to the Web site for your state's Department of Education.) The textbooks used in elementary classrooms may also prove useful to you, since they also present the material you need to know. Rely on standard school and college introductory textbooks and other professionally prepared materials, rather than on information provided by friends or from searching the Web. Neither of these sources is as uniformly reliable as textbooks.

- **Work through your study plan.** You may want to work alone, or you may find it more helpful to work with a group or with a mentor. Be able to define and discuss the topics in your own words rather than memorizing definitions from books. If you are working with a group or mentor, you can also try informal quizzes and questioning techniques.

- **Proceed to the practice questions.** Once you have completed your review, you are ready to benefit from the Real Practice Questions starting on page 451.

- **Answer the Real Practice Questions at the end of this chapter.** Make your own test-taking conditions as similar to actual testing conditions as you can. Work on the practice questions in a quiet place without distractions. Remember that the practice questions are only examples of the way the topics are covered in the test. The test you take will have different questions.

- **Score the practice questions.** Go through the detailed answers in Answers and Explanations, and mark the questions you answered correctly and the ones you missed. Look over the explanations of the questions you missed and see if you understand them.

- **Decide whether you need more review.** After you have looked at your results, decide if there are areas that you need to brush up on before taking the actual test. (The practice questions are grouped by topic, which may help you to spot areas of particular strength or weakness.) Go back to your textbooks and reference materials to see if the topics are covered there. You might also want to go over your questions with a friend or teacher who is familiar with the subject.

- **Assess your readiness.** Do you feel confident about your level of understanding in each of the subject areas? If you feel ready, complete the checklist on page 451 to double-check that you've thought through the details.

REAL QUESTIONS FOR PRACTICE

The questions that follow indicate the kinds of questions in the test. They are not, however, representative of the entire scope of the test in either content or difficulty. Answers with explanations follow the questions.

Directions: Each of the questions or statements below is followed by four suggested answers or completions. Select the one that is best.

I. Language Arts/Reading

1. Which of the following is an example of internal conflict?

    (A) "All the way home, Emilio felt angry with himself. Why couldn't he have spoken up at the meeting? Why was he always so shy?"

    (B) "Juanita and Marco disagreed about where they should take the money they had found."

    (C) "In the high winds, the crew was barely able to keep the sails from dipping sideways. Each time the wind accelerated, the crew almost lost the boat."

    (D) "Celine struggled to walk through the cold, blowing wind."

Question 2 is based on the following poem.

The fallen leaves are cornflakes
That fill the lawn's wide dish,
And night and noon
The wind's a spoon
That stirs them with a swish.

Excerpted from "December Leaves" in Don't
Ever Cross a Crocodile by *Kaye Starbird.*
Copyright © 1963, 1991 Kaye Starbird.

2. Which of the following devices or figures of speech appears most frequently in the poem?

    (A) Foreshadowing
    (B) Personification
    (C) Metaphor
    (D) Hyperbole

We came back to the city Labor Day Monday—us
and a couple million others—traffic crawling, a
hot day, the windows practically closed up tight to
keep Cat in. I sweated, and then cat hairs
stuck to me and got up my nose. Considering
everything, Pop acted quite mild.

I met a kid up at the lake in Connecticut who had skin-diving equipment. He let me use it one day when Mom and Pop were off sight-seeing. Boy, this has fishing beat hollow! I found out there's a skin-diving course at the Y, and I'm going to begin saving up for the fins and mask and stuff. Pop won't mind forking out for the Y membership, because he'll figure it's character building.

Meanwhile, I'm wondering if I can get back up to Connecticut again one weekend while the weather's still warm, and I see that Rosh Hashanah falls on a Monday and Tuesday this year, the week after school opens. Great. So I ask this kid— Kenny Wright—if I can maybe come visit him that weekend so I can do some more skin diving.

  I. First-person narrative
 II. Use of slang
III. Use of dialect
IV. Anthropomorphism

3. The selection contains which of the above?

  (A) I and II only
  (B) II and IV only
  (C) I, III, and IV only
  (D) I, II, III, and IV

II. Mathematics

4. Which of the following numbers is least?

  (A) 0.103
  (B) 0.1041
  (C) 0.1005
  (D) 0.11

5. The Statue of Liberty casts a shadow 37 meters long at the same time that a vertical 5-meter pole nearby casts a shadow that is 2 meters long. The height, in meters, of the Statue of Liberty is within which of the following ranges?

  (A) 115 m to 120 m
  (B) 105 m to 110 m
  (C) 90 m to 95 m
  (D) 60 m to 65 m

III. Social Studies

6. What major geographic feature in North America separates the rivers and streams that flow toward the Pacific Ocean from those that flow toward the Atlantic Ocean?

(A) Appalachian Mountains
(B) Continental Divide
(C) Great Plains
(D) San Andreas Fault

IV. Science

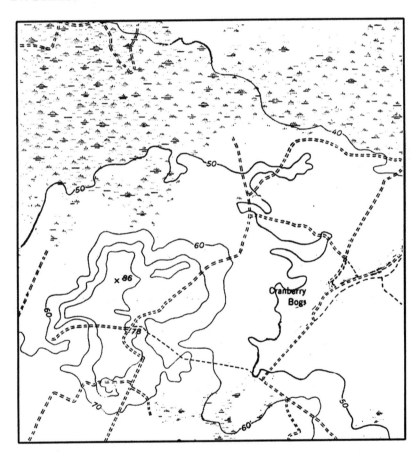

7. What do the solid lines on the map above represent?

(A) Levels of snow accumulation
(B) Lines above which certain trees do not grow
(C) Elevation of land above sea level
(D) The advance of glaciers in the region

8. "As altitude increases, atmospheric pressure decreases, but not at a constant rate." Which of the following graphs best represents this relationship?

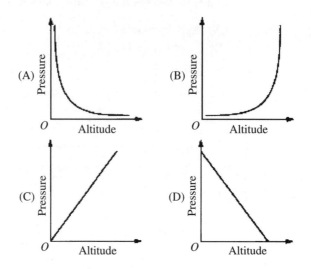

Question 9 refers to the following model.

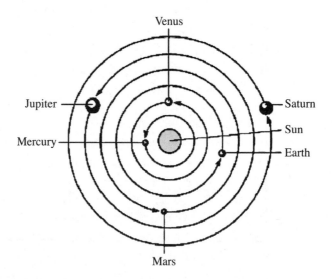

9. A model of the solar system is shown above. Which of the following is LEAST accurately shown in the model?

(A) The relative distance of each planet from the Sun
(B) The order of the planets from nearest to the Sun to farthest from the Sun
(C) The direction of the planetary orbits
(D) The shapes of the planetary orbits

10. A rock picked up on a hillside was found to contain tiny pieces of seashells. Which of the following is the best explanation of how this rock was formed?

(A) It was formed when sediments sank to the bottom of an ancient sea and were subjected to great pressure for long periods of time.

(B) It was formed on or near Earth's surface from magma or lava that flowed during a volcanic eruption.

(C) It was formed when minerals deep inside Earth were subjected to great heat and pressure.

(D) It was formed by seafloor spreading and erosion of the mid-ocean ridge deep in the ocean.

Answers and Explanations

1. This question asks you to recognize an example of a particular literary element. Internal conflict is a struggle between opposing forces in the mind of a single character. Choice A is the only choice where conflict is taking place in the mind of a character; accordingly, choice A is the correct answer.

2. This question asks you to apply your knowledge of figures of speech. A metaphor is a figure of speech that vividly describes a thing by identifying it directly with something else (for example, in line 4, "The wind's a spoon"). In line 1, the poet identifies fallen leaves with cornflakes. In line 2, the poet identifies the lawn with a wide dish. In line 4, the poet identifies the wind with a spoon. Therefore choice C is the correct answer.

3. This question asks you to apply your knowledge of narrative, structural, and stylistic elements to the selection. The narrator constantly says "I," and so the selection is written in first-person narrative. The narrator also uses slang (for example, "this has fishing *beat hollow*!" and "forking out for the Y membership"). There is no particular dialect represented, nor is the cat in the passage portrayed anthropomorphically—that is, as having human qualities. The correct answer, therefore, is choice A.

4. This question tests your knowledge of decimal values. Without the decimal, 1041 would be the greatest number and 11 would be the least, but because these are decimals, the position in relation to the decimal point is crucial in determining the value. It is helpful to work from left to right to determine which number is least. In this case, 0.1005 is the least number, and choice C is the correct answer. Another way to approach this kind of problem is to add a zero to the end of 0.103 in choice A, and two zeros to the end of 0.11 in choice D so that all four choices represent so many ten-thousandths. This does not change the numbers' values, but makes it easier to determine that choice D is the greatest, being equal to 1,100 ten-thousandths, and choice C is the least, being equal to 1,005 ten-thousandths. Again, choice C is the correct answer.

5. This question can be solved by setting up a proportion. The ratio between the height of the Statue of Liberty and the length of its shadow is equal to the ratio between the height of the pole and the length of its shadow. The proportion will look like this (where L represents the height of the Statue of Liberty):

$$\frac{L}{37} = \frac{5}{2}$$

Multiplying both sides by 37 and then simplifying both sides of the equation give you $L = 92.5$ m. Note that other proportions can be set up, such as: Statue height *(L)* divided by pole height (5 meters) equals statue shadow length (37 meters) divided by pole shadow length (2 meters). This will also give the correct result. Therefore, choice C is the correct answer.

6. This question tests your knowledge of important geographic features of North America. The Continental Divide is the series of mountain ridges extending from Alaska to Mexico that forms the watershed of North America. Most of the Divide runs along peaks of the Rocky Mountains. In the United States, it is often called the Great Divide. The correct answer, therefore, is choice B.

7. This question asks you to identify the purpose of a feature in a common topological map. This kind of map has contour lines, one line for each major level of elevation. All the land at the same elevation is connected by a line. These lines often form circles or ovals—one inside the other. If contour lines are very close together, the surface is steep. If the lines are spread apart, the land is flat or rises very gradually. The correct answer is choice C.

8. In this question, you are asked to interpret graphs and match the correct graph with a relationship expressed in words. Choices B and C are wrong, because they show that as altitude increases (i.e., left to right), pressure *increases* rather than decreases. Choice D is wrong because, although pressure does decrease (i.e., high to low), the relationship is linear and therefore *constant* rather than not constant. Choice A shows that as altitude increases pressure decreases, but not at a constant rate: the degree of decrease gets smaller as altitude increases. The correct answer, therefore, is choice A.

9. This question asks you to put together your knowledge of the solar system with a simple model representing part of the solar system. Models such as this are often found in textbooks, and it is important to distinguish what each model represents well and what each one represents poorly. In this model, the order of the planets going outward from the Sun is correct, as is the direction of the planetary orbits. The shapes of the planetary orbits are represented by circles. While the orbits are actually elliptical, the eccentricities of most of the orbits are so small that they are nearly circular. Even in a correctly scaled diagram, the small elongations of the orbits may not be discernable, thus the circular representation is close to being accurate. The relative distance of each planet from the Sun is inaccurate, since the inner four planets are significantly more closely spaced than the two outer planets shown. The correct answer, therefore, is choice A.

10. This question asks you to apply your knowledge of rock formation and the processes of Earth's history to a single sample, a rock containing tiny pieces of seashells. The presence of seashells in a rock on a hillside indicates that the hillside was under water many years ago. During the time that the ancient sea existed, shells, which are the "houses" of sea creatures, would have fallen to the seabed when the animals died. The pressure of the water over very long periods of time would have compacted and cemented the shells and sediment into rocks that were later exposed when the sea dried up. The correct answer, therefore, is choice A.

CHAPTER 19

Elementary Education: Content Area Exercises

The *Praxis Elementary Education: Content Area Exercises* test is designed to measure how well prospective teachers of students in the elementary grades can respond to extended exercises that require thoughtful, written responses. The exercises pose challenging, complex problems to assess examinees' in-depth understanding of elementary education.

The test is designed to reflect current standards for knowledge, skills, and abilities in teaching elementary education. ETS works in collaboration with teacher educators, higher education content specialists, and accomplished practicing teachers in the field of education to keep the tests updated and representative of current standards.

PREPARING FOR THE CONTENT AREA EXERCISES TEST

The *Elementary Education: Content Area Exercises* test consists of four essay exercises set in the context of a subject area (or integrated subject areas) and in the context of a classroom situation. The essays are graded on how well they answer all parts of the exercise and demonstrate understanding of the subject matter and pedagogy required by the exercise.

Elementary Education: Content Area Exercises

Test at a Glance

Time	2 hours	
Format	Four 30-minute exercises pose problems requiring extended responses.	
Content Categories	Approximate Number of Questions	Approximate Percentage of Examination
I. Reading/Language Arts	1	25%
II. Mathematics	1	25%
III. Science or Social Studies	1	25%
IV. Interdisciplinary Instruction	1	25%

The *Elementary Education: Content Area Exercises* test is not intended to test teaching skills. Its main purpose is to ensure that candidates who pass the test possess fundamental knowledge of the subject areas that they may be required to teach in elementary school.

Preparing on Your Own

If you are working by yourself to prepare for the *Elementary Education: Content Area Exercises* test, you may find it helpful to copy and fill out the Study Plan Sheet on page 443. This work sheet will help you to focus on what topics you need to study most, identify materials that will help you study, and set a schedule for doing the studying.

Preparing with a Study Group

Here are some ways to use this book as part of a study group:

- **Plan the group's study program.** Parts of the Study Plan Sheet can help to structure your group's study program. By filling out the first five columns and sharing the work sheets, everyone will learn more about your group's mix of abilities and about the resources (such as textbooks) that members can share with the group. In the sixth column ("Dates planned for study of content"), you can create an overall schedule for your group's study program.
- **Plan individual group sessions.** At the end of each session, the group should decide what specific topics will be covered at the next meeting and who will present each topic.
- **Prepare your presentation for the group.** When it's your turn to present, prepare two or three original questions to pose to the group. Writing sample test questions can help you better understand the topics covered as well as the types of questions you will encounter on the test. It will also give other members of the group extra practice at answering questions.
- **Take the practice question together.** The idea of the practice questions are to simulate an actual administration of the test, so scheduling a test session with the group will add to the realism and will also help boost everyone's confidence.
- **Learn from the results of the practice questions.** Score each other's responses. Then try to follow the same guidelines that the test scorers use to score each other's responses.

  Be as critical as you can. You're not doing your study partner a favor by letting him or her get away with an answer that does not cover all parts of the question adequately.

  Be specific. Write comments that are as detailed as the comments made in Chapter 16. Indicate *where and how* your study partner is doing a poor job of answering the question. Writing notes in the margins of the response may also help.

Be supportive. Include comments that point out what your study partner got right and that therefore earned points.

Then plan one or more study sessions based on aspects of the questions on which group members performed poorly. For example, each group member might be responsible for rewriting one paragraph of a response in which someone else did an inadequate job of answering the question.

Whether you decide to study alone or with a group, remember that the best way to prepare is to have an organized plan. The plan should set goals based on specific topics and skills that you need to learn, and it should commit you to a realistic set of deadlines for meeting these goals.

REAL QUESTIONS FOR PRACTICE

Question 1

Directions: Read the following scenario and then answer parts (A), (B), and (C) of this question on the lined pages in the space provided.

Scenario: A third-grade class is exploring the theme of friendship in language arts.

One of the stories the class will be reading is *Angelina and Alice* by Katharine Holabird. The book is about friends who help each other learn gymnastic tricks to perform at the town fair. The friends learn that by working together and helping each other, they not only improve their performance but also become closer friends.

Use the story *Angelina and Alice* as the core of a lesson on friendship. Be sure to explain why each activity or technique you suggest is appropriate.

Here is a summary of the story:

> Two young mice meet at school and become friends because they enjoy doing gymnastics. They are both good at most gymnastic tricks, but Alice can do a perfect handstand, while Angelina always falls over when she tries. The other mice in their class laugh at Angelina and call her names, and Alice joins the other mice and doesn't play with Angelina anymore. One day their gymnastics teacher announces that the class will put on a gymnastics show at the town fair and asks the students to practice for the show with a partner. Alice comes up to Angelina and asks her to be her partner. The two mice begin practicing, and Alice teaches Angelina how to do handstands. Angelina and Alice become very good friends again, and all their practicing makes their act the best at the show.

(A) Describe a prereading activity for this third-grade class. The activity should be age-appropriate and should reflect the friendship theme of the book that the students will be reading. The activity you describe should be focused and detailed and should demonstrate an understanding of the principles of reading instruction as well as an understanding of how children learn.

(B) Describe an instructional technique or strategy that you would use during the reading of the story to enhance the children's comprehension. Explain how you would determine whether the strategy did enhance comprehension.

(C) Describe an after-reading activity that would be an extension of the theme of friendship. The activity you describe should be focused and detailed. Carefully explain why you would develop the activity; your explanation should demonstrate an understanding of principles of literacy instruction as well as an understanding of how children learn.

Begin your response to Question 1 here.

(Question 1—*continued*)

(Question 1—*continued*)

(Question 1—*continued*)

Question 2

Directions: Read the following scenario and then answer parts (A), (B), and (C) of this question on the lined pages in the space provided.

Scenario: Suppose that you have a second-grade class with 25 students in a small elementary school. It is the first month of a new school year. Your objective is to teach addition of two- and three-digit numbers without regrouping, but you find that 10 of your students do not know basic addition facts (0 to 18) and do not understand place value. The remaining 15 students know the basic addition facts well and understand place value and would very likely be bored by a lesson in which you reteach these concepts.

(A) Describe three different activities that would help the 10 children who need help with addition facts. The activities should help the children develop conceptual understanding and familiarity with the basic facts as well as the ability to recall the facts with speed and accuracy. Provide examples of what the children would be doing during the activities and, to justify your choices, explain what is known about how children learn mathematics.

(B) Describe three different activities that would help the 10 children who do not understand place value. Provide examples of what the children would be doing during the activities, and explain how you would assess their understanding of place value after they have completed the activities.

(C) Describe two activities that would reinforce and extend the skills of the 15 children who do not need reteaching. Provide examples of what the children would be doing during the activities and, to justify your choices, explain what is known about how children learn mathematics.

Begin your response to Question 2 here.

(Question 2—*continued*)

(Question 2—*continued*)

(Question 2—*continued*)

Sample Responses and Commentary

Question 1

Response that would receive a score of 6

Learning the importance of friendship is vital to any child. I would begin my lesson with the following prereading activity. Together as a class, we would complete a K-W-L chart on the chalkboard. I would write the word "friendship" at the top to designate our area of interest for the length of this unit.

I would allow the children to raise their hands and name one aspect of "friendship" that we know. I would list these under the "K" column. Then we would collectively list the aspects about friendship that we want to know under the column marked "W." Finally, I would explain to the children that the column marked "L" stands for what we have learned through this unit. The children would be asked throughout the length of this unit to keep a personal list of what he/she has learned. At the end of the unit, we would list these on the board together and note how much we had learned. An example of a K-W-L of friendship might be:

Friendship

K	W	L
1. We all have friends	1. Why do we have to be nice to everyone?	1. Kindness is part of kind makes us better friendship and being citizens
2. Friends are kind		

Using a K-W-L chart as a prereading activity would be effective because it gets the children to thinking. Each child has to critically decide what he/she knows about friendship, wants to know, and evaluate what he/she has learned when the entire reading activity is completed. This activity is appropriate because it carries the children through; it foreshadows some of the learning that will take place throughout the unit. It also aids the teacher in knowing exactly where the children's interests lie. Their interests may or may not correlate with the teacher's objectives; however, by knowing their interests, the teacher is given an advantage. She can better keep their attention and promote further comprehension when she incorporates the children's interests into her important objectives.

During the reading of the story, the children need to be reading for comprehension. It is the obligation of the teacher to encourage that this is a main goal for each child. In order to do this, I would have the children read it separately then I would assign the children into groups of four and ask them to complete a list of vital notes from the story. Each child must contribute at least one fact. One child will naturally assume the role of the leader. When the children are finished I would allow them to stay in their groups and orally share with the rest of the class the points they listed. As each group shares, I would point out similarities and differences to the class as they are noticed. We would discuss the completed list as a class.

This during reading activity is appropriate because it is not fully teacher directed. They read the book separately, quietly at first. This enables each to read unintimidated at his/her own pace. In their groups, one child will naturally become the leader. They are not asked to reread the material, implying that they had read the book the first time they were asked. They must each contribute one fact from the book which causes each child to summarize and think critically to decide on what the important aspects of the book were as I list the aspects on the board. By having the compiled list on the board, the visual learners have the material reinforced. As we orally discuss similar and different facts each group gave, the audial learners have the material reinforced. Therefore, the teacher would know that comprehension was enhanced.

After this activity, we would summarize the lesson by allowing each child to write his/her own story about friendship. It could be factual or fiction. By allowing the children to complete their own story, they are reinforcing their reading skills. Reading and writing go hand in hand. They complement each other. The children would be using very high levels of thinking. They have now moved from listing facts to summarizing to applying their knowledge from comprehending the book. We would share these as a class and possibly hang them on the walls or in the hall to show pride in each child's work.

Commentary on the above response

This well-organized and coherent response addresses all three parts of the question and reflects a thorough understanding of the principles of reading instruction. All the activities are developmentally appropriate for third-grade students. The response describes the reading activities in detail and explains how and why each activity enhances students' reading comprehension. The first part of the response (the K-W-L chart) offers a focused activity that presents students with a clear purpose for reading, involves all children, and reflects the friendship theme. The response directly explains how the individual and group strategies used during reading provide for enhanced comprehension. The response also demonstrates how the after-reading summary activity would extend student knowledge and allow the teacher to assess comprehension and reinforce the theme.

Response that would receive a score of 5

Before reading ANGELINA AND ALICE I would ask my students to think of some characteristics that a friend should have. In small groups I would have them share their characteristics with group members and agree on the top five characteristics. I then would ask each group to tell me their five most important characteristics and list them on the board. A discussion of why the listed characteristics are so important in a friend would conclude the prereading activity. I believe this activity is appropriate because it stimulates the children's thoughts on friendship and may introduce a concept.

During the reading of ANGELINA AND ALICE I would pose questions to the students at key times to enhance comprehension. One example may be, "why do you suppose Alice joined in with the others and decided not to be Angelina's friend anymore?" Another may be "what kind of characteristic is Alice showing when she asks Angelina to be her partner for the show?" Yet another may be "Why do you suppose that the two mice had the best act?" Each of these questions should stimulate good conversation about what is happening in the story and therefore should enhance comprehension.

As an extension to the reading I would have the students write about a friend that they might have. Their writing should include some characteristics that they like about the friend and why the characteristics are something the student values in a friend. If they choose I would allow them to write in the form of a letter to that specific friend so that the friend may know as well. Later, in a whole group session, I would ask if anyone would like to share their paper and I would read my own paper about a friend I had. I believe this extension activity is appropriate for the theme of friendship because it asks students to write about their own friend and to reflect on why that friend is special.

Commentary on the above response

All three activities are developmentally appropriate, and the descriptions show a good understanding of the principles of reading instruction. The choice of activities, however, is less directly focused on the specific goals of the unit. The prereading activity—listing the characteristics of a friend—introduces the concept of friendship, but does not explain how the introduction of that concept will assist the students' reading development. Also, the discussion of how the chosen activities reflect the principles of literacy instruction and pedagogy is less well developed than in the response rated a 6. The postreading activity accomplishes the goal of extending the theme through a creative activity that requires higher-order thinking skills. The response, however, does not directly explain why the letter-writing activity contributes to the children's growth or extends their academic and social knowledge. If the activities had been more diverse and the explanations had been better developed, this response would have received a higher score.

Response that would receive a score of 4

Before I read the book to the children I would have them think about what being a friend means and what they think the qualities of a friend are. I would have them write them down and then discuss and share their thoughts as a class. As I read the story I would stop periodically and ask them questions about what was going on in the story, such as "Do you think that those who were laughing at Angelina were her friends? Why or why not?" I would also have them predict what is going to happen at the end of the story. After reading the story we would then discuss what happened in the story. So I could see if they understand it and if they understood the sequence of story beginning, middle and end etc. After we talk about the story and have discussed friendship then they will write their own story about their friend(s) and an experience of how they became friends or something that a friend did for them.

I would develop this activity to enhance the students' writing and have them use their own experiences to relate to the story and what happened in it. This helps them open up about their background/prior knowledge of friendship, the sequence of story and shows them that they can relate stories to their own lives.

Commentary on the above response

This response adequately describes three activities that are developmentally appropriate and enhance students' development, but offers only a partial explanation of why the activities are effective. While an explanation of part (C), the extension of the theme, is provided, similar explanations for parts (A) and (B) would have raised the score. The response also lacks clear paragraph organization to show the distinction between the three separate activities. The response demonstrates an accurate, if limited, understanding of the principles of reading instruction.

Response that would receive a score of 3

I believe that it is very important for children to learn about the interactions between friends and the qualities that promote friendship. As a teacher doing a unit on friendship, I would focus on forming a community of learners that would appreciate and understand the overall theme of friendship.

During the reading of the story Angelina and Alice, I would set up cooperative learning groups. Through these groups children can take control of their own learning and enhance their comprehension of the story. I would choose heterogeneous groups to form small literature circles. In these groups, I would have the children discuss their observations and reflections. The children would be free to discuss the book and form their own understanding. In order to assess this strategy I would observe the groups and make anecdotal notes on their progress. Through this authentic assessment I could gain an understanding as to the level of comprehension that the children had developed from the book.

(C) After reading the book, I would have the children take part in an interesting, interactive learning activity. The children would be instructed to interview people in their families, communities, etc. to find out what qualities people look for in a friend. This is important for children to see the many commonalities that form the basis of a friendship. After the children have interviewed several people, I would call the class together and discuss their findings. As a group we would list and discuss the qualities of friendship found. The class would then be broken into several groups to develop an advertisement for a friend. This advertisement should include the specific details that one would look for in a friend. After the students have developed ideas, they will be able to complete their projects with any necessary materials. The groups will then be able to share with the class their advertisements. Through this activity, children will see the basic fundamental qualities that form a friendship.

Commentary on the above response

This response does not provide a prereading activity or explanation for part (A). The omission of this part automatically limits the score to 3 or a below. The reading activity for part (B) is adequate, although more explanation of the activity would help clarify its instructional purpose. The activity described for part (C), extension of the theme, reflects a good understanding of principles of learning and human growth and development. Unfortunately, the overall score can be no more than 3 because part (A) is missing.

Response that would receive a score of 2

The prereading activity would be for the students to go to the library and check out a book relating to a friendship. When the students return to class, they will have 20–25 minutes to read their book silently. After the students have read their books, they will tell the class the title of their book, what the book is about, and why they chose that book. Then the class as a group will discuss the meaning of the word "friendship". Students will tell who their best friends are and how long they have been friends. This activity will develop listening skills and cooperating learning.

The teacher will have 2 students in the class to play the role of best friends. One friend will say something to hurt the other one's feelings. Then that student will tell how she is feeling and why did it hurt her feelings. Then the class will have the other student say something nice to her to make her feel better. This demonstrates just because they are your best friend they still have feelings too.

Commentary on the above response

The response omits both parts (B) and (C), and part (A) is answered only partially. The prereading activity described reflects a limited understanding of reading instruction at the third-grade level. Because of these omissions and lack of demonstrated knowledge of reading pedagogy, no score above 2 can be awarded.

Response that would receive a score of 1

(A) The prereading activity would be to ask students their knowledge on gymnastics. This would be appropriate because third graders love to move around.

(B) The instructional technique would be to "act out." I would have a number of selected students to act like gymnasts. This would give the students a visual idea of the story.

(C) The technique would be a discussion with the students. This is the only idea I can come to you with as far as postreading.

Commentary on the above response

The response does not adequately answer any part of the question, and demonstrates a serious lack of understanding about reading instruction at the third-grade level. The activity for part (A) focuses on neither reading nor friendship, and the explanation provided does not demonstrate knowledge of reading pedagogy. The activity for part (B) would lead to serious classroom management difficulties and raises possible safety issues. The activity for part (C) is not clearly defined or explained. Because of the inappropriateness of the activities and lack of supporting details, no score above a 1 can be awarded.

Question 2

Response that would receive a score of 6

We will now look at scored responses to Question 2 and see comments from the scoring leader about why each response received the score it did.

(A) The children need to understand what the abstract numbers represent before they can begin performing mathematical operations. In this case, they need to understand numbers as individual entities before they can begin to add two- and three-digit numbers without regrouping (and eventually, with regrouping). Before advancing to addition, I would first call together the group of 10 students who do not know basic addition facts and discuss numbers with them. I would ask the children, "What does 12 mean? Could you show me 12 with the counting chips?" We could discuss how to arrange the chips to make it easier to count, such as, placing them in groups of 2s to show 12 or groups of 5s to show 10. Each child would be given a container of counting chips and would practice showing abstract numbers in the concrete forms. Once the children understand the concept of numbers, it is appropriate to advance to basic addition facts. Write a problem on the board and ask the children to show the fact with counting chips (e.g., 5 + 7 =). Discuss strategies used to determine the answer to the number model. Repeat this process with several more problems. Then give the students a number fact that they know automatically (e.g., 2 + 2 =). Allow them to use the number chips to solve the problem. Discuss which method is quicker, using the number chips or knowing the answer automatically. Tell them that a goal for second grade is to be able to answer facts quickly and correctly.

Before beginning the games, remind the children of all the facts that they probably know. Begin with the facts for 10 and ask the children to tell you facts they know where the answer is 10 (e.g., 5 + 5 or 9 + 1). As the children give you the facts, add them to a list on the board. Discuss facts that are doubles (5 + 5) or turn around facts (if you know 8 + 2, then you also know 2 + 8). Extend the list to include all the doubles facts (2 + 2, 3 + 3, etc.) and then discuss near doubles facts (if you know that 7 + 7 = 14, then what would 7 + 6 equal?).

It is important to provide the children with models of all the information that they know. This provides the children with the proper mindset for retrieving the information independently when they are playing the games with their peers. It is important in second grade that the children know the facts fluently as well as accurately. The following three activities will help children gain fluency.

1. Addition Top It (this game is played in pairs)—the children are given a pile of cards with numbers (initially, the children can use cards with the numbers 0 to 9). Each child takes 2 cards from the pile and says the complete number model (e.g., child one gets cards with a 5 and 6 and says "5 plus 6 equals 11"; child two gets 8 and 7 and says "8 plus 7 equals 15; 15 is higher than 11 so I win this round of Top It"). The children continue until the pile is gone. Children may use counting chips or number grids to solve difficult problems or to verify an answer.

2. Domino Addition (this game is played in pairs)—the children are given a pile of dominoes with the dots facing down. One child takes a domino and gives two number models for the fact (e.g., if the domino has 3 dots on one half and 5 dots on the other half, the child says "3 + 5 = 8 and 5 + 3 = 8"). The other child takes a domino and gives two number models (e.g., if the domino has 3 dots on one half and 3 dots on the other half, the child says "3 + 3 = 6 and the turn around fact is the same, 3 + 3 = 6 and that is less than 8 so you get my domino"). The children continue until the pile is gone.

3. Computer Programs—this may be done individually or in pairs. Children solve math problems on the computer at adaptive sites such as www.funbrain.com or Accelerated Math.

(B) It is also important that the children understand the concrete representation of abstract numbers for place value. The Base-10 Blocks are valuable in visually representing numbers. First we would discuss as a group what the different blocks represent (the cubes represent ones, the longs represent tens). Then we would discuss how the blocks would represent numbers (e.g., 27 would be 2 longs and 7 cubes). It is also important to discuss how to exchange blocks (e.g., 10 cubes would be exchanged for one long). The following three different activities will help the children to understand place value:

1. Reach 1,000 (played in pairs)—The children are given a pile of Base-10 Blocks, a Place Value Mat and a die. As each child takes turns rolling the die, the child takes that number of cubes, making exchanges when possible (e.g., a child has 1 flat, 4 longs and 8 cubes on the Place Value Mat and rolls a 6 on the die; the child takes 6 cubes and adds those to the 8 already on the mat; then the child exchanges 10 of those cubes for a long, resulting in 1 flat, 5 longs and 4 cubes on the Place Value Mat; the child then has to identify how many blocks are on the mat by saying "I have 154 blocks"). The game continues until one of the children reaches 1,000.

2. Base-10 Blocks (this is played in pairs)—The child places any combination of flats, longs and ones on the Place Value Mat and then the child turns over a card that says "hundreds place", "tens place" or "ones place". The child must identify how many blocks are in that place. For example, if the child has placed 6 flats, 5 longs and 9 cubes on the Place Value Mat and then turns over a card that says "tens place" the child would say "I have 659 blocks and there are 5 tens."

3. Show the Number (this is played in pairs)—the child turns over cards with riddles and must show the number with Base-10 Blocks. For example, the riddle says, 1 ten and 3 ones. The child shows that with Base-10 Blocks and says "1 ten and 3 ones is 13". Call the children together as a group and give a large number such as 173. Ask which number is in the ten's place. Advance to basic addition without regrouping, asking the children to solve problems, such as 23 + 31 using the Base-10 Blocks. Observe how the children arrange the blocks to determine understanding of place value.

(C) As the 10 children above are strengthening their understanding of basic addition facts and place value, the 15 remaining students will reinforce and extend their skills through the following activities:

1. The children will be invited to create number problems involving two- and three-digit numbers. The students will create number problems by reviewing the aspects of number stories (unit, story, question, solution, number model, and illustration). The stories will be shared with the class, placed in a class number story book and used as models for other students. These students will then write a number story that their classmates will answer. This time the number story should have three components (unit, story and question) and the classmates will provide the other three components (solution, number model and illustration). Children learn from peer interaction

and by encouraging students to solve number stories that were developed by classmates. Two important functions are being accomplished: the child writing the story must present information clearly and the child solving the story must use that information, along with problem solving strategies, to determine a solution.

2. Have students create their own fact triangles with higher facts. Fact triangles are triangles in which the answer is placed at the highest point and the two numbers that are added together to get that number are placed in the two lower corners. Once the children have made 20 fact triangles with more complex facts, they can join a partner and play the fact triangle game. It is important to challenge students who have acquired basic facts and build on the basic foundation in order to advance learning to higher levels. Children learn best when they are actively involved and are completing new and exciting activities that require problem solving but are within their understanding.

Commentary on the above response

This response shows that the test taker has a superior understanding of the subject matter and pedagogy required by the question. The response provides good strategies for helping students develop mathematical understanding (Base-10 Blocks, Show the Number) and then offers explanations for why these strategies work for different populations of children. These activities extend and generalize learning in a social context.

Response that would receive a score of 5

The first activity I would do with my students would be to play math bingo addition. The students' card has addition facts only. The teacher calls out the number. For Ex: The number is "14." The students that have addition facts that equal that number place a token on their card. The students who cover the board get bingo.

The second activity that I would have my students play would be "Do or Die." For example, I give the students a math addition fact sheet. The students are timed. The table that has the most answers correct is the winner. The third activity I would have my students play is a card game, and they have a magic number. For example, 4 students per deck of cards. The magic number is "13." Each person would take a card and they would go counterclockwise. When one student who had two cards that equaled "13" they lay those cards down. The students keep going until the deck is gone. The student who has laid down the most cards win. These three different activities build accuracy and speed. This allows the student to become familiar with addition fact families. It also speeds up their process of learning: when you give them a timed test. I also encourage my students to try, because it gets easier everyday. To help my students learn place value, the first activity we do is a calendar activity. How many days we have been in school? 72 days. I have straws and containers. The student would come up and be the teacher and ask, "What place is the "two" in?" The student would reply, " The one's column." The teacher-student would then ask, "What place is the seven in?" The students would reply, " The ten's column." Then the students would place the straws in the correct column.

The second activity would be to give the students a sheet that has place value. The students must write the number in the correct place value that the teacher calls out. The third activity would be to write a number on the board. For example, 1,753. Call students up to the board and ask them to write the number that is in the hundred column. If they did it correctly they would write "7." I would be able to assess these types of activities very quickly. The student would also get immediate feedback. If the student still didn't understand, then I would do different activities using Cuisinart rods to show place value. One activity I would do for the 15 students who didn't need reteaching is peer tutoring. I find that my students enjoy working together to help their classmates. So the student who needs help would get w/ a student who doesn't and drill that student.

The second activity would be for the students who didn't need any help. I would give them enrichment problems that would expand their level of thinking. Students who do very well in math are sometimes analytical thinkers. Therefore, I always like to have a challenging math and problem solving center they can go to.

Commentary on the above response

This response answers all parts of the question clearly, but some of the explanations lack depth and detail. Part (A) represents the strongest part of the response; each of the three basic addition activities listed is supported with clear examples. While part (B) clearly describes three place value activities, the explanation of assessment as done "very quickly" is vague; it does not offer a description of how assessment would be accomplished. Part (C) describes the two enrichment and reinforcement activities only in very general terms; no specific details are offered, and there is no evidence for how problems would "expand their level of thinking." Although the response often lacks such reflection and analysis, the activities described do demonstrate a strong understanding of the subject matter and pedagogy required by the situation.

Response that would receive a score of 4

The first thing I would do with children who are having trouble with Basic math facts is pull out the unifix cubes. I need to be sure they know what it is they are doing in a concrete manner. We would complete simple addition problems using the blocks to demonstrate that 1 block and 2 blocks is 3 blocks etc. I would also use everyday items such as pencils or books. Once the students seem comfortable with the concept of adding I would teach them about fact families in order to help them see the relationship as well as aid in recall of the basic facts. When students understand that and are the same their speed and accuracy will increase. Finally, a fun way to help increase speed and accuracy is to play addition bingo. The student must recognize the facts quickly but because it is presented as a game it is an enjoyable activity that helps with memorization of facts.

These activities will be effective because children must start with concrete, manipulative activities moving on to more abstract activities. As knowledge builds their speed and accuracy follow. This holds true for all areas of math education so for students needing help with place value, I would again turn to manipulatives. I would have them begin with unit blocks to complete simple addition problems. Next I would discover how the units must stay in the tens. They would work problems until they were clearly comfortable left moving onto flats of 100. This process of manipulating concrete objects would be repeated until students demonstrate the ability to transfer the information to the abstract. Another activity I would do with these blocks is play a game called "First to Fifty". Children work as teams or as individuals by rolling dice and taking a block for every roll.

When necessary they trade in units for rods and try to be the first to reach 50. Finally I would ask them to make up problems of their own to use with each other in order to assess their understanding of what they are doing. At any time during these activities I can do individual spot assessments and correct any misconceptions I see.

The students who have a solid understanding of these concepts can center to increase speed and accuracy of the facts by playing the same game as the others but at a higher level. For example they can increase place value concepts by playing 'First to One Hundred' or 'First to One Thousand' etc. the same method of assessment and evaluation can be used. Also they can play math Bingo like the others but use higher level of facts for the game. This will allow the more advanced students to be challenged while their peers receive needed help.

Commentary on the above response

While this response answers all parts of the question, the activities, examples, explanations, and assessment are not fully developed. The three activities provided for part (A) need more detailed description and explanation of how and why the activities would achieve the instructional goal. The first activity described in part (B) is more appropriate for simple addition than for place value. Also, there is no explanation of how the rods, blocks, and flats will be used in the place value activities. The third activity described in part (B) is appropriate, but the description of its assessment lacks depth. Part (C) only briefly describes two enrichment and reinforcement activities; neither is explained in detail, and more analysis of why these activities are effective is needed. The lack of detail and analysis shows an accurate but limited understanding of the subject matter and pedagogy required by the question.

Response that would receive a score of 3

(A) One activity that the 10 children who need help with basic addition facts could participate in would be a flash card game. (The students would be in a circle). I would choose one student to hold up the flash card to the first person, if that person gets the answer right, he/she gets another problem to figure out—if he/she misses the problem, the card is shown to the next person. The most cards one individual student can answer correctly is 3 in one turn, then the next person automatically gets a turn. The "card holder" would switch after each round. Everyone would get practice during this activity, even if it wasn't their turn, because they would realize that if someone missed the problem they would be next. The cardholder gets practice just by looking at the flash cards. I would also pass out an "addition fact" worksheet time test to these students. Just by seeing the problem over and over, they will learn them, and learn to do the problem with speed and accuracy. I would also have those 10 students answer addition problems with manipulatives. (for ex: counting bears, cubes, etc.). I feel that it is very important for children to understand what they are actually doing. Children learn math many different ways. Some have to actually visualize what is happening in the problem, until you show them with counting bears. On the other hand, some students memorize the problems right away and don't care to see visuals. Everyone learns differently and teachers need to be able to accommodate every type of learner.

(B) One activity that would help the 10 children with place value would be to give them a piece of paper with a line down the middle and labeled 10's on the left side and ones on the right side. Each student would have several individual straws and some grouped in tens with rubber bands. I would tell them that the group is 10 straws. Then I'd show an example: "If I called out the number 22, I would put 2 groups of 10's on the 10's side and 2 ones (individual straws) on the right side. Following that activity I would give them a worksheet with place value problems on it. (For ex- The problem may say "if a number has two 10's and three 1's, what is it?" Another activity that you could use would be to group the students into partners and have one student say a number, (for ex, 15), and the other partner would say one 10's and five 1's. They would switch off turns. I would be constantly monitoring.

(C) While the 10 students were working on worksheets, I would hand out a tougher worksheet on addition and place value for them to be working on. If the 10 students still don't seem to be catching on after a few days, I would go ahead and start the 15 students on the new harder material. They could also be assisting me in helping out the other students (flash cards, straw games). This would help the 10 students out greatly plus enrich their understanding of the material better (as a review.)

Commentary on the above response

The test-taker answers some parts of the question adequately and shows some understanding of the subject matter and pedagogy required by the exercise. However, the activities, examples, explanations, and assessment are not fully developed. While the first activity in part (A) is explained in detail, the second and third activities are not fully developed, and the explanation as to why these activities were chosen is only adequate. For part (B), once again the first activity is explained in detail, but the second and third activities are weakly explained, and no mention of assessment is provided. The explanations for the two activities listed in part (C) are very weakly developed. More supporting details are needed throughout the response to receive a higher score.

Response that would receive a score of 2

(A) <u>Activity 1</u>
Working in pairs, and with unifix cubes, or any other manipulatives, students will practice their addition facts with each other. The manipulatives provide the students with concrete examples.

<u>Activity 2</u>
Pairing students with the 15 other children and having them practice basic facts together with manipulatives. This allows the students to learn from each other, and also helps with reinforcing skills in 15 other children.

Activity 3
Testing students everyday basic facts, with worksheets, and verbally. Develop a game where the teacher passes around a beach ball that has basic facts written on them, and the students catches it and gives the answer to one of the basic facts that are on the ball. This allows students to have fun and math don't be so stressful and helps with speed.

(B) Activity 1
Having each student use a roll of toilet paper, I would have write their numbers 0 to 18 on the paper as it unrolls. This would give them a visual picture of place value: Ex.

Activity 2
Have students make place cards showing place value. This provides another concrete example.

Activity 3
With worksheets, students will do math problems, using manipulatives to represent problems.

(C) Activity 1
Students will work in pairs with students who need additional help. This would reinforce these students math skills and provide them an opportunity to help other students.

Activity 2
Students will work by themselves on higher order math skills.

Commentary on the above response
The response demonstrates a weak understanding of the subject matter and pedagogy required by the question. In part (A), the response does not provide examples for each of the activities, and the descriptions lack supporting details and depth of analysis. Part (B) is particularly weak; the few examples provided lack clarity, are not fully developed, and do not mention assessment practices. Part (C) provides only very brief descriptions of the activities, and does not offer any explanation of how the activities extend and reinforce math skills. No part of the question is answered adequately because supporting details are underdeveloped or omitted.

Response that would receive a score of 1
Children who don't understand math need lots of hands on exposure.

First thing is using manipulatives having children group different things. If children can touch it and move it they have a better understanding.

2nd is board games. Playing in sm groups with each other. I would also have the ones that did understand help the students who didn't.

3rd I would have a sm group w/ dry erase boards. And we would go over math. I would be there to help them one-to-one.

Commentary on the above response

Many parts of the question are not answered in this response. Only three activities are described, and it is unclear to which parts of the question they apply. No examples of how the activities would be used are given. Explanations of assessment are also missing. This response does not reflect an understanding of the subject matter and pedagogy.

PART VI

Praxis II: Subject Assessments

Your Goals for This Part:

- Identify the format and content of 34 popular Subject Assessments.
- Learn what kinds of questions are asked on Subject Assessment tests and how to answer them correctly.

CHAPTER 20

All About the Subject Assessments

Praxis Subject Assessments are designed to assess your knowledge of specific subject areas. They test your grasp of the actual content you will be expected to teach once you are licensed. This chapter and the three following chapters describe 34 assessment tests. They provide sample questions to help you become familiar with the question formats that will actually appear on the test and answer explanations to help you understand the kinds of knowledge and reasoning you will need to apply to choose correct answers.

To determine which test or tests you need to take, consult Appendix A: State-by-State Certification Testing Requirements or contact your state's teacher licensing commission, usually located in the state department of education.

Praxis II: Subject Assessments include two types of tests: multiple-choice tests, for which you select your answer from a list of choices, and constructed-response tests, for which you write a response of your own. Multiple-choice tests measure a broad range of knowledge across your content area. Constructed-response tests measure your ability to provide in-depth explanations of a few essential topics in a particular subject area.

This chapter covers the following Subject Assessments:

- Fundamental Subjects: Content Knowledge
- Education of Young Children
- Special Education: Application of Core Principles Across Categories of Disability
- Educational Leadership: Administration and Supervision
- School Psychologist
- School Guidance and Counseling
- Library Media Specialist

FUNDAMENTAL SUBJECTS: CONTENT KNOWLEDGE (0511)

2 hours   100 multiple-choice questions

The Fundamental Subjects: Content Knowledge examination assesses candidates' skills and understanding broadly across four subjects:

- English Language Arts
- Mathematics
- Citizenship and Social Science
- Science

Questions are arranged by subject, with approximately 25 questions in each topic area. An index on the back page of the test book identifies the page locations where each subject can be found. Candidates may answer the questions in any order they choose.

The content of the examination is *not* predicated on the assumption that the candidates should be experts in all the subjects. Since the purpose of this examination is to assess knowledge and skills in subject matter that may lie outside an individual candidate's teaching specialization, the questions in each subject focus on key indicators of general knowledge and understanding. The questions require examinees to use fundamental skills that are founded upon broad concepts in each of the subjects.

EDUCATION OF YOUNG CHILDREN (0021)

2 hours   Part A—60 multiple-choice questions

                 Part B—6 short constructed-response questions

The Education of Young Children test is intended primarily for prospective teachers of preschool through primary grade students. It is based on a teaching approach that emphasizes the active involvement of young children in a variety of play and child-centered activities that provide opportunities for choices, decision-making, and discovery. The test is designed to assess the examinee's knowledge about pedagogy and content, the relationship of theory to practice, and how theory can be applied in the educational setting. Also included are multicultural influences, diversity, variations in development, including atypical development, and how they affect children's development and learning. Each of the six constructed-response questions will focus on one of the following areas: the learning environment, working with families, instruction, assessment, professionalism, and diversity.

The test was designed to align with the National Association for the Education of Young Children's *NAEYC Standards for Early Childhood Professional Preparation* (2001).

SPECIAL EDUCATION: APPLICATION OF CORE PRINCIPLES ACROSS CATEGORIES OF DISABILITY (0352)

1 hour   50 multiple-choice questions

The Special Education: Application of Core Principles Across Categories of Disability test is designed for examinees who plan to teach in a special education program at any grade level from preschool through grade 12. The 50 multiple-choice questions assess the knowledge and understanding of applying the basic principles of special education in a wide variety of settings for students with disabilities. Some of these questions are based on a case study related to the teaching of students with disabilities. Extensive knowledge of individual specialty areas, such as education of students with visual impairments or hearing impairments, is not required.

EDUCATIONAL LEADERSHIP: ADMINISTRATION AND SUPERVISION (0410)

2 hours   120 multiple-choice questions

The Educational Leadership: Administration and Supervision test is intended to assess a candidate's knowledge of the functions of an administrator or supervisor, including the background information needed to implement these functions. The examination is intended primarily for those who are candidates for master's degrees or who already possess a master's degree and are seeking first appointments as administrators or supervisors. This assessment instrument reflects the most current research and professional judgment and experience of educators across the country. The test is designed to capture what is essential about the role of a school leader—what makes the difference in whether a school community can provide experiences that ensure all students succeed.

The 120 multiple-choice questions cover five content areas: determining educational needs, curriculum design and instructional improvement, staff development and program evaluation, school management, and individual and group leadership skills. The test questions are structured to measure knowledge and cognitive skills in application, analysis, synthesis, and evaluation as described in *Bloom's Taxonomy of Educational Objectives*. For example, some questions emphasize knowledge of trends, principles, and theories; others require interpretation of data and identification of implications or consequences. Still others emphasize ability to generalize, determine priorities and relationships, integrate knowledge of theory to produce new information or patterns, and judge the value of a process or product on the basis of logical consistency

SCHOOL PSYCHOLOGIST (0400)

2 hours   120 multiple-choice questions

The School Psychologist test is designed for 60-hour master's- and specialist's-degree-level candidates wishing to serve as school psychologists in educational settings. The test assumes that candidates have had some form of supervised practicum or internship experience.

The 120 multiple-choice test questions focus on both content and process issues that are relevant to the school setting. Note that certain areas relevant to the practice of a school psychologist are not assessed in this examination because they do not lend themselves readily to multiple-choice assessment. It is assumed that candidates' competence in these other areas will have been evaluated using other methodologies during the course of academic training. The main content areas of the test include diagnosis and fact finding, prevention and intervention, psychological foundations, educational foundations, and ethical and legal issues. In measuring the five content areas, a variety of contexts are used as settings: consultation, assessment, intervention, research, professional standards, and in-service.

SCHOOL GUIDANCE AND COUNSELING (0420)

2 hours   120 multiple-choice questions, 40 based on the listening section

The School Guidance and Counseling test is intended primarily for persons who are completing master's-level programs for counselors and intend to become counselors in the public schools. It measures knowledge and skills required of the professional school counselor in relation to those developmental areas that constitute most of the work of the counselor. The test is designed to measure counselor functions and skills related to the primary and secondary school levels. A number of questions are applicable across school levels; other questions are especially applicable to the elementary school level, the middle or junior high school level, or the high school level. The content of the test is focused on questions that relate to the following four major categories: counseling and guidance, consulting, coordinating, and professional issues.

The 120 multiple-choice questions generally are intended to measure how the counselor skills and functions are applied to the following areas of student development:

- Identity and self-concept, covering student intrapsychic factors such as identity development, self-appraisal, and internal conflicts regarding the individual's actions, decisions, and values.
- Interpersonal, including the full range of interpersonal relationships, with emphasis on the student's relationships with peers, adults within the family, and adults outside the family, such as teachers.
- Career and leisure, covering the exploration and broadening of the student's options in planning such career and leisure activities as locating occupational information, interviewing for a job, and finding recreational facilities.
- Academic and cognitive, focusing on learning in the classroom and other educational contexts, with particular attention to the individual student's needs, abilities, and approach to the learning situation.
- Health and physical well-being, including student concerns about such matters as physical maturation, sexuality, fitness, injury and disease, handicapping conditions, chemical dependency, eating disorders, stress, abuse, and neglect.

The test is divided into two sections, one of which is based on a CD. Approximately 40 questions require listening to this CD and then responding to written questions. The CD includes brief client responses, client statements followed by counselor responses, and extended client–counselor interactions. The questions based on the CD cover such counseling processes as identifying client feelings, identifying client problems or critical issues, and identifying the appropriateness of various counselor responses. Consisting of interactions between clients and counselors, the questions emphasize the knowledge and skills included in counseling and guidance content but may also include material related to consulting, coordinating, and professional issues content.

During the test, examinees will have 40 minutes to work on the taped questions and will see only the questions and/or possible choices. The script of the CD does not appear in the test book.

LIBRARY MEDIA SPECIALIST (0310)

2 hours   120 multiple-choice questions

The Library Media Specialist test is designed to measure the knowledge and abilities of examinees who have had preparation in a program for school library media specialists, grades K–12. Because programs in school librarianship are offered at both the undergraduate and graduate levels, the test is appropriate for examinees at either level. The test content is aimed at the level of knowledge appropriate for the person who is responsible for administering the library media program at the individual school level. The material in the test, therefore, would not be suitable for those in systems with differentiated staffing or for those at the district level. The 120 multiple-choice questions cover program administration; collection development; information access and delivery; learning and teaching; and professional development, leadership, and advocacy.

REAL QUESTIONS FOR PRACTICE

The following real test questions illustrate the types of items on the actual exams. Answers and explanations follow the last question.

> **Directions:** Each of the questions or statements below is followed by four (or five) suggested answers or completions. Select the one that is best.

Fundamental Subjects

1. The following excerpt is from a speech by William Safire.

> Is the decline of the written word inevitable? Will the historians of the future deal merely in oral history? I hope not. I hope that oral history will limit itself to the discovery of toothpaste and the invention of mouthwash. I don't want to witness the decomposing of the art of composition, or be present when we get in touch with our feelings and lose contact with our minds.
>
> It can be inferred from the passage that the author believes that, in contrast to oral history, the written word is

(A) able to convey emotions more accurately

(B) a more intellectual exercise

(C) doomed to describe mundane historical events

(D) already obsolete

2. To make 36 5-inch pancakes, mix 4½ cups of water with 2 pounds of pancake mix.

When Mark goes shopping at Food Warehouse, he often buys food in large quantities in order to save money. A problem that sometimes arises is that large packages give directions for making food for large groups. Last week he brought home pancake mix with the directions shown above. If Mark wants to make 10 5-inch pancakes, how many cups of water should he use?

(A) $4\frac{1}{20}$ cups
(B) 1¾ cups
(C) 1½ cups
(D) 1¼ cups

3. Which of the following is true for both Martin Luther King, Jr. and Mahatma Gandhi, shown above?

(A) They based their movements for social change on Christian faith.
(B) They led mass movements based on nonviolent civil disobedience.
(C) They believed in achieving their goals by any means necessary.
(D) They urged their followers to cooperate with the rules laid down by established authorities.

4. During the nineteenth century, some bird species, such as starlings, were introduced into the United States from Europe. Since then they have spread throughout the country and become a nuisance, or pest species, especially in urban areas. They often drive native birds out of their habitats. Factors that have contributed to the starling's success in the United States most likely include all of the following EXCEPT

(A) appropriate locations for nesting
(B) suitable range of temperatures
(C) an abundance of natural predators
(D) availability of a variety of food sources

Education of Young Children

5. The portfolio a teacher keeps on each child in a class for assessment purposes needs to include all of the following EXCEPT

(A) dated work samples accompanied by teacher commentary
(B) anecdotal records and records of systematic observations
(C) checklists, rating scales, and screening inventories
(D) weekly classroom lesson plans and curriculum goals

6. Kate and Marc are working in the art center making a bird using paper-towel rolls, Styrofoam, feathers, sequins, scissors, scraps of material, and glue. The children are engaged in which type of play?

(A) Dramatic
(B) Constructive
(C) Exploratory
(D) Parallel

Special Education

7. For a special education teacher, which of the following is the best example of collaborative goal setting?

(A) Developing IEP goals with the regular classroom teacher and then presenting the completed goals to the student's parents
(B) Reaching a consensus on goals by consulting with parents and the multidisciplinary team
(C) Allowing parents to choose from goals designed by the multidisciplinary team
(D) Encouraging students to select goals for IEP inclusion from teacher-approved lists

Educational Leadership and Supervision

8. The primary role of the supervising or cooperating teacher in the education of the student teacher is most appropriately described as

(A) setting a good example for the student teacher to follow
(B) helping the student teacher develop effective ways of teaching
(C) determining the educational philosophy to be implemented by the student teacher
(D) providing the student teacher with information on classroom management techniques
(E) facilitating the proper placement of the student teacher in his or her initial position

School Psychologist

9. The decisions in *Tarasoff v. Board of Regents of California* (1974, 1976) establish which of the following principles regarding confidentiality in counseling relationships?

(A) Duty to warn and protect
(B) Responsibility to maintain privacy
(C) Need to obtain informed consent
(D) Need to maintain accurate records
(E) Duty to limit access to student records

School Guidance and Counseling

10. When should the counselor inform a student about conditions that may require the provision of more than routine counseling?

(A) At a time halfway through the counseling relationship
(B) Only when an ethical issue arises during the counseling relationship
(C) Only while giving the student advice on which the counselor expects the student to act
(D) Near the close of the counseling relationship
(E) At or before the time the student enters the counseling relationship

Library Media Specialist

11. All of the following awards recognize excellence in children's literature EXCEPT

(A) Michael Printz Award
(B) John Newbery Medal
(C) Randolph Caldecott Medal
(D) Mildred Batchelder Award
(E) Coretta Scott King Award

Answers and Explanations

Fundamental Subjects

1. The correct answer is choice B. In the final sentence of the passage, Safire suggests that if we stop engaging with the written word ("the art of composition"), we may also "lose contact with our minds," or miss out on the intellectual rewards of the written word.

2. The correct answer is choice D. According to the recipe, 36 5-inch pancakes require 4½ cups of water. The proportion of the number of pancakes to the number of cups of water is

$$\frac{\text{Number of 5-inch pancakes}}{\text{Number of cups of water}} = \frac{36}{4\frac{1}{2}} = \frac{36}{\frac{9}{2}} = \frac{72}{9} = \frac{8}{1}$$

Since Mark is using the same recipe to make 10 5-inch pancakes, the proportion of the number of pancakes to the number of cups of water is still

$$\frac{\text{Number of 5-inch pancakes}}{\text{Number of cups of water}} = \frac{8}{1}$$

The number of cups of water needed to make 10 5-inch pancakes is

$$\frac{\text{Number of 5-inch pancakes}}{\text{Number of cups of water}} = \frac{8}{1} = \frac{10}{\text{Number of cups of water}}$$

$$\text{By cross-multiplying,} = \frac{8}{1} = \frac{10}{\text{Number of cups of water}}$$

can be written as: Number of cups of water = 10/8, which is equal to 1¼ cups of water.

3. The correct answer is choice B. Both Gandhi and Martin Luther King, Jr. led movements for social change based on principles of nonviolence. King was a Christian minister, but Gandhi did not base his movement on Christian faith (choice A). "By any means necessary" (choice C) is a phrase often associated with Malcolm X, another civil rights leader in the United States in the 1960s. Choice D is incorrect: both King and Gandhi urged their followers to conduct nonviolent acts of civil disobedience when faced with unjust laws or policies.

4. The correct answer is choice C. The European starling was introduced into the United States in 1890. Environmental conditions in the United States were appropriate for the reproduction and survival of this species. However, as happens with many exotic species, there are few if any natural predators or competitors in their new habitats. This allowed starlings to thrive in their new ecosystems and reduce populations of native species. An abundance of predators would have kept the number of starlings from increasing greatly and, therefore, choice C would *not* be a factor that contributed to their success.

Education of Young Children

5. The correct answer is choice D. Choices A, B, and C are types of items that may be found in a portfolio kept to assess student progress. Weekly lesson plans and curriculum goals are items that do not need to be in such a portfolio.

6. The correct answer is choice B, the students are constructing a bird sculpture. Because Kate and Marc have a goal in mind and are using the materials to create a specific structure, it would be incorrect to characterize their behavior as simply exploratory play (choice C). Additionally, as the two are working together with a shared focus, this would not be considered parallel play (choice D). Dramatic play (choice A) may occur after the students have completed their project but is not described in the given scenario.

Special Education

7. The correct answer is choice B, since collaborative goal setting requires the sharing of ideas among all those involved with the student—educators, parents, related services providers, etc. It is not appropriate in collaborative goal setting for one person or group to present previously prepared goals to the student and his or her family. There must be collaboration among all concerned to develop appropriate goals for the student.

Educational Leadership and Supervision

8. The correct answer is choice B. The primary role of a supervising teacher regarding the education of a student teacher is to help develop effective ways of teaching. Among the choices provided, choice B is the only answer that addresses this point and is also the only choice that focuses on the development of the student teacher, not on the control exercised by the cooperating teacher.

School Psychologist

9. The correct answer is choice A. Choices B through E are good ethical practices but were not decided in the Tarasoff case.

School Guidance and Counseling

10. The correct answer is choice E. According to the American School Counselors Association, the counselor must inform the client of the purposes, goals, techniques, rules of procedure, and limitations that may affect the relationship at or before the time the counseling relationship is entered. Issues of violating the rights of clients are raised when counselors fail to provide adequate information that may affect the clients' welfare.

Library Media Specialist

11. The correct answer is choice C. The Randolph Caldecott Medal is awarded in recognition of outstanding illustration in a children's book.

CHAPTER 21

Reading, English, Language Arts

This chapter covers the following Subject Assessments:

- Middle School: English Language Arts
- English Language, Literature, and Composition: Content Knowledge
- English Language, Literature, and Composition: Essays
- English Language, Literature, and Composition: Pedagogy
- English to Speakers of Other Languages
- Reading Across the Curriculum: Elementary
- Reading Across the Curriculum: Secondary

MIDDLE SCHOOL: ENGLISH LANGUAGE ARTS (0049)

2 hours   90 multiple-choice questions (Part A)
              2 constructed-response questions (Part B)

The Middle School: English Language Arts test is designed to assess whether an examinee has the knowledge and competencies necessary for a beginning teacher of English Language Arts at the middle school level. The 90 multiple-choice questions constitute approximately 75 percent of the examinee's score and fall into three categories: knowledge of concepts relevant to reading and literature study, knowledge of the development and use of the English language, and knowledge of concepts relevant to the study of composition and rhetoric. The two equally weighted constructed-response questions constitute approximately 25 percent of the examinee's score and emphasize the use of critical-thinking skills. One question will ask examinees to interpret a piece of literary or nonfiction text and/or to discuss an approach to interpreting text; the other question will ask examinees to discuss the rhetorical elements of a piece of writing. The sections are not separately timed. However, examinees should allow about 90 minutes for the multiple-choice section and about 15 minutes for each essay question (for an approximate total of 30 minutes on the constructed-response portion).

ENGLISH LANGUAGE, LITERATURE, AND COMPOSITION: CONTENT KNOWLEDGE (0041)

2 hours   120 multiple-choice questions

The English Language, Literature, and Composition: Content Knowledge test is designed to assess whether an examinee has the broad base of knowledge and competencies necessary to be licensed as a beginning teacher of English in a secondary school. The 120 multiple-choice questions are based on the material typically covered in a bachelor's degree program in English and English education. The test covers literature and reading (55 percent), the English language (15 percent), and composition and rhetoric (30 percent).

ENGLISH LANGUAGE, LITERATURE, AND COMPOSITION: ESSAYS (0042)

2 hours   4 essay questions

The English Language, Literature, and Composition: Essays test is designed for those who plan to teach English at the secondary level. The test addresses two key elements in the study of literature: the ability to analyze literary texts and the ability to understand and articulate arguments about key issues in the study of English. The test consists of four essay questions, which are weighted equally. Two questions ask examinees to interpret literary selections from English, American, or world literature of any period. The first question always focuses on a work of poetry, while the second always features a work of prose. The third question asks examinees to evaluate the argument and rhetorical features of a passage that addresses an issue in the study of English. The fourth question asks examinees to take and defend a position on an issue in the study of English, using references to works of literature to support that position. The issue questions may deal with such matters as the nature of literary interpretation, the value of studying literature, the qualities that define the discipline of literary study, the kinds of literary works we choose to read and teach and why we make those choices, and so on.

ENGLISH LANGUAGE, LITERATURE, AND COMPOSITION: PEDAGOGY (0043)

1 hour   2 constructed-response questions

The English Language, Literature, and Composition: Pedagogy test is designed for those who plan to teach English at the secondary school level. The test assesses how well examinees can perform two tasks that are required of a teacher of English: teaching literature and responding to student writing.

The first question presents a list of literary works commonly taught at the secondary level and asks examinees to choose one work from the list as the basis for their response to the three-part question. The parts of this question are as follows:

1. Identify two literary features of the particular work that are central to teaching the work.
2. Identify two obstacles to understanding that students might experience when encountering the work.
3. Describe two instructional activities that could be used to help students understand the literary features and/or overcome obstacles to understanding.

Examinees should be sure to include specific examples from the work in their discussion. A general discussion of problems students tend to have when encountering any work of literature would be inappropriate; similarly, a discussion that does not demonstrate familiarity with the work and its literary features would be unacceptable. In responding to this question about teaching literature, examinees should show that they understand the various kinds of knowledge, abilities, and skills that students bring to the English classroom; that they can identify important literary features central to teaching a particular work of literature; that they can anticipate likely obstacles for students encountering a work of literature; and that they can plan and describe relevant instructional activities.

The second question requires examinees to read an authentic piece of student writing and then assess the strengths and weaknesses of the writing, identify errors in the conventions of standard written English, and create a follow-up assignment that addresses the strengths or weaknesses of the student's writing. Responses that focus on too general a strategy (e.g., "revise the essay"), identify only minor problems, or merely rewrite portions of the essay for the student, would not meet the demands of the task. In responding to this question about student writing, examinees should demonstrate how well they can assess student writing and design instructional activities that take into account student abilities. Examinees should also show that they can determine appropriate objectives for teaching composition while at the same time demonstrating their understanding of the knowledge, skills, and abilities that different students bring to the English classroom.

The suggested time for each question is 30 minutes. Each question represents one-half of the total test score.

ENGLISH TO SPEAKERS OF OTHER LANGUAGES (0360)

2 hours, with a 30-minute listening section

120 multiple-choice questions, with 20 based on the listening section

The English to Speakers of Other Languages (ESOL) test is designed to measure basic pedagogical knowledge within the context of teaching ESOL in elementary or secondary schools. The test consists of two timed 15-minute listening sections and a 90-minute writing section.

Taped Portion: Section I, Parts A and B

- The 20 questions in Section I, Parts A (Oral Grammar and Vocabulary) and B (Pronunciation), are on an audio recording.
- The recorded questions in Section I are based on speech samples recorded by ESOL students who are not native speakers; examinees will be asked to identify errors in the students' speech. Therefore, before taking the test, they should be familiar with the speech of nonnative speakers who are learning English.

- Each of the recorded speech samples is printed in the test book. Examinees should mark the students' errors directly on the printed version of the speech samples to help focus their listening.
- After each speech sample, there will be a pause to allow examinees to choose and mark their answer. Examinees must answer within the time provided. The speech samples in Part A will be played one time only. The speech samples in Part B will be played twice.

Section I, Part C, and Section II

- After the recorded portion, examinees have 90 minutes to answer the remaining 100 questions in the test: Section I, Part C (Writing Analysis), and Section II (Language Theory and Teaching). Although there is a suggested time for each section, examinees will be able to work at their own pace. Those who finish the test before time is called can use any extra time to check their answers in either Section I, Part C, or Section II.
- The questions in Section I, Part C (Writing Analysis), are based on writing samples produced by ESOL students who are not native speakers; examinees will be asked to identify errors in the students' writing. Therefore, before taking the test, examinees should be familiar with the writing of nonnative speakers who are learning English.

READING ACROSS THE CURRICULUM: ELEMENTARY (0201)

2 hours   60 multiple-choice questions (Part A)
              3 constructed-response questions (Part B)

The Reading Across the Curriculum: Elementary test is designed for persons completing teacher training programs with at least two or three courses in reading who are planning to teach at the elementary level or persons who are currently teaching and have the option of taking this test in lieu of state-mandated course work. The 60 multiple-choice questions and the 3 constructed-response questions assess knowledge of the content and skills necessary to be an effective teacher of reading as well as the ability to apply knowledge of content and skills in the teaching of reading to all students. The multiple-choice questions and the constructed-response questions each constitute about one-half of the total test. The test questions involve the selection and application of ideas and practices to reading instruction from the earliest stages of language acquisition through the development of literacy skills across the curriculum. The content is based on categories and competencies developed by the Professional Standards and Ethics Committee of the International Reading Association.

READING ACROSS THE CURRICULUM: SECONDARY (0202)

2 hours   60 multiple-choice questions (Part A)
                 3 constructed-response questions (Part B)

The Reading Across the Curriculum: Secondary test is designed for persons completing teacher training programs with at least two or three courses in reading who are
planning to teach at the secondary level or persons who are currently teaching and
have the option of taking this test in lieu of state-mandated course work. The 60
multiple-choice questions and the 3 constructed-response questions assess knowledge
of the content and skills necessary to be an effective teacher of reading as well as
the ability to apply knowledge of content and skills in the teaching of reading to
all students. The multiple-choice questions and the constructed-response questions
each constitute about one-half of the total test. The test questions involve the
selection and application of ideas and practices to reading instruction from the
different stages of language acquisition through the development of literacy skills
across the curriculum. The content is based on categories and competencies developed by the Professional Standards and Ethics Committee of the International
Reading Association.

REAL QUESTIONS FOR PRACTICE

The following real test questions illustrate the types of items on the actual exams.
Answers and Explanations follow the last question.

> **Directions:** Each multiple-choice question below is followed by four
> suggested answers or completions. Select the one that is best. For ques-
> tions that are not multiple-choice, follow the directions given.

Middle School English

1. Freewriting, brainstorming, clustering, and idea mapping are most
important during which stage of the writing process?

(A) Prewriting
(B) Drafting
(C) Revising
(D) Proofreading

English Language, Literature, and Composition: Content Knowledge

Questions 2 and 3 refer to the following paragraphs.

I. On a dark, secluded street stood three abandoned houses. The first had
broken shutters and shattered windows. Next to it stood a dilapidated

structure badly in need of paint. Adjacent, amid debris, stood a shack with graffiti scrawled across the door.

II. Weeks before they decided on their destination, the seniors had already begun a massive fundraising project to help finance their class trip. When they were offered the choice between Rome and London, an overwhelming majority chose Rome. Then preparations began in earnest. In the months that followed, the students' enthusiasm escalated until the day the plane finally took off, carrying them toward an experience they would remember forever.

III. Selecting a new car requires each buyer to weigh a number of factors. First to be considered is the car's appearance. Next, and even more critical, are the car's performance and safety ratings. Most significant to any prospective buyer, however, is the car's price.

> **2.** Which of the following best describes the organization of paragraph II?
>
> (A) Chronological order
> (B) Spatial order
> (C) Cause and effect
> (D) Order of importance

> **3.** Which of the following best describes the organization of paragraph III?
>
> (A) Chronological order
> (B) Spatial order
> (C) Cause and effect
> (D) Order of importance

English Language, Literature, and Composition: Essays Interpreting Literature

Below is a sample of the first question in this test, which presents a poem and asks examinees to analyze some of the literary elements in the poem. The second question in the test is similar in format, except that it will ask examinees to analyze literary elements in a prose selection instead.

> **4.** Read carefully the following poem by Louis MacNeice. Then discuss how MacNeice uses imagery and diction to convey the qualities of what the narrator calls "world." Be sure to use at least THREE specific examples from the poem to support your points about MacNeice's use of imagery and diction.

Snow

The room was suddenly rich and the great
bay-window was
Spawning snow and pink roses against it
Soundlessly collateral and incompatible:
World is suddener than we fancy it.
World is crazier and more of it than we think,
Incorrigibly plural. I peel and portion
A tangerine and spit the pips and feel
The drunkenness of things being various.
And the fire flames with a bubbling sound for world
Is more spiteful and gay than one supposes—
On the tongue on the eyes on the ears
in the palms of one's hands—
There is more than glass between the snow
and the huge roses.

From *The Collected Poems of Louis MacNeice*, ed. by E. R. Dodds, Copyright © 1966 by The Estate of Louis MacNeice. Reprinted by permission of Faber & Faber Ltd. and David Higham Associates, agent for The Estate of Louis MacNeice.

English Language, Literature and Composition: Pedagogy Teaching Literature

5. Assume you are teaching a literature unit to a ninth-grade class. Your overall goal is to help your students recognize and understand important literary features of the works they read. Your choices of literary works to use as part of this unit are

William Golding, *Lord of the Flies*
Lorraine Hansberry, *A Raisin in the Sun*
S. E. Hinton, *The Outsiders* **or** *That Was Then, This Is Now*
William Shakespeare, *Romeo and Juliet* **or** *Macbeth*
John Steinbeck, *The Grapes of Wrath* **or** *The Pearl*
Amy Tan, *The Joy Luck Club*
Mark Twain, *The Adventures of Huckleberry Finn*

Choose ONE of the works listed above. Choose a work that you know well enough to identify and cite examples of its central literary features. Such features include, but are not limited to, specific methods of characterization and narration; characteristics of specific genres and subgenres; specific literary devices; and specific poetic techniques. Once you have chosen the literary work, answer the following three-part question.

A. Identify and describe TWO literary features central to the work that you would want ninth-grade students to be able to recognize and understand. In your discussion
- be specific about what students should know about each literary feature
- include specific examples from the work that are relevant to each literary feature
- be sure the literary features are appropriate for teaching to ninth-grade students

B. Identify and describe TWO obstacles to understanding this work that you anticipate these students might have. In your discussion
- explain **why** each obstacle is likely for ninth-grade students encountering the particular work; include specific examples from the work that are relevant to each obstacle

C. Describe TWO instructional activities you would use while teaching this particular work that would help students understand the literary features you described in Part A and/or overcome the obstacles to understanding you described in Part B. In your discussion
- present clear, well-formulated activities in which students are actively involved
- explain **how** each activity would help students understand the literary features and/or overcome the obstacles of the particular work
- describe activities that are appropriate for ninth-grade students

English to Speakers of Other Languages

Questions 6 and 7 are based on the following section of a table of contents in an ESOL textbook.

CONTENTS

Lesson 1 Try Our Special Offer . . . . Page 1
WHAT: to describe specific people and things; to give reasons; to emphasize; to show uncertainty
HOW: relative clauses

Lesson 2 An "Excellent Opportunity". . . . . Page 8
WHAT: to read an ad; to write a letter of application
HOW: paragraph construction

Lesson 3 Buying a Computer . . . . Page 35
WHAT: to discuss the future; to read ads; to describe features of a computer; to use some language of contemporary technology
HOW: collective nouns; "the" with plural and mass nouns; "the" with the names of places

---

6. For which of the following students is this text most appropriate?

    I. Preschool
    II. Elementary
    III. Secondary
    IV. Postsecondary
    (A) I and II only
    (B) III and IV only
    (C) I, II, and III only
    (D) II, III, and IV only

7. For which of the following programs would this text be most appropriate?

    (A) English for Academic Purposes
    (B) Coping Skills in ESOL
    (C) English for Science and Technology
    (D) ESL Current Events

Reading Across the Curriculum: Elementary

8. According to research, effective vocabulary instruction integrates new information with the familiar. Students are most likely to achieve that integration by

    (A) using a dictionary
    (B) developing a semantic map
    (C) analyzing word structure
    (D) memorizing words

9. A teacher is leading a Directed Reading–Thinking Activity while using a piece of informational text with the class. The teacher is most likely to ask the students which of the following questions initially?

    (A) What part of the text gave you a clue about the writer's purpose?
    (B) What do you think the writer intended to say?
    (C) How do you know what references the writer used?
    (D) How might the information in the text be used?

Reading Across the Curriculum: Secondary

10. According to research, effective vocabulary instruction integrates new information with the familiar. Students are most likely to achieve that integration by

    (A) using a dictionary
    (B) developing a semantic map
    (C) analyzing word structure
    (D) memorizing words

11. A teacher is leading a Directed Reading-Thinking Activity while using a piece of informational text with the class. The teacher is most likely to ask the students which of the following questions initially?

(A) What part of the text gave you a clue about the writer's purpose?
(B) What do you think the writer intended to say?
(C) How do you know what references the writer used?
(D) How might the information in the text be used?

Answers and Explanations

Middle School English

1. The correct answer is choice A. The terms mentioned are processes and devices associated with generating new ideas and organizing them. These processes and devices would not be associated with proofreading (choice D). While they might be part of drafting (choice B) or revising (choice C), they are most important during the prewriting stage of the writing process.

English Language, Literature, and Composition: Content Knowledge

2. The correct answer is choice A. Paragraph II describes a series of events that take place over the course of several months. Words and phrases such as "weeks before," "when," "then," and "in the months that followed" relate events sequentially.

3. The correct answer is choice D. The organization of paragraph III reflects an order of increasing importance. The features of the car are arranged from the one that should least affect the prospective buyer's decision (appearance) to the one that should most influence the buyer's decision (price). Words such as "more" and "most" help establish the comparative importance of each feature.

English Language, Literature, and Composition: Essays Interpreting Literature

4. Sample response that received a score of 3

In the poem "Snow," by Louis MacNeice, the narrator uses conflicting imagery and unusual diction to draw a picture of a strange and contradictory world. Throughout the poem, the narrator uses conflicting images to create his "world." The first is the description of snow and roses at a single bay-window. This image confuses the sense of season. Snow normally falls in the winter, while roses bloom in the summer months. Then the narrator remarks that the two are "collateral and incompatible," again employing conflicting imagery. Another example of the narrator's use of conflicting imagery is his description of the fire bubbling. Usually, fire is expected to crackle and water is expected to bubble; people usually talk about "fire and water" as if they are two conflicting things. The narrator's use of imagery and description in the poem gives the reader a greater concept of the contradictory world he is describing. This world is full of contradictions and incompatible things. While the images illustrate the poem, it is the narrator's use of language that brings it to life. In this poem, the narrator uses vivid but odd diction in order to add life to his idea of "world." For example, he never refers to "a world" or "the world," but only "world," like it is something strange and new. The elaborate language creates an illustration of what the narrator is describing. For example, he refers to feeling the "drunkenness of things being various." Not only do things change in "world," but the changes are sharp and quick, enough so that one can feel intoxicated by the experience. The language even sounds intoxicated when it says, "On the tongue on the eyes on the ears . . . ." The narrator also uses a variety of vivid and surprising verbs throughout the poem. This tactic avoids stale, repetitive language that can often bore readers. In one case, the window in the first stanza was said to be "spawning snow and pink roses." While the idea is physically impossible, the word choice creates an unmistakable picture for the reader. It also emphasizes the idea that "world" is contradictory and strange. The overall effect of the narrator's use of imagery and diction was brilliant. The elaborate descriptions, verb variance, and conflicting images created a beautifully "crazy" world for the reader.

English Language, Literature, and Composition: Pedagogy Teaching Literature

5. Sample Response That Received a Score of 6

Work Chosen: John Steinbeck's *The Pearl*

A. One literary feature of *The Pearl* is its form as a modern-day parable of Everyman and ultimately Everyman's quest for the "American dream." The protagonist Kino is an Everyman who must deal with his new-found promise of wealth and the false hope it instills in him. In an allegory/parable such as this one, a simple style is used to represent characters who often have very little individual personality but who embody moral qualities and other abstractions. In this way, the novel's significance as a universal fable can be appreciated. Symbolism is another important feature of *The Pearl*. Symbols are used in literature to reveal abstract ideas or truths. Steinbeck's hero, Kino, finds The Pearl of the World, an object that promises hope and prosperity. Kino believes that with the money the pearl will earn him, he will be able to legitimize his family (with a real wedding) and provide better for them (his son will attend school, he will purchase a new rifle). But as the piece unfolds, the pearl ironically becomes a symbol of greed and evil that steals the prosperity and joy that Kino actually did enjoy as peasant husband, father, and provider. He loses his ability to provide for his family, and his first son is killed. Kino's real hope for the family's future is destroyed. The pearl as a symbol of false hope and greed is at the center of the novel.

B. Students might find the simple style of this novel to be an obstacle. Steinbeck strips down the narrative by using short, repetitive sentences and plain language. For example, he often begins sentences with "And" several times in a row. Students might miss the point that simple language is used to make the parable clearer. Another obstacle for students might be the archetypal characters. Not only are the main family members described as predictable types but also the doctor, the priest, and the pearl buyers are all developed as stick figures. Again, students might miss the depth of the text because they do not get to know well-rounded, fully developed characters.

C. One instructional activity that I might use to help students understand the story as a fable would be to read a fable before reading *The Pearl*. This could help them anticipate the style. They would also be prepared for understanding the theme better. I would read the fable and ask them to write a short reflection in their journals or notebooks. We would then engage in a small-group discussion about this question: Why is the fable told so simply? I would then bring them into a large-group discussion and lead them to an understanding of the concept of allegory and universal application. The concept of simplicity of style would help them to understand allegory. An instructional activity I might use to help students become interested in the seemingly "flat" characters in the novel would be to show the purpose of archetypal characters in a narrative. I'd ask the students to discuss common TV/movie characters: policeman, hero, queen, newspaper reporter under deadline, president. Then I'd have them determine the values, beliefs, or actions of their characters. Then I might pose the question: when is an archetypal character a useful character in a movie? Can you think of any examples? Then I'd pull the discussion into the concept of universal application again.

Rationale for the score

This response earned a 6 on a scale of 0–6. Points were awarded as follows:

- **Part A:** 2 points awarded. The examinee identifies two central literary features (the form of the allegory/parable and symbolism) and clearly connects those objectives to specific examples from the novel.
- **Part B:** 2 points awarded. The examinee identifies two obstacles to understanding (the simple style and flat characterization), explains why they would likely pose problems for student understanding, and cites specific examples from the novel.
- **Part C:** 2 points awarded. The examinee describes two instructional activities that are appropriate for the grade level and that address the literary features and obstacles to understanding. The instructional activities are designed to help students understand specific elements of the novel.

English to Speakers of Other Languages

6. The correct answer is choice B. The text would necessarily use and require language of both lexical and syntactic complexity greater than that which is likely to be possible or appropriate for levels I and II. The contexts or situations are more appropriate for teenagers and adults.

7. The correct answer is choice B. The lessons described in the table of contents would be most appropriate for a life skills or coping skills program (applying for a job, making purchases, etc.).

Reading Across the Curriculum: Elementary

8. The correct answer is choice B. A semantic map is a visual representation of ideas and the relationships among them. It usually has a key word or concept at the center, with other information radiating outward. It may be used before, during, and after reading to represent what students already know about a topic, to keep ongoing notes, to reorganize information, and to review and enhance information because of new information gained.

9. The correct answer is choice B. A Directed Reading–Thinking Activity is a guided reading method in which the teacher divides the text into shorter segments and then leads the students in predicting; reading silently to confirm predictions; discussing to refine and clarify predictions; and then formulates the new predictions about the remainder of the text. The process is repeated until the reading of the text is completed.

Reading Across the Curriculum: Secondary

10. The correct answer is choice B. A semantic map is a visual representation of ideas and the relationships among them. It usually has a key word or concept at the center, with other information radiating outward. It may be used before, during, and after reading to represent what students already know about a topic, to keep ongoing notes, to reorganize information, and to review and enhance information because of new information gained.

11. The correct answer is choice B. A Directed Reading-Thinking Activity is a guided reading method in which the teacher divides the text into shorter segments and then leads the students in predicting; reading silently to confirm predictions; discussing to refine and clarify predictions; and then formulates the new predictions about the remainder of the text. The process is repeated until the reading of the text is completed.

CHAPTER 22

Social Studies, Math, Science

This chapter covers the following Subject Assessments:

- Social Studies: Content Knowledge
- Citizenship Education: Content Knowledge
- Mathematics: Content Knowledge
- Middle School: Science
- Middle School: Social Studies
- Middle School: Mathematics
- Biology: Content Knowledge
- Chemistry: Content Knowledge
- Earth and Space Sciences: Content Knowledge
- Physics: Content Knowledge

SOCIAL STUDIES: CONTENT KNOWLEDGE (0081)

2 hours   130 multiple-choice questions

The Social Studies: Content Knowledge test is designed to determine whether an examinee has the knowledge and skills necessary for a beginning teacher of social studies in a secondary school. The test requires the examinee to understand and apply social studies knowledge, concepts, methodologies, and skills across the fields of United States history (22 percent); world history (22 percent); government/civics/political science (16 percent); geography (15 percent); economics (15 percent); and the behavioral science fields of sociology, anthropology, and psychology (10 percent).

A number of the questions are interdisciplinary, reflecting the complex relationships among the social studies fields. Answering the questions correctly requires knowing, interpreting, and integrating history and social science facts and concepts.

The 130 equally weighted multiple-choice questions consist of no more than 60 percent knowledge, recall, and/or recognition questions and no less than 40 percent higher-order thinking questions. Some questions are based on interpreting material such as written passages, maps, charts, graphs, tables, cartoons, diagrams, and photographs. Between 10 and 15 percent of the questions contain content reflecting the diverse experiences of people in the United States as related to gender, culture, and/or race, and/or content relating to Latin America, Africa, Asia, or Oceania.

Note: This examination uses the chronological designations B.C.E. (before the common era) and C.E. (common era). These labels correspond to B.C. (before Christ) and A.D. (anno Domini), which are used in some world history textbooks.

CITIZENSHIP EDUCATION: CONTENT KNOWLEDGE (0087)

2 hours   115 multiple-choice questions

The Citizenship Education: Content Knowledge test is designed to determine whether an examinee has the knowledge and skills necessary for a beginning teacher of citizenship education in a secondary school. The test requires the examinee to understand and apply knowledge, concepts, methodologies, and skills across the fields of United States history (25 percent); world history (25 percent); government/civics/political science (18 percent); geography (16 percent); and economics (16 percent). A number of the questions are interdisciplinary, reflecting the complex relationships among the social studies fields. Answering the questions correctly requires knowing, interpreting, and integrating history and social science facts and concepts.

The 115 equally weighted multiple-choice questions consist of no more than 60 percent knowledge, recall, and/or recognition questions and no less than 40 percent higher-order thinking questions. Some questions are based on interpreting material such as written passages, maps, charts, graphs, tables, cartoons, diagrams, and photographs. Between 10 and 15 percent of the questions contain content reflecting the diverse experiences of people in the United States as related to gender, culture, and/or race, and/or content relating to Latin America, Africa, Asia, or Oceania.

MATHEMATICS: CONTENT KNOWLEDGE (0061)

2 hours   50 multiple-choice questions, graphing calculator required

The Mathematics: Content Knowledge test is designed to assess the mathematical knowledge and competencies necessary for a beginning teacher of secondary school mathematics. Examinees have typically completed a bachelor's program with an emphasis in mathematics or mathematics education. The examinee will be required to understand and work with mathematical concepts, to reason mathematically, to make conjectures, to see patterns, to justify statements by using informal logical arguments, and to construct simple proofs. Additionally, the examinee will be expected to solve problems by integrating knowledge from different areas of mathematics, to use various representations of concepts, to solve problems that have several solution paths, and to develop mathematical models and use them to solve real-world problems.

The test is not designed to be aligned with any particular school mathematics curriculum, but it is intended to be consistent with the recommendations of national studies on mathematics education, such as the National Council of Teachers of Mathematics (NCTM) *Principles and Standards for School Mathematics* (2000) and the National Council for Accreditation of Teacher Education (NCATE) *Program Standards for Initial Preparation of Mathematics Teachers* (2003). Graphing calculators without QWERTY (typewriter) keyboards are required for this test. Some questions will require the use of a calculator. Because many test questions may be solved in more than one way, examinees should first decide how to solve each problem and then decide whether to use a calculator. On the test day, examinees should bring a calculator they are comfortable using. Selected notations, formulas, and definitions are printed in the test book.

MIDDLE SCHOOL: SCIENCE (0439)

2 hours   90 multiple-choice questions (Part A)
                 3 constructed-response questions (Part B)

The Middle School: Science test is designed to measure the knowledge and competencies necessary for a beginning teacher of middle school science, such as knowledge of scientific principles, facts, methodology, philosophy, scientific concepts, and an ability to integrate basic knowledge from all the sciences. Teachers need to understand the subject matter from a more advanced viewpoint than is actually presented to the students. Accordingly, some questions of a more advanced nature are included. These questions deal with topics typically introduced in freshman college-level courses in chemistry, physics, life sciences, and earth/space sciences. The questions require a variety of abilities, including definition of terms, comprehension of critical concepts, application, and analysis, to address and solve problems. Some questions may require the examinee to integrate concepts from more than one content area.

The constructed-response questions assess the examinee's ability to use and analyze critical concepts in science and to integrate knowledge from science, technology, and society. One question deals with a topic in the physical sciences (chemistry/physics), the second with a topic in the life sciences, and the third with a topic in the earth/space sciences. One question will assess an examinee's understanding of concepts and models; the second will assess skills in data analysis, experimental design, and investigations; and the third will assess understanding of the patterns and processes that occur in natural systems. In addition, one of the questions will contain a component that assesses the ability to deal with issues concerning science, technology, and society.

The 90 multiple-choice questions make up 75 percent of the total score. The 3 equally weighted constructed-response questions make up 25 percent of the total score. Examinees should plan to allow about 90 minutes for the multiple-choice section and about 30 minutes for the constructed-response section.

MIDDLE SCHOOL: SOCIAL STUDIES (0089)

2 hours   90 multiple-choice questions (Part A)
               3 constructed-response questions (Part B)

The Middle School: Social Studies test assesses the knowledge and skills necessary for a beginning middle school social studies teacher. The test is based on the understanding and application of social studies knowledge, concepts, methodologies, and skills across the fields of U.S. History, world history, government/civics, geography, economics, sociology, and anthropology. Some of the multiple-choice and all the short essay questions are interdisciplinary, reflecting the complex relationship among the social studies fields. Some questions are based on interpreting stimulus material such as written passages, maps, charts, graphs, tables, cartoons, diagrams, and photographs.

The three equally weighted short-answer/essay questions will focus on important historical events and issues as well as on fundamental social studies concepts. These questions, which should take about 10 minutes each to complete and will together comprise 25 percent of the examinee's score, will emphasize the exercise of critical-thinking skills, requiring the reading and interpreting of social studies materials (such as maps, charts, quotations), drawing inferences from such materials, and placing these materials in their historical, geographical, political, and economic contexts. The 90 equally weighted multiple-choice questions will constitute 75 percent of the examinee's score. Examinees should plan to spend about 90 minutes on the multiple-choice section and about 30 minutes on the constructed response section.

MIDDLE SCHOOL: MATHEMATICS (0069)

2 hours   40 multiple-choice questions (Part A)
               3 short constructed-response questions (Part B)

The Middle School: Mathematics test is designed to certify examinees as teachers of middle school mathematics. Examinees have typically completed a bachelor's program with an emphasis in mathematics education, mathematics, or education. Course work will have included many of the following topics: theory of arithmetic, foundations of mathematics, geometry for elementary and middle school teachers, algebra for elementary and middle school teachers, the big ideas of calculus, data and their uses, elementary discrete mathematics, elementary probability and statistics, history of mathematics, mathematics appreciation, and the use of technology in mathematics education. The examinee will be required to understand and work with mathematical concepts, to reason mathematically, to make conjectures, to see patterns, to justify statements using informal logical arguments, and to construct simple proofs.

Additionally, the examinee will be expected to solve problems by integrating knowledge from different areas of mathematics, to use various representations of concepts, to solve problems that have several solution paths, and to develop mathematical models and use them to solve real-world problems.

The 40 multiple-choice questions make up 67 percent of the total score. The 3 constructed-response questions make up 33 percent of the total score. Examinees should plan to spend 80 minutes on the multiple-choice section and 40 minutes on the constructed-response questions.

Examinees are allowed to use a four-function, a scientific, or a graphing calculator during the examination; however, calculators with QWERTY keyboards will not be allowed. More information on the calculator use policy for *Praxis* tests can be found at www.ets.org/praxis/prxcalc.html. The test is not designed to be aligned with any particular school mathematics curriculum, but it is intended to be consistent with the recommendations of national studies on mathematics education such as the National Council of Teachers of Mathematics (NCTM) *Principles and Standards for School Mathematics* (2000) and the National Council for Accreditation of Teacher Education (NCATE) *Program Standards for Initial Preparation of Mathematics Teachers* (2003).

BIOLOGY: CONTENT KNOWLEDGE (0235)

2 hours   150 multiple-choice questions

The Biology: Content Knowledge test is designed to assess whether an examinee has the knowledge and competencies necessary for a beginning teacher of biology in a secondary school. The development of the test questions and the construction of the test reflect the National Science Education Standards and recognize that there are conceptual and procedural schemes that unify the various scientific disciplines. The 150 multiple-choice questions are derived from topics typically covered in an introductory college-level biology course. They cover the following content categories: basic principles of science (8 percent); molecular and cellular biology (25 percent); classical genetics and evolution (15 percent); diversity of life, plants, and animals (35 percent); ecology (15 percent); science, technology, and society (7 percent). Within these content areas, the test questions require a variety of abilities and knowledge, including definition of terms, comprehension of critical concepts, and application and analysis, to address and solve problems.

CHEMISTRY: CONTENT KNOWLEDGE (0245)

2 hours   100 multiple-choice questions

The Chemistry: Content Knowledge test measures the knowledge and competencies necessary for a beginning teacher of chemistry in a secondary school. Examinees have typically completed or nearly completed a bachelor's degree program in chemistry, with appropriate course work in education. The 100 multiple-choice questions address examinees' breadth of knowledge of the physical and philosophical bases of chemistry, and issues related to laboratory practice (including data manipulation and analysis) and the importance of science in the community.

The test covers the following seven broad content areas: matter and energy; heat and thermodynamics and thermochemistry (16 percent), atomic and nuclear structure (10 percent), nomenclature; the mole, chemical bonding, and geometry (14 percent), periodicity and reactivity; chemical reactions; biochemistry and organic chemistry (23 percent), solutions and solubility; acid/base chemistry (12 percent), history and nature of science; science, technology, and social perspectives (11 percent), and mathematics, measurement, and data management; laboratory procedures and safety (14 percent).

Topics are typically covered in introductory college-level chemistry and physical science courses, although some questions of a more advanced nature are included because secondary school instructors must understand the subject matter from a more advanced viewpoint than that presented to their students.

Examinees are not permitted to use calculators in taking this test. Test books contain a periodic table and a table of information that presents various physical constants and a few conversion factors among SI units. Whenever necessary, additional values of physical constants are printed with the text of the question.

EARTH AND SPACE SCIENCES: CONTENT KNOWLEDGE (0571)

2 hours   100 multiple-choice questions

The Earth and Space Sciences: Content Knowledge test is designed to assess whether an examinee has the knowledge and competencies necessary for a beginning teacher of Earth and Space Sciences in a secondary school. The 100 multiple-choice questions address the examinee's knowledge of fundamental scientific concepts, methods, principles, phenomena, and interrelationships.

Questions are derived from topics typically covered in introductory college-level courses in the Earth and Space Sciences, including geology, meteorology, oceanography, astronomy, and environmental science. The questions require a variety of abilities, including an emphasis on the comprehension of critical concepts, analysis to address and solve problems, and an understanding of important terms. Some questions may require the examinee to integrate concepts from more than one content area.

The test covers the following six broad content areas: basic scientific principles of Earth and space sciences (8–12 percent), tectonics and internal Earth processes (18–22 percent), Earth materials and surface processes (23–27 percent), history of the Earth and its life-forms (13–17 percent), Earth's atmosphere and hydrosphere (18–22 percent), and astronomy (8–12 percent). In addition, a substantial number of the questions require knowledge and/or abilities listed under the content area of History and Nature of Science.

PHYSICS: CONTENT KNOWLEDGE (0265)

2 hours   100 multiple-choice questions

The Physics: Content Knowledge test measures the knowledge and competencies necessary for a beginning teacher of physics in a secondary school. Examinees have typically completed or nearly completed a bachelor's degree program in physics, with appropriate course work in education. The 100 multiple-choice questions address examinees' breadth of knowledge in physics, embracing scientific principles, facts, methodology, and philosophy in the following content areas: mechanics (32 percent), electricity and magnetism (23 percent), optics and waves (17 percent), heat and thermodynamics (8 percent), modern physics, atomic, and nuclear structure (8 percent), and history and nature of science; and science, technology and social perspectives (STS) (12 percent). Topics are typically covered in an introductory college-level physics course, although some questions of a more advanced nature are included since secondary school instructors must understand the subject matter from a more advanced viewpoint than that presented to their students.

Examinees are not permitted to use calculators in taking this test. The test books contain a periodic table and a table of information that presents various physical constants and a few conversion factors among SI units. Whenever necessary, additional values of physical constants are printed with the text of the question. Also, since a major goal of science education is to have students develop an understanding of science and the impact of science and technology on the environment and human affairs, these areas are included in the assessment. The questions include definition of terms, comprehension of critical concepts, application, analysis, and problem solving.

REAL QUESTIONS FOR PRACTICE

The questions that follow illustrate the types of questions in the test. Answers and Explanations follow the questions.

> **Directions:** Each of the questions or statements below is followed by four suggested answers or completions. Select the one that is best in each case.

Social Studies: Content Knowledge

1. Demographic transition

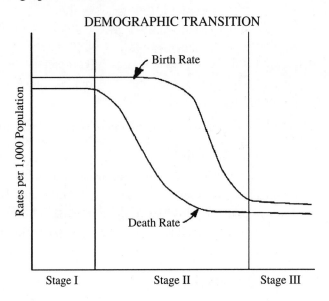

DEMOGRAPHIC TRANSITION

The graph above indicates that rapid population growth is most likely to occur in

(A) stage I only
(B) stage II only
(C) stages I and III only
(D) stages II and III only

Citizenship Education: Content Knowledge

2. Which of the following people would benefit most if the value of the U.S. dollar increased relative to the Japanese yen?

(A) A United States car dealer importing Japanese cars
(B) A Japanese tourist vacationing in the U.S.
(C) A worker in the United States beer industry
(D) A Japanese baker buying U.S. wheat

Mathematics: Content Knowledge

3. Given the recursive function defined by

$f(1) = -3,$
$f(n) = f(n-1) - 6 \quad for \; n \geq 2$

what is the value of $f(4)$?
(A) −2
(B) −9
(C) −10
(D) −21

4. For lines in the plane, the relation "is perpendicular to" is

(A) reflexive but not transitive
(B) symmetric but not transitive
(C) transitive but not symmetric
(D) both symmetric and transitive

Middle School: Science

5. Which of the following is most directly involved with controlling levels of sugar in blood?

(A) Hemoglobin
(B) Calcitonin
(C) Thyroid-stimulating hormone
(D) Insulin

Middle School: Social Studies

6. "I was adamant about getting fathers into the labor room and into the delivery room. I was insistent about fathers attending parenting classes. The only way I would take parents was as couples. I wrote an article for a family magazine and encouraged them to put a father holding a baby on the cover. Today we see fathers pushing baby strollers, carrying babies on slings. We see men doing commercials for diapers and showing tender loving care. There have been tremendous changes. It is no longer considered 'unmasculine' to be affectionate." The quote above is from a 1987 interview with an obstetrician who has been practicing medicine for decades. The changes mentioned by the obstetrician refer to changes in social

(A) regulations
(B) norms
(C) policies
(D) instincts

ROBIN'S TEST SCORES

88, 86, 98, 92, 90, 86

7. In an ordered set of numbers, the median is the middle number if there is a middle number; otherwise, the median is the average of the two middle numbers. If Robin had the test scores given in the table above, what was her median score?

(A) 89
(B) 90
(C) 92
(D) 95

Biology: Content Knowledge

8. A visual representation of an individual's chromosomes that have been stained, photographed, enlarged, and arranged in order of size from largest to smallest is known as a

(A) karyotype
(B) linkage map
(C) pedigree chart
(D) DNA fingerprint

Chemistry: Content Knowledge

9. The solubility product, K_{sp}, for $Mg(OH)_2$ is 1.0×10^{11}. What is the concentration of Mg^{2+} in a saturated solution of this base?

(A) $\sqrt[2]{5.0 \times 10^{-12}}$ M
(B) $\sqrt{1.0 \times 10^{-11}}$ M
(C) $\sqrt[3]{2.5 \times 10^{-12}}$ M
(D) $\sqrt[3]{1.0 \times 10^{-11}}$ M

10. When 0.50 mol of octane, C_8H_{18}, is burned completely and the reaction products are brought to 10°C and 1 atm, the products include approximately

(A) 18 mol of water
(B) 100 L of carbon dioxide
(C) 200 L of carbon dioxide
(D) 220 L of water vapor

Earth and Space Sciences: Content Knowledge

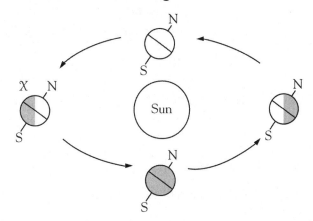

11. In the illustration above of the Earth's orbit about the Sun, which of the following is true of the Earth at location *X*?

(A) The spring equinox occurs.
(B) The fall equinox occurs.
(C) It is winter in the northern hemisphere.
(D) It is summer in the northern hemisphere.

12. Which of the following has provided evidence that the Sun's atmosphere contains sodium atoms?

(A) Stars with the same spectral class as the Sun are made mostly of sodium.
(B) The Sun gives off energy produced by the nuclear fusion of sodium in its core.
(C) Light from the Sun has absorption lines that are consistent with the presence of sodium.
(D) Solar samples returned to Earth by the Voyager spacecraft contained sodium.

Physics: Content Knowledge

13. In a test of an automobile air bag, a mannequin with a mass of 70 kilograms hits a stationary air bag. The velocity of the mannequin at the instant of impact is 25 meters per second. After 0.25 second the mannequin has come to a complete stop and the air bag has deflated. The average force on the mannequin during this interval is most nearly

(A) 70 N
(B) 700 N
(C) 7,000 N
(D) 70,000 N

14. If electrons have a velocity of 4.0×10^6 meters per second at right angles to a magnetic field of 0.20 newton per ampere-meter, what is the magnitude of the force on a single electron?

(A) 1.3×10^{-13} N
(B) 1.6×10^{-14} N
(C) 6.4×10^{-19} N
(D) 3.2×10^{-26} N

Answers and Explanations

Social Studies: Content Knowledge

1. The correct answer is choice B. In stages I and III, birth and death rates are approximately equal. Therefore, the rate of natural increase (population growth) would be quite low, even in the first stage in which the birth rate is high. In stage II, a decline in the death rate precedes a decline in the birth rate. It is in this middle stage that rapid and dramatic population growth would occur.

Citizenship Education: Content Knowledge

2. The correct answer is choice A. Appreciation in the value of the dollar results in a decline in the relative cost of importing foreign goods. An importer of foreign goods would thus benefit. U.S. goods would be relatively more expensive, so choices B and D are incorrect. Choice C is also incorrect; a change in the value of the dollar would have no beneficial effect on a worker in the U.S. beer industry.

Mathematics: Content Knowledge-Check Mathtype Symbols

3. The correct answer is choice D. Given the recursive function defined in the question, in order to find $f(4)$, you need first to find $f(2)$ and $f(3)$. [$f(1)$ is given.]

$$\text{Since } f(1) = -3 \text{ and } f(n) = f(n-1) - 6$$
$$f(2) = -3 - 6 = -9$$
$$\text{for } n \geq 2, \text{ then } f(3) = -9 - 6 = -15$$
$$f(4) = -15 - 6 = -21$$

4. The correct answer is choice B. To answer this question, you must read each answer choice and find the statement that correctly describes the properties of the relation defined as "is perpendicular to." You can see that each answer choice includes two of three properties: reflexivity, symmetry, or transitivity. It may be most efficient to first consider each of these properties and then find the statement that describes these properties correctly for the given relation. The definition of these properties can be found in the Notation,

Definitions, and Formulas pages that are included in this document and at the beginning of each of the Mathematics: Content Knowledge tests.

A relation $\mathfrak{R}$ is reflexive if $x \mathfrak{R} x$ for all x. In this case, a line cannot be perpendicular to itself, so the relation given in the question is *not* reflexive. A relation $\mathfrak{R}$ is symmetric if $x \mathfrak{R} y \rightarrow y \mathfrak{R} x$ for all x and y. In this case, if line j is perpendicular to line k, it follows that line k is perpendicular to line j. So this relation is symmetric. A relation $\mathfrak{R}$ is transitive if $(x \mathfrak{R} y$ and $y \mathfrak{R} z) \rightarrow x \mathfrak{R} z$ for all $x, y,$ and z. In this case, if line j is perpendicular to line k and line k is perpendicular to line l, then lines j and l either are the same line or are parallel to each other. Thus, line j is not perpendicular to line l. So this relation is not transitive. The answer choice that correctly describes the relation "is perpendicular to" is choice B, "symmetric but not transitive."

Middle School: Science

5. The correct answer is choice D. In response to rising levels of glucose in the blood, cells in the pancreas secrete the hormone insulin. Circulating insulin lowers blood sugar levels by enhancing the transport of glucose and other simple sugars into body cells, especially muscle cells.

Middle School: Social Studies

6. The correct answer is choice B. The obstetrician is discussing changes in people's learned behavior made through education, encouragement, and example. No actions by government or another official body are mentioned, therefore eliminating regulations (choice A) and policies (choice C). Instincts (choice D) are not learned behavior but rather are innate and would not be affected by the obstetrician's actions. "Norms," society's often unwritten and unspoken rules, serve to guide and control proper and acceptable behavior and can be affected by the type of actions that the obstetrician describes taking.

Middle School: Mathematics

7. The correct answer is choice A. The problem gives a set of test scores and the definition of median. The first part of the definition tells you to order the scores, that is, to arrange them in order from smallest to largest. Here are the numbers ordered from smallest to largest:

$$86, 86, 88, 90, 92, 98$$

Because there are an even number of scores (6), there are two middle numbers in the set, 88 and 90, and the average of the two middle numbers is

$$\frac{88+90}{2} = \frac{178}{2} = 89$$

Thus the median of Robin's scores is 89 and the answer is choice A. (Notice that the median of a set of numbers need not be one of the numbers in the set.)

Biology: Content Knowledge

8. The correct answer is choice A. A karyotype is basically a pictorial representation of the chromosomes contained in a cell.

Chemistry: Content Knowledge

9. The correct answer is choice C.
The K_{sp} of a salt is the product of the ion concentrations in a saturated solution. In the present case, $K_{sp} = [Mg^{2+}] [OH^-]^2$.
Since $[OH^-] = 2[Mg^{2+}]$, $K_{sp} = [Mg^{2+}] (2[Mg^{2+}])^2 = 4[Mg^{2+}]3 = 1.0 \times 10^{-11}$.
Solving for $[Mg^{2+}]$, one obtains $[Mg^{2+}] = [1 \times 10^{-11}/4]^{1/3}$.

10. The correct answer is choice B.
The balanced equation for the reaction is
$2C_8H_{18} + 25O_2 \rightarrow 16CO_2 + 18H_2O$.
0.5 mol octane produces 4 mol of CO_2, which at 10°C STP, occupies

$$\frac{(4\,mol \times 22.4\,L/mol)\,293\,K}{273\,K} = 96\,L \cong 100\,L$$

Earth and Space Sciences: Content Knowledge

11. The correct answer is choice D. When the Earth is at location X, the northern hemisphere receives the most direct rays of the Sun and experiences the greatest number of daylight hours. Under these conditions, it is summer in the northern hemisphere.

12. The correct answer is choice C. The chemical composition of the Sun's atmosphere has been inferred primarily from absorption lines observed in the solar spectrum.

Physics: Content Knowledge

13. The correct answer is choice C.
The average force $\bar{F}$ is equal in magnitude to the change in the momentum of the mannequin divided by the elapsed time, or

$$\bar{F} = \frac{m\,\Delta V}{\Delta t} = \frac{(70\,kg)(25\,m/s)}{0.25s} = 7,000\,N$$

14. The correct answer is choice A.
According to the Lorentz force law, $F = qvB = (1.6 \times 10^{-19}\ C) (4.0 \times 10^6\ m/s) (0.20\ N/Am) = 1.3 \times 10^{-13}\ N$

CHAPTER 23

Other Subjects

This chapter covers the following Subject Assessments:

- Spanish: Content Knowledge
- French: Content Knowledge
- German: Content Knowledge
- Business Education
- Art: Content Knowledge
- Physical Education: Content Knowledge
- Health Education
- Audiology
- Speech-Language Pathology
- ParaPro Assessment

SPANISH: CONTENT KNOWLEDGE (0191)

2 hours   120 multiple-choice questions based on recorded and printed materials in Spanish

The Spanish: Content Knowledge test is designed to assess the knowledge and competencies necessary for a beginning or entry-year teacher of Spanish. The 120 multiple-choice questions measure the test-takers' competence in various language skills and their knowledge of the cultures of Spanish-speaking regions. The test contains the following four sections: I. Interpretive Listening (27 percent), II. Structure of the Language (28 percent), III. Interpretive Reading (26 percent), IV. Cultural Perspectives (19 percent). In the first, third, and fourth sections, all questions and answer choices are in Spanish. All the questions in the Interpretive Listening section as well as the first part of the Structure of the Language section are based on recorded materials.

FRENCH: CONTENT KNOWLEDGE (0173)

2 hours   120 multiple-choice questions based on recorded and printed materials in French

The French: Content Knowledge test is designed to assess the knowledge and competencies necessary for a beginning or entry-year teacher of French. The 120 multiple-choice questions measure the test-takers' competence in various language skills and their knowledge of the cultures of France and French-speaking regions.

The test contains the following four sections: I. Interpretive Listening (27 percent), II. Structure of the Language (28 percent), III. Interpretive Reading (26 percent), IV. Cultural Perspectives (19 percent). In the first, third, and fourth sections, all questions and answer choices are in French. All the questions in the Interpretive Listening section, as well as the first part of the Structure of the Language section, are based on recorded materials.

GERMAN: CONTENT KNOWLEDGE (0181)

2 hours   120 multiple-choice questions based on recorded and printed materials in German

The German: Content Knowledge test is designed to assess the knowledge and competencies necessary for a beginning or entry-year teacher of German. The 120 multiple-choice questions measure the test-takers' competence in various language skills and their knowledge of the cultures of Germany and German-speaking regions. The test contains the following four sections: I. Interpretive Listening (27 percent), II. Structure of the Language (28 percent), III. Interpretive Reading (26 percent), IV. Cultural Perspectives (19 percent). In the first, third, and fourth sections, all questions and answer choices are in German. All the questions in the Interpretive Listening section, as well as the first part of the Structure of the Language section, are based on recorded materials.

BUSINESS EDUCATION (0100)

2 hours   120 multiple-choice questions

The Business Education test is intended primarily for persons planning to teach in business education programs at the high school level. The test concentrates on the core of knowledge and cognitive skills common to all business teachers, including content that contributes to business and economic literacy. Also included are questions about professional information related to business education in general and questions about areas of specialization within business education. Because of the variations among business education programs, some questions may refer to areas that may not have been studied. Therefore, no one is expected to answer all the questions on the test correctly. In general, the topics concern areas broadly defined as business and economic literacy; professional business education, including knowledge, comprehension, and application of pedagogical techniques; and business specialization, including specific background and application knowledge considered essential for a business education teacher.

The examination is typically taken by examinees who have completed a bachelor's degree program in education with appropriate course work in business education. Examinees are allowed to use a calculator during the examination. Calculators with QWERTY keyboards will not be allowed.

ART: CONTENT KNOWLEDGE (0133)

2 hours   120 multiple-choice questions

The Art: Content Knowledge test is intended primarily for individuals completing teacher training programs who plan to become art teachers. The multiple-choice test questions focus on those concepts that are considered central to the subject matter of art. The test measures knowledge of the traditions in art, architecture, design, and the making of artifacts (36 percent); art criticism and aesthetics (25 percent); and the making of art (39 percent). Illustrations may be included with some of the questions. The majority of these illustrations are printed in color. Test-takers have typically completed a bachelor's degree program in art or art education.

PHYSICAL EDUCATION: CONTENT KNOWLEDGE (0091)

2 hours   120 multiple-choice questions

The Physical Education: Content Knowledge test is designed to measure the professional knowledge of prospective teachers of physical education in elementary through senior high schools. The test assesses whether an examinee has the knowledge and competencies necessary for a beginning teacher of physical education.

The 120 multiple-choice questions cover knowledge of fitness, fundamental movements, and sports that comprise the content of physical education classes; knowledge of areas in the natural and social sciences that provide the foundation for teaching these activities; and knowledge of crucial topics in health and safety. Knowledge of these subject areas enables teachers to understand the nature and purpose of the activities in the physical education curriculum; to evaluate and interpret the physical characteristics and performances of students in physical education classes; and to make decisions about the ongoing conduct of physical education classes and the needs of students in those classes. Questions will test knowledge of essential facts, including the meaning of terms and placement of content elements in proper categories; understanding of relationships between and among areas of content; and the ability to apply concepts appropriately.

HEALTH EDUCATION (0550)

2 hours   120 multiple-choice questions

The Health Education test is designed to measure the professional knowledge of prospective teachers of health education in elementary schools, junior high schools, and senior high schools. The questions invite examinees to recall basic knowledge and to apply education and health principles to real-life situations. The content is appropriate for examinees who have completed a bachelor's degree program in health education. The 120 multiple-choice questions cover health education as a discipline (15 percent), promoting healthy lifestyles (30 percent), community health advocacy (10 percent), healthy relationships (20 percent), disease prevention (15 percent), and health education pedagogy (10 percent).

AUDIOLOGY (0340)

The Audiology test measures examinees' academic preparation in and knowledge of the field. The examination is typically taken by examinees who are in or who have completed a master's or doctoral degree program that prepares individuals to enter professional practice. Recognized as the national examination in audiology, the test is one of several requirements for the Certificate of Clinical Competence issued by the American Speech-Language-Hearing Association (ASHA). Some states use the examination as part of the licensure procedure. Examinees may obtain complete information about certification or licensure from the authority (ASHA, 10801 Rockville Pike, Rockville, MD 20852) or the state or local agency from which certification or licensure is sought.

The 120 multiple-choice test questions focus on the following content areas: basic human communication processes (26 percent), prevention and identification (10 percent), behavioral assessment and interpretation (13 percent), electrophysiological measurement and interpretation (8 percent), rehabilitative assessment (11 percent), rehabilitative technology (11 percent), rehabilitative management (11 percent), and professional issues/ psychometrics/research (10 percent). Case studies assess the candidate's knowledge of possible applications to clinical situations and issues. Research articles are included to assess the examinee's ability to synthesize information and to apply it to specific examples. The distribution of the test questions across the areas of practice was based on a national survey, commissioned by ASHA, of audiologists in a variety of employment settings. The Audiology test evolves slowly in order to incorporate new developments in this rapidly changing field while still maintaining comparability of scores from one year to the next.

SPEECH-LANGUAGE PATHOLOGY (0330)

2 hours   120 multiple-choice questions

The Speech-Language Pathology test measures examinees' academic preparation in and knowledge of the field. The examination is typically taken by examinees who are in or who have completed a master's degree program. Recognized as the national examination in speech-language pathology, the test is one of several requirements for the Certificate of Clinical Competence issued by the American Speech-Language-Hearing Association (ASHA). Some states use the examination as part of the licensure procedure. Examinees may obtain complete information about certification or licensure from the authority (ASHA, 10801 Rockville Pike, Rockville, MD 20852), or the state or local agency from which certification or licensure is sought.

The 120 multiple-choice test questions focus on the following content areas: basic human communication processes (17 percent), phonological and language disorders (19 percent), speech disorders (13 percent), neurogenic disorders (19 percent), audiology/hearing (5 percent), clinical management (19 percent), and professional issues/psychometrics/research (8 percent). Case studies assess the candidate's knowledge of possible applications to clinical situations and issues. Research articles are included to assess the examinee's ability to synthesize information and to apply it to specific examples. The distribution of the test questions across the areas of practice was based on a national survey, commissioned by ASHA, of speech-language pathologists in a variety of employment settings. The Speech-Language Pathology test evolves slowly in order to incorporate new developments in this rapidly changing field while still maintaining comparability of scores from one year to the next.

PARAPRO ASSESSMENT (0755)

2 ½ hours   90 multiple-choice questions

The ParaPro Assessment for prospective and practicing paraprofessionals measures skills and knowledge in reading, mathematics, and writing, as well as the ability to apply those skills and knowledge to assist in classroom instruction. The test consists of 90 multiple-choice questions across the three subject areas of reading, mathematics, and writing. Approximately two-thirds of the questions in each subject area focus on basic skills and knowledge, and approximately one-third of the questions in each subject area focus on the application of those skills and knowledge in a classroom context. Fifteen of the questions in the test (five in each subject) are pretest questions and do not count toward the examinee's score. The test questions are arranged by subject area, with reading first, then mathematics, and finally writing.

REAL QUESTIONS FOR PRACTICE

The following real test questions illustrate the types of items on the actual exams. Answers and explanations follow the last question.

> **Directions:** Each of the questions or statements below is followed by four or five suggested answers or completions. Select the one that is best in each case.

Spanish: Content Knowledge

1. Un magnífico ejemplo de la arquitectura Inca es:

(A) Chichén Itzá
(B) Machu Picchu
(C) Tikal
(D) Teotihuacán

French: Content Knowledge

2. À quelle heure les gens ont-ils le plus de chance de dîner en France?

(A) 15h30
(B) 16h30
(C) 20h00
(D) 23h00

German: Content Knowledge

3. Welches der folgenden Länder grenzt an Österreich?

(A) Polen
(B) Rumänien
(C) Ungarn
(D) Frankreich

4. Das Ruhrgebiet ist allgemein bekannt

(A) für seinen Weinanbau
(B) als populäres Ferienziel
(C) für seine Milchwirtschaft
(D) als Industrieregion

Business Education

5. In connection with the purchase of a house, the term "abstract" refers to a document that

(A) transfers the title of the property from one party to another
(B) provides a history of the ownership of the property
(C) quits a claim against a property that one may have held at any time
(D) guarantees that there is no encumbrance against the property
(E) certifies that the records of the property have been examined

6. The flowchart symbol ∇ means that data are

(A) collated
(B) displayed
(C) sorted
(D) stored off-line
(E) handled manually

Art: Content Knowledge

7. In painting, which of the following techniques generally makes the objects in a composition appear closer to the viewer?

    (A) Drawing the objects as relatively large compared with other objects in the composition.

    (B) Drawing the objects in three-point rather than two-point perspective.

    (C) Using analogous colors for all the objects that are in the foreground.

    (D) Outlining the objects in black or dark colors.

8. In storing printmaking supplies, it is most important to store which of the following separately from the other materials?

    (A) Acetic acid

    (B) Rosin powder

    (C) Nitric acid

    (D) Solvents

Physical Education: Content Knowledge

9. Which of the following practice alternatives would best promote motor learning and safety for potentially injurious sports such as pole vaulting and downhill skiing?

    (A) Whole

    (B) Part

    (C) Progressive-part

    (D) Distributed

10. All of the following are direct physiological consequences of warm-down (cool-down) activities following vigorous physical activity EXCEPT

    (A) preventing blood from pooling in the legs

    (B) increasing the rate of lactic acid removal from the blood and skeletal muscle

    (C) promoting the reduction of cholesterol in the blood

    (D) reducing the risk of cardiac irregularities

Health Education

11. Amniocentesis is most often used to

(A) facilitate artificial insemination
(B) measure immune response capability in transplant recipients
(C) determine the presence of certain disorders in the fetus
(D) estimate the mother's potential for maintaining a pregnancy to term

12. Compared to younger women, women over age 35 have an increased risk of giving birth to children with which of the following genetic disorders?

(A) Cystic fibrosis
(B) Down syndrome
(C) Hemophilia
(D) Sickle cell anemia

Audiology

13. In the measurement of real-ear sound-pressure levels with a probe-tube microphone system, insufficient probe-tube depth will tend to

(A) increase the high-frequency response
(B) decrease the high-frequency response
(C) decrease the response at all frequencies
(D) decrease the low-frequency response
(E) increase the low-frequency response

14. Click-evoked otoacoustic emissions are most likely to be recorded from the ears of which of the following individuals?

(A) A person with a profound hearing loss.
(B) A person with severe presbycusis.
(C) A person with an upper brain stem lesion.
(D) A person with otitis media.
(E) A person who has ingested large quantities of aminoglycosides.

Speech-Language Pathology

15. A speech-language pathologist is behaving ethically if he or she does which of the following?

(A) Refuses to deliver professional services on the basis of a client's sexual orientation.

(B) Offers to provide speech or language services solely by correspondence for an individual whose handicapping condition prevents easy access to the professional's office.

(C) Diagnoses a speech disorder solely through correspondence as long as the correspondence is thorough and careful.

(D) Offers general information of an educational nature by correspondence.

(E) Indicates the specific duration of the therapeutic program.

16. Which of the following statements best characterizes the ethics of formulating prognoses for clients with speech and language disorders?

(A) No assessment is complete until a precise statement can be formulated regarding the prognosis.

(B) Since offering a favorable prognosis is essentially equivalent to guaranteeing the results of a therapy program, it is unethical to make specific statements regarding prognosis.

(C) The extreme complexity of speech and language processes and behaviors makes it impossible to formulate prognoses.

(D) After an assessment has been completed, it is usually appropriate to make some general statements about prognosis.

(E) A clinician's ability to make prognostic statements depends on the availability of standardized tests to quantify the severity of a speech and language disorder.

ParaPro Assessment

Questions 17 and 18 are based on the following rough draft written by a student.

How to Teach Your Dog to Sit by Kiara

(1) First hold a dog biscuit so the dog pays attention. (2) Say "Sit!" (3) When you say it, use a loud and firm voice. (4) Move the hand holding the biscuit over the dog's nose, don't let him grab it. (5) You may have to give a light backwards tug on the dog's leash. (6) When the dog sits down, give him the treat and lots of praise. (7) Repeat this a few times, and he'll probably understand the command.

17. Kiara is writing an introductory sentence that summarizes the main points of the paragraph. What sentence would be the strongest introductory sentence for the paragraph?

(A) Dogs are naturally very intelligent and obedient.

(B) Your dog probably likes some dog biscuits better than others.

(C) It is easy to teach your dog the command "Sit!"

(D) Nobody likes a dog that can't play catch.

18. Kiara is learning how to use transition words (words that clarify the relationships between ideas). What transition word or words should Kiara use before the word "don't" in sentence 4 in order to clarify the meaning of the sentence?

(A) "but"
(B) "because"
(C) "for example"
(D) "so"

Answers and Explanations

Spanish: Content Knowledge

1. The correct answer is choice B. Machu Picchu was built by the Incas.

French: Content Knowledge

2. The correct answer is choice C. "Le dîner" (dinner) generally takes place around *"20 heures"* (8 o'clock in the evening). The other choices (3:30 p.m., 4:30 p.m., 11:00 p.m.) are not likely times for French people to have dinner.

German: Content Knowledge

3. The correct answer is choice C because Hungary borders Austria.

4. The correct answer is choice D because das Ruhrgebiet is the largest industrial area in Germany.

Business Education

5. The correct answer is choice B. An abstract of title provides a listing of the transfers of title to land. It is often obtained by a buyer as a means of protection, but it is not a guarantee.

6. The correct answer is choice D. The shape pictured is the standard symbol for off-line storage.

Art: Content Knowledge

7. The correct answer is choice A. Relative size is a powerful tool for making objects appear closer or farther away in pictorial space. The other techniques listed do not affect the viewer's impression of the nearness of the objects.

8. The correct answer is choice C. Nitric acid is an oxidizing agent that can react with any of the other supplies to cause an explosion or fire.

Physical Education: Content Knowledge

9. Choice C describes a method of practice that involves working on specific elements of a skill in isolation. Because this method allows those elements of a skill that present the greatest risk of injury to be mastered under controlled conditions before the skill is attempted "whole" and under real conditions, choice C is the correct answer.

10. The correct answer is choice C. This question is based on a standard textbook discussion of the rationale for warm-down following vigorous physical activity, which clearly establishes choices A, B, and D as real effects of proper warm-down procedures. Choice C is not such an effect and is thus the correct answer.

Health Education

11. The correct answer is choice C. Amniocentesis involves the removal and examination of a small sample of cells from the amniotic cavity, enabling doctors to detect genetic disorders.

12. The correct answer is choice B. The incidence of Down syndrome increases with the age of the mother. In the United States, for example, among mothers in the age range 20 to 30, about 1 in 800 newborns has Down syndrome, whereas the incidence of Down syndrome in newborns of mothers over age 40 is 1 in 100.

Audiology

13. The correct answer is choice B. Probe tubes for measuring real-ear sound-pressure levels (SPLs) should be inserted as close to the tympanic membrane as possible, since it is the SPL at the tympanic membrane that is being measured. If the probe tube is too far from the tympanic membrane, high-frequency sound waves bounced off the eardrum will dissipate before reaching the probe, but low-frequency sound waves, which do not dissipate as easily, will be essentially unaffected. The overall effect will thus be a decrease only in the high-frequency response.

14. The correct answer is choice C. Upper brainstem lesions do not always interfere with otoacoustic emissions, so otoacoustic emissions can be recorded from the ears of persons with upper brain stem lesions. Choices A, B, and E are incorrect because severe or profound hearing loss and ototoxic medications such as aminoglycosides cause a loss of spontaneous emissions. Choice D is incorrect because transmission of emissions is poor when the impedance of the middle ear is abnormal, as in cases of otitis media.

Speech-Language Pathology

15. The correct answer is choice D. According to the 1995 Code of Ethics of the American Speech-Language-Hearing Association (ASHA), the best answer, choice D, is allowed. The other choices are not approved and are discussed in Principle of Ethics I, Rule C, Rule F, and Rule G, among others.

16. The correct answer is choice D. According to the 1995 ASHA Code of Ethics, Principle of Ethics I, Rule F, a speech-language pathologist can make general statements about a client's prognosis. The other choices are contrary to the spirit of this ethical position.

17. The correct answer is choice C. Kiara's paragraph is concerned with discussing what steps to take when teaching a dog to sit. Choice A is too general, choice B concerns a minor element of the paragraph, not its primary focus, and choice D concerns playing catch, which is not discussed in the paragraph at all.

18. The correct answer is choice A. The word "but" is used to emphasize the contrast expressed in the sentence: "Move the hand holding the biscuit over the dog's nose, **but** don't let him grab it."

APPENDIX A

State-by-State *Praxis* Passing Scores

The Praxis Series™ Passing Scores by Test and State

This list shows the minimum/passing scores of user states/agencies for **The Praxis Series** tests. To determine if you passed a test in a particular state, compare your test score with the score listed for the state in which you are interested and read all related footnotes. If your scaled score equals or exceeds the printed score for that state, you have passed. (**Note:** Number in parentheses following the test name is the test code.) **These scores are current as of January 1, 2008.**

PRAXIS I®: ACADEMIC SKILLS ASSESSMENTS
PRE-PROFESSIONAL SKILLS TEST: MATHEMATICS (0730)
COMPUTERIZED PPST®: MATHEMATICS (5730)

AK -173	AR -171	CT -171	DC -174	DE -174
HI -173ᵃ	IN -175	KY -+	LA -172	MD -177ᵈ
ME -ᶜ	MN -171	MS -169	NC -173ᶠ	ND -170ᵍ
NE -171	NH -172ᵉ	NJ -174	NV -172	OH -172
OK -171	OR -175	PA -173ʲ	SC -172	TN -173
VA -178ᵏ	VT -175ʲ	WI -173	WV -172	DODEA - 175
GUAM - 170	VI -171			

PRE-PROFESSIONAL SKILLS TEST: READING (0710)
COMPUTERIZED PPST: READING (5710)

AK -175	AR -172	CT -172	DC -172	DE -175
HI -172ᵃ	IN -176	KY -+	LA -174	MD -177ᵈ
ME -ᶜ	MN -173	MS -170	NC -176ᶠ	ND -173ᵍ
NE -170	NH -174ᵉ	NJ -175	NV -174	OH -173
OK -173	OR -174	PA -172ʲ	SC -175	TN -174
VA -178ᵏ	VT -177ʲ	WI -175	WV -174	DODEA - 177
GUAM - 173	VI -173			

PRE-PROFESSIONAL SKILLS TEST: WRITING (0720)
COMPUTERIZED PPST: WRITING (5720)

AK -174	AR -173	CT -171	DC -171	DE -173
HI -171ᵃ	IN -172	KY -+	LA -173	MD -173ᵈ
ME -ᶜ	MN -172	MS -172	NC -173ᶠ	ND -173ᵍ
NE -172	NH -172ᵉ	NJ -173	NV -172	OH -172
OK -172	OR -171	PA -173ʲ	SC -173	TN -173
VA -176ᵏ	VT -174ʲ	WI -174	WV -172	DODEA - 174
GUAM - 170	VI -172			

PRAXIS II: PRINCIPLES OF LEARNING AND TEACHING (PLT)
PLT: EARLY CHILDHOOD (0521)

AR -159	HI -158	KS -161	LA -172	MD -169
MN -164	OH -166	SD -160	TN -155	UT -160

PLT: GRADES K–6 (0522) ** ROE: 185

HI -163	ID -161	KS -161	KY -161	LA -161
ME -166	MN -159	MS -152	ND -162	NV -169
OH -168	RI -167	SC -165	SD -153	TN -155
UT -160	VI -162	WV -165	DODEA - 156	

PLT: GRADES 5–9 (0523) ** ROE: 184

AR -164	HI -157	ID -162	KS -161	KY -161
LA -154	MN -155	MO -160	MS -152	OH -168
SC -165	SD -153	TN -154	UT -160	WV -159
WY -157	DODEA - 153			

PLT: GRADES 7–12 (0524) ** ROE: 184

AR -164	HI -157	KS -161	KY -161	LA -161
MD -162	ME -*	MN -157	MO -160	MS -152
NV -161	OH -165	RI -167	SC -165	SD -153
TN -159	UT -160	WV -156	WY -161	DODEA - 158

PRAXIS II®: SUBJECT ASSESSMENTS/SPECIALTY AREA TESTS
AGRICULTURE (0700)

AL -460	AR -510	DE -530	ID -510	KS -470
KY -520	LA -510	MN -490	MO -520	SD -480
TN -530	UT -*	WA -520	WI -510	WV -430
WY -*				

AGRICULTURE (CA) (0900)

OR -590

AGRICULTURE (PA) (0780)

PA -520

ART MAKING (0131)

AR -146	CT -148	KY -154	NC -ᶠ	NV -154
SC -155	TN -155	VT -148		

ART: CONTENT KNOWLEDGE (0133)

AK -155	AL -150	AR -157	CT -157	DE -161
HI -166	ID -155	IN -149	KS -156	KY -158
LA -155	MD -159ᵈ	ME -151	MN -164	MO -153
MS -139	NC -ᶠ	ND -146	NJ -150	NV -156
OH -157	OR -156	PA -161	SC -149	SD -143
TN -150	UT -*	VA -159	WA -155	WI -155
WV -160	WY -*			

ART: CONTENT, TRADITIONS, CRITICISM, & AESTHETICS (0132)

AR -140	CT -130	HI -135	MD -145ᵈ	OR -145
TN -140				

AUDIOLOGY (0340)

State Departments of Education: CO - 600   ID -600   MS -610
NC -590   OH -600   VT -600
ASHA and All State Boards of Examiners - 600

BIOLOGY & GENERAL SCIENCE (0030)

IN -560   OH -560   SC -570

BIOLOGY: CONTENT ESSAYS (0233)

NH -143   TN -146   VT -150

BIOLOGY: CONTENT KNOWLEDGE, PART 1 (0231)

HI -161   NV -154   OR -155   PA -156   WV -148

BIOLOGY: CONTENT KNOWLEDGE, PART 2 (0232)

OR -148   PA -137

BIOLOGY: CONTENT KNOWLEDGE (0235) ** ROE: 179

AK -139	AL -143	AR -142	CT -152	DC -150
DE -157	ID -139	IN -154	KS -150	KY -146
LA -150	MD -150	ME -150	MN -152	MO -150
MS -150	NC -ᶠ	ND -153	NH -153	NJ -152
OH -148	PA -147	SD -147	TN -148	UT -149
VA -155	VT -151	WA -152	WV -152	WY -*

* = Test required – passing score not set – verify with state.
** = Target score for ETS Recognition of Excellence.
+= Each preparation program may have different requirements. Before registering for Praxis I, please contact your advisor/program coordinator to determine your requirements.

‡ = Multiple scores required – verify with state.
a–k = See state notes at end of this section.

KEY TO AGENCIES:	ASHA = American Speech-Language-Hearing Association BCASP = British Columbia Association of School Psychologists	NASP = National Association of School Psychologists DODEA = Department of Defense Education Activity

BUSINESS EDUCATION (0100)

AL -570	AR -550	CT -620	DE -600	HI -570
ID -580	IN -480	KS -590	KY -590	LA -570
MD -590	ME -560	MN -610	MO -590	MS -560
NC -580	NJ -580	NV -560	OH -610	OR -600
PA -560	SC -540	SD -560	TN -570	UT -*
VA -590	WA -560	WI -580	WV -570	WY -*

CHEMISTRY: CONTENT ESSAYS (0242)

CT -140	NH -140	NV -145	VT -150

CHEMISTRY: CONTENT KNOWLEDGE (0241)

HI -144	OR -136

CHEMISTRY: CONTENT KNOWLEDGE (0245) ** ROE: 184

AK -139	AL -150	CT -151	DC -152	DE -158
ID -139	IN -151	KS -152	KY -147	LA -151
MD -153	MN -152	MO -152	MS -151	NC -ᶠ
ND -147	NH -153	NJ -152	NV -151	OH -152
PA -154	SD -135	TN -152	UT -151	VA -153
VT -160	WA -152	WV -157	WY -*	

CHEMISTRY, PHYSICS, & GENERAL SCIENCE (0070)

AL -560	MD -520	OH -520	OR -540	SC -540
UT -*				

CITIZENSHIP EDUCATION: CK (0087)

PA -148	RI -160

COMMUNICATION (0800)

PA -530

COOPERATIVE EDUCATION (0810)

PA -770

DRIVER EDUCATION (WV) (0867)

AL -149	WA -150	WV -141	WY -*

EARLY CHILDHOOD EDUCATION (0020)

IN -510	OR -580	PA -530	WV -530

EARLY CHILDHOOD: CONTENT KNOWLEDGE (0022)

AR -157	CT -156	KY -165	MD -160	MN -155
NC -155	ND -158	NH -161	NJ -159	RI -169
WY -143				

EARTH AND SPACE SCIENCES: CONTENT KNOWLEDGE (0571)

AK -144	AL -150	AR -145	CT -157	DE -150
ID -144	IN -150	KS -150	KY -145	MD -152
MN -149	MO -147	NC -136	ND -149	NH -148
NJ -153	OH -151	PA -157	SD -150	TN -146
UT -153	VA -156	VT -158	WA -150	WY -*

ECONOMICS (0910)

AK -460	AL -520	ID -460	ND -510	SD -500
TN -530	UT -560	WY -*		

ED. LEADERSHIP: ADMINISTRATION & SUPERVISION (0410)

AL -610	GA -620	KS -590	LA -620	NC -590
NV -590	OH -610	OR -600	PA -580	SC -590
SD -590	UT -*	WV -570		

EDUCATION OF DEAF & HARD OF HEARING STUDENTS (0271)

AR -160	ID -162	KS -163	KY -167	LA -160
MO -161	MS -151	OH -158	OR -144	PA -164
SC -161	TN -163	UT -*	WA -167	

EDUCATION OF EXCEPTIONAL STUDENTS: CORE CONTENT KNOWLEDGE (0353)

CT -158	DC -146	HI -152	ID -156	IN -150
KS -160	KY -157	LA -143	MD -148ᵈ	ME -157
MN -158	MO -160	MS -136	PA -136	SC -150
SD -150	TN -144	UT -155	VI -148	WA -152
WV -146				

EDUCATION OF EXCEPTIONAL STUDENTS: LEARNING DISABILITIES (0382)

SC -158	WV -133

EDUCATION OF EXCEPTIONAL STUDENTS: MILD TO MODERATE DISABILITIES (0542)

ID -168	IN -156	KS -169	KY -172	LA -141
MO -172	NC -159	SC -165	TN -164	UT -155
WV -153				

EDUCATION OF EXCEPTIONAL STUDENTS: SEVERE TO PROFOUND DISABILITIES (0544)

KS -159	KY -156ᵇ	LA -147	MO -153	NC -144
SC -148	TN -155	UT -*	WV -*	

EDUCATION OF YOUNG CHILDREN (0021)

CT -158	DC -174	HI -160	ID -169	KS -172
ME -166	MO -166	MS -165	OH -166	RI -171
SC -158	SD -166	TN -155	UT -168	WA -170

ELEM ED.: CONTENT AREA EXERCISES (0012)

CT -148	DC -148	HI -135	MD -150	NC -ᶠ
NV -135	RI -148	SC -145	UT -150	

ELEM ED.: CONTENT KNOWLEDGE (0014) ** ROE: 181

AK -143	AL -137	CO -147	DC -145	DE -151
IA -142	ID -143	KY -148	LA -150	MD -142
ME -145	MN -145	MS -153	MT -*	NH -148
NJ -141	OH -143	RI -145	SD -140	TN -140
UT -150	VA -143	VI -140	VT -148	WA -141
WI -147				

ELEM ED.: CURRICULUM, INSTRUCTION, & ASSESSMENT (0011)

AK -156	CT -163	HI -164	IA -151	IN -165
KS -163	MO -164	MS -158	NC -ᶠ	ND -158
NE -159	NV -158	PA -168	SC -164	TN -159
WV -155	WY -160			

ENGLISH LANG., LIT., & COMP.: CONTENT KNOWLEDGE (0041) **ROE: 192

AK -158	AL -151	AR -159	CO -162	CT -172
DC -142	DE -163	HI -164	ID -158	IN -153
KS -165	KY -160	LA -160	MD -164	ME -160
MN -157	MO -158	MS -157	NC -ᶠ	ND -151
NH -164	NJ -162	NV -150	OH -167	OR -159
PA -162	SC -162	SD -154	TN -157	UT -168
VA -172	VI -161	VT -172	WA -158	WI -160
WV -155	WY -*			

ENGLISH LANG., LIT., & COMP.: ESSAYS (0042)

AK -160	AR -150	CT -160	KY -155	NH -155
OR -145	SC -150	UT -*	VT -160	

ENGLISH LANG., LIT., & COMP.: PEDAGOGY (0043)

AR -145	DC -150	HI -150	LA -130	MD -155
NC -ᶠ	NV -140	TN -145	UT -*	

ENGLISH TO SPEAKERS OF OTHER LANGUAGES (0360)

AL -540	DC -520	HI -510	ID -580	KS -500
KY -620	MD -570	ME -540	MN -600	NC -520
OH -420	OR -510	SC -540	TN -530	UT -*
VI -570	WA -580	WI -530	WY -*	

* = Test required – passing score not set – verify with state.
** = Target score for ETS Recognition of Excellence.
+ = Each preparation program may have different requirements. Before registering for Praxis I, please contact your advisor/program coordinator to determine your requirements.

‡ = Multiple scores required – verify with state.
a–k = See state notes at end of this section.

KEY TO AGENCIES:	ASHA = American Speech-Language-Hearing Association	NASP = National Association of School Psychologists
	BCASP = British Columbia Association of School Psychologists	DODEA = Department of Defense Education Activity

ENVIRONMENTAL EDUCATION (0830)

PA - 600

FAMILY AND CONSUMER SCIENCE (0120)

AL - 530	AR - 560	CT - 630	HI - 560	ID - 580
IN - 540	KS - 600	KY - 600	LA - 510	MD - 590
ME - 570	MN - 600	MO - 600	MS - 560	NC - 540
NJ - 550	NV - 610	OH - 540	OR - 630	PA - 600
SC - 540	SD - 550	TN - 580	UT - *	VA - 550
WA - 500	WI - 590	WV - 530	WY - *	

FOREIGN LANGUAGE PEDAGOGY (0840)

ID - 158

FRENCH: CONTENT KNOWLEDGE (0173)

AK - 162	AL - 148	AR - 158	DC - 155	DE - 157
HI - 158	ID - 157	IN - 160	KS - 166	KY - 159
LA - 156	MD - 161^d	ME - 157	MO - 161	NC - ^{f}
ND - 156	NJ - 156	NV - 152	OH - 160	OR - 146
PA - 170	SC - 160	SD - 150	TN - 160	UT - 161
VA - 169	VT - 157	WA - 158	WI - 156	WV - 131

FRENCH: PRODUCTIVE LANGUAGE SKILLS (0171)

AK - 171	AR - 167	DC - 173	DE - 168	HI - 164
MD - 170^d	MN - 158	MS - 161	NC - ^{f}	NV - 162
OR - 160	SC - 166	TN - 165	VT - 163	

FUNDAMENTAL SUBJECTS: CONTENT KNOWLEDGE (0511)

DE - 155	MS - 142	NC - 148	PA - 150	RI - 160
UT - 161				

GENERAL SCIENCE: CONTENT ESSAYS (0433)

AK - 145	CT - 145	NH - 135	NV - 135	TN - 130
VT - 145				

GENERAL SCIENCE: CONTENT KNOWLEDGE, PART 1 (0431)

AK - 155	HI - 150	NV - 150	OR - 145	TN - 145

GENERAL SCIENCE: CONTENT KNOWLEDGE, PART 2 (0432)

AK - 149	OR - 143	WV - 149

GENERAL SCIENCE: CONTENT KNOWLEDGE (0435) ** ROE: 185

AK - 149	AL - 147	CO - 152	CT - 157	DC - 157
DE - 160	ID - 149	LA - 156	MO - 154	NC - ^{f}
ND - 150	NH - 147	NJ - 152	OH - 149	PA - 146
SD - 143	UT - *	VI - 154	VT - 157	WA - 153
WI - 154				

GEOGRAPHY (0920)

AK - 590	AL - 560	ID - 600	ND - 530	SD - 520
TN - 580	UT - *	WY - *		

GERMAN: CONTENT KNOWLEDGE (0181)

AK - 153	AL - 142	HI - 148	ID - 159	IN - 147
KS - 158	KY - 157	LA - 151	MD - 153^d	ME - 156
MO - 161	NC - 153	ND - 150	NJ - 157	OH - 165
OR - 156	PA - 165	SC - 151	SD - 143	TN - 149
UT - 153	VA - 162	VT - 148	WA - 160	WI - 153
WV - 132				

GERMAN: PRODUCTIVE LANGUAGE SKILLS (0182)

AK - 178	HI - 169	MD - 164^d	MN - 179	MS - 160
OR - 160	SC - 181	VT - 169		

GIFTED EDUCATION (0357)

AR - 156

GOVERNMENT/POLITICAL SCIENCE (0930)

AK - 610	AL - 570	ID - 610	ND - 490	SD - 540
TN - 600	UT - *	WY - *		

HEALTH EDUCATION (0550)

AL - 580	CT - 680	HI - 560	ID - 630	IN - 420
KS - 620	KY - 630	MD - 630	MN - 580	MO - 620
NC - 640	NV - 600	OH - 480	OR - 690	PA - 650
SC - 680	SD - 580	TN - 570	UT - *	WI - 610
WV - 640	WY - *			

HEALTH & PHYSICAL EDUCATION: CONTENT KNOWLEDGE (0856)

AR - 144	NJ - 151	NV - 159	PA - 146	VA - 151
WA - 149				

INTRODUCTION TO THE TEACHING OF READING (0200)

IN - 510	NC - 540	NJ - 560	NV - 560	OH - 540
SC - 560				

LATIN (0600)

AL - 590	KY - 700	MD - 610	ME - 610	ND - 500
PA - 610	TN - 540	UT - 610	VT - 580	WV - 480

LIBRARY MEDIA SPECIALIST (0310)

AL - 600	AR - 610	HI - 610	ID - 620	IN - 530
KS - 630	KY - 640	LA - 560	ME - 590	MN - 630
MO - 630	MS - 590	NC - 610	OH - 610	OR - 610
PA - 620	SC - 620	TN - 600	UT - *	WA - 600
WV - 570	WY - *			

LIFE SCIENCE: PEDAGOGY (0234)

AR - 146	DC - 147	HI - 139	MD - 144	NC - ^{f}
NV - 150	UT - *			

MARKETING EDUCATION (0560)

AL - 500	AR - 570	ID - 630	MO - 660	MS - 590
NC - 690	NJ - 630	OH - 440	OR - 660	PA - 550
TN - 640	UT - *	VA - 570	WA - 640	WI - 600
WV - 600	WY - *			

MATHEMATICS: CONTENT KNOWLEDGE (0061) ** ROE: 165

AK - 146	AL - 126	AR - 116	CO - 156	CT - 137
DC - 141	DE - 141	HI - 136	ID - 119	IN - 136
KS - 137	KY - 125	LA - 130	MD - 141	ME - 126
MN - 135	MO - 137	MS - 137	NC - ^{f}	ND - 139
NH - 127	NJ - 137	NV - 133	OH - 139	OR - 139
PA - 136	SC - 131	SD - 124	TN - 136	UT - 138
VA - 147	VI - 125	VT - 141	WA - 134	WI - 135
WV - 133	WY - *			

MATHEMATICS: PEDAGOGY (0065)

AR - 135	DC - 135	HI - 135	MD - 145	NC - ^{f}
NV - 135	TN - 125			

MATHEMATICS: PROOFS, MODELS, & PROBLEMS, PART 1 (0063)

AK - 171	AR - 144	DC - 154	KY - 141	NH - 140
OR - 144	SC - 137	UT - *	VT - 154	

MIDDLE SCHOOL: CONTENT KNOWLEDGE (0146)

AK - 140	AL - 141	AR - 139	SD - 141	TN - 150
WI - 146	WY - 150			

MIDDLE SCHOOL ENGLISH LANGUAGE ARTS (0049)

AK - 154	AL - 148	CT - 164	DE - 161	HI - 160
IN - 152	KS - 165	KY - 157	LA - 160	MD - 160
ME - 155	MN - 161	MO - 163	MS - 145	NC - 145
ND - 157	NH - 155	NJ - 156	NV - 158	OH - 156
OR - 159	PA - 163	RI - 162	SC - 155	SD - 150
TN - 145	VA - 164	VT - 154	WA - 158	WV - 147
WY - 160				

---

* = Test required – passing score not set – verify with state.
** = Target score for ETS Recognition of Excellence.
+ = Each preparation program may have different requirements. Before registering for Praxis I, please contact your advisor/program coordinator to determine your requirements.

‡ = Multiple scores required – verify with state.
a–k = See state notes at end of this section.

KEY TO AGENCIES:	ASHA = American Speech-Language-Hearing Association	NASP = National Association of School Psychologists
	BCASP = British Columbia Association of School Psychologists	DODEA = Department of Defense Education Activity

MIDDLE SCHOOL MATHEMATICS (0069)

AK -145	AL -149	CT -158	DE -148	HI -143
ID -145	IN -156	KS -158	KY -148	LA -148
MD -152	ME -148	MN -152	MO -158	MS -140
NC -141	ND -148	NH -151	NJ -152	NV -139
OH -143	OR -156	PA -151	RI -158	SC -149
SD -140	TN -143	VA -163	VT -161	WA -152
WV -148	WY -152			

MIDDLE SCHOOL SCIENCE (0439)

AK -136	AL -142	CT -162	DE -146	HI -148
IN -137	KS -149	KY -139	LA -145	MD -145
ME -142	MN -150	MO -149	MS -135	NC -134
ND -145	NJ -145	NV -143	OH -144	OR -148
PA -144	RI -154	SC -145	SD -138	TN -135
VA -162	VT -157	WA -145	WV -151	WY -147

MIDDLE SCHOOL SOCIAL STUDIES: (0089)

AK -147	AL -149	CT -160	DE -164	HI -152
IN -153	KS -155	KY -149	LA -149	MD -154
ME -153	MN -151	MO -154	MS -140	NC -149
ND -152	NH -153	NJ -158	NV -148	OH -151
OR -146	PA -152	SC -150	SD -145	TN -140
VA -160	VT -165	WA -157	WV -151	WY -153

MUSIC: ANALYSIS (0112)

AR -150	MD -147d	OR -167

MUSIC: CONCEPTS & PROCESSES (0111)

AR -145	CT -150	HI -145	KY -145	NC -f
NV -150	SC -145	TN -145	VT -150	

MUSIC: CONTENT KNOWLEDGE (0113)

AK -148	AL -150	AR -150	CT -153	DE -155
HI -139	ID -148	IN -140	KS -152	KY -154
LA -151	MD -154d	ME -151	MN -149	MO -151
MS -139	NC -f	ND -149	NJ -153	NV -149
OH -154	OR -162	PA -158	SC -151	SD -150
TN -150	UT -*	VA -160	VT -153	WA -150
WI -150	WV -155	WY -*		

PARAPRO ASSESSMENT (PAPER & PENCIL) (0755); (WEB-BASED) (1755)

AR -457	AZ -459	CO -460	CT -457	DC -461
DE -459	HI -459	ID -460	IL -460	IN -460
KS -455	LA -450	MA -464	MD -455	ME -459
MI -460	MN -460	MO -458	ND -464	NE -456
NJ -456	NM -457	NV -460	OH -456	OR -455
RI -461	SC -456	SD -461	TN -456	UT -460
VA -455	VI -466	VT -458	WA -461	WY -462

PHYSICAL ED.: CONTENT KNOWLEDGE (0091)

AL -141	AR -141	CT -154	DE -152	HI -155
ID -143	IN -150	KS -148	KY -147	LA -146
MD -153	ME -149	MN -143	MO -153	MS -138
NC -158	NJ -148	NV -154	OH -153	OR -156h
SC -146	SD -140	TN -152	UT -*	VT -147
WI -150	WV -150	WY -*		

PHYSICAL ED.: MOVEMENT FORMS-ANALYSIS & DESIGN (0092)

AR -150	CT -154	HI -145	KY -151	NV -149
OR -141h	TN -148	UT -*	VT -154	

PHYSICAL ED.: MOVEMENT FORMS-VIDEO EVALUATION (0093)

MD -155	OR -145h	SC -160

PHYSICAL SCIENCE: CONTENT KNOWLEDGE (0481)

AK -145	AR -145	DE -154	HI -149	ID -145
ME -147	NH -148	SD -143	UT -*	WV -142
WY -*				

PHYSICAL SCIENCE: PEDAGOGY (0483)

AR -145	DC -145	HI -151	MD -151	NC -f
NV -147				

PHYSICS: CONTENT ESSAYS (0262)

CT -135	NH -140	TN -135	VT -150

PHYSICS: CONTENT KNOWLEDGE (0261)

DE -136	HI -144	OR -139

PHYSICS: CONTENT KNOWLEDGE (0265) ** ROE: 177

AK -129	AL -138	CT -141	ID -129	IN -149
KS -141	KY -133	LA -141	MD -143	MN -137
MO -141	MS -139	ND -132	NH -146	NJ -141
OH -132	PA -140	SD -130	TN -144	UT -136
VA -147	VT -140	WA -140	WV -126	WY -*

PRE-KINDERGARTEN EDUCATION (0530)

IN -390	WV -590

PSYCHOLOGY (0390)

AL -550	ID -600	KS -550	NV -550	SC -720
SD -520	TN -560	UT -*	WY -*	

READING ACROSS THE CURRICULUM: ELEMENTARY (0201)

MD -173	TN -151	VI -149	WY -*

READING ACROSS THE CURRICULUM: SECONDARY (0202)

WY -*

READING SPECIALIST (0300)

AL -530	AR -560	DE -560	HI -540	ID -480
KS -560	ME -530	MN -590	NC -570	OR -610
PA -570	TN -510	WA -540	WV -520	

SAFETY/DRIVER EDUCATION (0860)

PA -520

SCHOOL GUIDANCE & COUNSELING (0420)

AL -520	AR -600	HI -580	KS -600	ME -570
MO -590	MS -580	NC -570	NV -610	OH -510
OR -600	PA -590	SC -550	TN -580	UT -*
WV -580				

SCHOOL PSYCHOLOGIST (0400)

State Boards of Education:

AL -520	AR -620	CO -660	KS -610	KY -630
MD -630	MO -610	MS -590	NC -620	NM -600
OH -630	OR -590	PA -560	SC -660	TN -590
UT -*	VT -660	WI -660	WV -550	

Boards of Psychology:

BCASP -660	FL -660	MA -660	NASP -660	OH -650
TX -660	WI -620			

SCHOOL SOCIAL WORKER: CONTENT KNOWLEDGE (0211)

WI -161

SOCIAL SCIENCES: CONTENT KNOWLEDGE (0951)

PA -*

SOCIAL STUDIES: ANALYTICAL ESSAYS (0082)

AR -140	NH -145

* = Test required – passing score not set – verify with state.
** = Target score for ETS Recognition of Excellence.
+ = Each preparation program may have different requirements. Before registering for Praxis I, please contact your advisor/program coordinator to determine your requirements.

‡ = Multiple scores required – verify with state.
a–k = See state notes at end of this section.

KEY TO AGENCIES:	ASHA = American Speech-Language-Hearing Association	NASP = National Association of School Psychologists
	BCASP = British Columbia Association of School Psychologists	DODEA = Department of Defense Education Activity

SOCIAL STUDIES: CONTENT KNOWLEDGE (0081) ** ROE: 184

AK -150	AL -153	AR -155	CO -150	CT -162
DC -145	DE -157	HI -154	ID -150	IN -147
KS -158	KY -151	LA -149	MD -154	ME -157
MN -146	MO -152	MS -143	NC -ᶠ	ND -153
NH -155	NJ -157	NV -152	OH -157	OR -153
PA -157	SC -158	SD -146	UT -*	VA -161
VT -162	WA -157	WI -153	WV -148	WY -158

SOCIAL STUDIES: INTERPRETATION AND ANALYSIS (0085)

OR -155

SOCIAL STUDIES: INTERPRETATION OF MATERIALS (0083)

KY -159	LA -152	SC -160	VT -165

SOCIAL STUDIES: PEDAGOGY (0084)

DC -169	HI -144	MD -164	NC -ᶠ	UT -*

SOCIOLOGY (0950)

AL -550	ID -570	SD -540	TN -540	UT -*
WY -*				

SPANISH: CONTENT KNOWLEDGE (0191)

AK -152	AL -147	AR -155	DC -153	DE -157
HI -171	ID -152	IN -159	KS -167	KY -160
LA -160	MD -162ᵈ	ME -158	MO -158	NC -ᶠ
ND -155	NJ -159	NV -160	OH -160	OR -161
PA -166	RI -156	SC -148	SD -135	TN -152
UT -161	VA -161	VT -163	WA -160	WI -158
WV -143				

SPANISH: PEDAGOGY (0194)

AR -160	DC -170	HI -150	UT -*

SPANISH: PRODUCTIVE LANGUAGE SKILLS (0192)

AR -141	DC -166	DE -156	MD -168ᵈ	MN -162
MS -155	NC -ᶠ	NV -156	OR -160	RI -174
SC -161	TN -154	UT -*	VT -165	

SPECIAL EDUCATION: APPLICATION OF CORE PRINCIPLES ACROSS CATEGORIES OF DISABILITY (0352)

AR -141	DE -139	HI -141	MD -147ᵈ	MS -139
NC -136	PA -144			

SPECIAL EDUCATION: KNOWLEDGE-BASED CORE PRINCIPLES (0351)

AR -150	NC -143	NV -150	OH -151	OR -147
PA -152				

SPECIAL EDUCATION: PRESCHOOL/EARLY CHILDHOOD (0690)

AR -610	ID -550	MO -620	OR -530	SD -550
TN -560	WA -550	WV -550		

SPECIAL EDUCATION: TEACHING STUDENTS WITH BEHAVIORAL DISORDERS/EMOTIONAL DISTURBANCES (0371)

MS -150	NC -147	SC -153	WV -156

SPECIAL EDUCATION: TEACHING STUDENTS WITH LEARNING DISABILITIES (0381)

NC -139

SPECIAL EDUCATION: TEACHING STUDENTS WITH MENTAL RETARDATION (0321)

ME -140	NC -144	SC -143

SPEECH COMMUNICATION (0220)

AK -560	AL -580	AR -550	ID -560	IN -490
KS -590	KY -580	LA -580	MO -530	MS -510
NC -560	NJ -560	NV -560	OR -620	SD -560
TN -570	UT -*	WV -600	WY -*	

SPEECH-LANGUAGE PATHOLOGY (0330)

State Boards of Education:

AR -600	CA -600	CO -600	GA -600	ID -600
KY -600	MO -600	MS -600	NC -550	NJ -550
NY -600	OH -600	OR -600	SC -530	TN -600
VT -600	WI -600	WV -600		

ASHA and All State Boards of Examiners: 600

TEACHING FOUNDATIONS: ENGLISH (0048)

CA -173

TEACHING FOUNDATIONS: MATHEMATICS (0068)

CA -153

TEACHING FOUNDATIONS: MULTI SUBJECTS (0528)

CA -155

TEACHING FOUNDATIONS: SCIENCE (0438)

CA -171

TEACHING FOUNDATIONS: SOCIAL STUDIES (0088)

CA -*

TEACHING SPEECH TO STUDENTS WITH LANGUAGE IMPAIRMENTS (0880)

ME -540	NV -500	PA -590

TEACHING STUDENTS WITH VISUAL IMPAIRMENTS (0280)

AR -690	ID -660	KS -710	KY -700	MO -660
MS -660	NC -550	OH -580	OR -730	PA -620
SC -690	TN -700	WV -660		

TECHNOLOGY EDUCATION (0050)

AL -540	AR -550	CT -640	HI -560	ID -590
IN -590	KS -570	KY -600	LA -600	MD -580
ME -570	MN -600	MO -570	MS -560	NC -580
NJ -570	NV -580	OR -620	PA -620	SC -570
SD -560	TN -580	UT -*	VA -610	WA -590
WI -590	WV -570	WY -*		

THEATRE (0640)

AK -560	AL -510	AR -580	ID -540	IN -*
KY -630	MD -560	MN -560	NJ -570	SD -540
TN -610	UT -*	WA -560	WI -600	WY -*

VOCATIONAL GENERAL KNOWLEDGE (0890)

ME -540	PA -560

WORLD & US HISTORY (0940)

NV -470

WORLD & US HISTORY (0941)

AK -*	AL -143	ID -141	ND -151	SD -135
TN -136	UT -156	WY -*		

* = Test required – passing score not set – verify with state.
** = Target score for ETS Recognition of Excellence.
+ = Each preparation program may have different requirements. Before registering for Praxis I, please contact your advisor/program coordinator to determine your requirements.

‡ = Multiple scores required – verify with state.
a–k = See state notes at end of this section.

KEY TO AGENCIES:	ASHA = American Speech-Language-Hearing Association	NASP = National Association of School Psychologists
	BCASP = British Columbia Association of School Psychologists	DODEA = Department of Defense Education Activity

HI Licensure for all areas requires (1) achieving a combined total score of 516 and meeting the minimum score of 170 on each of the three tests or (2) meeting the passing score of 173 for PPST or CPPST Mathematics (0730, 5730), meeting the passing score of 172 for PPST or CPPST Reading (0710, 5710), and meeting the passing score of 171 for PPST or CPPST Writing (0720, 5720).

ETS no longer offers the CBT tests; however, the scores for the CBT tests are reportable for ten years. Hawaii allows combining the PPST/CPPST scores with CBT scores to meet passing score requirements. The options are as follows:

(a) Combining two PPST/CPPST tests with one CBT test: Meeting a composite score of 647 and meeting the minimum score of 170 on the PPST/CPPST tests and a minimum score of 300 on the CBT test.

(b) Combining one PPST/CPPST test with two CBT tests: Meeting a composite score of 778 and meeting the minimum score of 170 on the PPST/CPPST test and a minimum score of 300 on the CBT tests.

(c) Combining three CBT tests: Meeting a composite score of 910 and meeting the minimum score of 300 on each of the three CBT tests.

b = KENTUCKY Notes

KY license for Moderate and Severe Disabilities – Please visit www.kyepsb.net/ for current requirements.

c = MAINE Notes

All Areas, K–12 (except Career and Technical Education) require (1) achieving a combined total score of 526 and meeting the minimum score of 172 on PPST or CPPST Mathematics (0730, 5730), meeting the minimum score of 173 on PPST or CPPST Reading (0710, 5710), and meeting the minimum score of 172 on PPST or CPPST Writing (0720, 5720) or (2) meeting the passing score of 175 for PPST or CPPST Mathematics (0730, 5730), meeting the passing score of 176 for PPST or CPPST Reading (0710, 5710), and meeting the passing score of 175 for PPST or CPPST Writing (0720, 5720).

Career and Technical Education requires

(1) achieving a combined total score of 513 and meeting the minimum score of 169 on PPST or CPPST Mathematics (0730, 5730), meeting the minimum score of 170 on PPST or CPPST Reading (0710, 5710), and meeting the minimum score of 165 on PPST or CPPST Writing (0720, 5720) or (2) meeting the passing score of 172 for PPST or CPPST Mathematics (0730, 5730), meeting the passing score of 173 for PPST or CPPST Reading (0710, 5710), and meeting the passing score of 168 for PPST or CPPST Writing (0720, 5720).

d = MARYLAND Notes

MD Initial Licensure (all areas) requires (1) achieving a combined total score of 527 for all three PPST or CPPST tests or (2) meeting the passing score of 177 on PPST or CPPST Mathematics (0730, 5730), meeting the passing score of 177 on PPST or CPPST Reading (0710, 5710), and meeting the passing score of 173 on PPST or CPPST Writing (0720, 5720). There are no minimum scores.

ETS no longer offers the CBT tests; however, the scores for the CBT tests are reportable for ten years. Therefore, the CBT test requirements were (1) achieving a combined score of 966 for all CBT tests, (2) meeting the passing score of 322 on CBT: Mathematics (0731), meeting a passing score of 325 on CBT: Reading (0711), and meeting the passing score of 310 on CBT: Writing (0721).

MD license for Art requires (1) a combined score of 304 from Art: Content, Traditions, Criticism and Aesthetics (0132) and Art: Content Knowledge (0133) or (2) meeting the passing score of 145 on Art: Content, Traditions,

Criticism and Aesthetics (0132) and meeting the passing score of 159 on Art: Content Knowledge (0133).

MD license for French requires (1) a combined score of 331 from French: Productive Language Skills (0171) and French: Content Knowledge (0173) or (2) meeting the passing score of 170 on French: Productive Language Skills (0171) and meeting the passing score of 161 on French: Content Knowledge (0173).

MD license for German requires (1) a combined score of 317 from German: Content Knowledge (0181) and German: Productive Language Skills (0182) or (2) meeting the passing score of 153 on German: Content Knowledge (0181) and meeting the passing score of 164 on German: Productive Language Skills (0182).

MD license for Spanish requires (1) a combined score of 330 from Spanish: Content Knowledge (0191) and Spanish: Productive Language Skills (0192) or (2) meeting the passing score of 162 on Spanish: Content Knowledge (0191) and meeting the passing score of 168 on Spanish: Productive Language Skills (0192).

MD license for Music requires (1) a combined score of 301 from Music: Analysis (0112) and Music: Content Knowledge (0113) or (2) meeting the passing score of 147 on Music: Analysis (0112) and meeting the passing score of 154 on Music: Content Knowledge (0113).

MD license for Special Education requires (1) a combined score of 295 from Education of Exceptional Students: Core Content Knowledge (0353) and Special Education: Application of Core Principles Across Categories of Disability (0352) or (2) meeting the passing score of 147 on Special Education: Application of Core Principles Across Categories of Disability (0352) and meeting the passing score of 148 on Education of Exceptional Students: Core Content Knowledge (0353).

e = NEW HAMPSHIRE Notes

NH initial licensure (all areas) requires (1) achieving a combined total score of 518 for all three PPST or CPPST tests and meeting the minimum score of 170 on PPST or CPPST Mathematics (0730, 5730), meeting the minimum score of 172 on PPST or CPPST Reading (0710, 5710), and meeting the minimum score of 170 on PPST or CPPST Writing (0720, 5720) or (2) meeting the passing score of 172 on PPST or CPPST Mathematics (0730, 5730), meeting the passing score of 174 on PPST or CPPST Reading (0710, 5710), and meeting the passing score of 172 on PPST or CPPST Writing (0720, 5720).

f = NORTH CAROLINA Notes

Entry into a teacher training program requires (1) achieving a combined total score of 522 for all three PPST or CPPST tests or (2) meeting the passing score of 173 on PPST or CPPST Mathematics (0730, 5730), meeting the passing score of 176 on PPST or CPPST Reading (0710, 5710), and meeting the passing score of 173 on PPST or CPPST Writing (0720, 5720). There are no minimum scores.

ETS no longer offers the CBT tests; however, the scores for the CBT tests are reportable for ten years. Therefore, the CBT test requirements for entry into teacher training programs are (1) achieving a combined score of 960 for all CBT tests, or (2) meeting the passing score of 318 on CBT: Mathematics (0731), meeting a passing score of 323 on CBT: Reading (0711), and meeting the passing score of 319 on CBT: Writing (0721).

NC license for Art requires a combined score of 322 from Art Making (0131) and Art: Content Knowledge (0133). There are no minimum scores.

NC license for Biology requires a combined score of 302 from Biology: Content Knowledge (0235); and Life Science: Pedagogy (0234). There are no minimum scores.

NC license for Chemistry requires a combined score of 307 from Chemistry: Content Knowledge (0245),

and Physical Science: Pedagogy (0483). There are no minimum scores.

NC license for Elementary K–6 requires a combined score of 313 from Elementary Education: Curriculum, Instruction, and Assessment (0011) and Elementary Education: Content Area Exercises (0012). There are no minimum scores.

NC license for English requires a combined score of 321 from English Language, Literature and Composition: Content Knowledge (0041) and English Language, Literature and Composition: Pedagogy (0043). There are no minimum scores.

NC license for French requires a combined score of 335 from French: Content Knowledge (0173) and French: Productive Language Skills (0171). There are no minimum scores.

NC license for Mathematics requires a combined score of 281 from Mathematics: Content Knowledge (0061) and Mathematics: Pedagogy (0065). There are no minimum scores.

NC license for Music requires a combined score of 299 from Music: Concepts and Processes (0111), and Music: Content Knowledge (0113). There are no minimum scores.

NC license for Science Comprehensive requires a combined score of 303 from General Science: Content Knowledge (0435) and Life Science: Pedagogy (0234), OR, a combined score of 305 from General Science: Content Knowledge (0435) and Physical Science: Pedagogy (0483). There are no minimum scores.

NC Social Studies Licenses (Anthropology, Economics, Geography, History, Political Science, Social Studies Comprehensive, and Sociology) require a combined score of 320 from Social Studies: Content Knowledge (0081), and Social Studies: Pedagogy (0084). There are no minimum scores.

NC license for Spanish requires a combined score of 327 from Spanish: Content Knowledge (0191) and Spanish: Productive Language Skills (0192). There are no minimum scores.

g = NORTH DAKOTA Notes

ND Licensure for all areas requires (1) achieving a combined total score of 516 and meeting the passing scores on any two of the three tests or (2) meeting the passing score of 170 for PPST or CPPST Mathematics (0730, 5730), meeting the passing score of 173 for PPST or CPPST Reading (0710, 5710), and meeting the passing score of 173 for PPST or CPPST Writing (0720, 5720).

h = OREGON Notes

OR license for Elementary Education requires achieving a combined total score of 299 for both tests by either (1) meeting the passing score of 142 on MSAT: Content Knowledge (0140) and meeting the passing score of 141 on MSAT: Content Area Exercises (0151) OR (2) meeting/exceeding the minimum score of 147 on Content Knowledge and meeting/exceeding the minimum score of 147 on Content Area Exercises.

OR Certification in Physical Education requires achieving a combined total score of 446 for three tests by either (1) meeting/exceeding the passing score of 156 on Physical Education: Content Knowledge (0091), or (2) meeting the passing score of 141 on Physical Education: Movement Forms - Analysis and Design (0092), or (3) meeting the passing score of 145 on Physical Education: Movement Forms - Video Evaluation (0093).

i = PENNSYLVANIA Notes

PA Initial Licensure (all areas) requires (1) achieving a combined total score of 521 for all three PPST or CPPST tests or (2) meeting the passing score of 173 and/or meeting or exceeding the minimum score of 171 on PPST or

---

KEY TO AGENCIES: ASHA = American Speech-Language-Hearing Association | NASP = National Association of School Psychologists
BCASP = British Columbia Association of School Psychologists | DODEA = Department of Defense Education Activity

STATE-BY-STATE *PRAXIS* PASSING SCORES ▶549

CPPST Mathematics (0730, 5730), meeting the passing score of 172 and/or meeting or exceeding the minimum score of 171 on PPST or CPPST Reading (0710, 5710), and meeting the passing score of 173 and/or meeting or exceeding the minimum score of 170 on PPST or CPPST Writing (0720, 5720).

j=VERMONT Notes

VT Initial Licensure (all areas) requires either (1) achieving a combined total score of 526 for all three PPST or CPPST tests or (2) meeting the passing score of 175 on PPST or CPPST: Mathematics (0730, 5730), meeting the passing score of 177 on PPST or CPPST: Reading (0710, 5710), meeting the passing score of 174 on PPST or CPPST: Writing (0720, 5720). There are no minimum scores.

k = VIRGINIA Notes

Entry into teacher training programs requires (1) achieving a combined total score of 532 for all three PPST or CPPST tests or (2) meeting the passing score of 178 on PPST or CPPST Mathematics (0730, 5730), meeting the passing score of 178 on PPST or CPPST Reading (0710, 5710), and meeting the passing score of 176 on PPST or CPPST Writing (0720, 5720). There are no minimum scores.

ETS no longer offers the CBT tests; however, the scores for the CBT tests are reportable for ten years. Therefore, the CBT test requirements for initial licensure were (1) achieving a combined score of 973 for all CBT tests, or (2) meeting the passing score of 323 on CBT: Mathematics (0731), meeting a passing score of 326 on CBT: Reading (0711), and meeting the passing score of 324 on CBT: Writing (0721).

KEY TO AGENCIES: ASHA = American Speech-Language-Hearing Association   NASP = National Association of School Psychologists
                     BCASP = British Columbia Association of School Psychologists   DODEA = Department of Defense Education Activity

70857-54449 • UNLOCKEDPDF18

For More Information

For more information about state teacher certification testing requirements, contact the agencies listed below.

Alabama
Teacher Education and Certification Office
State Department of Education
P.O. Box 302101
Montgomery, L 36130-2101
Internet: www.alsde.edu

Alaska
Alaska Teacher Certification

Arkansas
Office of Professional Licensure
Arkansas Department of Education
#4 State Capitol Mall—Rooms 106B/107B
Little Rock, AR 72201

California
California Commission on Teacher Credentialing (CCTC)
Information Services Unit
P.O. Box 944270
1900 Capitol Avenue
Sacramento, CA 94233-2700
Telephone: 916-445-7254 or 888-921-2682, 12:00 p.m. to 4:45 p.m. (PST)
E-mail: credentials@ctc.ca.gov

Colorado
Educator Licensing
Colorado Department of Education
201 E. Colfax Avenue, Room 105
Denver, CO 80203-1799
Telephone: 1-303-866-6628
Internet: www.cde.state.co.us/index_license.htm

Connecticut

Connecticut State Department of Education
Bureau of Certification and Teacher Preparation
PO Box 150471—Room 243
Hartford, CT 06115-0471
Telephone: 860-713-6969
Fax: 860-713-7017

Delaware

Delaware Educator Data System

District of Columbia

District of Columbia Public Schools
Educational Credentialing and Standards Branch
825 North Capitol Street, NE—6th Floor
Washington, DC 20002
Telephone: 202-442-5377

Georgia

The Georgia Professional Standards Commission
Two Peachtree Street, Suite 6000
Atlanta, GA 30303
Telephone: 1-404-232-2500 in Georgia
1-800-869-7775 (outside metro Atlanta)

Hawaii

Hawaii Teacher Standards Board
ATTN: Licensing Section
650 Iwilei Road, Suite 201
Honolulu, HI 96817
Telephone: 1-808-586-2600
Fax: 1-808-586-2606

Iowa

Internet: www.iowacte.org

Idaho

Specific *Praxis II* information is found at:
http://www.sde.state.id.us/certification/praxisinfo.asp
For more information on Idaho certification requirements, refer to the following
Web sites:
http://www.sde.state.id.us/certification
http://www.sde.state.id.us/certification/certmanual.asp

Indiana

Indiana Professional Standards Board
251 East Ohio Street, Suite 201
Indianapolis, IN 46204-2133
Telephone: 1-317-232-9010

Kansas

Kansas Certification and Teacher Education

Kentucky

Kentucky Education Professional Standards Board.

Louisiana

For further information about education and teacher licensing in Louisiana visit the Louisiana State Department of Education or the Teach Louisiana Web site.

Maine

For further information about education and initial certification visit the Maine Certification Office.

Maryland

For further information visit Maryland State Department of Education or call the Maryland Certification Information Line at 1-410-767-0412.

Minnesota

Minnesota Department of Education
Personnel Licensing Team
1500 Highway 36 West
Roseville, MN 55113-4266
Telephone: 1-651-582-8691

Mississippi

For further information about education and teacher licensure in Mississippi, visit the Mississippi Department of Education at http://www.mississippi.gov/frameset. jsp?URL=http%3A%2F%2Fwww.mde.k12.ms.us%2F.

Missouri

Visit the Missouri Department of Elementary and Secondary Education.

Nebraska

Teacher Education and Certification
Nebraska Department of Education
301 Centennial Mall South
P.O. Box 94987
Lincoln, NE 68509
Telephone: 1-402-471-2496
Fax: 1-402-471-9735 or 8127

Nevada

Nevada Department of Education
1820 East Sahara, Suite 205
Las Vegas, NV 89104-3746
Telephone: 1-702-486-6455

New Hampshire

For more information visit the New Hampshire Department of Education.

New Jersey

New Jersey Department of Education
Office of Licensing and Credentials
CN 500
Trenton, NJ 08625-0500
Telephone: 1-609-292-2070

New Mexico

For further information, visit the New Mexico Department of Education.

New York

For further information, visit the New York Office of Teaching.

North Carolina

Department of Public Instruction
Licensure Section
301 North Wilmington Street
Raleigh, NC 27601-2825
Telephone: 1-919-807-3310

North Dakota

Internet: http://www.nd.gov/espb/

Ohio

For additional information, visit the Ohio Department of Education, Center for the Teaching Profession.

Oklahoma
Oklahoma Department of Education
Professional Standards Section
Hodge Education Building, Room 211
2500 North Lincoln Boulevard
Oklahoma City, OK 73105
Telephone: 1-405-521-3337

Oregon
Visit Oregon's Teacher Standards and Practices Commission.

Pennsylvania
Bureau of Teacher Certification and Preparation
Pennsylvania Department of Education
333 Market Street
Harrisburg, PA 17126-0333
Telephone: 1-717-787-3356

Rhode Island
Please refer to the Rhode Island Web site for the most current information.

South Carolina
Division of Educator Quality and Leadership
South Carolina Department of Education
3700 Forest Drive, Suite 500
Columbia, SC 29204
Telephone: 1-803-734-8446 or
1-877-885-5280 (toll free in-state only)
between 1:00 p.m. and 4:30 p.m. each business day
Fax: 1-803-734-2873

South Dakota
South Dakota Department of Education
Office of Accreditation and Teacher Quality
700 Governors Drive
Pierre, SD 57501
Telephone: 1-605-773-3553

Tennessee
Office of Teacher Licensing
State Department of Education
5th Floor, Andrew Johnson Tower
710 James Robertson Parkway
Nashville, TN 37243-0377
Telephone: 1-615-532-4885

Texas

Texas State Board for Educator Certification.

Utah

Certification and Personnel Development
Utah State Office of Education
250 East 500 South
Salt Lake City, UT 84111
Telephone: 1-801-538-7500

Vermont

For questions concerning teacher licensure call 1-802-828-2445 or visit Vermont Department of Education.

Virginia

Virginia Department of Education.

Washington

Professional Educator Standards Board
Old Capitol Building
P.O. Box 47236
Olympia, WA 98504-7236
E-mail: pesbassessment@k12.wa.us
Telephone: 1-360-725-6275
Fax: 1-360-586-4548
TTY: 1-360-664-3631

To obtain additional information about teacher certification, please contact:
OSPI Office of Professional Education and Certification
Telephone: 1-360-725-6400
E-mail: cert@k12.wa.us

West Virginia

Office of Professional Preparation
West Virginia Department of Education
1900 Kanawha Blvd. East
Building 6, Room 252
Charleston, WV 25305-0330
Telephone: 1-304-558-7826

Wisconsin

Teacher Education, Professional Development and Licensing Team
Wisconsin Department of Public Instruction
125 South Webster Street
P.O. Box 7841
Madison, WI 53707-7841
Telephone: 1-800-266-1027
E-mail: tcert@dpi.state.wi.us

Wyoming

Wyoming Professional Teaching Standards Board.

Test Name	Test Code	NC	ND	OH	OK	OR	PA	RI	SC	SD	TN	VI*	UT	VT	VA
Psychology	0390								X	X	X	X			
Reading Across the Curriculum: Elementary	0201										X				
Reading Specialist	0300	X				X	X		X		X				
Safety & Driver Education	0860						X								
School Guidance and Counseling	0420	X		X		X	X		X		X				
School Leaders Licensure Assessment	1010	X									X				X
School Superintendent Assessment	1020														
School Psychologist	0400	X		X		X	X		X		X			X	
School Social Worker: Content Knowledge	0211														
Social Sciences: Content Knowledge	0951	X					X								
Social Studies: Content Knowledge	0081	X	X	X		X	X		X				X	X	X
Social Studies: Analytical Essays	0082														
Social Studies: Interpretation of Materials	0083								X					X	
Social Studies: Interpretation and Analysis	0085					X									
Social Studies: Pedagogy	0194	X											X		
Sociology	0950									X	X				
Spanish: Content Knowledge	0191	X	X	X		X	X	X	X	X	X		X	X	X
Spanish: Productive Language Skills	0192	X				X	X	X	X	X	X		X	X	
Spanish: Pedagogy	0194												X		
Special Education: Knowledge-Based Core Principles	0351	X		X		X									
Special Education: Preschool/Early Childhood	0690					X				X	X				

(Continued)

Test Name	Test Code	NC	ND	OH	OK	OR	PA	RI	SC	SD	TN	VI*	UT	VT	VA
Special Education: Application of Core Principles Across Areas of Disability	0352	X													
Special Education: Teaching Students with Learning Disabilities	0381	X													
Special Education: Teaching Students with Behavioral Disorders/ Emotional Disturbances	0371	X							X						
Special Education: Teaching Students with Mental Retardation	0321	X							X						
Speech Communication	0220	X				X			X	X	X		X		
Speech-Language Pathology	0330	X		X		X			X	X	X			X	
Teaching Foundations: English	0048														
Teaching Foundations: Mathematics	0068														
Teaching Foundations: Multiple Subjects	0528														
Teaching Foundations: Science	0438														
Teaching Foundations: Social Science	0088														
Teaching Speech to Students with Language Impairments	0880						X								
Teaching Students with Visual Impairments	0280	X		X		X	X		X		X				
Technology Education	0050	X				X	X		X	X	X		X		X
Theatre	0640									X	X				
Vocational General Knowledge	0890						X								
World History and United States History: Content Knowledge	0941		X						X	X	X		X		

VI = U.S. Virgin Islands

Praxis II

Test Name	Test Code	WA	WV	WI	WY
Agriculture	0700	X	X	X	
Art: Content Knowledge	0133	X	X	X	
Art: Content, Traditions, Criticism, and Aesthetics	0132				
Art Making	0131				
Audiology	0340				
Biology: Content Knowledge	0235	X	X		
Biology: Content Knowledge, Part 1	0231		X		
Biology: Content Knowledge, Part 2	0232				
Biology: Content Essays	0233				
Biology & General Science	0030				
Business Education	0100	X	X	X	
Chemistry: Content Knowledge	0241, 0245		X		
Chemistry: Content Essays	0245				
Chemistry, Physics, and General Science	0070				
Citizenship Education: Content Knowledge	0087				
Communication	0800				
Cooperative Education	0810				
Driver Education	0867	X	X		
Earth and Space Sciences: Content Knowledge	0571	X			
Economics	0910				
Early Childhood Education	0020		X		
Early Childhood Education: Content Knowledge	0022				
Educational Leadership: Administration and Supervision	0410		X		
Education of Deaf and Hard of Hearing Students	0271	X			
Education of Exceptional Students: Core Content Knowledge	0353	X	X		

(Continued)

Test Name	Test Code	WA	WV	WI	WY
Education of Exceptional Students: Learning Disabilities	0382		X		
Education of Exceptional Students: Mild to Moderate	0542		X		
Education of Exceptional Students: Severe to Profound Disabilities	0544		X		
Education of Young Children	0021	X			
Elementary Education: Content Knowledge	0014	X		X	
Elementary Education: Content Area Exercises	0012				
Elementary Education: Curriculum, Instruction, and Assessment	0011	X	X		X
English Language, Literature, and Composition: Content Knowledge	0041	X	X	X	
English Language, Literature, and Composition: Essays	0042				
English Language, Literature, and Composition: Pedagogy	0043				
English to Speakers of Other Languages	0360	X		X	
Environmental Education	0830				
Family and Consumer Sciences	0120	X	X	X	
Foreign Language Pedagogy	0840				
French: Content Knowledge	0173	X	X	X	
French: Productive Language Skills	0171				
Fundamental Subjects: Content Knowledge	0511				
General Science: Content Knowledge	0435	X		X	
General Science: Content Knowledge, Part 1	0431				
General Science: Content Knowledge, Part 2	0432		X		
General Science: Content Essays	0433				
Geography	0920				
German: Content Knowledge	0181	X	X		
German: Productive Language Skills	0182			X	

Test Name	Test Code	WA	WV	WI	WY
Government/Political Science	0930				
Health Education	0550		X	X	
Health & Physical Education: Content Knowledge	0856	X			
Introduction to the Teaching of Reading	0200				
Latin	0600		X		
Library Media Specialist	0310	X	X		
Life Sciences: Pedagogy	0234				
Marketing Education	0560	X	X	X	
Mathematics: Content Knowledge	0061	X	X	X	
Mathematics: Proofs, Models, and Problems, Part 1	0063				
Mathematics: Pedagogy					
Middle School: Content Knowledge	0146			X	
Middle School English Language Arts	0049	X	X		
Middle School Mathematics	0069	X	X		
Middle School Science	0439	X	X		
Middle School Social Studies	0089	X	X		
Music: Analysis	0112				
Music: Content Knowledge	0113	X	X	X	
Music: Concepts and Processes	0111				
Physical Education: Content Knowledge	0091	X	X	X	
Physical Education: Movement Forms–Analysis and Design	0092				
Physical Education: Movement Forms–Video Evaluation	0093				
Physical Science: Content Knowledge	0481		X		
Physical Science: Pedagogy	0483				
Physics	0260				
Physics: Content Knowledge	0265	X	X		

(Continued)

Test Name	Test Code	WA	WV	WI	WY
Physics: Content Essays	0262				
Pre-Education Kindergarten	0530		X		
Principles of Learning & Teaching: Early Childhood	0521		X		
Principles of Learning & Teaching: Grades K–6	0522		X		X
Principles of Learning & Teaching: Grades 5–9	0523		X		X
Principles of Learning & Teaching: Grades 7–12	0524		X		
Psychology	0390				
Reading Across the Curriculum: Elementary	0201				
Reading Specialist	0300	X	X		
Safety & Driver Education	0860				
School Guidance and Counseling	0420				
School Leaders Licensure Assessment	1010				
School Superintendent Assessment	1020				
School Psychologist	0400		X	X	
School Social Worker: Content Knowledge	0211			X	
Social Sciences: Content Knowledge	0951				
Social Studies: Content Knowledge	0081	X	X	X	
Social Studies: Analytical Essays	0082				
Social Studies: Interpretation of Materials	0083				
Social Studies: Interpretation and Analysis	0085				
Social Studies: Pedagogy	0194				
Sociology	0950				
Spanish: Content Knowledge	0191	X	X	X	
Spanish: Productive Language Skills	0192				
Spanish: Pedagogy	0194				
Special Education: Knowledge-Based Core Principles	0351				
Special Education: Preschool/Early Childhood	0690	X	X		
Special Education: Application of Core Principles Across Areas of Disability	0352				

Test Name	Test Code	WA	WV	WI	WY
Special Education: Teaching Students with Learning Disabilities	0381				
Special Education: Teaching Students with Behavioral Disorders/Emotional Disturbances	0371		X		
Special Education: Teaching Students with Mental Retardation	0321				
Speech Communication	0220		X		
Speech-Language Pathology	0330		X	X	
Teaching Foundations: English	0048				
Teaching Foundations: Mathematics	0068				
Teaching Foundations: Multiple Subjects	0528				
Teaching Foundations: Science	0438				
Teaching Foundations: Social Science	0088				
Teaching Speech to Students with Language Impairments	0880				
Teaching Students with Visual Impairments	0280		X		
Technology Education	0050	X	X	X	
Theatre	0640	X		X	
Vocational General Knowledge	0890				
World History and United States History: Content Knowledge	0941				

For More Information

For more information about state teacher certification testing requirements, contact the agencies listed below.

Alabama
Teacher Education and Certification Office
State Department of Education
P.O. Box 302101
Montgomery, L 36130-2101
Internet: www.alsde.edu

Alaska
Alaska Teacher Certification

Arkansas
Office of Professional Licensure
Arkansas Department of Education
#4 State Capitol Mall—Rooms 106B/107B
Little Rock, AR 72201

California
California Commission on Teacher Credentialing (CCTC)
Information Services Unit
P.O. Box 944270
1900 Capitol Avenue
Sacramento, CA 94233-2700
Telephone: 916-445-7254 or 888-921-2682, 12:00 p.m. to 4:45 p.m. (PST)
E-mail: credentials@ctc.ca.gov

Colorado
Educator Licensing
Colorado Department of Education
201 E. Colfax Avenue, Room 105
Denver, CO 80203-1799
Telephone: 1-303-866-6628
Internet: www.cde.state.co.us/index_license.htm

Connecticut

Connecticut State Department of Education
Bureau of Certification and Teacher Preparation
PO Box 150471—Room 243
Hartford, CT 06115-0471
Telephone: 860-713-6969
Fax: 860-713-7017

Delaware

Delaware Educator Data System

District of Columbia

District of Columbia Public Schools
Educational Credentialing and Standards Branch
825 North Capitol Street, NE—6th Floor
Washington, DC 20002
Telephone: 202-442-5377

Georgia

The Georgia Professional Standards Commission
Two Peachtree Street, Suite 6000
Atlanta, GA 30303
Telephone: 1-404-232-2500 in Georgia
1-800-869-7775 (outside metro Atlanta)

Hawaii

Hawaii Teacher Standards Board
ATTN: Licensing Section
650 Iwilei Road, Suite 201
Honolulu, HI 96817
Telephone: 1-808-586-2600
Fax: 1-808-586-2606

Iowa

Internet: www.iowacte.org

Idaho

Specific *Praxis II* information is found at:
http://www.sde.state.id.us/certification/praxisinfo.asp
For more information on Idaho certification requirements, refer to the following
Web sites:
http://www.sde.state.id.us/certification
http://www.sde.state.id.us/certification/certmanual.asp

Indiana

Indiana Professional Standards Board
251 East Ohio Street, Suite 201
Indianapolis, IN 46204-2133
Telephone: 1-317-232-9010

Kansas

Kansas Certification and Teacher Education

Kentucky

Kentucky Education Professional Standards Board.

Louisiana

For further information about education and teacher licensing in Louisiana visit the Louisiana State Department of Education or the Teach Louisiana Web site.

Maine

For further information about education and initial certification visit the Maine Certification Office.

Maryland

For further information visit Maryland State Department of Education or call the Maryland Certification Information Line at 1-410-767-0412.

Minnesota

Minnesota Department of Education
Personnel Licensing Team
1500 Highway 36 West
Roseville, MN 55113-4266
Telephone: 1-651-582-8691

Mississippi

For further information about education and teacher licensure in Mississippi, visit the Mississippi Department of Education at http://www.mississippi.gov/frameset.jsp?URL=http%3A%2F%2Fwww.mde.k12.ms.us%2F.

Missouri

Visit the Missouri Department of Elementary and Secondary Education.

Nebraska

Teacher Education and Certification
Nebraska Department of Education
301 Centennial Mall South
P.O. Box 94987
Lincoln, NE 68509
Telephone: 1-402-471-2496
Fax: 1-402-471-9735 or 8127

Nevada

Nevada Department of Education
1820 East Sahara, Suite 205
Las Vegas, NV 89104-3746
Telephone: 1-702-486-6455

New Hampshire

For more information visit the New Hampshire Department of Education.

New Jersey

New Jersey Department of Education
Office of Licensing and Credentials
CN 500
Trenton, NJ 08625-0500
Telephone: 1-609-292-2070

New Mexico

For further information, visit the New Mexico Department of Education.

New York

For further information, visit the New York Office of Teaching.

North Carolina

Department of Public Instruction
Licensure Section
301 North Wilmington Street
Raleigh, NC 27601-2825
Telephone: 1-919-807-3310

North Dakota

Internet: http://www.nd.gov/espb/

Ohio

For additional information, visit the Ohio Department of Education, Center for the Teaching Profession.

Oklahoma

Oklahoma Department of Education
Professional Standards Section
Hodge Education Building, Room 211
2500 North Lincoln Boulevard
Oklahoma City, OK 73105
Telephone: 1-405-521-3337

Oregon

Visit Oregon's Teacher Standards and Practices Commission.

Pennsylvania

Bureau of Teacher Certification and Preparation
Pennsylvania Department of Education
333 Market Street
Harrisburg, PA 17126-0333
Telephone: 1-717-787-3356

Rhode Island

Please refer to the Rhode Island Web site for the most current information.

South Carolina

Division of Educator Quality and Leadership
South Carolina Department of Education
3700 Forest Drive, Suite 500
Columbia, SC 29204
Telephone: 1-803-734-8446 or
1-877-885-5280 (toll free in-state only)
between 1:00 p.m. and 4:30 p.m. each business day
Fax: 1-803-734-2873

South Dakota

South Dakota Department of Education
Office of Accreditation and Teacher Quality
700 Governors Drive
Pierre, SD 57501
Telephone: 1-605-773-3553

Tennessee

Office of Teacher Licensing
State Department of Education
5th Floor, Andrew Johnson Tower
710 James Robertson Parkway
Nashville, TN 37243-0377
Telephone: 1-615-532-4885

Texas

Texas State Board for Educator Certification.

Utah

Certification and Personnel Development
Utah State Office of Education
250 East 500 South
Salt Lake City, UT 84111
Telephone: 1-801-538-7500

Vermont

For questions concerning teacher licensure call 1-802-828-2445 or visit Vermont Department of Education.

Virginia

Virginia Department of Education.

Washington

Professional Educator Standards Board
Old Capitol Building
P.O. Box 47236
Olympia, WA 98504-7236
E-mail: pesbassessment@k12.wa.us
Telephone: 1-360-725-6275
Fax: 1-360-586-4548
TTY: 1-360-664-3631

To obtain additional information about teacher certification, please contact:
OSPI Office of Professional Education and Certification
Telephone: 1-360-725-6400
E-mail: cert@k12.wa.us

West Virginia

Office of Professional Preparation
West Virginia Department of Education
1900 Kanawha Blvd. East
Building 6, Room 252
Charleston, WV 25305-0330
Telephone: 1-304-558-7826

Wisconsin

Teacher Education, Professional Development and Licensing Team
Wisconsin Department of Public Instruction
125 South Webster Street
P.O. Box 7841
Madison, WI 53707-7841
Telephone: 1-800-266-1027
E-mail: tcert@dpi.state.wi.us

Wyoming

Wyoming Professional Teaching Standards Board.